Operations Strategy

Competing in the 21st Century

Operations Strategy

Competing in the 21st Century

Sara L. Beckman, PhD
Haas School of Business
University of California, Berkeley

Donald B. Rosenfield, PhD
Sloan School of Management
Leaders for Manufacturing Program
Massachusetts Institute of Technology

McGraw-Hill
Irwin

Boston   Burr Ridge, IL   Dubuque, IA   Madison, WI   New York   San Francisco   St. Louis
Bangkok   Bogotá   Caracas   Kuala Lumpur   Lisbon   London   Madrid   Mexico City
Milan   Montreal   New Delhi   Santiago   Seoul   Singapore   Sydney   Taipei   Toronto

 **McGraw-Hill Irwin**

OPERATIONS STRATEGY: COMPETING IN THE 21ST CENTURY

Published by McGraw-Hill/Irwin, a business unit of The McGraw-Hill Companies, Inc., 1221 Avenue of the Americas, New York, NY, 10020. Copyright © 2008 by The McGraw-Hill Companies, Inc. All rights reserved. No part of this publication may be reproduced or distributed in any form or by any means, or stored in a database or retrieval system, without the prior written consent of The McGraw-Hill Companies, Inc., including, but not limited to, in any network or other electronic storage or transmission, or broadcast for distance learning.

Some ancillaries, including electronic and print components, may not be available to customers outside the United States.

This book is printed on acid-free paper.

1 2 3 4 5 6 7 8 9 0 DOC/DOC 0 9 8 7

ISBN   978-0-07-250078-3
MHID   0-07-250078-6

Editorial director: *Stewart Mattson*
Executive editor: *Scott Isenberg*
Editorial assistant: *Katie Jones*
Marketing manager: *Kelly M. Odom*
Project manager: *Jim Labeots*
Senior production supervisor: *Carol A. Bielski*
Lead designer: *Matthew Baldwin*
Lead media project manager: *Cathy L. Tepper*
Cover design: *Matthew Baldwin*
Cover image: *© Getty Images*
Typeface: *10/12 Times New Roman*
Compositor: *International Typesetting and Composition*
Printer: *R. R. Donnelley*

Library of Congress Cataloging-in-Publication Data

Beckman, Sara Lynn.
 Operations strategy : competing in the 21st century/Sara L. Beckman, Donald B. Rosenfield.
  p. cm.
 Includes index.
 ISBN-13: 978-0-07-250078-3 (alk. paper)
 ISBN-10: 0-07-250078-6 (alk. paper)
 1. Business logistics. I. Rosenfield, Donald B., 1947- II. Title.
HD38.5.B43 2008
 658.5'03—dc22   2007006141

www.mhhe.com

To my parents, Victor and Frostine Beckman. S.L.B.
To my wife, Nancy Rosenfield. D.B.R.

Brief Contents

Contents

Chapter 7
Business Process–Focused Strategies and Organizational Design   253

Chapter 8
Coordinating the Supply Chain   292

Chapter 9
Information Technology   320

About the Authors

Sara L. Beckman Sara Beckman teaches new product development and operations management at the University of California's Haas School of Business. Since joining the faculty in 1987, she developed, institutionalized, and directed the school's Management of Technology Program and initiated new courses on design, entrepreneurship in biotechnology, new product development, and work and workspace design. She has also taught for Stanford University's Department of Industrial Engineering and Engineering Management and been a visiting faculty member at MIT, where she taught in the Leaders for Manufacturing (LFM) program.

Dr. Beckman also worked for Hewlett-Packard Company, most recently as director of the Product Generation Change Management Team. This group was responsible for supporting strategic decision making, workforce planning and design, manufacturing education and training, and environmental, health, and safety management throughout the company. Before joining HP and the Haas School, Dr. Beckman worked in the Operations Management Services practice at Booz, Allen and Hamilton where she developed manufacturing strategies with companies in industries ranging from pharmaceuticals to aerospace.

Dr. Beckman has BS, MS, and PhD degrees from the Department of Industrial Engineering and Engineering Management at Stanford University and an MS in statistics from the same institution. She serves on the boards of Building Materials Holding Corporation and the Corporate Design Foundation. She lives in Marin County, California, with her husband, Chip, and sons, Charley and Alexander. Her stepdaughters, Caroline and Elizabeth, live in New York and Texas.

Donald B. Rosenfield Donald Rosenfield is a senior lecturer in operations management at the MIT Sloan School of Management and is director of the Leaders for Manufacturing (LFM) Fellows program (a dual degree master's program run by the School of Management and the School of Engineering in partnership with leading global corporations). He has served at MIT since 1980 as lecturer, senior lecturer, and visiting associate professor. He has taught at Harvard Business School, the State University of New York, and Boston University. Dr. Rosenfield has helped make the Leaders for Manufacturing program a groundbreaking program in manufacturing education. Prior to joining MIT, Dr. Rosenfield served on the staff of Arthur D. Little, Inc., from 1976 to 1988, focusing in the areas of logistics and manufacturing strategy.

Dr. Rosenfield focuses on the areas of operations strategy and supply chain management. He has written articles for *Harvard Business Review, Operations Research, Management Science,* and *Sloan Management Review,* as well as a number of other journals. He is the coauthor of one previous book, *Modern Logistics Management.*

Dr. Rosenfield has a BS in mathematics, an MS in operations research and an EE degree from MIT, and a PhD in operations research from Stanford University. He lives in Lexington, Massachusetts, with his wife, Nancy, and son Adam and has two other children, Jennifer of Newport Beach, California, and Todd of New York.

Preface

The global economy is changing and the face of operations is changing along with it. Reduced barriers to trade are allowing smoother flow of goods, services, capital, and labor across geographic boundaries and thus more efficient allocation of resources globally. Technological advancements, particularly in information technology, are creating new opportunities for companies to compete in different ways. Reduced transportation and communication costs are facilitating placement of operations activities around the world to access required resources and cost structures. In this highly complex global environment, countries compete on the basis of both macroeconomic factors—institutions, infrastructure, health and primary education, higher education and training, and market efficiency—and microeconomic factors—technological readiness, business sophistication, and innovation.[1]

Operations strategy, the topic of this book, addresses both questions of how a company should structure itself to compete in the complex global economy and of how it can develop the capabilities that underlie technological readiness, business sophistication, and innovation. It addresses major capital decisions such as whether and how much to vertically integrate, what types of process technologies to employ, how much capacity to carry, and where to locate facilities. It also addresses adoption of information technology, development of a strong supply base and the supply chain that supports it, design of production and service delivery processes, and nurturing of the talent to design and deliver sophisticated products and services. The aptitude of a company to make these types of decisions, and thus plan and execute its operations effectively, is critical to both its competitiveness and to the competitiveness of the countries in which it operates. National competitiveness—for any country—depends upon improving productivity. Operations—manufacturing and service—is at the heart of the productivity improvement effort.

We define operations to include both manufacturing activities and service operations. Manufacturing activities range from one-of-a-kind shipbuilding to high-volume production of consumer products like shampoo or laundry detergent to continuous-flow operations such as those at oil refineries. Service operations include healthcare management, business and leisure travel, fast food delivery, and the back-office operations at financial institutions. Service operations often accompany production operations in the form, for example, of supply chain services such as retailing and transportation. Advanced economies tend to focus more of their resources in service operations, while developing economies focus more on agriculture or manufacturing.

The evolution of the U.S. economy is illustrative. In the 1800s, agriculture and food production dominated the U.S. economy. Since that time, significant improvements in productivity were made as farms were consolidated to achieve economies of scale, investments were made in equipment and technology, and those working in the farming sector became more knowledgeable and skilled. As the United States became more productive in agriculture and food production, the standard of living in the United States rose, even as

---

[1] See http://www.weforum.org/pdf/Global_Competitiveness_Reports/Reports/gcr_2006/chapter_1_1.pdf, November 25, 2006.

these sectors declined as a fraction of the overall economy. The resources freed were applied to the development of manufacturing-based businesses, which commenced to improve productivity of their operations in turn. Today, the U.S. standard of living still depends on productivity improvements in agriculture and manufacturing, even as the freed resources are being applied to service operations.

According to the World Bank (1995), high-income economies like the United States' devote only 4 percent of their working population to agriculture, while low-income economies devote 62 percent of theirs. Exhibit 1 shows employment figures for different levels of economic development. Low-income economies, for example, employ only 23 percent of their working population in services, while high-income economies employ 66 percent in services. The more advanced the economy, the fewer resources are typically devoted to agriculture and industry. It is difficult for a society, however, to devote the majority of its resources to services unless it has already become productive in agriculture and manufacturing. Thus, the evolution that the United States has gone through is followed by most developing economies around the world.

EXHIBIT 1   **Percentage of Working Population Employed by Sector**

Source: World Bank, 1995.

Percentage of the Working Population Employed in:	High-Income Economies	Middle-Income Economies	Low-Income Economies
Agriculture	4%	31%	62%
Industry (manufacturing)	30%	27%	15%
Services	66%	42%	23%

The advancement of an economy through these stages affects the development and deployment of operations throughout the rest of the world, resulting in frequent and significant changes in global production and distribution patterns. When a country initially industrializes, advancing from an agriculturally based economy to an industrially based one, it starts by taking advantage of its low labor costs to compete in global markets with low-cost products. Typically these are commodity markets, where the basis of competition is cost rather than quality, availability, features and innovativeness, or environmental performance. Over time, however, as investments are made to improve productivity, labor costs rise (and concurrently the standard of living), eventually making the country uncompetitive on the basis of cost alone. To remain competitive it must commence producing value-added goods that compete on something other than cost. When this occurs, production of the low-cost and commodity goods moves to a new location where labor costs are still low. The cycle then repeats itself.

This pattern has manifested itself in numerous countries. In Japan in the 1950s and 1960s labor costs were very low compared both to Japanese labor costs today and to labor costs in the more developed countries at that time. Japanese goods were thus competitive on the basis of cost. As Japanese companies became increasingly productive, Japanese labor costs increased significantly and Japan shifted its focus to compete on quality instead. The global markets sought to source commodities and other low-cost goods elsewhere. The pattern then repeated itself in the "four tigers"—South Korea, Taiwan, Singapore, and Hong Kong.

All started out as sources of low-cost labor and associated goods, but then evolved to sources of more sophisticated goods.

More recently, Thailand, Malaysia, Indonesia, and Mexico have begun the transition, but the more significant source of development has been China. Like the many countries that preceded it, China started off as a source of low labor costs. China is so large, however, that the entire country is not developing at the same pace. To some, China represents an inexhaustible supply of labor and will remain a low-cost source for many years to come, as production will simply move from region to region within China to achieve lower costs. The coastal regions of China, for example, have already seen increased costs and have changed their basis of competition to higher-value-added products, while the inland regions still have labor surpluses that allow them to deliver at low cost.

The patterns that have played themselves out in the production of goods are beginning to play out in services as well. India, for example, started out as a source of low-cost labor for services such as call centers and computer programming. As it has increased its productivity, enhanced the skill sets of its workforce, and improved the efficiency of its processes, it has shifted some portion of its work to higher-value-added activities. The global market is likely to start sourcing some of the low-cost or commodity services it has sourced from India elsewhere.

Where do these cycles end? Will products and services that left the United States return in the future? What is the next frontier after services? Some believe that innovation is the only self-sustaining driver of growth for countries that have reached the high-tech frontier.[2] They argue that developing countries can take advantage of existing technologies or incremental change to improve their productivity, but advanced economies must come up with cutting-edge products and processes to maintain a competitive edge. As a result, many advanced economies today, such as Singapore, place innovation policy—to establish an environment that promotes entrepreneurship and innovation—at the very center of their economic policy.

When manufacturing and service operations in advanced economies are uncompetitive, exchange rate adjustments cause costs to come down, and the standard of living is reduced. For less developed societies, investment in manufacturing and service operations provides a mechanism for creating jobs and raising the standard of living. In both cases, proficiency in operations sets the value of factor inputs, particularly the cost of labor and the standard of living. Some argue that advanced economies should outsource their operations to lower cost locations and focus their efforts on gaining competitive advantage through branding or marketing. Others (e.g., Cohen and Zysman 1987 and, more recently, Fingleton 2003) debate and question this notion and continue to emphasize the importance of operations to a national economy.

There is no doubt that the ability of a country to manage its operations—manufacturing or service—and to improve its productivity over time is critical to the competitiveness of that country. The evolution over time from agriculture to services and from low-cost provider to high-value-added provider is achieved only through continuous improvement of productivity. Operations strategy and management are at the core of that ability. The role of operations in the evolution of the global economy is not to be taken lightly. As companies

[2] http://www.weforum.org/pdf/Global_Competitiveness_Reports/Reports/gcr_2006/chapter_1_1.pdf, November 25, 2006.

shift operations around the world to access lower costs, better skills, or required technologies, people in their home markets are displaced. This raises a number of social, ethical, and political issues as companies and countries together determine how to move people to new careers and jobs and how to keep people current in such fluid environments. Globalization and the evolution we have described are inevitable. It is left to operations managers worldwide to deal gracefully and constructively with them.

Perhaps notions of national competitiveness are too abstract and not a good enough reason to believe that operations matter. If so, consider the simple list of benefits customers seek when procuring a product or a service. They examine the cost, quality, availability, features and innovativeness, and, increasingly, environmental performance of the product or service. Operations plays a critical role in delivering against each of these dimensions. Certainly the design or development organization sets the parameters for the production of a product or delivery of a service, and certainly marketing ensures that the product or service is properly presented to the customer. But, in the end, operations delivers the product or service. If operations is not capable, does not work closely with design or development in the creation of the product or service, or does not coordinate with marketing about promises made to the customer, customer satisfaction is extremely hard to achieve.

Operations—service and manufacturing—is thus core to national competitiveness as well as to simply satisfying customers. Decisions about operations must thus be made in a rigorous, thoughtful, and systematic manner. This book describes the important decisions that operations strategists must make and provides a number of methods for making them. We hope that it is helpful to all those prospective managers and executives who hold the future health of the global economy in their hands.

References   Cohen, Stephan S., and John Zysman. *Manufacturing Matters: The Myth of the Post-Industrial Economy.* New York: Basic Books, 1987.
Fingleton, Eamonn. *Unsustainable: How Economic Dogma Is Destroying American Prosperity.* New York: Thunder's Mouth Press, 2003.
World Bank Development Report. World Bank, 1995.

Acknowledgments

We are very grateful to the many people and organizations that have contributed to this book. We have been the beneficiaries of people who were willing to spend a great deal of their valuable time speaking to us to share their experiences, insights, and data and provide us a rich diversity of cases and examples. Many others reviewed sections of the manuscript and completed background reviews.

We are especially grateful to the Leaders for Manufacturing (LFM) program at MIT, a joint program of the Sloan School of Management, the MIT School of Engineering and the Engineering Systems Division, and leading multinational corporations. The LFM program supported the work on this book, underwrote a wide range of projects that are a major part of this book, and set an intellectual direction for the importance of manufacturing that led us to this project. Kent Bowen of Harvard and Tom Magnanti of MIT founded the LFM program and provided this direction. Bill Hanson and Paul Gallagher of LFM helped us scope the project and formulate some of the concepts. Many faculty and senior research staff at MIT, particularly those associated with the Operations Management group, supported the projects that are the source of the ideas in this book and reviewed our concepts. These include Steve Graves, Steve Eppinger, Gabriel Bitran, Charlie Fine, Jan Klein, Jeremie Gallien, Thomas Roemer, John Sterman, Nelson Repenning, Retsef Levi, Larry Lapide, Tom Allen, Ron Slahetka, David Simchi-Levi, and Roy Welsch.

The students of the LFM program made a number of contributions. The 42 students of the LFM class of 1999, including Harrison Smith, who tragically passed away shortly after graduation, were part of a capstone course in Operations Strategy and provided us many ideas while as students and during their subsequent careers. We are particularly grateful to Tom Blake, Gary Tarpinian, Rob Mosher, Bob Bliss, Roberta Braum, Adam King, Alison McAfree, Chris Ogden, Earl Jones, John Tagawa, Maria Alvarez, Shafali Rastogi, Eric Selvik, Greg Kandare, Adam Kohorn, Carey Mar, and Mike Milby and non-LFM students Jim Duda and Jochen Linck.

Many LFM graduates provided examples, cases, and data for this book from their internships and theses. These include Jeff Goldberg, Elizabeth Kao, Tony Newlin, Alison Page, Rob Hacking, Mindy Hsu, Bob Kelly, Tom Chandler, Tammy Greenlaw, Carl Ryden, Stephan Schmidt, Lynne Haupt, and Brad Householder, along with Bindiya Vikal, a graduate with a master's of engineering in logistics.

A number of LFM students made other valuable contributions while they were enrolled in the program. Kerry Person, Jessica Dolak, and Dave Penake of the class of 2006 reviewed and edited major portions of the manuscript, and Dan Walsh of the class of 2008 helped in research.

We are grateful to the corporate partners and other associates of LFM who were very generous with their time and willingness to share their stories. These include George Chamillard (Teradyne), Mike Bradley (Teradyne), Gary Cowger (General Motors), Jeff Wilke (Amazon), Dick Hunter (Dell), Mike Splinter (then of Intel), Blair Okita (Genzyme), Jim Miller (Cisco), Vah Erdekian (Cisco), Corey Billington (then of HP), Mary Puma (Axcelis), Steve Kalenik (Celestica), Bert Anderson (then of Celestica), Janet

Cramer (Polaroid), Tim Copes (Boeing), Gary Bass (Boeing), Eric Rohrbacher (UTC), Steve Nelson (UTC), Jeff Lucchesi (Building Materials Holding Corporation), and Rafael de Jesus (ABB). Other companies also contributed. We are grateful to Ron Drabkin (JRG Software), Alex Kandybin (Booz, Allen and Hamilton), Chris Richard (PRTM), and Kevin Schwartz (PRTM).

We are very grateful to Rodolfo Duran of McKinsey, at the time a student at the MIT Operations Research Center, and Henrik Jorgenson of Aalborg University, who both assisted in research, and Nuran Acur of Bilkent University, who reviewed the entire first draft and gave us a number of very good ideas.

We also benefited greatly from the reviews of Joy Fields of Boston College, Roy Shapiro of Harvard Business School, Eric Johnson of Dartmouth, Gary Scudder of Vanderbilt, John McCreery of North Carolina State University, John Mills of Cambridge University, Steve Nahmias of Santa Clara University, Yehuda Bassok of USC, Kingshuk K. Sinha of the University of Minnesota, Jan Van Mieghem of Northwestern University, and Kathy Stecke of the University of Texas at Dallas. We very much appreciate their support. We thank our editors Scott Isenberg of McGraw-Hill/Irwin and Robin Reed of Carlisle Publishing Services. We are also grateful to Jim Labeots, Katie Jones, Kelly Odom, Matthew Baldwin, Carol Bielski, and Cathy Tepper of McGraw-Hill/Irwin. All of these people were far more patient than we had a right to deserve. We appreciate the support of the LFM staff and the Engineering Systems Division. These include Jon Griffith and Jeff Shao. Nancy Young-Wearly of LFM spent a great deal of time incorporating revisions.

There is one person who deserves special thanks. Cara Cherson prepared the manuscript for submission, obtained all permissions, edited the references, helped revise exhibits, and edited some sections of text. Without Cara's patience and perseverance, we would not have been able to complete this book.

Finally there are our families, who unselfishly provided love and support throughout this project. Chip, Caroline, Elizabeth, Charley, and Alexander Gow, and Nancy, Jennifer, Todd, Runa, and Adam Rosenfield all sacrificed many hours and days that they were entitled to so that we could complete our work.

Sara L. Beckman
Berkeley, California

Donald B. Rosenfield
Cambridge, Massachusetts
November 2006

Chapter 1

Business Strategy Context for Operations Strategy[1]

Introduction

Axcelis Technologies, Inc., a 2000 spin-off of Eaton Corporation, is a $365 million producer of ion implantation equipment used in the fabrication of semiconductors. Its business, as that of others in the semiconductor equipment industry, fluctuates significantly from year to year as the fortunes of the semiconductor industry and its customers in the electronics industry wax and wane. While the growth rate of GDP fluctuates only modestly, the growth rate of the semiconductor industry overall fluctuates between negative 32% and plus 46% annually and growth rates in the semiconductor equipment sector fluctuate from negative 43% to plus 114% (Exhibit 1.1).

As a result of these regular fluctuations, Axcelis must adopt a strategy that allows it to react efficiently to business conditions, while still retaining an edge in providing the latest technological solutions to its customers. Its business strategy—to be innovative and flexible in response to industry demands—builds on three key elements: technology leadership, operational excellence, and customer partnerships. This strategy, in turn, guides the key decisions constituting Axcelis' operations strategy.

- Axcelis limits its *vertical integration* to those activities that are critical to the final assembly and test of its complex and technical equipment, thus minimizing its investment in fixed capacity. This allows Axcelis to deliver on its technology promise, as it maintains key technological equipment and knowledge—the basis of its key capabilities—in house. At the same time, it can suffer declines in demand without having to cover significant fixed costs. Its suppliers, in turn, aggregate demand across multiple customers, thus smoothing requirements for their own fixed assets.

- Given its vertical integration strategy, Axcelis selectively invests in *process technology* to improve the organization of the workflow on its factory floor and the integration of its

[1] We are grateful to Rob Mosher, Chris Ogden, and Earl Jones, Leaders for Manufacturing graduates, and Jim Duda for their thoughtful integration of many concepts in the business and operations strategy literature. We have used much of their work in writing this chapter.

EXHIBIT 1.1   Growth Rate Fluctuations in the Semiconductor Industry

Source: Data drawn from Semiconductor Industry Association. *2002 Annual Databook, Review of Global and US Semiconductor Competitive Trends* 1978–2001, pp. 6, 7, and 39, and online sources http://www.globalfinancialdata.com, http://www.eia.doe.gov/, http://www.sia-online.org, and http://wps2a.semi.org/wps/portal/_pagr/135/_pa.135/679, June 18, 2006.

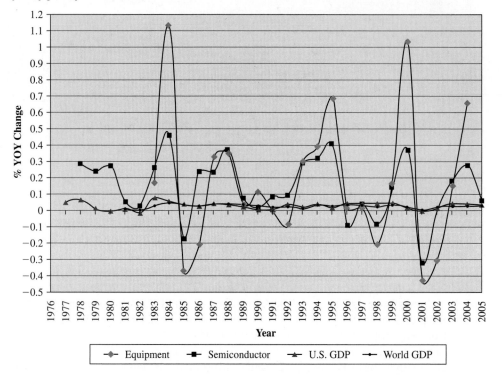

suppliers onto the factory floor. These investments allow Axcelis to maintain its technology edge and improve its operational performance.

- *Capacity* management is critical to Axcelis as it tracks the ups and downs of the business cycle. Attention to forecasting future trends in the industry allows Axcelis to work with limited space and labor buffers, thus maximizing its ability to respond to changes in demand at the lowest possible cost.

- Axcelis focuses its *facilities* on specific product lines or geographic regions. Its two U.S.-based plants focus on different product lines, while its Japan-based plant services the Asia-Pacific region. This allows Axcelis to develop focused technology expertise at each facility and provide local access to its large customers and markets.

- As Axcelis increases the amount of its business that it outsources and extends its geographic reach, it fine-tunes its *sourcing* policies to manage an increasingly wide range of suppliers. It segments its suppliers and defines different operational strategies for dealing with each segment. It strives to integrate its suppliers with its lean manufacturing agenda to maintain operational excellence.

- Axcelis carefully manages its *business processes and policies* for product and service generation, order fulfillment, and service and support to efficiently and effectively bring new technology solutions to the market and deliver them to customers as promised. The highly technical nature of Axcelis' equipment forces it to tightly integrate product development with manufacturing process development to ensure that new products can actually be built.

- Not only does Axcelis strive to integrate its internal activities through a business process focus, but it also works closely with suppliers to streamline its *supply chain,* allowing it to, for example, ship direct to customers from supplier sites where possible.
- Axcelis' investments in *information technology* focus on integration across the supply chain, including tools for customers to order and configure the complex products Axcelis offers, and tools for managing spare parts service and inventory. Such information technology investments support both the quest for operational excellence, and closer customer partnerships.
- Finally, Axcelis directs much of its effort to the development of *organizationwide capabilities* in lean manufacturing, quality management, and flexibility. The techniques it employs include work cells on the shop floor, Six Sigma quality programs, and cycle time reduction.

Axcelis makes decisions in each of these areas in an integrated way, so the decisions support each other and the overall business strategy. Its choice to outsource, which reduces its degree of *vertical integration,* works only because of increased attention to *sourcing* management and tighter relationships with suppliers. Managing *capacity* to follow the ups and downs of the industry requires that Axcelis' *business processes and policies* support use of contract workers and overtime to grow and shrink the workforce as needed while still allowing Axcelis to retain critical technical knowledge. The focus of its *organizationwide capabilities development* on lean manufacturing has implications for most of the decision categories including *supply chain coordination* that streamlines the flow of parts and materials to Axcelis.

Over the years, Axcelis fine-tuned both its business and operations strategies as it developed within Eaton Corporation and was subsequently spun out. In doing so, it had to answer the following questions:

- What businesses are we in?
- How will we gain competitive advantage in each of those businesses?

  - What market segment(s) do we wish to serve?
  - How will we satisfy our customers with respect to the cost, quality, availability, features/innovativeness, and environmental performance of our product and/or service families in each of those segments?
  - How will we work with our partners (customers, suppliers, competitors, those who offer complementary products and services, and others) to collectively satisfy our customers' needs?
  - What are our capabilities? How should we leverage the capabilities we have? What capabilities should we develop?

- How do our operations need to be structured to create competitive advantage? Specifically, what choices do we make with respect to

  - Vertical integration
  - Process technology

- Capacity
- Facilities
- Sourcing
- Business processes and policies
- Supply chain coordination
- Information technology
- Organizationwide capabilities

- How will the decisions we make about operations fit with decisions made in the other functional areas—marketing, research and development, finance and accounting, human resources—to synergistically create competitive advantage?

This book addresses these questions. Chapter 1 defines what we mean by strategy and how it is made, describes the corporate and business context in which operations strategy is made, and briefly introduces the areas of operations strategy that will be covered in this book.

What Is Strategy?

Strategic thinking has its origins in the strategy of war and is defined formally as "1: an elaborate and systematic plan of action [syn: scheme] 2: the branch of military science dealing with military command and the planning and conduct of a war." In the same context, tactics are defined as "the branch of military science dealing with detailed maneuvers to achieve objectives set by strategy" (Dictionary.com).

The earliest known writings on strategy are over 2,000 years old. Sun Tzu (2003), who wrote around 400 B.C. and whose book *The Art of War* was first translated from Chinese around 1910, captured critical strategic ploys such as what is known today as *first mover advantage:* "Generally, he who occupies the field of battle first and awaits his enemy is at ease; he who comes later to the scene and rushes into the fight is weary" (Mintzberg et al. 1998, p. 86). Carl von Clausewitz, who lived from 1780 to 1831 and whose book *On War* was first published in 1832, captured much of what we think about in strategy-making today when he argued that:

> [S]trategy depends on basic building blocks, which are used in attack, defense, and maneuver. Strategy making relies on finding and executing new combinations of these blocks. In every age, technology and social organization limit the combinations. After some time, these limits seem inevitable and hence natural. Strategists cease to question received wisdom and confine themselves to variations on accepted themes. It is therefore left to the great commanders, such as Napoleon, to innovate strategically by recognizing and bringing about new combinations" (Mintzberg et al. 1998, pp. 88–89).

That this view from 200 years ago is still relevant today is evident in recent work showing that companies seeking "blue oceans," or untapped market spaces outside the traditional bounds of their industry, in which to compete outperform those that stay within those bounds (Kim and Mauborgne 2005). In other words, the "great commanders" still succeed by questioning the rules of the game and finding new ways to play. Early writings by Sun Tzu and von Clausewitz have been highly influential on both the theory and practice of strategy, which to this day reflect a significant military flavor.

Over the years, strategy-thought leaders adapted these military definitions to fit business environments where the battles were fought among competing firms:

> What business strategy is all about—what distinguishes it from all other kinds of business planning—is, in a word, competitive advantage. Without competitors there would be no need for strategy, for the sole purpose of strategic planning is to enable a company to gain, as efficiently as possible, a sustainable edge over its competitors. Corporate strategy thus implies an attempt to alter a company's strength relative to that of its competitors in the most efficient way (Ohmae 1982, p. 36).

Today, there is a considerable body of academic and practitioner literature on strategy—both its content and the process of making it—and two points of view have emerged as most prominent.

The first, the field of competitive strategy, grew largely out of the military strategy literature and focuses on positioning a firm in the right way within the right industry. The second, the resource-based view of the firm, focuses on the capabilities of the firm and how those capabilities can be leveraged to obtain competitive advantage. We examine both in some detail before integrating them into the strategy-making framework we will use in this book.

Competitive Strategy: The Positioning View

The key concepts of the competitive strategy paradigm evolved directly from early military-based thinking and formed the basis of strategy teaching, research, and practice for over 20 years. The underlying premise of competitive strategy is that there are good industries and bad industries in which to play, and that one should seek to become a dominant player in a good industry (Porter 1980).

Industries comprise suppliers, buyers, potential new entrants, incumbent competitors, and possible substitutes. These five sets of players constitute what came to be known as the *five forces model* (Exhibit 1.2), as each player has different means by which it can gain or retain competitive advantage in the industry (Porter 1980). New entrants might, for example, be kept out if incumbent competitors maintain sufficient barriers to entry. Suppliers might make a strong position in the industry even stronger by forward integrating into the industry competitors' businesses. An ideal industry in this model might have very few competitors, thousands of competing suppliers that could be pitted against one another to reduce prices and improve quality and service, millions of eager customers, no possible substitutes, and high barriers to entry for new participants. Upon finding such an industry, a firm would contrive to become the dominant player in that industry.

In the competitive strategy view there are limited options for how a firm might position itself to gain that dominant position:

- Cost leadership: A firm could aim to be the low-cost provider in an industry.
- Differentiation: A firm could stand out by delivering a set of unique products and/or services—those providing higher quality, better performance, and/or distinctive features.
- Focus: A firm could serve a narrow segment of the market, focusing on particular customer groups, product lines, or geographic segments.

Within these three generic positions, firms might choose to further distinguish themselves by choosing one of the following three orientations (Porter 1996):

EXHIBIT 1.2   Five Forces Model

Source: Adapted from Porter, *Competitive Strategy: Technique for Analyzing Industries and Competition,* The Free Press, 1980.

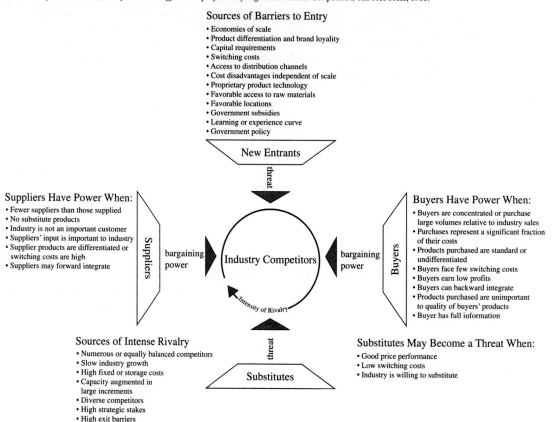

- **Variety-based:** These firms tailor their activities to deliver particular products, features or services across a range of customer groups, thus meeting a subset of customer needs. Examples include Southwest Airlines, offering no-frills service, and Jiffy Lube, offering low-cost, quick oil changes across all customer segments.

- **Needs-based:** These firms tailor their activities to meet the particular needs of a distinct customer group or purchasing occasion. IKEA, for example, serves young first-time homebuyers and the like with a complete range of home and office furnishings.

- **Access-based:** These firms tailor their activities to reach differently accessible customers with similar needs. Carmike Cinemas, for example, operates theaters in cities and towns with populations under 200,000.

Ultimately, in the competitive strategy view, the key is to identify a desired position in the industry and then structure the activities and develop the capabilities of the firm to match or fit the requirements of that position.

A popular approach to strategy development that arose from the competitive strategy view is the now classic SWOT (strengths, weaknesses, opportunities, threats) analysis

EXHIBIT 1.3
SWOT
Analysis
Approach to
Strategy
Design

Source: Adapted from
Porter, *Competitive
Strategy: Technique
for Analyzing
Industries and
Competition,* The Free
Press, 1980, and
Mintzberg, Ahlstrand,
and Lampel, *Strategy
Safari: A Guided Tour
through the Wilds of
Strategic Management,*
The Free Press, 1998.

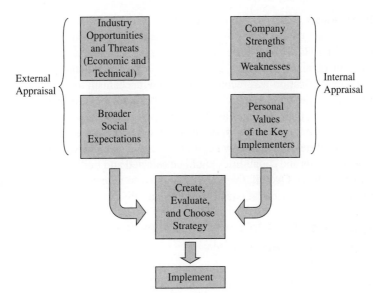

depicted in Exhibit 1.3. In a SWOT analysis, firms assess the threats and opportunities present in the external environment and, by creatively matching them with the strengths and weaknesses of the organization, determine where they should be positioned to obtain competitive advantage. They assess alternative strategies for internal consistency (whether the resulting goals and policies mutually reinforce one another) and for fit with both the external environment (whether they exploit opportunities and deal with threats) and internal resources (whether they leverage existing or planned strengths or avoid calling upon weaknesses of the firm).

Critics of the competitive strategy view argue that it

- Is too narrowly focused on industry and product economics rather than, for example, customer economics as the locus of competition.
- Allows too few options for positioning a firm. Indeed, looking at the conflicts among positions could well lead to creative new positioning options.
- Relies too much on analytical tools for strategy identification and assessment.
- Does not acknowledge the need for learning and adaptation over time.

Such criticisms gained strength in the 1980s, as researchers struggled to explain the rising power and global competitiveness of Japanese industry and the success of certain Japanese companies whose competitive advantage could not be explained simply by a positioning argument. Some Japanese companies, in fact, not only changed their competitive positioning rapidly over time—from, for example, low cost to high precision to flexibility to innovativeness—but transformed the nature of competition in the industry altogether (Hayes and Pisano 1996).

In part as a result of the desire to better understand the Japanese threat and Japan's approach to business and operations strategy development, the resource-based view of strategy gained attention and credibility. Various arguments were put forth. The main one was the notion that the focus of strategy development should shift from market positioning and industry forces (the five forces model) to identifying unique sets of capabilities and resources that could be developed and exploited to provide long-term profitability (Wernerfelt 1984). Firms were urged to identify, focus, and build on their "core competences" to obtain competitive advantage in a variety of markets (Prahalad and Hamel 1990). Diversification was recommended as a mechanism to extract additional value from those capabilities and resources (Teece 1980 and 1982, Wernerfelt and Montgomery 1988). In short, the academics argued that firms should be viewed not just as portfolios of assets and separable businesses, or even just as bundles of human resources and organizational capabilities. Instead, they suggested that firms be viewed as sets of mechanisms by which new skills and capabilities could be selected and built dynamically over time (Teece and Pisano 1994). Overall, the conversation led to renewed emphasis on and definition of the resource-based view of strategy (Hayes and Pisano 1996).

Capabilities Development and Leveraging: The Resource-Based View

While the competitive strategy view suggests that industry structure plays the central role in creating opportunities for superior profitability, the resource-based view argues that competitive advantage is derived from the firm's development of its resources and capabilities. In this view, firms occupy different market positions because they possess unique bundles of resources and capabilities that are *valuable* (allow the firm to improve its market position relative to competitors), *rare* (in relatively short supply), and *inimitable* (difficult and costly to imitate or replicate). Resources and capabilities are difficult to replicate when they are protected by intellectual property laws or are costly to learn and develop.

Often the relationship between a set of resources and capabilities and the success of a firm is not clear to those outside the firm, so those resources or capabilities are not immediately sought or copied. This can leave the firm with a competitive advantage for some time (Hoopes et al. 2003). Even when it is obvious that a firm's capabilities are providing it competitive advantage, its competitors often delay developing similar capabilities because they are wed to their own approaches to structuring operations. Companies with large-scale facilities, for example, might view smaller operations as inefficient, or companies that have invested heavily in automation might dismiss worker-intensive operations as unreliable or outdated. Many companies put too much faith in the power of their size, asset base, and market position and assume that they can replicate anything a competitor can do at a reasonable cost when needed. Numerous examples have proven these assumptions incorrect (Hayes and Upton 1998).

To more fully understand the resource-based view, we define the terms *resources* and *capabilities*. A resource is "an observable (but not necessarily tangible) asset that can be valued and traded—such as a brand, a patent, a parcel of land, or a license" (Hoopes et al. 2003, p. 890). It is "an asset or input to production (tangible or intangible) that an organization owns, controls, or has access to on a semi-permanent basis" (Helfat and Peteraf 2003, p. 999). Resources are the technologies, methodologies, and skills that are available to the firm that, when combined, can be used to create competitive advantage. The sustainability of this advantage depends on the ease with which the resources can be imitated or substituted. Resources can be classified as tangible (physical, technology, financial), intangible (communication and information systems, reputation, culture, brands), and human (specialized skills and knowledge, communication and interaction, motivation) (Lowson 2002).

A *capability*, on the other hand, is "not observable (and hence necessarily intangible), cannot be valued, and changes hands only as part of its entire unit" (Hoopes et al. 2003, p. 890). Capabilities are the processes, activities, or functions performed within a system and reflect the ability of an organization to perform a coordinated set of tasks, utilizing organizational resources, for the purpose of achieving a particular end result. Competencies refer to the fundamental knowledge—know-how, experience, innovation and unique information—owned by the firm, while capabilities reflect an organization's ability to use its competencies (Lowson 2002). Capabilities are enacted through a mixture of people and practices and are represented in such systems as American Airlines' yield management system, Wal-Mart's docking system, and Dell's logistics system. (See the sidebar "Capabilities Development" for further description of these examples.) A capability can be valuable on its own or enhance the value of a resource. Nike's marketing capability, for example, increases the value of its brand (a resource) (Hoopes et al. 2003).

In short, capabilities are developed through a firm's experience, focus, and effort over time. As firms learn, they tune their capabilities, giving them a competitive advantage that is difficult to replicate without going through the same long-term learning process. Because the notion of capabilities can be somewhat vague, it is helpful to identify specific types of capabilities a firm might choose to develop, or find it already has. Although there are many possible ways to think about a firm's capabilities, here are four dimensions along which they might be framed: process-based, coordination-based, organization-based (Hayes and Upton 1998) and network-based capabilities (Lowson 2002).

Process-Based Capabilities

Process-based capabilities are anchored in the activities a firm undertakes to transform material or information into products and/or services. These capabilities are often focused on achievement of cost and quality outcomes. McDonald's has invested significant research in developing its process for delivering low-cost, highly consistent fast food throughout the world. Note that, in developing this capability, it excludes itself from doing other things well: McDonald's has a much more difficult time allowing its customers to "have it your way" than does Burger King, for example. Nonetheless, McDonald's has terrific command of the burger-making process—command that has allowed it to successfully replicate the process around the world with a high degree of consistency. Fidelity Investments, through investments in state-of-the-art image and audio capture technology, can enter information into its systems accurately and retrieve that information instantaneously when customers inquire about a previous transaction. Although it lags competitors in other dimensions of performance, these capabilities allow it to attract and retain customers seeking superior service (Hayes and Upton 1998).

Systems- or Coordination-Based Capabilities

Coordination-based capabilities derive from a firm's skill in seamlessly executing multiple elements of its internal product or service delivery process to deliver high-quality customer experiences, short lead times, a broad range of products or services, customization on demand, or rapid new product introduction. A firm might have a *process-based capability*— for example, a technology that none of its competitors have been able to imitate—that is not necessarily well integrated or coordinated with other activities in the firm, but nonetheless provides competitive advantage. Firms with *coordination-based capabilities*, on the

YIELD MANAGEMENT AT AMERICAN AIRLINES

American Airlines began developing its yield management capability in the 1960s when it pioneered a sophisticated reservation management system that was subsequently embodied in the Semi-Automated Business Research Environment (SABRE) that allowed American to centrally control the activities of reservation agents around the country. To this day, the SABRE group is a leader in both the methodology and technology of reservations management.

One of the critical elements of SABRE is the automated overbooking process; American estimates that, without overbooking, 15% of the seats on sold-out flights would otherwise be unused. The introduction of super-saver discount fares in 1977 and the deregulation of schedules and fares in 1979 created new opportunities for SABRE to "sell the right seat to the customer at the right time." SABRE took on the task of allocating seats to each fare category and then dynamically adjusting the allocation as actual demand materialized. For example, it retains a number of full-fare seats for those customers who make reservations close to the departure date and for whom price is less critical. To accomplish this, SABRE's sophisticated forecasting model must take into account such complexities as the hub and spoke nature of its system and thus the links between connecting flights.

The net impact of the Dynamic Inventory and Maintenance Optimizer (DINAMO) when it was first implemented was estimated at about $1.4 billion in additional revenue over a three-year period, with only about 3% empty seats on sold-out flights. The capabilities that American developed through SABRE were of such significant value that its American Airlines Decision Technologies Group began applying yield management to other industries including lodging, car rental, railroad, and broadcasting with significant benefits as well (Smith et al. 1992; www.optims.com/UK/hight_profits.html, August 15, 2005).

The importance of the SABRE capability grew at American throughout the years. In 1993, AMR Corporation (American Airlines' parent) formed the SABRE Technology Group, which included AMR Information Services, SABRE Travel Information Network, SABRE Computer Services, SABRE Development Services, and AMR Project Consulting and Risk Assessment. In 1996, AMR announced that the SABRE Group was filing for an initial public offering, and in 2000 completed its spin-off into an independent company (www.aa.com/content/amrcorp/corporate Information/facts/history.jhtml, August 20, 2005). Today, SABRE Holdings is an S&P 500 company that contains Travelocity.com, an online travel service; SABRE Travel Network, which offers electronic services to travel agencies, travel suppliers, corporations, and government agencies; and SABRE Airline Solutions, which offers solutions and services to optimize operations and reduce costs for airlines, airports, and government agencies (www.sabre.com, August 20, 2005).

Meanwhile, American continues to leverage the capabilities SABRE caused it to develop. In March 2000 it received *CIO Magazine*'s 2000 Web Business 50/50 Award for its website, and in September 2002 it announced an EveryFare program that provided traditional travel agents with the option to access and sell the low fares previously only available on American's own website. In exchange, travel agents provided American with long-term distribution cost savings through a cost-sharing arrangement.

Although these capabilities have clearly not been sufficient to keep American profitable through recent years, they provided the company with significant advantages over the years and have continued to be valuable in their new form at SABRE Holdings.

WAL-MART'S DOCKING SYSTEM

In 1979, Kmart was king of the discount retailing industry with 1,891 stores and average revenues per store of $7.25 million. Its size provided it with economies of scale in purchasing, distribution, and marketing that made it a formidable competitor. Wal-Mart, on the other hand, was a small niche retailer in the South with only 220 stores and average revenues about half those of Kmart stores. By 1989, however, Wal-Mart had transformed itself and the discount retailing industry; growing nearly 25% a year, the company achieved the highest sales per square foot, inventory turns, and operating profit of any discount retailer. Its 1989 pretax return on sales of 8% was nearly double that of Kmart.

Wal-Mart's success was attributed to its focus on a small set of goals: to provide customers access to quality goods, to make these goods available when and where
(continued)

customers want them, to develop a cost structure that enables competitive pricing, and to build and maintain a reputation for absolute trustworthiness. One of the key ways in which the company sought to meet these goals was through its inventory replenishment system that involved cross-docking. In this system, goods are delivered to Wal-Mart's warehouses, sorted, repacked, and sent out to its stores without sitting in inventory. This allows Wal-Mart to purchase full truckloads of product but avoid the inventory and handling costs associated with storing the goods, which in turn allows it to offer lower prices, which in turn allows it to avoid promotions that lead to large inventory fluctuations.

While cross-docking is a relatively common concept today, it was not in the 1980s when Wal-Mart started it. To make cross-docking work and obtain all of its advantages, Wal-Mart had to make significant investments in information systems that linked its distribution centers, suppliers, and point-of-sale systems through a private satellite-communications system and a fast and responsive transportation system of its own dedicated fleet of trucks. These investments were matched with a human resource management system that encouraged cooperation among stores, distribution centers, and suppliers and a strong sense of ownership by middle management for operating the business.

The capabilities Wal-Mart developed to support and leverage its cross-dock system yielded it $244.5 billion in revenues for 2002, or four times what the number two retailer, Home Depot, sells in a year. Wal-Mart now does more business than Target, Sears (now owned by Kmart), Kmart, J.C. Penney, Safeway, and Kroger combined, taking in 7.5 cents of every dollar spent in any store (other than auto-parts stores) in the United States (Fishman 2003). Kmart, meanwhile, declared bankruptcy in 2002 (http://money.cnn.com/2002/01/22/companies/ kmart/, August 20, 2005).

Considerable controversy surrounds Wal-Mart today as people question the effects of Wal-Mart's tough negotiations on the U.S. supply base (Fishman 2003) and document the status of Wal-Mart employees (Ehrenreich 2001). Nonetheless, much has been learned from observation of the capability set it developed around its inventory management system.

DELL'S LOGISTICS SYSTEM

The Dell Direct Model, launched when Michael Dell founded Dell Computer Corporation in 1984, has five underlying tenets (www.us.dell.com/content/topics/global.aspx/corp/background/en/directmodel?c=us&l=en&s=corp, August 20, 2005):

1. Most efficient path to the customer—a direct relationship with no intermediaries.

2. Single point of accountability—Dell coordinates all resources required to meet customer needs.

3. Build-to-order—a custom configuration and ordering system that minimizes inventories and lead times.

4. Low-cost leader—through investment in continuous improvement of a highly efficient supply chain.

5. Standards-based technology—that allows Dell to access low-cost technologies quickly, and mix and match them in its highly modular products.

With this system, Dell strives to balance supply and demand, holding as little inventory as possible to meet its customers' needs. Dell controls its value chain from procurement through the delivery of the finished product, eliminating the middleman, which allows it to exert greater control over cost, quality, and time. Its logistics process is quintessential just-in-time. Supplies and components are pulled through the value chain allowing Dell to operate on only eight days of inventory. Dell's shared logistics centers (SLCs) are the hubs that hold the inventory for its factories, which can pull material in from the SLCs within minutes of receiving a customer order. The factories hold only about six hours of inventory, so the SLCs play a critical role in buffering against fluctuations in demand.

Dell uses Internet technology to make its logistics function efficient and effective, providing customers with online order status information, and to work real time with suppliers and customers to engage in collaborative product development. Dell is able to receive feedback from suppliers regarding their capacity to produce certain quantities of components, and information on inventories in their supply lines, as well as current cost structures. Dell can also manage and smooth demand through active management of its sales through its own website.

Dell's corporate culture reflects its highly efficient logistics system. Transmission of information both internal and external to the organization is done real time, revolutionizing the way suppliers, manufacturers, and customers interact. Product designs can be developed in a matter of days, incorporating efforts of engineers

(continued)

around the world. Shared goals—to reduce inventory costs throughout the value chain—breed cooperative efforts between Dell and its suppliers.

According to Dell executives, the advantages of Dell's innovative supply-chain management system translate directly to the consumer (Vargus 2003):

- Customers have immediate access to the latest, most relevant technology.
- Suppliers get their products to market quickly.
- Quality is improved with fewer touches.
- Communication is immediate and accurate.
- Cost-savings and efficiencies are passed on to its customers.

Since its IPO in 1989, Dell's annual revenues have grown from $0.3 billion to nearly $50 billion (www.us.dell.com/content/topics/global.aspx/corp/investor/en/history?c=us&l=en&s=corp&~ck=mn, August 20, 2005). Its capabilities in logistics management continue to be held up as an outstanding example.

other hand, integrate activities across the firm to achieve competitive advantage. The Ritz-Carlton Hotel Company, for example, coordinates its activities—reception, housekeeping, dining, and banquet services—to provide guests a quality experience from arrival to departure (Heching 1998). Southwest Airlines coordinates the multiple activities associated with low-cost air travel—from ticketing to seat assignments to beverage and snack delivery to luggage handling—better than its competitors. With this capability, it has outperformed much of the airline industry despite attempts by a number of its competitors—such as Continental, which offered Continental Lite—to imitate its offerings.

Organization-Based Capabilities

Firms sometimes described as learning organizations or good at knowledge management are said to have organization-based capabilities. These firms have developed organization-wide skills to master new technologies, product designs, or processes and bring them online significantly faster than their competitors. Nucor Steel, a steel recycling company whose business has grown nearly 20% per year since its entry into steel making in 1973, prides itself on its mastery of steel-making processes. It learns from various sources including universities, competitors, equipment manufacturers, and its own operations and applies that knowledge to run its facilities highly efficiently. (See the sidebar "Organization-Based Capabilities at Nucor.") Organization-based capabilities are particularly difficult for others to replicate, as they are embedded in the routines and tacit knowledge of the organization. As such, they make particularly formidable competitive weapons.

Information technology and management can also be key to the development of organization-based capabilities. The primacy of information—whether about customers, competitors, technologies, or suppliers—in today's business environment suggests that managing information is a potential source of competitive advantage. Firms may develop capabilities in information awareness, decision architecture, knowledge/information architecture, organizational focus on information collection and use, and information network management that will provide them a competitive edge (Mendelson and Ziegler 1999). Consulting firms such as Accenture are well aware that the knowledge they bring to bear in their consulting assignments is a critical capability of their firm. They guard that knowledge carefully and have built sophisticated information systems to capture and manage it. Intuit, provider of Quicken and TurboTax personal financial management tools, has deep knowledge of its

Organization-Based Capabilities at Nucor*

Nucor Corporation is arguably the most innovative and fastest growing steel company in the world with annual compounded sales growth of 17%, profit margins consistently above industry medians, and average annual returns to shareholders in excess of 20% for the past 30 years. Its success cannot be explained by external factors: It is not in a growth industry, there are few critical barriers to entry for the business, and it has little brand recognition or market power in the commodity steel marketplace.

Instead, Nucor's success has come about because of its "social ecology"—the social environment in which its people operate—which in turn supports strongly effective knowledge management. Nucor excels in all of the key elements of the knowledge management process:

- Knowledge creation because of its

  - Superior human capital, which it accesses by locating plants in rural areas with an abundance of hard-working, mechanically inclined people and then invests in training.

  - High-powered incentives in which employees can earn large incentive bonuses for productivity and quality gains.

  - High degree of empowerment, which includes both a high tolerance for failure and a high degree of accountability.

- Knowledge acquisition, because employees motivated by the desire to improve performance continually scan the outside world for new technology developments and are willing to take risks in implementing them.

- Knowledge retention because it does not lay people off in downturns and cultivates a high degree of loyalty and commitment among its personnel.

- Knowledge identification through systematic performance measurement at all levels of the organization, which allows comparison and sharing of performance gains and ways to achieve them.

- Knowledge outflow because the incentive system is structured to encourage not only productivity gains at the local level, but across the organization.

- Knowledge transmission both within plants, which are kept small to encourage regular communication, and across plants using performance metrics, group meetings of plant managers, and plant visits.

- Knowledge inflow, again driven by the incentive system to take in any and all new information that is useful to improving performance.

*Based on Gupta and Govindarajan 2000.

---

customers and how they manage their finances. This knowledge has allowed Intuit to retain a competitive lead over Microsoft's Money and other comparable products.

Network-Based Capabilities

Finally, network-based capabilities are those that reach outside the bounds of a single organization and encompass the entire value chain or supply network. Firms with strong network-based capabilities are able to guide, or at the very least work well with, the other players in their value chain to improve the efficiency of the value chain overall. Zara, the clothing manufacturer, distributor, and retailer, coordinates its supply chain—a large centralized warehouse with tightly integrated production facilities, a well-coordinated transportation network, and tight information integration with its retail outlets—to deliver a high mix of products with short life cycles at relatively low cost. Dell's renowned logistics management system integrates product design with supplier management with internal assembly operations with a strong sales information system to provide efficient design, production, and delivery of computers and related products.

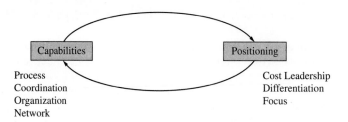

EXHIBIT 1.4
Strategy-Making Process with Traditional Positioning Options

Capabilities

Process
Coordination
Organization
Network

Positioning

Cost Leadership
Differentiation
Focus

Integrating the Competitive Strategy and Resource-Based Views

Despite the sometimes acrimonious debate between the competitive strategy and resource-based views, we integrate them in this book, as we believe strategy comes about through an iterative process that employs both perspectives (Mintzberg et al. 1998; Hax and Wilde 2001). On the one hand, firms may choose a position in the marketplace and then develop the capabilities they need to take that position. When Southwest Airlines was founded, for example, it chose a market segment in which to compete and then developed the coordination capabilities to excel in that market. In the long run, as its competitors attempted to move into its market, they found it extremely difficult to imitate Southwest's capabilities as they were much farther down the learning curve (Hayes and Upton 1998). On the other hand, firms may examine their capabilities and choose to leverage them in identifying new businesses or market segments in which to compete. Amazon.com, for example, started by selling books but determined that its capabilities in selling via the web might be applied in other sectors as well. Thus, it seeks new market opportunities, such as warehousing and selling toys for Toys "R" Us or household merchandise for Target, that allow it to leverage the capabilities it has built.

Strategy, in short, is deciding where you want your business to go and how you want to get there. It is an iterative process of examining the marketplace for opportunities and leveraging the firm's ever changing capabilities in new and interesting ways. Exhibit 1.4 captures this iterative process in the beginning of a framework we will build on later in this chapter.

How Strategy Is Made: Intended, Emergent, and Realized Strategy

Thus far, the view we've presented of strategy-making suggests that managers can assess, perhaps rather analytically, their organizations' positions in the marketplace and their capabilities, devise a strategy, and then implement it. This view of strategy as a plan or set of guidelines to take the organization into the future is not a fully accurate representation of the use of the word *strategy* in business today. In fact, if you ask someone to describe the strategy of his or her own organization, or that of a competitor, what you most often hear about is not what that organization intended to do, but what it actually did. The cover of Eagle Materials' 2004 annual report, for example, proclaims it to be "absolutely, positively a low-cost producer with high-margin products" and proceeds to describe the ways in which the company reduced costs during the year (http://ir.eaglematerials.com/ downloads/ar2004.pdf). Thus, we think of strategy not only in terms of planning a future direction, but as reflecting the pattern of decisions an organization has made over time.

Consider, for example, the cereal manufacturer whose stated operations strategy was to be highly flexible and thus able to respond to changes in demand from the marketplace as well as to marketing requirements for all kinds of special promotions such as putting an action figure in the cereal box. While the manufacturing manager was quite clear about this focus and showed supporting strategic planning documents, manufacturing engineers on the shop floor were using very different criteria to justify investments in new capital equipment. When asked how to best justify an equipment purchase, the engineers explained that they had to show how the investment would pay for itself in reduced labor and floor space costs. Showing that the new equipment would improve the plant's flexibility was inadequate. Although this organization's stated strategy was to be flexible, the pattern of decisions made by those actively managing and changing plant operations was to reduce cost.

So, in fact, organizations have both *intended* strategies, which are generally conceived by the top management team, typically through a process of negotiation, bargaining, and compromise among many individuals in the organization, and *realized* strategies, which reflect the actual pattern of decisions they have made over time. But even this representation is overly simplistic. In practice it is extremely difficult—impossible, really—to execute an intended strategy fully as laid out. But, if an organization accomplishes some portion of that strategy, its realized strategy will at least partially match its intended strategy. The portion of an organization's intended strategy that reaches fruition is sometimes called a *deliberate* strategy, while the portion that does not is called an *unrealized* strategy (Mintzberg et al. 1998).

There is yet another path to a realized strategy. *Emergent strategy* arises from the day-to-day patterns of decisions that managers make as they both interpret the intended strategy and accommodate the many changes that arise from the external environment. Individual actions may, over time, evolve into a consistent pattern of decisions that leads the organization in a new direction. Thus, the realized strategy of the organization may, at least in part, emerge from a pattern of unintended decisions made by the organization. Capabilities are sometimes discovered in this way. A company may not be aware of the full potential of the capabilities it is developing until a sudden insight or fortuitous incident reveals how they can be exploited. Thus, strategies based on capabilities are as likely to be emergent as they are to be the product of traditional strategic planning (Hayes and Upton 1998).

Organizations rarely follow just one of these paths to their realized strategy (Exhibit 1.5). Rather, they set forth plans for the future (intended strategies) and at the same time engage in an experimentation and learning cycle that allows them to adapt to the changing realities of the environment in which they operate. This provides some balance between the control provided by executing against an intended strategy and the real-time responsiveness provided by allowing an emergent strategy to evolve. The appropriate balance is determined by the industry in which the organization plays. In rapidly and unpredictably changing industries, it is difficult to envisage which industries, competencies, or strategic positions will be viable and for how long, and the key strategic challenge becomes how to cope with ongoing and rapid change. At the extreme, such organizations define strategy as "the creation of a relentless flow of competitive advantages that, taken together, form a semi coherent strategic direction. The key driver of superior performance is the ability to see change. Success is measured by the ability to survive, to change, and ultimately to reinvent the firm constantly over time" (Brown and Eisenhardt 1998).

In this book, we focus on the key decisions that make up an operations strategy and provide tools that are useful to both extremes in strategy-making. We support the planning strategist—the senior manager providing long-term direction to his or her organization—

EXHIBIT 1.5
Types of Strategies

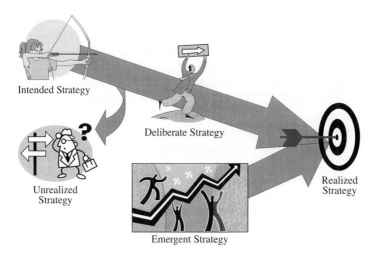

Intended Strategy

Deliberate Strategy

Unrealized Strategy

Realized Strategy

Emergent Strategy

and the emergent strategist—the individual making a seemingly stand-alone decision that may well have far-reaching effects throughout the organization.

Corporate, Business, and Functional Strategies

Strategy is defined at multiple levels in the organization as depicted in Exhibit 1.6 (Hofer and Schendel 1978). At the *corporate level,* decisions are made about the scope of the firm, including the choice of industries and markets in which it will participate. At the *business level,* decisions entail choosing specific market segments in which the firm will compete, deciding how the firm will position its products and services to compete in those markets, and determining which of the firm's capabilities to leverage and how. In effect, decisions made at this level determine how the firm will obtain and/or retain competitive advantage

EXHIBIT 1.6   Levels of Strategic Planning

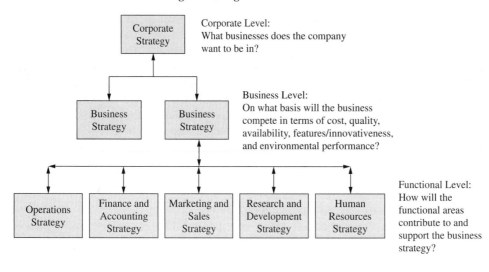

Corporate Strategy

Corporate Level:
What businesses does the company want to be in?

Business Strategy

Business Strategy

Business Level:
On what basis will the business compete in terms of cost, quality, availability, features/innovativeness, and environmental performance?

Operations Strategy

Finance and Accounting Strategy

Marketing and Sales Strategy

Research and Development Strategy

Human Resources Strategy

Functional Level:
How will the functional areas contribute to and support the business strategy?

or how it will shift the competitive dynamics of the industry to form new opportunities. At the *functional level,* decisions are made about how to synergistically structure the activities in operations, finance and accounting, marketing and sales, research and development, and human resources to support or create competitive advantage. The functions, individually or collectively, may offer resources, capabilities, and competencies from which new sources of competitive advantage may be derived, and on which new business strategies may be developed. This book focuses on the functional level, specifically on strategy for the operations function. We examine each level of strategy-making here, however, to provide a sense of the broader context in which operations strategy is made.

Corporate Strategy

Corporate strategy identifies the industries and markets in which a firm will compete. Corporate strategists make decisions that implement these choices, including investment in and divestment of businesses as well as allocation of resources among existing businesses. In essence, they manage the portfolio of businesses in which the firm participates, investing more or less in those businesses as needs shift in the broader market. See the sidebar "Corporate Strategy at Eaton Corporation" for a detailed description of the evolution of a corporate strategy over time.

As the Eaton example suggests, corporate strategy entails forming and reforming the corporation's portfolio of businesses over time in response to both the needs of the businesses in the portfolio and the pressures of the external environment. Corporate strategists may seek synergies among the businesses they manage that will allow the company to obtain a better position in the marketplace, or they may simply seek improved financial performance through an acquisition or divestiture. They will set performance expectations and determine appropriate levels of investment in the businesses in the existing portfolio. The financial strategy of the company is clearly a critical part of corporate strategy setting, as the company seeks funds for investment or from divestiture. Further discussion of corporate strategy—its content and how it is developed and executed—is beyond the scope of this book.[2] It is important to understand, simply, that operations strategy is typically determined within the broader context of corporate strategy.

Business Strategy

Business strategy is focused at the level of the individual business or business unit within the firm, and is concerned with where the business positions itself within a particular industry or market as well as with how and with what capabilities the business will win customers, cooperatively and/or in competition with other players in its industry. Empirical evidence from a study of over 100 companies found that those companies that engaged in system level thinking (Sterman 2000) about their business strategies significantly outperformed those that focused at the product level. Specifically, the study (Hax and Wilde 2001) differentiated three views a firm might take in setting strategy:

1. Best Product: This view comes from the classic competitive strategy field of thought. Simply, it focuses on beating the competition by positioning the firm's products or

---

Corporate Strategy at Eaton Corporation

Eaton Corporation, the former parent of Axcelis, is a large global, diversified industrial manufacturer. It defines its four primary businesses as fluid power systems, industrial and commercial controls, automotive, and truck. Within each of these primary businesses, it defines a number of secondary businesses or divisions, each focused on a particular product, technology, and/or market. Its corporate strategy, however, has evolved continually since its founding as a gear and axle company in 1911 (Exhibit 1.7). In the early years of the

corporation, much of the corporate strategy focused on diversification and growth through acquisition, and it expanded from axles and gears into springs, bumpers, valves, transmissions, and power devices. Its interest in ion implanters, the products that Axcelis makes today, came about in 1983 when Eaton formed a joint venture with Sumitomo. In recent years, Eaton divested a number of businesses to focus more tightly on a smaller number of industries and markets. Axcelis Technologies was spun out of Eaton in this divestment process in 2000.

EXHIBIT 1.7
Evolution of Eaton's Corporate Strategy through Investment and Divestment

Source: Data drawn from Eaton Corporation: http://eaton.com/NASApp/cs/ContentServer?pagename=EatonCom%2FPage%2FEC_T_TwoThirdsBodyNav&c=Page&cid=1008110157919 (accessed August 20, 2005).

Era	Acquisitions	Divestitures
1920s	Axles	
	Chassis leaf springs	
	Bumpers	
1930s	Engine valves, tappets, valve seat inserts, hardened and ground engine parts	
	Coil springs	
	Engine valves	
1940s	Eddy current power devices	
1950s	Heavy-duty transmissions	
	Axles	
	Forging	
1960s	Marine products	Marine products
	Locks, hardware, material-handling equipment	
	Appliance and automotive valves	
	Clutches, brakes, and compound rubber golf club grips	
	Overhead conveyor cranes and stackers	
	Fasteners	
	Automotive parts distribution	
	Micro-miniature connectors for electronics and communications industries	
1970s	Hydraulic motors for agriculture and industrial equipment	
	Industrial control and power distribution, aircraft, commercial, appliance, and semiconductor	
1980s	Joint venture in hydraulic motors and transmissions	Materials handling
	Joint venture in ion implanters	
	30% interest in industrial controls	
	Hydraulics	
1990s	Industrial control and power	Appliance Controls
	Engineered components for industrial, aerospace, and automotive markets	Worldwide Axle and Brake business
2000	Sumitomo Heavy Industries Ltd.'s interest in fluid power joint venture	Axcelis Technologies, Inc.
		Automotive Vehicle Switch/Electronics Division

services as low cost, having a unique set of features, or targeting a focused or niche segment in the market.

2. Total Customer Solutions: This view puts the customer, not the competitor, front and center. It argues that deep understanding of customers and the subsequent development of close relationships with those customers to support them in creating their own economic value is the best way to succeed. Firms competing with this focus organize their supply chains to be responsive in providing a family of products and/or services that closely match customer requirements.

3. System Lock-In: This view includes the extended enterprise—the firm, the customers, the suppliers, and most importantly those firms whose products and services enhance the strategy-making firm's own product and service portfolio. The key to success in this view is to identify, attract, and nurture those firms whose products and services are complementary, engaging them in a collective effort to please the customer.

In this study, firms engaged in "system lock-in" far outperformed those employing "total customer solutions" or "best product" strategies in both Market Value Added (MVA) and Market-to-Book Value (Exhibit 1.8).

Thus, to develop business strategy, the firm must think about its positioning not only in terms of its competitors, but also in terms of its customers, suppliers, and potential "complementors." The firm must develop and nurture an integrated value chain, paying particular attention to those firms whose products and services complement its products and services, with the intent of working closely with those firms to provide better solutions to customers than any other set of firms can. Underlying this system-level view of the firm's business environment is a clear understanding of the customers and users of the firm's products or services.

Keeping an Eye on the Customer

For over 30 years, research on the success and failure of products has shown lack of understanding of customer and user needs to be a critical failure mode (Rothwell 1972, Zirger and Maidique 1990). Today, increasingly, we appreciate that understanding customers is core to strategy development and execution. There are many different frames with which one might look at customer and user needs. The Kano Method (Stein 1996) recognizes the sometimes nonlinear relationship between fulfilling a need and satisfying a customer. It defines four types of needs:

1. Must Haves: A must have will never make a customer happy; it is simply expected that the product will have this feature.

EXHIBIT 1.8   **Relative Performance of Three Positioning Strategies**

Source: Hax and Wilde, *The Delta Project: Discovering New Sources of Profitability in a Networked Economy,* Palgrave, 2001.

Strategy	Number of Firms in the Study Employing This Strategy	Relative Market Value Added Performance	Relative Market-to-Book Value Performance
Best product (classic positioning strategy)	74	1.0	1.0
Total customer solutions	67	1.6	1.2
System lock-in	16	4.0	2.0

2. Linear Satisfiers: A linear satisfier is a characteristic that, when improved, improves customer satisfaction in linear fashion. There is typically a minimum threshold for the performance of the feature, and anything better than that threshold is considered good.

3. Delighters: A delighter can only have a positive effect on customer satisfaction, and its absence never creates customer dissatisfaction.

4. Neutrals: Things about which the customer is neutral will not change his or her level of satisfaction with the overall product or service if this feature is lacking or included.

A simplified version of this framework suggests that there are order qualifiers and order winners. Order qualifiers include those criteria that a company must meet for a customer to even consider it as a possible supplier. Order winners are those criteria that will win the order (Hill 2000).

In this book, we use a framework that has been used in various forms in the operations strategy literature for some time (Dangayach and Deshmukh 2001) but adapt it to reflect, at the business strategy level, the expectations customers place on a firm's output. We focus on understanding customer needs along the dimensions of cost, quality, availability, features/innovativeness, and environmental performance (Hayes and Wheelwright 1984) and define these multidimensional attributes as summarized in Exhibit 1.9.

Cost   We define cost as the cost of the product or service to the customer. Cost thus includes not only the purchase price of the product or service, but the cost of ownership as well. Customers, and thus companies, emphasize different aspects of the cost dimension depending on what industry they are in. Customers procuring products such as shampoo or shaving cream are likely to focus their assessment of the cost of the product to them on its purchase price. Customers of products such as manufacturing equipment, automobiles, or airplanes, on the other hand, are likely to consider the product's cost of ownership along with its purchase price including costs to install, run, maintain, and dispose of the product.

EXHIBIT 1.9
Customer Requirements—Cost, Quality, Availability, Features, and Environment

Dimension	Definition
Cost	Purchase price to the customer
	Cost of ownership—lifetime cost of owning, using, and maintaining the product or service
Quality	Tangible characteristics:
	Aesthetics
	Reliability, durability, and safety
	Serviceability
	Intangible characteristics:
	Competence, courtesy, understanding, and communication
	Access and security
Availability	For purchase: Off-the-shelf or make-to-order
	Of new products: Rapid cycle or planned evolution
	Range of products available: Degree of customization
Features/ innovativeness	Inherent characteristics of a product or service
	Degree of innovation
Environmental performance	Degree to which process that produces and delivers the product or service is environmentally sound
	Degree to which the product or service itself is environmentally sound and reusable or recyclable

EXHIBIT 1.10   **Tangible and Intangible Dimensions of Quality**

Sources: Data drawn from Garvin, *Managing Quality: The Strategic and Competitive Edge*, The Free Press, 1988, and King, "A Framework for a Service Quality Assurance System," *Quality Progress,* 1987.

Tangible Quality Dimensions	Intangible Quality Dimensions
Reliability: probability of successful operation, consistency of performance Durability: length of usefulness, dependability Safety: for end user Serviceability: ease of repair Aesthetics: pleasing to the senses	Competence: possession of skills and knowledge required to perform the service Courtesy: politeness, respect, consideration for property, clean/neat appearance Credibility: trustworthiness, believability Understanding: of customer needs and wants Communication: educating and informing consumers Access: approachability and ease of contact Security: freedom from danger, risk, doubt

Companies may choose to compete primarily along this cost dimension. Retail outlets such as Wal-Mart, for example, focus on providing goods at the lowest possible cost to the consumer. Wal-Mart in particular has developed network-based capabilities that allow it to achieve low-cost performance throughout its supply chain. Valero and ARCO focus on providing (relatively) inexpensive gasoline to consumers. JetBlue focuses on providing low-cost air travel.

Quality   Customers evaluate the quality of the products and/or services they procure along many dimensions and integrate these assessments into an overall assessment of the quality of their experience with the organization. In examining quality, it may be important to differentiate assessments of the actual quality delivered from the quality perceived by the customer. Ultimately, some argue, perception has the most effect on a customer's short-term buying decision; in the longer run actual quality experienced by the customer may matter more. A customer's overall assessment of quality judges both the tangible outputs gained as well as the intangible aspects of the purchasing or service experience (Exhibit 1.10).[3]

The tangible aspects of quality include the aesthetics of the product, or output of the service, how reliable it is over 2 period of time, whether or not it is safe, and how straightforward it is to service or repair. The intangible aspects of quality—which may be assessed in making a purchase decision about a product or a service—include the competence, courtesy, and credibility of the people involved in the process, as well as the degree to which those people understand the customers' needs and communicate well with the customers. They also include assessments of the environment surrounding the purchase process or service, including considerations such as accessibility and security.

Business strategists must decide where they want to position their businesses along these various dimensions of quality. The Ritz-Carlton hotel chain, for example, is quite

[3] Note that some authors include product features/innovativeness as a dimension of quality. We choose to include features/innovativeness as a separate category. Responsiveness (willingness or readiness to provide service) is also sometimes included as a dimension of quality. We include responsiveness in our definition of availability.

clear in its specification of a very high quality experience for its customers. The credo for the hotel spells this out:

> The Ritz-Carlton is a place where the genuine care and comfort of our guests is our highest mission. We pledge to provide the finest personal service and facilities for our guests who will always enjoy a warm, relaxed, yet refined ambience. The Ritz-Carlton experience enlivens the senses, instills well-being, and fulfills even the unexpressed wishes and needs of our guests (www.ritzcarlton.com/corporate/about_us/gold_standards.asp).

The Ritz invests heavily in quality management programs to offer a quality experience across all of the dimensions described in Exhibit 1.10. Not only does it offer high-quality tangible outputs ("the finest personal service and facilities"), but the intangibles ("a warm, relaxed, yet refined ambiance") made possible by well-trained Ritz "Ladies and Gentlemen" (as Ritz calls its employees) are high quality as well (Heching 1998).

Availability   The emphasis on time in today's markets is captured in the availability dimension. Customers expect products or services to be available when they want them and/or when they were promised. Availability requirements clearly vary by business. Grocery store customers expect products to be available on the shelves when they go shopping. An out-of-stock item is a lost sale for a particular brand or product in most instances, although it may not be a lost sale for the store itself. Airlines buying airplanes, on the other end of the spectrum, do not expect to buy their products off the shelf, but they do expect delivery when promised. Plans are made months ahead of projected delivery to put the new aircraft into service immediately upon delivery, possibly retiring and replacing another aircraft. Late deliveries can cause great disruption to an airline's entire schedule. Service customers also have different demands for the execution of a service. Customers at McDonald's expect to receive their meals within two to three minutes of ordering, while customers at upscale restaurants expect a longer wait for their meals.

Availability applies to new product introductions as well. Some industries such as consumer electronics focus on fast time-to-market for new products. Others have longer product development and introduction cycles but must deliver new products when promised. Semiconductor equipment manufacturers such as Axcelis, for example, average 2 to 3 years to develop and introduce new products and introduce new platform products about every 10 years. They must, however, meet the requirements of the semiconductor fabricators for new generations of equipment as new generations of semiconductor chips are developed. Although their product development cycles are not as rapid as those of the consumer electronics manufacturers, they must have predictable completion dates.

Finally, availability refers to the variety of products a company offers. There is a wide spectrum of ways in which companies offer customized products or services to their customers. On one end of the spectrum, McDonald's and FedEx offer a moderate range of options to their customers that allow the customers to choose products or services that best meet their needs. On the other end of the spectrum, large-scale projects such as the space shuttle are fully custom designed to the customer's specifications. In between lie companies such as Dell that assemble standard components to customer orders and tailors who cut and assemble parts from standard patterns to customer order. Thus, availability describes the firm's ability to deliver the variety of products or services its customers want when they want them.

Features and Innovativeness Customers also look at the features that are offered by a product or a service and at the level of innovativeness of the product or service. Features are the inherent characteristics of the product or service. One can buy a highly featured car, such as a high-end BMW or Mercedes, or a less featured car, such as a stripped-down Toyota or Saturn. One can buy highly featured services, such as business class fares on full-service airlines like United and American, or less featured services, such as passage on Southwest Airlines' "no frills" flights or JetBlue's "younger, fresher, more innovative, but simpler" airline.

We distinguish the features and innovativeness dimension from the quality dimension. Take the car industry, for example. Some would argue that a BMW is a higher quality car than a Toyota or a Saturn because it is more fully featured and employs more innovative technology. But Toyota often outperforms BMW in minimizing number of defects per vehicle. Thus, we argue that BMW competes better on the features and innovativeness dimension, while Toyota competes better on at least some dimensions of quality. Similarly, some would argue that the experience in business class on United is of higher quality than the experience on JetBlue because it offers more features. They might agree, on the other hand, that the competence, courtesy, and credibility of the gate agents checking them in for their flights—whether on United or JetBlue—are equivalent. Thus, the airlines could be said to be differentiating themselves on the features they offer, while the quality of their services is similar. Alternatively, some would argue that their experience with JetBlue is of higher quality than that with United or American, even though fewer features are offered. Then, differentiation might be based on the quality of key features of the offering, rather than on a full set of features. Because features and innovativeness do not always track directly with quality, we differentiate the two dimensions of performance.

Innovativeness is closely related to features. High-end cars often include advanced technologies—global positioning systems, back-up warning systems, and the like—that represent innovativeness on the part of the organization developing them. Amazon.com's innovative approach to capturing information about visitors to its site and using that information to customize the site to each customer's preferences allows it to offer a more highly featured service.

Environmental Performance Increasing regulation as well as pressure from environmental activists is forcing companies to pay more and more attention to environmental performance as one of the key dimensions along which they understand and deliver against customer requirements.

Environmental performance may apply to the product (or tangible output of a service) itself, or to the process by which that product was made or service delivered. *Design-for-environment programs* focus on products and aim to improve the environmental performance (e.g., energy consumption) of the product during its useful life as well as the reusability or recyclability of the product once its useful life is over. Interface, Inc., a provider of modular carpet, broadloom carpet, panel fabrics, and upholstery fabrics, for example, makes sustainability central to its strategy with its stated goal: "To be the first company that, by its deeds, shows the entire industrial world what sustainability is in all its dimensions—people, process, product, place and profits—and in doing so we will become restorative through the power of influence" (www.interfaceinc.com, January 23, 2007). It designs its products to reuse various materials in their production, and to be readily recycled after use. *Environmental management systems* focus on processes and aim to reduce the environmental impact (e.g., hazardous waste generation) of the processes used to make the products or deliver the services. ISO 14000 and the European Eco-Management & Audit Scheme (EMAS, www.quality.co.uk/emas.htm) are but two of several structures or frameworks for firms to follow to improve environmental performance. Thus, one might assess the environmental soundness of a product or of the process used to make a product or service.

Market Positioning and Making Trade-offs

As business strategists examine the market segments in which they choose to compete, they decide where they want to be positioned along each of these five dimensions—cost, quality, availability, features/innovativeness, and environmental performance. Axcelis Technologies, for example, places strong emphasis on its technology and the resultant feature set it will be able to offer to its customers both in terms of how its products will perform technically as well as how well they support the overall process of manufacturing semiconductors. Quality, particularly in terms of product performance and reliability over the life of the product, is also critical. While Axcelis places great emphasis on delivering new technologies to its market quickly, it does not offer them off-the-shelf. Instead, customers accept a certain lead time to receive their customized products. Customers do expect predictability in those lead times, as they expect to be able to install the equipment when planned. Axcelis emphasizes cost of ownership, not just purchase price, for its customers, as it provides solutions to maximize the uptime, throughput, and yield of its customers' processes. And Axcelis worries about the environmental performance of its products, as its customers are concerned about the environmental performance of the production processes in which they employ Axcelis equipment.

There are trade-offs inherent in managing performance along each of these five dimensions. Some suggest, for example, that the greater the number of innovative features in a product, or the higher its functionality, the more costly it will be. Others suggest that the more highly customized a product is to a particular customer's specifications, the longer the lead time to provide the product will be. Great disagreement exists both in academic literature and in practice about the true nature of the trade-offs. There is evidence that companies trade-off cost with quality, cost with degree of customization, and cost with delivery (availability), but that other types of trade-offs vary by type of organization. Batch facilities trade off cost with delivery, while continuous flow shops that make higher volumes of more standardized products trade-off quality with customization. The reverse is not true, as batch shops do not trade-off quality and customization, nor do continuous flow shops trade-off cost and delivery (Safizadeh et al. 2001). Nonetheless, there are a few issues on which there does seem to be agreement (Da Silveira and Slack 2001):

- Trade-offs do exist and are dynamic, and their relative importance and sensitivity vary among companies.
- Trade-offs are seen as compromises primarily between competitive objectives such as cost, quality, availability, features/innovativeness, and environmental performance, though other types of trade-offs, such as those among the various functional groups in an organization, also exist.
- The *importance* of trade-offs is determined by external—market and strategy—factors. But some trade-offs are seen by managers as existing more in people's perceptions than in reality.

EXHIBIT 1.11
Trade-offs and Performance Frontiers

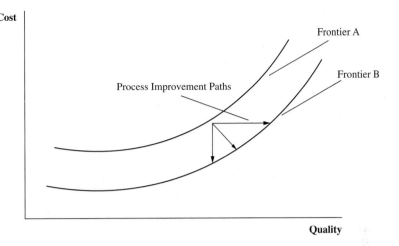

- The *sensitivity* of trade-offs is determined by internal variables—resources, capabilities, and attributes—and different trade-offs may have common or similar sources.
- Trade-offs are easier to visualize in less complex systems.

Much of the literature on trade-offs suggests that one can improve but not eliminate trade-offs (Hayes and Pisano 1996). This literature depicts a series of performance frontiers as shown in Exhibit 1.11 that reflect the trade-offs inherent in the business but allow for improved performance over time.

In this case, the firm trades off cost and quality but can invest in improvements to its processes that allow it to shift from Frontier A to Frontier B, where it still trades off cost and quality, but with better overall performance. It might improve cost performance with no change in quality, quality performance with no change in cost, or achieve some improvement in each. Investments in lean manufacturing techniques, for example, are thought to allow companies to move their performance frontiers and thus lessen the effects of making trade-offs. Thus, there is value in questioning the validity of trade-offs and in understanding opportunities for improving performance along multiple dimensions simultaneously. Rather than make trade-offs among static performance dimensions, business strategists must think through the dynamics of trade-offs over time as they are affected by the development and exploitation of superior capabilities.

We integrate these concepts into our developing model of business strategy in Exhibit 1.12. Now firm positioning is considered not only in the context of the firm's own industry but also in the context of those firms whose products or services complement the firm's own offerings. Firm positioning also requires a deep understanding of what customers want in terms of cost, quality, availability, features/innovativeness, and environmental performance.

Functional Strategy

Functional strategies are the sets of decisions made in each of the functional areas of an organization that determine how it will play in the overall business strategy of the firm. Marketing managers make decisions about product and service positioning, advertising and promotion, and customer relationship management. Research and development managers

EXHIBIT 1.12
Strategy-
Making
Process in
System
Context

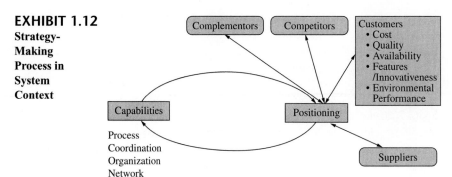

make decisions about technology use, engineering resource allocation, product development process, research and development skills and organization, product prototyping and testing approaches, and involvement of customers in product development. Human resource managers make decisions about organizational structure, workforce skill management, hiring and firing policy, reward and evaluation systems, and pay. Finance and accounting managers make decisions about sources of funding, resource allocation, accounting principles, currency hedging, and internal auditing structure.

Collectively, the decisions made in these various functions make up the overall business strategy of the organization. Successful companies drive synergistic decision making among the functions in support of an overall business strategy and leverage cross-functional capabilities to create and/or support business strategy direction. Exhibit 1.13 integrates this concept in our strategy framework and inserts the strategists' notion of "fit." Each individual functional area may develop its own capabilities that in turn serve the business strategy, or the functional areas may work in concert with one another to create overarching capabilities.

EXHIBIT 1.13   Strategy-Making Framework

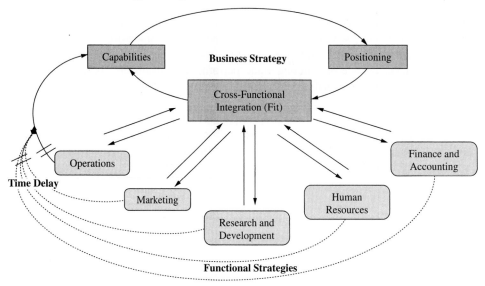

A business strategy is best supported, or created, when the activities undertaken by the functional areas and/or the capabilities they develop complement one another and work together to achieve the goals of the business (Fine and Hax 1985). We refer to this requirement as cross-functional integration or fit.

While the focus of this text is on the decisions made by operations managers about strategic operations issues, we nonetheless emphasize the need for operations managers to work with their functional counterparts in developing, creating, and supporting overall business strategy. Throughout the book we will emphasize the relationship between operations and the new product or service development organization, as these two functions must work closely to develop and deliver successful products and services. With this background on strategy-making, and the fit among corporate, business, and functional strategy, we now turn to a specific discussion of operations strategy, the topic of the remainder of this book.

Operations Strategy

Operations strategists may respond to the requirements of the business strategy by setting their own performance targets or goals. Or they may contribute to the business strategy by developing and exploiting capabilities that allow the business to perform in the areas critical to customers, enter new markets, or exploit new opportunities (Skinner 1969 and 1974). Here we describe the operations goals that follow from the dimensions of performance for the business strategy, the set of decisions operations strategists make, and the way in which these goals and decisions play together in a coherent operations strategy.

Operations Strategy Goals

Exhibit 1.14 shows the five dimensions of customer requirements and maps them against operations performance measures. In each case, operations can affect some, but not all, of the firm's performance along that dimension (Fine and Hax 1985).

Cost

Operations directly affects the cost of the product or service and thus its purchase price (assuming that products are priced to achieve some profit) through its direct or indirect control of the supply chain. It can also affect the product's cost of ownership through joint efforts with engineering (research and development) and/or marketing in the design of the product or service.

Quality

Operations also directly controls the quality of the product or service, again through its direct or indirect control of the supply chain. This is often thought of as a "conformance to specifications" task as operations strives to have all products and services delivered meet the specifications set forth by the developers on behalf of the customers. Operations can also influence the design of a product or service so that it can be produced or delivered with higher quality. It does so, again, in joint efforts with research and development and marketing.

Availability

Operations is primarily responsible for the availability of products or services already in the market and often determines make-to-order versus make-to-stock strategies. Operations'

EXHIBIT 1.14
Business and Operations Strategy Performance Dimensions

Source: Data drawn from Fine and Hax, "Manufacturing Strategy: A Methodology and an Illustration," *Interfaces* 15, no. 6 (November–December 1985).

Dimension	Customer Concerns	Operations Influence
Cost	Purchase price Cost of ownership	Costs of: • Materials • Production • Delivery • Distribution Capital productivity Inventory turnover Design for cost Cost objectives are measured using labor, materials, and capital productivity; inventory turnover; unit cost.
Quality	Tangible characteristics • Aesthetics • Reliability, durability, and safety • Serviceability Intangible characteristics: • Competence, courtesy, understanding, and communication • Access and security	Quality of: • Materials • Production • Delivery • Distribution Design for quality Quality measures include percent defective or rejected, frequency of failure in the field, cost of quality, and mean time between failures.
Availability	For purchase: Off-the-shelf or make-to-order Of new products: Rapid cycle or planned evolution Variety of range of products available: Degree of customization	Availability • Timeliness of delivery of product or service • Ability to respond to volume fluctuations • Timeliness of new product introductions Delivery performance is measured by percentage of on-time shipments, average delay, expediting response time. Flexibility is measured by product mix and range, volume, and lead time for new products.
Features/ innovativeness	Inherent characteristics of a product or service Degree of innovation	Process capability • Capabilities for more featured and innovative products and services • Process knowledge and ability to extend it Design and development capabilities Measures of process capability assess the types of products or services that can be delivered.
Environmental performance	Degree to which process that produces and delivers the product or service is environmentally sound Degree to which the product or service itself is environmentally sound and reusable or recyclable	Environmental performance • Managing environmental performance of suppliers or other partners in the supply chain • Managing the environmental performance of internal production or service delivery operations Environmental performance measures include both emissions measures (water, air, and solid waste) as well as measures of product reuse and recyclability.

flexibility[4] and process knowledge are critical in determining both the variety of features and the availability an organization can offer. The ability of operations to control the supply chain and the timeliness with which products or services can be delivered directly affects availability. The determination of how much flexibility operations can offer is a joint decision with marketing and research and development.

Features/Innovativeness

Generally, features are the purview of the marketing and research and development organizations, although the operations function is influential in determining the range of products, services, or features the firm will be able to provide based on its own ability to deliver them. Process knowledge and innovation are key to the organization's ability to customize output to specific customer needs, to embed new innovations, and to allow research and development to create novel products and services.

Environmental Performance

Finally, operations owns the environmental performance of both internal and external operations throughout the supply chain. It either works with suppliers to achieve adequate environmental performance in their facilities or works to achieve it in internal operations or both. Operations may also influence research and development to design products that are more environmentally sound (e.g., easier to disassemble and recycle).

Operations Goals in Practice

Researchers have identified many alternative categorizations of these operations performance dimensions over the years (Dangayach and Deshmukh 2001). Some identify many categories such as the following 11: low cost, design flexibility, volume flexibility, quality conformance, product performance, speed of delivery, dependability of deliveries, after-sales service, advertising, broad distributions, and broad product line (Miller and Roth 1994). Others summarize the characteristics in fewer categories defined as follows (Spring and Boaden 1997):

- Cost: produce and distribute product (or service) at low cost.
- Quality: manufacture or deliver product or service with high quality or performance standards.
- Delivery dependability: meet delivery schedules.
- Delivery speed: react quickly to customer orders to deliver fast.
- Flexibility: react to changes in product, changes in product mix, modifications to design, fluctuations in materials, and changes in sequence.

Yet others link clusters of operations performance characteristics into stylized business strategies such as those of caretaker, marketer, and innovator (Miller and Roth 1994).

---

[4] Some (Hayes and Wheelwright 1984) include flexibility as one of the dimensions of operations performance. We prefer dimensions that more directly reflect *customer* needs or requirements. Flexibility need not be the cornerstone of product differentiation since it is most often of direct benefit to the producer rather than the customer. A firm may, for example, provide product or service differentiation in expensive ways such as by carrying considerable inventories. For this reason, we think of flexibility as an operations capability that can enhance or enable a differentiation strategy rather than serving as the sole basis of differentiation (Ward et al. 1996).

Some researchers have examined similarities and differences in emphasis on these performance categories by industry, by geography, and over time. One study, for example, found that computer and electronics companies rate high product quality as their most important competitive factor, but computer companies rate innovative features and designs more highly than do electronics companies, while electronics companies place more emphasis on short lead times than do computer companies (Lau 2002). Others have found important differences among various countries or geographies in the emphasis they place on these characteristics. After achieving a high level of quality, for example, Japanese manufacturers turned their focus to time-based competition and innovative products, while the U.S. and Europe continued to rank quality as a critical objective (Kenney and Florida 1993). The Manufacturing Futures Survey, which collected longitudinal data over many years, found that lasting improvements in manufacturing can only be achieved by first building quality, followed by delivery reliability, then flexibility and responsiveness, and then technological leadership. At each step of the progression, cost efficiency is pursued for the given capability set, culminating with an overall focus on cost leadership (Roth et al. 1989, Miller et al. 1989).

Operations Decision Categories

Creating an operations strategy essentially entails making a set of decisions about the structure and infrastructure of operations (Exhibit 1.15) (Skinner 1969, Hayes and Wheelwright 1984). Structural decisions deal with the vertical integration of the operations, its facilities, capacity, and process technology, whereas infrastructure decisions focus on organizational and human resource policies, sourcing and supply chain management practices, quality management systems, planning and control systems, and information technology. Infrastructure is developed over time through persistent day-to-day practice, top management commitment, and cross-functional efforts to create capabilities that support and leverage the firm's structure. Infrastructure decisions usually deal with less tangible outcomes than do structural decisions, but it is the effective integration and synthesis of structural and infrastructural decisions that create long-term operations excellence (Dangayach and Deshmukh 2001).

In making decisions in each of these categories, operations managers strive to ensure that the decisions are mutually supportive and consistent with one another. Further, they aim to

EXHIBIT 1.15
Operations Strategy Decision Categories

Structural Decisions	Infrastructural Decisions
Vertical integration	Sourcing
Process technology	Business processes and policies
Capacity	Product and service generation
Facilities	Order fulfillment
	Service and support
	Workforce and organizational design
	Supply chain coordination
	Information technology
	Capabilities development
	Lean operations
	Quality
	Flexibility

have the collection of decisions support or facilitate the overall business strategy. We describe each of the decision categories briefly here. Each is the subject of a chapter of the book.

Structural Decisions

Vertical Integration   Vertical integration decisions answer questions about how much of the value chain a firm should own. Should they own more or less of the value chain reaching back to their suppliers? Should they own more or less of the value chain reaching forward to their customers? Issues considered include cost of the business to be acquired or entered; degree of supplier reliability; the proprietary or nonproprietary nature of the product or process to be brought in house; transaction costs of contracting through market versus nonmarket mechanisms; and impact on risk, product quality, cost structure, and degree of focus. Chapter 2 will address these questions.

Process Technology   Process technology decisions relate to the firm's investment in the technology it uses to transform materials and/or information into products and/or services. Evaluation of this investment requires a firm to address several questions: Should its process be more labor intensive or more automated? Should it purchase technology or develop it in house, or use some combination thereof? Should it be a follower or a leader in process technology investment? How does its process technology investment fit with its product technology development strategy? Chapter 3 addresses these questions.

Capacity   Capacity decisions establish how much capacity the firm will carry in order to manage both short-term fluctuations in demand and longer-term growth opportunities. Capacity may be added gradually or in large chunks. How should the firm deal with cyclical demand? Should the firm add capacity before it is needed, as it is needed, or after it is needed? Different types of capacity may be added at different times. How should the firm use capacity to influence its competitors' decisions or actions? Decisions about capacity are covered in Chapter 4.

Facilities   Facilities decisions are often closely related to capacity decisions, as firms may add or close facilities in response to a need for more or less capacity, but are often longer-term. In thinking through its facilities decisions, a firm will answer questions about how many facilities it should have, where they should be located, and what they should do. Facilities issues become even more crucial in a global environment as firms decide whether to locate facilities near the local market to increase share in that market, to access local technologies, to reduce costs, or to leverage local talent. These decisions are the focus of Chapter 5.

Infrastructural Decisions

Sourcing   Sourcing decisions follow closely from vertical integration decisions. Once a firm has decided not to own certain parts of its value chain, it must determine what types of relationships it should have with the entities outside the boundaries of the firm. Should the suppliers be managed with the five forces competitive-strategy framework suggested by Porter in this chapter, or with the more cooperative approach modeled by the Japanese *keiretsu?* Chapter 6 will address these questions.

Business Processes and Policies   Business processes, such as product and service generation, order fulfillment, and service and support, cut across functional boundaries in an organization and are critical in serving the customer. Business process decisions include determining and defining critical processes, setting performance goals for each, and then choosing an appropriate organizational design to meet those goals. Some of the organizational design questions include: How should the operations organization be structured? What are the roles of the line and staff organizations? What skills are required in operations? How should those skills be developed and retained? How should operations personnel be rewarded? Chapter 7 focuses on business processes and on the workforce and organizational design as it supports a business process focus.

Supply Chain Coordination While business process management focuses inside the organization, operations management today often requires management of multiple sources, markets, and flows outside the firm as well. Thus, operations managers face strategic decisions about the structure of the supply chains in which they operate and choices of policies with which to operate those supply chains. Should they co-locate their own operations with those of their suppliers? How many layers should they have in their distribution networks? What modes of transportation are appropriate for which links in the supply chain? How should flows of goods among the various entities in the supply chain be monitored? These and other questions are the subject of Chapter 8.

Information Technology Information technology and process technology decisions are closely related, but process technology decisions relate to the physical equipment with which products and services are made and delivered, while information technology refers to the system that moves information around the operations function, between operations and the other functional areas in the firm, and among the players in the broader supply chain. There are a number of decisions operations managers make about their information technology. How automated should information processing be? Should information systems be purchased or developed internally? Should the firm be a follower or a leader in the development and/or use of state-of-the-art technology? How does the information technology investment fit with other investments the firm is making? These questions are the subject of Chapter 9.

Operations Capabilities Development There is some evidence that traditional operations improvement programs such as lean manufacturing, just-in-time, total quality management, focused factories, and the like are misused by managers. Often hastily adopted as an industry best practice or in emulation of a competitor, these programs can yield poor results, wasted effort, and missed opportunities for an organization. When thoughtfully and fully implemented, however, they can be enormously successful. In developing operations strategy, managers must examine such programs and consider the capabilities required to develop and implement them. In Chapter 10, we examine three such programs—lean operations, quality management, and flexibility—and the implications of investing in their development and implementation.

Consistency and Contribution

The concept of consistency or fit in strategy development and implementation is strongly influenced by the population ecology school of thought. It emerged as one of the foremost concepts in the strategic management and organizational theory literature in the particular context of contingency theories linking context or environment, industry and firm structure, and performance. This literature suggests that the critical elements to be aligned are (a) internal to the firm, where the *implementation* of strategy focuses on obtaining fit between the strategy and the organizational structure, (b) external to the firm, where the strategy *formulation* process seeks a fit between the firm's strategy and the environment in which it operates, and (c) internal-external fit, where the *formulation* and *implementation* of strategy are considered to be interactive elements (Nath and Sudharshan 1994).

Business strategy is "integrated actions in the pursuit of competitive advantage" with functional strategies as the supportive activities essential for translating the core strategy into an effective guide for action (Day 1984). To be effective, each functional strategy must support the competitive advantage sought through a specific and consistent pattern of decisions (Hayes and Wheelwright 1984). Just as there is good integration between the business strategy and the functional strategies, there must be consistency and fit among the key elements of an operations strategy as well. The key decisions made in developing an operations strategy must be consistent both internally, in that the decisions made in the various categories (vertical integration, process technology, capacity, facilities, sourcing, business processes and policies, supply chain coordination, information technology, and operations capabilities development) are mutually supportive, and externally, in that the collective set of decisions supports the overall business strategy.

Good operations strategies also contribute to business strategy, directing attention to new business opportunities and providing the needed capabilities to execute them. The philosophy of strategic choice is based on a need to attain internal and external consistency. Failure to match with external business, product, and customer factors can lead to a mismatch with the market and consequently erosion of market share (Chatterjee 1998).

Nucor Steel is an excellent example of a company that has a highly consistent operations strategy that has contributed significantly to the company's business strategy and success over the years. Nucor started as a joist manufacturing company. It developed manufacturing capabilities that it thought it could apply in steel making, and backward integrated to ensure a steady supply of steel for its joist products. It soon learned that its capability to make low-cost steel could be leveraged in the steel market itself, and it began selling steel, thus launching a business that has grown steadily over many years. Its operations strategy thus facilitated entering new businesses.

Nucor's operations strategy is also highly internally consistent. Nucor locates, for example, in rural areas (facilities strategy), which allows it to use nonunion labor (business policy), which allows it to use employees flexibly throughout the facility, thus engendering communication, sharing, and innovation (operations capability). Nucor not only fulfills its own internal requirements for steel, but sells on the outside (capacity strategy), which allows it to sustain a productivity-based incentive program (business policy) that creates an environment of learning and continuous improvement (organizational capability). Nucor buys standard off-the shelf equipment but applies engineering skills (business policy) to that equipment to have it run over rated capacity (process capability) in many cases.

Operations strategy requires understanding the implications of the business strategy for performance in cost, quality, availability, features/innovativeness, and environmental performance. It then requires making structural decisions about degree of vertical integration, size, location, and focus of facilities, what types of capacity to add and when, and what types of process technology are needed. It also requires the development and exploitation of capabilities in cross-functional process management, sourcing and supply chain management, quality and flexibility management, and lean operations as well as appropriate investments in information technology. The development of these capabilities and the structural choices must be made in such a way that they are consistent with one another, with the other functional strategies, and with the business strategy of the firm. Over the years, this has been expressed succinctly by various authors in different ways. Operations strategy is

- Exploiting certain properties of the operations function as a competitive weapon (Skinner 1969).
- A consistent pattern of decision making in the operations function, which is linked to the business strategy (Hayes and Wheelwright 1984).
- A coordinated approach, which strives to achieve consistency between functional capabilities and policies for success in the marketplace (Hill 2000).
- A tool for effective use of operations' strength as a competitive weapon for achievement of business and corporate goals (Swamidass and Newell 1987).
- A collective pattern of decisions that acts upon the formulation and deployment of operations resources. To be most effective, the operations strategy should act in support of the overall strategy directions of the business and provide for competitive advantage (Cox and Blackstone 1998).

Summary: Operations Strategy in Its Business Strategy Context

Strategy is about deciding where you want your business to go and figuring out how to get there. It entails balancing controlled or planned actions (intended/deliberate strategy) with uncontrolled or unplanned patterns of actions (emergent strategy). Operations strategy is developed in the context of both corporate and business strategy. Corporate strategy dictates what businesses an organization will be in, while business strategy determines the market segments in which the business will compete; the partnerships it will leverage in providing solutions to its customers; and the sources of competitive advantage in terms of cost, quality, availability, features/innovativeness, and environmental performance the firm will gain in each segment. The process of developing an operations strategy requires substantial analysis of the market in which the firm operates as well as technical understanding of the operations. Operations strategists must understand the evolution of the industry over time, detect changes in the structure of the industry, and identify competitive challenges and opportunities. Two important sources of information involve benchmarking competitor performance from a customer perspective to reveal standards, gaps, and opportunities and benchmarking competitors' practices to understand how current performance levels are being met and find ways to challenge accepted practices (Bennigson 1996). These activities must be undertaken with open-minded inquiry and thoughtfulness about the appropriate framing of the industry boundaries and opportunities.

The highly iterative process of strategy-making, summarized in Exhibit 1-16, entails *understanding what position the firm wants to or can take in the marketplace, which in turn requires deep understanding of*

- Competitors within the industry
- Suppliers to the industry
- Complementary product or service offerings and the firms offering them
- Spaces outside the industry into which the firm might expand
- Customers and what they want in terms of:
  - Cost

EXHIBIT 1.16 **Integrated Strategy-Making Framework**

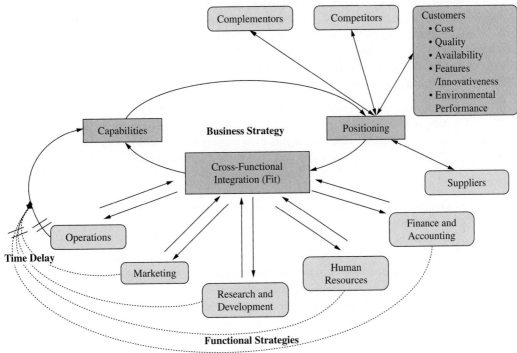

- Quality
- Availability
- Features/innovativeness
- Environmental performance

Methodologies such as conjoint analysis and market segmentation that have not been tra-ditionally applied to operations are increasingly understood to provide important insights into the positioning question and thus into the operations strategy development process (Berry et al. 1991).

The process of strategy-making also entails *understanding what capabilities the firm has to offer or can or should develop both within and across the key functional areas of the firm:*

- Operations
- Marketing
- Research and development
- Human resources
- Finance and accounting

It is the understanding, development, and application of capabilities that is thought to pro-vide the greatest opportunity for strategic advantage in today's markets.

Strategy-making further entails *integrating or synthesizing the activities and capabili-ties of the functions to achieve a coherent strategy or fit in support of a desired strategic direction, or in pursuit of a new strategic direction.*

Product and service realization start with research and development; include design, engineering, procurement, and production; and culminate with distribution, customer service, and warranty management. Thus, operations strategy cannot focus solely on operations-related issues but must encompass the entire chain (Skinner 1996) and support substantial cross-functional analytical, problem-solving, and design activity.

Operations strategy, as one of the functional strategies that support or make up the business strategy, both executes the business strategy and contributes to it.

- Operations managers make decisions about vertical integration, sourcing, capacity, facilities, process technology, information technology, business processes, operations capabilities, and supply chain management to support the business strategy. Specifically, they make decisions in these categories that allow the firm to achieve its desired *position* in the eyes of its customers in terms of cost, quality, availability, features/innovativeness, and environmental performance.
- Operations managers not only respond to the needs of the market as expressed through the business strategy, but they contribute to the creation of the business strategy through investment in capability development both within operations itself as well as with operations' functional counterparts. The continuous improvement of *operations capabilities* creates new business opportunities to be considered by the business strategists.
- Operations managers work closely with their functional counterparts in marketing, research and development, human resources, and finance/accounting to ensure that the decisions they make and capabilities they develop are not only *consistent* but also mutually reinforcing. Often they work together on overarching decisions such as vertical integration, information technology, new product management, and supply chain management decisions to ensure that the best possible *fit* of decisions is made to support the business strategy.

The strategic decision-making process plays a critical role in the success of world-class operations (Dangayach and Deshmukh 2001). World-class firms place a formal emphasis on strategic planning, communicate strategy to all stakeholders, have a long-term orientation, and are clear about the strategic role of operations in their strategy. These organizations also stress continuous improvement efforts, supplier-customer integration, development of human resources, and proper alignment and use of information technology.

Strategy entails more than just finding and emulating best practice. It requires firms to search out new practices by exploring questions such as "What if our competitor had new capabilities with which it could attack our company at its weak points?" and "How would we respond if we were attacked?" It entails seeking out and studying fast-growing competitors to learn about the innovative operational methods they have developed (Hayes and Upton 1998). And it may entail looking beyond the traditionally defined boundaries of the industry to seek new opportunities. Instead of focusing on existing competitors and ways to beat them according to the rules of the currently defined game, companies may seek growth opportunities that require expansion of the bounds of the industry or redefinition of the rules of the game. Only 14% of new business launches look for such game-changing opportunities but derive 38% of their revenue and 61% of their profits from having done so (Kim and Mauborgne 2005).

Conventional planning operates on the premise that managers can extrapolate future results from a well-understood and predictable platform of past experience. Companies adhering to conventional planning practices are often subject to the following errors in planning (McGrath and MacMillan 1995):

1. The company has little or no hard data but, once a few key decisions are made, proceeds as though its assumptions were facts.
2. The company has all the hard data it needs to check its assumptions but fails to see the implications of incorrect assumptions.
3. The company possesses all the data it needs to determine that a real opportunity exists but makes implicit and inappropriate assumptions about its ability to implement.
4. The company starts off with the right data but implicitly assumes a static environment and thus fails to notice that a key variable has changed until it is too late.

"Discovery-driven planning" systematically converts assumptions into knowledge as a strategic venture unfolds using such tools as (McGrath and MacMillan 1995):

1. Reverse income statements that model the basic economics of the business and start with required profits.
2. Pro forma operations specs, which lay out all the activities required to produce, sell, service, and deliver product or service to the customer and then use industry standards to build a realistic picture of what the business has to look like to be competitive. They spell out clearly and realistically where the venture will have to match existing industry standards and in which one or two places managers expect to excel and how they expect to do so.
3. Key assumptions checklist, which is used to ensure that assumptions are flagged, discussed, and checked regularly as the venture unfolds.
4. Milestone planning chart, which specifies assumptions to be tested at each project milestone. Major commitments of resources are postponed until evidence from the previous milestone event signals that the risk of taking the next step is justified.

For operations managers to participate in the radical reinventions that can emerge from these processes, they must engage in revolutionary rather than evolutionary change in many cases. Continuous improvement (evolution), like the benchmarking of best practices, is a prerequisite for success in a competitive world. But incremental change is not sufficient when competitive conditions or new market opportunities dictate a redeployment of operations resources. Successful redeployment of operations resources requires rapidly and simultaneously (Bennigson 1996):

- Changing the mind-set of people in the firm about customer needs, competitive standards, what operations policies and practices are possible or feasible, and how operations should work.
- Changing the strategy itself and specifically how resources are deployed for technology, capacity, vertical integration, and global facilities as well as for the internal development of skills, values, and organizational capabilities and the external supply network for products and services.
- Changing the actions people take from day-to-day as they identify priorities, solve problems, and develop and manage working relationships both within operations and among the functions.

Because of the comprehensive nature of the changes involved in implementing operations strategy in many cases, implementation program teams must pay close attention to gaining understanding and buy-in at every level of the organization and make a heavy investment in communication throughout the process (Bennigson 1996).

At Axcelis, operations plays a critical role in the achievement of the company's business objectives: technology leadership, operational excellence, and customer partnerships. Operations managers have carefully balanced decisions to outsource noncritical activities with the need to reliably deliver leading-edge technology to the marketplace. Through implementation of lean manufacturing concepts throughout the supply chain, they have reduced costs and increased the flexibility of the organization to respond to downturns in the economy. Investments in information technology have brought them closer to their customers. These decisions, made by operations managers about the allocation and use of operations resources, have both implemented the Axcelis business strategy and supported the development of additional capabilities to be leveraged in the future. Making these decisions and achieving these performance outcomes is what this book is all about.

References

Barney, J.B. *Gaining and Sustaining Competitive Advantage.* Reading, MA: Addison-Wesley Co., 1997.

Bennigson, L.A. "Changing Manufacturing Strategy." *Production and Operations Management* 5, no. 1 (Spring 1996), pp. 91–102.

Berry, W.L., T. Hill, J.E. Klompmaker, and C.P. McLaughlin. "Linking Strategy Formulation in Marketing and Operations: Empirical Research." *Journal of Operations Management* 10, no. 3 (1991), pp. 294–302.

Brown, S.L., and K.M. Eisenhardt. *Competing on the Edge: Strategy as Structured Chaos.* Boston, MA: Harvard Business School Press, 1998.

Chatterjee, S. "Delivering Desired Outcomes Efficiently: The Creative Key to Competitive Strategy." *California Management Review* 40, no. 2 (Winter 1998), pp. 78–95.

Cox, J.F., III, and J.H. Blackstone. *APICS Dictionary,* 9th ed. Falls Church, VA: APICS, 1998.

Dangayach, G.S., and S.G. Deshmukh. "Manufacturing Strategy: Literature Review and Some Issues." *International Journal of Operations & Production Management* 21, no. 7 (July 2001), pp. 884–932.

Da Silveira, G., and N. Slack. "Exploring the Trade-off Concept." *International Journal of Operations & Production Management* 21, no. 7 (July 2001), pp. 949–964.

Day, G.S. *Strategic Market Planning: The Pursuit of Competitive Advantage.* St. Paul, MN: West Publishing, 1984.

Dictionary.com. *WordNet® 2.0,* Princeton University. http://dictionary.reference.com/browse/ (accessed May 4, 2006).

Ehrenreich, B. *Nickel and Dimed. On (Not) Getting By in America.* New York: Metropolitan Books, 2001.

Fine, C.H., and A.C. Hax. "Manufacturing Strategy: A Methodology and an Illustration." *Interfaces* 15, no. 6 (November–December 1985), pp. 28–46.

Fishman, C. "The Wal-Mart You Don't Know." *Fast Company* 77 (December 2003), p. 68.

Garvin, D.A. *Managing Quality: The Strategic and Competitive Edge.* New York: The Free Press, 1988.

Grant, R.M. *Contemporary Strategy Analysis: Concepts, Techniques, Applications.* 3rd ed. Oxford: Blackwell Publishers Inc., 1998.

Gupta, A.K., and V. Govindarajan. "Knowledge Management's Social Dimension: Lessons from Nucor Steel." *Sloan Management Review* 42, no. 1 (Fall 2000), pp. 77–80.

Hax, A.C., and D.L. Wilde II. *The Delta Project: Discovering New Sources of Profitability in a Networked Economy.* New York: Palgrave, 2001.

Hayes, R.H., and G.P. Pisano, "Manufacturing Strategy: At the Intersection of Two Paradigm Shifts." *Production and Operations Management* 5, no. 1 (Spring 1996), pp. 25–41.

Hayes, R.H., and D.M. Upton. "Operations-Based Strategy." *California Management Review* 40, no. 4 (Summer 1998), pp. 8–25.

Hayes, R.H., and S.C. Wheelwright. *Restoring Our Competitive Edge: Competing through Manufacturing.* New York: John Wiley and Sons, 1984.

Heching, A. "The Ritz-Carlton Hotel Company: The Quest for Service Excellence." Columbia Business School, 1998.

Helfat, C.E., and M.A. Peteraf. "The Dynamic Resource-Based View: Capability Lifecycles." *Strategic Management Journal* 24, no. 10 (2003), pp. 997–1010.

Hill, T.J. "Teaching Manufacturing Strategy." *International Journal of Operations & Production Management* 6, no. 3 (1987), pp. 10–20.

Hill, T. *Manufacturing Strategy: Text and Cases.* 3rd ed. Boston, MA: Irwin McGraw-Hill, 2000.

Hofer, C.W., and D.E. Schendel. *Strategy Formulation: Analytical Concepts.* St. Paul, MN: West, 1978.

Hoopes, D.G., T.L. Madsen, and G. Walker. "Guest Editors' Introduction to the Special Issue: Why Is There a Resource-Based View? Toward a Theory of Competitive Heterogeneity." *Strategic Management Journal* 24 (2003), pp. 889–902.

Kenney, M., and R. Florida. *Beyond Mass Production: The Japanese System and its Transfer to the United States.* New York: Oxford University Press, 1993.

Kim, W.C, and R. Mauborgne. "Blue Ocean Strategy: From Theory to Practice." *California Management Review* 47, no. 3 (Spring 2005), pp. 105–121.

King, C.A. "A Framework for a Service Quality Assurance System." *Quality Progress* 20, no. 9 (September 1987), pp. 27–32.

Lau, R.S.M. "Competitive Factors and Their Relative Importance in the U.S. Electronics and Computer Industries." *International Journal of Operations & Production Management* 22, no. 1 (January 2002), pp. 125–135.

Lowson, R.H. "Operations Strategy: Genealogy, Classification and Anatomy." *International Journal of Operations & Production Management* 22, no. 10 (October 2002), pp. 1112–1129.

McGrath, R., and I.C. MacMillan. "Discovery-Driven Planning." *Harvard Business Review* (July–August 1995), pp. 44–54.

Mendelson, H., and J. Ziegler. *Survival of the Smartest: Managing Information for Rapid Action and World Class Performance.* New York: Wiley and Sons, 1999.

Miller, J.G., A. Amano, A. De Meyer, K. Ferdows, J. Nakane, and A.V. Roth, "Closing the Competitive Gaps." In *Managing International Manufacturing,* ed. K. Ferdows. Amsterdam North Holland: Elsevier Science Publishers B.V., 1989, pp. 153–168.

Miller, J.G., and A.V. Roth. "A Taxonomy of Manufacturing Strategy." *Management Science* 40, no. 3 (1994), pp. 285–304.

Mintzberg, H. "Five P's for Strategy." *California Management Review* 30, no. 1 (1987), pp. 11–24.

Mintzberg, H. "The Fall and Rise of Strategic Planning." *Harvard Business Review* (January–February 1994), pp. 107–114.

Mintzberg, H., and A. McHugh. "Strategy Formation in an Adhocracy." *Administrative Science Quarterly* 30 (1985), pp. 160–197.

Mintzberg, H., B. Ahlstrand, and J. Lampel. *Strategy Safari: A Guided Tour through the Wilds of Strategic Management.* New York: The Free Press, 1998.

Nath, D., and D. Sudharshan. "Measuring Strategy Coherence Through Patterns of Strategic Choices." *Strategic Management Journal* 15, no. 1 (January 1994), pp. 43–61.

Ohmae, K. *The Mind of the Strategist: The Art of Japanese Business.* New York: McGraw-Hill Book Company, 1982.

Porter, M.E. *Competitive Strategy: Techniques for Analyzing Industries and Competitors.* New York: The Free Press, 1980.

Porter, M.E. "What Is Strategy?" *Harvard Business Review* 74, no. 6 (November–December 1996), pp. 61–78.

Prahalad, C.K., and G. Hamel. "The Core Competence of the Corporation," *Harvard Business Review* 68, no. 3 (May–June 1990), pp. 79–93.

Prahalad, C.K., and G. Hamel. *Competing for the Future*. Boston, MA: Harvard Business School Press, 1994.

Roth A., A. De Meyer, and A. Amano. "Global Manufacturing Strategies: An International Comparison." In *Managing International Manufacturing,* ed. K. Ferdows. Amsterdam North Holland: Elsevier Science Publishers B.V., 1989.

Rothwell, R. "Factors for Success in Industrial Innovations." *Project SAPPHO—A Comparative Study of Success and Failure in Industrial Innovation*, S.P.R.U., 1972.

Safizadeh, M.H., L.P. Ritzman, and D. Mallick. "Revisiting Alternative Theoretical Paradigms in Manufacturing Strategy." *Production and Operations Management* 9, no. 2 (2001), pp. 111–127.

Skinner, W. "Manufacturing—Missing Link in Corporate Strategy." *Harvard Business Review* 47, no. 3 (May–June 1969), pp. 136–145.

Skinner, W. "The Focused Factory." *Harvard Business Review* 52, no. 3 (May–June 1974), pp. 113–121.

Skinner, W. "Three Yards and a Cloud of Dust: Industrial Management at Century End." *Production and Operations Management* 5, no. 1 (Spring 1996), pp. 15–24.

Smith, B.C., J.F. Leimkuhler, and R.M. Darrow. "Yield Management at American Airlines." *Interfaces* 22, no. 1 (1992), pp. 8–31.

Spring, M., and R. Boaden. "One More Time, How Do You Win Orders: A Critical Reappraisal of Hill's Manufacturing Strategy Framework." *International Journal of Operations & Production Management* 17, no. 4 (1997).

Stalk, G., P. Evans, and L.E. Shulman. "Competing on Capabilities: The New Rules of Corporate Strategy." *Harvard Business Review* 70, no. 2 (March–April 1992), pp. 57–69.

Stein, E. "Product Development: A Customer-Driven Approach." Cambridge, MA: Harvard Business School Publishing, 1996.

Sterman, J.D. *Business Dynamics: Systems Thinking and Modeling for a Complex World*. New York: Irwin McGraw-Hill, 2000.

Swamidass, P.M., and W.T. Newell. "Manufacturing Strategy, Environmental Uncertainty and Performance: A Path Analytic Model." *Management Science* 33, no. 4 (April 1987), pp. 509–524.

Teece, D.J. "Economics of Scope and the Scope of the Enterprise." *Journal of Economic Behavior and Organization* 1, no. 3 (1980), pp. 223–247.

Teece, D.J. "Towards an Economic Theory of the Multiproduct Firm." *Journal of Economic Behavior and Organization* 3 (1982), pp. 39–63.

Teece, D.J., and G. Pisano. "The Dynamic Capabilities of Firms: An Introduction." *Industrial and Corporate Change* 3, no. 3 (1994), pp. 537–556.

Tzu, S. *The Art of War*. Philadelphia, PA: Running Press Book Publishers, 2003.

Vargus, A.M. *Cook Discusses Dell's Demand/Supply Balancing Act.* 2003, http://esd.mit.edu/HeadLine/cook_discusses.html (accessed August 20, 2005).

von Clausewitz, C. *On War*. London: Everyman's Library, 1993.

Ward, P.T., D.J. Bickford, and G.K. Leong, "Configurations of Manufacturing Strategy, Business Strategy, Environment and Structure." *Journal of Management* 22, no. 4 (Winter 1996), pp. 597–626.

Wernerfelt, B. "A Resource-Based View of the Firm." *Strategic Management Journal* 5, no. 2, (April–June 1984), pp. 171–180.

Wernerfelt, B., and C. Montgomery. "Tobin's Q and the Importance of Focus in Firm Performance." *American Economic Review* 78, no. 1 (1988), pp. 246–250.

Zirger, B.J., and M.A. Maidique. "A Model of New Product Development: An Empirical Test." *Management Science* 36, no. 7 (July 1990), pp. 867–883.

Chapter 2

Vertical Integration

Introduction

When Hewlett-Packard (HP) started in 1939, it was difficult to find competent suppliers of Class A painted sheet metal enclosures for the company's early instrumentation products. As a result, the company built its own internal sheet metal bending and painting capabilities. As the company grew, it invested in many different types of manufacturing so that by the late 1970s it had become a highly vertically integrated company. HP not only bent its own sheet metal, but plastic-injection molded its own calculator keypads, wound its own transformers, die cast frames for instruments, and fabricated and assembled its own printed circuit boards as well as assembled and tested its end products. It was clear that for HP to control the cost, quality, availability, features/innovativeness, and environmental performance of its product offerings, it had to own these capabilities.

In the mid-1980s, HP's competitive landscape changed, and it began to question its investments in these manufacturing capabilities. A number of new, less vertically integrated companies such as Apple and Sun Microsystems drew HP's focus from the older, more vertically integrated competitors like Digital Equipment Corporation (DEC) and International Business Machines (IBM). A reliable, efficient network of suppliers grew to support the computer and electronics industry with sources of basic sheet metal and plastic parts as well as other electronic components and subassemblies. Customers demanded more integrated products and services. HP began to consider divesting itself of some of the manufacturing processes it felt it no longer needed in order to free up capital for investment in some of the activities that would bring it closer to its end users. In essence, HP asked itself the following questions:

- What core capabilities were required to serve HP's target markets? How should HP get these core capabilities? Should it develop them internally? Or access them from external sources?
- What should HP do with the activities it owned that were no longer core to achieving competitive advantage in its target markets?

In short, HP faced questions that make up the vertical integration decision. This chapter defines vertical integration, describes the factors to be considered in making a vertical integration decision, suggests alternative means of achieving the benefits of vertical integration without full ownership, and outlines a process for making vertical integration (or disintegration) decisions. Although vertical integration decisions can be made for any activity in the business (marketing, research and development, human resources, finance, and accounting), we focus primarily on vertical integration decisions for those areas most related to operations management, product or service design, and delivery. Nevertheless, the frameworks and concepts presented can be more broadly applied.

Defining Vertical Integration

A simplified version of a value chain is shown in Exhibit 2.1. Raw materials (e.g., iron ore) are extracted from their sources, converted to production materials (e.g., sheet metal), fabricated into parts or components (e.g., enclosures), assembled into products (e.g., instruments), delivered to distributors or retailers, and ultimately sold to end users at which time the products enter the reverse supply chain in which the products or components are reused, recovered, or recycled. Service industry value chains are similarly structured. In the fast food value chain, for example, raw materials (e.g., beef and potatoes) are grown and harvested, processed into intermediary materials (e.g., hamburger meat), converted to parts or components (e.g., hamburger patties), assembled into end products (e.g., Big Macs), and delivered to end users. Some value chains are more complex, such as the one that connects banks, credit card companies, merchants, and consumers.

The activities in the value chain take on different characteristics depending on where they are located (Exhibit 2.2). The *upstream* activities, those closest to the raw material sources, are typically capital-intensive processes that require long production runs. The products made in these processes tend to be more standardized, and the product lines relatively narrow. The capital intensity of the upstream processes in many industries results

EXHIBIT 2.1
Generic Value Chain

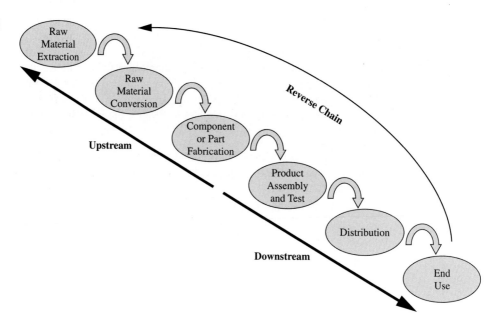

EXHIBIT 2.2 **Comparison of Upstream and Downstream Activity Characteristics**

	Upstream Activities Tend to	Downstream Activities Tend to
Products	Produce a *narrower* line of *more standardized* outputs.	Produce a *broader* line of *more specialized* outputs.
Processes	Employ more *automated, capital-intensive* processes that require *longer production runs* and have *higher break-even* points.	Employ less automated, more *labor-intensive* processes that allow for *shorter production runs* and *lower break-even* points.
Economics	Have *higher break-even* points resulting in *lower responsiveness to market downturns* and *higher profit variability*.	Have *lower break-even* points resulting in *higher responsiveness to market downturns* and *lower profit variability*.

in a high break-even point, which makes it difficult to respond to large fluctuations in the market. Companies focusing on these processes typically have to reduce prices in market downturns and suffer relatively high profit variability with market changes. The steel industry, which is part of many value chains from cars to computers, is a classic example of an upstream operation. Steel mills are large, capital-intensive facilities that tend to produce standardized products and whose economics are driven by the ups and downs of commodity markets for steel products.

Downstream activities, those closest to the end user, are typically, although not always, more labor-intensive processes that allow shorter setup times and thus shorter production runs. The products made in these processes can be less standardized, allowing for broader product lines. The low capital intensity of these processes results in lower break-even points, making it easier to respond to fluctuations in the market. Companies performing these processes can often reduce output during market downturns and suffer less profit variability than their upstream counterparts. Most computer manufacturers today invest relatively small amounts of capital in their final assembly and test processes. Computers are largely manually assembled. Dell Computer is most well known for its ability to offer many custom configurations of computers to its customers at low cost. It can manage its capacity, by hiring and firing workers, fairly closely in market upturns and downturns. Further downstream, distribution operations, while often capital intensive, are usually highly flexible and can handle a wide range of products.

Companies that choose to move upstream and own more of the supply end of their value chain are said to be *backward integrating*. Those companies choosing to move downstream and own more of the customer end of the value chain are said to be *forward integrating*. Companies may also decide to *vertically disintegrate,* shedding upstream or downstream operations by outsourcing them. In our introductory example, HP vertically disintegrated, shedding manufacturing activities such as sheet metal production and printed circuit board assembly, which provided capital for the company to forward integrate into system integration and service activities that brought it closer to its end users. These vertical integration decisions, shown in Exhibit 2.3, shift the boundaries of the organization, changing what activities the organization will perform internally and the nature of its relationships with the resulting suppliers and customers.

Historically, companies have embraced a wide range of vertical integration decisions, ranging from the almost complete vertical integration that Ford Motor Company

EXHIBIT 2.3
Vertical
Integration
Decisions

Source: Printed with
permission from
PRTM, a global man-
agement consulting
firm. Copyright 2006
PRTM, Inc.

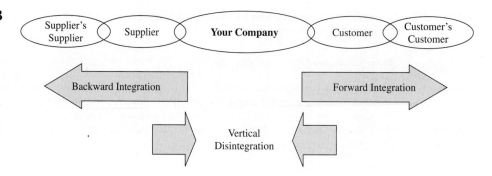

implemented in the 1920s (Womack et al. 1990, and Abernathy and Wayne 1974) to the models of nearly full outsourcing practiced by companies such as Cisco in the telecommunications networking sector. Some companies, such as Hewlett-Packard, have significantly shifted the extent to which they are vertically integrated over their lives.

In addition to vertical integration decisions, some companies choose to make *horizontal integration* decisions. These companies continue to perform the same set of activities they have always performed, but do so in a different industry or market. Contract manufacturers in the electronics industry like Celestica, SCI, Solectron and Flextronics have both vertically and horizontally integrated as they have developed their electronics manufacturing services (Exhibit 2.4). They have, for example, expanded from their initial focus on printed circuit board assembly and test to include materials sourcing and final product assembly and test in their repertoire of activities, thus vertically integrating. At the same time, they have expanded the number of different markets they serve with their printed circuit board assembly business from computer manufacturers to, for example, telecommunications

EXHIBIT 2.4
Contract
Manufacturer
Integration
Moves

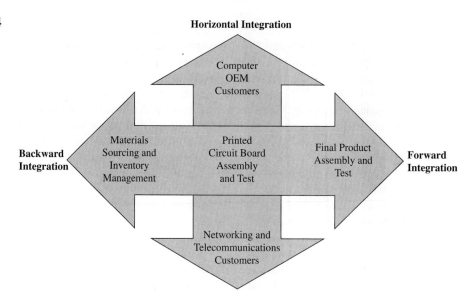

equipment manufacturers, thus horizontally integrating. This chapter will focus largely on vertical integration and disintegration decisions.

The Vertical Integration Decision

The vertical integration decision is complex, but one of the most fundamental and critical decisions a firm makes. Because industries are dynamic and marketplaces are constantly changing, firms must develop the ability to make vertical integration decisions regularly and thoughtfully. The vertical integration decision essentially boils down to answering the following questions:

- How much of the value chain should the company own, i.e., which principal activities will be performed in house? For each of the activities that will be performed in house, will the company have sufficient capacity to meet all internal demand, or will some fraction of work be outsourced?
- Under what conditions should the company change the amount of the value chain it owns? In what direction—toward its suppliers or toward its customers—should it make those changes?

Answering these key questions constitutes making a *vertical integration* decision. A related set of questions about how the company should manage the parts of the value chain that it does not own will be covered in Chapter 6.

There are four sets of factors to be considered in making a vertical integration decision: strategic factors, including whether or not an activity is critical to developing and/or sustaining the core capabilities of a firm; market factors, which focus on the dynamics of the industry in which the firm resides; product, service, and technology factors, which relate technology, product, or service architecture and product or service development to operations; and economic factors, which balance the costs of owning an activity with the costs of transacting for it instead. Some researchers believe that market factors and economic factors are the most important of the four (e.g., Stuckey and White 1993). They argue that what we call strategic factors are subsumed in industry dynamics and thus covered by the market factors. Therefore different frameworks exist for thinking about these issues. We proceed here to provide a detailed description of all four sets of factors.

Strategic Factors

If supplier markets were perfectly reliable and efficient, rational companies would own only those capabilities that would allow them to achieve a unique competitive edge and would outsource all others. Understanding a firm's core capabilities—both existing and needed in the future—and determining whether or not those core capabilities must be owned in order to remain core thus constitute the critical first steps in the vertical integration decision process.

Core Capabilities

In Chapter 1 we describe the notion of a firm as a locus of competitively distinctive, or core, capabilities. Core capabilities are the sets of activities that the company performs better than any other enterprise. They are the sets of skills and systems that a company does at best-in-the-world levels and through which a company creates uniquely high value for customers today and in the future (Quinn 1999). Clearly, the development and preservation of such capabilities is a motive for internalizing them. Core capabilities are often derived not from individual skill sets or systems, but from their integration with and reinforcement by other skills sets or systems. Vertical integration decisions, thus, must address capabilities as *sets* of skills, activities, and systems and take care not to segment critical pieces (Hayes and Pisano 1996). Further, the development and use of capabilities is dynamic, so vertical integration decisions must not only consider current capabilities or needs for capabilities, but future requirements as well. There also may be some essential, but noncore, activities that a firm will choose to internalize because customers have asked for them or because they are needed to defend the core activities. All other activities are outsourcing candidates. In short, if a set of capabilities is critical to future success, then a firm needs to either develop it in house or develop close relationships with the suppliers providing it.

In addition to capabilities, a firm may address its positioning on the cost, quality, availability, features/innovativeness, and environmental performance dimensions in making its vertical integration decisions. If the company is competing on availability, for example, and needs highly flexible operations, it might vertically disintegrate to keep from being saddled with assets it cannot easily use or change when needed. If the company is competing on costs, it may choose to vertically disintegrate and allow its suppliers to gain economies of scale, which in turn will reduce its costs. Recently, firms have been accused of vertically disintegrating to avoid taking responsibility for environmental performance. Conversely, a company may choose to gain control over any one or all of its cost, quality, availability, features/innovativeness, and environmental performance dimensions by owning key operations itself.

As HP approached its vertical integration decision, it determined that control over final product assembly and test was core to providing high-quality products to its customers. Bending sheet metal, fabricating printed circuit boards, and winding transformers, however, were determined to no longer be core. These activities became candidates for outsourcing. A great concern at the company, however, as cries of "hollow corporations" in the United States reverberated in the press, was whether or not the loss of production and manufacturing activities would affect HP's design capability. Indeed, as the years have progressed, the design and development of new products or services, or at least of large chunks of those products and services, has been solicited by the very firms that took over the manufacturing functions some years ago. As more and more firms face the question of whether or not to follow the outsourcing of manufacturing with the outsourcing of design, they must make sure that their core capabilities lie elsewhere (Vakil 2005).

Immediate Access to Capabilities and Capacity

It may not always be possible for a firm to develop core capabilities internally as quickly as it needs them. Firms pursuing new market opportunities or employing new product or process technologies, for example, may need access to a new capability immediately. When the needed capability requires significant time to develop internally, a firm must outsource it to a competent supplier in the short term. Often, this is a transient situation, as the firm will strive to acquire the capability through investment of appropriate time and financial resources in the longer term. Even when the company has some capacity in a capability, the company may want to continue to access that capability externally as well in order to have surge capacity when needed. In short, outsourcing may provide a capability when the internal capability is either not available or has insufficient capacity.

From a strategic perspective, firms ideally own only the activities that are core, essential, or critical and outsource all others. They may, in the short run, need to source certain key capabilities from outside suppliers while building their own, but otherwise will choose to own them. Unfortunately, vertical integration decisions are not quite this simple, as supplier markets are far from reliable and efficient. Economists talk about market reliability and cases of vertical market failure in describing other reasons why firms may choose to own certain capabilities. We turn now to some of those market factors.

Market Factors

Vertical integration decisions inevitably require an understanding of the industry in which the firm resides and the market structure and dynamics of that industry. The literature on industrial organization suggests that there are two classic approaches to organizing: markets and hierarchies. Markets, which apply in vertically disintegrated environments, rely on self-interested exchanges (buying and selling) on the part of buyers and suppliers to coordinate the completion of work. The presence of viable market structures mitigates the need to vertically integrate and provides the advantage of efficient markets and possibly of economies of scale. Hierarchies, on the other hand, rely on the authority associated with legal ownership to assign work to subsidiary entities and monitor its completion (Williamson 1975). Vertical integration to create hierarchies protects a firm against unreliable markets, market control, and dependency risks. In reality, these represent two extremes on a spectrum of options from which firms may choose. We address four major market factors to be considered in choosing where on the spectrum to position a firm: market reliability, economies of scale, market power, and asset specificity and dependency risk.

Market Reliability

Market reliability refers to the ability of a supply base to perform along cost, quality, availability, features/innovativeness, and environmental dimensions. In some cases, creating competition among suppliers encourages improved performance (using market mechanisms), while in other cases direct control over an activity (using hierarchical mechanisms) is required.

Ensuring Performance through Competition   Competition among suppliers has been a cornerstone of free market economies for hundreds of years, as it is seen to drive improvement in supplier performance. In fact, the performance of external suppliers often surpasses that of internal, captive operations that are frequently structured as cost centers and do not themselves compete for work. Lack of interest in noncore operations often leads to underinvestment internally and thus to substandard performance. Obtaining competitive performance is thus a significant driving force for outsourcing those noncore or nonessential operations. When there are many players in the market competing with one another to provide a good or a service, the advantages of providing that good or service internally diminish.

Ensuring Performance through Control   Sometimes, however, such competitive supply markets do not exist. When the supply base underperforms, economists describe it as a case of vertical market failure. Firms operating with unreliable supplier markets may instead choose to vertically integrate to gain control over their own performance. For example, a firm may feel it can better control its **cost** structure by vertically integrating to gain access to cost data and to better understand critical leverage points in controlling costs. A vertically integrated firm might be able to invest in special tools or equipment to improve **quality,** or it might be able to better manage communication of quality information internally among various steps of a production process. It might be able to create better collaborative, cross-organizational problem-solving groups to address particular quality issues. A vertically integrated firm might also be able to more closely manage delivery schedules and coordinate production to achieve improved **availability** performance. It could shorten the supply chain by reducing transportation and delivery times—which can be quite long for distant sites—through co-locating activities in a single facility. A firm seeking to improve its **features/innovativeness** might choose to own its design process and to optimize the links between design and operations. And a firm concerned with **environmental performance** might choose to own the processes that create the biggest environmental issues, as well as the process engineering and possibly equipment design activities associated with those processes in order to minimize their environmental impact.

Ownership of the full supply chain, or at least of the critical parts of the chain, can ensure supply as well as secure channels for output in times of uncertainty. Nucor Steel, now a well-known producer of various types of steel products, first chose to backward integrate into steelmaking in the early 1970s to assure itself a regular supply of steel for its joist manufacturing business. At the time, it consumed very small amounts of steel relative to other buyers and was subject to the capriciousness of the commodity steel markets. Nucor not only successfully eliminated the uncertainty in steel supply to its joist business, but leveraged its steel manufacturing capabilities to become a very profitable player in the steel market itself.

Vertical integration may also be critical to the ability of a firm to offer customized products or services. Dell Computer, for example, owns those processes that are critical to its build-to-order strategy: product final assembly and test, and the direct sales channel. Ownership of these activities gives Dell ready access to good information about its markets and customers and control over the process of getting the end products put together to meet customer needs. Dell chooses not to own the processes involved with manufacturing the components and subassemblies for the computers; these are all standard parts readily available in the market and do not need to be altered to offer custom products to Dell's customers.

There are many ways other than full vertical integration, including different ways of managing or interacting with suppliers, that allow firms to gain the control we discuss here. Use of the Internet is facilitating rapid communication and sharing of information that improves supply chain performance and reduces the impetus for vertically integrating. Nevertheless, there may be times when a company finds it can better control the activities involved in delivering its goods or services by owning them.

Economies of Scale

Economies of scale are achieved when the unit cost of producing a good or delivering a service decreases as the volume of that good or service increases. Scale effects accrue as a result of spreading the fixed costs of an operation over increasing volumes, being able to invest in higher volume equipment that runs at lower cost, or aggregating purchasing volumes to obtain price discounts and the like. We discuss economy of scale curves in more depth in Chapter 4 but point out the relevance of understanding economies of scale to the vertical integration decision here.

Obtaining Scale from Multiple Sources   A supplier providing goods or services to many customers can typically achieve greater economies of scale than can a customer providing its own goods or services to itself, because the supplier produces or delivers in greater volumes than does the customer. Based on data from industry sources, for example, Hewlett-Packard developed an economy of scale curve for printed circuit board assembly (PCBA). In PCBA, components are inserted either manually or automatically onto a raw printed circuit board and then soldered to the board. The data showed a clear scale relationship, exemplified by Exhibit 2.5, between the cost per insertion and the total number of insertions made at each facility.

Firms operating at higher volumes had a clear cost advantage over firms operating at lower volumes. HP learned, after plotting its own sites on the curve, that not only was the company operating at lower volumes, but it was operating on the portion of the curve where small reductions in volume could send cost per insertion soaring. Worse, some of its small operations were not as efficient as those on the industry curve. It became clear to HP after performing this analysis that it either had to outsource PCBA or reduce the number of internal facilities it had performing PCBA to obtain available economies of scale.

Obtaining Scale by Reducing the Effects of Variability and Uncertainty   When a supplier can aggregate demand across customers that experience different demand profiles, that supplier can effectively reduce the effects of variability and uncertainty in demand as well. In Exhibit 2.6, manufacturers A and B have very different demand profiles for sheet metal production.

Although their individual demand profiles fluctuate greatly, when added together (because they are negatively correlated) overall demand (aggregate demand A + B) is smooth. Were A and B to perform their own sheet metal fabrication internally, they

EXHIBIT 2.5
Typical Economies of Scale Curve

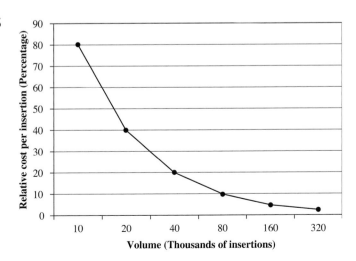

EXHIBIT 2.6
Demand
Variability
Aggregation
Effects

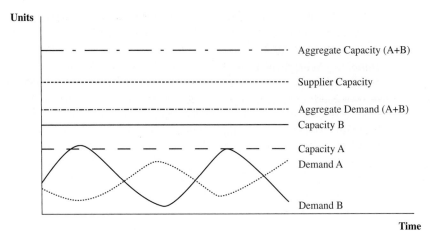

would each likely invest in capacity to cover their individual demand profiles with a little buffer for unpredicted spikes in demand (capacity A and capacity B), resulting in turn in aggregate capacity A + B. Were they both to outsource to a single supplier, however, that supplier would be able to safely cover the aggregate demand with significantly less capacity. Aggregation of demand works both when the demand is relatively predictable and when there is high uncertainty in demand. When multiple customers are all subject to highly uncertain demands, pooling their demands results in reduced uncertainty on a percentage basis. A supplier serving the multiple customers can take advantage of the reduced uncertainty in the pooled demand to invest in less capacity to provide the same service level. In Chapter 4 we show the specific formulas that allow calculation of the required capacities in these cases. The decreased investment in capacity and associated higher capacity utilization rates would in turn allow the supplier to do the work at lower cost.

Aggregating volume improves cost performance through better scale economies and improves responsiveness to variability. It can also provide a company sufficient critical mass to invest in quality improvement, time reduction, feature development, innovation, and environmental improvement efforts that a smaller operation cannot. To achieve the benefits of aggregated demand, however, there has to be some degree of standardization in the goods or services that are being produced or delivered. If there is not, it may not be possible to sufficiently standardize the underlying processes to achieve the desired benefits. There are many examples of suppliers, such as ITT Automotive (Pisano and Rossi 1994) in the antilock braking system business, who work with their customers (in this case the automakers) to standardize products across the industry, allowing them in turn to standardize their own processes and gain economies of scale. The possibility of demand aggregation is dependent on the industry structure; there must be fewer suppliers than customers for demand to be greater at the supply site than at a customer site.

Market Power

Economists talk about where market power resides in a given value chain by looking at the number of players and their relative sizes and profitability. When most of the competitors in an industry are vertically integrated, it can be difficult for nonintegrated players to enter the market. Thus, the vertically integrated players hold the power. When there are few buyers and/or sellers in a market, monopoly or oligopoly conditions exist that concentrate power in the hands of a few. In less vertically integrated industries, there may be certain stages of the value chain in which companies are able to achieve abnormally high returns (known as economic surpluses), suggesting that they wield market power over other stages in the chain. In all of these situations, it may be attractive for participants with less market power (the dominated industry) to enter the dominating industry, thereby shifting the market power balance and in some cases capturing the excess returns. It is not always trivial to make these moves, however. In the computer and bicycle industries, for example, suppliers such as Intel and Shimano have wielded enough power to keep other parts of the value chain from effectively entering their part of the chain.

Asset Specificity and Dependency Risk

Dependency risk arises whenever at least one party in a transaction adapts its process in some way to accommodate the demands of the other party. A manufacturer might, for example, alter its production equipment to accommodate the unique part design of one of its suppliers. A supplier might invest in capacity dedicated to a particular manufacturer. Or both parties might choose to co-locate their production facilities to reduce production or service delivery lead times. When such an accommodation is made, economists say that the relationship entails some degree of asset specificity. In other words, one or both parties make investments in assets—people, equipment, or physical facilities—at the behest of the other party and are unlikely to be able to redeploy those assets for use in another application or with another party. Ultimately, a high degree of asset specificity in a relationship creates dependence or interdependence and, in effect, reduces the number of manufacturers or suppliers who can enter into that specific transaction, thus concentrating market power. The more market power is concentrated, the closer the industry moves to a hierarchical rather than a market-driven structure and the higher the degree of vertical integration.

There are six types of asset specificity: *Site specificity* occurs when buyers and sellers locate fixed assets, such as beet growing fields and sugar beet refining plants, in close proximity to minimize transport costs and maximize assets, as in sugar content recovered from the beets. *Dedicated assets* are discrete investments in general-purpose plant and equipment that are made at the behest of a particular customer and in essence represent capacity that is dedicated to that customer. *Physical asset specificity* occurs when one or both parties to a transaction invest in equipment or tooling (specialized dies) specific to that transaction and with a low value in alternative uses. *Human capital specificity* occurs when employees develop skills that are specific to a particular buyer or customer relationship. *Brand name capital* entails investments in brand building, and *temporal specificity* refers to investments made that link the two parties at a particular point in time.

Vertical integration decisions depend not only on asset specificity, but also on the frequency of transactions between two parties (Exhibit 2.7). When both transaction frequency and asset specificity are high, such as in the development and manufacturing of specialized components, vertical integration is likely to look more attractive than when transaction frequency and asset specificity are both low, such as in office lease contracts where detailed, standardized contracts will do. When asset specificity is low but transaction

EXHIBIT 2.7   Vertical Integration Options Based on Transaction Frequency and Asset Specificity

Source: Adapted from Stuckey and White, "When and When Not to Vertically Integrate," *MIT Sloan Management Review* 34, no. 3 (Spring 1993), pp. 71–83.

	High Asset Specificity	Low Asset Specificity
High Transaction Frequency	Vertical integration	Standardized transactions not necessarily requiring contracts
Low Transaction Frequency	Detailed, probably unique contracts	Detailed, standardized contracts

frequency is high, such as in many retail operations, standardized transactions are likely to be sufficient. On the other hand, when transaction frequency is low and asset specificity high, such as in a major construction project, contracts are needed and are likely to be unique to the specific relationship (Stuckey and White 1993).

In summary, vertical integration decisions must address the market factors of market reliability, economies of scale, and market power.

Product, Service, and Technology Factors

There are also product-, service-, and technology-related factors to consider in making vertical integration decisions. The first two have to do with how the firm wants to manage its intellectual property, particularly that surrounding core products, services, and technologies. An integration decision can also provide an advantage or differentiation for a specific technology. Finally, a great deal has been made of whether a design is modular or integral. Vertical integration will have the advantage of possibly providing a technology advantage. On the other hand, it could have a disadvantage of insourcing a modular part of the design that could be efficiently outsourced.

Intellectual Property

Whenever a firm outsources an activity, particularly an activity associated with critical technologies, products, or services, it runs the risk that the intellectual property associated with that activity will be given to its competitors. Product secrets could conceivably be lost. Thus, intellectual property must be considered in making a vertical integration decision and managed carefully through the implementation of that decision. This issue is particularly relevant to growing companies with new products such as semiconductor companies and biotech companies. Intellectual property can also be a process issue if a particular process is proprietary, in which case a company needs to be careful about licensing its manufacturing.

Technology Differentiation

Vertical integration can be a way to achieve technological differentiation and to rapidly accommodate technological change. Conversely, vertical integration can lock a firm into a technology base, making it harder for the firm to adopt new technologies quickly when needed. As we discussed in the section on strategic factors, a firm may decide that a particular technological capability is core and will ultimately seek to develop and own that technology. But the firm must also remain aware of the risk of having core capabilities turn into what have been called core rigidities (Leonard-Barton 1994) and must remain ready to divest itself of old technologies to make way for new.

Divesting a technology that has been vertically integrated can be very difficult as doing so may have grave consequences. Kodak, for example, over its 100-year history cycled multiple times from being highly vertically integrated to being less so and back again (The History of Kodak 2005). Kodak's focus for many years was the production of film and paper, which it managed internally from start to finish including the ossification of cow bones to make its own gelatin. In 1994, at the dawn of the digital revolution in photography, however, Kodak began to reduce its investments in U.S. film and paper operations, moving many overseas, exiting some, and consolidating several in Rochester to increase its focus on digital imaging solutions. At the same time it began acquiring firms such as Ofoto to increase its presence in the digital photography space. The size and scope of Kodak's operations made it difficult to react quickly in a rapidly changing marketplace. Kodak's chief U.S. competitor, Polaroid, did not fare as well in the transition, in part because it was slow to decide what to do with some of its highly technical operations.

Making vertical integration decisions for the operations function requires understanding the interrelationships among research (which develops the knowledge about the technology), product or service development (which applies the knowledge to specific outputs), and operations (which produces or delivers the outputs). The product and technology factors take these interrelationships into account.

The first question a firm typically asks is whether or not it should own the development of a particular technology, usually requiring an investment in research. To make this determination, the firm must ask two other questions. First, do the technological capabilities in question exist, or do they have to be developed? When the capabilities exist outside the firm, it is likely best to establish some relationship short of full ownership with the technology provider to access the capabilities. Second, is the technology stand-alone or modular, or is it an integral part of a larger system? When a technology is separable from the rest of a product or system, it is easier to substitute alternative technologies without affecting the performance of the whole. When, on the other hand, the technology is integral to the product or system, it is important to have a closer relationship with the provider as the use of that technology will have a significant effect on the ultimate performance of the product or system. Exhibit 2.8 provides a matrix of the likely choices to be made as these questions are answered. An integral technology that still must be developed is the most risky to a firm and thus the most likely candidate for ownership. A stand-alone technology that has already been developed, on the other hand, is the least risky and a candidate for external ownership.

Companies should also ask how well the technology in question fits their current capabilities. A small company might not want to vertically integrate into a set of operations

EXHIBIT 2.8   **Technology Access Vertical Integration Decisions**

Source: Adapted from Chesbrough and Teece, "When is Virtual Virtuous? Organizing for Innovation," *Harvard Business Review*, 74, no. 1 (1996) pp. 65–73.

	Capabilities Exist Outside	Capabilities Must Be Developed
Autonomous or Stand-Alone Technology	Do not vertically integrate	Ally with technology developer or bring technology in house
Systemic or Integrated Technology	Ally with technology provider with caution	Vertically integrate, bringing technology development in house

with vastly different technologies and skill sets. A larger company may have a broader range of operations, but there is still a strategic question as to whether a particular set of capabilities is a good match for the others.

Modular or Integral Product Architecture

A decision to own the development of a technology may or may not suggest ownership of the operations associated with that technology. Product architectures are described as modular or integral (Ulrich and Eppinger 2004). A modular product architecture is one in which each element or component of the product plays a separate function, with one-to-one mapping between the components and those functions. A Swiss Army knife is an excellent example of modular product architecture, as each component of the knife (e.g., corkscrew, scissors, knife) plays a different and separate function. A second example that is often cited is the personal computer, as microprocessors, power supplies, and optical and hard drives are easily substituted within designs. Modular architectures are favored when a company wants to be able to easily produce, customize, and/or service its products. Modules are easily swapped to change the features of a product or to repair it.

Integral architectures on the other hand have a one-to-many mapping of components and functions. Integral architectures are used primarily to increase product performance. In effect, no efficiency or effectiveness is lost in the clear separation of functions. Rather, all parts of the product work together to optimize performance. High-performance motorcycles are examples of integral products. BMW motorcycles, for example, use similar parts to those used in other bikes, but the parts are very much tuned to work with each other. In automobiles, parts such as interior panels are highly dependent on the design of other parts of the vehicles.

The more integral a part is to a product or service design, the more likely the organization will be to own the capability for producing that part. This depends, however, on the extent of the organization's dependence on the outside supplier. If it is dependent for capacity only, it is more likely to outsource. If it is dependent for knowledge as well, it may choose to insource or form a close alliance (Exhibit 2.9).

Technology and product factors are particularly important in decisions about vertical integration of design functions. When design activities are the focus of a vertical integration decision, the firm should ask how core that design activity is to its strategy, whether there is a viable market of providers of the requisite design services, and what economies of scale an external firm might offer, particularly on highly standardized designs. These decisions also depend heavily on the architecture of the firm's products or services and the degree of modularity in that architecture (Ulrich and Ellison 2005). In simple terms, product design has two elements: component design and system design. Component design focuses on the parts or subassemblies that make up the product or system, and system

EXHIBIT 2.9 Part Access Vertical Integration Decisions

Source: Adapted from Fine, *Clockspeed: Winning Industry Control in the Age of Temporary Advantage,* Perseus Books, 1998.

	Dependent for Capacity Only	Dependent for Knowledge and Capacity
Autonomous, Stand-Alone, or Modular Item	Best outsourcing opportunity	A potential outsourcing trap—consider vertical integration
Systemic or Integral Item	Can live with outsourcing	Worst outsourcing situation—should vertically integrate if possible

EXHIBIT 2.10
Conditions Under Which Pairs of Design and Production Activities Should Be Integrated and Jointly Managed

Source: Adapted from Ulrich and Ellison, "Beyond Make-Buy: Internalization and Integration of Design and Production," *Production and Operations Management,* 14, no. 3, (2005), pp. 315–330.

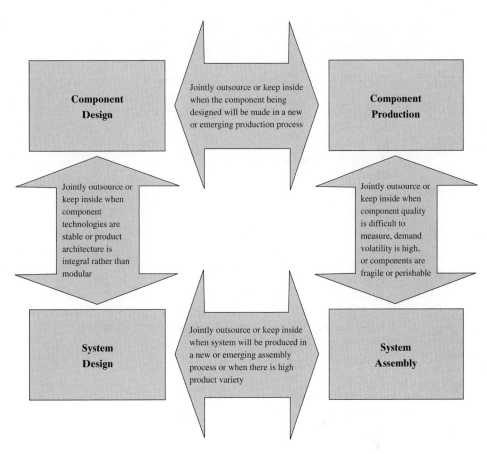

Component Design

Jointly outsource or keep inside when the component being designed will be made in a new or emerging production process

Component Production

Jointly outsource or keep inside when component technologies are stable or product architecture is integral rather than modular

Jointly outsource or keep inside when component quality is difficult to measure, demand volatility is high, or components are fragile or perishable

System Design

Jointly outsource or keep inside when system will be produced in a new or emerging assembly process or when there is high product variety

System Assembly

design integrates the parts or subassemblies. Similarly, the production or service delivery task can be split into component production and system assembly. There are specific conditions under which one would choose to keep some or all of these activities together, either inside the firm or outsourced together to the same supplier. Exhibit 2.10 presents recommendations for vertical integration for pairwise combinations for components, systems, design, and production. For example, keep component design and component production together when the component being designed will be made in a new or emerging production process. Keep system design and system assembly together when the system being designed will be produced in a new or emerging process or when there is a high degree of product variety.

Thus, although we focus largely on operations decisions in this chapter, it is critical to assess the relationships between operations activities and other activities in the firm including not only research and development, but marketing as well. In this case, understanding whether or not a particular technology is important to the firm may suggest that the firm not only develop that technology, but maintain the capability to produce it as well. Further, product architecture—whether integral or modular—suggests different vertical integration choices. Finally, there may be circumstances under which a firm wants to keep a design and production pair together, whether internally or externally, to maximize communication and management of uncertainty.

Economic Factors

The strategic, market, and product and technology factors we have discussed so far focus on the intangible considerations in a vertical integration decision. These intangible factors often determine the vertical integration choice, but it is helpful to understand the economics of the decision as well. An economic analysis of a vertical integration decision involves understanding the costs of producing the product or delivering the service both internally and at the supplier site. It requires understanding the costs of transacting and coordinating with the supplier as well as the costs of transporting goods from the supplier to the buyer. Finally, it requires understanding the investment that would have to be made to develop the capability internally.

Investment Costs

A firm's decision to acquire or develop a capability internally must consider the investment costs associated with that decision. If the capability is acquired, there is the cost of buying another company or part of a company. If the capability is developed in house, there are likely to be capital costs (for equipment and space), people costs (for hiring and training), systems development costs, and inventory costs (for the initial investment in inventory). Conversely, a firm's choice to vertically disintegrate requires the firm to invest in shedding one or more operations (e.g., layoffs, facility shutdown, and sale). It seeks a return on this investment in reduced design, production, service delivery, and transaction costs.

Design, Production, and Delivery Costs

The firm that chooses to vertically disintegrate substitutes the direct costs of designing, making, and/or delivering the product or service—the materials, labor and overhead costs—for the cost of procuring that design work, product, or service from an outside vendor. The purchase price for a design, product, or service will cover the vendor's materials, labor, and overhead costs and will include a profit for the vendor as well. Materials and labor costs are typically fairly straightforward to compare. A vendor may achieve economies of scale in the materials area as well as in production as discussed earlier by aggregating demand and making higher-volume purchases from its vendors. Labor cost advantages may exist due to the vendor's location. Location in low-wage countries, for example, will decrease labor costs as long as productivity is about the same.

Overhead costs are the most difficult to compare, as decisions must be made about what to include in the calculations and what costs will actually go away if a process is outsourced. Design, production, and service delivery overhead (the cost of supervisors and managers, equipment depreciation, and floor space), procurement overhead (the cost of purchasing, materials engineering, and purchasing management), and process engineering (the cost of process engineers and engineering management) must all be considered. There may be information technology costs that are affected by the decision as well.

In addition to the costs of actually making a product or delivering a service, there are costs for transporting goods from the supplier to the buyer's facilities. These costs vary widely depending on the locations of the buyer and supplier. Because transportation costs can be significant, many buyers seek suppliers who have facilities in close proximity to the buyers' facilities or are willing to relocate.

Transaction Costs

The costs that are most often missed in analyses of vertical integration decisions are transaction costs, and they can be significant (Williamson 1975). Transactions can be structured in a wide range of ways from standard arm's length contracts to contracts that are more specific to the given pair of firms. Lately a growing trend has been to include arrangements such as revenue-sharing agreements and buybacks. The structure of the transaction itself will affect the magnitude of the associated transaction costs. Transaction costs include the costs of searching for, contracting with, controlling, and recontracting with suppliers, most of which are incurred by the procurement or partnership management organizations. Transaction costs also include the costs of coordinating with a supplier to do engineering, forecasting, scheduling, and information sharing. Clearly, transaction costs rise with the frequency of transactions. The more transactions two firms execute, the higher the cost of the partnership. While transaction costs may be reduced by investments in information technology that speed communication of forecast, planning, and engineering data across both national and international boundaries, they are still significant.

Both contracting and coordinating costs increase significantly when there is uncertainty in markets or when suppliers are unreliable. It is virtually impossible to write a contract with a supplier that is robust enough to anticipate and cope with all possible contingencies, particularly in highly uncertain markets. Contract renegotiation when a major issue arises unexpectedly is a near certainty. Unfortunately, contract renegotiation is often limited to the two parties on the original contract rather than considering the full range of possible suppliers available at the time of the first negotiation. This effectively concentrates market power, creating what economists refer to as the *small-numbers bargaining problem.* Even when contracts are not renegotiated, time and money are spent communicating and resolving the unexpected situation.

The costs a firm must consider in making a vertical integration decision are summarized in Exhibit 2.11. While numbers may not drive the decision, they are helpful as they allow the implementers to develop budgets and target performance for the new capability or new outsourcing relationship. If, for example, a firm expects to save $1 million a year by outsourcing production of a particular part, it will want to set a budget based on that cost savings and do an audit of the results of the outsourcing action after it is complete.

A Spectrum of Options

So far, we have focused on ownership as the key variable in making a vertical integration decision. In fact, a firm may choose to *virtually integrate* by developing relationships with its suppliers or customers that fall short of complete ownership. There is a wide spectrum of such relationships. At one end of the spectrum, a firm has an arm's length relationship with a supplier. At the other end is full ownership of the company. In between are a range of other relationships such as joint ventures, alliances, and so forth. While we will cover these types of relationships in more detail in Chapter 6, it is important to point out here that there are alternatives to vertical integration. Long-term contracts, joint ventures, strategic alliances, technology licenses, and asset ownership, for example, may provide many of the benefits of vertical integration, while avoiding the inherent risks of owning a capability outright.

EXHIBIT 2.11 Comparison of Costs for Internal Ownership versus Outsourcing

Type of Cost	Cost of Owning an Activity	Cost of Outsourcing an Activity

Design, production, or service delivery costs	Materials
	Labor (Direct)
	Overhead
	   Production
	   Procurement
	   Engineering
		Purchase cost includes:
		   Labor (Direct)
		   Materials
		   Overhead
		   Vendor profit

Transportation and logistics costs	Cost of moving output from site of creation to site of use	Cost of moving output from vendor's location to buyer's site of use
Investment costs	Capital (equipment and space) People resources (hiring, training) System development Inventory	
Transaction costs		Contracting costs including purchasing, sales, marketing, taxes, legal Coordination costs including engineering, forecasting, production scheduling

Summary of the Factors For and Against Vertical Integration

The factors for and against vertical integration are summarized in Exhibit 2.12. A firm will vertically integrate to control activities it considers core or essential, to cope with unreliable supplier markets, to change the structure of its industry, to control technologies, particularly those that are integral to its products or systems, and to minimize transaction and

EXHIBIT 2.12 Factors for and Against Vertical Integration

	Vertically Integrate to:	Vertically Disintegrate to:
Strategic Factors	Develop and retain core and essential capabilities	Access a core or essential capability externally while working on its development internally
Market Factors	Control cost, quality, availability, features/innovativeness and environmental performance in unreliable markets Shift power relationships in the industry Reduce dependency (due to asset specificity) on suppliers	Leverage competition among suppliers to access best-in-class performance Aggregate demand at suppliers thus generating economies of scale and improved responsiveness to variability in demand
Product and Technology Factors	Control integral or critical technologies Integrate design and production or service delivery under uncertain conditions	Access current technologies not available internally Obtain leverage available from modular product architectures
Economic Factors	Minimize transportation and logistics costs Minimize transaction (contracting and coordination) costs	Access lower production or service delivery costs Minimize investment costs

Vertical Integration Decision-Making at Genzyme

Genzyme Corporation is a diversified biotechnology company with 2005 revenues of $2.7 billion (www.genzyme.com, September 1, 2005). In 2004, Genzyme grappled with two vertical integration decisions, each considering the adoption of a new production process (Haupt 2005). The first, encapsulation, is the process for making capsules. Biopharmaceutical companies generally prefer capsules to tablets during development and early stage clinical trials because they require less formulation than tablets, so more easily accommodate frequent formulation changes. The second is the process of manufacturing high-potency compounds. High-potency compounds are active pharmaceutical ingredients or intermediates that are capable of exerting strong chemical or physiological effects. These compounds are important building blocks for the development and production of many end products.

Genzyme's company strategy is to vertically integrate where possible, as it believes that it derives competitive advantage from its investment in process technology. So, it approached these two decisions predisposed to invest in in house capability. In each case, however, there were complicating strategic, market, product and technology, or economic factors that made the decision less clear.

In the short run, there were two major arguments against acquiring *encapsulation* process technologies. First, from a strategic perspective, Genzyme did not view encapsulation as a core competency and did not want to divert resources from other more core activities. Second, from a market perspective, there were plenty of capable outside suppliers who could work with Genzyme to achieve its time-to-market objectives. While Genzyme could catch up and be competitive with those suppliers in the long run, it would take some time to ramp up its own processes to achieve similar performance. It was thus difficult to make a short-term case for

investment in encapsulation. A long-run argument could be made, however, to invest in encapsulation in support of the design and development of future products that were core to Genzyme's strategy. The turnaround time needed to support the design and development process for these core products might best be achieved with internal operations. Availability of products in the current pipeline, however, was best assured by continuing to employ subcontractors.

The question of whether to build the *high-potency compound* processes came about as a result of an acquisition Genzyme made of a company that had been outsourcing production of its compounds. Following its corporate policy of vertically integrating in processes where possible, it began an investigation of the possibility of taking on high-potency compound production for its new subsidiary. High-potency compounds have significant safety implications including major constraints and requirements for containment, isolation, and protection of workers. The market for high-potency compounds is a niche market, but highly lucrative. There are high barriers to entry and many companies outsource their production.

An evaluation of the contract manufacturers that could provide high-potency compounds identified market and economic issues. From a market perspective, there were capable external suppliers for the compounds. From an economic perspective, a new facility at Genzyme would be significantly underutilized in the beginning until new products could be brought in. Although it appeared that the first product produced in the internal facility could be highly profitable, it could be made even more profitably through a contractor. Although in this case the factors were not clear, the company had time to continue its outsourcing arrangements and further examine the risks and benefits of vertically integrating as it watched the markets develop and potential volume materialize.

transportation costs. Conversely, a firm will choose to contract with an external supplier to access a capability it does not have time (in the short run) to develop internally, to take advantage of competition among suppliers and the benefits of aggregated demand, to access a variety of technologies, and to reduce costs and minimize investment.

Making a vertical integration decision requires carefully assessing the pros and cons associated with each of these factors. See the sidebar "Vertical Integration Decision-Making at Genzyme" for an illustration of how the factors might be applied.

Making a Vertical Integration Decision

Making a vertical integration decision is not simply a matter of applying the set of factors in Exhibit 2.12. It entails an industry analysis and a clear understanding of the company's strategy. In addition, the vertical integration decision is not as simple as choosing between keeping an activity in house or having a supplier do it. There is a spectrum of options from which to choose. We suggest the following process for making a vertical integration or dis-integration decision:

1. Apply the core capabilities screen.
2. Assess the industry context and dynamics to identify opportunities.
3. Identify alternative value chain structures.
4. Assess alternatives and choose one.
5. Implement.

Step 1: Apply Core Capabilities Screen

Use the list of core and essential capabilities identified in the firm's business strategy to determine which activities to own and which are candidates for outsourcing. Identifying what a firm's core capabilities should be is difficult enough in a static world. With rapidly changing industry structures, the task is more difficult. Companies today are advised to constantly review their ideas about what is core and noncore and to react accordingly in thinking through ownership decisions.

Our introductory example about Hewlett-Packard illustrates the dynamic nature of core capabilities. In the 1980s, HP identified a new set of core capabilities that were more customer focused, and determined that many of its manufacturing activities were no longer core as they once had been. The manufacturing activities that remained core or essential were those associated with specific technologies, such as those in the delicate sensors in medical instrumentation. Later, HP determined that its instrumentation businesses in general were not core to the computing side of the business and spun them off as Agilent Technologies. As the computing, communications, and information technology markets continue to evolve, HP continues to reassess what is core and what is not.

Step 2: Assess Industry Context and Identify Opportunities

Prepare a flowchart of the company's value chain showing the flow of materials and/or services from the raw material sources to delivery to the end user. Exhibit 2.13, for example, depicts Dell's value chain with its major suppliers for plastic, metal, and electronic parts and subassemblies.

Activities should be disaggregated to natural business or work units that cannot reasonably be further disaggregated from an ownership perspective. In the computer industry, for example, disaggregating printed circuit board fabrication into smaller work units does not make sense, but disaggregating integrated circuit design and fabrication from assembly and test is reasonable.

The flowchart should also be annotated with information about:

- Number of players at each stage of the value chain (e.g., number of disk drive manufacturers)

EXHIBIT 2.13
Dell Computer's Value or Supply Chain Map

Source: Data drawn from Kraemer and Dedrick, "Dell Computer: Organization of a Global Production Network," Working paper, Center for Research on Information Technology and Organizations, 2002.

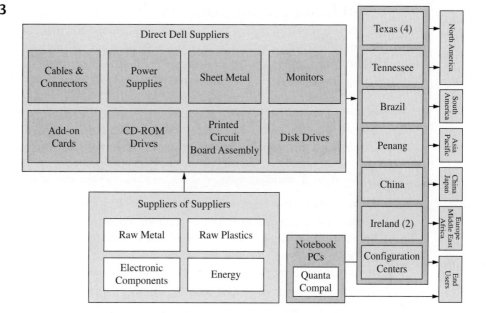

- Sizes of players at each stage of the value chain (e.g., annual sales volume per disk drive manufacturer).
- Types of transactions between players (e.g., spot market purchases of electronic components, long-term contracts for design and production of disk drives).
- Frequency of transactions between players (e.g., weekly transactions, annual contract negotiations).
- Volumes of transactions between players (e.g., dollar volume of disk drives flowing from Seagate to Dell).
- Ownership connections (e.g., joint venture relationships, equity stakes).

Use the flowchart to identify weaknesses and opportunities in the value chain that might be exploited with a vertical integration move. Stuckey and White (1993) suggest the following steps in making that assessment:

Perform a Static Analysis of the Industry

1. Search for existing cases of supply uncertainty.
   - Assess and, where possible, measure degrees of dependency or asset specificity.
   - Identify bilateral monopolies/oligopolies where market power is concentrated in the hands of a few companies.
   - Measure transaction frequency (e.g., number of deals/year).
   - Measure degree of uncertainty (e.g., variance over time in demand, output).
   - Examine information flows, seeking weak links.
2. Search for existing market power defense/creation reasons to integrate.
   - Measure economic surplus by stage of the industry chain or business system.

- Identify cases of sustained market power asymmetry (monopoly, oligopoly).
- Test if vertical integration by weak participants would add more value to them than it would cost them.
- Test if vertical integration by powerful participants would strengthen their positions (e.g., raise barriers to entry, allow price discrimination).

Perform a Dynamic Analysis

The locus of market power in the value or supply chain is dynamic. In the computer industry, for example, the considerable power once held by the vertically integrated computer suppliers is held today by their suppliers. Understanding the potential for such shifts is the objective of the dynamic analysis, which aims to predict changes in industry structure.

1. Predict changes in market power due to changes in industry structure.
2. Predict future changes in industry structure. Focus on changes in power symmetry between stages, numbers/sizes of buyers and sellers, asset specificity (e.g., due to technological change), transaction frequency.
3. Infer changes in supply uncertainty and instances of market power asymmetry.
4. Predict any changes in vertical behavior by other participants.

The objective of the static and dynamic industry analyses is to identify both opportunities for strengthening the firm and weaknesses in the firm's value chain that might be exploited.

Step 3: Identify Alternatives

From an understanding of where the firm wants to focus its resources (on its core capabilities) and of where opportunities lie in the industry value chain structure, identify options for making vertical integration moves. Then, realistically identify practical options for acquiring or shedding a capability. HP, for example, considered several options for shedding its sheet metal operations that ranged from full outsourcing to partial ownership options as shown in Exhibit 2.14. To be useful, the final set of alternatives identified

EXHIBIT 2.14
Options Considered by Hewlett-Packard to Vertically Disintegrate Sheet Metal Operations

Option Type	Characteristics
Full outsourcing	Find outside suppliers for all sheet metal parts Close down internal sheet metal operations Offer employees other jobs within HP or voluntary severance packages
Sale of business	Find potential buyer for sheet metal business Sell entire operation, employees included Contract with buyer for ongoing production of some or all sheet metal parts
Partial outsourcing and consolidation	Find outside suppliers for some sheet metal parts Consolidate internal sheet metal operations within a region Offer employees other jobs within HP or voluntary severance packages
Partial ownership	Identify a partner—could be a competitor who needs sheet metal parts as well, or someone who is or wants to be in the business Negotiate a contract to share ownership of the business

EXHIBIT 2.15   **Assessing a Vertical Integration Option—Questions to Ask**

Performance Dimension	If the Firm Vertically Integrates	If the Firm Vertically Disintegrates
Cost	How much will it have to invest to acquire the target activity? How much will it cost to operate the target activity annually? How does this cost compare to the cost of buying the goods or services from an external supplier? What is the return on investment for owning this activity?	How much capital will it save by not having to invest in the target activity? How much will it save in operating costs from not having to operate the target activity? How does this savings compare to the cost of buying the goods or services from an external supplier? What is the return on investment for divesting this activity?
Quality	What type of quality management system will be needed to ensure quality output from the new activity? How will the quality management system for the new activity integrate with the existing quality management system(s) at the firm? Can the firm create additional value by integrating the quality management systems?	What kind of quality management systems do the potential suppliers of the goods or services have? How well do the potential suppliers perform against appropriate quality metrics? How will the firm work with potential suppliers to manage or improve quality? Will the potential suppliers' quality management systems feed data to or integrate with the firm's quality management system?
Availability	How will ownership of the target activity affect the firm's availability performance (i.e., will lead time through the value or supply chain be shorter or longer)? How will availability management in the target activity be integrated with availability management across the firm?	How will outsourcing the target activity affect the firm's availability performance (i.e., will lead time through the value or supply chain be shorter or longer)? How will the firm work with potential suppliers to manage availability?
Features/ Innovativeness	What new product or service features will be facilitated by ownership of the target activity? What is the value to the firm of the new product or service features?	What product or service features are affected by the target activity and how will their delivery be affected by outsourcing that activity? What type of ongoing relationship does the firm want to have with the potential suppliers to facilitate ongoing provision of product or service features (new or existing)?
Environmental Performance	What are the environmental effects of the activities to be internalized? What risks do they represent to the firm? How will the firm manage those risks? What additional design for environmental activities would be possible were the process internal?	Are the suppliers competent at performing environmental management? What are the legal, political, and social risks associated with having the supplier underperform?

should be realistic and achievable. For example, if partial ownership is truly an option, a set of potential partners should be identified.

Step 4: Assess the Alternatives and Select One

Assess each of the alternatives against the cost, quality, availability, features/innovativeness, and environmental performance criteria. Exhibit 2.15 lists specific questions that can be asked. A matrix showing the cost, quality, availability, features/innovativeness, and environmental performance of each alternative will allow for easy comparison of options.

Finally, make a choice. Although it would be nice if there were a straightforward, analytical means of making the choice—for example, weighting all the decision criteria and calculating a single "returns" number for each alternative—it is our experience that these choices are made by teams of managers who meet to evaluate the information they have been given, integrate it with their knowledge about the business, and come to an agreement about the appropriate direction for the firm.

Step 5: Implement

Quinn (1999) describes the outcome of a process of vertical disintegration. "As companies disaggregate intellectual activities internally and outsource more externally, they rapidly approach a true virtual organization with knowledge centers interacting largely through mutual interest and electronic—rather than authority—systems. Each node of their organization form becomes a knowledge source; some nodes are internal, and some external." This description highlights the changes and risks an organization undertakes when it chooses to change its degree of vertical integration, many revolving around people, information management and communication, and intellectual property management.

It is sometimes helpful for firms that are actively managing their vertical integration strategy to divide their organizations (internal and external value chains) into different groups that can be considered as different knowledge centers. In doing so, they highlight the role that knowledge and intellectual property play in today's organizations and are thus more likely to explicitly and actively manage these critical assets. Some of the major risks associated with outsourcing an activity—in addition to those associated with supplier underperformance—include loss of skills that can be very difficult to rebuild and loss of intellectual property that is sold or leaked from the firm's new suppliers. Internally, the firm may suffer backlash from its own employees who see outsourcing as a threat to their security, and may lose its ability to perform cross-functional tasks when one of the functions is not performed internally.

Conversely, there are risks associated with bringing an activity in house including longer-term risks of becoming too inwardly focused and missing an innovation that would obsolete the firm's own technology, or diverting focus from the activities that are most critical to the firm's competitive performance. A firm that chooses to vertically integrate reduces the number of external partnerships it has to manage, but at the same time widens internal management spans of control and the number of different skill sets that must be hired, trained, managed, and evaluated within the firm.

All of these are risks that must be managed once an outsourcing decision is implemented. The vertically disintegrating firm must improve its ability to manage external relationships, shed the overhead associated with owning the outsourced activity, and put in place ongoing monitoring, performance measurement, and feedback systems to manage its new supplier network. The vertically integrating firm, on the other hand, must restructure its organization, typically increasing management span of control; hire, train, manage, and evaluate a new set of skills; develop systems to integrate the new activity with the other activities internal to the firm; and retain the capability to scan the external environment for new technical and product or service knowledge that might be useful.

Possible Outcomes of the Vertical Integration Decision

Any organization considering a vertical integration or disintegration decision should go through the analytical process described in this chapter, as there are no generic answers that fit all situations. Even within single industries, and sometimes within single firms, we find different answers to the vertical integration question.

In the notebook computer industry, for example, we find firms that perform both design and production internally (Toshiba), firms that perform their own design, but outsource production (Apple), and firms that outsource both design and production (as Compaq—now part of HP—did with Mitac). Each of these firms, presumably using logic similar to that presented in this chapter, came up with different answers to the question of how vertically integrated they should be. Their choice of different bases on which to compete in the marketplace may well be the driving force behind their choices.

An extreme outcome of vertical disintegration or outsourcing is the virtual corporation (Davidow and Malone 1992, De Meyer 1993), a company whose primary function is to coordinate the activities of a network of suppliers. Although the virtual corporation has advantages of flexibility and the ability to select from a wide range of external capabilities, it runs the risk that overreliance on external suppliers of manufacturing, service delivery, and technology will cause it to degenerate into the proverbial hollow corporation decried in the pages of the popular management press in the 1980s as manufacturing was transferred out of the United States to overseas locations. Even though incremental moves to outsource individual activities can be justified on the basis of cost efficiency, in the long run, unless a company focuses on developing and maintaining its own core capabilities, it can lose the ability to innovate and perform its own activities at best-in-class levels.

Summary

The vertical integration decision is one of the most critical decisions a company must make in setting business as well as operations strategy. In effect, vertical integration is simply a means of coordinating the stages of the firm's value chain when bilateral trading is not economic or reliable. Firms making vertical integration decisions ask these questions:

- How much of the value chain should my company own, and for the owned activities, how much should be performed in house?
- Under what conditions should my company change the amount of the value chain it owns? In what direction—toward my suppliers or toward my customers—should I make those changes?

There are four sets of factors that must be taken into account when making a vertical integration decision:

1. Strategic factors link the vertical integration decision to the firm's choice of core capabilities on which it will compete. A firm will typically choose to own the activities associated with its core capabilities and may outsource all other activities if possible.
2. Market factors address the reliability of the available supplier markets for the activities the firm chooses not to own, and consider the structure and dynamics of the industry in which the firm resides. A firm may choose to own an activity to control its performance,

gain market power, or reduce dependence on an outside supplier. A firm may choose to outsource to improve process economics and performance.

3. Product and technology factors relate an operations decision to outsource to technology strategy and product architecture. A firm may choose to own a process if the technology underlying that process is new or is integral to the firm's products, or there is uncertainty associated with the product/process relationship. It may, on the other hand, outsource a process if the underlying technology development is also outsourced and/or the technology is used in a modular product architecture making it easy to separate from the product.

4. Economic factors provide tangible data about the cost of a vertical integration decision. A firm may choose to own an activity if it can perform that activity at lower cost, the investment required is reasonable, and the transaction costs associated with procuring the output of the activity from outside are high. A firm may outsource when it cannot achieve these economies.

We recommend the following steps in making vertical integration or disintegration decisions:

1. Apply the core capabilities screen identifying which activities should be retained in house and which are potential candidates for outsourcing.

2. Assess the industry context and dynamics, identifying weaknesses and opportunities that might be exploited through a change in vertical integration.

3. Identify alternative value chain structures, realistically naming practical options for acquiring or shedding a capability.

4. Assess alternatives and choose one based on the cost, quality, availability, features/innovativeness, and environmental performance of each alternative as well as its strategic contribution.

5. Implement the chosen alternative, remaining aware of the cost targets to be achieved and the associated risks.

References

Abernathy, William J., and Kenneth Wayne. "Limits of the Learning Curve." *Harvard Business Review* (September–October 1974), pp. 109–119.

"A Transatlantic Tussle Over Automation." *Fortune* (November 11, 1996).

Chesbrough, Henry W., and David J. Teece. "When Is Virtual Virtuous? Organizing for Innovation." *Harvard Business Review* 74, no. 1, (1996), pp. 65–73.

Davidow, W. H., and M. S. Malone. *The Virtual Corporation: Restructuring and Revitalizing the Corporation for the 21st Century*. New York: Harper Collins, 1992.

Dedrick, Jason, and Kenneth L. Kraemer. "Globalization of the Personal Computer Industry: Trends and Implications." Working paper, Center for Research on Information Technology and Organizations, University of California, Irvine, 2002.

De Meyer, Arnoud. "Creating the Virtual Factory." Working paper, Fontainebleau: INSEAD, 1993.

Fine, Charles. *Clockspeed: Winning Industry Control in the Age of Temporary Advantage*. Reading, MA: Perseus Books, 1998.

Grant, Robert M. "Vertical Integration and the Scope of the Firm." *Contemporary Strategy Analysis: Concepts, Techniques, Applications*. 3rd ed. Malden, MA: Blackwell Publishing, 1998, pp. 315–330.

Haupt, Lynne. "Vertical Integration and Strategic Sourcing in the Biopharmaceutical Industry." Masters thesis, MIT, 2005.

Hayes, Robert H., and Gary Pisano. "Manufacturing Strategy: At the Intersection of Two Paradigm Shifts." *Production and Operations Management* 15, no. 1 (Spring 1996), pp. 25–41.

The History of Kodak; http://www.kodak.com/global/en/corp/historyOfKodak/chronology.jhtml?pq-path=2217/2687/2695 (accessed 2005).

Kraemer, Kenneth L., and Jason Dedrick. "Dell Computer: Organization of a Global Production Network." Working paper, Center for Research on Information Technology and Organizations, University of California, Irvine, 2002.

Leonard-Barton, Dorothy A. "Core Capabilities and Core Rigidities." In *The Perpetual Enterprise Machine: Seven Keys to Corporate Renewal through Successful Product and Process Development,* H. Kent Bowen, Kim B. Clark, Charles Holloway, and Steven Wheelwright, eds. New York: Oxford University Press, 1994.

Pisano, Gary P., and Sharon Rossi. "ITT Automotive: Global Manufacturing Strategy." Harvard Business School Publishing, 1994, 9-695-002.

Quinn, James Brian. "Strategic Outsourcing: Leveraging Knowledge Capabilities." *Sloan Management Review* 40, no. 4 (Summer 1999), pp. 9–21.

Quinn, James Brian, and Frederick G. Hilmer. "Strategic Outsourcing." *Sloan Management Review* 35, no. 4 (Summer 1994), pp. 43–55.

Quinn, James Brian. "Outsourcing Innovation: The New Engine of Growth." *Sloan Management Review* 41, no. 4 (Summer 2000), pp. 13–28.

Sanders, Matthew R. "Responsible Outsourcing: Risk Assessment in Electronics Contract Manufacturing." Masters thesis, MIT, June 2001.

Stuckey, John, and David White. "When and When Not to Vertically Integrate." *Sloan Management Review* 34, no. 3 (Spring 1993), pp. 71–83.

Ulrich, Karl T., and David J. Ellison. "Beyond Make-Buy: Internalization and Integration of Design and Production." *Production and Operations Management* 14, no. 3 (2005), pp. 315–330 .

Ulrich, Karl T., and Steven D. Eppinger. *Product Design and Development,* 3rd ed. New York: McGraw-Hill/Irwin, 2004.

Vakil, Bindiya. "Design Outsourcing in the High-tech industry and its Impact on Supply Chain Strategies." Master's thesis, MIT, 2005.

Williamson, Oliver E. *Markets and Hierarchies: Analysis and Antitrust Implications.* New York: The Free Press, 1975.

Womack, James P., Daniel T. Jones, and Daniel Roos. *The Machine that Changed the World.* New York: Simon and Schuster, 1990.

Chapter 3

Process Technology

Introduction

In 1971, Intel Corporation designed the first dynamic random access memory (DRAM) chip, the Intel 1103, and held a significant technological advantage for the next decade as it continued to design and introduce new DRAM products, such as the CMOS (complementary metal oxide semiconductor) DRAM, introduced in 1983. Then, despite its technological leadership, it gradually lost ground to Japanese integrated circuit (IC) competitors and eventually exited the DRAM business in 1985.

This was a major blow to Intel, and much of the blame was placed on the difficulties Intel faced in replicating and ramping up its production facilities. The rollout of its 1μm process technology is illustrative (Exhibit 3.1). The process development facility, or "fab" as it is known in the industry, worked for many months to improve die yields (the percentage of good die per wafer) of the new 1μm process, and engineers at the first 1μm production fab worked alongside those from the development fab, closely replicating the process. As the second and third fabs were rolled out, however, the process deviated increasingly from the original design, causing yield performance to revert to levels seen only in the earliest months of the development fab's work. The so-called improvements undertaken at the second and third fabs actually resulted in up to a 10x *reduction* in die per wafer (Natarajan et al., 2002).

Loss of the DRAM business, along with increasing fabrication equipment costs and shrinking technology life cycles, motivated a thorough review of Intel's process technology strategy (Hayes and Mathur 1995). In 1986, Intel created the Process Equipment Development (PED) department to centralize and coordinate the selection and implementation of new generations of IC process equipment and subsequently launched a program known as Copy Exactly!. Under Copy Exactly!, "everything which might affect the process, or how it is run" is copied across all fabs, down to the finest detail, unless it is either physically impossible to do so or there is an overwhelming competitive benefit to introduce a change (McDonald 1997).

Intel completed adoption of Copy Exactly! in 1996 and credits it with enabling the company to bring factories online quickly with high-volume practices already in place, thus decreasing time-to-market and increasing yields (www.intel.com, accessed July 15,

EXHIBIT 3.1
Die Yields for Introduction of Intel's 1μm Production Process

Source: Reprinted with permission from Natarajan et al. "Process Development and Manufacturing of High-Performance Microprocessors on 300mm Wafers," *Intel Technology Journal*, 6, no. 2 (2002).

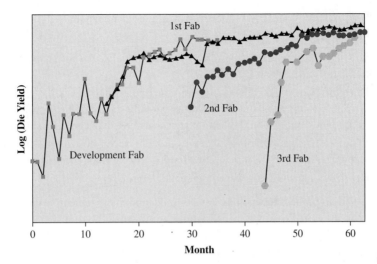

2005). Exhibit 3.2 shows die yield performance for the introduction of five recent processes at Intel. In almost all cases, the performance of the production fabs closely tracks that of the development fab (Natarajan et al. 2002).

For Intel, and for many other companies, process technology and how it is managed provide significant competitive advantage (Hayes et al., 1988, Leonard-Barton 1992, Pavitt 1990, and Pisano 1996). Choice of a process technology can directly affect product or service cost and quality; the speed with which new products or services can be brought to market; the firm's innovativeness; ability to provide variety appropriate to the market-place, and environmental soundness. Technology, while not necessarily the creator of value for a company, can be a key driver of the strategies that do cause the rise or fall of a company (Collins 2001).

EXHIBIT 3.2
Die Yield Matching with Copy Exactly!

Source: Reprinted with permission from Natarajan et al. "Process Development and Manufacturing of High-Performance Microprocessors on 300mm Wafers," *Intel Technology Journal* 6, no. 2 (2002).

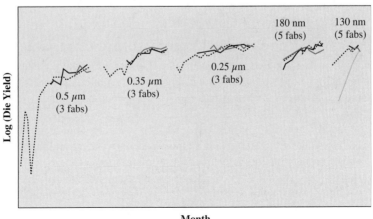

This chapter focuses on the critical strategic decisions to be made about process technology:

- To what degree should the product or service delivery process be automated, and how flexible should the process be?
- Does the firm want to be an innovator, leading in the development of process technology, or a follower, using technologies already used and/or proven by other organizations? How much should the company invest in advanced technologies?
- Should the firm develop its own process technology with in-house engineering resources, or should it purchase technology from other companies?
- How does the company want to manage its process technology?
  - Should process technology development and management be centralized (as Intel did in the mid-1980s with PED) or decentralized?
  - Should the company standardize technology across all of its operations, as Intel did with Copy Exactly!, or allow individual operations to vary? If process technologies vary by site, which technologies should be implemented at which sites?

We first briefly describe what we mean by process technology and then present two important models or frameworks for thinking about process technology strategy: the experience curve and the product-/service-process matrices. We then apply these models to address each of the critical process technology strategy questions raised above. We close with a six-step approach to developing process technology strategy.

What Is Process Technology?

Process technology is the technology used to produce products or provide services. While process technology is tightly integrated with information technology, we address information technology strategy in another chapter and focus here on the hardware, systems, and procedures used to deliver products or services. We describe process technology for manufacturing and service companies in this section to give the reader a feel for what process technology looks like and a better understanding of the magnitude of investment in process technology in some industries.

Process Technology in Manufacturing Companies

For a manufacturing company such as Intel, process technology may include basic production equipment and/or more advanced processes. At Intel, process technology is highly specialized to the semiconductor fabrication process, technologically advanced, very expensive, and used in an extremely complex process (Exhibit 3.3). A new wafer fabrication facility costs $2–3 billion, 60% of which is spent on production equipment and 25% of which is spent on the facility and support systems to house and run the equipment. A single piece of production equipment, such as a lithography tool, can cost up to $30 million, and a new fab might use 15 to 20 such tools (Silverman 2003).

Automotive companies also have complex processes that employ expensive equipment. The total cost can run up to $1 billion to build an average speed plant that makes medium-sized cars. The paint shop alone (Exhibit 3.4) can cost $250 million and has historically been one of the largest sources of environmental issues in automobile production. The body

EXHIBIT 3.3
The Semiconductor Production Process

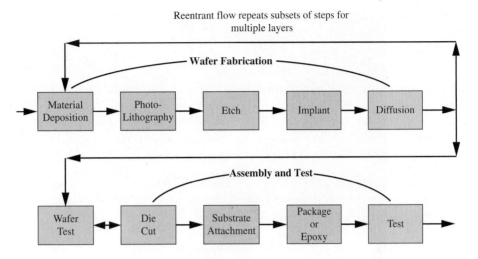

Reentrant flow repeats subsets of steps for multiple layers

— Wafer Fabrication —

Material Deposition → Photo-Lithography → Etch → Implant → Diffusion

— Assembly and Test —

Wafer Test ↔ Die Cut → Substrate Attachment → Package or Epoxy → Test

shop, where the parts for the car are fabricated using large stamping presses and other such equipment, can easily cost over $250 million. The final assembly line itself, which is often tailored to the particular car model it is building, costs about $150 million (Exhibit 3.5). The full cost to establish a new automobile production facility is nearly as high as that for semiconductor fabrication. Toyota Motor Manufacturing, for example, invested $1.5 to 2.9 billion to set up each of its Canadian facilities, such as the one in Cambridge, Ontario, pictured in Exhibit 3.6. The great expense of this equipment causes automobile producers to strive to keep their plants busy at all times.

Even chocolate manufacturing requires investments in process technology. Specialty chocolate maker Scharffen Berger (recently purchased by Hershey) uses a *mélangeur*

EXHIBIT 3.4   **Auto Body Paint Shops—Manual and Robotic**

Sources: Left photo: Reprinted with permission from Dallas Auto Painting & Collision Repair.
Right photo: Reprinted with permission from Carnegie Mellon University, Biorobotics Lab.

EXHIBIT 3.5
Automobile Body Shop and Final Assembly Line at General Motors

Source: Reprinted with permission from General Motors Corporation.

(*mixer* in French) that was manufactured in Dresden, Germany, in the 1920s to grind the insides of the cacao seeds into a thick paste called chocolate liqueur. Although more modern equipment exists to perform this task, Scharffen Berger believes that its mélangeur operates in a special way, and that it in turn produces better chocolate than other manufacturers

EXHIBIT 3.6
Toyota Motor Manufacturing Canada

Reprinted with permission from JAMA Canada.

can with newer equipment. In short, it believes it has a competitive advantage in producing better quality chocolate as a result of owning this mélangeur (Exhibit 3.7).

Clearly, process technology is core to converting inputs to outputs in manufacturing businesses, sometimes allowing the firm to differentiate its products or services from its competitors and often requiring a sizable capital investment. (Visit Stanford University's collection of manufacturing videos at http://manufacturing.stanford.edu/ accessed January 29, 2007 to learn more about process technology and see manufacturing in action at a range of companies.)

Process Technology in Service Companies

For retailing and distribution companies, process technology comprises the equipment used to move and manage the massive flow of materials throughout the supply chain.

EXHIBIT 3.7
Mélangeur at Scharffen Berger Chocolate

Source: Reprinted with permission from Scharffen Berger Chocolate Maker.

EXHIBIT 3.8
Sortation Equipment at Amazon

Source: Reprinted with permission from Amazon.com.

Amazon.com, for example, has five warehouses in the United States[1] and ten outside, each requiring an initial investment of about $50 million. The warehouses are completely computerized, requiring as many lines of code to run each warehouse as to support Amazon.com's website. The physical equipment is impressive as well (Exhibit 3.8). Each warehouse is reputed to have 10 miles of conveyor belts, "forests" of bookshelves, and metal bridges for navigating the floor. Central to warehouse operations is a $25 million Crisplant sorting machine that reads the bar codes on items as they are passed through the machine and routes them into one of 2,100 chutes, each representing an order (Hansell 2002). Amazon.com's ability to run these warehouses extremely efficiently has provided it with a capability that it has been able to leverage into numerous applications other than selling new books. Jeff Bezos, Amazon.com's founder and CEO says, "In the physical world it's the old saw: location, location, location. The three most important things for us are technology, technology, technology" (Vogelstein 2003).

The most obvious investments in technology for those who travel by air are the aircraft themselves and the information systems used to purchase tickets and check in, but there are significant behind-the-scenes process technology investments in the industry as well. The cost of the baggage system connecting a main terminal building with two satellite buildings for the new Terminal 5 campus at Heathrow international airport is projected to cost $500 million, $185 million of which will be spent on purchase and installation of equipment (e.g., screening machines, conveyor belts, baggage racks, gantries such as those

---

[1] These warehouses are for multiple-item orders. There are a number of others that supply only case- or pallet-sized items.

EXHIBIT 3.9
Baggage Conveyors and Sorting Equipment

Source: Reprinted with permission from Vanderlande Industries.

shown in Exhibit 3.9) and $280 million of which will be spent on development and installation of the associated controls system. Airport designers had to choose from a range of technologies, each of which had different implications for how the airport would be run and how effective its operations would be. For the 20 screening machines to be installed, for example, they had to choose from machines that ranged from a simple X-ray screening machine with 2-D imaging that cost only $555,000 to a sophisticated CT-scan machine with 3-D imaging that cost $1.85 million. It will take about five years to procure and install the entire baggage handling system in the airport, two of which will be spent in testing and commissioning the equipment itself. The equipment has a life of about 10 years, at which time the airport can choose to replace or upgrade it (Gil 2006).

Many other services use expensive technologies as well. Amusement parks employ expensive technology in their rides and attractions. Banks and financial institutions invest in information technology as well as the physical structures (e.g., automated teller machines) that facilitate delivery of their services. Logistics management companies, like FedEx and UPS, maintain huge truck fleets, cargo sorting and storage centers, and fleet maintenance facilities. In short, process technology is the physical hardware—often accompanied by or inextricably intertwined with information technology or software—that facilitates the creation and delivery of goods or services.

We now turn to two models that help frame the process technology decisions. The first, the experience curve model, helps us understand the cost trade-offs made in technology choice. The second, the product/service process matrix, helps us match process choices to product or service requirements.

The Experience Curve

The *experience curve* is a relationship between *unit cost* (e.g., the cost to produce one car, the cost to package one customer order, or the cost to handle one telephone call) and total volume (e.g., total number of cars made to date, total number of orders processed, or total

EXHIBIT 3.10
Typical Experience Curve

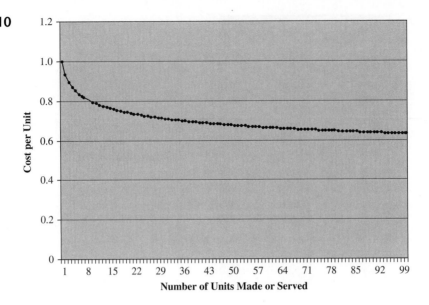

number of calls handled). The principle behind the experience curve is that as total volume increases, *unit cost* decreases in a predictable way (Exhibit 3.10). Intuitively what this suggests is that as a firm's experience in making a product or delivering a service increases over time, the firm will find ways to reduce the unit cost of the product or service.

The *learning curve* is a closely related concept but narrower in scope than the experience curve. Learning curves show the relationship between number of *labor hours per unit* and total number of units produced. Because labor hours per unit and cost per unit are closely related in some industries, specifically those that are highly labor intensive, the experience and learning curves are sometimes used interchangeably. The theory of the learning curve, however, is based on the notion that reductions in labor hours per unit arise from learning on the part of the workers themselves. This learning is of two types: conceptual learning happens as workers optimize the process by adjusting known control parameters, while operational learning involves experimentation with new theories (e.g., of cause-effect relationships not yet understood) to find ways of improving performance (Lapre and Van Wassenhove 2002).

While learning can have a major impact in reducing costs over time, it is not the only way to do so; there are many ways in which companies can reduce unit costs. That these collective improvements result in the experience curve effect was shown in the late 1960s with empirical research by the Boston Consulting Group (1972). This list describes improvements a firm might expect to make:[2]

- Labor efficiency improvement: As workers throughout a process become physically more dexterous and/or mentally more confident, they spend less time hesitating and making mistakes. Over time, they learn shortcuts and improvements that increase their efficiency.

[2] List adapted in part from http://en.wikipedia.org/wiki/learning_curve, July 15, 2005.

- Standardization, specialization, and methods improvement: As processes, parts, products, and services become more standardized, employees can specialize in and learn a limited number of tasks well and perform them at a faster rate. Over time, employees also come to understand the process better and can make changes to the process in a reasoned and logical way to achieve higher yields and efficiency gains.
- Process automation: Automating production and/or service delivery tasks can make them more efficient; this is often the basis on which investments in automation are justified.
- Product or service redesign: Investment in design for manufacturability programs for products, or design for delivery programs for services, provides product or service designers increased awareness of the processes that will produce or deliver their products. Increased awareness allows them to design or redesign products and services to be more efficiently produced or delivered.
- Increased scale and volume: As more volume is put through a facility, the fixed costs associated with that facility will be spread over more units, thus decreasing cost per unit.
- Value chain improvement: Suppliers and distributors can also take advantage of experience curve effects. As they move down their own experience curves, the improved efficiencies and reduced costs may be passed along to their customers.
- Shared experience effects: When two or more products or services share the same production or delivery process, learning or improvements from one product or service may be applied to the other, thus leveraging improvements across all products or services in that process.

While the experience curve is largely focused on cost reduction, experience also may lead to improvements in yield and hence quality, product or service performance, environmental performance, and so forth. These improvements may in turn lead to cost improvements. While we focus on cost reduction, the reader should also be aware of these other potential benefits of experience.

Experience Curve Formulation

The mathematical relationship that describes the experience curve is

$$C_x = C_1 x^{-b}$$

where

C_x = cost of the xth unit produced or delivered

x = cumulative volume

b = experience curve parameter

C_1 = cost of the first unit produced or delivered

and $b = \log r / \log 2$

where r = rate of learning

For instance, if a company estimates that it can achieve a cost reduction that is 5% of the new cost with each doubling of volume, then $r = 1.05$, and the learning curve parameter, b, is 0.07. Exhibit 3.11 compares learning curves for improvement rates of

EXHIBIT 3.11
Experience Curves for Improvement Rates of 5%, 10%, and 20%

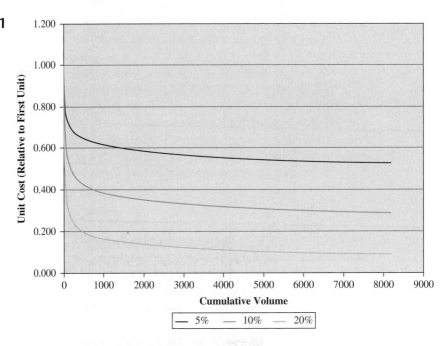

5%, 10%, and 20% (and r values of 1.05, 1.10, and 1.20, respectively), calculating cost per the formulas given above.

Using the same variables, another way to express the experience curve relationship is logarithmically, as depicted in Exhibit 3.12 and as shown here:

$$\log C_x = \log C_1 - b \log x$$

It is sometimes easier to look at this linear relationship to estimate the experience curve parameter (the slope of the line, b) and to assess the strength of the experience curve relationship using linear regression analysis.

Although there is no theoretically based derivation of the mathematical relationship underlying the experience curve, it is a phenomenon that has been observed in repeated industry studies, the first of which were in the airframe industry (e.g., Rohrbach 1927, Wright 1936). There is sound empirical support for the relationship, which has proven robust in approximating performance in a wide range of industries.[3]

Using the Experience Curve

The existence of the experience curve effect has a number of important implications. First, there are implications for the firm's position in the market. Costs are negatively correlated with market share; as market share increases, costs should go down, and vice versa. Gaining share is thus good for achieving cost reductions. Similarly, as a firm grows, it should move down the experience curve. If the firm grows faster than its competitors, its relative cost position should improve. In fact, by using a combination of

[3] http://www.bcg.com/this_is_bcg/mission/experience_curve.html, February 11, 2007.

EXHIBIT 3.12
Logarithmic
Experience
Curve

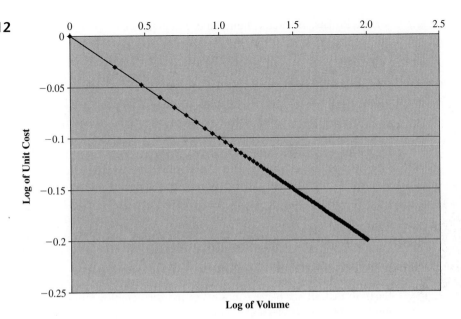

market elasticity curves, which show the quantity of product that customers will purchase based on the market price, and experience curves, the firm should be able to assess
its profitability and the size of its potential market over time. Exhibit 3.13 shows how
total market volume, company share of that volume, prices, costs, and profits change
with time based on these relationships. Annual market and company volumes are shown
on the left-hand *y*-axis, while unit costs, prices, and profits are shown on the right-hand

EXHIBIT 3.13
Relationship of
Market Volume,
Company
Volume, Price,
Cost, and Profit
as a Function of
Experience

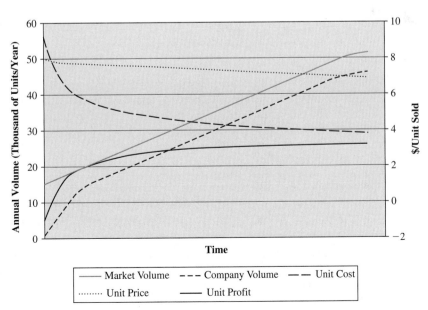

y-axis. Profits, market volume, and company share go up while prices and costs go down. A leading company would ultimately be able to develop a commanding position with significant profits.

The experience curve is also useful for making internal product or service design and cost control decisions. When the experience curve is in effect, cost declines are predictable and can thus be used for forecasting, management, and evaluation. Product or service design alternatives can be assessed, at least in part, on the basis of whether or not they will leverage existing experience to reduce initial production or delivery costs. The value of increasing product or service line variety can also be based on whether or not the new products or services will leverage or contribute to experience curve effects.

Finally, understanding experience curve effects can be helpful in value chain structuring and vendor management decisions. Firms making vertical integration or make-or-buy decisions may need to evaluate their positions on the experience curve relative to those firms to which they are considering directing work. Similarly, a firm may set expectations for a vendor based on where it thinks that vendor resides on the experience curve, and thus what cost targets the vendor might be expected to hit.

Let's look at a hypothetical example of an industry that illustrates some of these points. Suppose that all six players in a given industry employ similar processes, and that they improve those processes at the same rate; that is, they all follow the same experience curve. We'll assume that rate to be 5%, and the cost to make the first unit to be $1. Given data on the market share of each participant and knowledge of the size of the market (16,000 units), we can calculate the quantity each produces or delivers as well as the cost per unit (Exhibit 3.14). For competitor F, for example:

$$x = \text{cumulative volume} = 256$$

$$r = \text{rate of learning} = 1.05$$

$$b = \text{experience curve parameter} = \log(1.05)/\log(2) = 0.07$$

$$C_1 = \text{cost of the first unit produced or delivered} = \$1$$

$$C_{256} = C_1 x^{-b} = \$1 * 256^{-0.07} = \$0.68$$

This simple analysis provides a number of insights for the various companies involved. Company D, for example, knows how much market share it must retain in order to maintain its cost advantage over companies E and F, and how much share it must gain to be able to compete with company C. Company A knows, for example, that if all the players in the industry retain their market share positions, it will retain the lead, even as all six companies

EXHIBIT 3.14
Sample
Competitive
Analysis with
Experience
Curve

Competitor	Market Share	Cumulative Quantity	Cost/Last Unit Produced
F	2%	256	$0.68
E	3%	512	$0.64
D	6%	1024	$0.61
C	13%	2048	$0.58
B	26%	4096	$0.56
A	51%	8192	$0.53

move down the experience curve. Companies like F, that are just entering the market, can use these calculations to set pricing, and determine when the company might expect to break even or become profitable. Company F might, for example, have to start pricing its products at the average market price and thus incur losses for some period of time. Alternatively, Company F might attempt an alliance of some sort with Companies A, B, or C to leverage their experience and associated cost structures.

In a real world example, Duke and Kammen (1999) describe the use of experience curves in the evaluation of three energy-sector market transformation programs: the Environmental Protection Agency's ongoing Green Lights program to promote on-grid efficient lighting, the World Bank Group's new Photovoltaic Market Transformation Initiative, and the federal grain ethanol study. They develop benefit-cost models for each of the programs that use experience curves to estimate unit cost reductions as a function of cumulative production, and a dynamic feedback model to adjust demand response to reduced prices. They show that, while the first two programs had sufficient benefit-cost ratios to justify subsidization, the third did not. Thus, the experience curve is a valuable tool, even in public policy decisions.

The experience or learning curve is particularly applicable in two important situations:

1. For a very new product or service that is undergoing frequent changes.
2. For production of large-scale projects or products that have high costs and relatively low volumes.

Very New Products or Services

Experience curve effects are often seen in the introduction of very new products or services, as there is less known about the effects at the start of the development process, and experience proves a valuable teacher during initial rollout. Cost improvements for very new products or services may arise from two sources. First, product or service design changes can translate into production or delivery efficiencies. For example, product designers may use fewer parts and assemblies, design in more standard subassemblies and parts, or develop a design that is more consistent with standardized methods. These approaches underlie "design for manufacturing" programs.

Similarly, service designers may streamline a service, reducing the number of elements of that service and standardizing others so that they are more easily executed. Second, process design changes may improve the performance of the production or delivery system itself. For example, process engineers may be able to develop a better layout, an improved assignment and allocation of labor, more efficient technology and methods, and so forth. McDonald's announced in 2005, for example, that it would employ call centers to take customer orders at its drive-through windows. The company discovered that a centralized call center covering a number of stores could be not only more efficient than having store personnel cover this task, but also more effective during periods of congestion. The change would thus improve the speed, quality, and cost of the order-taking process.

The interaction between product or service and process design is most evident at the time of product or service launch. Prior to launch, it can be difficult to get developers to pay sufficient attention to process costs and efficiencies, as there is greater focus on getting the product or service to market. As launch occurs, however, flaws in the product or service design become apparent, particularly when they cause inefficiency in the process.

As product or service developers and process designers work through launch issues, they improve process yields and drive costs down, creating the experience curve effect. Many companies aim to identify these issues early and avoid steep experience curve effects. Intel's Copy Exactly! program, for example, was established to eliminate start-up effects across fabs. Once the new product or service is launched, scale effects may kick in. Simply, as volumes improve, unit costs go down because fixed costs are allocated over a larger base, and because higher volumes allow use of technologies that are better matched (and hence more efficient) for the higher volumes.

Although it can be difficult to predict experience curve effects accurately and quantitatively, it is important to understand them nonetheless. Understanding that they occur is the best first step to reducing any adverse effects of them. Concurrent engineering (where product/service and process designers work together to simultaneously design and optimize product/service and process) and design for manufacturability programs (where product or service designers consider manufacturing or service delivery systems' limitations and costs in the process of design) are important to reducing early and steep experience curve effects. Thus, even without quantitative data to estimate experience curve effects, understanding them and where they come from can be important to successful and efficient introduction of new products and services.

Production of Large-Scale Projects

The experience curve effect also appears on large-scale projects where costs are high and production volumes low. A classic example of a large-scale project is commercial airframe manufacturing. Indeed, the earliest uses of the experience curve were in this industry. Other examples include defense contracts (aircraft, radar systems, etc.), aircraft engines, and power plants. As for very new products and services, there is an adjustment period as the first products are built. During this time there is a stream of Engineering Change Orders (ECOs) and sometimes radical restructuring of the production or assembly process to accommodate engineering changes and to streamline the process. The size and complexity of these projects makes predicting and planning the production process difficult. Because these projects are large and complex, it can be quite difficult to predict what the production or assembly process should look like. Engineers at Boeing, for example, tell stories about "part interference"—when different parts are unknowingly planned to go into the exact same place in the aircraft—that was not identified until the first plane was assembled. Thus, considerable adjustment to the process is often required. The experience curve helps predict the effects of early iteration of the product and process design, as well as the later effects of economies of scale as the process smoothes and volumes increase.

Exhibit 3.15 gives an example of a *learning* curve (labor hours only) from Boeing Company for one of its commercial aircraft projects; note that it is plotted on a log-log scale, so we expect to see a straight-line relationship. While the data do not fit a perfect line, there is clearly a decrease in labor content as total volume increases. Boeing's engineers fitted two different curves to the data. For all 333 aircraft the best fit yields a learning curve parameter, b, of 0.127. This implies an overall learning rate of 9.2% ($r = 1.092$), or a 9.2% reduction in labor hours per unit with each doubling in volume. A second curve fit to the data for aircraft 93 through 333 had a much higher rate of learning ($b = 0.514$) and a reduction in labor hours per aircraft of 42.8% with each doubling of volume. While a single learning curve did not fit all of the data for the full production cycle of the aircraft,

EXHIBIT 3.15 **Boeing Experience Curve Example for Aircraft Project**

Source: Gary J. Bass, reprinted with permission from The Boeing Company, 2001.

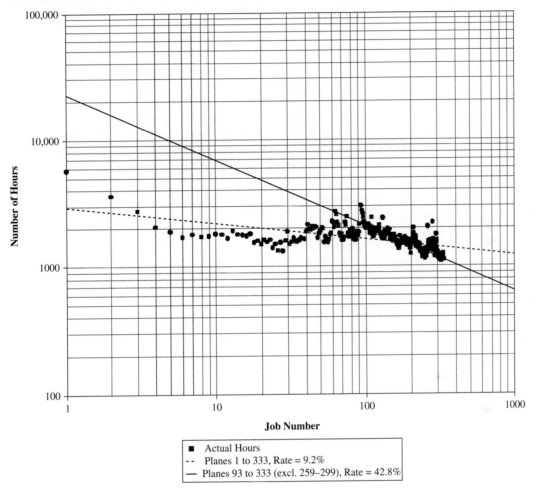

learning curve effects were clearly present and were important considerations for production planning and cost management.

Boeing and other large-scale project-based companies must make pricing decisions that take experience curve effects into account. They must project future costs (in this case based on labor hours per aircraft) and when they will achieve those costs and then decide at what price to sell the initial products and when price reductions might take effect. Clearly, the company's strategic choices and profitability can be directly affected by its assumptions about experience curve effects and thus cost structure (Hirshmann 1964). Pricing policy, for example, can be used in conjunction with the predicted cost decreases from experience curve data to obtain competitive advantage (Hayes and Wheelwright 1984). Such decisions can be a major factor in the long-term health of a company.

Potential Issues with the Experience Curve

There are certainly detractors of the experience curve model. Some question the use of these analyses because getting good data to put into the model requires uncertain projections of how markets will develop, what pricing strategies will be employed, and how competitors will react. Others argue that, with today's rapid product life cycles, cumulative experience with a given product may be limited and thus not relevant. They further argue that, because production is outsourced, the locus of learning or accumulating experience will be with a subcontractor and that the subcontractor's cumulative experience may not be with a single product, but with a number of different products. Of course, the subcontractor's cumulative experience should pay off in lower costs, and therefore prices, on all of its products for all of its customers. It is important to remember that a narrow focus on cost reduction, a strategy suggested by the experience curve, can lead to a loss of flexibility. A classic example of such a loss of flexibility is Ford Motor Company in the 1920s as the company increased production of the Model T (Abernathy and Wayne 1974). While continued investments in capital equipment and scale lowered the costs of the Model T, the company was unable to obtain flexibility to produce variants of its products. General Motors gained market share by having multiple models while Ford needed to close its major plants for an extended period to change to the newer Model A. Finally, some have argued that cost reduction, the focus of the experience curve, is not the only possible strategy; firms must balance their investments in cost reduction with those in quality, availability, features/innovativeness, and environmental performance.

Application of the Experience Curve in Industry

There are nonetheless compelling examples of the experience curve in effect in, for example, the dynamic high-technology industry today. In 1962, Canon started research on using lasers to write text and applied for related patents. It was unable to develop a practical laser light source at that time, however, so suspended research until the 1970s, when the Canon Central Research Institute succeeded in fine-tuning the technology. The first laser-based printer was subsequently shown in the United States in May 1975. A strong response from the U.S. market prompted Canon to pursue the project, producing both its own laser beam printers and entering into OEM (original equipment manufacturer) agreements to provide printer engines for various other companies as well. Today, Canon has produced over 15 million units of laser printer engines.[4] Canon has far outproduced any other manufacturer of laser-based print engines in the world, positioning it far down the experience curve. Although many OEMs outsource laser-based print engine production to Canon, they benefit from Canon's significant experience in lower costs to them. To this day, Canon holds a leading position on the experience curve that is very difficult for other manufacturers to reach.

Product-Process and Service-Process Matrices

The product-process and service-process matrices are tools that facilitate the matching of processes to product or service needs. The product-process matrix focuses on the trade-off between flexibility and efficiency, while the service-process matrix identifies degree of

---

[4] http://www.bubblejet.canon.com.my/product/laser_beam/laser_beam.htm, July 15, 2005.

interaction and customization and labor intensity as critical characteristics. Here we explore each of these matrices in turn. We start with a description of the types of processes (production or service delivery) and then place these types of processes in matrices that match them to the products or services they deliver.

Product-Process Matrix

The concept underlying the product-process matrix is that the relative flexibility or rigidity of a process should match the needs of the products it is to build, and that as flexibility increases, process efficiency decreases (Hayes and Wheelwright 1979a). The product-process matrix is built around the six basic types of production processes.

Project

Projects entail high-cost, complex sets of activities and produce very few items. Shipbuilding and large-scale construction are examples of project-based processes. These processes are relatively labor intensive and employ general-purpose equipment that can be used across multiple projects. The construction industry, for example, uses earthmovers, cement mixers, and welding equipment that can be used on a variety of large-scale building projects. The labor force for project-based work is often specialized by function. On a building project, for example, different specialists pour concrete, construct the steel structure, install the electrical systems, and so on. The information needs in project-based work are around managing project specifications and the changes to those specifications over time, planning and scheduling the many activities and tasks to be completed, and tracking actual costs (labor and materials) over the course of the project. Most of the inventory associated with project-based work is work-in-process (WIP) inventory, although some amount of raw materials inventory may be staged at the site.

Job Shop

A job shop produces a wide variety of items in single lots—therefore a large number of lots per year. Job shops are characterized by flexible equipment and highly skilled workers expert at translating customer specifications into production work. Job shops employ standard, general-purpose equipment such as mills, lathes, and drills that can be adjusted to do a variety of work, although not generally at the same rates that more specialized equipment can. Similar equipment is grouped together on the shop floor, which focuses the flow on individual processes or process steps. Equipment utilization is generally low, as the job shop carries excess capacity to be responsive to a wide variety of customer needs. Workers in job shops are often competent on multiple, different types of equipment and managed in a decentralized fashion. Information systems in job shops are used to track the location and progress of work in the shop, plan and control the flow of the work, and collect cost data (mostly equipment and labor applied to a production run). Job shops can build-to-order or build-to-stock; those that build-to-order carry primarily WIP inventory, while those that build-to-stock also carry some finished goods inventory (FGI). Job shops have high variable costs and moderate fixed costs.

Batch

Firms that employ batch production techniques manufacture products in higher volumes than do job shops, or can group their orders into larger quantities to form economical production batches. In general, they build more standardized products to fill recurring customer orders.

They are quite similar to job shops in their use of equipment, human resources, and information technology but can use somewhat more specialized equipment, may lay out the equipment in product-focused cells or groups, and may require skilled labor only to change equipment setups while less skilled labor runs production. WIP is still high, and FGI may also be high if batch sizes are large relative to customer orders.

Repetitive and Continuous Flow

Repetitive and continuous flow processes make standardized products in long production runs at very low cost. Repetitive processes make discrete items such as bottles of shampoo and automobiles, while continuous flow processes handle nondiscrete materials such as oil or cranberry juice. These highly efficient processes rely on specialized equipment and materials transfer processes and employ workers less skilled in the technology of the products themselves than in troubleshooting and problem solving to keep the line up and producing quality output. Often the products that are produced in repetitive flow processes are designed modularly so they can be easily changed without significantly affecting the production process. The information systems for these processes focus less on where a specific product is in the process at any given time and more on how much the process needs to make in a period of time and whether or not materials are available to produce that much. These factories tend to be more capital intensive and thus have high fixed costs, which causes them to drive for high utilization in order to achieve economies of scale and low per-unit product costs.

Mass Customization

Finally, mass customization processes aim to achieve the same low cost per unit as repetitive or continuous flow processes, sometimes known as mass production processes, while producing a wide variety of products (Pine 1993). To achieve mass customization, engineering, design, marketing, operations, and logistics personnel must work closely together to design products that can be easily customized according to customer desires. They rely on modular designs, low setup times, and effective scheduling to achieve rapid throughput at low cost. Mass customization requires specialized but flexible equipment; in particular, low changeover times are required. The people who work in mass customization environments have troubleshooting and problem-solving skills similar to those in the repetitive flow settings, but must apply them to a broader variety of products. These tend to be capital intensive plants; high utilization in these plants implies that the plant is producing high volumes, but not of the same product. Instead of achieving economies of scale, some say that these facilities achieve economies of scope (Lei et al. 1996).

Manufacturing Process Summary

Exhibit 3.16 summarizes the characteristics of these six processes. They differ radically in the type of equipment used, skills sets employed, information systems required, inventory held, and costing approaches used.

Matching Product Needs with Process Capabilities

As suggested in our descriptions of these processes, each is good at producing a particular type of product. The product-process matrix (Hayes and Wheelwright 1979a and 1979b) suggests that product plans and process choice should be linked. Product plans,

EXHIBIT 3.16 Types of Manufacturing Processes

	Project	Job Shop	Batch	Repetitive Flow	Continuous Flow	Mass Customization
Equipment	General purpose, flexible	General purpose, flexible	Some specialized equipment, sometimes organized in groups or cells	Special purpose	Special purpose	Specialized, but allows for rapid changeover
Operators	Specialized by function, often within subcontractors	Broadly skilled	Less broadly skilled; may need technical skills for changeovers	Troubleshooting and problem-solving skills	Troubleshooting and problem-solving skills	Flexible operators
Information Requirements	Coordination and planning, specification management, costing	Product specifications, job tracking, planning and scheduling, job costing	Batch tracking, planning and scheduling, materials planning	Output rate planning, materials planning, quality management	Output rate planning, materials planning, quality managemen	Customer requirements, materials planning, process flow and scheduling
Inventory Requirements	Mostly WIP (work-in-process), some RMI (raw material inventory)	Mostly WIP	Mostly WIP, sometimes some FGI (finished goods inventory) if build-to-stock	Mostly RMI and FGI; fast process so little WIP	Low levels of RMI to feed process; may have FGI if make-to-stock	Low levels of RMI to feed process; little FGI as is made-to-order
Costs	Fixed low to moderate; variable high	Fixed low; variable high	Fixed moderate; variable moderate	Fixed high; variable low	Fixed high; variable low	Fixed high; variable low
Job or Part Costing	Time and materials by task	Time and materials per job	Time and materials per batch	Dependent on capacity utilization and allocation of overhead	Dependent on capacity utilization and allocation of overhead	Dependent on capacity utilization; dynamic and difficult to determine

EXHIBIT 3.17
Product-Process Matrix Applied to Cake-Making

Source: Adapted from Hayes and Wheelwright, *Restoring Our Competitive Edge: Competing Through Manufacturing*, John Wiley and Sons, 1984.

Process Types	Product Characteristics				
	One-of-a-Kind Products	Low Volume, Many Products	Moderate Volume, Multiple Products	High Volume, Some Product Variety	High Volume, Standardized, Commodity Products
Project	Guinness World Book of Records Cake				
Job Shop		Woodlands Market Bakery			
Batch			Grace Baking		
Repetitive Flow				Entenmann's	
Continuous Flow					Hostess Twinkies

generated by the marketing and strategic planning organizations, determine the degree of product customization and volume required. Process choices, generally made by the production or operations organization, must accommodate these product plans. There are also times when the converse is true; product plans are sometimes made to accommodate existing process choices. Across the top of the matrix, depicted in Exhibit 3.17, are five general product categories ranging from one-of-a-kind to high-volume, standardized, commodity products, and down the side of the matrix are the first five types of processes we just introduced.

We'll deal with mass customization processes separately, as they do not fit on the chart. The highlighted cells along the diagonal of the matrix indicate preferred positions:

- Guinness World Records Cake: Were one to choose to build the world's largest cake, the best process with which to build it would be a project structure with general-purpose equipment and highly skilled, specialized labor.[5]
- Woodlands Market Bakery:[6] Woodlands Market is an upscale independent grocery store with its own in-store bakery that makes many different products but produces them in low volumes. It is best served by a job-shop structure with general-purpose equipment and skilled pastry chefs.
- Grace Baking:[7] An example of a regional baker, Grace Baking serves about 250 upscale restaurants and grocery stores with multiple products that it builds regularly in moderate volumes. Batch production is likely to be a good fit for Grace Baking, as it maintains some degree of flexibility in its processes, while it gains some efficiency.

[5] The world's largest wedding cake weighed 6,818.40 kg (15,032 lb) and was made by chefs at the Mohegan Sun Hotel and Casino, Uncasville, Connecticut, and displayed at their New England bridal showcase on February 8, 2004. (http://www.guinnessworldrecords.com/, August 19, 2005).

[6] http://www.woodlandsmarket.com/, August 22, 2005.

[7] http://www.gracebaking.com, July 15, 2005.

- Entenmann's:[8] One of the largest bakeries in the United States, Entenmann's produces significant volumes of products, such as breakfast pastries and cakes, for which it is likely to find a repetitive flow process most efficient. If it has sufficient volumes of any given product, it may even dedicate entire production lines (and possibly even entire facilities) to the production of that product.
- Hostess Twinkies:[9] Twinkies, known by children and adults around the world, are produced at the rate of 1,000 per minute; 500 million are sold a year. Although discrete products, they are made in a highly standardized fashion in what approximates a continuous flow process, using dedicated equipment.

Moving diagonally down the matrix from the upper left corner (project, one-of-a-kind) toward the lower right corner (continuous flow, high volume, standardized), the processes become more rigid and specified and flexibility decreases. Competitive priorities are also different for each section of the matrix. In a job-shop organization, for example, customization and high-performance design are the principle competitive priorities, while in a continuous flow shop high efficiency and consistent quality are paramount. These competitive priorities drive the choice of production technology, skills sets, and methods employed in the facilities.

Proponents of the product-process matrix argue that an organization should choose a position on the diagonal, although some off-diagonal positions may be viable. A batch shop wishing to offer more flexibility (a broader range of products) might choose to operate slightly left of the diagonal, while a batch shop wishing to compete on costs might operate to the right of the diagonal. Such positions might prove quite lucrative in serving the needs of a particular niche market. Positions far away from the diagonal have, historically, been harder to justify. With the advent of lean production methodologies and flexible technologies (Browne et al. 1984, Sethi and Sethi 1990), however, more extreme off-diagonal excursions have become viable. Lean production methods streamline inventories so that a wider variety of materials can be managed and handled without significantly increasing overall inventory investments. Flexible technologies allow for reduced changeover or set-up times and support multiple, different process or tools, which in turn facilitate production of smaller lot sizes. This adds flexibility without significantly increasing capital costs. These methods and technologies allow organizations to move off the diagonal and still compete effectively, providing increased variety at similar costs or decreased costs for similar variety.

These new approaches argue for a different view of the product-process matrix that accommodates off-diagonal positions. Exhibit 3.18 shows product volumes on one dimension and product variety on the other. In this depiction, according to advocates of the product-process matrix structure, project-based organizations operate at the intersection of one-of-a-kind products and very low volumes, while repetitive or continuous flow shops operate at the intersection of very low product variety and very high volumes. The traditional structures operate along the diagonal of this matrix, while the new structures—such as mass customization—operate off the diagonal; a mass customization process serves one-of-a-kind or high product variety at the same time that it handles a high volume of production.

---

[8] http://entenmanns.gwbakeries.com, July 15, 2005.
[9] http://www.hostesscakes.com, July 15, 2005.

EXHIBIT 3.18
Matching
Process to
Product
Requirements

	Low ← Total Process Volume → High			
High Variety of Products	Project			
↑		Job shop		Mass customization
Range of Product Mix			Batch	
↓				Continuous or repetitive flow
Low Variety of Products				

To continue with our cake-making analogy, photo cakes with a photograph printed in the icing of a cake might best be produced in large quantities in a mass customization environment with highly flexible, but efficient processes. If the cakes were made in much smaller volumes, as they are at some local bakeries and Baskin-Robbins stores, then they would best be produced using a job-shop structure.

Although flexible technologies and methods are starting to be implemented, resulting in off-diagonal choices by a number of firms, there is empirical evidence of adherence to the matrix (Safizadeh et al., 1996) showing that: firms chose positions that lie on or near the diagonal of the matrix; the competitive priorities for the product lines produced in those facilities are consistent with the plant's process choice; and firms positioned on or close to the diagonal outperform those that choose extreme off-diagonal positions. Further, it shows that all five types of organizations rate quality as critically important to their competitive success but differentiate themselves on other competitive dimensions. Job and batch shops, for example, focus on product flexibility, repetitive flow shops on responsiveness to new designs and design changes, and continuous flow shops on delivery time and dependability.

Using the Product-Process Matrix

The product-process matrix can be utilized in a number of ways. It can be used to structure operations in a single facility, creating what some call "a plant within a plant" to handle disparate product types in a single facility. It can be used to test the fit between product and process for an existing facility and cause the organization to change processes or products. Finally, it can be used to determine the appropriate level of flexibility and efficiency for a new plant or to develop a portfolio of plants with differing levels of these traits. In making these choices, however, it is important to understand that products rarely have the same requirements throughout their life cycles.

Mapping Processes to Product Requirements over Time

Many products follow the classic four-stage product life cycle depicted in Exhibit 3.19. In this model, products are introduced, go through a stage of rapid growth, mature, and then decline and often die. We describe the main characteristics of each of these stages in turn.

Introduction In the introduction stage, the firm seeks to build product awareness and develop a market for the product or product family. The number of different products it offers is likely to be limited, and their designs focused on rapid adoption. The firm may sell its products at a low price to penetrate the market and build share quickly. Distribution is usually selective or exclusive, while providing sufficient margins to justify heavy promotion. Target customers include innovators and early adopters. The desired production process accommodates low volumes and considerable and frequent change, and because

EXHIBIT 3.19
Product Life Cycle

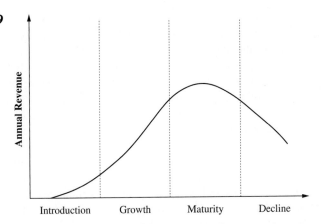

The product life cycle chart with "Annual Revenue" on the vertical axis and stages labeled along the horizontal axis: Introduction, Growth, Maturity, Decline.

the firm has little experience building the products, it will incur the high costs of being on the steep slope of a nascent experience curve. An example of this is the cellular phone market, where manufacturers release the newest phones at high prices through exclusive retailing agreements with service providers, generally targeting early adopters.

Growth   In the growth stage, the firm seeks to build brand preference and increase market share. Product designs are likely to be modular to accommodate multiple customer needs and allow for rapid expansion of the product line. The firm grows its distribution channels, aiming its promotions at a broader audience. It maintains pricing levels as high as possible as long as possible before significant competition enters the market. Production at this stage focuses on keeping up with company growth and moving down the learning curve. There may be some emphasis on standardization and on upgrading production technologies to do so. In this stage, a cellular phone company focuses on adding accessories such as chargers, adapters, and GPS navigation to its line to support its base phone product. Early software and hardware issues are identified and remedied.

Maturity   In the mature stage, strong sales growth diminishes and competition increases. The firm's objective in this stage is to defend its market share while maximizing profits. The firm is likely to be forced to reduce prices (and thus costs) in response to competitive threats and may have to find ways to differentiate itself from the competition. Production at this stage focuses on efficiency, attempting to take advantage of experience curve effects to reduce production costs. A cellular phone in the maturity stage of its life cycle would be used as an inexpensive promotional phone for attracting new cellular contracts.

Decline   As sales decline, the firm may decide to maintain the product, possibly adding new features or finding new applications for it; harvest the product, reducing its costs and offering it to a loyal niche market; or discontinue the product, either stopping production altogether or selling it to another firm. Distribution, promotion, and production of the product are phased out. At this stage the production facility is likely to be highly flexible again but also focused on cost management. As purchases of the cellular phone decrease, it is phased out of production and replaced with newer, better models.

The product life cycle maps quite clearly to the product-process matrix. In the introductory phase, a company adopts a flexible process—like a job shop—to best accommodate frequent product and process design changes. As the business matures and the product design evolves, the basis of competition moves from innovation to cost and the product design becomes standardized, which requires a less flexible, more efficient process. Over time, as the product moves from introduction through growth and into maturity, it moves from the upper left-hand corner of the matrix towards the lower right-hand corner and thus requires commensurate changes in process design; eventually the product moves back to the left-hand corner as it transitions into decline and requires more flexible processes once again.

There are a number of strategic implications of product life cycles for organizations making technology choices. For example, an organization with only one production facility may want to change its production process as its product needs evolve. Alternatively, it may choose to focus its facility on a specific stage of the product life cycle and either constantly redesign its products to leverage its process or subcontract production at other stages. Some contract manufacturers, for example, choose to focus on products only *after* they achieve a certain level of stability, allowing them to capitalize on efficient technology investments. Organizations that outsource their production may need different suppliers to support the different phases of their product life cycles.

Summary—Product-Process Matrix

In summary, the product-process matrix represents a strategic way of thinking about (1) efficiency and flexibility trade-offs, (2) the range of process choices available, (3) how a company may align a set of plants, and (4) how competitors in an industry align their offerings.

Service-Process Matrix

The product-process matrix, conceived as a tool for manufacturing operations, has applicability to service operations as well (Exhibit 3.20). The design and implementation of a customized information system requires a project-based process with many of the same characteristics as project manufacturing. Similarly, the back-office operations of banks require processes with many of the characteristics of a continuous flow operation.

There are other ways to look at services and to match service requirements to the processes used to deliver them. No single model stands out as definitively as the product-process matrix, nor is there much empirical research on the existence of patterns in service-process matching. But these frameworks provide a useful start.

Types of Service Processes

Services can be broken into three distinct groups that are defined primarily in terms of how customers interact with them (Metters et al. 2006). *Demand-sensitive services,* such as banks, restaurants, and retail stores, are those customers visit in person. *Delivered services,* such as fire and police protection, postal and package delivery, emergency medicine, and some repair services, are delivered to the customer's location. *Quasi-manufacturing services,* such as back-office processing centers of banks and insurance companies, warehouses, hotel reservation centers and other call centers, and many firms in the wholesaling industry, are not immediately visible to customers and often have no direct interaction with a customer.[10]

---

[10] Another model, the "customer contact model of services" (Chase 1978), differentiates *pure services,* such as medical centers, restaurants, and transportation services that have high customer contact, from *mixed services,* such as branch offices, and from *quasi-manufacturing services,* such as back offices and distribution centers that have very low customer contact.

EXHIBIT 3.20   Product-Process Matrix for Services

Process Types	Product Characteristics				
	One-of-a-Kind Products	Low Volume, Many Products	Moderate Volume, Multiple Products	High Volume, Some Product Variety	High Volume, Commodity Products
Project	Designing and implementing a customized information system				
Job shop		Operating a hospital emergency room			
Batch			Universities processing students through a variety of classes		
Repetitive Flow				Service desks processing applicants for new driver's licenses	
Continuous Flow					Processing checking account transactions

Service-Process Matrix Examples

The service-process matrix describes a spectrum of services ranging from those with a low degree of interaction and customization to those with a high degree of interaction and customization, and service processes ranging from those with a low degree of labor intensity to those with a high degree of labor intensity. As can be seen in Exhibit 3.21, the service-process matrix is much simpler than the product-process matrix. A service factory has both

EXHIBIT 3.21
Service-Process Matrix

Source: Adapted from Schmenner, "How Can Service Businesses Survive and Prosper?" *MIT Sloan Management Review* 27, no. 3 (1986).

	Low Degree of Interaction and Customization	High Degree of Interaction and Customization
Low Degree of Labor Intensity	**Service Factory** Airlines Trucking Hotels	**Service Shop** Hospitals Auto repair Other repair services
High Degree of Labor Intensity	**Mass Service** Retailing Wholesaling Schools Retail aspects of commercial banking	**Professional Service** Doctors Lawyers Accountants Architects

low interaction and customization and low labor intensity. Hotels are a good example in that, with a few notable exceptions, they do little to customize their services to individual customers and incur large capital expenses to build and maintain their facilities. Service shops, such as auto repair services, similarly incur relatively significant capital expenses to maintain their facilities, but do more customization of their services to individual customer needs than do service factories. Professional services, like architectural design firms, are highly customized to specific client needs, and are highly labor intensive. Finally, mass services, like retail stores, customize to about the same degree as service factories but have a higher degree of labor intensity in their service processes.[11]

Just as the various types of production processes differ in their use of technology, people, information systems, and cost management approaches, service organizations differ in the priorities managers must have in running them (Schmenner 1986). Managers of *low labor intensity* operations, for example, concern themselves with making capital investment decisions, staying current with technological advances, and scheduling service delivery with particular attention to managing peak demand times. Just as for managers of highly capital intensive production operations, minimizing fixed costs and highly utilizing fixed assets are important to these organizations. Managers of *high labor intensity* operations, on the other hand, focus on hiring, training, and general employee welfare, on designing and implementing flexible methods for executing the work, and on scheduling the workforce to cover peaks and valleys in workload.

Operations with a *high degree of interaction and customization* require managers to closely monitor and maintain quality, adapt to changing customer needs and expectations, and provide employees with the freedom to make appropriate decisions in their interactions with clients. Operations with a *low degree of interaction and customization,* on the other hand, must work to make the service feel friendly and comfortable for the customer, often through appropriate investments in the physical setting in which the service is delivered. They must also strive to standardize service delivery methods to ensure customers have similar experiences in their interactions at different times and locations.

The fact that these four quadrants require quite different management attention and focus suggests that service delivery processes must be properly matched to the requirements of the service. A traditional hospital should be managed differently than a specialty clinic such as hernia repair specialist Shouldice Hospital.[12] A traditional law firm should be managed differently than a legal services chain like Jacoby & Meyers, which specializes in personal injury cases (Metters et al. 2006). A firm that wants to provide two very different services may want to consider housing them in different organizations. A firm that wants to change its offerings may need to consider changing its processes, as McDonald's had to do in moving to provide customers more menu choices. The company redesigned its cooking system to make cooking burgers one at a time (instead of in

---

[11] Note that, within any given quadrant of the matrix, there may still be a variety of degrees of customer interaction, customization, and labor intensity. Service Factory A, for example, might have a high degree of interaction with its customers and a low degree of customization, while relatively speaking Service Factory B has a low degree of interaction and a high degree of customization. To apply the matrix in some situations, it may make sense to think of it as three dimensional, separating degree of interaction and degree of customization. Current approaches, however, combine these two dimensions.

[12] http://www.shouldice.com/, July 15, 2005.

batches) more efficient and did away with the heat-lamp systems so that food would be made-to-order instead of substantially made-to-stock.

Implications of Product-Process and Service-Process Matrices

Our descriptions of the product-process and service-process matrices make clear that process technology choices have implications for other choices a firm makes as well: The type of skills needed, the degree of fixed (e.g., capital) costs versus variable (e.g., labor) costs, the amount and type of inventory carried, and the relationship between the technology and the information systems used to run the process are all determined at least in part by the choice of process technology. Failure to understand the relationships among these decisions can lead to a situation where the performance of the technology does not meet expectations.

The product-process and service-process matrices make clear the strategic implications of process technology choices. The choices a firm makes about the characteristics of its products or services are typically driven by the strategic priorities of the business. Firms providing a wide range of products or services, for example, may be particularly focused on features and availability. Firms providing commodity products or services, on the other hand, may be more concerned with cost and quality. Ideally, the firm would choose its process technologies to match the needs of its products or services. The firm may already have processes in place, however, that may restrict its set of choices of new products or services. Thus, process technology choice plays a critical role in achievement of a firm's overall objectives. In the next section, we dig further into process technology choice.

Process Technology Strategy Decisions

Armed with two important tools for thinking about process technology strategy, the experience curve and the product/service-process matrix, we turn now to the strategic decisions we highlighted at the beginning of the chapter. To what degree should the process be automated, how flexible should it be, and what economies of scale should it be able to achieve? Does the firm wish to be a leader or follower in process technology? Should the firm make or buy its process technology? Finally, how does the firm want to manage process technology development and deployment?

All of these decisions are made in the context of the company's business strategy and competitive environment. In some industries, process technology provides little competitive advantage, as the technology employed is largely the same across companies. In other industries, companies may differentiate themselves on the basis of the process technologies themselves, on the basis of how the technologies are implemented, or on the basis of how they are managed across multiple locations. Dell, for example, differentiates itself on delivery time and product flexibility by implementing common technologies effectively. While much of the process technology it employs is equally available to its competitors, Dell configures that technology in flexible assembly lines that are highly responsive to its key business requirements. Where needed, it invests in streamlining processes—such as product test, which it streamlined with an online testing system—to achieve low assembly and delivery times. It links its process technology strategy closely to its product design strategy; modular product designs allow for rapid product configuration and reconfiguration. By deploying the equipment in this way and making significant investments in information technology to schedule and run the equipment, Dell gains a competitive advantage in availability and product variety.

In short, companies must choose process technologies, configure them, and in some cases manage them across multiple sites in support of their business strategies. The firm must determine which process technology choices are appropriate to support the position it wishes to take in cost, quality, availability, features/innovativeness, and environmental performance, and what capabilities the firm can exploit or should develop to execute the business strategy. In all cases, the company will make these choices not only for its own internal operations but will seek partners who make these choices as well.

We turn now to the first of the process technology strategy decisions these firms must make, whether in support of their business strategies or as a contribution to them.

Choosing an Appropriate Technology

In choosing an appropriate technology, firms grapple with four questions: How automated should the process be? How flexible should the process be? How scalable is the process, and what degree of scale should the process achieve? What are the economic returns to investing in the technology?

Labor Intensive versus Automated Processes

The product-process and service-process matrices provide some hints for answering the question of how automated a process should be. The farther down the diagonal of the product-process matrix a process is, the higher the level of automation will be. While projects are generally executed with a high proportion of labor content, continuous/repetitive flow and mass customization shops generally have a smaller proportion of labor content. Similarly, service factories (e.g., airlines) and service shops (e.g., hospitals) are likely to have more automation than do mass service (e.g., retail stores) and professional service (e.g., law firms) organizations. Thus, choice of the level of automation of any given process is driven in part by the type of product or service the firm is offering.

That said, there are still choices firms must make about how much they will automate, even within a specific position on the product/service-process matrix. In very mature industries, such as repetitive flow automobile manufacturing, where process technologies are fairly standard and choices limited, firms may still choose to automate to different degrees in different markets, or to automate different parts of the process for specific competitive purposes. Within a given industry, one is likely to find more automated processes in Germany, Japan, or the United States, where labor costs are quite high, and less automated processes in Mexico, Brazil, and Thailand, where labor costs are lower.

Some companies in an industry may choose to automate a process, or portion of a process, more than their competitors in order to achieve a specific strategic goal. An automobile manufacturer, for example, may choose to automate its paint shops to eliminate workers and thus the health issues associated with handling paint. Or, the same manufacturer might choose to automate specific part-handling tasks—such as moving a fully assembled seat into position in the car—to reduce worker injuries. A semiconductor fabricator could fully automate material handling to reduce cost and throughput time, thus improving both cost and availability. An insurance provider might choose to automate its payment receipt process to improve accuracy and speed.

So, while the product-process and service-process matrices provide general guidance as to the degree of automation of the process, there is still space for firms to differentiate themselves and make choices. There are four sets of issues that firms should consider when making decisions about how much to automate: business, operational, social and political, and regulatory issues (Goldberg 2001).

Business Issues Business issues link the automation decision to the overall business, focusing on return on investment, flexibility, timing, and competitiveness of the automation. In the pharmaceutical industry, for example, firms only own exclusive rights to produce and sell a drug for the life of the patent(s) they have on the drug. Thus, it is critical to get new processes up and running as quickly as possible once it is clear that the drugs will receive Food and Drug Administration (FDA) approval. Any delays in bringing a new product to market result directly in lost revenues to the firm. Thus, timing of the automation and its ability to deliver new products quickly is a key concern in the industry.

Operational Issues Operational issues are associated with the technological and physical constraints placed upon the process by its inputs and outputs as well as by the humans and machines involved. The operational capabilities of the process to perform from a cost perspective (e.g., appropriate economies of scale), quality perspective (e.g., adequate precision and repeatability), availability perspective (e.g., fast enough), features/innovativeness perspective (e.g., can handle the variety of technologies, products, and services to be put through it), and environmental perspective (e.g., acceptable volume of pollutants generated) must all be considered. The firm may have other technological, scientific, engineering, and management goals as well that dictate investments in automation to, for example, collect and analyze data and respond to aberrant conditions. In the pharmaceutical industry, for example, each batch of product must meet stringent quality guidelines or it cannot be sold, so information systems are required to track each batch produced, including the raw materials that went into it.

Social and Political Issues Social and political issues address both the way in which the automation decision is made by the organization and the way in which automation might affect the organization and its human resources. Some organizations have cultures that thrive on being "high tech" and employing the latest and greatest technologies. These organizations are often dominated by engineering personnel who drive the automation decision process. While it may not always make sense to forge ahead with automation, at least these organizations are comfortable with technology. Other organizations may not have as deep a bench of technical strength and may be more cautious about adopting higher levels of automation. Degree of automation also has significant implications for the skill sets of the employees. It may mean fewer operators are needed, leading to concerns about job security, or it may require significant retraining efforts. Thus, an organization's culture, decision-making process, and management of front-line employees can have a significant effect on automation decisions.

Regulatory Issues Finally, regulatory issues are of particular concern in the pharmaceutical industry, as the Food and Drug Administration (FDA) in the United States and comparable agencies around the world wield considerable control over the industry. The FDA's good manufacturing practice (GMP) standards set strict guidelines for pharmaceutical manufacturing processes, and companies must be requalified each time they change their processes. But regulation is not unique to the pharmaceutical industry; virtually all companies are subject to some regulatory requirement whether from the Environmental Protection Agency (EPA), Occupational Safety and Health Administration (OSHA), Underwriters Laboratories (UL), Federal Communications Commission (FCC), or their

EXHIBIT 3.22
Considerations in Making Automation Decisions

Source: Adapted from Goldberg, "*Process Automation at Genzyme*," MIT masters thesis, 2001.

Business Issues	**Operational Issues**
Fit with business strategy	Effect on cost
Competitiveness vs. peers	Effect on quality/reliability
Return on investment	Repeatability of process
Cost savings	Precision of process
Direct labor cost reduction	Effect on availability
Flexibility and adaptability	Effect on features/innovativeness
Time to implement and ramp up	Effect on environmental performance
Safety	Ability to meet internal goals (e.g., for data
	collection, tracking)
	Security
Social/Political Issues	**Regulatory Issues**
Organizational culture	Regulatory compliance
Comfort with technology	Change control
"Cool tech factor" for engineers	Data collection, analysis, and reporting
"Cool tech factor" for customers	Perception
Not-invented-here syndrome	
"That's the way we do things here" syndrome	
Decision-making dynamics	
Decision-maker bias	
Workforce implications	
Skill requirements	
Simplification of operator tasks	
Job security (reality and perceptions)	

equivalents in other countries. Thus, all automation decisions must take into account the regulatory standards that must be met.

Exhibit 3.22 summarizes the business, operational, social and political, and regulatory issues a firm should consider when deciding on new automation. The degree to which a firm must consider any or all of these issues depends in part on its business strategy and also in part on what the key drivers are for the automation decision it is making. It is likely that the final decision will entail only a few of the most critical issues for the firm's specific situation.

Flexible versus Rigid Processes

The product-process and service-process matrices also provide guidance for deciding how much flexibility a process must have. On the product-process matrix, moving down the diagonal from project-based organization to repetitive and continuous flow organizations, flexibility decreases and efficiency increases. A mass customization process returns flexibility to the process while retaining the efficiency of a repetitive or continuous flow structure. Similarly, service shops and professional services offer more customization and thus must have more flexibility than service factories and mass services. The degree of flexibility in the process is thus largely dictated by the types of products and/or services the firm wishes to offer.

Nonetheless, as in deciding how much to automate a process, businesses must make choices about how much flexibility to develop, even within a single position in the product- and service-process matrices. At the heart of the decision is a trade-off between flexibility and efficiency. Generally, there is some cost to attaining flexibility, whether due to investments in smarter equipment, a wider range of tooling for the equipment, more sophisticated information technology, or more highly cross-trained people. Thus, organizations wishing to add flexibility to respond to demands in the marketplace must understand the costs of attaining that flexibility, particularly those related to investments in process technology.

Mass customization firms, however, break this mold and seek to optimize flexibility and efficiency simultaneously. Dell, for example, revolutionized the personal computer industry by implementing a series of flexible assembly lines that can easily produce a broad range of products according to customer demand. It retains efficiency, however, through finely tuned processes, close management of inventories, and control over the range of options offered (which in turn limits the amount of flexibility needed). As with many mass customization companies, Dell learned that it could offer more flexibility than its mass production counterparts, while retaining efficiency near mass production levels.

The ability to attain increased flexibility without sacrificing efficiency is due in part to the advent of more flexible advanced technologies (Lei et al. 1996) as well as to the increased use of subcontracting or outsourcing to manage the business. Some of the commonly used means of increasing flexibility at low cost include:

- Investment in flexible manufacturing systems (FMS) and other advanced technologies. Motorola's award-winning Bandit facility, which produced Motorola's alphanumeric radio pagers in lot sizes of one, had the remarkable ability even in 1990 to begin producing a customized pager within 20 minutes of a salesperson entering a rush order.
- Modular product and service design, as Dell has, which allows customers to configure products or service to their own needs and allows production and/or delivery to operate efficiently by easily swapping modules in and out.
- Postponement strategies (see Chapter 8) that delay differentiation of a product or service until as late as possible in the production or delivery process, thus allowing the early stages of that process to operate as efficiently as possible. Hewlett-Packard adds country-specific information to its products just before they are shipped, allowing it to produce and store undifferentiated "vanilla" products at low cost.
- Set-up or changeover time reduction, often through investment in flexible process technologies and/or information technologies to control those processes. Single minute exchange of die (SMED), for example, led to reductions in the set-up time for producing sheet metal car parts from hours to less than 10 minutes (Shingo 1992).
- Just-in-time or lean manufacturing techniques to reduce inventories throughout the supply chain, thus making the supply chain more responsive to a wider range of requirements at lower cost.

All of these approaches, and others, increase the flexibility of an operation often without investment in different process technologies. Thus, any given process technology may have a range of flexibility it can offer. Nonetheless, that range may be limited, and other investments or trade-offs may be required to increase flexibility outside that range.

Thus, firms must first determine how much flexibility is required of them and then decide how to go about obtaining that flexibility. In the auto industry, for example, manufacturers do extensive market research to determine which option bundles are most popular or will please the customers most. Even customers ordering custom vehicles are limited to these choices. Boeing and Airbus have always provided a wide range of options—in seating, cabin layout, and so on—to their airline customers but are now considering limiting those options as they seek to streamline and reduce the costs of their production facilities. Thus, companies continue to assess flexibility/efficiency trade-offs as they develop their process technology strategies.

Scalability and Degree of Scale Achievable

In addition to deciding how much to automate a process and how flexible to make it, firms must decide how scalable a process should be. In other words, firms need to understand how well a process technology will be able to accommodate growth in product or service output, and what economies of scale are achievable when the facility is operating at full production or service delivery rates.

Companies that are introducing new products and then ramping them to high-volume production face not only the question of what economies of scale they need to be able to achieve, but how scalable their processes are. When their products are young, and being produced in low volumes, they may prefer a flexible job-shop type of process. As the products age, however, the company may require high-volume production facilities. In this situation, the firm may choose technologies that scale well to higher volumes, even though they are not optimal for the low volumes at introduction. Alternatively, they may choose to have two processes: one that supports the job-shop activities of new product introduction, and one that takes on the products as they grow in volume.

Services that intend to grow must also consider whether or not the technologies they employ are scalable, or whether they should invest in different types of facilities for new service introduction rather than for volume service delivery. For example, Bank of America chooses not to differentiate the facilities in which it tests and introduces new services from regular mass service operations expressly because it wants to learn about the performance of the new services as they interact with real customers in real settings (Thomke 2003).

In production as well as in services, scalability questions generally encompass more than just the scalability of the technology itself. When McDonald's considers expanding the capacity of a single location, it must address all elements of the operating system, including not only the food preparation technologies (e.g., grills, fryers), but also staffing, inventory policies, customer flow patterns, meal assembly methods, and the like.

So, the type of product or service the organization wishes to offer, and thus its position on the product/service-process matrices, suggests the degree of scale it might choose. A firm's decision will also be influenced by the steepness of the scale curve. Suppose, for example, that a firm had three process technologies from which to choose, each with a different scale curve, as shown in Exhibit 3.23. If the firm wanted to be able to achieve reasonable costs throughout the life of a product, but not necessarily the lowest possible costs, it might choose technology A. If, on the other hand, it needed to be able to compete at the lowest possible cost when producing or delivering at full volume, it might choose technology C. Finally, it might be willing to tolerate slightly higher costs at low volume in order to achieve reasonable costs at high volume later and thus select technology B. Scale alternatives are a function of the technology alternatives available to the company. The company should fully understand these alternatives and the range of possible scales in developing a strategy.

EXHIBIT 3.23
Comparison of
Three
Technology
Scale Curves

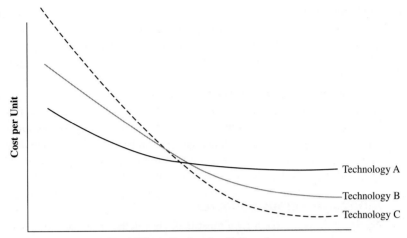

Economic Evaluation of Technology Options

So far, the considerations we have discussed are largely qualitative. But it is possible in many cases to do a straightforward economic analysis of the process technology options. Costs to develop or procure and implement new process technology include not only the obvious costs of the research and development hours to develop the equipment or the purchase cost of the equipment, but also installation, training, debugging, and ramp-up costs. The benefits associated with the new process technology may include floor space reductions, productivity increases, quality improvements, lower costs of environmental compliance, and reduced employee headcount. They may also include less tangible benefits, such as the ability to produce a broader range of products or services, the ability to respond to market changes more quickly, and the ability to learn about new process technologies. These intangible benefits can often far outweigh the more tangible benefits.

The costs and benefits of the new process technology as well as a risk-adjusted expected rate of return can all be put into a net present value (NPV) calculation to determine the NPV of the technology as follows:

$$NPV = -\,\text{Initial cost} + \sum_{i=1}^{n} \frac{(\text{Benefits}_i - \text{Costs}_i)}{(1 + r)^i}$$
$$+ \frac{\text{Salvage value}}{(1 + r)^n}$$

where

r = risk-adjusted rate of return expressed as a percentage

While NPV calculations often underestimate the full benefits of investment in a new process technology (Kaplan 1986), they provide useful numbers for comparison of alternative technologies and are a meaningful input to the decision process.

Summary: Choosing an Appropriate Technology

Choosing an appropriate process technology for an organization is largely a question of identifying the position the firm wants to occupy on the product-process or service-process matrix. Position on the matrix will suggest appropriate degrees of automation, flexibility, and scale. Within any given position on the matrix, however, firms still have choices. To make choices about degree of automation, they must consider business, operational, social and political, and regulatory issues. To make choices about degree of flexibility, they must fully understand what customers want from them and make appropriate trade-offs with efficiency. To make choices about scale, they must assess their alternatives and identify the most cost-effective choice. Net present value calculations provide information about the potential cost or return to the company of investing in the technology.

Innovator versus Follower

A related decision that a firm must make is whether it wishes to use proven, well-understood technologies or newer, more innovative ones. Will the company be a follower, employing technologies that have been used and at least partially debugged by others, or will the firm be a leader, using technologies that have not been tried before? Between these options lies a range of choices. A company may use proven technologies in most process steps and experiment with groundbreaking technologies in others, or it may use proven technologies, but modify them significantly (e.g., through continuous improvement efforts) for its own purposes.

Taking a leadership position by investing in innovative technologies may provide the firm with significant competitive advantage. Advanced technologies can provide economies of scope, promote strategic flexibility by "facilitating integration of stakeholders," and provide flexibility for future growth. However, investment in advanced technology is not necessarily the only way to achieve a competitive performance target. Flexibility can, as we noted, be obtained through means other than investment in advanced technologies (Narasimhan and Das 1999). In fact, investments in advanced technology do not always result in improved performance (Boyer et al. 1996), suggesting that the risks associated with investing in advanced technologies sometimes outweigh the benefits, especially when equivalent benefits can be achieved in other ways.

Investments in proven technologies arguably have lower risk and more certain returns, but may not by themselves provide significant competitive advantage. Firms employing standard, readily available technologies may instead seek competitive advantage through the ways in which they use the technology to facilitate cost reductions, quality improvements, better availability, more innovation or features, or improved environmental performance. Chaparral Steel, for example, uses standard steel-making technologies in its facility, but it invests significant time and effort in refining that equipment to operate faster, at lower cost, and sometimes with capabilities that other steelmakers are unable to replicate.

Continuous Improvement and Process Technology Choice

Continuous improvement of the use of proven technologies is an important strategic option for achieving competitive advantage through process technology. Improvements may be based on innovative methods and techniques surrounding the use of the process technology such as planning methods for materials replenishment and movement, procedures for assembly, or the way workers perform a certain task. Improvements may be made in the processes that feed or support the process technology, such as in order processing or new product development. Or improvement might come from better control over environmental factors such as temperature, which allow the process to operate within tighter parameters.

Investments in continuous improvement activities are almost always justified, but some companies make them core to achieving competitive advantage. Amazon.com, for example, employs largely standard technologies that can be purchased by anyone in the distribution or materials handling business. But it focuses considerable attention on continuous improvement, sweating "every last drop of productivity out of the warehouses."[13] It increased the capacity of its Fernley, Nevada, warehouse by 40%, for example, when it redesigned the bottleneck between the picking and sorting operations. Between 1999 and 2003, Amazon tripled the volume it could handle at its warehouses and dropped the cost of operating them from nearly 20% of Amazon's revenues to less than 10%. Amazon's efficiency at running its warehouses has won it major contracts to handle the e-commerce business of other retailers such as Target.

Continuous improvement efforts, however, can be limited by product or service design. Various studies have shown that close to 80% of the cost and quality of a product is determined by choices made in the design of the product, leaving only 20% of the cost available for reduction by manufacturing. In the auto industry, for example, the vehicles that are easiest to assemble are those with the simplest designs. Easy assembly leads to low defect rates as well (e.g., Womack et al. 1990). Similarly, the design of a financial product or service dictates to a large degree the efficiency and effectiveness with which it can be delivered.

While continuous improvement efforts are often a way to achieve competitive advantage, as they allow a firm to get more out of a given investment in process technology than its competitors, innovation in products or services often requires more than just continuous improvement of process technologies. Mature industries often focus on continuous improvement as a means of reducing cost in products or services that are in decline. Industries that are earlier in the life cycle, however, may need to seek improvement through investment in new process technologies.

Product Innovation and Process Technology Choice

Often, innovative process technologies are used to facilitate development and delivery of innovative products or services. Indeed, process innovation is often tightly tied to process and/or service innovation (Wheelwright and Clark 1992). Exhibit 3.24 maps product or service innovation against process innovation, with degree of process change on one axis and degree of product or service change on the other. In the upper left corner of the matrix are projects that entail significant product or service change and significant process change; these are sometimes referred to as *breakthrough projects* or *technologies*. In the center of the matrix are projects that entail investment in either next generation processes or next generation products or services, or both. These are referred to as *platform projects*. In the lower right-hand corner of the matrix are *derivative projects* that require incremental changes in products, services, or processes. Companies use the matrix in planning investments in development projects and often attempt to strike a balance across breakthrough, platform, and derivative projects.

---

[13] http://www.mutualofamerica.com/articles/Fortune/May03/fortune.asp, August 19, 2005.

EXHIBIT 3.24   Mapping Change in Process to Change in Product or Service

Source: Adapted from Wheelwright and Clark, 1992.

		More ⟵ Degree of Product or Service Change ⟶ Less			
		New core product or service	Next generation product or service	Addition to product or service family	Derivatives and enhancements
More ↑ **Degree of Process Change** ↓ **Less**	New core process	Breakthrough projects			
	Next generation process		Platform projects		
	Change to a small set of activities			Derivative projects	
	Incremental change (e.g., to a single activity)				

The argument that generally follows from the use of this matrix is that firms cannot generate new streams of products or services without generating periodic breakthrough projects, or at least investing in new product, service, or process platforms. Without new platforms on which to build families of derivative products or services, companies eventually run out of new paths to follow in product or service innovation. Thus, there might be a time when investment in innovative process technologies is appropriate, as it will allow the firm to launch a new series of products or services. In these cases, the new process may also offer the firm a proprietary advantage over other firms, as the company will own the intellectual property associated with the breakthrough innovation. Many companies will, however, try to avoid significant changes in product or service and in process simultaneously, investing in major change in only one area at a time.

Intel, clearly a leader in both product and process innovation, carefully manages its investments to limit the amount of change it makes at any given time. When it introduces a new process technology (e.g., 300 nm capability), it uses that new technology initially to build existing products. Conversely, the company introduces its new products on existing or proven process technologies. In this way, it continues to innovate in both product and process, while minimizing risks associated with introducing too many changes at once. Intel also reduces risk in its new processes by reusing equipment from existing processes as much as possible. It trades off the benefits of investing in state-of-the-art technologies with the risks of implementing new, unproven technologies in its highly complex production process. In this way, Intel acts as an innovator where innovation is important to achieving its performance goals, and as a follower where following allows it to reduce risks.

When it is possible to develop multiple families of products or services that leverage a single process platform, a company may gain competitive advantage as it gains significant experience in the chosen process technology (Meyer and Utterback 1993). The notion of using a single process platform across multiple generations of products or services is displayed graphically in Exhibit 3.25. Here the initial peak investment in process innovation

EXHIBIT 3.25
Process Innovation and Multiple Product Generations

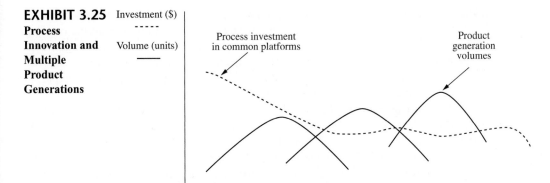

occurs with the launch of the first generation product or service. Follow-on products or services benefit from the initial investment, requiring less and less process technology investment per launch.

Develop In House or Outside?

Closely related to the decision about how innovative to be is the question of whether to develop process technology in house or not. The factors to be considered in making this decision are similar to those associated with making a vertical integration decision in general. (See Exhibit 2.14 for a summary of these factors.) The firm must decide whether or not development of the process technology is critical to achieving competitive advantage, and whether that advantage is in cost, quality, availability, features/innovativeness, or environmental soundness. Developing the process in house could also build critical capabilities on which the firm could build a competitive advantage. Most companies' core competencies and sources of competitive advantage lie outside the process development area, so there is not a clear advantage for them to develop technologies in house. There are, however, important exceptions.

If the company's source of competitive advantage is a new or unique technology that is difficult to find in the marketplace, it may make sense for the company to develop the technology itself or at least have significant control over its development. In this way it gains access to early knowledge of how the technology works and how it may be used. This can be critical for developing products or services that leverage the new technology. Finally, in situations where the technology needs to be adapted to specific needs, the company may need to develop expertise in the technology in order to fully adapt it to the specific situation.

The semiconductor industry, once again, provides an interesting example of vendor technology development. Although Intel holds a major position in the semiconductor market and thus has significant leverage over the technology vendors in its industry, it still engages in industrywide consortia[14] that set joint standards for equipment development. In this way, Intel can avoid customization charges from its vendors for requesting features that are slightly different from those requested by its competitors. In general, companies with major market positions, such as Intel, can dominate technology vendor

---

[14] e.g., SEMI, www.semi.org, July 15, 2005.

relationships and thus get technology developed to their standards without developing it in house. Companies in these positions must, however, take care to ensure the ongoing health of their vendor base. Boeing, for example, often uses engines from two engine suppliers on an aircraft to help ensure that both companies survive and can continue to experiment with new technologies. Intel, similarly, uses multiple equipment vendors in part to ensure that they all stay in business.

The way in which a company improves process performance over time may also be a determinant of the choice of developing technology in house or outsourcing it. A company that derives process improvement from new process methods and techniques may choose to outsource its development, and focus its internal engineering efforts on continuous improvement. A company that improves process performance through technological means may choose to focus its internal engineering efforts on process technology development. To do so, however, it must have a sufficient need for the technology, so that it can afford the significant up-front investment. External equipment developers can often amortize the research and development costs for equipment over sales to many different organizations, making it difficult for an in house development organization to compete. Of course, any time equipment development is outsourced, all competitors in an industry can access the same technology; differentiation in this case reverts to the ways in which the competitors use the technology.

The question of whether to develop in house or not can be linked to the question of how innovative to be in process technology. A company may be innovative by developing its own process technologies internally or by purchasing them. Similarly, a company may be a follower by developing its own technology internally or by purchasing it. Exhibit 3.26 shows these four options. The alternative of developing proven technologies in house is relatively rare, as it is generally more cost-effective to simply purchase them, but the other three combinations are more common.

There are sometimes interesting competitive or market dynamics associated with these choices. In the semiconductor industry, for example, U.S. companies tend to look to external sources for process technology development and engage in a range of innovation from follower to leader. Japanese companies, on the other hand, tend to be innovators who develop their process technology in house (Egelhoff 1993). Over time, the Japanese semiconductor companies have become the major suppliers of photolithography equipment to the semiconductor industry, which means that U.S. companies are faced with purchasing equipment from their direct competitors. In some cases, this leaves the U.S. manufacturers

EXHIBIT 3.26
Process Technology Development and Acquisition Choices

	Lead Using Innovative Process Technologies	Follow Using Well-Proven Process Technologies
Develop Process Technology In-House	Expensive, but can lead to significant competitive advantage	Rare. Not much benefit in re-inventing something that is already readily available.
Purchase Process Technology from Outside Vendors	May be difficult to retain competitive advantage as vendors share technology with other customers.	Common. Often companies purchase standard technologies and then adapt them to their own internal use.

at a competitive disadvantage, as they cannot access new technology as quickly as the Japanese manufacturers that developed it. It can thus be important to examine market competition when making technology innovation, sourcing, and positioning decisions.

Managing Technology in Multisite Networks: Degrees of Standardization and Centralization

All of the decisions we have addressed so far—about type of process technology, whether to be a follower or a leader, and whether to develop in house or not—are made more complex in multisite networks. While this issue is addressed in more detail in Chapter 5, we highlight a couple of important choices here. When a firm has more than one production or service delivery location, it must address the question of whether it wants to standardize its processes across all locations and, if not, which sites will use which technologies. There are many reasons why a firm might choose to let its process technologies vary across sites. A high-volume facility, for example, might employ a higher degree of automation or more specialized technology than a low-volume facility. A facility in a developed country with relatively high labor rates might choose a higher degree of automation than a facility in a less developed country with lower labor costs. A facility producing for or delivering to a mature market might invest in more rigid technologies that allow it to operate at very low cost, while a facility producing for an emerging market might invest in more flexible technology that allows it to be more responsive to the changing market.

A firm with multiple sites may either let each site make its own process technology decisions, choosing an appropriate level of automation, degree of innovation, and extent of internal development itself, or it may choose to standardize processes across the company. Often, companies that want to standardize their production or service delivery processes firmwide centralize process technology development and management. Decentralized process technology development and management structures make process standardization extremely difficult, but centralized structures do not by themselves ensure standardization. In many firms, processes that start out standardized diverge from one another over time as the various locations that employ them make changes. Also, a firm may wish to centralize process technology development to gain control over development costs and ensure some degree of standardization (e.g., in equipment choice), but not worry about divergence in the process once deployed. Another firm may wish to control the process after deployment as well. The four paths a company might follow are summarized in Exhibit 3.27.

Intel's Copy Exactly! program, described in the sidebar "Intel's Copy Exactly! Approach," is a widely cited example of both centralization and standardization of process technology across multiple sites. Intel standardizes equipment, methods, process parameters, maintenance procedures, training, and specifications across all of its fabrication sites worldwide and is increasingly standardizing its assembly and test processes as well. To implement Copy Exactly! Intel manages the development of new processes centrally in a single technology development fab and employs joint engineering teams with representatives from each of the sites at which the process is to be implemented to ensure precise replication. Furthermore, a joint control change board is required to approve any process changes recommended by the sites.

Copy Exactly! allows Intel to ramp up new facilities quickly, provides Intel's customers products that are the same regardless of where they are produced (which reduces qualification times), and facilitates learning and resource sharing across sites. Intel recognizes that this

Intel's Copy Exactly! Approach

In many manufacturing companies new processes and equipment technology are first developed and tested in a research laboratory setting. The lab setting allows highly talented engineers and technologists to develop and fine-tune the new process and equipment unimpeded by the everyday distractions of a high-volume production environment. The fully engineered process is then transferred to the actual production facility where a new set of engineers modifies it to produce at volume. This two-phase development process has some downsides: It often delays process ramp-up to full volume as the process has to be reworked to operate properly at high volume, and the resulting process is often quite different from the original one, thus limiting the extent to which learning can be shared across the two plants.

It is this dilemma that drove Intel to adopt the Copy Exactly! strategy in the mid-1980s. In Intel's highly complex semiconductor fabrication process, small differences in equipment and process may create dozens of ill-understood interactions that can significantly reduce yields. When small changes to the process are made as it is rolled out from the technology development fab to the high-volume manufacturing fabs, yields go down and Intel is unable to leverage learning from one site to another.

The Copy Exactly! approach dictates that all fabs running a given process technology be matched as closely as possible. Matching includes not only selecting the same equipment and using the same process output parameters but also the physical inputs to the process—facilities, clean rooms, equipment, chemicals, gases. Even suppliers and training methodologies are replicated across plants. Organizationally, this has required managers from high-volume manufacturing facilities to become more involved earlier in the development of new processes at the technology development fabs. Also, Intel must increase its investment in coordination among its facilities to ensure ongoing consistency.

Intel gains three major benefits from its Copy Exactly! policy:

First, it is able to ramp up new high-volume production facilities more quickly, which increases yields and decreases Intel's time-to-market for new technologies and new products. It also allows Intel to respond more quickly to changing market demands as it can bring on new facilities more quickly in the face of unexpected demand growth.

Second, it allows Intel to run a "flexible virtual fab" in which wafers can be started at one facility and completed at another without significant yield losses. This allows Intel to not only quickly rebalance production schedules globally as needed but also to respond quickly to any catastrophic event at a single plant by immediately moving production away from that facility.

Third, Intel leverages its significant investment in technical resources as engineers can readily share knowledge across like facilities, thus speeding their learning cycles. Performance-enhancing changes identified at one site can be quickly transferred to and implemented at the other sites.

Intel claims significant returns on its investment in the Copy Exactly! strategy. Between 1985 and 1995, when the program was fully implemented, revenues per manufacturing employee increased from $114,000 to $461,000; revenues increased three times, while the number of factory workers declined by 30%.

Source: www.intel.com/pressroom/kits/manufacturing/copy_exactly_bkgrnd.htm, June 23, 2006.

system creates additional bureaucracy and increases the time to gain approval of changes among the appropriate constituencies and implement changes across multiple sites, but does its best to ameliorate these problems with a streamlined decision-making process. Regardless, the company believes that the advantages of the program far outweigh its disadvantages.

There are five key considerations to be made in deciding whether or not to standardize process technology in a multisite network: how standard the company's products are, how stable its process technology is, what the basis for process learning and improvement is, what the differences in volume among the facilities are, and what the differential effects of labor in different locations are. We address each of these in turn.

EXHIBIT 3.27   **Centralization and Standardization Options**

	Standardized Processes	Nonstandardized Processes
Centralized Process Development and Management	Reduces start-up costs, as each site can learn from those that have gone before it Facilitates cross-plant learning, as a central organization gathers and communicates knowledge Reduces initial capital outlays, as a single pilot facility can test and fine-tune the process before rollout	Captures some of the efficiencies of standardized processes, while allowing local sites to adapt the processes to local needs in a controlled fashion
Decentralized Process Development and Management	Extremely difficult to do, unless a good deal of overhead is spent on coordination and sharing	Allows the local site to respond to site-specific conditions such as: Market differences Labor differences Supplier differences Eliminates the overhead associated with coordination across the corporation

Product and Service Standardization

The degree to which a company can standardize its processes across multiple facilities depends in part on whether or not the products to be produced or services to be delivered by those facilities are also standardized. When products and/or services are standardized, standard processes are possible. When variations of the products or services are created for local markets or distribution channels, process standardization may be more difficult. Intel uses the same microprocessors in products around the world, which facilitates standardization of its processes worldwide. The auto industry, on the other hand, localizes its products based on specific market requirements. While there is a relatively high degree of standardization in some of the components that go into the cars, (e.g., engines and transmissions), even these vary by market. The U.S. market, for example, generally requires engines that are larger and more powerful than those required in Europe and Latin America. To the degree that products or services are different, different processes may be needed to produce or deliver them. In some situations, a company may produce a standard product or service with local variations. In this case, a standardized process can be used for much of the production or delivery process, with either local variations in other facilities or by using a standard flexible operation that can be adapted for each market.

Stability of Technology

In an industry where process technology is stable, a standardization strategy may be easier to implement and manage across multiple sites. Indeed, Intel identifies this as a factor in its process technology strategy. In situations where technology tends to advance significantly and new generations of technology can leapfrog others, standardizing technology across multiple sites may be more difficult and companies may be better off allowing some independently managed technologies. Even though individual sites can respond more quickly on

their own, a centralized process technology organization could still lead technology introduction but allow for different rates of adoption at different sites. Or it may introduce a new
technology at one site, debug and integrate it at that site, and then release it to other sites.
A centralized structure may make more sense when change needs to be coordinated and
happen rapidly across the whole organization.

Basis for Learning and Improvement

Competitive advantage is often based on companies making significant and frequent
improvements in their production processes. The sources of such improvement might be
procedures and methods in the factory or a new generation of technology. When learning
is technology-based, it makes more sense to standardize technology across sites so that
changes and improvements in technology can be implemented at all sites. Learning in this
case arguably occurs at the development site rather than at one of the remote locations and
is applied to each new generation of process equipment developed (Exhibit 3.28a).

On the other hand, when improvements are methods- and procedures-based, the sources
of improvements will often come from the individuals on the front lines running the
process, creating the traditionally defined learning curve effect (Exhibit 3.28b). In this case,
it is important to give the sites autonomy to improve processes as they see fit and then to
filter improvement ideas up to a central development organization or across to other sites.
For the individual sites to have this autonomy, the company may need to minimize process
standardization. Whether most learning occurs via the family of curves in Exhibit 3.28a or
via that in Exhibit 3.28b is not clear. Most organizations will have both types of learning
and will have to sort out which is most important to advancing process performance quickly.

EXHIBIT 3.28   **Comparison of Learning Approaches**

Source: Adapted from Pisano, "ITT Automotive: Global Manufacturing Strategy," teaching note, Harvard Business School, 1994.

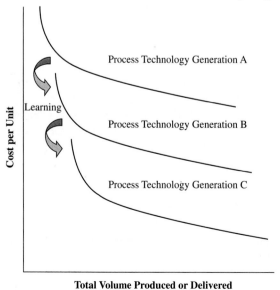

(a) Learning in a centralized process-development context

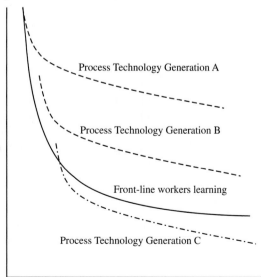

(b) Learning by front-line workers in a facility

Different Levels of Volume and Scale

The degree to which a process can be standardized across facilities in a multisite network also depends on the volumes to be produced or delivered from each of the facilities. Facilities of very different sizes within one company may each need different technology and different scale. In the auto industry, assembly plants are geared to local markets, with very little shipment of complete automobiles from country to country. Plant sizes thus reflect local market sizes and dictate in turn which process technologies must be employed. Assembly plants producing less than 20,000 cars per year to serve small markets look different from high-volume assembly lines serving larger markets. When a company has facilities whose size and volume are essentially similar, standardization becomes more of an option. In the semiconductor industry, wafers and assembled microprocessors are typically delivered across borders. There is thus no reason to tailor the factory size to the local market size, and a company like Intel is free to design factories as big (or as small) as it desires, making it easier to standardize wafer and assembly manufacturing across different sites.

Labor Force Impacts

Labor costs and the availability of skilled labor may also have an effect on the decision to standardize processes globally. Companies whose processes require a high degree of automation and have low-labor content will find little advantage in modifying the technology to take advantage of low-labor costs. These processes might well remain standardized regardless of location. In the semiconductor business, for example, processes are highly capital intensive and automated, so global standardization makes sense. Companies that can choose from a range of processes with different degrees of labor intensity, however, may find it beneficial to fine-tune the process to leverage labor rates in specific locations, using more labor-intensive processes in locations with inexpensive labor, and more capital-intensive processes in those with more expensive labor. In these situations one might see a range of process technologies and less standardization.

Access to skilled labor may also dictate choice of process technologies. Advanced process technologies often require sophisticated operators. When Steve Jobs (CEO of Apple Computer and Pixar) started his computer company, NeXT, for example, his highly automated production facility boasted more PhDs than did the research and development group. This facility was expected to produce computers untouched by human hands. Located in the United States, the facility had ready access to well-educated process engineers but faced high labor rates; this situation suggested a high level of automation. Were the facility located in a developing country with fewer engineering resources, it might have made more sense to have less sophisticated robotic technology and more human hands assembling the computers.

Multisite Network Process Technology Management Summary

Firms managing multiple sites around the world must decide to what extent they will standardize the processes used at each of those sites and to what degree they will centrally manage the development and deployment of process technologies. To answer these questions they must consider the degree of standardization of their products or services, the stability of the process technologies they use, the basis for learning and process improvement, variability in volumes produced or delivered at their facilities, and availability and cost of labor in their local markets.

Competing in an Environment of Dynamic Technological Change

Occasionally a technology will come along—a radical new type of product, service, or process—that can completely change the dynamics of an industry (Christensen 1997 and Drejer 2001). These so-called *disruptive technologies*, which sometimes lead to poorer short-term performance before they shift the entire industry to a new, improved level of performance, are distinguished from sustaining technologies, which lead to better short-term performance but may plateau at a level below that achievable with disruptive technology. The electric car, introduced in the 1980s but only recently made popular through the introduction of the Toyota Prius, is an example of a disruptive product technology (Christensen 1998).

Disruptive process technologies (Christensen 2001) can create an entirely new scale curve such as that shown in Exhibit 3.29. In this case, there is little advantage to higher volumes on the new scale curve, which eliminates the possibility of competing on economies of scale and makes operations at different volumes equally efficient. For example, the Toyota Production System (TPS) radically altered scale economies for automobile manufacturing, and the Human Genome Project significantly changed the scale economies of developing new pharmaceuticals. Disruptive process technologies may also improve the economics of mass customization. In the heavy equipment industry, for example, Caterpillar (http://www.cat.com/) was known for providing a full line of products and for dealerships that stocked a full range of parts. Its competitor, Komatsu, disrupted the industry by applying flexible design and assembly techniques to produce an even broader range of products and then using faster transportation modes to allow local dealers to supply these products without carrying large inventories of the resultant wide range of spare parts. Komatsu, in effect, streamlined the process of providing a wide range of products, making it nearly as cost-effective as that for providing a narrow range of products.

Companies most often seek disruptive product, service, or process technologies in markets where customers' needs cannot be fully met by the functionality of existing products or services. By creatively examining the problem the customer is trying to solve and

EXHIBIT 3.29
Disruptive Technology Flattening of a Scale Curve

Source: Based on Christensen 2001.

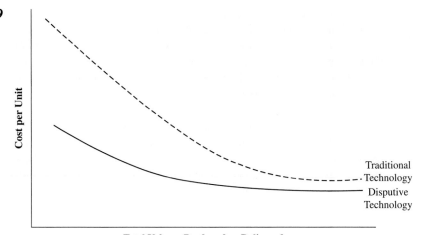

Total Volume Produced or Delivered

applying alternative technologies to its solution, companies find new and better ways of meeting customer needs. Technology investments must be driven by an understanding of where the firm is positioned relative to such industry dynamics. When customers across an industry are dissatisfied with what they are getting or new entrants to the industry are experimenting with radically different solutions, it is time for the company to think about investing in the development of different and new technologies.

Chapter Summary and Approach to Developing Process Technology Strategy

This chapter has presented a number of frameworks for examining process technology investment decisions, including the economies of scale curve, the product-process matrix, and the service-process matrix. It has also examined the key strategic questions that must be answered by a process technology strategy. We close the chapter with a six-step plan for developing a process technology strategy.

Step 1: Understand the Business Strategy and Competitive Environment

The firm must understand where the business is to be positioned relative to cost, quality, availability, features/innovativeness, and environmental performance. A company focused on *cost* and *efficiency* might, for example, try to exploit economies of scale; standardize its processes across locations; automate heavily; select rigid technologies that are highly efficient; allow less product variety; and locate in low labor cost sites. A company focused on *quality* might choose highly automated processes that deliver consistent output over time, specialized equipment that can be fine-tuned to achieve specific performance targets, and advanced measurement and test equipment to assess and improve process performance. A company focused on *availability* might invest in reducing set-up or changeover times or in high-speed equipment that reduces the amount of time a product or service will take to produce or deliver. A company seeking to be highly *innovative* or provide a wide variety of *features* might choose technologies that are flexible and have short set-up or changeover times. Finally, a company wanting to stand out as being *environmentally sound* will pay close attention to the environmental performance of its process equipment, possible working with equipment vendors to reduce its environmental impact.

Management must understand the capabilities the firm wishes to develop or sustain as well. A rapid response capability implies highly integrated information and process technologies that together react rapidly to customer requirements. A firm might also develop deep knowledge in a specific technical area, requiring ongoing investment in that technology. Nucor Steel, for example, became so good at steel fabrication that it was able to leverage this skill into markets beyond the joist market it had originally launched its business to serve. Amazon.com has developed expertise in purchasing, warehousing, and shipping products, allowing it to offer more than just books. In both cases, the companies parlayed their investments in process technology, configuration, and means of management into new business opportunities.

The firm's business strategy—where it wishes to be positioned and what capabilities it has or wishes to develop—is likely to dictate general guidelines for its process technology strategy. This is made clear in the use of the product-process and service-process matrices.

The types of products and/or services the firm wishes to offer determine to a large degree the types of processes it should employ. In other cases, the firm's process technology strategy may suggest a strategic direction in which the firm might head. Amazon.com, for example, leveraged its process and information technology capability to sell not only books but myriad other products as well.

The process technology strategy must not only support or be consistent with the firm's business strategy, but it must also be consistent with the other functional strategies, such as the research and development and marketing strategies, as well as with the other operations choices made. In particular, within operations strategy, process technology choices must be consistent with: vertical integration choices, as the firm decides whether or not to develop process technologies itself and whether or not to own them; facilities location choices, particularly where labor costs are an important factor and a simultaneous choice of process technology and facility location must be made; capacity choices, as different technologies offer different amounts of capacity with different scale economies; information technology strategies, supply chain strategies, and business processes strategies, as decisions are made how to organize and use the equipment; and human resource management choices, as technologies dictate required skill sets in the company. A key element of an operations strategist's work is to clearly understand the interactions and dependencies among the choices made in the decision categories addressed in this book.

Step 2: Understand the Technology Trends in the Industry

This step scans the external environment to find out what technologies the competition is using, what technologies the vendors have under development, and how satisfied customers are with the output of the existing technology base in the industry. In general, it seeks to evaluate the stability of the process technologies used in the industry; to identify important technological trends and assess their impact on the industry, market, and firm; and to surface any potentially disruptive technologies.

Although this evaluation is generally focused on competitors and technology vendors within the industry, it may also examine technologies outside the industry for potential use within the industry. There are numerous case studies (e.g., Henderson 1993) of industries that were surprised by the application of a technology from outside the industry to their work. In the photolithography equipment industry, for example, the next generation technologies were regularly developed and launched by newcomers to the industry rather than by its incumbents. Thus, it is critical to examine alternative technologies to the ones being used in an industry, as they may well be sources of disruption.

Technology can be the source of unique competitive advantage for a firm, particularly when it is not easily copied (West 2000). Understanding where that advantage might lie—whether in the proprietary nature of the technology, in its ability to achieve greater economies of scale, or in its ability to disrupt the industry along some other dimension—is a critical step in developing a technology strategy.

Step 3: Understand the Internal Capabilities of the Organization

Understanding the internal capabilities of the organization around process technology development and management is equally critical. What technologies does the organization have now? What expertise does the organization have to develop and/or manage the technologies? Is the firm good at continuous improvement? Is it good at adopting new technologies and using them effectively? What types of relationships does the firm have with its technology vendors? How much leverage does it have with its technology vendors? Is process technology development managed centrally or is it dispersed throughout the organization? Understanding of how the firm presently manages the development, implementation, and improvement of its process technologies is an important input to the technology strategy decision-making process.

Step 4: Identify and Assess Process Technology Investment Alternatives

Once the organization has a good sense of its business strategy, the external technology environment in which it operates, and its internal capabilities, it can develop alternative process technology investment options and assess them for strategic fit and returns using the frameworks presented in this chapter.

The full complement of process technology options will potentially include: a range of technologies, some that are being developed within the industry and others from outside; a range in degree of automation, from highly labor intensive to highly capital-intensive processes; a range of achievable economies of scale, including technologies that allow for very flat or very steep scale curves; and a range of ways to manage the technologies, particularly in multisite operations, including degree of standardization and degree of centralization.

The choice of possible process technologies in which the firm might invest will be bounded by the position the firm chooses to take on either the product-process or service-process matrix, and by the projected life cycle of the product or service the firm offers. Once a reasonable set of alternatives is identified, they can be assessed both qualitatively and quantitatively: What degree of automation is desired? How flexible do the processes need to be? How scalable are the processes? What are the economics? What economies of scale can be achieved? Where will that position the company competitively? Will the technology put the company in a leadership position? Answering these questions will lead the company to a choice of process technology appropriate to its situation and needs.

The company still needs to decide whether it will develop the technology in house or procure it from an outside vendor and whether it will centralize and/or standardize the development and implementation of the technology or let individual sites make their own decisions.

Step 5: Develop an Implementation Plan

Implementation planning for new process technologies can be a significant project itself. Intel, for example, dedicates entire organizations to monitoring the development of equipment at its suppliers, planning and overseeing the construction of the infrastructure to support the technology, managing the vendor workforce onsite to implement and troubleshoot the new technology, training Intel personnel, and measuring the performance of the new technology to ensure it meets targets.

The implementation plan for any new process technology must take into account three critical issues (Maffei and Meredith 1995):

- Role of the operator: Successful technology implementations engage the operators in ongoing monitoring of the new technology, elicit from them a high degree of problem solving, and provide operator control of the prove-out process.

- Structure of the planning systems that support the new technology: Materials planning and scheduling needs to be carefully integrated with the new process technology.
- Integration of the technology with the organization: Any new technologies have to be accepted and understood by other parts of the organization such as sales, marketing, and design, where they may be leveraged in selling to customers or designing new products and services.

Even new technologies that are not disruptive may present the firm with major management and strategic challenges. For example, the new technology may require organizational or skill level changes throughout the organization or involve a different level of scale, requiring changes in the facility network leading to fewer but larger facilities. The corporation must make sure that the organization, infrastructure, and other strategic choices are aligned with the new technologies and the pace of technological change in products, services, or processes.

Step 6: Implement, Assess, and Measure Results

The firm must implement the process technology strategy as planned, measure outcomes, and check against the original plan. Were the planned economies achieved? Did the plan achieve the desired business goals for cost, quality, availability, features/innovativeness, and environmental soundness? Is the plan consistent with other elements of the operations strategy (e.g., with the facilities and vertical integration strategies)? Is the plan consistent with and/or supportive of other functional strategies (e.g., marketing, human resources, information technology, and engineering)? The firm should prepare a post mortem report on the process technology planning process and feedback to be used to improve the process in the future.

Summary   Technology is a critical strategic decision category, and technology strategy development requires an integrated and careful approach.

- Process technology can be a major driver of strategy in that the capabilities it provides can be the basis of competitive advantage,
- Process technology is closely intertwined with many other decisions and thus the evolution of technology must be carefully managed in terms of these decisions, and
- Advanced technologies in particular provide both major opportunities and risks.

To develop a process technology strategy, a company needs to review the external technology environment, develop a good understanding of internal process capabilities, and answer the specific process technology questions: What is the appropriate technology? Should the firm be an innovator or a follower? Should the technology be developed in house or not? How should internal technology development be managed?

Technology strategy development can and should be reciprocal. While strategy development influences and often dictates technological development, technological choices can also influence strategy.

References   Abernathy, William J., and Kenneth Wayne. "Limits of the Learning Curve." *Harvard Business Review* 52, no. 5 (September–October 1974), pp. 109–119.
Boston Consulting Group. *Perspectives on Experience.* 1972.

Boyer, Kenneth K., G. Keong Leong, and Peter T. Ward. "Approaches to the Factory of the Future: An Empirical Taxonomy." *Journal of Operations Management* 14, no. 4 (1996).

Browne, J., D. Dubois, K. Rathmill, S.P. Sethi, and K.E. Stecke. "Classification of Flexible Manufacturing Systems." *The FMS Magazine* (April 1984), pp. 114–117.

Chase, R. "Where Does the Customer Fit in a Service Operation?" *Harvard Business Review* 56, no. 6 (November–December 1978), pp. 137–142.

Christensen, Clayton. *The Innovator's Dilemma: When New Technologies Cause Great Firms to Fall.* Boston: Harvard Business School Press, 1997.

Christensen, Clayton. "Why Great Companies Lose Their Way." *Across the Board* 35, no. 9 (October 1998), pp. 36–41.

Christensen, Clayton. "The Past and Future of Competitive Advantage." *MIT Sloan Management Review* 42, no. 2 (Winter 2001), pp. 105–109.

Collins, Jim. *Good to Great, Why Some Companies Make the Leap, and Others Don't.* New York: Harper Business, 2001.

Drejer, Anders. "Innovation and Manufacturing—Separate Entities." *Proceeding of the IFIP WG 5.7 International Working Conference on Strategic Manufacturing,* 26–29 August 2001, Aalborg University, Aalborg, Denmark, pp. 125–136.

Duke, Richard, and Daniel M. Kammen. "The Economics of Energy Market Transformation Programs." *The Energy Journal* 20, no. 4 (1999), pp. 15–64.

Egelhoff, William G. "Great Strategy or Great Strategy Implementation—Two Ways of Competing in Global Markets." *Sloan Management Review* 34, no. 2 (Winter 1993), pp. 37–50.

Gil, Nuno. "The T5 Project: Single Terminal "Occupancy Change (A)." Case study, Manchester Business School, University of Manchester, 2006.

Goldberg, Jeffrey. "Process Automation at Genzyme." MIT master thesis, 2001.

Hansell, Saul. "Amazon Ships to a Sorting Machine's Beat." *The New York Times,* January 22, 2002, C3.

Hayes, R., and G. Mathur. Intel-PED, Harvard Business School case, 5-693-057, 1995.

Hayes, R., G. Pisano, D. Upton, and S. Wheelwright. *Operations, Strategy, and Technology: Pursuing the Competitive Edge.* New York: Wiley, 2005.

Hayes, Robert H., and Steven C. Wheelwright. "Link Manufacturing Process and Product Life Cycles." *Harvard Business Review* 57, no. 1 (January–February 1979a), pp. 133–140.

Hayes, Robert H., and Steven C. Wheelwright. "The Dynamics of Process-Product Life Cycles." *Harvard Business Review* 57, no. 2 (March–April 1979b), pp. 127–136.

Hayes, Robert H., and Steven C. Wheelwright. *Restoring Our Competitive Edge: Competing through Manufacturing.* New York: John Wiley and Sons, 1984.

Hayes, Robert H., Steven C. Wheelwright, and Kim B. Clark. *Dynamic Manufacturing: Creating the Learning Organization.* New York: The Free Press, 1988.

Henderson, Rebecca. "Underinvestment and Incompetence as Responses to Radical Innovation: Evidence from the Photolithographic Industry." *Rand Journal of Economics* 24, no.2 (Summer 1993).

Hirshmann, W. "Profit from the Learning Curve." *Harvard Business Review* 42, no. 1 (January–February 1964), pp. 125–139.

Kaplan, Robert S., "Must CIM be justified by faith alone?" *Harvard Business Review* 64, no. 2 (March–April 1986), pp. 87–95.

Lapre, Michael A., and Luk N. Van Wassenhove. "Learning Across Lines, The Secret to More Efficient Factories." *Harvard Business Review* 80, no. 10 (October 2002), pp. 107–111.

Lei, David, Michael A. Hitt, and Joel D. Goldhar. "Advanced Manufacturing Technology: Organization and Strategic Flexibility." *Organization Studies* 17, no. 3 (1996), pp. 501–523.

Leonard-Barton, Dorothy. "Core Capabilities and Core Rigidities: A Paradox in Managing New Product Development." *Strategic Management Journal* 13 (Summer Special Issue 1992), pp. 111–125.

Maffei, Mary Jo, and Jack Meredith. "Infrastructure and Flexible Manufacturing Technology: Theory Development." *Journal of Operations Management* 13, no. 4 (1995), pp. 273–298.

McDonald, C. "Copy Exactly! A Paradigm Shift in Technology Transfer Method." IEEE/SEMI Advanced SEMiconductor Manufacturing Conference and Workshop, 1997, pp. 414–417.

Metters, Richard, Kathryn King-Metters, Madeleine Pullman, and Steve Walton. *Successful Service Operations Management,* 2nd ed. Boston, MA: Thomson Higher Education, 2006.

Meyer, Mark H., and James Utterback. "The Product Family and the Dynamics of Core Capability." *Sloan Management Review* 34, no. 3 (Spring 1993), pp. 29–47.

Narasimhan, Ram, and Ajay Das. "An Empirical Investigation of the Contribution of Strategic Sourcing to Manufacturing Flexibilities and Performance." *Decision Sciences* 30, no. 3 (1999), pp. 683–718.

Natarajan, Sanjay, Melton Bost, Derek Fisher, David Krick, Chris Kenyon, Chris Kardas, Chris Parker, and Robert Gasser, Jr. "Process Development and Manufacturing of High-Performance Microprocessors on 300mm Wafers." *Intel Technology Journal* 6, no. 2 (May 16, 2002).

Pavitt, Keith. "What We Know about the Strategic Management of Technology." *California Management Review* 32, no. 3 (Spring 1990), pp. 17–26.

Pine, Joseph. *Mass Customization: The New Frontier in Business Competition.* Boston: Harvard Business School Press, 1993.

Pisano, Gary. *The Development Factory: Unlocking the Potential of Process Innovation.* Boston: Harvard Business School Press, 1996.

Pisano, Gary. "ITT Automotive: Global Manufacturing Strategy (1994)." Teaching note, Harvard Business School, Number 5-696-040, 1995. For instructors only.

Rohrbach, Adolph. "Economical Production of All-Metal Airplanes and Sea Planes." *Journal of the Society of Automotive Engineers* 20 (1927), pp. 57–66.

Safizadeh, M., Larry P. Hossein, Deven Sharma Ritzman, and Craig Wood. "An Empirical Analysis of the Product-Process Matrix." *Management Science* 42, no. 11 (November 1996), pp. 1576–1591.

Schmenner, Roger. "How Can Service Businesses Survive and Prosper?" *Sloan Management Review* 27, no. 3 (1986), pp. 21–32.

Sethi, A.K., and S.P. Sethi. "Flexibility in Manufacturing: A Survey." *International Journal of Flexible Manufacturing Systems* 2, no. 4 (1990), pp. 289–328.

Shingo, S. *The Shingo Production Management System: Improving Process Functions.* Cambridge, MA: Productivity Press, 1992.

Silverman, Peter. "Who Can Afford Advanced Lithography?" *Microlithography World* (November 1, 2003).

Thomke, Stefan. "R&D Comes to Services: Bank of America's Pathbreaking Experiments." *Harvard Business Review* 81, no. 4 (April 2003), pp. 70–79.

Vogelstein, Fred. "Mighty Amazon." Fortune, May 12, 2003 (http://www.mutualofamerica.com/articles/Fortune/May 03/fortuneasp), accessed August 12, 2005.

West, Jonathan. "Module Overview: Sustaining Growth through Operations." Harvard Business School case study, 5600-103, 2000.

Wheelwright, S.C., and K.B. Clark. "Creating Project Plans to Focus Product Development." *Harvard Business Review* 70, no. 2 (March–April 1992), pp. 67–83.

Womack, James P., Daniel T. Jones, and Daniel Roos. *The Machine That Changed the World.* New York: Simon and Schuster, 1990.

Wright, T.P. "Factors Affecting the Cost of Airplanes." *Journal of Aeronautical Science* 3 (1936), pp. 122–138.

Chapter 4

Capacity Strategy[1]

Introduction

Boeing Corporation's commercial airplane business is both complex and dynamic.[2] Just a few statistics illustrate the complexity of Boeing's commercial market as well as of the supply chain it has in place to serve that market. In a 24-hour day, 3 million passengers board 42,300 flights on Boeing aircraft that take them to nearly every country on earth. In the same 24 hours, more than 15,000 Boeing suppliers in 81 countries provide parts and services for Boeing products and the infrastructure that designs, builds, and supports them. The Commercial Airplane Group employs about 55,000 people who design, build, and support aircraft such as the 747 that has over 10,000 parts.[3]

Other statistics illustrate the volatile nature of the business and the long time frames over which Boeing must plan. Boeing's commercial airplane business delivered a high of 620 airplanes in 1999 and a low of 281 in 2003 (Exhibit 4.1). During the same time frame, it ceased production of the classic 737 and all McDonnell-Douglas airplane models while launching production of the 717 and the next generation 737, creating large shifts in product mix (Exhibit 4.2).

Boeing predicts a robust market during the next 20 years that will double the world's commercial airplane fleet by 2024 and accommodate a forecasted 4.8 percent annual increase in passenger air traffic growth. It expects that airlines will take delivery of 3,900 regional jets, 15,300 single-aisle airplanes, 5,600 midsize, twin-aisle airplanes, and 900 large aircraft over the next 20 years, each to serve a different market. Single-aisle planes allow airlines to offer more frequent and nonstop domestic service and short-haul international flights, while midsize twin-aisle planes service long-haul markets.

In the face of this considerable complexity and uncertainty, Boeing's Commercial Airplane Group closely manages its capacity to design, produce, and service airplanes,

---

[1] We are grateful to Maria Alvarez and John Tagawa, Leaders for Manufacturing graduates, for their review of various concepts in the capacity strategy literature (Alvarez and Tagawa 1999). We have drawn upon their work in this chapter.

[2] Data and information in these paragraphs has been taken from various places on Boeing's website, http://www.boeing.com, July 8, 2005.

[3] See http://manufacturing.stanford.edu, January 25, 2007 (Stanford University, produced by Design4x, 2003) for a video of the airplane manufacturing process.

EXHIBIT 4.1
Boeing Commercial Airplane Deliveries from 1997–2005

Source: Data drawn from http://www .boeing.com, annual press releases, 1997–2005.

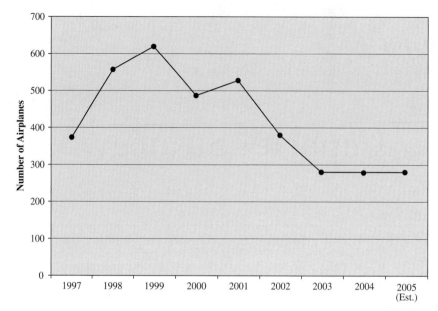

adjusting its workforce as needed. It employed a high of 117,950 employees in 1998 and a low of 52,669 at the end of 2004 closely tracking the delivery of commercial aircraft (Exhibit 4.3). It introduced lean production techniques at its Renton, Washington, facility, allowing it to reduce work-in-progress inventory by 55 percent and stored inventory by 59 percent, and to assemble a 737 in 11 days, half of what it used to take. These changes

EXHIBIT 4.2
Boeing Commercial Airplane Group Deliveries by Year and Type

Source: Data drawn from http://www .boeing.com, annual press releases, 1997–2005.

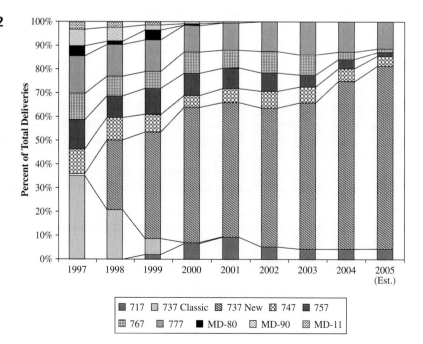

EXHIBIT 4.3
Boeing
Corporation
Commercial
Airplane
Group
Employment
and Deliveries

Source: Data drawn
from http://www
.boeing.com, annual
press releases and
employment data,
1997–2005.

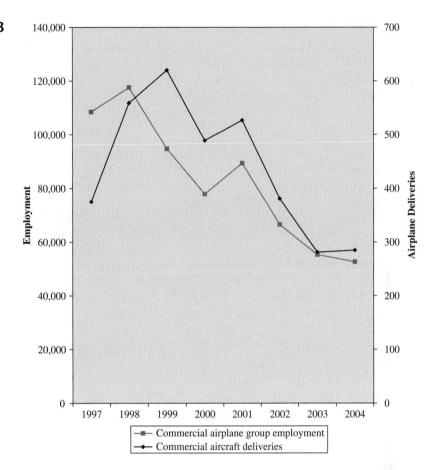

not only free considerable floor space at Boeing's facilities, but also increase its flexibility to respond to customer decisions about aircraft configuration closer to the delivery date.

In the context of considerable complexity, a dynamic and uncertain market, and a formidable competitor, Airbus, Boeing must forecast the demand for its products, determine the rate at which it will build aircraft over several years, and decide what triggers or trends should determine when to change the rates. Decisions about production rates in turn affect the amount and type of capacity Boeing maintains, as well as what it expects its suppliers to maintain. It maintains both base capacity and reserve, or surge, capacity to respond to unplanned or unexpected increases in demand. Here are the questions Boeing must ask as it makes capacity strategy decisions:

- What is the forecasted demand for the company's products or services in the short, intermediate, and long term? How will demand grow or shrink over time?
- How much capacity should the company have to cover expected demand? What service level does the company want to offer? How much reserve capacity does the company wish to have to buffer against unexpected fluctuations in demand?

- In what increments and when, or at what intervals, should the company add capacity?
- What type of capacity should the company add? Human resources? Process and information technology? Facilities? Can the company extract more output from its existing resources, thereby increasing its capacity? How will it trade off short-, intermediate-, and long-term investments in capacity?
- Where in the value chain, internal and/or external to the company, should capacity be added?

In this chapter, we address the development of capacity strategy in the context of the business and operations strategies. We first define the terms used in capacity planning and management including the types of capacity and how capacity is managed in the short, intermediate, and long term. We describe the trade-offs inherent in making capacity strategy decisions and introduce a set of models that are helpful in making those trade-offs. The lead, lag, or stay-even model suggests three strategic options for managing capacity and provides a strategic framework for the use of the more analytical models. Three analytical models provide insights into the costs associated with having too much and too little capacity. We review the importance of capacity decisions to the development of flexibility and the competitive dynamics that affect capacity strategy. We close the chapter with a step-by-step approach to developing a capacity strategy.

The Capacity Decision

Defining Capacity

Capacity is the volume of output per period of time that a business or facility can produce. Boeing might measure capacity by the number of aircraft its final assembly facility can complete in a month. A bank might measure capacity in number of transactions its call center can handle per hour. A hotel might measure capacity in number of rooms available or number of meals it can serve in its banquet facilities in an evening. Capacity is not as trivial to measure at it might seem at first glance. The capacity of a facility depends entirely upon what you make in that facility. Imagine a conversation with a handful of people about the capacity of their kitchens. Some might define that capacity in terms of the number of TV dinners they can produce in 15 minutes, others might describe capacity in terms of the number of people who can fit in the kitchen for a meal, and yet others might use their ability to produce a large holiday meal as a proxy for capacity. Product and service mix vary widely in many organizations: Boeing, for example, might build three 747s and two 777s one month and one 747 and six 777s another. A financial institution might process 650 stock trades and open 40 new accounts one month, and 740 stock trades and 30 new accounts in another. Finding a common base unit in which to measure capacity (e.g., hours of production) is often a critical first task in capacity management.

Capacity may be measured in different ways (e.g., Melnyk and Denzler 1996): *Maximum or design capacity* defines the highest rate of output that a process or activity can theoretically achieve. When process equipment is designed, for example, it is rated to run at a certain output rate. That design rating is often taken to be the maximum, or design, capacity. Maximum theoretical capacity is rarely achieved in reality, so two other measures of capacity are commonly used. *Effective or planned capacity* identifies the output rate that managers expect to get for a given activity or process. They may base their expectations on past performance, or on the performance of an average person or piece of equipment for a given product or service mix. Standard costs are often based on effective or planned capacity measures. Finally, *demonstrated capacity* deals with actual rather than planned production and measures the actual level of output for a process or activity over time.

Capacity utilization is the percentage of the facility's capacity that is used by actual production and can be determined using either the maximum or effective measure of capacity. (Capacity utilization measured against demonstrated capacity will, by definition, be 100 percent.) Boeing might, for example, have effective capacity to build four aircraft per month but have built only three in the past month. Its capacity utilization for that month would be 75 percent (or the output of 3 divided by the capacity of 4). Hotels regularly measure utilization by occupancy rate, or the percentage of rooms occupied in a given night. Some organizations refer to the capacity utilization ratio as *efficiency* and strive for performance close to 100 percent. Other organizations set capacity utilization or efficiency goals at well under 100 percent, implying that they hold some *reserve capacity,* generally for unplanned or unexpected events. When organizations operate at less than full capacity, they have excess capacity, or *slack,* in their production or service delivery systems. The amount of reserve capacity or slack a company chooses to maintain should be directly related to its business strategy and goals. A company focused primarily on low cost is likely to minimize its excess capacity, while a company focused on high availability is likely to have more.

Types of Capacity

Capacity comes in many different forms including people, process technology or equipment, information technology, and facilities, internally or externally owned. Firms can increase or decrease capacity by adding or getting rid of these resources—hiring or firing people, buying or selling equipment and facilities, or expanding or shrinking business with external vendors. Firms can also increase or decrease capacity by changing how they use existing resources (e.g., increasing production yield, decreasing the cycle time of a bottleneck operation, changing product mix, improving quality control). There are pros and cons, costs and benefits to each approach.

The capacity of *human resources* is critical in most industries, particularly those with labor-intensive processes. As demand fluctuates, managers decide how much to change human resource levels and what types of human resources (temporary, permanent, overtime) to use. Tangible costs associated with making changes in human resources include hiring, firing, training, and overtime costs. Less tangible costs include training time, workforce flexibility, and the effects of changing the workforce on the quality of its output. Human resources can be more flexible than other types of capacity, however, as workforce levels can be readily increased or decreased, allowing a firm to quickly match changing demand patterns. As seen earlier, Boeing adjusts its workforce in line with changes in its demand. Package delivery companies like UPS, FedEx, and DHL hire additional workers during the holiday season to handle the peak in shipping demand.

Investment in *process and/or information technology* is another way to add capacity. Faced with demand *increases,* managers may choose to purchase or lease additional production or information process equipment or may trade out existing equipment for equipment better suited to higher volumes. Faced with demand *decreases,* they may choose to do the converse. Google, Yahoo!, and other such Internet companies make decisions to invest in additional servers as the volume of visits to their websites increases. Kraton Polymers,[4] the world's leading manufacturer and supplier of styrenic block copolymer, expanded the capacity of its Paulinia, Brazil, plant by 25 percent by selectively investing in additional equipment at its bottleneck processes. When making such decisions, managers choose from alternative technologies ranging from those that are specific to certain products or services to those that are general purpose and can produce or deliver a wide range of products or services. Compared to human resource capacity expansion investments, technology capacity expansion investments typically require capital expenditures, are larger investments, have longer lives, and are harder to change in a short time frame.

Facilities investments (or divestments) are a third way to expand (or contract) capacity. Projections of significant demand growth, or of demand growth in new locations, may cause a firm to add on to existing facilities or to build new. Similarly, projections of declining demand may cause managers to close down entire facilities or to sublet parts of facilities. Facilities may be built to house a single product, service, or process or to be capable of delivering a wide range of outputs. Oshkosh Truck Corporation,[5] a specialty truck maker, planned to invest $18.5 million to expand its manufacturing facilities in Wisconsin by 130,000 square feet. It purchased additional manufacturing facilities near its headquarters and began upgrading them in response to strong demand for its fire and rescue and military equipment.[6] Amazon.com opened a second fulfillment center in the United Kingdom to handle an increase in sales of 80 percent between 2003 and 2004. Adding (or taking away) facilities often goes hand in hand with adjustments to human resources, process equipment, and information technology capacity. Facilities investments are generally the most capital intensive, longest term, and least flexible of the capacity expansion options in the sense of being most difficult to change quickly.

Finally, firms may use *suppliers and subcontractors* as a source of external capacity to buffer the effects of demand variability on their own internal resources, or to simply provide an alternative to internal capacity. In fact, outsourcing decisions are often in response to a need to offload demand on internal resources. Firms may place expectations on external sources to keep in place human resources, process and information technology, and/or facilities to handle the firms' demands when needed. The growth of the contract manufacturing industry to support electronics manufacturing (e.g., with firms such as Solectron, Celestica, and Flextronics) and the growth of the software development industry in India are both examples of the use of external contractors to supplement or replace investments in internal capacity. The costs of using external resources may include premiums paid to contractors and the costs of moving work in and out of the firm. The benefits include reduced risk of having excess capacity and sometimes reduced costs due to improved economies of scale at the contractor.

So far, we have focused on increasing or decreasing internal resources—human, technology, and facilities—or using external sources as a means of increasing or decreasing capacity. There are also ways of managing resources that are already in place to increase

---

[4] http://www.kraton.com/, July 8, 2005.

[5] http://www.oshkoshtruckcorporation.com/, July 8, 2005.

[6] http://fleetowner.com, July 8, 2005.

or reduce capacity (e.g., by training people to work faster, streamlining the process, or speeding slow operations). Quality improvement and process optimization are two general approaches to increasing capacity.

Quality improvement increases capacity by reducing the amount of waste and rework generated by a process, which frees time to generate additional good output. The semiconductor industry, for example, invests heavily in improving production yields. Initial yields from a new semiconductor production process can be as low as 30–40 percent. Increasing yields to 60–80 percent effectively doubles the output of these $2–$3 billion facilities. Software development engineers strive to reduce the defect (bug) rate in new software development projects, thus reducing the amount of time spent debugging and fixing the software and increasing the effective output of the software design and development group. Quality improvement efforts aim to ensure high-quality inputs (materials, components, instructions, and people) as well as to control production and service delivery processes to perform against required standards.

Process optimization around a particular product or service mix also increases capacity (Anupindi et al. 1999). Software packages such as those from jda[7] and i2[8] and approaches such as Goldratt's (2004) theory of constraints help companies optimize operations and increase capacity without investments in human resources, technology, or facilities. Some employ relatively simple techniques, such as sequencing products to minimize the amount of set-up time required between them. Some rely on more sophisticated analytical models, for example, to optimize the use of the bottleneck operations. The major types of capacity investment (human resources, process and information technology, facilities, and external contractors) as well as the capacity improvement approaches (quality improvement and process optimization) may be undertaken in different ways in the short, intermediate, and long term.

Short-, Intermediate-, and Long-Term Capacity

Short-term capacity is managed through the day-to-day decisions organizations make in response to short-term fluctuations in demand and usually entails human resource adjustments or investment in quality improvement or process optimization. Process and information technology and facilities investments are generally infeasible in the short term. Automobile manufacturers, for example, use overtime to increase production as needed. In 2002, about a third of workers in the motor vehicle and parts manufacturing industry worked, on average, more than 40 hours per week. Overtime is especially common during periods of peak demand.[9] A 2000 Bureau of Labor Statistics report makes the magnitude of the temporary workforce clear: "Of the 13 million workers in alternative work arrangements, independent contractors compose the majority—8.5 million—with temporary workers accounting for another 1.3 million."[10] These workers are widely used throughout industry to fill short-term capacity needs.

Intermediate-term capacity decisions are made on a month-to-month basis in response to, for example, seasonal fluctuations in demand and, as for short-term capacity decisions,

[7] http://www.jda.com/, February 28, 2007.

[8] http://www.i2.com/, July 8, 2005.

[9] http://stats.bls.gov/oco/cg/cgs012.htm, July 8, 2005.

[10] http://www.bls.gov/opub/ooq/2000/Summer/art04.pdf, July 8, 2005.

EXHIBIT 4.4
U.S. Retail
Employment
by Year and by
Month

Source: Bureau of
Labor Statistics,
http://data.bls.gov/,
2005.

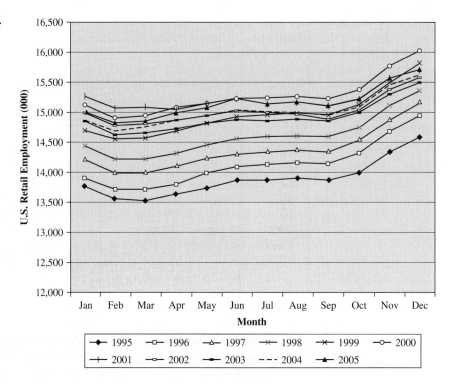

usually entail adjustments to human resources—hiring, firing, overtime, and subcontracting—as well as quality improvement and process optimization. Toy manufacturers, for example, plan for increased holiday demand for products by building inventories ahead of demand and increasing production labor to cover peak demand. Aggregate planning tools (see, e.g., Melnyk and Denzler 1996, pp. 666–674) are used to assess the cost trade-offs among hiring and firing, carrying inventory, and incurring lost sales for firms making intermediate-term capacity decisions. Retail businesses regularly hire temporary employees to handle seasonal changes in demand (Exhibit 4.4).

Long-term capacity decisions, which are the primary concerns of this chapter, rely on projections about highly uncertain future demand and the strategic moves of competitors and involve sizable investments in resources—such as process and information technology and physical facilities—that take some time to put in place. Competitively, companies can choose to make preemptive moves, investing in capacity ahead of their competitors, or may lose out in a market with aggregate overcapacity. For example, semiconductor fabrication facilities, which cost about $3 billion, are planned for one to two years before construction begins, take another two to three years to build, and then often take 6–18 months to "debug" and get to full production capacity. When semiconductor companies add long-term capacity, they do so in very large increments. This can lead to gaming among the semiconductor producers as they try to postpone adding capacity until they think they have sufficient demand to make their investments pay off quickly but at the same time build before their competition. Over the years, this has caused some producers to make false announcements of plans to build new facilities, as well as significant overages and underages of capacity

EXHIBIT 4.5 Capacity Planning in the Long, Intermediate, and Short Term

Long-Term Capacity Planning	Intermediate-Term Capacity Planning	Short-Term Capacity Planning
Greater than a one-year planning horizon	Six- to eighteen-month planning horizon	One-day to six-month planning horizon
Usually done in yearly increments	Usually done in monthly or quarterly increments	Usually done in weekly increments
Deals with strategic resource allocation (e.g., product/ service selection, facility size/location, equipment investment, facility layout)	Attempts to optimize the use of resources (e.g., labor, inventory, output)	Results in detailed resource schedule (e.g., jobs, workers, equipment)

in the industry at large. Similarly, the airlines make decisions about how many and what type of aircraft to buy or lease based on short- and long-term forecasts of demand. Theme parks and ski resorts decide how many rides or ski lifts they need, and how much local lodging is required to support them. The call center industry decides how many new facilities to build, where to place them, and what information and communications technology to equip them with to support global demand.

Exhibit 4.5 summarizes capacity planning in the three time horizons. Although we describe them as separate decisions, capacity management requires understanding all three and making appropriate trade-offs among them. A firm might choose not to invest the capital to build a new facility (a long-term capacity decision) but to hire people for a second shift to build capacity instead (an intermediate capacity decision) or to use overtime only when needed to meet demand (a short-term capacity decision). For example, a hospital could expand its capacity by staffing its clinics 16 hours a day rather than just 10, or by building and staffing another facility. Staffing costs in both cases might be roughly the same, but the capital costs for the new building would be significant and it could take years to build. Kaiser Permanente's new 1.2 million square foot Santa Clara (California) Medical Center, for example, will cost about $375 million and take about six years to complete.[11] Although doubling staff in an existing facility is not an insignificant task, it is likely to take less time than building and staffing a new facility. Exhibit 4.6 depicts alternative combinations of these approaches. In Alternative A, the firm chooses to add a long-term capacity (e.g., a new facility) then expand with intermediate-term capacity (e.g., adding a second shift operation at the facility) and then short-term capacity (e.g., overtime, external contractors). In Alternative B, the firm chooses to get along as long as possible by adding smaller increments of short-term capacity (e.g., temporary labor) until it must add long-term capacity (e.g., a new facility or process line).

The existence of these different ways to expand capacity—using human resources, technology, and/or facilities expansion and the interactions among choices that can be made in the short-, intermediate-, or long-term—complicates the question of how much of what type of capacity to add when. To make a decision about expanding (or contracting) capacity, a firm must consider all the possible ways in the short-, intermediate-, and long-term that it might add (or reduce) capacity and assess the costs and benefits of each.

[11] http://california.construction.com/features/archive/0405_Feature8.asp, July 15, 2005.

EXHIBIT 4.6
Capacity
Expansion
Using Short-,
Intermediate-,
and Long-
Term Options

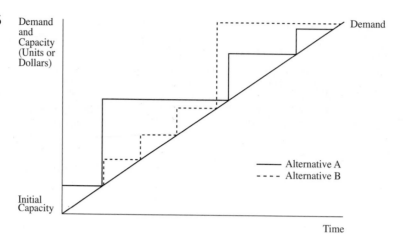

Capacity Strategy Models

Firms consider a number of issues or trade-offs in setting their capacity strategies. They must think about how much capacity they wish to have to cover expected demand, possibly including reserve capacity to cover unexpected fluctuations in demand. This requires balancing service level with cost. They must think about the size of the increments in which they want to add capacity, which in turn determines the frequency with which they will add capacity. This requires understanding the economics of each increment size, as well as the value of investments over time. They must think about different capacity expansion options, in the short, intermediate, and long term, and the costs and benefits of each. This includes understanding the intangible effects of the expansion options, including the degree of flexibility afforded by each.

This section of the chapter describes a set of models that are useful to companies considering these issues to make capacity strategy decisions. We start with the stylized lead, lag, or stay-even model that offers three options for capacity management and insights into the important trade-offs. We then present analytical models that integrate economies of scale and the cost of capacity over time, hedging models that directly account for the uncertainty in demand and provide a way of thinking about reserve capacity levels, and dynamic decision-making models that allow assessment of multiple capacity expansion options under uncertainty and over time. These models facilitate

- Exploration of multiple capacity expansion (or contraction) scenarios.
- Quantification of the sensitivity of the answer to varying market assumptions.
- Use of discounted cash flow techniques to quantify the costs of various capacity expansion timing policies.
- Evaluation of competitive responses to capacity changes.

The Lead, Lag, or Stay-Even Model

The lead, lag, or stay-even model takes a relatively simple perspective of long-term capacity management based on the fact that long-term capacity is added (or taken away) in relatively large increments. If a new factory is needed, it is difficult to add anything less than a full factory. If a new hospital is needed, it is difficult to build anything less than a full hospital. In the short run, capacity can be added through additional shifts, new capital equipment, and the like. But, in the long run, these options are exhausted and the decision to expand capital facilities is undertaken. In some industries, such as semiconductor and biotech manufacturing, capacity increments have become extremely expensive as the production equipment has become highly sophisticated, and very expensive controls and environmental health and safety systems are needed in the facilities. Other industries have seen a scaling down of capacity increments. Nucor and Chaparral Steel found ways to make steel with much smaller facilities, or "minimills," than so-called Big Steel had employed previously. Nonetheless, even when scaled down, long-term capacity is added in large increments relative to those in which short-term capacity can be added (e.g., a few hours of overtime).

The challenge, then, is to decide when to put in place an increment of capacity—before there is enough demand to fill it, after there is sufficient demand to fill it, or at some point in between. This set of stylized and simplified options adapted from Hayes and Wheelwright (1984) and Hayes et al. (2005) includes:

- **Lead—Try not to run short.** As shown in Exhibit 4.7, with a lead policy, capacity is added before it is needed, so on average there is excess capacity and demand is always met. Companies adopting a lead strategy are more responsive to shifts in demand and, as a result, capture additional revenue. The downside of the lead strategy is that the company carries on average a half increment of capacity more than needed and, in doing so, incurs some cost.

- **Lag—Maximize capacity utilization.** In the lag strategy, also depicted in Exhibit 4.7, average demand is never fulfilled and the company holds less than necessary capacity. This is the most conservative approach to increasing capacity, where no excess capacity is ever developed; the company always runs with insufficient capacity. If other short-term capacity options cannot be used to handle demand, revenues are lost, and in the long run, customers are likely to seek more reliable suppliers, so long-term business

EXHIBIT 4.7
Lead and Lag Policies

Source: Adapted from Hayes and Wheelright, *Restoring Our Competitive Edge, Competing through Manufacturing,* Wiley, 1984.

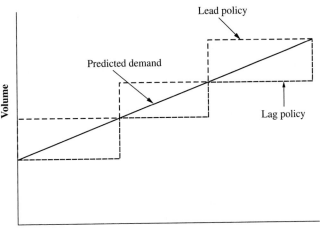

EXHIBIT 4.8
Stay-Even
Policy

Source: Adapted from
Hayes and Wheelright,
*Restoring Our
Competitive Edge,
Competing through
Manufacturing,* Wiley,
1984.

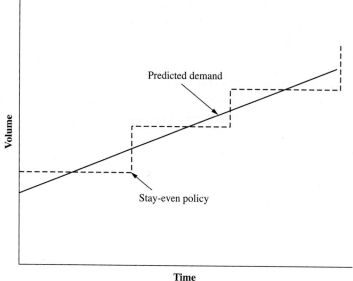

will be lost. But the capital cost of the lag strategy is lower than for the lead or stay-even strategies because significant investments are postponed.

- **Stay even—Build to forecast.** In the stay-even policy, average demand is met, but as seen in Exhibit 4.8, the company has excess capacity half of the time and too little capacity the other half of the time. Thus, 50 percent of the time, the company pays for excess capacity, and 50 percent of the time it loses revenues due to insufficient capacity. If the shortfalls can be made up using short- and medium-term capacity expansion strategies such as overtime or subcontracting, it may be possible to recoup some of the revenue losses, making this a good strategy to follow. Generally this policy will be less expensive than the lead strategy.

These policies are all depicted under circumstances of a growing market. One could just as easily draw declining demand curves and choose from among three similar strategies:

1. Reduce capacity ahead of a reduction in demand, particularly if capacity reductions must be made in large increments, and excess capacity would be carried for some time before it is depleted (lead).

2. Reduce capacity after the reduction in demand, in effect eliminating resources (e.g., closing plants) as they become unutilized (lag).

3. Choose a strategy in between, sometimes meeting demand and sometimes foregoing it (stay even). The same basic trade-offs exist: The cost of fully meeting demand is the cost of excess capacity; the cost of not keeping excess capacity is lost revenue.

To choose among the three strategy expansion (or contraction) options, a firm must take a number of things into account, including: the competitive dynamics of the industry, and how customers will react to capacity shortages; the innovativeness of the industry, and the flexibility required to respond to rapid changes; and investments in capacity throughout the value chain, and the degree of balance required.

Capacity and the Nature of the Market

The competitive dynamics of the industry in which the firm serves often dictate the choice to lead, lag, or stay even. Firms are likely to choose a lead strategy if they are competing in industries with:

- Commodity products with limited functional differentiation.
- A large number of competitors.
- Time-sensitive customers.

Customers in these industries exert considerable power over their suppliers, and insufficient capacity will lead to lost sales. In these industry structures, pricing is highly competitive and customers are likely to source from the lowest-cost, most readily available source. There is little or no loyalty between customer and supplier, and lack of capacity will result in a lost sale. Personal computer manufacturers, with the exception of Apple, increasingly fall in this category as their products have become commoditized and buyers readily substitute one for another. If a firm is in this type of industry and market share is critical to success, then a lead strategy is important: Capacity should be put in place before it is needed.

Companies in markets with high switching costs and rapid growth in demand are also best served by a lead strategy. If the firm doesn't have sufficient capacity to meet demand, it loses customers who are unlikely to come back later, given the high switching costs. A lead strategy allows the firm to increase market share and its control over the market in the long run. Many telecommunications products, from telephones to large communications networks, are in this category; once customers commit to a product it is costly to make a change.

Finally, in industries that obtain most or all of their profitability through an aftermarket strategy (e.g., shaving equipment such as razors and blades, turbine engine manufacturers such as engines and spare components, and inkjet printers and cartridges), a lead strategy may also be appropriate. For each product sold, the majority of the profits come from the aftermarket products rather than the initial sale. In an industry exhibiting this type of profit structure, advance implementation of capacity is preferable for the initial product. Because a lost sale will lead to the loss of greater downstream revenues, the firm must ensure availability of the initial product.

Companies in industries with few players, those that compete on functionality and/or intellectual property rights, those with strong brand equity, and those with large numbers of customers have more power over the market and can likely afford a stay-even or lag strategy. In these situations, customers are more willing to backlog orders for products, and a strategy that implements capacity only as it is needed allows the firm to maximize its return on investment (in process and information technology and facilities) while still retaining market share in the short run. Products like the iPod and the Prius fell, at least temporarily, in this category when demand far outstripped supply, but customers postponed their purchases until product was available. On the other hand, firms with significant market power may also be able to charge customers extra when they do carry extra capacity, so may find a lead strategy equally worthwhile.

Thus, the structure of the market in which a firm competes and the resulting competitive market dynamics suggest appropriate choices of capacity management strategy.

Innovation and Capacity

In highly innovative industries, products, services, processes, and technologies change rapidly, creating considerable uncertainty about both the size and make-up of the demand against which the firm must deliver in the future and for which it must plan. In general, firms competing in such industries will want to maintain enough excess capacity to react to unpredicted events, but not invest too much in capacity that will shortly become obsolete.

Firms such as those in the consumer electronics and fashion industries compete on their ability to produce and introduce new or different products and services quickly. The apparel company, Zara, for example, introduces 10,000 new styles a year, each of which has an average life of only four to six weeks (Helft 2002). These firms will likely adopt a lead strategy and maintain sufficient excess capacity to respond to new products or service plans and changes in demand for new products or services from the market. Many product firms in this category must produce all of the demand for a new product and fill distribution channels before the first product is ever sold. HP, for example, often fills its distribution channels with product and shuts down production of new personal computer models before the first unit is sold by a retailer (Cargille et al. 2005). Its production facilities must therefore be sized to produce high quantities in short bursts. A lead strategy allows innovative companies to ensure product or service availability during very short life-cycle windows. A stay-even or lag strategy would likely cause the organization to lose sales or have fewer products to offer, which in turn could cause the organization to have less revenue to fund its R&D activities and ultimately innovate less.

Conversely, in industries where process or information technology evolves rapidly, such as the semiconductor, biotech, and Internet industries, the risk of technology obsolescence is high. In these industries, a stay-even or lag strategy in which the firm waits to procure the latest technology may be preferable. This ensures that the new technology is state-of-the-art and minimizes the risk of obsolescence. This also applies to industries where the cost of equipment is rapidly decreasing; deferring purchase as late as possible allows the firm to take advantage of price decreases.

Thus, innovative companies will choose capacity strategies that support their ability to continue innovating. Their choice will, in part, depend upon whether the source of innovation is the products and services they offer or whether it is the processes and/or information technology in which they invest.

Managing Capacity Across Internal and External Value Chains

Rarely can a firm make a capacity decision about a particular facility or location without considering the effects on other locations in the firm's value chain, inside or outside of the firm. First, there is a question of balance throughout the value chain. The entire chain will only be able to operate at the rate of the lowest capacity step in the chain. Second, there is a question of whether capacity should be incremented inside the firm or with outside resources.

There are multiple perspectives on whether or not capacity should be balanced throughout the value chain. An assembly line such as is used to build automobiles, for example, is based on the premise that each stage of the process has approximately the same amount of capacity. Others suggest structuring the value chain around the bottleneck,[12] which is

---

[12] The bottleneck of a process is the rate-limiting step in that process. It is the step that has the lowest capacity. Bottlenecks can be difficult to find, as they can move about with changes in product mix, or can be an overarching resource (e.g., a given skill set) rather than a specific process step.

commonly the most expensive piece of equipment or facility in the value chain, to maximize efficiency and ease of management (Goldratt 2004). If one stage of a process or value chain is considerably more expensive than the others (e.g., a semiconductor fabrication facility, the engineering group in a software development process), it makes sense to limit investment in that stage and carry excess capacity at the other, less expensive, stages so that the bottleneck is not starved and operates smoothly at the highest possible rate (Kurz 1995). This only makes sense, however, when there are large discrepancies in the costs of the different steps.

Intel faces this issue internally in its assembly and test facilities, where it has followed a policy of investing in 10 percent excess capacity for its most expensive pieces of equipment, 15 percent for the next most expensive, and 20 percent for the cheaper stages. In this way it expects to minimize its investment in process equipment but facilitate flow through the production process by keeping the bottleneck fed. However, a more effective approach for Intel (and others) considers the service level it wishes to achieve with its process. A 95 percent service level for a particular piece of equipment, for example, means that the equipment will meet the demands placed upon it 95 percent of the time. This approach suggests that Intel build enough capacity at the most expensive piece of equipment (the bottleneck) to achieve a certain service level (e.g., 95 percent) and then use the remaining capital budget to target higher levels of service (e.g., 98 percent) at the other stages (Newlin 2000). This approach takes into account inherent uncertainty in demand, places a practical limit on the investment in the expensive equipment, and still ensures efficient use of that equipment.

Clearly, one of the dilemmas in managing capacity across a value chain is that not all steps of the value chain are necessarily owned by the same organization, and it can be difficult to negotiate appropriate investments in capacity by the various players in the value chain. Some members of a value chain may prefer lead strategies, while others choose to lag. Without coherence in strategies across the value chain, imbalances are likely to occur. Companies deal with this regularly when they have chosen to outsource some or all of their production or service delivery processes.

The ability of a company to outsource suggests different choices for the management of its internal capacity. If a production or service delivery process is outsourced easily, then a company may choose to maintain limited in-house capacity (adopting, for example, a lag strategy in house) and use subcontractor or supplier capacity to ensure product or service availability. This assumes that it has a reasonable relationship with its contractor and that the contractor is willing to maintain sufficient capacity and tolerate demand volatility. If, on the other hand, outsourcing a process takes considerable resources or time, diminishes competitive advantage in some way (e.g., through release of intellectual property), or is limited by market conditions, then a company may choose to maintain enough capacity in house to adequately serve its customers (i.e., employing the lead strategy). Chapter 2 addresses these choices more fully.

If a company fully outsources its work, it will likely want to at least understand and possibly help develop the capacity management strategies of its suppliers or subcontractors. If, for example, service and responsiveness are critical to its success, the company will want its suppliers to add capacity in anticipation of demand (or adopt a lead strategy). If cost control is more critical, the company might encourage its suppliers to follow a lag strategy, adding capacity only when it is clear that capacity can be filled

EXHIBIT 4.9
Considerations in Choosing Among Lead, Lag, and Stay-Even Strategies

Strategic Consideration	Lead	Stay Even	Lag
Nature of the Market			
Commodity products with little feature differentiation?	X	X	
Time-sensitive customers?	X		
High switching costs for customers?	X	X	
Many suppliers (so customers have choices)?	X	X	
Supplier controls the market (e.g., unique offerings)?			X
Aftermarket sales are important?	X		
Innovativeness			
Short product life cycles?	X	X	
High velocity of technology change?			X
Value Chain Balance			
Product easily outsourced?		X*	X*
Product difficult to outsource?	X*		

* Indicates appropriate internal capacity management strategy. It may be appropriate to ask suppliers or subcontractors to adopt the opposite strategy.

economically.[13] Chapter 6 suggests alternative means of working with suppliers to achieve goal congruence or simply compliance with guidance, such as how much capacity to carry.

Thus, choice of an appropriate capacity strategy is based on a broad view of the company's value chain and depends on the degree of balance the company wishes to maintain, what external resources are available to it, and what goals it wishes to reach with its external suppliers and subcontractors.

Summary of Strategy Alignment Issues

In sum, there are three stylized models for thinking about capacity strategy: lead demand in the implementation of new capacity, lag demand, or try to stay even with demand. While most situations are nowhere near as simple as the linear demand growth models depicted here, these simple ways of thinking about the strategic options can be quite useful. Exhibit 4.9 summarizes the considerations a firm might make in choosing from among these options, and what choices are suggested for each.

An Analytic Model for Sizing Long-Term Capacity Increments

The lead, lag, or stay-even model addresses the timing of long-term capacity additions but implicitly assumes that the amount of the increment is fixed. Determining how much capacity to add in each of these increments is not easy. On one hand, scale considerations suggest that the increments be as large as possible. Large increments are likely to provide

[13] Note that more efficient capacity management can be a key driver in outsourcing decisions. A supplier aggregates demand from many customers. In doing so, it can reduce the uncertainty in that demand when the various demand profiles in its portfolio do not all move in tandem. To achieve the same service level, the supplier can carry less overall capacity than the total capacity that would have been carried by its customers.

greater economies of scale and thus lower unit costs, as they entail technologies that operate at lower cost for higher volumes. Large increments also increase the length of time the company can operate without making another expansion decision. On the other hand, opportunity cost considerations suggest that the increments be as small as possible. Small increments can be added as demand grows, keeping the firm's investment in excess capacity to a minimum. Small increments require small investments, and the return on those investments can be recouped fairly quickly as the capacity is filled. If capacity is not filled quickly, returns are spread out over a long period of time, reducing overall return on investment. The model we present in this section calculates an appropriate capacity increment size, taking into account both economies of scale and opportunity cost.

Achieving Economies of Scale

Economies of scale are achieved whenever the fixed costs associated with an activity can be spread over increased volume of output from that facility, thus reducing average cost per unit. In simple terms, for a single facility, economies of scale are achieved when a product's unit cost decreases as production of the product increases. Consider the two basic elements of a product's cost: (1) Variable costs typically include the direct labor and materials costs associated with making the product. These costs remain fixed on a per-unit basis regardless of how many units are made, causing *total* variable cost to increase linearly with volume. (2) Fixed costs typically include indirect labor, facilities cost depreciation, insurance, and taxes. *Total* fixed cost remains fixed regardless of how many units are produced, but the allocation of fixed costs on a per-unit basis declines as volume increases. Exhibit 4.10 shows the behavior of total cost as volume increases: Fixed cost remains flat even as volume grows, while variable cost increases linearly with volume. The curve shown in Exhibit 4.11 represents the behavior of unit cost (total fixed and variable costs divided by total volume) as volume increases. The sum of variable costs and amortized fixed costs decreases as production volumes increase, creating the well-documented economies of scale effect.

Economies of scale do not necessarily grow unlimited; at some point diseconomies of scale may set in. These occur due to increased bureaucracy, confusion, and vulnerability to risk that in turn cause an increase in cost per unit. They may also occur when the firm runs

EXHIBIT 4.10
Fixed and Variable Production Costs

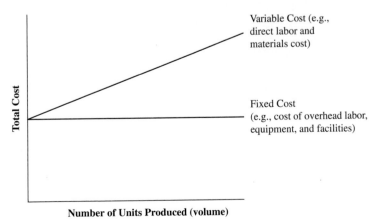

Variable Cost (e.g., direct labor and materials cost)

Fixed Cost (e.g., cost of overhead labor, equipment, and facilities)

Total Cost

Number of Units Produced (volume)

EXHIBIT 4.11
Economy of
Scale Curve

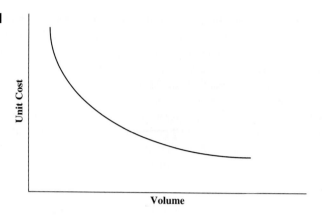

out of technology alternatives that allow it to produce at even lower cost. Exhibit 4.12 shows what the curve might look like as diseconomies of scale occur. The average unit cost of the product decreases as more units of the product are produced up to point A. Between points A and B unit costs change very little, and after point B diseconomies of scale show up. While the absolute minimum cost occurs at some specific point between A and B, the shallow rate of change in that region implies that any point between captures most of the scale effects.

The following two models embed economies of scale concepts with opportunity cost assessments to determine appropriate capacity increment size (1) when demand is known or certain, and (2) when demand is unknown or uncertain.

Sizing Capacity Increments When Demand Is Known or Certain

This model assumes that capacity can be procured in any size increment and that the cost per increment declines at some rate as increment size grows. In technical terms, this means that the plot of increment size versus increment cost (Exhibit 4.13) is a concave function. For this particular curve, the cost of an increment of 700 units is $5 million, while the cost of an increment of 1,400 units is only about $8 million. The cost

EXHIBIT 4.12
Diseconomies
of Scale

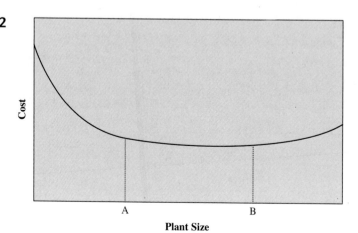

EXHIBIT 4.13
Relationship between Increment Size and Cost per Increment

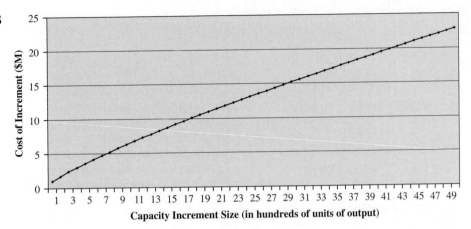

of an increment of capacity may include the costs of constructing a new facility, the costs of procuring process equipment and/or information technology, and/or the costs of staffing a facility to allow it to operate minimally. It would generally *not* include costs that are variable with the amount of volume put through the facility such as direct labor costs.

The assumption that capacity expansion costs decrease per unit of output as the size of the increments goes up is a reasonable one. First, capital costs associated with new construction generally do not increase linearly with the size of the facility. There are some fixed costs associated with constructing a new facility that are incurred regardless of its size. Second, operational costs also do not increase linearly with the size of a facility. There are certain overhead costs, related, for example, to the size of the management team, that increase at a slower rate than the size of the facility. As a result, typically, the larger the size of the facility is, the smaller the cost per unit of capacity is. We call the improvement in cost for each doubling of capacity the *scale factor*. Suppose that a hospital can expand in increments of 400 beds or 800 beds. A scale factor of 41.4 percent says that if it costs $1 million to build the 400-bed expansion, it will cost $1,414,000 (or $1,000,000 × 1.414) to build the 800-bed expansion.

The model also assumes that capacity is added at regular intervals, and that it is added at the rate at which demand is growing. In other words, it is added in a fixed increment once every fixed time period at a rate sufficient to cover demand. Suppose, for example, that the hospital needed 20 additional beds every year. In this model it chooses among options such as adding 400 beds every 20 years or 40 beds every 2 years. The model takes into account the time value of money, calculating the present value of the stream of future investments implied by the choice of increment size. In the case of the addition of 400 beds every 20 years and a 20-year planning horizon, it would simply calculate the net present value of the one-time investment 20 years hence. If capacity is added once every two years, the model calculates the net present value of 10 future investments in 40-bed expansions. These net present value calculations, accounting for the time value of money, increment size, and timing, can yield an optimal solution for the size of the increment to be added. (See the sidebar "Choosing the Optimal Size of a Capacity Increment When Demand Is Known and Certain" for detailed development of this model.)

Choosing the Optimal Size of a Capacity Increment When Demand Is Known and Certain

This model employs the economies of scale notion and defines the cost of building a capacity increment of size x as $F(x)$. There are many reasonable ways to represent the increment size cost function, but a common way is

$$F(x) = cx^a$$

where x = size of capacity increment
  c = constant
  a = the degree of economies of scale (must be strictly less than 1)

The critical parameter in this formulation is what we will call the *scale factor*, which represents how much the cost of a capacity increment increases with each doubling of size. Suppose, for example, that we have an opportunity to expand a hospital in increments of 400 beds or 800 beds. A scale factor of 41.4 percent says that if it costs $1million to build the 400-bed expansion, it will cost $1,414,000 (or $1,000,000 × 1.414) to build the 800-bed expansion. (This represents what is referred to as the square root law, which says that total cost is proportional to the square root of the rate at which capacity is being increased. In this case, we are doubling capacity, so its cost increases at the rate of the square root of two or 1.414.) A scale factor of 41.4 percent corresponds to a value of $a = 0.5$. Exhibit 4.14 shows how total costs and costs per unit of capacity change as capacity doubles for $a = 0.5$ and $c = \$100$. In this case, c is the cost of one unit of capacity. When capacity is doubled from 1 unit to 2 units, the *total cost* of that capacity goes from $100 to $141, and the *cost per unit* of capacity drops from $100/unit to $71/unit.

While a scale factor of 41.4 percent results in costs going up fairly quickly with increases in capacity, a scale factor of 10 percent suggests that costs go up more slowly. With a scale factor of 10 percent, the 800-bed facility costs only $1.1 million, which is a 90 percent cost reduction for the second increment of capacity over the first. A scale factor of 90 percent suggests only a 10 percent cost savings from increment to increment and that total costs go up quickly, in this case to $1.9 million for the 800-bed hospital.

The model also assumes that capacity is added at the rate it is needed or, in other words, is added at the same rate demand is growing and is added at regular intervals.[14] We represent demand growth as D, measured in units of demand per unit of time (e.g., 200 units per year). Demand growth is assumed to be both known and constant for the purposes of this model. We represent the length of time between capacity investments as L, measured in units of time (e.g., one year). The size of the capacity increment then is D * L (e.g., 200 units per year * one year = 200 units). Using the generic capacity increment cost function, we then determine the cost of the capacity increment as $F(DL)$.

Finally, the model assumes that costs incurred and revenues received in future time periods are discounted at some fixed rate to present-day costs. We represent the discount rate as r, which in practice is usually the cost of capital to the firm or the opportunity cost to the firm of making an investment. To determine the net present value of a future investment we discount it by the discount rate, r. The present value of an expenditure made a year from now is

[14] This assumption has been proven optimal under conditions of constant demand growth and constant discount rate. When these hold true, it is optimal to employ identically sized capacity increments and to implement them at identical intervals (Manne 1967).

EXHIBIT 4.14
Costs of Capacity with Scale Factor of 41.4% and $a = 0.5$

X	Total Cost of Capacity $F(x)$	Cost per Unit of Capacity (c)
1	100	100
2	141	71
4	200	50
8	283	35
16	400	25
32	566	18
64	800	13
128	1,131	9

(continued)

(continued)

EXHIBIT 4.15
Relationship between Time between Capacity Increments, *L*, and Cost

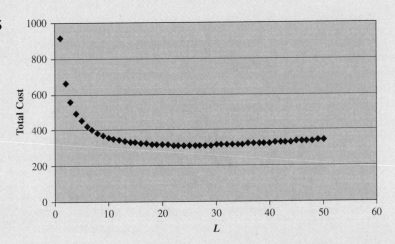

$$PV = FV_1 / (1 + r)$$

where PV = present value
FV_1 = future value
r = discount rate

So, for example, if the discount rate is 5 percent, $100 invested one year from now will have a present value of $95.24. Or $95.24 invested today at an expected return of 5 percent will yield $100 a year from now. The more general form of the present value equation is

$$PV = FV_N / (1 + r)^N$$

where N = the year in which the investment is made

Our model assumes that equal capacity increments of size DL are made every L time periods in the future, so to calculate total cost we must calculate the present value of each future capacity increment and then sum those present values together. The first capacity increment is not discounted; the next is discounted by e^{-rL}, the next by e^{-2rL} and so forth. This forms a sum of an infinite series, which has a well-known closed form $1/(1 - e^{-rL})$ and thus the total discounted investment is

$$Total\ cost = F(DL)/(1 - e^{-rL})$$

where D = demand growth rate
L = time interval between capacity increments
r = discount rate
$F(x)$ = cost function, which could be as described above

Examine what happens to total cost as L increases (Exhibit 4.15). For some period of time, total cost decreases, but then it begins to increase again. Both the numerator $[F(DL)]$ and the denominator $(1 - e^{-rL})$ increase as L increases (Exhibit 4.16), but do so at different rates, creating this overall effect.

There are two ways to find the minimum of the total cost curve. One is to solve the total cost equation for many values of L, seeking the lowest-cost solution. Alternatively, if one assumes the cost function described above, it is possible to show that the minimum cost occurs for the L that solves this equation:

$$a = rL/(e^{rl} - 1)$$

EXHIBIT 4.16 **Relationship between *L* and *F(DL)* and between *L* and $1 - e^{-rL}$**

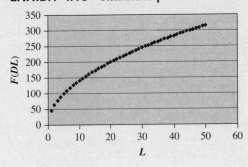

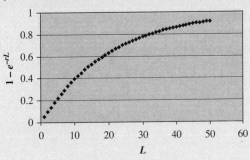

139

EXHIBIT 4.17
Optimal
Expansion
Intervals by
Discount Rate
and Scale Factor

		Discount Rate				
Scale Factor	Cost Savings per Increment	10%	15%	20%	30%	40%
10%	90%	31.8	21.2	15.9	12.7	8.0
20%	80%	22.6	15.1	11.3	9.0	5.7
30%	70%	17.1	11.4	8.6	6.8	4.3
40%	60%	13.1	8.7	6.5	5.2	3.3
50%	50%	9.9	6.6	5.0	4.0	2.5
60%	40%	7.3	4.9	3.7	2.9	1.8
70%	30%	5.1	3.4	2.6	2.0	1.3
80%	20%	3.2	2.1	1.6	1.3	0.8
90%	10%	1.5	1.0	0.8	0.6	0.4

In practice it can be difficult to compute or develop the detailed mathematical relationship between capacity size and cost the model requires. Fortunately, the model can be used to develop the set of heuristic guidelines provided in Exhibit 4.17. These guidelines suggest optimal capacity expansion intervals as a function of the discount factor and the scale factor. With a discount factor of 10 percent per year and a scale factor of 10 percent, for example, the optimal expansion interval is 31.8 years, meaning that the company should add capacity every 31.8 years and add enough capacity to cover demand growth over the upcoming 31.8 years. (If we use monthly discount factors, we can interpret the optimal expansion intervals in terms of months.) Alternatively, if we increase the discount factor to 15 percent and hold the scale factor constant at 10 percent, we reduce the interval between expansions to 21.2 years. On the other end of the spectrum, a scale factor of 90 percent with the same discount factor of 10 percent suggests expansion only once every 1.5 years. For high scale factors and high discount rates, optimal expansion intervals are very short, frequently less than one year.

A couple rules of thumb arise from examining the table:

1. As discount rates rise, add capacity in smaller increments. With higher discount rates, future expenditures are relatively less expensive, and delaying expenditures by adding smaller increments in the future is more economical.

2. As scale factors rise, add capacity in smaller increments. As the scale factor goes up, the cost savings per increment of capacity goes down, and making larger investments in capacity up front is not worth the modest savings that would be gained.

We have described this model as it might be applied to internal capacity management decisions, but it can be applied to external capacity management as well. Outsourcing, for example, sometimes requires long-term investment, such as commitment to a contract factory overseas, or may offer a different scale curve than internal expansion. A company can compare its options for building capacity internally and externally by using the tools we have presented so far. For example, suppose that the cost to add capacity increments internally follows the solid curve in Exhibit 4.18, and the cost to add capacity increments externally (e.g., at a subcontractor) follows the dashed curve in Exhibit 4.18. Then the best capacity expansion strategy when the amount of capacity needed is less than point A is to add it externally, while the best expansion strategy when the amount of capacity needed is more

EXHIBIT 4.18
Comparison of
Capacity
Increment Costs
Internal to the
Firm and at a
Subcontractor

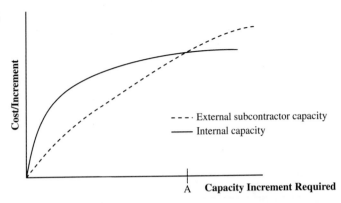

than point A is to add it internally. This might logically make sense in the case in which a supplier already has capacity in place (e.g., a facility and a number of production or service delivery processes) and simply has to increment that capacity by a small amount (e.g., one production line or one service delivery process), leveraging infrastructure already in place. When the capacity needed, however, requires an additional facility, it might be more cost-effective to make the addition internally than to have a supplier do so.

This model for determining increment size (or duration between expansions) assumes a known and constant growth rate. In reality, however, growth rates are rarely constant or known, particularly over the long lead times associated with capacity expansion decisions. While there are extensions of this model that handle uncertainty in growth rate (Manne 1967 and Bean et al. 1992), we will turn to other more general models to do so.

Analytical Models for Hedging Individual Capacity Expansion Decisions

Underlying the capacity decision is the fundamental problem that a firm must forecast inherently uncertain demand. Companies generate demand forecasts in many different ways, from simply extrapolating from past experience to using very sophisticated analytical models. It is beyond the scope of this book to discuss specific techniques for demand forecasting. What is important is the fact that there is considerable uncertainty in most demand forecasts. We must consider that uncertainty in making capacity investment decisions.

In the lead, lag, or stay-even model, we assumed that demand grew at a constant rate over time, that we knew the size of a capacity increment, and that we knew exactly how long it would take to bring that increment of capacity online. When these assumptions hold, it is relatively straightforward to see when to make a capacity investment. If one wants to have capacity come online just as needed, then one must start building it one lead time before it is needed (Exhibit 4.19). For example, if a new hospital is needed seven years from now based on projections of known demand and it takes five years to build, then we should start construction two years from now. However, uncertainty affects this capacity decision in a number of ways. There may be uncertainty about the size of the ultimate demand the capacity is serving. There may be uncertainty about the lead time required to bring a new increment of capacity online. There may be uncertainty about the actual capacity the added resources will be able to deliver in the end. Strategies for dealing with these issues are similar to those for inventory management under uncertainty.

EXHIBIT 4.19
Capacity Expansion under Deterministic Conditions

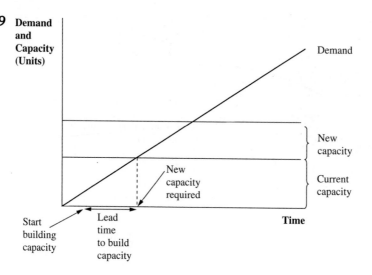

There is a wide variety of approaches that might be used to deal with these issues (e.g., Van Miegham 2003). We highlight three for hedging capacity expansion. The first is how to hedge to handle short-term demand variation. The second is how to hedge to handle uncertainty in the long-term growth rate. The third is how to hedge against potential and major shifts in long-term conditions. In all three cases, we confront the issue of uncertain demand.

Demand Forecasts and Uncertainty

Most companies represent their forecasts as a set of numbers like that shown in Exhibit 4.20 for a hypothetical manufacturer of men's suits. A forecast for a product/service or product/service family predicts the number of units the firms expects to sell and/or the revenue the firm expects to generate from those sales. This view of the demand forecast is misleading, however, as all numbers in the table appear equally certain. Alfani and Lauren, for example, have roughly equivalent demand–around 2,500 units. Without any other information, we would feel equally comfortable building 2,500 units of capacity to make "Alfanis" or "Laurens."

Suppose, however, in addition to forecasting average demand, we assessed the expected variability in that demand forecast. There are a number of ways of doing this including, for

EXHIBIT 4.20
Demand Forecast for a Men's Suit Manufacturer

Style	Forecasted Demand for the Next Year in Number of Units
Mino Lombardi	4,022
Alfani	2,525
Armani	2,147
Sean John	3,309
Lauren	2,383
Hugo Boss	1,347
Bill Blass	1,013
Calvin Klein	1,042
Collezione Italia	1,095
Joseph Abboud	1,117
TOTAL	20,000

EXHIBIT 4.21
Demand
Forecast for
Men's Suits
with Standard
Deviations

Style	Average Demand Forecast (Number of Units)	Standard Deviation of Demand Forecast
Mino Lombardi	4,022	1,125
Alfani	2,525	680
Armani	2,147	804
Sean John	3,309	2,086
Lauren	2,383	1,394
Hugo Boss	1,347	472
Bill Blass	1,013	391
Calvin Klein	1,042	646
Collezione Italia	1,095	753
Joseph Abboud	1,117	1,064
TOTAL	20,000	

example, estimates of high, expected or average, and low demand. Here we use the standard deviation of demand as a measure of its uncertainty (Exhibit 4.21). This new information may cause us to think differently about Alfani and Lauren. The standard deviation of demand for Alfani is 680 units, while the standard deviation for Lauren is 1,394 units, so we are much more uncertain about the demand for Laurens than that for Alfanis. With this new information, we are likely to feel differently about building 2,500 units of capacity for Lauren than we are for Alfani; we are less certain that we can fill all 2,500 units with orders for Lauren than we are with orders for Alfani. We will return to this example later in this section.

Throughout this section, we assume that the mean and standard deviation of the demand forecasts are known and that demand follows a normal distribution (truncated at zero), such as those pictured for Alfani and Lauren in Exhibit 4.22. (Note that according to this

EXHIBIT 4.22
Demand for
Alfani and
Lauren Suits

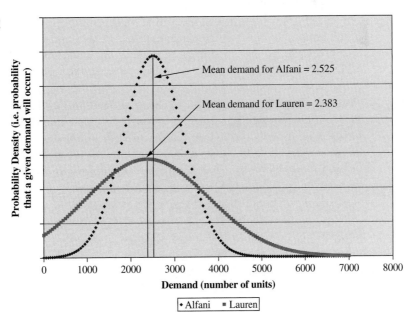

distribution there is a relatively significant probability that we will not sell any Laurens at all—the area under the curve that lies below zero—while we are relatively certain to sell at least a few Alfanis.) Further, we assume stationary uncertainty, meaning that the expected variation in demand (or its standard deviation) does not change over time. This assumption may be difficult to verify and not always true, but using an average estimate of variation still significantly improves capacity decisions.

A Model to Set Capacity Levels to Meet Short-Term Fluctuations in Demand

When demand is uncertain, companies may adopt a number of different strategies, all of which take into account short-, intermediate-, and long-term options for increasing demand, and consider the costs of carrying too much capacity versus having too little to meet demand.

- They may choose to invest in enough capacity to meet the average demand, knowing that half the time they will have too much capacity and half the time they will have too little. In this case, they may be able to build inventory or expand capacity through short-term means (e.g., overtime, part-time workers, use of contractors, short-term equipment rentals) to meet demand when it is above average. Or they may be able to shift demand to smooth the output from the operation. Back-room operations at banks, for example, may be able to postpone work from hour to hour, thus smoothing its effect on the operation.

- They may choose to invest in enough capacity to meet peak demand or the highest level of demand they expect to experience in a given month, day, hour, or even minute. Fast food restaurants adopt this model, investing in significantly more than average capacity because when they don't have enough capacity to meet demand, that demand is lost. Although short-term capacity adjustments may be made (e.g., through appropriate work schedules), the size of the physical facility is set to serve peak demand loads and as a result is underutilized much of the time. One case study (Sasser and Rikert 1980) suggests that the grill at McDonald's is used only about 13 percent of the time on average, and 40 percent of the time during the peak lunch hour. Why? Because there is the possibility of a peak during a five-minute interval, and McDonald's wants to be ready to meet its targeted two-minute delivery time in the face of that peak demand.

- They may choose to invest in enough capacity to meet demand a certain percentage of the time or to provide a certain level of service. Call centers do this when they size their facilities to answer a certain percentage of calls in a certain amount of time (e.g., 98 percent of calls within one minute). Build-to-order companies, such as Dell, target delivery of a certain percentage of their orders in a specified lead time. They must size their assembly facilities to meet this target.

The model we present in this section is based on similar models for planning inventory. It assumes that demand is uncertain, but normally distributed with known mean and standard deviation, and calculates required capacity to meet a given service level. A service level of 90 percent implies the organization will have sufficient capacity to meet demand 90 percent of the time. A 99 percent service level implies demand will be met 99 percent of the time. Meeting demand 99 percent of the time is generally much more

EXHIBIT 4.23
Capacity Hedging Model Choices for Alfani Suit

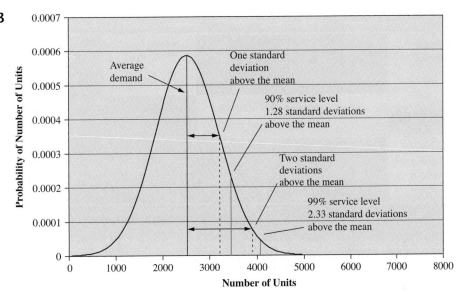

expensive than meeting demand 90 percent of the time. The formulation of the model is as follows:

$$\text{Required capacity} = \text{Average demand} + (z \times \text{Standard deviation of demand})$$

where z is the number of standard deviations from the mean implied by the chosen service level.[15] Sometimes we refer to the portion of required capacity represented by $z \times$ Standard Deviation of Demand as reserve capacity or a "safety stock" of capacity. It is the capacity required above the average demand to handle uncertainty in demand.

Exhibit 4.23 shows the model graphically for the Alfani suit. For a service level of 90 percent, we must provide capacity equal to the area under 90 percent of the curve. This equates to the area under the curve that is below 1.28 standard deviations above the mean.

[15] An easy way to find the value of z is to use the NORMSINV function in Excel, with the service level as the argument of the function. The reader should be aware that equating the percentile of the distribution to the desired service level involves some simplifying assumptions. There are multiple definitions of service level that depend on factors such as whether the impact of a shortage depends on the length of that shortage. Here we use what is known as type I service (see, for example, Hopp and Spearman 2001), which simply looks at the probability of a stockout and sets it to a target level. This is appropriate for the newsvendor formulation described later in this chapter where the target is based on balancing the costs of underage and overage. However, when one examines periodic increases in capacity and uses what is known as *fill rate,* or percentage of demand satisfied from capacity, the appropriate target service level depends on the relative values of the capacity increments and the standard deviation of demand during the capacity implementation lead time. In simple terms, the larger the capacity increments, the lower the target service level needs to be. Readers interested in this should explore a treatment of advanced inventory models. For the purpose of this analysis, the type I service level or a newsvendor approach with a target service level is a reasonable way of thinking about reserve capacity.

EXHIBIT 4.24
Capacity
Required as
Service Level
Increases

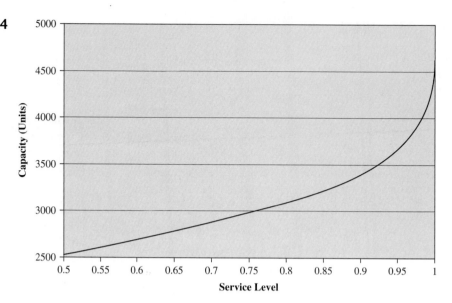

Similarly, for a service level of 99 percent, we must provide capacity equal to the area under 99 percent of the curve, which is the area that is below 2.33 standard deviations above the mean. The formula above yields the following results. Average demand for the Alfani suit is 2,525 and its standard deviation of demand is 680. A 90 percent service level yields a z value of 1.28. Putting these values into the formula yields:

Alfani required capacity at 90 percent service level = 2,525 + (1.28 × 680) = 3,395 units

Similarly, a service level of 99 percent ($z = 2.33$) requires 4,109 units of capacity.

The relationship between service level and capacity required is not linear. The amount of capacity increases sharply as service level approaches 100 percent. Exhibit 4.24 plots the capacity requirements by service level for the Alfani suit. This suggests that the cost of achieving a service level of 100 percent or 100 percent coverage of demand is likely to be prohibitive. In such cases, firms are likely to have to select an affordable service level and live with the cost of unmet demand.

Establishing a designated service level is one way of handling this problem. An alternative formulation explicitly considers the costs of having too much or too little capacity and is known as the *newsvendor model.* The classic newsvendor model assumes that the newsvendor has only one chance to decide how many newspapers he or she will sell each day. At the end of the day, he or she will either sell out and wish for more newspapers to meet demand or have too many newspapers and have to either sell them at a discount or scrap them. Commercial real estate developers similarly must decide at the start of an office building project how many square feet of space to build. Once the building is completed, they will either run out of space to lease and wish they had built more to meet demand or have too much space and have to lease it at a discount. Winemakers make decisions about how many vines of each type to plant five to seven years before they will be able to harvest grapes from those vines to make wine. If they plant too few vines, they will run short of wine to meet demand; if they plant too many vines, they will have too much wine and will have to sell some at a discount or use the grapes in other wine formulations that may make less profit.

In all of these cases, demand is known but uncertain and is assumed to follow a normal distribution with mean μ and standard deviation σ. We also assume that we know the cost of overage, Co, or the cost of having one too many units of capacity, and the cost of underage, Cu, or the cost of having one too few units of capacity. Generally, Co is the opportunity cost associated with having invested in that unit of capacity and Cu is the lost profit on the sale of an additional unit. When these costs are known, the solution to the newsvendor problem is to find the point on the normal distribution, z, such that the area under the normal distribution equals

$$Cu/(Co + Cu)$$

Using Excel, this means finding z = NORMSINV $[Cu/(Co + Cu)]$. This z is then used in the formulation

Required Capacity = Average Demand + (z × Standard Deviation of Demand)

to find the required capacity increment.

To apply the newsvendor formulation, not only must demand, Co, and Cu be known, but it must be a situation in which the capacity expansion decision is being made only once. In other words, another decision cannot be taken to increase or decrease capacity before this decision is played out. This is often a good assumption in capacity expansion decisions, as it is difficult to change them in the short term.

This formulation is useful when the costs of underage and overage are known. Often they are difficult to generate, in which case making an assumption about desired service level is an easier way to establish capacity levels. This model also works well in situations where average demand is relatively constant and the firm wishes to size its facility to meet that average demand and deal with variability around the average. In addition, the model provides a useful way to think about the costs of exceeding and falling short of capacity. When demand is growing or changing over time, however, we use a somewhat different model.

A Model for Setting Capacity Levels to Meet Long-Term Growth Expectations

This model integrates uncertainty in the growth of demand with uncertainty about how long it will take to bring new capacity online. In essence, the model seeks the upper bound on how much demand could be during the uncertain lead time to implement new capacity. The model looks very similar to the one we just used to determine the appropriate capacity level in the face of fluctuating demand; just the inputs to the model are different.

In this model, we must find the standard deviation of growth during the lead time and will use it along with a desired service level to determine reserve capacity. The calculation of that standard deviation follows.

Suppose expected growth in demand is g and the nominal lead time is L. Then the variance and standard deviation in the demand growth during the lead time is

$$\sigma^2_{gL} = E(L) \times \sigma^2_g + (E(g))^2 \times \sigma^2_L$$

$$\sigma_{gL} = SQRT (E(L) \times \sigma^2_g + (E(g))^2 \times \sigma^2_L)$$

where $E(L)$ = expected lead time
σ_L = standard deviation of lead time
$E(g)$ = expected growth in demand
σ_g = standard deviation of growth

Once we know the standard deviation of the growth during the lead time, we can plug it into our newsvendor formula to calculate the required capacity growth or increase:

Required capacity increase = Expected demand growth over the lead time + $(z \times \sigma_{gL})$

where z = the number of standard deviations from the mean implied by the chosen service level

Suppose, for example, demand is growing 10 percent per year, the average lead time to bring on a new facility is two years, and the standard deviation of demand growth during the lead time, σ_{gL}, is 4 percent. Suppose further that the firm wants to be assured that it will be able to handle additional growth with a probability of 98 percent, which corresponds to a z value of 1.96. Then the expansion will need to be:

Required capacity increase = (2 years $\times$ 10%/year) + (1.96 $\times$ 4%) = 27.84%

This is much more than might be required under the case of no uncertainty. To hedge the uncertainty in both growth and lead time, management should add a capacity reserve of 7.84 percent over the 20 percent increment it needs to serve expected demand growth. Management may choose to be more or less aggressive in adding capacity to meet demand by testing alternative service levels. Alternatively, it can try to reduce uncertainty by identifying and managing the factors that create the uncertainty.

This model can be modified for situations in which the size of the capacity increment is fixed and the question becomes how long ahead of need should the capacity be brought online. Generally, the more uncertainty in the demand growth, the earlier the company would choose to start building to reduce the chances that it will run out of capacity before the new increment is brought online. In general, the model highlights the need to consider uncertainty—in demand, in lead time, and in the ability of the new capacity (e.g., process, facility) to deliver as planned—when making capacity expansion decisions.

The models we've presented so far deal with covering the uncertainty in day-to-day, week-to-week, or month-to-month demand, and the uncertainty in longer-term growth rates of demand as well as uncertainty in lead time to bring new capacity online. They provide some intuition and guidance for individual capacity expansion decisions when made more or less in isolation. Often capacity planning is more complex, requiring consideration of multiple facilities placed around the globe at one time, or considering and reconsidering decisions made as new information becomes available. The dynamic decision-making methods of the next section help with these more complex decisions.

Decision Analysis and Dynamic Decision-Making Methods

Dynamic decision-making models are useful in situations where demand growth rates change in unanticipated ways, or where a company has opportunities to revisit an expansion decision at some future date (Eppen et al. 1998). The simplest of these models lays out capacity expansion alternatives and possible outcomes and evaluates each alternative with each outcome to identify the best choice. More complex multistage models evaluate capacity expansion decisions over time, including such alternatives as procuring options to expand capacity once more is known about demand. We start by describing the simple model and then expand to the multistage version.

Single-Stage Decision Tree Models   In a single-stage decision model, all possible alternatives are mapped along with all possible outcomes in a decision tree structure. In Exhibit 4.25, we show n capacity expansion alternatives, which could represent, for example, a range of options from full expansion to very little expansion, or a set of different means of expanding capacity (e.g., internally, through contractors). For each of the n alternatives we show the m possible outcomes that could happen and the probabilities that each could happen. These could simply represent different growth scenarios (e.g., high, medium, low) or could include more complex assessments of market dynamics (e.g., including competitive moves). For each option-outcome pair (e.g., high-capacity option with demand outcome 1), we calculate the return based on the specific revenues and costs associated with that scenario. Once the decision tree is fully populated with data, we calculate the expected value of each capacity expansion alternative or option as the sum of the returns times their respective probabilities:

$$\text{Expected return (Option 1)} = \sum_{i=1}^{m} (\text{Return for Option 1 and outcome } i \times \text{probability of outcome } i)$$

We then choose the expansion alternative that has the highest expected return.

EXHIBIT 4.25
Single-Stage
Decision Tree

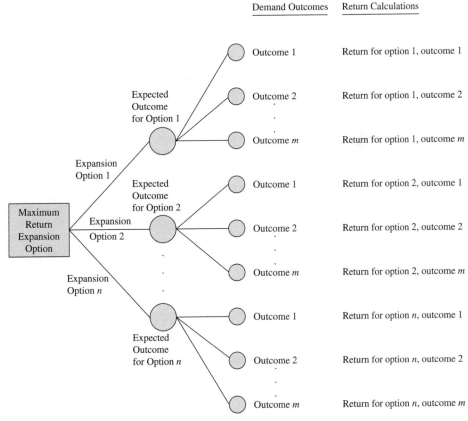

Demand Outcomes	Return Calculations
Outcome 1	Return for option 1, outcome 1
Outcome 2	Return for option 1, outcome 2
Outcome m	Return for option 1, outcome m
Outcome 1	Return for option 2, outcome 1
Outcome 2	Return for option 2, outcome 2
Outcome m	Return for option 2, outcome m
Outcome 1	Return for option n, outcome 1
Outcome 2	Return for option n, outcome 2
Outcome m	Return for option n, outcome m

Maximum Return Expansion Option

Expansion Option 1

Expansion Option 2

Expansion Option n

Expected Outcome for Option 1

Expected Outcome for Option 2

Expected Outcome for Option n

Application of Decision Tree Analysis at UTC[16]

United Technologies Corporation's Fuel Cells business (UTCFC), now called UTC Power, has been designing and manufacturing fuel cells for the space industry for nearly 40 years. In 1991, it introduced the PC25, a 200kW phosphoric acid fuel cell that became the first commercially available fuel cell in the world. In 2002, UTC was working on the launch of the PC35, a next generation commercial fuel cell based on proton exchange membrane (PEM) technology that was expected to sell at much lower cost and higher volume than its predecessor. The highly dynamic fuel cell market, buffeted by sporadic technological advances, shifting government incentives, and unpredictable customer adoption, posed a significant challenge to those at UTCFC who were planning the capital investments required to build and deliver the fuel cell products. While there was consensus that there would be significant demand growth, no one could forecast it accurately, and there were many alternative capacity expansion scenarios to examine.

UTCFC employed a computer-based methodology called Dynamic Strategic Planning (DSP) to apply decision analysis techniques to clearly illustrate and analyze the alternative strategies and possible outcomes. The project was formulated to address the location of a new plant as well as its size or capacity. In the first phase of the project, planners developed a short list of possible locations that met a series of qualitative criteria. (See Chapter 5 for a full description of what such criteria might be.) The five finalists included South Windsor, Connecticut (the current location of UTCFC manufacturing and operations); Milwaukee, Wisconsin; Columbus, Georgia; San Antonio, Texas; and City of Industry, California. In the second phase, costs were developed for each alternative location. Assuming that assembly, raw materials, facility layout, and capital equipment costs would be comparable from site to site, the analysis focused on costs that would differ:

- Labor costs.
- Energy costs and availability.
- Real estate and construction costs.
- Local tax and business incentives.
- Inbound and outbound freight costs.

For each candidate location, for example, the model computed distances from that location to each major supplier and to each potential set of customers. Based on these distances and a freight rate database, the model computed total freight cost.

With all of these calculations, the model could evaluate relevant costs for each location and suggest an optimal choice given a particular market situation. It had yet, however, to deal with uncertainty in market size or in any cost factors. Some costs, such as freight, could be assumed to change linearly, with changes in market size; others were nonlinear. The most important nonlinear effect was building cost, where significant economies of scale might be achieved with larger buildings. To deal with this uncertainty, in the third phase, UTCFC created three possible building scenarios: high capacity (the largest building possible), medium capacity, and low capacity (the smallest building possible). For each of these scenarios, UTCFC determined:

- Production line size.
- Physical product size.
- Expected life of the building.
- Required space for nonmanufacturing activities such as administration.
- Relevant costs associated with each.

In addition, despite great uncertainty about their estimates, the planners identified appropriate probability distributions for different demand scenarios. For simplicity, the planners assumed three scenarios: high demand that they expected to occur with 20 percent probability, medium demand that they expected to occur with 48 percent probability, and low demand that they expected to occur with 32 percent probability.

The planners then computed the costs, revenues, and net present value (NPV) for each combination of facility location, facility size (capacity), and demand scenario, including a penalty if demand exceeded capacity, and represented all of the data in a single-stage decision tree. Exhibit 4.26 depicts just the branch of the tree for Site (Location) D. For each site, the expected value of each capacity expansion option was calculated allowing UTCFC to choose an expansion option for each site, and then the results for each site were compared to identify the best combination of site and capacity expansion option. At the end of the first pass analysis, South Windsor appeared to be the low-cost option, but UTCFC vowed to reevaluate as further information on the product design and potential capacity needs developed. The tool provided planners a quick way to examine alternatives in the rapidly changing fuel cell market and yielded numbers to guide their strategy discussions.

[16] This example is drawn from Beabout, "Strategic Facility Siting in a Highly Variable Demand Environment," MIT master's thesis, 2002.

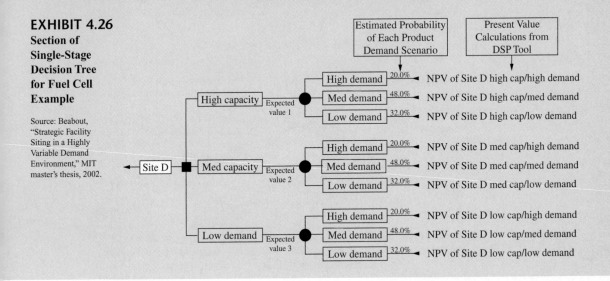

EXHIBIT 4.26

Section of Single-Stage Decision Tree for Fuel Cell Example

Source: Beabout, "Strategic Facility Siting in a Highly Variable Demand Environment," MIT master's thesis, 2002.

As long as all capacity expansion scenarios and possible outcomes can be fully enumerated and analyzed, this approach is feasible. The process of mapping alternatives and outcomes leads to a better understanding of how the alternatives may play out and can allow for early elimination of unfavorable and/or unlikely options. The sidebar "Application of Decision Tree Analysis at UTC" describes how this approach was used to evaluate both facilities location and capacity sizing options at United Technologies Corporation's Fuel Cells Division.

Multistage Decision Analysis Models Multistage decision models are helpful when there is an opportunity to revisit a capacity expansion decision at some point in the future. This could happen when it is necessary to hedge a decision in a way that allows easily adding capacity in the future as needed, or when it is possible to procure an option on a chunk of capacity that does not have to be exercised if demand does not increase as anticipated. Options are sometimes available through suppliers or subcontractors when they, for example, have a facility that might be easily converted to produce the required products or services. Options are sometimes available for purchasing production equipment for processes that are done in house. Options are sometimes available in the form of easily expanded facilities—the option to lease additional square footage, the purchase of sufficient land to allow for facility expansion, and the like. In such cases, it can be worth paying something for the option—a fee to the subcontractor to hold available capacity, a fee to an equipment vendor to commit to potential delivery—which in turn allows the firm to adjust its capacity expansion decision in reaction to actual demand. We represent such options by a second stage in the decision tree.

Suppose that we have three capacity expansion options at the start of a two-year horizon: full expansion, partial expansion with an option for completion, and no expansion. While we have to choose one of these options now, the partial expansion option allows us to revisit our decision after watching demand for a year and updating our expectations for the second year. Under the partial expansion option, at the end of the first year we can choose to either complete the expansion or not. During the second year, the firm may once again

EXHIBIT 4.27 **Multistage Decision Tree**

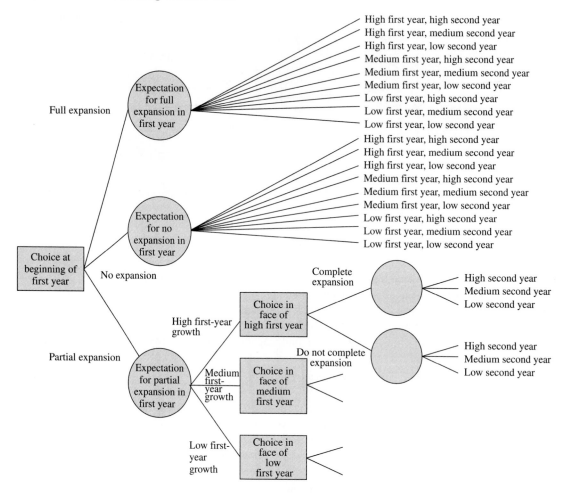

experience high growth, medium growth, or low growth. These options and outcomes are displayed in the decision tree in Exhibit 4.27.

To analyze this decision tree, we must first calculate the net present value for each branch. This entails estimating the cost of each option (i.e., full expansion, no expansion, partial expansion, and each of the second year options) and the returns from each option-outcome combination (e.g., full expansion, high growth in first year, and low growth in second year). Returns may be limited by the choice of capacity option; some capacity expansion alternatives (e.g., no expansion) may not be able to meet the demand of some outcomes (e.g., high growth). Once we have all the returns data for each branch of the tree, we can analyze the options and choose one. Analysis of the full expansion and no expansion options is straightforward, as it is the same as for the single-stage decision tree. For each option we sum the net present values times the probabilities with which they are associated to get an expected value for that option. The expected value for the full expansion

EXHIBIT 4.28   **Partially Solved Multistage Decision Tree**

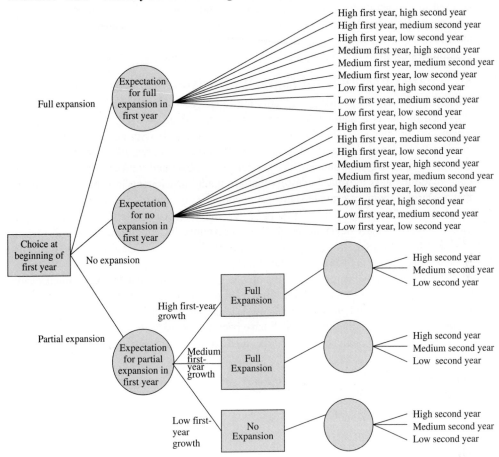

option, for example, is the sum of the net present values for each of the nine option-outcome combinations times the probabilities of those outcomes.

The partial-expansion option analysis involves backwards analysis to account for the fact that there is an option to reevaluate after the first year. We start with the decisions to be made at the end of the first year and find the best choice in each case. If we experienced high growth in the first year, for example, we have the options of completing the expansion or not. By calculating the expected value of each of those options, we determine the best choice given that we experienced high growth in the first year. Exhibit 4.28 illustrates a possible solution to this problem where the best alternative under high growth or medium growth is to fully expand, and under low growth is to not expand. Once we have determined the best choices to be made in the second year, we can compute the expected value of partial expansion in the first year and compare it to the options of full expansion and no expansion to determine which is best for the organization. In short, we can determine whether or not buying an option on capacity expansion is worth it to gain additional demand information in the first year.

Decision analysis has two very important applications for capacity strategy. First, it can be used to enumerate a limited set of outcomes and strategies. Second, it can be used to evaluate real options and the value of information. Even if a formal analysis is not undertaken, management should be fully aware of the range of outcomes and strategies, and the possibilities of options and hedging.

Summary of Models for Capacity Decision Making

We have presented five models for examining capacity strategy decisions. The lead, lag, or stay-even model is a qualitative model that presents three stylized options for capacity expansion: add capacity ahead of demand, after demand, or with demand. It is useful in placing the capacity management decisions in the broader context of the business strategy and the competitive environment. The economies of scale and return on investment models provide insights into the trade-offs that are made in investing in capacity increments that are large enough to provide significant economies of scale, but too large to be used in the short run. The hedging models indicate how much reserve capacity is required to provide a desired service level in the face of uncertainty in demand and demand growth. Decision tree analysis allows full examination of all capacity expansion (or contraction) options across a range of potential outcomes.

Each of these models provides a different perspective on the capacity expansion decision. The choice of models to use depends on the specific situation of the firm at the time it is making the decision and on what it most needs to understand about that decision. In addition to cost and service (availability), which have been the primary focus of the models, a firm must also consider the effect of capacity on its flexibility. We turn to this question next.

Capacity and Flexibility

A company's capacity strategy must be developed in the context of the business strategy it intends to support, meeting the cost, quality, availability, features/innovativeness, and environmental performance goals of the organization as well as supporting the development of chosen capabilities. In many companies one of the specific operational goals—in support of the business goals of availability and features/innovativeness—is the development of flexibility. There are several different types of flexibility that a firm might develop; the most commonly discussed are volume flexibility and product/service mix flexibility. Volume flexibility is used to respond to variability in demand quantity, while product or service mix flexibility is used to respond to changes in the mix of products or services the firm offers.

Firms wishing to increase volume flexibility will most likely follow a lead strategy that provides a capacity buffer ahead of predicted demand. They will likely use the hedging models to establish a level of reserve or excess capacity that provides responsiveness to changes in demand, whether short-term fluctuations or longer-term growth. Carrying reserve capacity is often an alternative to carrying reserve inventory; either allows the firm to respond quickly to unexpected demand spikes. Many firms use a combination of capacity and inventory to buffer demand fluctuations. Service companies, of course, cannot carry inventory so must establish capacity reserves to handle demand as it arrives.

Firms wishing to increase product/service mix flexibility generally need some reserve capacity to handle the variability in product or service mix over time. But they must also consider alternative types of capacity that will allow them to handle a broad product or service mix. Capacity can very specifically target certain products or services (e.g., Shouldice Hospital targets hernia patients only), or it can be built to accommodate a wide range of products or services (e.g., as does the Mayo Clinic). Facilities that are targeted specifically at individual products or services (or families of product or services) may be highly efficient in production or delivery of those specific products or services but are unable to handle any other products or services the firm offers. Thus, they are highly efficient but limit the firm's flexibility. On the other hand, facilities that can handle many different products or services may be less efficient due to the amount of time spent in setup and changeover between products or services but may provide more flexibility for the firm to move activities around among sites. When a firm is unable to move products or services among sites, its availability may suffer as it cannot meet demand with the capacity it has in place even though capacity in one facility may be underutilized.[17]

How flexible should capacity be? The answer lies in understanding the cost structures of the flexible and specialized facilities. First, the capital costs of flexible and specialized facilities may differ. It is difficult to predict which will be more expensive. In some cases, general-purpose equipment and processes may be less expensive to buy off-the-shelf than specialized equipment and processes. In other cases, much higher investments may be required to obtain equipment that is easily changed over from activity to activity. Second, the ongoing operating costs, typically measured in cost per unit, may differ. We generally think of operating costs in flexible facilities as being higher, as there is cost associated with changing over between activities, but it is possible that operating costs could be lower in a flexible facility as well. The only way to answer these questions is to collect the data on capital, operating, and inventory costs for both levels of flexibility and compare them. These costs must be balanced against the service level implications of the different alternatives to get an overall picture of costs and benefits. This is particularly true in multisite facilities where the firm must consider the costs and benefits of flexibility in determining the focus of each facility. Using the inventory models introduced earlier, a company can compare the costs of a single flexible facility, where it can protect against multiple risks (risk pooling), with the costs of multiple specialized facilities. The next section provides an example of this type of analysis.

Assessing the Value of Flexibility in a Multisite Network

The hedging model we discussed earlier quite clearly shows the value of flexible capacity in managing a multiplant network. Suppose, for example, we have the following two choices for our men's suit company: (1) Build two facilities, one focused on producing Alfani suits and one focused on producing Calvin Klein suits. (2) Build one flexible facility[18] capable of making both Alfani and Calvin Klein. Suppose, further, that we want to achieve a 99 percent service level regardless of scenario. For option (1), we treat the two products separately and find that the Alfani plant needs capacity to make 4,109 suits as calculated earlier and the Calvin Klein plant needs capacity to build 2,547 (1,042 + 2.33 × 646) suits for total

---

[17] See Rosenfield et al., "Baker Precision Instruments," Harvard Business School, 2002, for an example of how product variety and changeover time issues create major barriers to flexibility.

[18] These calculations are valid for two flexible or more flexible plants as well. As long as production can be easily moved among the facilities, the capacity is fungible and the calculations apply. There may be other costs, however, to having multiple facilities that are not considered here.

EXHIBIT 4.29
Capacity Calculations for Alfani and Calvin Klein Production

	Alfani	Calvin Klein	Total Separate Facilities	Total Flexible Facility	Savings Due to Flexibility
Mean Demand	2,525	1,042	3,567	3,567	
Standard Deviation	680	646	na	938	
z value for 99% Service Level	2.33	2.33	2.33	2.33	
Reserve Capacity Required	1,584	1,505	3,089	2,186	903
Total Capacity Required	4,109	2,547	6,656	5,753	903

capacity of 6,656 suits. Reserve capacity in this case is 1,584 (2.33 × 680) for Alfani and 1,505 (2.33 × 646) for Calvin Klein for a total of 3,089 units. For option (2), we pool the demand for Alfani and Calvin Klein suits for total demand of 3,567 suits. If sales of these two suit models are independent, then we can assume that the peaks and valleys in demand for one suit are offset to some degree by the peaks and valleys in demand for the other. When this is the case, the overall uncertainty in demand will decrease when we pool the demand and can be calculated as the square root of the sum of the squares of the two respective standard deviations or SQRT $(646^2 + 680^2) = 938$. Our calculations then tell us that we only need capacity to build 5,753 [3,567 + (2.33 × 938)] suits, which includes reserve capacity of 2,186. These calculations are summarized in Exhibit 4.29. Why do we need less capacity? Because the facilities can be used flexibly to meet the demand, allowing us to move production between them as needed, taking advantage of offsetting peaks and valleys in demand and minimizing unused capacity.[19] We can compare the savings in reduced capacity required against other possibly greater capital and operating costs of the flexible plant. This same type of approach can be used in assessing other investments in flexibility, such as flexible equipment.

Organization of a multisite network may well be more complicated than this example indicates. Instead of choosing between fully specialized and fully focused facilities, the firm might choose a mixture of the two. It might, for example, have a couple of specialized facilities that focus on specific product or service families along with a single flexible facility that can produce or deliver all products or services. The specialized facilities offer high efficiency and low costs, while the flexible facility contributes just enough flexibility to the firm overall to improve its effectiveness despite the higher operational costs of that facility. The calculations can be more complex in this situation, but any plant that can be flexible for multiple products or services provides the system with effective pooling for all those products or services.

The notion of having partial flexibility was addressed by Jordan and Graves (1995) in a model that they later applied to General Motors assembly plants. The objective of the

---

[19] As a first order approximation, reserve capacity increases roughly as the square root of the number of distinct types of reserve capacity required. In this case, two plants with specialized capacity for Alfani and Calvin Klein will require about 41.4 percent more reserve capacity than a single plant that can handle both (i.e. 3,089 ≅ 1.414 × 2,186).

model was to maximize sales subject to a capacity constraint for a system with 10 sites and 10 products, which in effect optimized availability. The model examined strategies where each plant could produce a limited set of products (as opposed to all products), but where the linkages between products and plants allowed a great deal of flexibility. By properly structuring the plants to each have limited but complementary flexibility, almost total flexibility was achieved and capacity utilization and sales increased almost 15 percent. The general lesson learned from their work is that significant flexibility can often be achieved in a multisite network with relatively modest investments in flexibility at any given site.

Flexibility is thus a critical consideration in making capacity decisions for responsiveness to variability in both demand volume and product or service mix.

Competition and Gaming with Capacity

Key capacity strategy decisions entail forecasting future demand, acknowledging uncertainty in that forecast, and then deciding the *amount* and *type* of capacity and the *timing* of capacity additions or reductions in response to the forecast. The models we have presented to make these decisions—the lead/lag/stay-even framework and all of the analytical models—have primarily focused on the firm itself and the effect of the capacity decisions on the firm. There are times, however, when competitors' moves must also be taken into account in making capacity strategy decisions.

In some industries, particularly those that are capital intensive, where there is a small number of players and capacity is added in large increments, competitive considerations in capacity decisions are paramount. Companies in these industries watch total industry capacity carefully and time their capacity expansion plans around industry capacity and expected competitive moves. When industry capacity is low, or a new process technology is ready for introduction, a company may choose to build capacity ahead of its competitors, thus preempting them and causing them to lose a chance to expand in the present expansion cycle. Having too much capacity in the industry can be good for consumers, as prices often go down, but it can be expensive for the producers as margins erode and they sit on excess capacity.

We can understand competitive dynamics using the basic concepts of game theory. Suppose, for example, there are two competitors considering capacity expansion. If neither expands, there is neither gain nor loss to either. If both expand, their success is determined by the total size of the market, which is uncertain at the time of the decision. If only one expands, it will "win" as it grows and gains market share. Exhibit 4.30 depicts the

EXHIBIT 4.30
Potential Outcomes of a Competitive Capacity Expansion Decision

	Company A Chooses NOT to Expand	Company A Chooses TO Expand
Company B Chooses NOT to Expand	No gain or loss for either firm	Company A "wins"
Company B Chooses TO Expand	Company B "wins"	Both firms "win" if the total market expands to utilize the new capacity Both firms "lose" if they must support significant excess capacity

outcomes of these four potential scenarios. When market growth can support expansion by both parties, the best solution is for both companies to expand. When market growth cannot support expansion by both parties, the situation is less clear. It may be that the adverse effects of both firms expanding outweigh the adverse effects of neither expanding, so they should not both expand. Or it may make sense for one of them to expand, but not be clear which one can or will do so. In these situations, assessing competitive moves is a critical part of the capacity expansion decision.

The airframe industry recently experienced such a classic game theory situation. In the market for large commercial transport planes, Boeing and Airbus were both planning to develop and build large passenger planes (the 747X and the A380, respectively), but the outcome depended significantly on what the other party did. Most experts agreed that the market could not absorb two such projects, so each company had to consider what the other would do. In the end, Airbus went forward with the A380, effectively preempting Boeing's short-term investment in the 747X. Boeing shifted its focus to the 787, a new midsize airframe, instead. The market could not sustain the tremendous investment required to bring two new aircraft to market from two companies.

When outsourcing is used to expand capacity, the interactions among competitors create an additional level of complexity. If market capacity is limited, for example, and multiple companies are sharing contractor capacity, capacity needs to be allocated and the different parties may attempt to inflate orders in order to win higher allocations. If the contractors do not create incentives against inflated orders, the dynamic of inflated orders followed by cancellations could continue period after period. Capacity contracts in general can address the interactions and risk sharing among multiple buyers and contractors, a topic we address further in Chapter 6.

Summary and Approach to Developing Capacity Strategy

This chapter has presented a number of models for analyzing and evaluating capacity strategy decisions. In this section, we return to the big picture view of how capacity strategy is made. We start with a description of how Intel approaches capacity planning to show how one organization structures itself to do capacity planning, and how and where the tools we have described fit into the overall capacity planning process. We then describe a more generic seven-step process to do capacity planning in any organization.

A Closing Example: Intel Corporation's Strategy Capacity Planning Process

Intel Corporation illustrates the type of approach that one might want to use for capacity planning and implementation (Page 2001). Intel's Strategic Capacity Planning (SCP) team is responsible for Intel's long-range strategic capacity roadmap and production facility investment decisions across all Intel product lines as well as fabrication, assembly, and test facilities. Its mission is to align Intel's supply networks (internal and external) to customer needs, while maximizing shareholder value.

Intel breaks its capacity planning activities down into three segments as depicted in Exhibit 4.31. The production build plan represents actual in-plant production plans zero to nine months into the future. It is updated monthly and includes weekly production

EXHIBIT 4.31

**Capacity
Planning
Horizons at
Intel**

Source: Adapted from
Page, "Forecasting
Mix-Sensitive
Semiconductor
Fabrication Tool Set
Requirements under
Demand Uncertainty,"
MIT master's thesis,
2001.

Long-Range Plan
Development of new fabrication facilities
Development of new assembly/test sites
Negotiation of subcontracting arrangements

Extended Build Plan
Assignment of products to facilities
External subcontracting use

Production Build Plan
Wafer start per week production schedules
Allocation of production to specific facilities
Assembly/test routing decisions

0 months 9 months 24 months 60 months

schedules, allocation of production to fabrication facilities, and assembly and test routing decisions. The extended build plan covers 9 to 24 months in the future and includes decisions about which products to produce at which plant and how much external contracting to do. The long-range plan is built against demand forecasts 9 to 60 months in the future and drives capital investment decisions including the development of new fabrication facilities and assembly and test sites as well as subcontracting arrangements. The three levels of planning are closely intertwined; decisions made for the long-range plan delimit the flexibility to make decisions for the extended build plan, and similarly, the extended build plan sets bounds on what can be done in the production build plan.

The SCP team consists of a Demand Information Team that works with the product divisions to forecast demand requirements, a Factory Capability Team that is responsible for assessing current and future factory capabilities (and thus capacities), and the Roadmap Analysis Team that incorporates the demand and factory capability forecasts to develop a five-year plan for the entire Intel manufacturing network. These three teams are supported by information technology, modeling, finance, and organizational development experts.

The basic process the team uses is depicted in Exhibit 4.32. They take the demand forecast and factory capability inputs and identify gaps or potential shortfalls in capacity. They then decide which markets they will support with existing capacity and how much capacity they are willing to add. This leads to the creation of a capacity roadmap that allocates capacity to forecasted demand and suggests appropriate capacity additions. The strategic questions they ask and answer in this process are detailed in Exhibit 4.33. The answers to these questions provide input to the analytical models that support their work, some of which are described throughout this chapter.

Intel updates its long-range plan on a quarterly basis to respond to the sometimes dramatic changes in demand in the semiconductor industry. The extended build plan and production build plan are updated monthly and allow fine-tuning of capacity to current market conditions. Critical interactions among these plans are handled smoothly by having all three managed in the same planning group.

EXHIBIT 4.32
Intel's Long-Range Planning Process

Source: Data drawn from Page, "Forecasting Mix-Sensitive Semiconductor Fabrication Tool Set Requirements under Demand Uncertainty," MIT master's thesis, 2001.

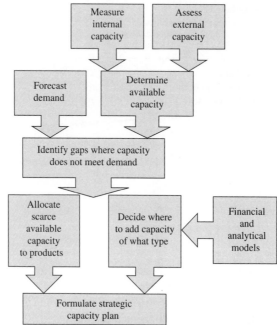

Seven-Step Capacity Planning Process

We close by describing a seven-step process for developing and planning implementation of a capacity strategy.

Step 1: Understand the Business Strategy and Competitive Environment

Understand where the business is to be positioned relative to cost, quality, availability, features/innovativeness, and environmental soundness. A low-cost strategy may imply a

EXHIBIT 4.33
Strategic Questions in Developing Capacity Strategy

Source: Page, "Forecasting Mix-Sensitive Semiconductor Fabrication Tool Set Requirements under Demand Uncertainty," MIT master's thesis, 2001.

Demand Assessment
Which products should be included in the forecast?
What is the base case (most likely) forecast of demand?
What other demand forecasts, or "what if" demand scenarios, should we test?
What are the forecasts for other product parameters (e.g., die size, yields, run rates) critical to the forecast?

Factory Capability Assessment
What in-house capacity is and will be available by type (e.g., fab, assembly, test)?
What external capacity is and will be available at subcontractors?
What is the flexibility of the capacity? On what range of products can it be used?
What are the forecasts of factory production parameters (e.g., yields, run rates)?
What is the most efficient product routing strategy?

Strategic Capacity Plan Determination
What are the probabilities of seeing each demand forecast scenario materialize?
What gaps exist between the forecasted demand and the factory capabilities?
If there are gaps, to which products or markets will we allocate scarce capacity?
If there are gaps, where should capacity be added? When? Of what type?
What are the financial effects of adding or shifting capacity? Of not supplying a product or market?

lag strategy of capacity expansion to minimize investment in excess capacity. A high-quality strategy could have a number of implications, including investing in a type of capacity (often automated) that allows for consistent high-quality performance. A high-availability strategy may imply investment in significant reserve capacity so that demand can be met on time all the time. A strategy focused on features and innovation may imply a need for flexible capacity that can be used in multiple applications. High levels of environmental soundness may imply investing in types of capacity that have lower environmental impact.

Understand the capabilities the firm wishes to develop. A rapid-order response capability may require excess capacity to deal effectively with fluctuations in demand. A rapid product introduction capability may require highly flexible capacity to handle a variety of innovations. Capability in certain process technologies will require investment in those technologies, perhaps on a global basis.

The firm's business strategy—where it wishes to be positioned and what capabilities it has or wishes to develop—is likely to dictate general guidelines for its capacity strategy. In some cases, the firm's capacity strategy may also suggest a strategic direction in which the firm might head. The firm may, for example, have excess capacity that it could fruitfully use in a new market or business. It might be particularly good at managing capacity, like many companies in the contract manufacturing business, and be able to leverage that capability into other business opportunities.

Finally, examine the firm's competitive situation. Is there too little or too much capacity in the industry? Which competitors are likely to add capacity soon? Are there competitors the firm would like to preempt by adding capacity early? What economies of scale are competitors likely to achieve with their capacity investments? How can the firm compete with firms that have better economies of scale?

Step 2: Develop a Demand Forecast

Develop forecasts of demand over the appropriate time horizons (weeks, months, years) and in the appropriate categories (by products/services, product/service families). When possible, collect data on forecast uncertainty as well, by determining not only mean or average demand per time period but the variability (measured in standard deviation or variance) of that demand as well. Demand forecasts are often made in numbers of units to be sold or in dollars of revenue expected. Often such forecasts have to be converted to units of capacity consumption such as hours. It may be important to collect such conversion data at this stage as well.

Step 3: Identify Capacity Expansion (or Contraction) Alternatives

Develop alternatives for capacity expansion (or contraction). These may include short-term (e.g., overtime), intermediate-term (e.g., hiring/firing), and long-term (e.g., facilities expansion/contraction) options. Some options may entail adding large increments of capacity (e.g., a new facility, a new production line, a new franchise) or smaller increments of capacity (e.g., a single new piece of equipment, a new person). They may include investing in additional capacity (e.g., people, equipment, facilities) or improving the efficiency of existing capacity (e.g., quality improvement programs). It is important to be as comprehensive as possible at this stage but practical going forward as to which options are actually feasible and can reasonably be undertaken by the firm.

EXHIBIT 4.34 **Capacity Strategy Analysis Models**

Model	Decision	Approach	Goal
Lead, lag, or stay even	Timing	Qualitative	Maps capacity strategy to business strategy and competitive environment
Competitive gaming	Timing and increment size	Qualitative	Maps competitive options for capacity expansion and relationships among them
Economies of scale and return on investment	Increment size and timing	Quantitative	Balances economies of scale achievable with larger increments with costs of carrying excess capacity
Hedging to cover demand fluctuations	Increment size	Quantitative	Determines how much reserve capacity should be made available to cover demand variability
Hedging to cover demand growth	Increment size	Quantitative	Determines how much reserve capacity should be made available to cover uncertain demand growth
Dynamic decision trees	Increment size, timing, and type	Quantitative	Allows examination of multiple capacity expansion (or contraction) alternatives

Step 4: Apply Relevant Models to Develop Capacity Strategy

Apply the relevant models (Exhibit 4.34) for determining the timing, size, and type of capacity expansions. In some cases, qualitative models such as the lead, lag, or stay-even and competitive gaming models may provide sufficient insight to make an expansion (or contraction) decision. When increment size is a given (e.g., production lines or service delivery systems only come in one size), capacity strategy may be determined through a strategic analysis of the company's business objectives and its competitive position. In other cases the analytical models will provide additional useful insights.

When demand or demand growth is uncertain, the hedging models can help firms decide how much capacity they should put in place to achieve desired availability or service levels. Firms may want to add even more capacity than is needed to cover demand and demand growth in order to achieve greater economies of scale. The economies of scale and return on investment model allows these firms to determine when they should try to achieve greater economies of scale and when they will carry too much excess capacity in doing so. When capacity decisions are complicated by concurrent facilities location decisions, extreme market uncertainty, or the possibility of capacity expansion options, dynamic decision analysis may be appropriate. This analysis allows the firm to lay out its options and possible outcomes and evaluate them as a whole.

While companies rarely make decisions on the output from analytical models alone, the models do provide important insights that inform decisions otherwise made on a qualitative basis.

Step 5: Assess Implications for Flexibility and Balance

Determine how flexible any new and existing capacity needs to be. Some of the analytical models provide insights into the value of flexible processes. The hedging models, for example, show how having reserve capacity increases responsiveness to uncertain demand, and the benefit of pooling demand in a single, more flexible facility over the construction of two, more focused facilities. Other dimensions of flexibility are harder to assess analytically. The firm must address questions of flexibility to handle multiple product or service configurations or the introduction of new technologies, products, or services in a more qualitative fashion and ensure that the demands of its business strategy are met.

Decide how to balance investment in capacity across process steps both internal to the firm and externally across the supply chain. For internal processes, find the bottleneck activity or process step, choose an appropriate level of capacity for that process step, and make investments in the other process steps that surround it to ensure the bottleneck is well fed and thus well utilized. For external processes, identify the capacity at each step of the supply chain. Expand internal capacity as necessary to balance the supply chain or negotiate with other members of the supply chain to do so.

Step 6: Develop an Implementation Plan

Develop an implementation plan. Generally implementation requires a project manager and team that will flesh out the details of acquiring new facilities and equipment as needed and implementing the new capacity. There are likely to be hiring (or firing) requirements, with potentially significant human resource and organizational implications. The team will need a project plan with a schedule and budget to complete the expansion (contraction) project as well. Consideration of implementation issues should have been made in the process of developing the capacity strategy, but in rare cases key implementation problems may not surface until this step of the process, causing the firm to reiterate the steps.

Step 7: Implement, Assess, and Measure Results

Implement the capacity strategy as planned. Measure outcomes and check against the original plan. Were the planned economies of scale achieved? Did the plan achieve the desired business goals for cost, quality, availability, features/innovativeness, and environmental soundness? Is the plan consistent with other elements of the operations strategy (e.g., with the facilities and vertical integration strategies)? Is the plan consistent with and/or supportive of other functional strategies (i.e., marketing, human resources, information technology, and engineering)? Prepare a post mortem report on the capacity planning process and feedback to be used to improve the process in the future.

Summary   In this chapter, we defined capacity and capacity utilization and how to measure them. We described types of capacity—human resources, process and information technology, facilities, and external contractors—as well as ways of increasing capacity through quality improvement and process optimization. We explained the types of choices firms make in managing short-term, intermediate-term, and long-term capacity investments, and the fundamental trade-offs of having too much or too little capacity.

We introduced a couple of qualitative models for thinking through capacity strategies—the lead, lag, or stay-even model and the competitive gaming model—as well as some quantitative models—around economies of scale, hedging, and decision trees—that allow more in-depth understanding of the trade-offs made in capacity strategy development. We discussed the implications of capacity decisions for achieving the business goals of cost, quality, availability, features/innovativeness, and environmental soundness and the operational goal of flexibility, as well as for building capabilities. We closed with a simple seven-step process for developing a capacity strategy, illustrated with an example from Intel.

Capacity strategy is clearly critical to the performance of many organizations. Boeing must manage its capacity closely in order to manage its cost structure. Disney must manage capacity at its amusement parks closely to ensure high availability and customer satisfaction. Call centers must manage capacity to balance responsiveness and cost. The concepts in this chapter can be helpful in thinking through capacity strategy and management in all these situations.

References

Ahmedi, Reza H. "Managing Capacity and Flow and Theme Parks." *Operations Research* 45, no. 1 (1997), pp. 1 –13.

Alvarez, Maria Jose, and John Tagawa. "Capacity Strategy." Report for MIT course 15.769, 1999.

Anupindi, Ravi, Sunil Chopra, Sudhakar D. Deshmukh, Jan A. Van Miegham, and Eitan Zemal. *Managing Business Process Flows.* Upper Saddle River, NJ: Prentice Hall, 1999.

Bakke, Nils Arne, and Roland Hellberg. "The Challenges of Capacity Planning." *International Journal of Production Economics,* 30–31, no. 8 (July 1993), pp. 243–264.

Beabout, Brent R. "Strategic Facility Siting in a Highly Variable Demand Environment." MIT master's thesis, 2002.

Bean, James C., Julia L. Higle, and Robert L. Smith. "Capacity Expansion under Stochastic Demands." *Operations Research* 40, supplement 2 (1992), pp. S210–S216.

Bradley, James, and Bruce B. Arntzen. "The Simultaneous Planning of Production, Capacity, and Inventory in Seasonal Demand Environments." *Operations Research* 47, no. 6 (1999), pp. 795–806.

Browne, J., D. Dubois, K. Rathmill, S.P. Sethi, and K.E. Stecke. "Classification of Flexible Manufacturing Systems." *The FMS Magazine* 2, no. 2 (April 1984), pp. 114–117.

Burcher, P.G. "Effective Capacity Planning." *Management Services* 36, no.10 (1992), pp. 22–25.

Cargille, Brian, Chris Fry, and Aaron Raphel. "Managing Product Line Complexity." *OR/MS Today,* June 2005, http://www.lionhrtpub.com/orms/orms-6-05/frcomplexity.html.

De Neufville, Richard, Joel Clark, and Frank Field. "Dynamic Strategic Planning Overview Course Notes." http://msl1.mit.edu/mib/dsp/curricula.mit.edu/~dsplan/Docs/Papers/dsppol.pdf, February 28, 2007.

Dornier, Philippe-Pierre, et al. *Global Operations and Logistics.* Hoboken, NJ: John Wiley & Sons, Inc., 1998.

Eppen, Gary D., Floyd J. Gould, Charles P. Schmidt, Jeffrey H. Moore, and Larry R. Weatherford. *Introductory Management Science.* 5th ed. Englewood Cliffs, NJ: Prentice Hall, 1998.

Goldratt, Elyahu M., and Jeff Cox. *The Goal: A Process of Ongoing Improvement.* 3rd ed. Great Barrington, MA: North River Press, 2004.

Hayes, R., and S. Wheelwright. *Restoring Our Competitive Edge: Competing through Manufacturing.* Hoboken, NJ: John Wiley & Sons, 1984.

Hayes, R., G. Pisano, D. Upton, and S. Wheelwright. *Operations, Strategy, and Technology: Pursuing the Competitive Edge.* Hoboken, NJ: John Wiley & Sons, 2005.

Hopp, Wallace J., and Mark L. Spearman. *Factory Physics.* 2nd ed. Burr Ridge, IL: Irwin McGraw-Hill, 2001.

Helft, Miguel. "Fashion Fast Forward." *Business 2.0,* 3, no. 5 May 1, 2002, pp. 61–66.

Jordan, W.C., and S.C. Graves. "Principles on the Benefits of Manufacturing Process Flexibility." *Management Science* 41, no. 4 (1995), pp. 577–594.

Kurz, M. "Selection of Operations Management Methodologies in Disparate Cost Environments." MIT master's thesis, 1995.

MacCormack A., L. Newman, and D.B. Rosenfield. "The New Dynamics of Global Manufacturing Site Location." *Sloan Management Review,* 35, no. 4 (Summer 1994), pp. 69–80.

Manne, Alan S., ed. *Investments for Capacity Expansion.* Cambridge, MA: MIT Press, 1967.

Melnyk, Steven A., and David R. Denzler. *Operations Management: A Value-Driven Approach.* Burr Ridge, IL: Irwin/McGraw-Hill, 1996.

Nahmias, Steven. *Production and Operations Analysis.* 5th ed. Burr Ridge, IL: Irwin McGraw-Hill, 2005.

Newlin, Anthony. "Equipment Protective Capacity Optimization Using Discrete Event Simulation." MIT master's thesis, 2000.

Page, Allison. "Forecasting Mix-Sensitive Semiconductor Fabrication Tool Set Requirements under Demand Uncertainty." MIT master's thesis, 2001.

Rajagopalan, S. "Capacity Expansion and Equipment Replacement: A Unified Approach." *Operations Research* 46, no. 6 (1998), 846–857.

Rosenfield, Donald, Kathryn E. Stecke, and Roy Shapiro. "Baker Precision Instruments, Inc." Harvard Business School Publishing, 9-687-052, 2002.

Sasser, W. Earl, and David C. Rikert. "McDonald's Corp.," (condensed). Harvard Business School Publishing, 681044, 1980.

Sethi, A.K., and S.P. Sethi. "Flexibility in Manufacturing: A Survey." *International Journal of Flexible Manufacturing Systems* 2, no. 4 (1990), 289–328.

Slack, Nigel, and Michael Lewis. *Operations Strategy.* Upper Saddle River, NJ: Prentice Hall, 2001.

Van Mieghem, Jan A. "Capacity Management, Investment, and Hedging: Review and Recent Developments." *Management and Service Operations Management* 5, no. 4 (2003), pp. 269–302.

Chapter 5

Facilities Strategy and Globalization[1]

Introduction

Motorola, a $37 billion provider of seamless mobility products and solutions across broadband, embedded systems, and wireless networks, has 320 facilities in 73 countries,[2] 11 of which are manufacturing plants. Over the past few years, Motorola has consolidated manufacturing into about half the number of Motorola-owned locations it used to have. It concentrates manufacturing for its Mobile Devices business, for example, in Tianjin, China, to serve the North American and North Asian markets; Jaguaríuna, Brazil, to serve Latin America; and Singapore to serve South Asia and parts of Europe and is opening a plant in India to serve that market.[3] Managing the configuration of its facilities is one of the critical challenges the company faces. With over 50 percent of its 2005 sales from regions outside the U.S.—19 percent in Europe, 17 percent in the Asia-Pacific region, 10 percent in Latin America, and 8 percent in other markets[4]—Motorola seeks ways to "supply each of its markets as efficiently as possible from a cost and cash perspective, in addition to having access to and presence within each of its markets to support short lead-time customer requirements, while addressing demand volatility and growth."[5] It must balance these global needs with those of serving its largest market, the United States, which represents 46 percent of its revenues.

Since factor costs, particularly labor, can be a major competitive factor, Motorola made large investments in low-cost countries such as Brazil and China[6] that allowed it to move handset production from its higher-cost facilities in the United States and Ireland.[7]

---

[1] Some short sections of this chapter are drawn from MacCormack et al. 1994.

[2] http://www.motorola.com/mot/doc/5/5332_MotDoc.pdf, July 7, 2006.

[3] Interview with Motorola, August 8, 2006.

[4] http://library.corporate-ir.net/library/90/908/90829/items/186361/MOT200510Ka.pdf, August 8, 2006.

[5] Interview with Motorola, August 8, 2006.

[6] Interview with Motorola, August 8, 2006.

[7] http://telephonyonline.com/news/telecom_motorola_lays_off/index.html, July 7, 2006.

At the same time, Motorola is cautious to avoid an overdependence on any one site in the event that capacity should be temporarily lost[8] and maintains flexibility in its facilities network to react to changes in costs over time. The evolution of Motorola's China strategy is illustrative. Motorola is described as a "China pioneer."[9] Its former Chairman, Christopher B. Galvin, first visited Shanghai in 1986 and met with Jiang Zemin before he became China's president. Since then Motorola has invested $3.4 billion in manufacturing and research and development facilities in China, more than any other Western company. In 1992, Motorola established Motorola (China) Electronics Ltd. as a major manufacturing base for mobile phones, two-way radios, wireless communications equipment, and automobile electronics to serve the Chinese market.[10]

Its investments were successful. In 2002, Motorola sold nearly 17 million cell phones in China, more than any other producer. It manufactured telecommunications and other equipment valued at $5.7 billion, roughly $2 billion of which it exported, making it one of China's top exporters and providing about 20 percent of the company's total revenues. And it employs about 10,000 people in China. But competitors are nipping at its heels. Nokia invested $2.4 billion in China and has a large complex to make cell phones and components near Beijing. Local Chinese handset makers have grown their share of the Chinese market from less than 3 percent of the market in 1999 to 26 percent of the market in 2003. Ningbo Bird, for example, added two new plants to increase its production capacity from 7 to 20 million in 2003. In contrast with Motorola, it buys technology off the shelf to develop and deliver products without highly vertically integrated manufacturing and R&D operations.[11]

New and growing competition, as well as the changing nature of the market, requires Motorola to remain flexible. It invested $1.5 billion in a semiconductor plant in Tianjin to make phone-handset chips that was described as one of the most advanced chipmaking factories in China. Demand for the output of the facility, however, did not materialize as planned. The factory was sold in 2004 to China's biggest chipmaker, Semiconductor Manufacturing International Corporation (SMIC). As part of the deal, Motorola took a stake in SMIC's business.[12] Motorola remains committed to "investing, transferring technologies, and building local manufacturing and R&D capabilities in China, which will provide China with advanced communications solutions."[13] It plans continued investment in the development of local management and supply chain infrastructure both on its own as well as in cooperation with joint venture and other such partners in the China market.

China is not the only place in which Motorola is making investments. It plans to spend $100 million on a manufacturing facility in India that will produce a wide range of handsets, as well as network base stations. The facility will supplement Motorola's current

---

[8] Interview with Motorola, August 8, 2006.

[9] http://www.businessweek.com/magazine/content/03_04/b3817010.htm, July 17, 2006.

[10] http://www.businessweek.com/technology/content/sep2003/tc20030923_8656_tc058.htm, July 7, 2006, http://www.motorola.com/cn/about/inchina/inchina_en.doc, July 7, 2006.

[11] http://www.businessweek.com/technology/content/sep2003/tc20030923_8656_tc058.htm, July 7, 2006.

[12] http://www.paulweiss.com/practice/servicedetail.aspx?firmService=29, August 8, 2006.

[13] http://www.motorola.com.cn/about/inchina/inchina_en.doc, July 7, 2006.

presence of 3,000 engineers at six R&D centers in India. In describing its motivation to locate the manufacturing facility in India, a Motorola executive says "India is a vitally important market for Motorola and as a strategic manufacturing hub offers a compelling value-proposition of best-in-class talent and strong cost efficiencies. Our decision to make an investment of this scale is a reflection of our continued global commitment to connect the next billion consumers."[14]

While global manufacturing operations are important for access to both low-cost and emerging markets, global R&D operations are also important. Motorola has 1,300 engineers in China doing research for products such as mobile-phone handsets, semiconductors for PCs, and speech software and recently announced a $100 million expansion of its R&D center in Beijing. Further, it is hiring more local designers to cater to China's increasingly savvy and trend-conscious market.[15]

Managing its far-flung global networks of facilities, both manufacturing and R&D, is a dynamic and ongoing issue. Motorola must consider the location and structure of its entire supply chain from research, design, and development through component production to final product assembly and test, and how to manage the many integration issues inherent in designing, developing, and then manufacturing new products across wide geographic distances.

Motorola's challenges are typical of the issues facing companies that have global supply or service facilities networks. Companies such as Motorola ask themselves four questions in configuring their facilities networks:

1. *How large should our facilities be?* Should we have some large and some small facilities, or should they all be the same size? Can we achieve economies of scale if volume is spread across multiple facilities?

2. *Where should our facilities be located?* Do we need presence in our key markets? How will plant location affect costs? What are the risks associated with a particular location? How, for example, might factor costs in that location be expected to change over time?

3. *What should each facility focus on doing?* Should all facilities be able to build all products or just a few products? Should each facility produce products to serve the global market or products to serve the local market? Should research and development facilities develop products and services for a local market or for the global market?

4. *Finally, given the focus of each of the facilities in the network and of each of the players in the broader supply chain, how will work across the network be coordinated and managed?* How will work be coordinated with external suppliers? How will work be coordinated with internal or external research and development functions?

This chapter addresses these questions and develops a framework to link facilities strategy with the firm's overall operations strategy. It commences with a description of the facilities decision and of the use of supply chain models to assess alternative facilities strategies. It then addresses each of the four questions we have raised here in turn: sizing facilities, locating facilities, choosing a facilities focus, and coordinating facilities in a

---

[14] http://www.motorola.com/mediacenter/news/detail.jsp?globalObjectId=6848_6803_23, July 17, 2006.

[15] http://www.businessweek.com/magazine/content/03_04/b3817010.htm, July 17, 2006.

global facilities network. The chapter closes with a framework for managers to develop a facilities strategy.

The Facilities Decision

Exhibit 5.1 depicts a typical multistage supply chain in which materials flow from suppliers to manufacturing facilities or plants to distribution centers and then to customers. Supply chains may be much more complex than that depicted here, as there may be multiple layers of suppliers (e.g., a raw materials extractor supplying materials to a steel mill that in turn supplies flat rolled steel to a stamping plant that furnishes stamped parts to an automobile assembly plant) or multiple stages of distribution (e.g., a food manufacturer may supply a grocery wholesaler who in turn delivers to the distributors who supply the retailers). At each stage of the supply chain there are likely to be multiple facilities supporting the activities of that stage: Suppliers may have facilities located around the world to support their global customers, manufacturers may choose to support multiple production facilities to serve global production demands, and distributors may maintain warehouses close to local markets around the world. Service organizations often represent their supply networks in similar fashion. A retail business, for example, may rely on an extensive network of manufacturers, wholesalers, and distributors. Other services may be modeled as information management networks; a bank, for example, may process transactions centrally but provide services at many discrete locations (e.g., automated teller machines) close to customers.

The challenge for any given player in the supply chain in creating a facilities strategy is to first establish the strategic goals for the operation of the supply chain and then determine how many facilities to have, where they should be located, what they should focus on doing, and how they should interact with the other facilities in the supply chain. A firm's ability to position itself along the cost, quality, availability, features/innovativeness, and environmental performance dimensions is driven in part by its facilities strategy. A strategy of availability, for example, might suggest a set of decentralized plants that can respond quickly to changes in local market conditions. A low-cost strategy, on the other hand, might concentrate production in a smaller number of larger facilities in low-cost regions of the world, but maintain flexibility to move should cost structures change. Facilities strategy can also support capabilities development: Often firms choose to locate in specific regions to access local technology or talent.

EXHIBIT 5.1
Multilocation
Supply Chain

Suppliers   Plants   Distribution Centers   Customers

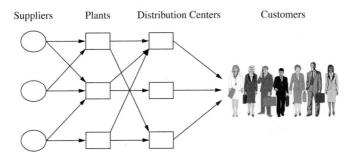

Using Supply Chain Models to Determine Optimal Facilities Configurations

One way to identify the optimal structure of a facilities network such as the one depicted in Exhibit 5.1 is to use supply chain models. These mathematical models can be used to optimize a network relative to a variety of strategic goals such as minimization of transportation or inventory costs or of time through the network. Supply chain models are increasingly used by companies to analyze tactical issues such as how to manage product flow on a short-term basis, as well as strategic issues such as where to position inventory in a supply chain, how product design affects supply chain cost, whether or not to co-locate with a supplier, or how large a manufacturing plant to build. The models can be used to assess a variety of strategic issues including vertical integration, capacity management, and supply chain design. Here we focus on their application to facilities strategy questions.

A cursory review of some of these basic supply chain models illustrates the considerations that must be made in facilities strategy design. Shapiro (2001) describes two types of models that are useful in doing integrated supply chain planning. The first, descriptive models, includes forecasting models that use historical data to predict such variables as product demand and raw material cost; cost relationship models, often derived from activity-based costing, that show how direct and indirect costs vary as a function of defined cost drivers; resource utilization relationship models that describe how the firm's activities consume critical resources; and simulation models that, given a set of input variables or parameters, allow the firm to observe the performance of its supply chain operations over time. The second type, normative models, includes mathematical programming or optimization models that support management decision making by suggesting optimal choices for supply chain structure for a particular outcome such as cost minimization or revenue maximization.

Descriptive Models

Descriptive models are frequently used to assess facilities strategy and supply chain structure in an organization. Hewlett-Packard (HP), for example, made a number of decisions to consolidate its manufacturing facilities in the late 1980s and early 1990s using descriptive modeling. In these projects, a set of production facilities producing similar products (e.g., mid-range computers) were targeted for potential consolidation. Individuals were selected from each of the sites to participate in the modeling effort, and each person was charged with fully understanding the cost structure of one function (e.g., purchasing, production engineering, production) across all the sites under consideration. By spreading responsibilities in this way, team members were forced to take a broad view and not just defend their own divisions. With detailed cost models, derived from activity-based costing data, the team was able to simulate different consolidation scenarios and predict potential cost savings due to plant closure. This approach to assessing the consolidation opportunities not only allowed HP to generate considerable savings from its new facilities configuration, but made implementation smoother because the study team had thoroughly understood the cost structures of the various sites and knew where consolidation savings were to be gained.

Normative Models

A simple normative model starts with a picture something like that in Exhibit 5.1. (Other more complex models and comprehensive treatments can be found in a variety of sources including Simchi-Levi et al. 2003, Shapiro 2001, and Cachon and Terwiesch 2006.) With a particular goal in mind, such as revenue maximization or cost minimization, a company collects data for each node and flow in the network. Specifically, data are typically required on the capacity for and costs of handling each product or product family at each node (e.g., manufacturing or distribution capacity) and along each arc (e.g., transportation capacity). Revenue or profit data could be required as well. A great deal of care must be taken in estimating these input parameters; since model solutions depend on how costs vary with inputs, it is important to understand which costs are fixed and which are variable. With this information, a company can formulate a linear programming problem (or other mathematical formulation) that allows it to determine how much of each product or product family should come from each facility and flow along each arc to minimize the total cost of the network subject to a set of constraints that might include the following:

- The quantity of product delivered to a customer or customer group must meet the market demand.
- The total activity at any facility or along any flow must not exceed its capacity, or more specifically the activity associated with a given product or product family may not exceed its capacity. The flow out of a facility cannot exceed the flow into that facility.

Constraints in a service environment might include specific customer requirements, such as a facility being within a certain distance of the customer location. Mathematical formulations of variants of this model can be found in Appendix A. The models' output guides decisions about how many facilities are needed, where the facilities should be located, what should flow along each of the arcs, how customer service requirements trade off against inventory and other facility costs, and how transportation costs trade off against facility costs. Answers to these questions are often derived by running the models with various different scenarios and then evaluating the results for each scenario against the others.

The case study of a pet food manufacturer (Kandybin and Furlong 1998) nicely illustrates the application of normative supply chain models. The company had a strategy of reducing costs in order to be more competitive in the marketplace, so it focused on improving efficiency in its factories, consolidating plants to realize economies of scale, and partnering with contract manufacturers. Its supply chain, based in the U.S., included 14 potential plant locations, including co-packers and 18 possible distribution centers. The company believed that significant consolidation would be possible, into either existing or new locations. Under consolidation, the company could realize economies of scale by leveraging the fixed costs of its facilities across more volume, but at the same time locate distribution facilities close to its customers' markets. The company used a network-based supply chain model to understand the full cost implications of specific scenarios of facility locations and to determine the effects of a reduced number of facilities. The optimized network had six plants and six distribution centers, and the result was a significant reduction in costs. The supply chain model was instrumental in developing this facilities strategy.

Summary of Facilities Models

Supply chain models are not limited to the analysis of a single manufacturing company or service operation but can be used to model flow for combinations of suppliers and manufacturers, manufacturers and distributors, and so on. Furthermore, supply chain modeling is not limited to companies involved in manufacturing, but is effective for designing retailer networks and delivery networks as well. Online retailers, for example, must determine the appropriate facilities or supply chain strategies for delivering goods to their customers. Models in these situations might include just a set of warehouses and the clusters of customers to be served from those warehouses, or they might be more complex and include major suppliers or major retail outlets from which customers might be served. Often they are simple single-stage models (warehouses only with inbound and outbound costs based on the locations) with very few and possibly only one product class that can be readily treated with the normative models described above. Rosenfield (1987) treats this problem in detail.

In addition to retailing and distribution, network models can also be used to develop a facilities strategy for locating spare parts facilities or service facilities or to find an optimal delivery route (e.g., for grocery delivery). Supply chain models for all of these cases can be used to suggest low-cost facilities configurations for serving given markets, or to assess inventory versus customer service trade-offs. These models work well for situations with static, unchanging factor costs without any uncertainty. However, additional factors such as duties, duty drawbacks, and varying taxation factors can be incorporated. An example of such a model developed for Digital Equipment Corporation can be found in Arntzen et al. (1995).

In conclusion, the flow of material within the supply chain is a major input in the development of the facilities strategy. If a given facilities strategy can be shown to fulfill strategic goals as based on the supply chain flow, then that particular facilities strategy should be an effective one. But these models take into account only those variables that can be reasonably and readily measured—costs, capacities, times, customer service levels. There are many other considerations to be made in determining a facilities strategy. We now turn to more detailed examination of how one might go about answering the four questions we raised in the Motorola case: How large should the facilities be? Where should they be located? What should they focus on doing? How should they be coordinated?

Facilities Sizing

The first question we address is how large the facilities in the firm's network should be. Here we are looking for insights into what the cost structures of different facilities might be, and how volume might be split across multiple facilities in a network. While we ask this question first, and in isolation, it will rarely be answered that way, as final determination of how large the facilities in a network will be depends as well on where the firm wishes to locate them and what they will focus on doing. We'll return to a discussion of the interactive nature of the four questions we have asked after discussing each in turn.

Economies of Scale and Scope

In Chapters 3 and 4 we presented the notion of economies of scale in some detail. In short, economies of scale or scope are achieved when the fixed costs of an operation can be spread over greater and greater volumes. Exhibits 5.2a and 5.2b summarize the dynamics of the economy of scale curve: As production or delivery volumes increase, cost per unit decreases. Variable costs per unit remain the same, but total fixed cost when divided by volume generated results in decreasing fixed cost per unit. As we have seen, economies of scale are an important consideration in making vertical integration, capacity, and process technology decisions; they are important in making facilities strategy decisions as well.

EXHIBIT 5.2   **(a) Fixed and Variable Production Costs and (b) Economy of Scale Curve**

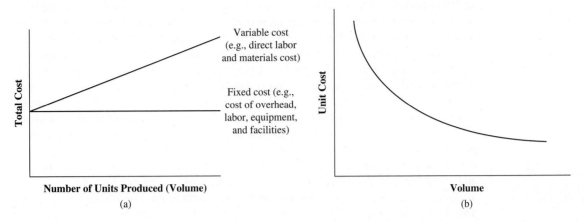

(a)   Number of Units Produced (Volume)

(b)   Volume

For any given facility, which will have a specific fixed and variable cost profile, economies of scale suggest that the firm will want to fill that facility with sufficient volume to operate as near as possible to the flat part of the curve. In a multifacility network, then, the firm will likely want to size facilities and allocate volume to those facilities so that they may all operate near the flat parts of their respective curves.

To design such a network is not trivial, for it requires the firm to understand the cost structures of all the various facilities configurations in which it might invest. Recent developments in both process technology and process infrastructure (e.g., just-in-time and lean concepts) have created a wider range of options from which firms can choose.

Lower-Scale Production and Service Systems

Emergence of lower-scale manufacturing and service technologies such as flexible-manufacturing systems facilitate more decentralized facilities networks. A flexible-manufacturing system (FMS) (Jha 1991) integrates computer-controlled equipment and materials-handling systems with centralized monitoring and scheduling. Such systems are most efficient when numerous, different parts need to be manufactured in relatively small batches and offer significant advantages over other manufacturing methods when the product requires customization.

Two dynamics explain the increasing attractiveness of scale-reducing technologies such as FMSs. First, product life cycles are rapidly declining, and customers increasingly prefer customized rather than generic products, forcing manufacturers to produce greater product variety in shorter lead times. Second, technical advances in FMSs and scale reduction are making these technologies increasingly attractive to low-volume producers, allowing them to be more competitive with the hard automation used by high-volume producers.

FMS technology is not the only approach to reducing the effects of scale. Just-in-time (JIT) and lean thinking offer a number of methodologies and approaches that allow smaller facilities to be constructed without the cost penalty of operation at lower volumes. Both JIT and lean thinking, for example, emphasize reduced changeover times to achieve small lot production. Single minute exchange of die (SMED), developed in Japan by Shigeo Shingo (1996), allowed automobile stamping plants to change over their equipment in minutes rather than hours, thus facilitating production of smaller lot sizes and greater variety. As a result of this and other changes in layouts and procedures, the automobile industry now has lower-scale and more focused assembly plants that are able to produce annual volumes on the order of 25,000 units with the efficiency of some of the older facilities that produced hundreds of thousands of units. Lean thinking is not just restricted to manufacturing operations; it has also led to scale reduction in software development, bank operations, and other services.

Through the productivity increases due to new management philosophies and improved production techniques, a facility is able to produce to the same demand with less overhead. Plant scale is thus reduced, which implies that smaller, more focused plants can satisfy demand. In addition, overhead reductions and the efficiency of newer technologies decrease labor costs as a percentage of overall product costs so that the cost structure of products is primarily determined by the other factor costs of material, capital, and energy. While low-cost labor is often a driver of facility location, the other costs tend to vary less by location, and thus these new approaches can provide more flexibility in facility location.

Although these methodologies can reduce dependence on low-cost labor, they rely heavily on workforce quality and skill. Thus, while the total number of production and lower-skilled labor employees may decrease, the remaining workforce must be highly qualified. FMSs are highly automated and thus reduce direct labor, relying instead on qualified engineers. In a typical system, engineers will significantly outnumber production workers. In considering a location for an FMS or other highly automated manufacturing facility, the company must therefore consider the local engineering labor pool.

Generating Economy of Scale Cost Curves

The world has undergone technological changes that allow smaller-scale operations and leaner manufacturing operations, reducing economy of scale effects. This does not make economies of scale, however, irrelevant. In designing a facilities network a firm may want to have multiple facilities that divide up the volume of a given product or service. To understand the implications of dividing up the volume, the firm needs to determine the scale impact at a number of locations. Doing so is not a trivial matter. To fully understand the implications of scale economies in a facilities configuration decision, a firm needs to develop scale curves for each of the potential technologies and/or facility options it is considering. The collection of such curves might be as shown in Exhibit 5.3a. Each of the

EXHIBIT 5.3 (a) Economy of Scale Curves for Technology Options for a Given Production or Delivery Task and (b) Technology Envelope for a Given Production or Delivery Task

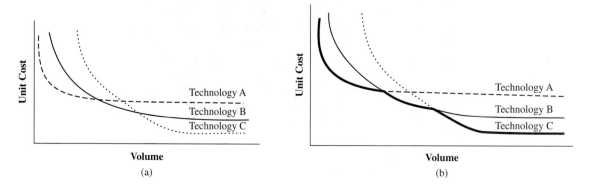

curves in this figure represents a different technology or infrastructure choice, and each provides the lowest-cost solution for a range of volumes. The lower bound of the curves creates what we call the technology envelope, or the overall economies of scale curve for a given task as depicted in Exhibit 5.3b.

Exhibit 5.4a represents another way to look at economy of scale cost curves. In this case, instead of cost per unit, each of the straight lines represents the total cost (fixed plus variable) for the use of an individual technology or infrastructure choice at any given volume. Exhibit 5.4b shows the technology envelope. At high volumes, the best technology is the one that has very low variable costs and high fixed costs, technology 2 in this case. At medium volumes, an intermediate technology, technology 1, with higher variable costs and lower fixed costs will do, and at low volumes, a curve with very high variable costs and low fixed costs, such as a subcontracting operation, is appropriate. Cost functions need not be linear as shown in this example and costs may not be strictly fixed or variable. Thus, a variety of types of cost curves might be developed to understand scale effects across various technologies.

Development of these scale curves requires both data for the individual technologies or infrastructures that the corporation already uses and data for the technologies or infrastructures that it could use. Collecting such data requires comparison of different plants with similar operations. Many companies have problems developing this data, because they may not have multiple plants doing similar operations, or they may not be able to appropriately compare the operations at two different plants because of differences in packaging or product standards. In addition, companies often do not have data for technologies that they do not use. Since such information lies elsewhere, evaluation requires benchmarking and exploration of outside technologies. Nonetheless, it is critical for companies to collect such data to establish an effective facilities strategy. Well-managed companies continually search to understand both technologies at alternate volumes as well as emerging technologies so they can develop the multiple-technology scale curve.

EXHIBIT 5.4   **(a) Total Cost Curves for Three Options and (b) Technology Envelope Formed by Three Total Cost Curves**

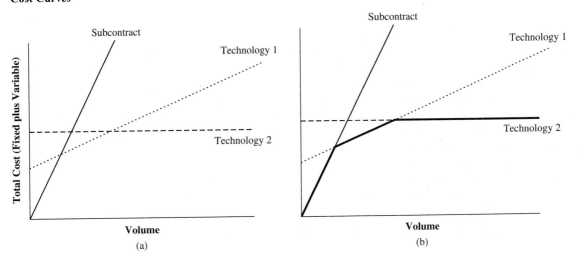

A company is always faced with a choice of technologies and must choose the best technology for the volume to be generated. When a company grows its volume, it gravitates toward a more efficient technology or infrastructure for that volume. Similarly, when it shrinks its volume it may scale back its technology or infrastructure to a more appropriate position. The scale relationship ultimately determines appropriate facility size and hence suggests the number of facilities that the company should have. Semiconductor fabrication companies, for example, generally invest in facilities of such large scale that they must significantly limit the total number of facilities they build. Steel mini-mills, on the other hand, are designed to operate at relatively low volumes, and companies such as Nucor Steel can thus afford to have many small facilities located close to important markets. The development of inexpensive automated teller machines (ATMs) has allowed banks to provide service in dozens of locations in a community rather than just one or two, thus providing improved customer service for simple transactions. For more complex transactions, they still need larger branch offices staffed with people. Their facilities strategies thus balance investment in ATMs with that in larger branch offices.

It is extremely important to understand economies of scale in making facilities decisions for both services and manufacturing operations. To do so, a firm needs to gather information about all the relevant technologies or infrastructure choices it has in designing its facilities network. Armed with the appropriate cost information, it can then develop economy of scale curves that suggest which technologies or infrastructure choices are appropriate at which volumes, and how many facilities of each type it may be able to support.

Leveraging Global Economies of Scale and Scope Outside Operations

Companies often try to sell internationally even when not operating globally. To do so effectively, they leverage economies of scale and scope on a global basis across their entire range of supply chain activities to undermine the competitive strength of local or domestic players. The emerging global markets, including expanding economies in Asia, Eastern Europe, and Latin America, underscore the need for doing so. As the fixed costs of manufacturing and operations have decreased, the fixed costs of other supply chain activities such as research and development and marketing have come to play a more prominent role. Firms must leverage these fixed costs across as much volume as possible globally. Here are a few examples.

In high-tech products, scale in research and development (R&D) has become more relevant than scale in manufacturing. Investment in R&D rose in the drive for rapid innovation, so industry players seek more markets across which to recoup research and development expenditures. Consider the pharmaceutical industry where the cost of drug development has increased from about $4 million in 1962 to something in the range of $450 to $700 million in 2000, according to industry averages reported to the Pharmaceutical Research and Manufacturer's Association.[16] As a result, the industry underwent substantial transformation through mergers, acquisitions, divestments, and globalization to increase scale. One of the countries courting investment from the pharmaceutical industry is India, whose low-cost economy and high-quality human resource base make it a sought-after destination for clinical

---

[16] http://www.netsci.org/scgi-bin/Courseware/projector.pl?Course_num=course1&Filename= slide07.html, July 16, 2006.

research outsourcing. Sixty percent of the country's earnings come from export of bulk drugs.[17]

Financial scale can also play a transformative role as it has in consumer products. Take Procter and Gamble (P&G), a nearly $57 billion company in 2005, that has three product categories—global beauty care; global health, baby, and family care; and global household care—and more than 20 brands that are billion-dollar sellers worldwide, including Actonel, Always/Whisper, Bounty, Charmin, Crest, Downy/Lenor, Folgers, Iams, Olay, Pampers, Pantene, Pringles, Tide, and Wella.[18] Its financial scale gives it significant advantage in managing cash flows between different product segments or national markets and allows P&G to gain entry into a local market by undercutting domestic competitors and investing heavily in promotion.

Global markets also enable the economies of scale in the product life cycle. Introducing products in secondary markets after they reach the maturity or declining phases of the life cycle in the first market can extend the product life cycle. (See Chapter 3 for a more complete description of a product life cycle.) For example, Japanese auto and consumer goods manufacturers often delay introduction of products in the United States until after they have been introduced in Japan. Leveraging global product volumes does not require that products be homogeneous across markets. Scale can leverage locally tailored products, differentiated products, or different product families. Honda, for example, has unique capabilities in the fast-cycle design and manufacture of engines. It uses this to great advantage globally across a line of businesses, from automobiles to powerboats to lawn mowers.

Facility Sizing Summary

In developing a facilities strategy, it is critical to consider (a) ways in which volumes may be built and then leveraged globally and (b) the economies of scale associated with breaking up that volume among facilities that have different technologies or infrastructures. Firms today have many choices of how to structure their facilities that often provide them a range of sizes they can consider from large to small. They must understand the individual scale curves for each of these options and use them to understand which choices best fit which volume requirements. Clearly understanding economies of scale and scope alone are not enough in completing a facilities strategy. The firm must also decide where it wants to locate its facilities and what those facilities will focus on doing. We turn now to the location decision.

Facilities Location

Facilities location is perhaps the most complex part of the facilities strategy decision. To think through facilities location, the decision makers must understand the global nature of today's businesses and the factors affecting them as they approach globalization. Then, they must consider the various reasons for choosing to locate a facility in a given location or region: market access, capabilities access (e.g., technology, materials, and skills), and low-cost access. We start with an in-depth exploration of globalization and its effects on

---

[17] http://www.netsci.org/scgi-bin/Courseware/projector.pl?Course_num=course1&Filename= slide07.html, July 16, 2006.

[18] http://www.hoovers.com/procter-&-gamble/–ID__11211–/free-co-factsheet.xhtml, July 16, 2006.

facilities location decisions and then turn to each of the factors to be considered in making location decisions.

Globalization Impacts and Strategies: Some Macroeconomic Trends

Globalization is one of the defining trends of our times and affects operations strategy and, specifically, facilities strategy significantly. There is no question that we are in an era of expanding global activity. While some argue that the growth in global trade since 1945 is simply a resumption of what was taking place before the era of protectionism and war that lasted from 1914 to 1945, recent activity stands in stark contrast to this era. Exhibit 5.5 shows the growth of world exports from 1950 through 2004.

The presence of more developed overseas markets suggests that there are large benefits of scope for firms who sell globally. Trends in trade and investment patterns, and the advent of lower-scale production and delivery technologies, suggest that the most effective way to serve the global market is often with a regional approach that provides presence in a number of marketplaces. This reduces costs, provides better customer feedback, and minimizes risk resulting from exchange-rate fluctuations and other political factors. However, access to the required capabilities—skills to run the new technologies, access to suppliers, transportation and communications infrastructure—may limit the number of feasible locations. It is this trade-off that is at the heart of the facilities strategy decision. We discuss the major macroeconomic factors affecting this decision—global markets, trade and investment patterns, and emerging economies—in turn in the following sections.

Global Markets

Overseas markets dictate a global presence for manufacturers, with some ability to tailor products to local tastes. Many countries once regarded as lesser developed or developing now constitute large markets for sophisticated, leading-edge, quality products. In Asia, Japan has long been one of the world's most developed markets, and Korea, Taiwan, Singapore, and Hong Kong are in the process of accomplishing a similar feat. In Latin America, countries such as Brazil and Chile are enjoying an economic renaissance.

EXHIBIT 5.5
Trends in Value of Worldwide Manufacturing Exports

Source: Data drawn from World Trade Organization, http://www.wto.org/english/res_e/statis_e/its2005_e/its05_longterm_e.htm 2005, April 21, 2006.

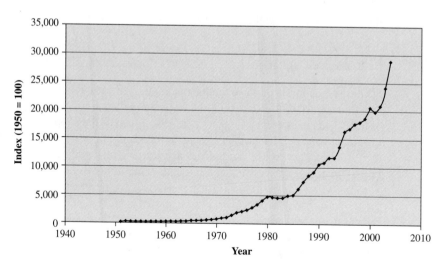

The world economic arena is no longer concentrated in North America, Japan, and Western Europe; it now includes China and large parts of Asia, Eastern Europe, and South America. In the future, additional emerging markets will command significant attention.

The growth of such large markets has led to the emergence of powerful global competitors, many of whom emphasize production for export markets. In Japan, for example, as domestic markets have become increasingly sophisticated, the cash flows generated at home have been used to fight market share wars in other regions. The growth of Japanese exports tells the story. In 1960, Japan exported $4.1 billion. During the 1960s exports grew at an average annual rate of 16.9 percent, and in the 1970s at an average annual rate of 21 percent. Growth slowed in the 1980s to only 11.3 percent per year on average, but by 1990 merchandise exports from Japan reached $286.9 billion and by 2004 stood at $566 billion.[19] To compete against such export-oriented firms, becoming global is crucial. Corporations cannot allow their competitors the luxury of cash-generating havens in untapped markets. Global competitors make aggressive moves to overcome regional or local barriers and play in all relevant markets.

Competing in global markets requires first understanding those markets and then engaging in rapid innovation of products and services to meet the needs of the specific markets. It is increasingly difficult to push products or services that have matured in developed markets into developing markets. Customers around the globe increasingly demand leading-edge, high-quality products. Product innovations introduced in the United States and other developed economies are copied, improved upon, and introduced to other markets within months. A firm's global facilities strategy must address opportunities in these many different markets.

Trade and Investment Patterns

Nontariff barriers (NTBs) are trading requirements that circumvent formal tariffs. They interfere with a firm's ability to export to a market by placing restrictions on local content, volumes, or market share. NTBs seek to shape the operations of foreign-owned companies that have set up facilities within a region and are forcing firms to localize production resources.

Nontariff barriers come in many forms. Regional trade agreements, such as the North American Free Trade Agreement (NAFTA) among Canada, the United States, and Mexico, and the European Union's attempts to reduce trade barriers within the European Market, are the more obvious forms of nontariff barriers. Such regionalized trading blocks, which are being created in Asia and Latin America as well, allow for relatively free internal movement of goods and production resources, common standards, and coordinated macroeconomic policies. When trade barriers are reduced or eliminated in one of these regional blocks, it is relatively more expensive to serve these countries from other regions of the world, making a decentralized facilities structure beneficial. Other types of nontariff barriers include product standards, such as how markets treat organic food products, foreign investment restrictions, labor standards, and local content requirements.

The evolution of a world trade system based on regional blocks creates incentives for firms to follow direct investment strategies that give them a presence in each region of significant demand and unrestricted trade. These trade policies also shape the nature of operations for companies already established in a region, forcing them to expand the scope of

[19] http://www.photius.com/countries/japan/economy/japan_economy_exports.html, http://www.wto.org/english/res_e/statis_e/its2005_e/section3_e/iii01.xls, July 16, 2006.

their local activities either by sourcing more from local suppliers or by increasing their own local value-added work. The more formally managed nature of trade between blocks means that firms using export-based strategies face additional administrative hurdles and potentially damaging regulatory barriers. Differences in trade policies among regions may cause companies to invest more in some regions than in others, as we see with emerging economies such as China.

Emerging Economies, Particularly China

In 2005 China exported $750 billion worth of goods, up from $266 billion in 2001. Much of this activity was through multinational companies that expanded their reach into China, either establishing facilities of their own or using suppliers. Many subcontract manufacturing operations established themselves in China, some developing major networks of multiple facilities (e.g., Flextronics) and others investing in a single location of major size and scale (e.g., Foxconn), to serve original equipment manufacturers (OEMs) in other countries. Some companies, such as Motorola, placed a major portion of their production in China, while others use China as one of several sources.

China is the latest, and perhaps largest, example of the development of an emerging economy. The general pattern for emerging economies is that they start by attracting manufacturing activity because they offer low labor costs. The producers they attract help them develop the required infrastructure, and as they develop, factor costs rise, pushing the original investors to seek newer emerging economies with lower factor costs. The original economies then focus on higher-value-added products. Exhibit 5.6 shows the difference between labor rates in the developed economies and those in the emerging economies as well as how labor costs tend to increase in the emerging economies over time. For comparison purposes, the hourly compensation rate for manufacturing labor in China averaged $0.57 on 2002.[20] Thus, after Japan and Korea developed, the products they produced moved to other countries such as Hong Kong, Singapore, Taiwan, Thailand, Malaysia, Mexico, and now China, and for services, India. The products produced in these newer economies are not necessarily all low-tech products, but sometimes include higher-value products with relatively cheap transportation costs, such as electronics.

The case of China is different from those of the other emerging economies. China is an enormous country with a very large source of labor; the manufacturing workforce alone was estimated at 100 million people in 2002.[21] There is virtually no limitation on the degree of economic activity that global players can locate within China. Furthermore, the trend of rising factor costs that takes place in other emerging economies will take a very long time to play out in China.[22] China is also different in that skills and manufacturing sophistication are relatively high. Thus it can provide the benefits of both low costs and high sophistication. Further, with the emergence of technologies that support relatively long transport links, it is possible for a global company to source a large amount of global production within China. At the same time, with lower-scale technologies they can maintain presence in other parts of the world as well.

[20] http://www.bls.gov/opub/mlr/2005/08/art3full.pdf, July 16, 2006.

[21] http://www.bls.gov/opub/mlr/2005/08/art3full.pdf, July 16, 2006.

[22] The pattern of increasing factor costs is playing out in China to some degree in that costs in coastal areas are increasing and some activity is moving inland. The move inland in turn has created issues of transportation and energy infrastructure and has also increased lead times.

EXHIBIT 5.6   **Hourly Labor Rates for Production Workers in Selected Developed and Emerging Economies in U.S. Dollars**

Source: Data drawn from U.S. Bureau of Labor and Statistics, ftp://ftp.bls.gov/pub/special.requests/ForeignLabor/ind3133naics.txt, July 16, 2006.

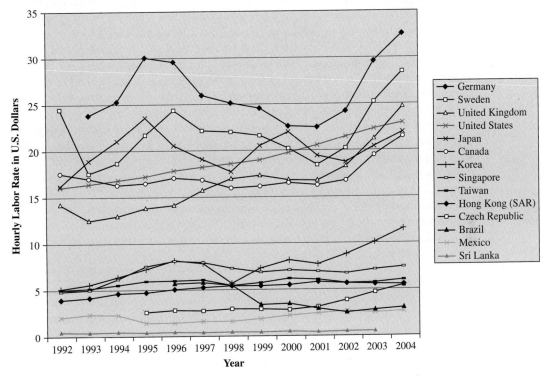

Considerations in Facilities Location Decisions

The development of global markets, regional trading blocks, and emerging economies, particularly China, is forcing companies to address globalization in all of the decisions they make. With these broader macroeconomic trends in mind, we now examine the major considerations in making facilities location decisions: market access, capabilities access (e.g., technology and skills), and low-cost access. Worldwide markets can be served in many ways: by export, local presence with final product assembly or service delivery only, or fully integrated production or service delivery. Each potential strategy has a unique cost structure, set of skill requirements, and ability to respond to local markets.

Market Access

As our discussion of trends in globalization makes clear, the markets in which companies compete today are global. Even markets such as the 4 billion people who subsist in this world on less than $2 a day are now thought to be accessible and of interest to global competitors (Prahalad 2004). Accessing the global market often requires companies to have presence in the countries or locales they wish to serve. This presence can take any of a number of forms, such as a sales office, a small marketing organization, or procurement personnel, but often manufacturing presence is required.

"Host governments have imposed domestic-content restrictions on the subsidiaries of foreign investors to enhance 'industrial deepening,' augment 'supplier creation,' and multiply 'backward linkages' in the hope of creating reasonably vibrant, productive and, ultimately, competitive indigenous industrial base."[23] Such restrictions, that often accompany foreign direct investment policies, have had mixed results over the years. Often they result in high local prices to cover fixed costs of small facilities or in the allocation of low-end products to those regions. Nonetheless, these types of regulatory requirements often drive companies wishing to access a market to invest in placing facilities there.

Local presence is also often required for a firm to gain understanding of customers and users in the target market. It is extremely difficult to understand local culture, norms, practices, and so on without actual presence in a market. While this does not necessarily require that manufacturing or service delivery operations be present in the market, it does generally require at least sales or marketing presence. Sales and marketing personnel in these situations are charged with both understanding the local market requirements and feeding that knowledge back to the research, design, and development organization and with tailoring advertising and product or service delivery to the local situation.

Finally, local presence may be dictated for logistics reasons. Transportation costs to a market may be significant enough that locating a facility in that market makes sense. The models discussed earlier in this chapter that minimize transportation costs are helpful in assessing whether or not this is the case.

Capabilities Access

Companies may also wish to locate facilities in certain regions in order to access the capabilities available to it in that location. A location might offer access to new technologies, such as Japan does in the development of semiconductor processing equipment. It might offer access to specific skill sets, such as those offered by India's software programming capabilities. It might offer connection to a supply base that is facile with just-in-time or lean manufacturing concepts. In all cases, location in a country or region allows a firm to build desired capabilities. Here we examine two capabilities that are particularly important in operations management, lean operations, and total quality management.

Lean Operations and JIT   In just-in-time (JIT) operations, parts and information are pulled through each process step based on a daily demand schedule, each step producing only what is demanded by the succeeding step. (See Chapter 10 for a more in-depth discussion of JIT and total quality management.) The process is thus better synchronized with customer demand, wasteful in-process inventories are avoided, and cycle times are reduced. One of the many benefits of JIT operations is that these advantages can be realized with very little investment and with wide applicability to a diversified industry base. Lean operations extend the notions of JIT to include product development, supplier management, and other areas as the following examples from service operations show.

Dell's service operations applied lean thinking in a customer-service initiative that used artificial intelligence software to provide telephone-based service agents responses to give customers to resolve problems with their computers. As a result, today 90 percent of customer calls can be handled with one phone call, product returns have declined, average call times have declined 8 percent, and more complicated repairs are handled on the phone

[23] http://www.iie.com/publications/chapters_preview/53/4iie258x.pdf, July 17, 2006.

(Nallicheri et al. 2004). Jefferson Pilot Financial (JPF), a life insurance and annuities firm, wished to establish itself as a preferred provider and so launched a program to reduce turn-around times on policy applications, simplify the submission process, and generally reduce errors. Applying lean practices, it created a "model cell"—a fully functioning microcosm of JPF's entire process—which allowed it to experiment and make needed changes while working toward an optimal design. The team applied lean manufacturing practices, including placing linked processes near one another, balancing employees' workloads, posting performance results, and measuring performance and productivity from the customer's perspective. JPF is now rolling out similar systems across many of its operations (Swank 2003).

Lean operations and JIT require strong infrastructure both in terms of the skills sets needed to run lean operations and in terms of the supplier infrastructure surrounding the operations. In making facilities location decisions for lean operations, firms must consider the capabilities of both the local workforce as well as of the local supplier base. We address each in turn. First, lean operations are highly dependent on the quality of front-line labor as well as the quality of process designers and engineers. Employees must be highly flexible and multiskilled as they perform tasks including preventive maintenance, repairs, and complex planning activities. Although some companies host extensive internal training programs, they must regard local employee skills as a key decision variable and support plant locations with a strong educational infrastructure as well as employee exposure to modern technology and practices.

Such factors suggest that progressive operations management practices will be more effective in developed regions that are close to sophisticated markets, rather than in less developed, low-labor-cost regions. The importance of labor skill and effective management philosophies has been corroborated in an empirical study comparing select mature industries in less developed countries (LDCs) to those in newly industrialized countries (NICs) (Mody et al. 1992). The authors demonstrated that the overall cost saved from locating in NICs exceeded the labor cost savings from locating in LDCs, in effect showing that NICs are more competitive than LDCs, as the skilled labor available in NICs outperforms the lower-cost labor in the LDCs.

The second major impact of lean operations and JIT policies is on the relationship between the manufacturer or service provider and its supplier network and support services. Reliable institutional and local infrastructures are both critical. Lean systems require a supplier base that is capable, reliable, and physically close (typically within about 100 miles). Such requirements suggest that existing industrialized regions will increasingly attract the investment of global manufacturing firms, particularly as they seek to rely on significant outsourcing during initial production while higher-value-added capabilities are developed.

In major industries like automobile production, it is possible to develop such an infrastructure, as Japanese automobile transplants in the United States demonstrated when they attracted component suppliers to the "transplant corridor" from Ontario, Canada, to Tennessee. BMW and Mercedes followed the same path for their facilities in South Carolina and Alabama, respectively. Similarly, when McDonald's first put its restaurants in Russia it had to set up its own farms and other sources of supply because it was not happy with the existing vendor infrastructure. However, most companies possess neither the scale nor the leverage to create their own supplier networks in new locations. It is generally easier to choose a location where infrastructure—capable suppliers, good transportation options, and well-developed communications systems—already exists, which is often in more industrialized regions.

Total Quality Management and Organizational Learning Like lean operations, total quality management (Walden and Shiba 2001) and organizational learning (Senge 1990) are highly skill dependent capabilities that many organizations wish to develop. At the heart of the total quality management (TQM) methodology is the concept of continuous improvement, which is based on the iterative "plan, do, check, act" technique. Within each iteration, the "plan" step identifies problems and suggests corrections, the "do" step implements corrections for evaluation, the "check" step confirms that the correction is effective, and the "act" step modifies the process.

Organizational learning takes the TQM philosophy one step further. Since technical positions can be easily copied and even built upon in today's global world, firms find that static advantage based on traditional competitive positions is no longer enough. Those firms that are capable of learning and disseminating knowledge faster than their competitors will achieve superior performance. Research in the shoe, bike, printed-circuit-board, and steel industries supports the view that establishing manufacturing excellence requires creating a learning organization capable of assimilating new production technologies (Mody et al. 1992). Companies that succeed not only garner cost advantages but are also better poised for further incremental improvement.

TQM and organizational learning affect facilities decisions in two ways. First, they require problem solving and learning skills in the workforce, suggesting that access to these capabilities be an important consideration in facilities location decisions. Second, a decentralized facilities network may well allow an organization to augment its learning and thus build its capabilities by accessing knowledge—new technological, market, and management trends—from many parts of the world.

In sum, the labor requirements of advanced systems and techniques are driving the need for a better educated direct-labor or front-line workforce. Advanced technologies and lean manufacturing systems place greater importance on the flexibility of workers and their ability to operate under growing autonomy. The increasing sophistication of product and process technologies has also increased skill requirements. Access to all of the capabilities underlying these shifts—the skills, the technologies and processes themselves, and supportive supply bases—is a critical consideration in facilities location decisions.

Low-Cost Access

Arguably, facilities location for either manufacturing or service firms should be based more on achieving access to markets and capabilities (skills, technologies, vendor networks) than on cost minimization. As new technologies and processes reduce the amount of direct labor in product cost, capital becomes proportionately more important. But capital costs are essentially the same the world over, so increasing the capital intensity of the production process often decreases its sensitivity to site location. Companies continuing to focus on direct labor cost savings may find transitory advantages, as our discussion of emerging economies suggested, when costs in the emerging economies rise. Given these factors, emphasizing market and capabilities access in facilities location decisions is likely to be increasingly important. Nonetheless, it is important to understand the cost implications of location decisions.

Factor costs include the costs of direct and indirect labor, capital, energy, and materials. These costs can be highly variable due to a variety of economic factors; changes in government regulations and tax systems can cause factor costs to increase or decrease from one period to another. The labor rate fluctuations that are shown in Exhibit 5.6 illustrate the degree of variability that can exist, even in developed economies. The development of a firm's facilities strategy must determine how important each of these factor costs are, identify locations that allow for minimization of the costs, and assess how much variability in the costs there might be.

For many industries, such as apparel, shoes, and toys, labor costs are a significant portion of production costs. Apparel makers are more likely to seek low labor cost locations to site production operations, potentially giving up some proximity to final markets. Alternatively, they might seek new production technologies or processes that reduce dependence on labor, allowing them to locate closer to their marketplaces, reducing transportation costs and providing increased market access. For other industries, such as semiconductors, capital and energy costs are far more important. They are more likely to seek locations that provide a ready source of water and energy and access to highly skilled technicians and engineers. Understanding the cost structure of an industry and the importance of minimizing costs to competitive success are thus critical starting points in assessing the cost structures and risks associated with facilities location strategy.

Factor Cost Variation   There is enormous variation in factor costs around the world. Just within the United States, hourly labor rates are lower in the south (about $14.49) than in the west (about $20.70) or northeast (about $20.12), driving companies to locate facilities in these regions.[24] Factor costs on a global basis are even more variable, with differences in labor costs between the highly developed countries (e.g., Germany at $32.53 per hour in 2004) and the less developed countries (e.g., Brazil at $3.03 per hour in 2004) often being one or even two orders of magnitude.[25] Labor is typically the most variable factor cost, although capital, energy, and materials costs can also vary. Factor costs vary not only due to regulatory and economic conditions in a region, but also due to exchange-rate variation.

Changes in exchange rates can suddenly and significantly change the economics of producing or of providing services (e.g., call centers, information technology) in a given country. In a 120-day period in 2006 for example, the Hungarian forint traded for as little as 187 forints to the U.S. dollar to as much as 217 forints,[26] a 16 percent rise from bottom to top. The Mexican peso traded for as little as 10.43 pesos to the dollar to as much as 11.46 pesos to the dollar,[27] nearly a 10 percent rise from bottom to top. A company buying materials, labor and/or energy in these locations with U.S. dollars, either for its own operations or through subcontractors, would thus experience relatively significant shifts in their costs, even as the labor, energy, and materials rates remained the same in the local currency.

Coping with Variable and Uncertain Factor Costs   Exposure to risk becomes critical as firms develop global networks with multiple facilities serving many markets. If a company sells in a particular market, not producing in that market exposes it to a risk of currency depreciation, thus lowering revenues. Conversely, having a large production site in a country exposes the firm to the risk of currency appreciation. From a financial and operational point of view,

---

[24] Sample data taken from reports found at http://www.bls.gov/ncs/ocs/compub.htm#Division, July 16, 2006.

[25] Sample data from ftp://ftp.bls.gov/pub/special.requests/ForeignLabor/ind3133naics.txt, July 16, 2006.

[26] http://www.x-rates.com/d/HUF/USD/graph120.html, July 16, 2006.

[27] http://www.x-rates.com/d/MXN/USD/graph120.html, July 16, 2006.

increased flexibility reduces these risks and can reduce average costs. Such flexibility can be gained in operations by having a number of facilities, either within the firm or in the firm's supply network, to serve demand with the ability to vary facility loadings according to factor cost and exchange-rate trends. If a company owns facilities around the world and maintains sufficient excess capacity in those facilities, it can shift production or service delivery as needed to take advantage of changes in factor costs. A company that outsources its work may also want to develop relationships at multiple locations that allow it to shift work as costs vary. In the apparel industry, for example, companies often develop a web of suppliers throughout Asia and coordinate production among them to manage the effect of factor cost fluctuations (Fung and Magretta 1998).

To develop a low-cost facilities strategy, then, a vertically integrated firm should first determine which factor costs contribute the most to its cost structure, and then seek sites that allow it to minimize those costs. When exchange rates, and thus factor costs, are highly variable, the firm might consider having more than one location, maintaining extra capacity, and shifting production or service delivery among those locations as factor costs vary. Similarly, a less vertically integrated company should choose its suppliers based first on the factor costs that it wishes to minimize and then, when factor costs are highly variable, choose multiple subcontractors among which work can be moved to optimize its cost structures at any given time. Companies that outsource can sometimes realize more flexibility in that it is often easier to change contractors than to move production or service delivery among internal facilities. For this reason, outsourcing may be more viable in situations where factor costs are more important, such as they are in the apparel and toy manufacturing sectors.

While it is clear that a firm does not want to shift production or services cavalierly around the world, chasing every fluctuation in exchange rate, moving *marginal* production can be useful. A firm can set up extra capacity through part-time or short-term labor contracts or through outsourcing, so that it can execute relatively small volume shifts easily. While it is clear that the option of extra capacity needs to be evaluated carefully and could be undervalued by some, the approach has both theoretical and empirical support. In a survey on this topic, 63 percent of foreign exchange managers cited having locations "to increase flexibility by shifting plant loading when exchange rates changed" as a factor in selecting international sites (Lessard 1990). A company needs to examine the complexities of multiple markets, sources, and production stages through sophisticated modeling approaches that account for the effects of exchange rates throughout the supply chain.

Operational Hedging Models   The operations management literature includes demonstrations of the use of operational hedging with extra facilities and capacity (Huchzermeir and Cohen 1996) and models that quantify the viability of flexibility (Rosenfield 1996). A firm with multiple facilities, for example, could find those with higher than average costs due to exchange rates at any given point in time and move production or service delivery from those facilities to ones with lower costs. Using a stochastic exchange-rate model, Rosenfield (1996) shows that the increased investment in capacity and, thus, flexibility required by such a scenario actually reduces expected costs.

Operational hedging, in this case in the form of an extra facility or investment in extra capacity, is a type of real option. In any circumstance of uncertainty, one can invest in a strategy, and the return for that investment depends on the uncertain outcome. With a real option, the strategy can be adjusted periodically as outcomes are observed to optimize returns. Real options in this context include contracts to procure capacity from a subcontractor or opportunities to purchase production or service delivery facilities. Implementing a modeling approach that accounts for different exchange-rate scenarios and strategy options is one of the more challenging modeling exercises in operations strategy. We briefly examine such models here.

Earlier in this chapter we described a normative approach to modeling facilities and the flows among them in a supply chain. In a more general model with uncertainty, each of the individual scenarios modeled with the supply chain model becomes one input. The mathematical formulation with all possible options, however, is quite sophisticated and complex and thus untenable in most situations. A more reasonable approach focuses on a limited number of probabilistic scenarios. The general modeling approach is as follows.

- Identify a limited set of major facilities strategy options or configurations (specific facility locations, as well as possible changes in levels of activity). These constitute the real options.
- For each of several exchange-rate scenarios, optimize the flow through the network using a normative supply chain model of the type introduced earlier.
- For a set of multiple-year exchange-rate scenarios, identify the facilities option that performs best, taking into account any period-to-period changes in exchange rates. Huchzermeir and Cohen (1996) give an example of the type of analysis that can be used for this.

Solving this problem entails working backward, optimizing each time period and scenario with a technique also referred to as *dynamic programming*. Thus, for a given facilities strategy, one would optimize flows in a given period and then look at possible outcomes in the other periods while taking into account any switching costs from, for example, changing plant capacities. One evaluates a strategy with respect to different paths of multiple-period exchange rates. For example, Exhibit 5.7 shows a set of structural options or facilities that one might consider for a given time period. In this example, there are three markets in Asia, the United States, and Europe. The facilities configuration options include having supply facilities in any or all of Asia, the United States, and Europe, having production facilities in any or all of Asia, the United States, and Europe, and which of the three markets to serve. Each option indicates with a black circle presence of a facility in a location or service of a market. The arcs indicate feasible flows in the network. Option two, for example, only serves the U.S. market with one production facility in the United States and supply facilities in all three regions. The code at the top of the option describes whether the supply, production, and market are local (L) or global (G). Local implies a single region of supply or single production source or that the market is served by a local production source.

Any one of these facilities options or configurations may be optimal under a given set of exchange-rate assumptions, so part of the analysis determines how each configuration performs under specific exchange-rate assumptions. The more difficult analysis comes in determining which options work best under a wide range of exchange-rate assumptions. The model takes into account a probability distribution of exchange rates and identifies a specific option as being superior. In short, the model finds a facilities configuration or option that performs well across a range of exchange rates or, in other words, that is robust in terms of exchange-rate fluctuations.

The approach also needs to allow for transitions from one option or configuration to another, such as between option 3 and option 7 in Exhibit 5.7. This comprehensive and formal approach using dynamic programming to examine all possible dyads and the

EXHIBIT 5.7 Example of Multiple-Period Exchange-Rate Scenarios That Could Involve Switching

Source: Huchzermeir and Cohen, "Valuating Operational Flexibility under Exchange Rate Risk," *Operations Research,* 1996. Reprinted with permission.

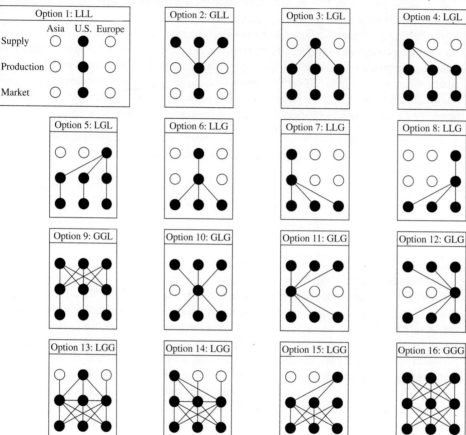

transitions between them, however, may be too difficult to implement, in which case one might examine a limited set of options using the following approach:

- Identify a set of configurations or options that work well under different exchange-rate assumptions.
- Identify the costs of changing from one configuration to another.
- Pose a set of rules for when one might move from one configuration to another based on knowing which configuration performs best under which set of exchange-rate assumptions.
- Simulate the proposed set of rules for various multiyear exchange-rate scenarios.

The general approach is depicted in Exhibit 5.8. The supply chain network model evaluates the network for a given set of facilities and a set of fixed exchange rates. The overall model examines how a company might change from configuration to configuration based on the range of possible exchange rates.

EXHIBIT 5.8   **Valuation Model for Facilities Strategy Subject to Exchange-Rate Uncertainty**

Adapted from Huchzermeir and Cohen, "Valuating Operational Flexibility under Exchange Rate Risk," *Operations Research,* 1996.

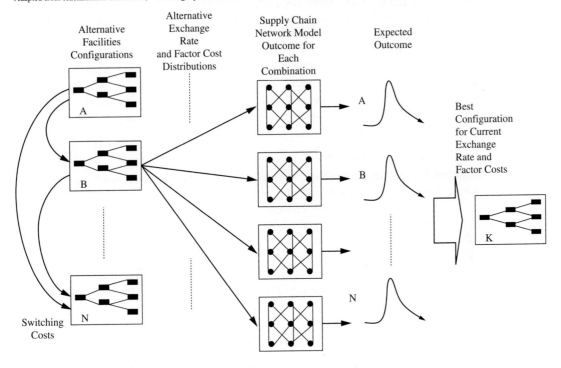

Risks in Facilities Location

We have discussed market, capabilities, and low-cost access considerations in making facilities location decisions, but we have not paid much attention to the risks inherent in choosing a particular location, with the exception of currency exchange risks. The risks a company must assess in thinking through the possibilities of any given location include political risks (government and the financial system stability), terrorism, environmental risks, natural disasters, labor force stability, and labor relations. A 2006 article, "iPod's Children" highlights some of these risks.[28] In the article a Foxconn Electronics facility in Longhua, China, that exported $20.7 billion in products in 2005 is taken to task for paying low wages and forcing workers to work long hours. Although Foxconn sells its electronics product assembly services to many companies including Cisco Systems, Dell, Hewlett-Packard, Intel, Nokia, and Sony, Apple received particular criticism as the ideals it sets forth for its own company are in stark contrast with those with which the workers are seen to be treated at Foxconn. Although it is difficult to know the truth of the allegations made, and Apple claims not to tolerate subpar working conditions at its suppliers, the negative publicity will come at some cost.

Depending on a single facility for most of global production can expose a company to currency exchange risks as well as the risks described here. In order to hedge against

[28] http://www.sfgate.com/cgi-bin/article.cgi?f=/c/a/2006/07/16/MNGAFK06MI1.DTL&hw=ipod+ children&sn=001&sc=1000, August 7, 2006.

these risks, companies may choose to have facilities in multiple locations and carry extra capacity at all of them. Maintaining multiple locations that are flexible enough that they can readily move work among them, however, is a nontrivial task. It is possible to gain flexibility in other ways, such as sourcing from a diverse supply base or investing in flexible process technologies. Sheffi (2005) suggests that companies catalog the risks they face, assess the severity of those risks, and put in place plans to deal with them. Those plans may include increasing buffers, postponing product differentiation until the last possible moment, and thoughtfully choosing facilities locations. In the face of the many possible things that can go wrong—tornados, hurricanes, grounded airplanes, supplier quality problems—he suggests enterprises consider how to develop their resilience.

Facilities Location Summary

Facilities location in a global economy is complex. Firms must consider the macroeconomic trends—global markets, development of trading blocks and nontariff trade barriers, and emerging economies. In this context, they must determine where they need facilities in order to gain access to a market, where they need facilities in order to tap needed capabilities (skills, technologies, supply base), and where they need facilities to obtain low or at least reasonable factor costs. They must consider the many risks associated with any given location, including currency exchange risks. These decisions are complicated by the dynamic nature of the global marketplace, a topic to which we return later.

Facilities Focus

We have discussed how to determine the appropriate size of a facility and how to decide where to locate that facility. We now turn to the question of what that facility should do or how it should be focused. Once again, while we address this question in isolation, there are clearly interactions among the choices made for a facility's focus and choices made for its size and location. We return to integrate these decisions with a set of examples at the end of the chapter.

It has been an article of faith for those in the field of operations management that companies should strive to achieve focus in each of their facilities or, in other words, that each facility in a network should be limited to a relatively small number of functions that it can perform well (Skinner 1974). In Chapter 1, we described the benefits of focus at the level of the firm when we discussed the limited set of positions a firm might take in the marketplace, and the importance of choosing just one of those positions. Strategy expert Porter (1996) specifically argues that strategy rests on a set of unique activities, that a sustainable strategic position requires trade-offs, and that fit among the specific activities a firm chooses to do drives its competitiveness. Similar arguments are made in Skinner's (1974) original treatise on the creation of focused factories: A factory cannot perform well on every yardstick, and simplicity and repetition breed confidence.

While focus is theoretically desirable, however, there is limited empirical evidence of its value (Hayes and Wheelwright 1984 and Huckman and Zinner 2005) and little known about what degree of focus is warranted. Nonetheless, it is clear that the roles of facilities in a network must be clearly defined. We approach the facilities focus question by first discussing the alternative dimensions along which a facility might be focused and then addressing how the roles of individual facilities in a global network might be defined and expected to evolve over time.

Dimensions of Focus

There are four dimensions along which facilities tend to be focused (Schmenner 1982). They might be focused around a process, or a specific stage in the manufacturing or service delivery process. They might be focused around a specific product or family of products or around a service or family of services. They might be focused on serving a specific market. Or they might be general-purpose facilities that are meant to be flexibly used in many different ways. We address each of these dimensions of focus in turn.

Process-Focused Facilities

The ways in which a firm chooses to separate the different stages of its manufacturing or service delivery process dictates to a great extent the choices it has for facilities focus. There are a couple of reasons a firm might be able or choose to separate stages of the process. First, the different stages might be characterized by greatly differing economies of scale. For example, in the computer industry, wafer fabrication is a much higher-scale operation than printed circuit board fabrication, which is a higher-scale operation than printed circuit board assembly or assembly and test of the final product. In the pharmaceutical industry, chemical synthesis is a much higher-scale operation than tablet making and packaging. It is advantageous to centralize the higher-scale operations to take maximum advantage of economies of scale and to decentralize the lower-scale operations, usually final product or service delivery operations, to minimize final transportation costs to customers, allow local customization, or be closer to the market. Second, when the different stages of a manufacturing or service delivery process have different levels of technological complexity, companies often prefer to separate them. Sometimes they do so to allow the separate operations to access needed technologies or skills in different locations.

Separation of the stages provides a firm with a number of potential advantages. First, it can locate each of the stages in a different place, allowing it to have presence in more of its markets, reduce factor costs specific to that stage of the process, access technologies or skills specific to that stage, or locate in one or more tax havens. Second, it can achieve some of the desired benefits of facilities focus, specifically the ability of each facility to do a small number of activities well and optimize that stage of the process. Finally, separation may facilitate an outsourcing strategy. The downside of separation, of course, is the resultant difficulty in integrating, streamlining, or optimizing the full process. We return to this topic later. To the extent that a company practices significant stage separation, such separation should be based on the overall operations strategy. For example, cost considerations may dictate centralizing some of the stages, or customer responsiveness may dictate locating final stages closer to customers.

Intel provides an interesting example. A new wafer fabrication facility costs Intel $2 to $3 billion, creating a steep and significant economies of scale curve and suggesting facilities centralization. The facilities have relatively little labor content, so can be located in relatively high-cost countries. Intel thus consolidates its semiconductor fabrication processing in 11 major facilities located in the United States, Israel, and Ireland. Intel's assembly and test facilities, on the other hand, are lower in cost and have higher labor intensity. As a result, Intel operates six assembly and test facilities in different, mostly low labor cost locations around the world, including, Malaysia, China, Costa Rica, and the Philippines. This enables Intel to focus its facilities on the technologies most relevant to it, take advantage of cost structures in the countries in which they are located as needed, and have manufacturing presence in a reasonable number of markets.

An obvious question arises when one separates facilities by process stage: How will the stages work together? Co-location is one solution that can provide advantages in terms of transportation cost and easier communications for such tasks as schedule synchronization. Co-location, however, limits the number of different countries or regions in which the company might otherwise gain presence and may be infeasible for other reasons. Differing scales may imply the optimum number of locations for the different stages varies, and the technologies used at different stages of the process may have different lives, making long-term coordination difficult. Intel, for example, shifts production among its fabrication facilities depending on whether a product needs newer or older production technology. Co-location of a fab with an assembly and test site may therefore only be valuable temporarily.

Process focus with highly specialized facilities optimized for a limited set of operations is particularly prominent today given the degree of outsourcing in many industries. Companies like Flextronics and Foxconn, for example, are able to optimize the printed circuit board assembly process to serve computer and electronics manufacturers around the world efficiently and effectively. Process-focused manufacturing facilities as they are implemented today tend to have a high degree of machine pacing, high economies of scale, a high level of automation, few variations in the sizes and shapes of the products they produce, and a small geographic reach compared to market- or product-focused facilities (Vokurka and Flores 2002).

Product- or Service-Focused Facilities

Product- or service-focused facilities are devoted to specific products or services, product or service families, or product or service types. Hewlett-Packard, for example, at one time dedicated each of its manufacturing facilities to a specific product; DeskJets were assembled in Vancouver, Washington, while LaserJets were assembled in Boise, Idaho. Banks focus the facilities in their consumer business on families of transactions: Automated teller machines process simple transactions such as deposits, withdrawals, and transfers, while its branch locations handle more complex transactions such as loan processing and opening and closing accounts. Some board assembly contractors have plants that are focused on high-volume product assembly and others focused on assembly of a broad mix of low-volume products.

Product-focused facilities might also be focused on families of products at different stages of their lives. The product-process matrix introduced in Chapter 3 is replicated in Exhibit 5.9 with a description of how facilities might be focused to serve each of the product-process combinations. Products that are early in their life cycles, or are in decline, might be produced in a low-volume/high-mix facility, while products that are reaching maturity might be produced in high-volume/low-mix facilities. Products that have sufficient volume to fill a facility might merit their own, while products with less volume might have to share. The length of time a product would spend in any given facility would depend on the length of its life; products with short life cycles will spend less time ramping up in a low-volume/high-mix facility and will move quickly into higher-volume plants or possibly be launched directly in high volume.

EXHIBIT 5.9
Matching Facilities to Product/ Process Pairings

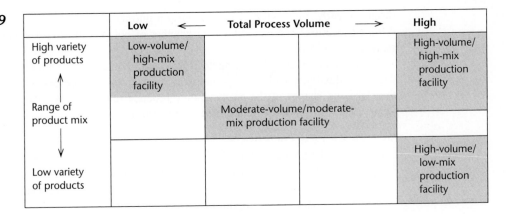

Firms need to be clear about the roles of plants in these situations; often high-mix/low-volume facilities are doomed by accounting practices that burden them with high overhead costs. When the costs are allocated to the products, decisions are sometimes made to reduce production further, which only increases the overhead burden on the remaining products. Often times, these types of plants need to be evaluated on a different basis. In the case study Wriston Manufacturing Corporation (Hammond 1997), an axle manufacturer had a plant devoted to low-volume products, many of which were early life-cycle products. The plant was a crucial part of its de facto strategy and an important part of product development. But because of inappropriate cost measures, the company sold the plant to a group of insiders, who then refurbished the plant and ended up selling product back to the company. The company did not understand the important role of this low-volume/high-mix plant in design, development, and operations strategy.

Product-focused manufacturing facilities as they are implemented today tend to produce many SKUs or end units, have relatively few setups (suggesting that the products they produce share similar designs), and have a large geographic shipment area with high variability in delivery requirements relative to facilities that are focused along other dimensions (Vokurka and Flores 2002).

Market-Focused Facilities

A focus on market implies that the facility serves a specific market. Markets can be defined as narrowly as a specific country or as broadly as an entire region. Global companies find that they generally have to have separate facilities to service the larger markets (e.g., North America, Europe, and Asia), but when they have more than one facility in a market, they can focus those facilities along product, process, or materials dimensions.

To compete in a local market, understand the needs of that market, and deal with trade barriers and local content requirements, companies increasingly need to have presence in those markets. The form of that presence may be small facilities focused on sales, marketing, product development for the local market (customization or localization), service delivery, or manufacturing. Often, if the facility is to do manufacturing, it does final assembly and test of products, sometimes customized to that market. Placing a facility in a local market may not be simply a matter of wanting access to the market; it may be the most cost-effective means of serving that market. The normative supply chain models discussed early in this chapter provide insight into the transportation cost implications of different locations and can tell a firm whether or not it is most cost-effective to serve a market with a local facility.

Market-focused manufacturing facilities, as they are implemented today, have a low degree of flexibility with few alternative routings in their processes and few variations in the sizes and shapes of the products they produce relative to facilities that are focused along other dimensions (Vokurka and Flores 2002).

General-Purpose Facilities

Some firms deliberately choose to maintain a small number of facilities that can be assigned any of a number of capabilities: product, process, market, or some combination thereof. While it violates some of the tenets of focus in that the plant is set up to do anything, it provides flexibility in the facilities network.

Choosing a Dimension of Focus

The choice of a dimension along which to focus should be driven by the objectives set by the overall operations strategy. A firm competing on low cost might choose a process-focused strategy that allows it to take maximum advantage of economies of scale for each stage of its production or service delivery process. Or it might combine a process-focused strategy to capture economies of scale for the early stages of the process with a market-focused strategy to minimize transportation costs in the later stages. A company competing on features and innovativeness might choose a product-focused strategy that marries product and process research and development in facilities to work jointly on new product development and introduction. Or it might choose a market-focused strategy to position itself close to its customers to gather information for innovation and ensure delivery of appropriate features for each of its markets. A firm focused on availability might choose a market-focused strategy as well to minimize lead times. A firm needing flexibility might have some general-purpose facilities that could quickly be converted to whatever task needed to be completed at the time.

Two surveys of the dimensions of focus chosen by U.S.-based companies show that general-purpose and process-focused plants have gained in popularity in the past 20 years or so (Exhibit 5.10). This may be an artifact of different approaches to sampling in the two surveys, or may be consistent with the outsourcing trend that has led to more process-focused facilities, or with the growth of companies such as Foxconn, Flextronics, Solectron, Celestica, and other electronics manufacturing companies that maintain flexibility to respond to the rapidly changing demands of their customers and thus may describe their facilities as general purpose.

EXHIBIT 5.10
Changes in Choice of Facility Focus over 20 Years

Dimension of Focus	Percentage of Plants of Each Focus in 1982 (Schmenner 1982)	Percentage of Plants of Each Focus in 2002 (Vokurka and Flores 2002)	Change
Product	58	64	10%
Market	30	7	−77%
Process	9	11	22%
General	3	19	533%

Often facilities focus decisions are not as clean as choosing just one dimension of focus. Many organizations structure their facilities networks along more than one of these dimensions. Hewlett-Packard used to have many product-focused facilities around the world, each of which served the global market. It then adopted a process focus for those stages of the process that demanded greater scale, and consolidated those activities to create plants (e.g., printed circuit board fabrication) that served several product-focused plants. Thus, it employed both a product and a process focus. IBM, on the other hand, chose to produce some of its high-volume products in a small number of plants located in large market regions. It used a combination of market and process focus to align its facilities.

It can also be difficult to cleanly separate the activities in a given facility to allow it to narrowly focus. Many manufacturing plants, for example, find themselves building some products in very high volumes and others in low volumes. While they would like to separate these two processes, because they require very different infrastructures to manage, it is not cost-effective to construct an additional facility. In these cases, they may choose to set up what some call a "plant within a plant," which allows the two processes to be run relatively independently but remain in the same facility.

Establishing Roles of Facilities in a Supply Chain

One of the important outcomes of making a facilities focus determination is a set of charters or roles for the facilities in a network. A facilities charter tells what products or services the facility will make or deliver, what processes it will support to do so, what markets it will serve, from whom it will source, and what information it is responsible for accessing from the local community, if any.

There are six strategic roles a facility might play in a global network that relate to the type of access it provides and the degree of competence it is asked to develop (Ferdows 1997):

1. Offshore facility: Established to gain access to low wages or other factors integral to low-cost production or service delivery.
2. Source facility: Like an offshore facility, chartered to gain access to low-cost production or service delivery, but with the resources and expertise to develop, produce, and/or deliver a part, product, or service for the firm's global market.
3. Server facility: A market-focused facility that supplies a specific regional or national market with products or services designed in another location.
4. Contributor facility: Like the server facility, a market-focused facility that serves a specific market, but that makes active contributions to the firm in product or service customization, modification or even development, and process improvement.
5. Outpost facility: Established to access capabilities—technologies, skills, knowledge—in a local market and feed them back into the firm.
6. Lead facility: With the strongest of the facility charters, has the ability, skills, and knowledge to innovate and create new products and services, processes, and possibly technologies for the company.

Exhibit 5.11 summarizes these facilities types.

These facilities may be internally owned, or these roles may be played by external subcontractors. Over time, low-competence facilities may develop additional competencies

EXHIBIT 5.11
Roles of Facilities in a Global Network

Source: Adapted from Ferdows, "Making the Most of Foreign Factories," *Harvard Business Review*, 1997.

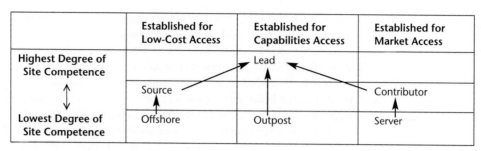

	Established for Low-Cost Access	Established for Capabilities Access	Established for Market Access
Highest Degree of Site Competence		Lead	
↕	Source		Contributor
Lowest Degree of Site Competence	Offshore	Outpost	Server

that allow them to grow into higher-competence roles. An offshore facility might evolve into a source facility, a server into a contributor facility, and an outpost into any of a source, lead, or contributor facility. A lead facility has the strongest facility charter of all and has a position many facilities strive to achieve.

Integrating and Managing a Dynamic Facilities Network

We have talked about the many forces that are driving companies today to disperse their operations in multiple facilities around the world: need for presence in multiple markets, value in separating the stages of the process to focus facilities on each, and required access to technologies and capabilities. As operations become more and more disintegrated and dispersed around the world, the obvious question becomes how can they be managed as an integrated whole so that the overall process works smoothly?

Co-locating facilities is one option, but as we discussed, there are a number of draw-backs to doing so. Information technology is clearly of great importance, and we will discuss it extensively in Chapter 9. There are also organizational solutions, discussed at greater length in Chapter 7, such as designating personnel as liaisons whose job is primarily to ensure integration between two steps of a process or two facilities. Cross-cutting performance measures such as time-to-breakeven for a new product or service and various order fulfillment metrics can also be used to drive integrative behavior.

In general, recognition that the processes a company must execute cut across organizational units and facilities is critical. In the early 1990s, Hewlett-Packard realized that it had to explicitly assign management responsibility for the two processes it performed that were most critical to its customers: product generation and order fulfillment. It assigned senior executives to the roles of "product generation manager" and "order fulfillment manager" and tasked them with ensuring that all pieces of the process worked well together toward a shared set of end objectives. We address the issue of managing these integrative processes more fully in Chapter 7, but highlight the importance of integrating product or service design and development here.

Product and Service Design and Development

One of the most critical processes for a firm's competitiveness today is new product and service design and development. In 2004, U.S. companies derived 28.0 percent of their revenues and 28.3 percent of their profits from products or services introduced in the last five years. High-tech companies derive an even greater percentage of revenues (60.5 percent) and profits (42.3 percent) from products introduced in the past five years, while service companies lag, deriving only 24.1 percent of revenues and 21.7 percent of profits from services introduced in the past five years (Griffin 1997). The frequency with which new products and services are introduced in this era of innovation has increased significantly. Product development times in the automobile industry, for example, have decreased from five to six years to around two years. Firm growth, indeed survival, is dependent on the ability of the firm to innovate.

New product and service development, while typically managed by the research and development function, is only successful when the new products and services can be efficiently and effectively rolled out by the operations function, and this requires tight integration of the research and development function with at least parts of, if not the whole, facilities network internal and external to the firm. In the process of developing a new product or service, decisions are made about which suppliers' components or services will be used, in which locations the products will be manufactured or services provided, and which markets will be served. All of these decisions require knowledge of the current facilities network configuration: which suppliers are available with which competencies, which facilities are focused on doing the kind of work the new product or service requires, and which markets are best served by which facilities.

Most operations functions have personnel dedicated to new product or service introduction who work closely with the research and development (R&D) organization to identify appropriate suppliers and contract with them if needed and determine which facilities will manufacture the product or deliver the service. They also provide information to help the R&D organization design the new product or service to take best advantage of existing operational capabilities; in manufacturing this is part of a process called *design for manufacturability (DFM),* and there is a similar process for service companies. They track the progress of the new product or service development process and prepare the supply base and internal facilities, as well as outbound distribution partners, for ramp-up and introduction. They coordinate with both suppliers and internal operations to obtain prototypes of components or products, order tooling if needed, and test the process before launch.

Accomplishing these tasks requires a good deal of communication between R&D and operations. Polaroid struggled to maintain needed communication links between R&D and manufacturing as it restructured its camera manufacturing supply chain in the mid-1990s (Rykels 1997 and Householder 1996). Under pressure to reduce costs and lessen import duties in overseas markets, Polaroid moved all of its camera production to Scotland, China, Russia, and India. R&D, however, remained in the original facility in the United States. Before production moved offshore, a close connection between R&D and manufacturing was maintained by moving personnel from the Norwood, Massachusetts, manufacturing facility into the Cambridge R&D center for the duration of the product development process. The personnel would return to Norwood at product launch, ensuring a smooth transition. When production in Norwood was shut down, much of the knowledge critical to managing smooth transitions between R&D and manufacturing was lost. Polaroid replaced the co-location policy with cross-functional teams that included R&D and manufacturing representatives, but these teams were not as effective as the co-located and experienced personnel.

Polaroid was not alone in its struggle. Even with the development of videoconferencing tools, groupware for shared design and development work, and clearer guidelines for product and service design, it is not trivial to manage the R&D–operations relationship across global divides. The relationships become even more complicated when there are multiple internal sites and external vendors involved in research and development, design, production, and service delivery. Within research and development itself, software, hardware, and firmware are often developed in separate organizations. When a call center or product repair facility, often an outsourced function, cannot resolve a customer issue, the R&D organization is called upon to take over the interaction. Thus, there are coordination requirements that cut across tasks within a function, across functions within an organization, and across company and geographic boundaries.

Increasing product differentiation and customization add to the coordination difficulties. Yahoo!, for example, localizes its products (e.g., search, e-mail) for dozens of locations around the world. In order to do so, it must understand the requirements of a local region—culture, language, and user interface preferences. Then those responsible for internationalization must work with the product managers, back-end engineers, marketing, and operations personnel for the specific product at the centralized product development site in California, as well as with product managers, front-end engineers, marketing, legal, editorial, and business operations personnel in the specific market. A quick comparison of the Korean Yahoo! site with the U.S. Yahoo! site, for example, gives some indication of the attention to detail required to perform the localization.[29]

In short, new product and service development are critical to the competitive success of almost all firms. Manufacturing or service delivery personnel must work closely with product or service design and development personnel to successfully transition new products or services from development to production or delivery. The development of facilities strategies must consider this critical relationship and decide where and when R&D should be co-located with operations to optimize the process, and what tools or organizational structures will be used when they are not co-located.

Facilities Network Dynamics

The role and criticality of R&D to a company change as the company moves through its life cycle, thus changing the optimal facilities configuration over time. Companies in the early stages of their life cycles tend to centralize their facilities networks to handle the rapid rate of change in product, service, and process technology and the uncertain or volatile nature of early customer demand. Early on, the technology involved in product or service development varies widely as the firm experiments with unknown or ill-understood options. As we discussed in Chapter 2, firms early in their life cycles employ flexible, general-purpose technologies and evolve over time to use more efficient and capital-intensive processes. Cost is likely to become increasingly critical as the company evolves, leading it to invest in lower factor cost locations. Close ties between R&D and operations are crucial in the early phases of development and can often be more easily handled remotely in later phases.

The environment of rapid change that characterizes the early stages of an industry's life cycle is also typical in many high technology firms where new products are introduced every six months, and the technology base continues to evolve rapidly. The challenge, then, is to design a facilities network that can react quickly to change. Often, firms initially limit the amount of decentralized manufacturing to a level below that expected in the long term. As the industry or business matures, the companies extend their facilities networks beyond the home market, retaining production for more sophisticated products and processes in

---

[29] http://kr.search.yahoo.com/search?fr=kr-front&KEY=&search_go=01&p=yahoo, http://www.yahoo.com/, August 10, 2006.

EXHIBIT 5.12
Evolution of Facilities Strategy of Specific Products

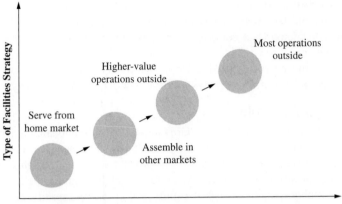

Maturity of Global Facilities Strategy for a Specific Product

the home country near the R&D organization, and moving more mature products to lower-wage locations. Eventually, they move the more advanced technologies to other markets as well (*The Economist,* 1998), as appropriate knowledge and skills are developed. Honda and Toyota, for example, initiated manufacturing in the United States with assembly plants and later imported more advanced technologies such as engine manufacturing.

The dynamics of industry evolution are mirrored at the product or service level; a company with a global network needs to be prepared to move products or services as they mature to outlying locations and possibly continue to produce the more sophisticated products or services in the home country. As the industry matures, all products or services may be produced at regional locations around the world, leaving the home organization to do only advanced research and development. This evolution is depicted in Exhibit 5.12. The implication is that a company has to maintain flexibility in its entire supply chain, and be prepared to change facilities in other markets to encompass a wider range of operations and reduce the scope of activities in the home country. This dynamic has occurred in the auto, advanced consumer electronics, and photography industries of Japan and the United States.

An Approach to Developing a Facilities Strategy

These days successful global companies need presence in each region of significant market demand. As a result, they tend to choose facilities that are small and flexible. Trade and investment incentives are exerting powerful pressures in this direction, and process technologies and methodologies facilitate it through reduced economies of scale and increased flexibility. Regional facilities can provide rapid customer feedback on product or service performance and exposure to multiple markets.

Once a presence is established in a market, the number of sites for serving the region becomes a function of the classic trade-off between scale benefits and transport costs. Where scale benefits are low, there is potential for multiple plants to serve a single region. As the number of major world markets expands beyond North America, Europe, and Japan, other regions, particularly China, will start to require presence as well. Requirements for facilities network configuration change over time as products, services, and industries mature, making facilities strategy development an ongoing process. We've addressed the multiple considerations a company must make in developing a facilities strategy to meet these challenges.

We close this chapter with an example that pulls together the issues we've addressed in the chapter and a four-step process for developing a facilities strategy.

A Closing Example

A consumer goods manufacturer (CGM) was faced with rationalizing the facilities strategy for its worldwide network. The company had 25 product groups and 10 production locations around the world. It had a wide variety of product values and weights, including over-the-counter health aids with a relatively low value and high weight, as well as very expensive and low-weight pharmaceuticals. It had a great deal of excess capacity, and its plants were not focused. It also had significant tax issues with its plants in Puerto Rico and elsewhere.

To address the problem, CGM did an analysis of its network and modeled the separate stages of the manufacturing process. This analysis was completed in the following steps:

1. Performed a cross-sectional analysis for different operations at different plants to develop scale curves. Exhibit 5.13 shows one of the scale curves generated for the process of making tablets. Each point on the curve represents one of CGM's tableting facilities.

2. Analyzed variable costs for production, inventory, transportation, handling costs, and the variable effects of taxes at each of the facilities.

3. Built a mathematical program to optimize variable costs.

4. Based on output of the model, did a detailed assessment of the impact of the recommended changes on fixed costs. If a product were moved from one plant to another, for example, CGM calculated the resultant change in fixed costs.

The mathematical program was for direct delivery from plant to market with no distribution centers and was extended to multiple products. It was not an overly complex formulation but did capture the key strategic considerations.

EXHIBIT 5.13
Tableting Cost Scale Curve for Pharmaceutical Manufacturer

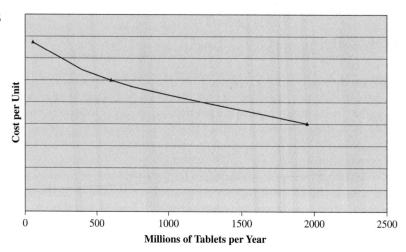

Cost per Unit

Millions of Tablets per Year

The resulting rationalization of the plants led to some general strategic principles for the business. First, it clearly illustrated the need to better focus the product groups. One of the facilities in the tax haven reduced its scope to focus on tableting, encapsulation, and packaging processes. The home plant, which formerly did tableting and encapsulation, narrowed its focus to chemical synthesis, product development, and production of over-the-counter goods. Second, it illustrated the principle of moving the lighter and higher-value products to the tax havens where they realized tax savings with only modest increases in operating and logistics costs. While no plants were closed, significant fixed costs were saved through movement of products out of some facilities and the reduction of space and equipment. Through this exercise, CGM also learned the value of separating stages of production so that earlier stages might be centralized to gain economies of scale. The analytical models helped it see where economies in the global network lay and how they might access them.

We turn now to a more generic process that firms might undertake to create a facilities strategy.

Five-Step Facilities Planning Process

A company developing a facilities strategy can take the following approach:

1. Based on the overall business and operations strategy, develop criteria for plant focus and charter.
2. Using cross-sectional data, benchmarking of other companies, and analysis of other technologies, develop the appropriate multiple-technology scale curves for the plants (in each geographical region for a global strategy).
3. If operating globally, identify the major options for the facilities network such as how the company will source and in which markets it should have operations presence.
4. Identify potential locations and major decision choices covering plant and process options, such as potential sizes, and separation of stages.
5. Analyze the detailed options for flow of materials and production, potentially using a computer model.

The five-step process is depicted graphically in Exhibit 5.14 and described below.

Step 1: Business and Operations Strategy and Plant Charters

Collect basic background and context information on the firm's corporate and business strategies, the availability of capital, the structure of the existing site network—which may include facilities outside as well as inside the company—and the company's growth strategy.

Understand where the firm wishes to be positioned with respect to cost, quality, availability, features/innovativeness, and environmental performance. When cost leadership is the competitive focus, location is only important as a driver for reducing transportation, labor, and inventory costs. For firms that emphasize the other factors more strongly, location has an expanded role: Quality leadership places higher demands on both the workforce and the supply network. Competing through features and innovativeness requires customer proximity, a coordinated design-manufacturing link, and local development resources. Competing on availability may require a very flexible facilities network, which may again require customer proximity and a different set of techniques and skills. Competing on environmental performance requires locating in a region where governmental controls on environmental performance are strong and well-enforced, and the local supplier network is in compliance.

EXHIBIT 5.14

Five-Stage Approach to Strategy Development

Source: Drawn from MacCormack et al. "The New Dynamics of Global Manufacturing Site Location," *Sloan Management Review,* 1994.

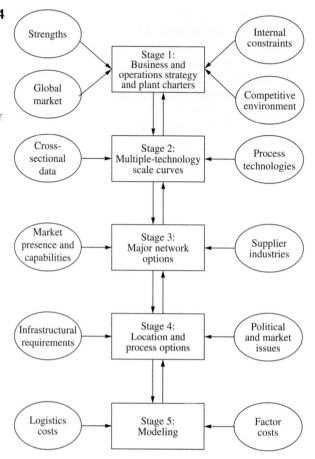

Understand what capabilities the firm has and what capabilities it wishes to develop. Global facilities location is increasingly important as a means of accessing capabilities specific to certain regions in the world. Japan, for example, has long been known for its prowess in semiconductor manufacturing equipment design as well as its general process management capabilities in, for instance, total quality management. India has developed a strong reputation for software programming. Singapore is developing a reputation in multimedia design. Companies wanting to develop capabilities in any of these areas will have to consider placing locations in these regions.

Choices of positioning and desired capabilities development also dictate decisions made in the other operations strategy decision categories. In particular, decisions made about appropriate process technologies and capacity expansion strategies will have a great effect on facilities strategy. It is critical, therefore, in this step to understand interactions with other operations strategy decisions and to take the implications of those decisions into account in making facilities strategy choices.

Forecast Industry Evolution Forecast the likely evolution of global market requirements for the industry. How will the competitors in the industry address global markets? How will global players compare with companies that primarily operate locally? To generate this forecast, examine three classic outcomes of industry evolution: (1) scale-driven consolidation in which the industry consolidates to obtain economies of scale; (2) scope-driven consolidation in which the industry consolidates, although perhaps along different lines, to achieve economies of scope; and (3) niche/local market-driven fragmentation in which the industry disintegrates, competing in smaller niche markets.

Managers must evaluate the drivers most likely to affect the industry's development—the strategies of competitors, the basis on which competition takes place, and the industry cost structure—and determine what degree of influence each will have. The presence, for example, of high economies of scale likely drives the need to leverage greater volumes, which in turn suggests ever-bigger facilities serving multiple markets. Economies of scope, on the other hand, are gained through scale in market access or capital resources. Large pharmaceutical companies, for example, have escalated research expenditures to levels that smaller companies cannot sustain. Those levels can be achieved only by serving many markets, across which investments are recouped. Market fragmentation happens when the basis of competition is customization and requires timely delivery to a local market. Service industries, such as McDonald's, for example, are able to leverage a consistent process design around the world but customize their offerings to the specific needs of a region. Often this requires that they source locally to cater to the tastes of the local market.

Identify Internal Constraints on Facilities Location Choices   Review the internal constraints that may limit a firm's ability to implement an optimal location strategy—primarily, the availability of investment capital and managerial resources. While industry dynamics may suggest that global scale is necessary for success, financial and managerial limitations may restrict the options available for expansion. In such cases, firms may seek alliances to increase product volumes.

The nature of a company's growth strategy may also have a substantial impact on location decisions. Building a coherent network of plants serving local markets can take more than 10 years. Any company that generates growth primarily through acquisition is likely to become a significantly different organization over such a long time frame. Location is unlikely to be a strategic priority for firms that rely on frequent asset trading to increase stakeholder value.

Finally, based on these strategic analyses, the company determines what the role and charter of each of its facilities will be. This might entail a specific focus for the global network (for example, plants for each global market) with further subfocus of facilities in those markets with multiple facilities.

The output of step one is a comprehensive assessment of industry dynamics, the basis on which the company competes within that industry, the company's growth strategy, and the resultant requirements for the company's operations and facilities strategies. The critical inputs to this assessment, as summarized in Exhibit 5.14, are understanding of the global market, the competitive dynamics within that market, the capacity factors (i.e., the expected evolution of the industry toward consolidation or fragmentation), the strengths of the company itself and the basis on which it chooses to compete, and any internal constraints it may have on capital and managerial resources. These factors are the primary determinants of the nature of the global operations network, the roles of individual facilities, and the degree to which such a network can generate and sustain competitive advantage.

Step 2: Develop Multiple Scale Curves

Establish the effect of process technologies on facility scale in order to define a reasonable number of sites per region, the range of volumes that could be supported by individual facilities, and the capacities required for each stage of the production or service delivery process. This process can be completed through analysis of cross-sectional data that compares similar operations at multiple plants, through benchmarking other companies and processes, and through the analysis of newer technologies that the company may not have. Identify the technology-scale envelope for the firm's processes. For a company competing on innovation and time-to-market, maximizing the number of plants subject to minimum scale may be appropriate. Companies adopting such a dispersed strategy, however, must weigh the costs of complexity against forecast market benefits. The output of this step will be a series of scale envelopes that might apply for different products and markets.

Step 3: If Operating Globally, Identify the Major Facilities Network Options

Develop the options for the facilities and supply chain strategy including how the company will source internally and externally, how suppliers are to be used, and the selection of markets in which to have operations presence. This step establishes where the company will have presence globally. If not operating globally, then the company is presumably locating its owned facilities in its home market, but it may still need to consider a global strategy for its suppliers. To complete this step:

- Examine the company's outsourcing strategy, including the degree to which it relies on outside suppliers, and understand the current regional network configurations of those suppliers. If suppliers have their major sources in particular regions of the world, this will suggest locating in those areas.
- Understand government regulations and market access requirements. To avoid tariffs and other nontariff trading restrictions, firms should locate within trading blocks. They should understand the nature and composition of these trading blocks, as well as their likely development. Market requirements for exempt status, such as local content stipulations, should be well defined. Firms should assess other political issues, such as incentives for local investment in facilities or contract offset agreements, for an overview of the political imperatives.
- Assess the degree of risk inherent in serving the regional markets and the options available for managing that risk. Forecast exchange-rate movements and develop alternative scenarios for service or product sourcing.
- Define the characteristics of regional demand including the level of homogeneity in customer requirements across a region, the size of demand in each region, and the forecast for future development of that region. When combined with the basis of competition, such characteristics will define priority areas of demand and suggest how many facilities it might be reasonable to support in which regions. Assess the options for serving demand from one point within a region versus those for serving it from multiple sources. In industries that place a premium on local differentiation, for example, multiple facilities, each with a high degree of flexibility, may better serve markets. Where customer needs are more homogeneous across a region, single facilities may be more cost-effective.

All of these factors must be set in the context of competitors' strategies. Many competitors will attempt to establish a global presence simultaneously. First movers often have advantages in tying up local joint-venture partners or establishing a "blue chip" distribution network. In fast-growing regions, such dynamics can lead to preemptive capacity expansion, committing investments to markets with less volume than appears economically viable. Based on assessment of all of these factors, this stage will yield a set of broad alternatives for siting facilities and for developing the supply chain.

Step 4: Narrow the Set of Potential Locations

Examine in more detail the relevant facilities network options surfaced in Step 3. Identify specific locations and analyze size and process options:

- Determine whether or not the process stages can be separated, and then, based on scale curves, determine the potential range of facilities sizes for each stage. Evaluate the amount of capacity to be carried at each site based on uncertainty in demand projections and the company's capacity strategy (discussed in detail in Chapter 4).

- Assess the applicability of alternative process technologies and methodologies for alternative locations and the implications for demands on the workforce, supplier base, and transportation and communication networks. Examine both the "hard" and "soft" site infrastructure requirements: Hard, or tangible, requirements relate to the physical availability of supplier, communication, and transport systems and are influenced by the nature of the production or service delivery system and the degree of vertical integration. Soft, or intangible, requirements relate to organizational and educational infrastructure, inherent workforce education levels, or suppliers with specific technical know-how, which are often the most important sources of future competitive advantage.

- Examine, on a pro forma basis, the levels of infrastructure development required for each option. For example, the need for trained technical staff might suggest a location near specific institutions or science parks. On this basis, the range of potential sites can be narrowed to specific areas in a region. The resulting options are those that best meet a range of infrastructural parameters, yet do not fail to meet any that are critical.

The output of this step is a narrowed set of potential options for facilities network configurations that have sufficient infrastructure to meet the firm's competitive needs. Chrysler Corporation, before the Daimler merger, undertook a detailed analysis of the sort described in this step for two potential site locations in Brazil (Kao 1997). The analysis explored a wide variety of factors, weighted the factors for their importance to the organization, and rated the facilities against those factors (Exhibit 5.15). The analysis showed a slight edge for Site B in its cost performance, human resource access, and ease of working with the local government.

Step 5: Analyze and Model to Identify Final Recommendation

Select a recommended facilities configuration describing specific locations, detailed flows, and expected changes over time with the possible use of computer models to optimize flow patterns. Start with a forecast and alternative scenarios for how the network might be configured in the future. Evaluate alternative factor-cost scenarios to develop a robust strategy where short-term adjustments can be made. The analysis may include the entire supply chain and facilities both within and outside the firm.

Apply appropriate models using the following inputs:

- Candidate facility locations.
- Potential size of each facility.

EXHIBIT 5.15

Chrysler Location Analysis for Brazil Plant

Source: Reprinted with permission from Kao, "Methodologies for Design of a Low-Volume, International Automotive Assembly Plant, with Emphasis on Site Selection and Body Shop," MIT master's thesis, 1997.

Fundamental Economic Factor			Site A	Site B
Comparison for Locations in Two Sites				
	Category	Individual	10 = Best	10 = Best
	Weight	Weight	1 = Worst	1 = Worst
A. Operating Costs	25%			
Logistics ($20M/yr for both)		40%	10	10
Labor Costs ($10 vs $7.5/hour)		40%	7	10
Energy ($40 vs. $33 Mwh)		10%	8	10
Inventory Carrying Cost diff. (1 week)		10%	10	8
Average			8.6	9.8
B. Logistics	25%			
Quality of road access		20%	8	5–8
Congestion/expeditious access		20%	5	8
Quality/proximity seaport/airport		30%	7	5
Proximity to suppliers/dealers		30%	9	5–7
Average			7.4	6.8
C. Human Resources	25%			
Labor climate/militant unions		20%	6	10
Work-ethic education		20%	7	10
Expat living conditions		20%	7	9
Skilled professional pool		20%	10	9
Quality of life		20%	6	8
Average			7.2	9.2
D. Manufacturing Site	15%			
Topography/soil quality		25%	10	10
Access		25%	10	10
Utilities/materials		25%	8	8
Corporate presence & all other		25%	7	8
Average			8.8	9
E. Other	10%			
Accessibility to state govt. to make things happen		50%	5	9
Timing to close transaction		25%	5	8
Proximity to commercial/financial center		25%	10	6
Average			6.3	8.0
Total fundamental economic factors			7.8	8.6

- Requirements for each market from each source.
- Sourcing and location of products and services.

   Then use these models to determine:

- Which candidate facility locations to use.
- Which production and service activities will be at each location.
- How each market requirement will be serviced.

   To address uncertainties due to exchange rates:

- Define activity levels for each facilities configuration for each scenario of exchange rates.
- Select the facilities configuration that is most robust under the alternative scenarios tested.

Develop, Implement, and Measure   Develop an implementation plan. Generally implementation requires a project manager and team that will flesh out the details of acquiring new facilities and equipment, contracting with new suppliers as needed, and implementing the new network configuration. There are likely to be hiring (or firing) requirements, with potentially significant human resource and organizational implications. The team will need a project plan with a schedule and budget. Consideration of implementation issues should have been made in the process of developing the facilities strategy, but in rare cases key implementation problems may not surface until this step of the process, causing the firm to iterate the steps again.

Implement the network configuration as planned. Measure outcomes and check against the original plan. Were planned economies realized? Was desired market access achieved? Did the plan achieve the desired business goals for cost, quality, availability, features/innovativeness, and environmental performance? Is the plan consistent with other elements of the operations strategy (e.g., with the capacity and vertical integration strategies)? Is the plan consistent with and/or supportive of other functional strategies (i.e., marketing, human resources, information technology, and engineering)? Prepare a post mortem report on the facilities planning process and feedback to be used to improve the process in the future.

Summary

In this chapter, we introduced the notion of a facilities network, including points of supply and flows among those points, and some simple models for understanding the costs of and optimizing such a network. We reiterated the importance of understanding economies of scale and scope introduced in earlier discussions of capacity and process technology management, and developed the notion of a process or technology-scale envelope that shows which type of technology or process is appropriate for which size facility. We used the technology-scale envelope to suggest means of assessing alternative facility sizes.

In an extensive discussion of globalization and its effects, we developed a set of criteria for thinking through facilities location issues: market access, capabilities access (technology, skills, and knowledge), and low-cost access. Companies needing to be close to their customers generally seek locations that will provide them with access to those markets. Companies needing to develop certain skill sets or access certain technologies seek locations near the sources of those capabilities. Companies driving for low cost find locations where factor costs are minimized. Factor cost minimization is complicated by variability in both the costs themselves and in exchange rates. We presented the broad outlines of models to evaluate the effects of uncertainty on facilities network configurations.

Finally, we presented alternative ways of defining the roles of facilities in the network. Facilities may be focused according to markets to be served, according to specific steps or stages of the production or service delivery process, on selected families of products or services, or around required components or materials. The roles of facilities may be defined according to their focus and/or according to the type of access they provide—market, capabilities, or cost. Facilities can be of "low" competence in providing access or can be allowed to develop "high" competence over time.

We highlighted the difficulties of and need for integration of a dispersed facilities network and, in particular, the need for links with a research and development or service design organization as production and service delivery are dispersed around the world.

The five-step process we closed with integrates the decisions about facilities size, location, and focus to determine an optimal network configuration.

Facilities strategy is clearly critical to the performance of many organizations. Motorola must manage its facilities network to carefully balance market access with a need for low-cost production. Dell and others have worked through call center location decisions in the past few years, attempting to balance cost with customer service. Foxconn and other such subcontractors adapt their facilities strategies to the rapidly changing needs of their customers and the markets those customers serve, opening and closing facilities as demand for specific products ebbs and wanes, and penetrating emerging economies such as China as infrastructure permits. The concepts in this chapter can be helpful in thinking through facilities strategy and management in all these situations.

Appendix A

Models for Facilities Network Optimization

The first model we consider is the case depicted in Exhibit 5.A1 where a company does not use warehouses to store finished goods. If we consider a single product, the mathematical formulation is:

$$\text{minimize} \sum_{i,j} c_{ij} x_{ij}$$

subject to

$$\sum_{j} x_{ij} \le K_i$$

$$\sum_{i} x_{ij} \ge D_j$$

where

x_{ij} = Amount of product supplied from facility i to market j

c_{ij} = Costs associated with supplying market j from facility i

K_i = Capacity at factory i

D_j = Demand in market j

The costs associated with the arc from i to j include production or service delivery, transportation, and inventory costs. Production and service delivery costs typically depend only on the origin node i, unless there is some customization cost that depends on j, but the others depend on both indices.

This model assumes a single product. With multiple products, there are capacity constraints for each product that may result in shared capacity at the factory. In this case, a factor is needed to denote the usage by each product of shared capacity. It can also be important to capture any fixed costs and economies of scale that arise when

EXHIBIT 5A.1
Simple Facilities
Network and
Supply Chain

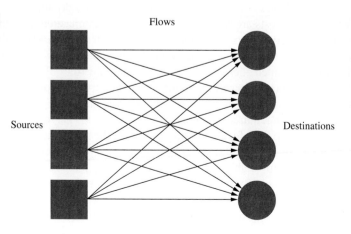

Flows

Sources

Destinations

considering a number of plants of different sizes. A nonlinear cost function is used to capture economies of scale, although in practice nonlinearity is usually approximated by a fixed cost and a variable cost. Accommodating fixed plant costs, the previous model becomes:

$$\text{minimize} \sum_{i,j} c_{ij} x_{ij} + \sum f_i y_i$$

subject to

$$\sum_j x_{ij} \le K_i y_i$$

$$\sum_i x_{ij} \ge D_j$$

where $y_i = \begin{cases} 0 & \text{if factory } i \text{ is not used} \\ 1 & \text{if factory is used} \end{cases}$

f_i = fixed cost of opening facility i

all other variables are as above

This model also works for co-locating suppliers to optimize transport cost. In an extended supply chain model that also looks at supplier cost, additional stages are required. When warehouses or distribution centers are added to capture transportation economies of scale or to allow for inventory positioning with multiple products, the model becomes:

minimize

$$\sum c_{ijk} x_{ijk} + \sum d_{jkl} z_{jkl} + \sum_i f_i y_i + \sum_j g_j w_j$$

subject to

$$\sum_j z_{jkl} \ge D_{kl}$$

$$\sum_{l,k} b_k z_{jkl} \le M_j w_j$$

$$\sum_{j,k} a_k x_{ijk} \le K_i y_i$$

$$\sum_i x_{ijk} \ge \sum_l z_{jkl}$$

where

x_{ijk} = amount of product k supplied from plant i to warehouse j

z_{jkl} = amount of product k supplied from warehouse j to market l

c_{ijk} = transportation, inventory, and variable facility costs associated with supplying product k from plant i to warehouse j

d_{jkl} = transportation, inventory, and variable facility costs associated with supplying market l with product k from warehouse j

$y_i = \begin{cases} 1 & \text{if plant } i \text{ used} \\ 0 & \text{otherwise} \end{cases}$

$w_j = \begin{cases} 1 & \text{if warehouse } j \text{ used} \\ 0 & \text{otherwise} \end{cases}$

f_i = fixed cost for plant i

g_j = fixed cost for warehouse j

D_{kl} = demand in market l for product k

a_k = unit usage of factory capacity for product k

b_k = unit usage of warehouse capacity for product k

K_i = capacity at plant i

M_j = capacity at warehouse j

The first set of constraints includes the demand requirements; the second, warehouse capacities; the third, plant capacities; and the fourth, conservation of flow at warehouses. Conservation of flow constraints ensure that what comes in must be at least as much as what flows out. Other constraints not shown in this formulation could include capacities for individual products or classes of products.

These types of models can be solved in a number of ways depending on their size and complexity. Simpler versions can be solved using optimization modules within spreadsheet programs such as Solver within Microsoft Excel. Larger and more complex formulations require more sophisticated algorithms offered by third-party firms. The models all assume that costs are known and that uncertainty will not affect the solutions and insights to any great degree. In a global environment, uncertainty can indeed have a significant impact, but including uncertainty is challenging for these types of models.

For facilities analysis, the major drawback with this formulation is that it does not address the concept of multiple stages of the manufacturing process, as manufacturing is represented as only one stage. There are often important strategic reasons for having different stages of the manufacturing process in different geographic locations. The mathematical approach for incorporating multiple stages is similar to that of adding a distribution or warehousing stage. The size and complexity of such problems can grow very quickly, but the techniques for analyzing them are identical to those presented here.

References   Arnold, D.J., and J.A. Quelch. "New Strategies in Emerging Markets." MIT *Sloan Management Review* 40:1 (Fall 1998), pp. 7–20.

Arntzen, B.C., G.G. Brown, T.P. Harrison, and L.L. Trafton. "Global Supply Chain Management at Digital Equipment Corporation." *Interfaces,* 25, no. 1 (1995), pp. 69–93.

Badri, M.A. "Combining the Analytic Hierarchy Process and Goal Programming for Global Facility Location-Allocation Problem." *International Journal of Production Economics* 62, no.3 (Amsterdam, September 1999), pp. 237–248.

Cachon, Gerard, and Christian Terwiesch. *Matching Supply with Demand: An Introduction to Operations Management.* Burr Ridge, IL: McGraw-Hill/Irwin, 2006.

Chakravarty, A., K. Ferdows, and K. Singhal. "Global Operations and Technology Management." *Production and Operations Management* 6, no. 2 (Summer 1997), pp. 99–101.

Central Intelligence Agency. *The World Factbook.* http://www.cia.gov/cia/publications/factbook/rankorder/2078rank.html, (accessed April 21, 2006).

The Economist. "Meet the Global Factory, A Survey of Manufacturing." June 20, 1998, pp. 1–18.

Eppinger, S., and K. Ulrich. *Product Design and Development.* 3rd ed. Burr Ridge, IL: McGraw-Hill, 2004.

Ferdows, K. "Making the Most of Foreign Factories." *Harvard Business Review* 75, no. 2 (March/April 1997), pp. 73–88.

Fine, C., *Clockspeed.* Reading, MA: Perseus Books, 1999.

Flaherty, M.T. *Global Operations Management.* Burr Ridge, IL: McGraw-Hill, 1996.

Friedman, Thomas. *The World Is Flat: A Brief History of the Twenty-First Century.* New York, NY: Farrar, Straus, and Giroux, 2005.

Fung, V., and J. Magretta. "Fast, Global, and Entrepreneurial: Supply Chain Management, Hong Kong Style: An Interview with Victor Fung." *Harvard Business Review* 76, no. 5 (September/October 1998), pp. 102–114.

Griffin, Abbie. "Drivers of NPD Success: The 1997 PDMA Report." Product Development Management Association, 1997, available at http://www.innovationforum.com/bookstore/drivers.html, (accessed August 10, 2006).

Hammond, Janice. "Wriston Manufacturing Corporation." Harvard Business School Publishing, 698-049, 1997.

Hayes, R., and S. Wheelwright. *Restoring Our Competitive Edge: Competing through Manufacturing.* Hoboken, NJ: Wiley, 1984.

Hayes, R., G., Pisano, D., Upton, and S. Wheelwright. *Operations, Strategy, and Technology: Pursuing the Competitive Edge.* Hoboken, NJ: Wiley, 2005.

Householder, W. "Adapting the New Product Introduction Process to Changes in a Global Manufacturing Network." MIT master's thesis, 1996.

Huchzermeier, A., and M. Cohen. "Valuating Operational Flexibility under Exchange Rate Risk." *Operations Research* 44, no. 1 (1996), pp. 100–113.

Huckman, Robert S., and Darren E. Zinner. "Does Focus Improve Operational Performance? Lessons from the Management of Clinical Trials." Harvard Business School, working paper, 05-073, 2005.

Jha, Nand K. *Handbook of Flexible Manufacturing Systems.* San Diego, CA: Academic Press, 1991.

Kandybin, Alex, and Chris Furlong. Booz Allen, Hamilton, presentation at MIT, 1998.

Kao, Elizabeth Emay. "Methodologies for Design of a Low-Volume, International Automotive Assembly Plant, with Emphasis on Site Selection and Body Shop." MIT master's thesis, June 1997.

Lessard, D.B. "Survey on Corporate Responses to Volatile Exchange Rates." MIT Sloan of School of Management, working paper, 1990.

Lessard, D.B., and J.B. Lightstone. "Volatile Exchange Rates Can Put Operations at Risk." *Harvard Business Review* 64, no. 4 (July/August 1986), pp. 107–114.

Levy, D.L. "Lean Production in an International Supply Chain." *Sloan Management Review* 38, no. 4 (Winter 1997).

MacCormack, A.D., L.J. Newman III, and D.B. Rosenfield. "The New Dynamics of Global Manufacturing Site Location." *Sloan Management Review* 35, no. 4 (Summer 1994), pp. 69–80.

McGrath, M.E., and R.W. Hoole. "Manufacturing's New Economies of Scale." *Harvard Business Review,* 70, no. 3 (May/June 1992), pp. 94–102.

Mody, A., R. Suri, and T. Sanders. "Keeping Pace with Change, Organizational and Technological Imperatives." *World Development* 20 (1992), pp. 1797–1816.

Motorola Annual Report, 2005.

Nallicheri, Narayan, T. Curt Bailey, and J. Scott Cade. "The Lean, Green Service Machine." *Strategy + Business,* November 18, 2004, http://www.strategy-business.com/resilience/rr00013, (accessed July 16, 2006).

Porter, Michael E. "What Is Strategy?" *Harvard Business Review,* 74, no. 6 (November–December 1996), pp. 61–78.

Prahalad, C.K. *The Fortune at the Bottom of the Pyramid: Eradicating Poverty through Profits.* Upper Saddle River, NJ: Wharton School Publishing, 2004.

Rosenfield, D.B. "The Retailer Facility Location Problem." *Journal of Business Logistics* 8, no. 2 (1987), pp. 95–114.

Rosenfield, D.B. "Global and Variable Cost Manufacturing Systems." *European Journal of Operational Research* 95 (1996), pp. 325–343.

Rykels, S. "Adapting Communication Structures for Globally-networked Manufacturing Organizations." MIT master's thesis, 1997.

Schmenner, R.W. "Look Beyond the Obvious in Plant Location." *Harvard Business Review,* 57, no. 1, (January–February 1979), pp. 126–132.

Schmenner, R.W. "Multiplant Manufacturing Strategies Among the Fortune 500," *Journal of Operations Management* 2, no. 2 (1982), pp 77–86.

Senge, P. *The Fifth Discipline.* New York, NY: Currency Doubleday, 1990.

Shapiro, Jeremy F. *Modeling the Supply Chain.* Pacific Grove, CA: Duxbury, 2001.

Sheffi, Yossi. *The Resilient Enterprise.* Cambridge, MA: MIT Press, 2005.

Shingo, Shigeo. *Quick Changeover for Operations: The SMED System.* New York, NY: Productivity Press, Inc., 1996.

Simchi-Levi, D., P. Kaminsky, and E. Simchi-Levi. *Designing and Managing the Supply Chain.* 2nd ed. Burr Ridge, IL: Irwin McGraw-Hill, 2003.

Skinner, W. "The Focused Factory." *Harvard Business Review,* 52, no. 3 (May–June 1974), pp. 113–121.

Swank, Cynthia Karen. "The Lean Service Machine." *Harvard Business Review* 81, no. 10 (October 2003), pp. 123–129.

Vokurka, Robert J., and Benito E. Flores. "Plant Charter Classifications and the Operating Homogeneity of U.S. Manufacturing Plants." *Industrial Management + Data Systems* 102, no. 8–9 (2002), pp. 406–416.

Walden, David, and Shoji Shiba. *Four Practical Revolutions in Management: Systems for Creating Organizational Capabilities.* New York, NY: Productivity Press, Inc., 2001.

World Trade Organization. *International Trade Statistics.* 2005, http://www.wto.org/english/res_e/statis_e/its2005_e/its05_longterm_e.htm, (accessed April 18, 2006).

Chapter 6

Sourcing

Introduction

Cisco Systems, founded in 1984 by two Stanford University computer scientists who wanted to figure out how to get two networks to communicate seamlessly, is one of the great growth stories of the 1990s. Its revenues climbed from $250 million in 1990 to $34,613 million in 2000, while employee headcount grew from 60 to 18,928 (Exhibit 6.1). The company became the leading producer of networking equipment through an aggressive acquisition strategy; in the 1990s it acquired 72 companies, which clearly drove its meteoric revenue growth of 175 percent per year (Exhibit 6.2).[1] While its growth and acquisition strategy were major topics of discussion in the media, there was another very important part of its strategy, which was outsourcing.

Cisco not only outsources manufacturing, but business processes such as order fulfillment and some product design as well. On the sales and distribution side, Cisco collaborates with over 200,000 people in 20,000 independent value-added resellers, systems integrators, and network consultancies worldwide that account for more than 90 percent of Cisco's worldwide commercial and enterprise revenue.[2] It retains, however, much of its research and development (R&D) capability, as innovation is core to its growth strategy (Exhibit 6.3). Cisco's outsourcing model facilitated its rapid growth, allowing quick capacity additions in key supply areas without investment in internal facilities and processes.

Cisco's outsourcing strategy was facilitated through significant investments in information technology (Nolan et al. 2005). Cisco invested heavily in enterprise resource planning (ERP) systems to link its suppliers to its own planning systems, in effect creating a single enterprise. Cisco integrated its product development activities through what are known today as product data management (PDM) systems that collect and manage data across the many functions involved in new product development. Cisco automated and standardized product testing procedures and developed approaches for direct fulfillment

---

[1] Data and a complete list of the acquisitions made can be found at http://newsroom.cisco.com/dlls/corporate_timeline.pdf, July 20, 2006.

[2] http://newsroom.cisco.com/dlls/company_overview.html, July 17, 2006.

EXHIBIT 6.1
Employee and Revenue Growth at Cisco

Source: Data drawn from http://newsroom.cisco.com/dlls/corporate_timeline.pdf, July 20, 2006.

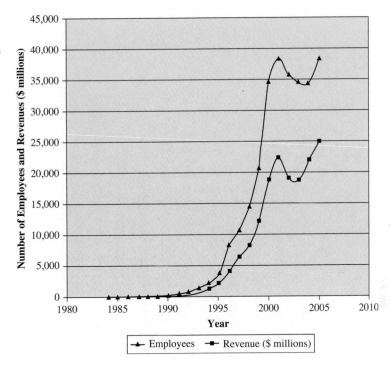

EXHIBIT 6.2
The Role of Acquisitions in Cisco's Growth

Source: Data drawn from http://newsroom.cisco.com/dlls/corporate_timeline.pdf, July 20, 2006.

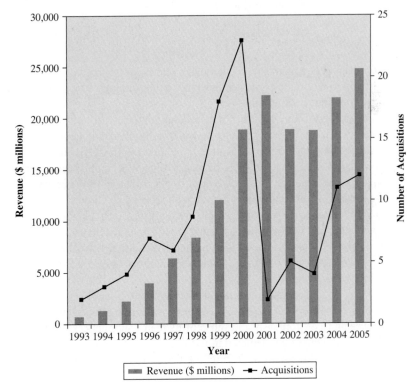

EXHIBIT 6.3
**Cisco's Patent
History**

Source: Data drawn
from http://newsroom
.cisco.com/dlls/
corporate_timeline.pdf,
July 20, 2006.

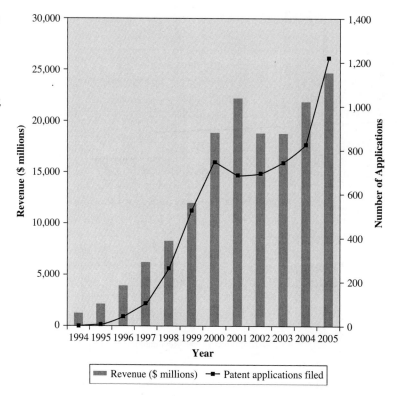

from suppliers so that these functions could be outsourced as well. Cisco thus developed systems so that manufacturing as well as other functions could be outsourced, but remain integrated in a seamless manner.

In addition to linking itself to its various sources with well-developed information technologies, Cisco also invested a great deal of effort in setting up organizational structures and guidelines for its interactions with its suppliers. To effectively manage its suppliers and supplier activities, Cisco classified them according to the significance of the activity to Cisco's strategy (i.e., whether it was core or not) and criticality of the activity to the completion of the process involved. The classification scheme helps Cisco set priorities for and structure its interactions with suppliers. Some are tight relationships with frequent interactions, and others, like that with Hewlett-Packard, entail strategic alliances across a number of product or technology areas. Some of the suppliers in Cisco's network are direct suppliers who work directly with Cisco, while many others are indirect suppliers who support the direct suppliers in some way.

Cisco's highly outsourced model is not without its challenges. The downturn in the electronics industry in 2002–2003, evident in Exhibit 6.1, surfaced significant differences between Cisco's forecasts and those of its major suppliers. The effect that ensued was the classic bullwhip effect depicted in Exhibit 1.1 in Chapter 1. Some suggest that Cisco's outsourced model made these differences harder to resolve (CIO Magazine 2001) and made recovery from the slump slower than it might otherwise have been.

A highly outsourced process makes it challenging to get all players onto the same information systems or, at the very least, able to synchronize all the different information systems involved. Cisco's investment in ERP and PDM systems put it well ahead of many of its suppliers, at least in the early days, forcing it to spend time bringing its suppliers up to speed or reconciling the output of different systems. Finally, as discussed in Chapter 2, outsourcing forces the company to compete in a market economy for the desired levels of output and performance from its suppliers. In the market downturn, Cisco received from its suppliers the large quantities it had ordered, leaving it in a significant overstock situation. When a market is constrained, sometimes companies will over-order in order to receive allocations. The possibility of such situations drives the structure of contracts and incentives with the supply base, including conditions for returns and cancellations, and a need to retain a big picture of the dynamics of the supply chain with as much information as possible at all times.

The Cisco outsourcing model poses a number of questions about how to structure its supply base and how to manage the suppliers in it:

- How many suppliers should be engaged? Under what conditions should the firm source from only one supplier for a specific part or commodity? Under what conditions should it choose to source from many suppliers? Should the firm set limits on the amount of any given supplier's business it wants to make up?

- What role should each supplier play? Is the supplier providing design services, a component or subassembly, or a complete product? Is the supplier giving the company access to a particular market or to a desired set of capabilities?

- Should overseas sourcing be used, and if so, how much should be sourced from overseas? In what ways must overseas suppliers be managed differently, if at all, from suppliers in the home country?

- How should the relationship be structured and managed, including any contracts and economic incentives? Are there ways to manage risks? How does the company create a mechanism for suppliers to improve performance? How should the supplier network be integrated with, for example, information technologies? What form should the integration take and how should it be implemented?

These are the questions addressed in this chapter. We start with a brief history of the evolution of supplier management, as thinking has changed significantly over the past 20 years, particularly with the increase in outsourcing. We then address each sourcing strategy question in turn: How many suppliers should the firm engage? What roles should they play? When and how should overseas sourcing be used? How should suppliers be managed?

Sourcing Strategy

For a typical manufacturing company today, total purchases account for roughly 50 percent of sales revenues.[3] Firms can source any number of tangible and intangible outputs from suppliers including:

---

[3] http://logistics.about.com/library/weekly/uc010101a.htm, July 17, 2006.

- Design of part or all of its product or service.[4] The original OXO GoodGrips products, for example, were designed by Smart Design at a time when the start-up could not afford to invest in its own internal design group.
- Manufacturing or delivery of a complete product or service. In the computing and electronics industry, final assembly and test are often conducted by subcontractors such as Jabil, which describes itself as a provider of design, manufacturing, and post-manufacturing services.
- Manufacturing or delivery of some or all of the components or modules of the product or service. Aircraft manufacturers may source anything from a fully assembled engine to the individual nuts and bolts that are used to assemble the airplane. Because of the complexity of final assembly and test, it is usually retained in house.
- Extraction and processing of raw materials. Sugar beet refiners source the raw sugar beets from the farmers who grow them. Dozens of industries source steel from the major steel producers, who in turn convert iron ore extracted from mines.
- Processing equipment for both manufacturing and services. Intel's complex manufacturing processes require a large internal group focused entirely on working with its semiconductor processing equipment suppliers.
- Logistics and supply chain services. UPS and FedEx provide logistics support services that range from the well-known delivery services to warehousing and document management.
- IT and other services. In 2003, Hewlett-Packard won a 10-year, $3 billion contract with Procter & Gamble to handle its IT infrastructure, data operations, desktop and end-user support, network management, and some applications development and management (McFarlan and Delacey 2004). The contract is not atypical today. Companies outsource various human resources management functions as well.

The wide range of products and services that are being sourced today has made procurement an increasingly important function, and the complexities of managing sourcing greater than ever.

Approaches to sourcing have evolved significantly over the years. Historically, sourcing was simply viewed as a means to procure needed components at the lowest price possible. An original equipment manufacturer (OEM) would complete the design work, including full specifications of the components of the design, and then put each component out to bid with a large number of competing suppliers. Generally, the lowest cost bidder was chosen, sometimes subject to performance qualifications for quality and delivery. There was very little information exchanged, outside the specifications of the part and perhaps expected production volumes, or any collaboration to improve quality or delivery performance.

Japanese companies were the leaders in engaging with their suppliers and structuring their supplier networks in very different ways. The Japanese automotive industry is illustrative. As far back as 1991, Japanese automobile manufacturers (Toyota, Nissan, and Mazda) had suppliers perform 30 percent of the engineering work for a new car model; in Europe suppliers were used for 16 percent of the work, and in the United States only 7 percent of the work (Clark and Fujimoto 1991). At the time, the U.S. automobile production

---

[4] http://www.designdirectory.com/, July 17, 2006, has a comprehensive list of the hundreds of design firms around the world that provide such services.

network consisted of highly vertically integrated assembly and component fabrication plants owned by the carmakers and a very flat hierarchy of a large number of small suppliers with whom the carmakers maintained arm's-length relationships. Carmakers and suppliers behaved as adversaries with little information exchange, as carmakers played suppliers off against one another in contests for one-year contracts.

The Japanese production network, on the other hand, featured assembly and component production plants with a much lower degree of vertical integration and a multi-tiered supplier network in which the first tier comprised a small number of large suppliers, most of which had engineering capability. Second-, third-, and fourth-tier suppliers supported the first tier in a very hierarchical system. The first-tier suppliers were called upon to provide relatively large subassemblies such as instrument panels and complete seats. They were provided with long-term guarantees but required to take significant responsibility in return. On the one hand, they would be compensated for undepreciated equipment costs in the face of lower than expected demand. On the other hand, they were expected to meet strict and ever more stringent cost and quality targets. The types of relationships set up between carmakers and first-tier suppliers in Japan fostered close communication and coordination and often involved sharing personnel and detailed information on costs and production processes.

As a result, in part, of much examination of and publication about the lack of competitiveness of the United States in the global automotive industry (e.g., Clark and Fujimoto 1991, Womack et al. 1990), supplier management in the United States began to change. U.S. car companies went through reductions in suppliers from the thousands to the hundreds. Companies outside the auto industry changed as well. Xerox reduced its number of suppliers by 90 percent and Motorola by 70 percent in the early 1990s. Today, the following are considered characteristic of a successful sourcing strategy:

- Limited numbers of suppliers.
- Functional specifications developed jointly with the suppliers doing the detailed design and development.
- Emphasis on quality, delivery, and other criteria rather than cost.
- More cooperative relationships and information exchange in a wide variety of areas such as planning and scheduling.

In sum, companies today rely on suppliers for an ever-expanding set of products and services, and as a result the roles of suppliers in the supply chain network have evolved significantly. It is in this context that we explore the four sourcing strategy questions, starting with how many suppliers a firm ought to have.

Choosing the Right Number of Suppliers

There are two questions a firm faces in examining the question of how many suppliers it should have: First, how many suppliers does it want to manage in total, and second, how many suppliers does it want to have for each subassembly, component, or service it sources? The answer to the first of these questions is inextricably tied up with the question of how the firm wishes to structure its supply network. Modern supplier management theory suggests using a small number of suppliers with which more structured and interactive relationships can be developed. This often implies that the firm sources larger chunks of work, whether larger subassemblies or larger sets of process activities, from a set of "first-tier" suppliers, and that the myriad other suppliers from which it sourced previously become lower-tier suppliers serving the first tier. There are pros and cons to developing such a hierarchical supply chain.

The answer to the second of these questions requires an assessment of the risks associated with sourcing from a single supplier. The viability of using a single supplier depends on its financial stability, market position, and strength and depends on what one is sourcing. For example, a company might procure relatively inexpensive commodities from a larger number of suppliers than it would use for expensive processing equipment or a critical subassembly. We address each of these questions in greater detail.

Total Number of Suppliers

There are many reasons why engaging with a smaller number of suppliers is advantageous and why so many companies went through supplier reduction programs. As firms established stronger links with their suppliers, with more information sharing and collaboration, dealing with a large supplier base became impractical. Indeed, the larger the supplier base, the more a firm is forced into interacting at arm's length about specified designs with decisions based on cost only and the more it cannot manage such tasks as scheduling with a just-in-time system, addressing joint quality issues, or allowing supplier autonomy in the design of outsourced modules. The advantages firms expect to derive from reducing their supplier base include:

- Lower cost and effort to manage relationships overall.
- Greater potential to coordinate designs.
- Increased capability to synchronize schedules.
- Increased capability to evaluate suppliers on multiple criteria, not just cost.
- Capabilities of procuring modules rather than parts.
- Ease of tracking performance.
- Ease of exchanging information.

In short, working with a smaller number of suppliers allows for more in-depth interactions along many fronts—design, scheduling, and process performance. But there are potential disadvantages to creating a hierarchical network of suppliers that often go along with the smaller number of suppliers, mostly having to do with loss of visibility into and control over what is happening throughout the supply chain. In the completely vertically integrated firm, information is readily available and negotiations can quickly solve an immediate problem, at least theoretically. To obtain complete visibility and quickly resolve issues in a hierarchical supply network requires excellent information systems and highly flexible contracts that allow for jointly acceptable resolution of problems. Neither, as we discuss later, are fully developed and effective in some supply chains today, although the better outsourced supply chains have developed these capabilities. As a result, the deepening hierarchy of some of today's supply chains can lead to a number of at least potential disadvantages:

- Lack of visibility over inventory leading to:
  - More stockouts as information is late to arrive from lower levels of the supply chain.
  - More inventory throughout the supply chain as each tier buffers against uncertainty.

- Increased cost of quality. The cost of quality is greatest for the OEM, as the most value has been added to the product or service by the time it reaches the OEM, making rework expensive. Without visibility into the performance of the entire supply network, poor quality is not identified until late in the process.
- Greater demand volatility. Small changes in demand at the OEM level get magnified as they propagate through the supply chain, creating the classic bullwhip effect (see Exhibit 1.1 in Chapter 1) and causing shortages and excess inventory.
- Diminished new product or service introduction performance including:
  - Increased cycle times for new product or service introduction. The many details associated with bringing a new product or service to market are difficult to manage across a complex supply network. Problems may surface late in the process, delaying introduction.
  - Less effective optimization of integral product or service architectures. Developing a highly integrated product or service requires intimate knowledge of the component and process technologies that will be used, which must be gathered from across the supply chain. Modular designs are better suited to these multilayer networks.

Significant investments in information systems can mitigate a number of these problems, but can be nontrivial to implement throughout a large supply network.

The information processing view of organizational design described in Chapter 7 provides an interesting lens through which to view the trade-offs a firm makes in designing a supplier network. When there is little uncertainty to be handled by a supply chain, it can be run hierarchically with rules and procedures and shared goals and objectives. Historically, this characterized the flat supply networks where suppliers were managed with arm's-length transactions. As uncertainty increases, however, exceptions to be handled increase, and thus, communication requirements increase. Under conditions of such uncertainty, supplier networks must be restructured and managed in different ways. First, work can be broken down into "self-contained" chunks and those chunks sourced from a single supplier or group of suppliers. This suggests that products and services be modularly designed, and that each module be sourced from a first-tier supplier that in turn works with a focused group of second- and third-tier suppliers. This minimizes information flows required among first-tier suppliers. Second, significant investments can be made in information technology to handle the increased information flows both vertically and laterally across the supply network. Firms today use a combination of these approaches.

In summary, a firm must weigh the advantages and disadvantages of a hierarchical supply network as it considers how many suppliers it wants to directly engage. In parallel, it must consider redesigning the architecture of its products or services to allow outsourcing of larger chunks or modules to first-tier suppliers if it wishes to move to such a structure. If the firm chooses to go with fewer direct suppliers in a hierarchical structure, it must invest in organizational structures and information technologies that facilitate communication throughout the network of design, as well as operational data. We now turn to the next question: For any given item, how many suppliers should a firm engage?

Number of Suppliers per Item Outsourced

While the strategic reasons for limiting suppliers are often compelling and clear, the question of whether to use a single source or small number of suppliers suggests some additional considerations and complexities. For example, there is a perception that the use of a single supplier is risky. If the single supplier were to face problems, the company sourcing from that supplier might not have any contingency options. There are, however, circumstances in which a company would want to use a single supplier, despite the risks involved. Intel's equipment procurement organization opted for the dual-supplier approach after weighing the pros and cons (Mathur and Hayes 1994a). Specific concerns about the ability of its current supplier to deliver a particular piece of equipment drove Intel's decision; it determined that it could better motivate the supplier to improve if it had competition. Some of the pros and cons of a multiple-supplier approach are presented in Exhibit 6.4.

In general, firms base their decisions about whether to single or multiple source on the following factors, which we cover in detail in the following sections:

- Uniqueness of sourced item or equipment.
- Viability and reliability of suppliers.
- Stability of the technology associated with the item being sourced.
- Significance of the buying company's business to the total business of the supplier.
- Branding implications of sourcing decision.
- Competitiveness of market.

Uniqueness of Sourced Item

There are situations in which the sourced item, whether a component, a subassembly, a product, a piece of processing equipment, or a process, is so unique or differentiated that it can only be provided by a single source. In this case, the firm has no choice but to rely on a single source. Some companies differentiate the notions of single sourcing and sole sourcing, using *single sourcing* to refer to the situation in which a company has the choice of multiple suppliers but chooses to go with just one and using *sole sourcing* to refer to the situation in which there is but one choice.

Often the need to sole source is driven by a design decision, frequently around a complex subassembly, piece of equipment, or process. If a final product or service design is not robust enough to handle variability in its subcomponents or in the process used to build or deliver it, then sole sourcing may be the only option. In most situations, however, variations in the item being sourced do not have much effect on product, process, or service

EXHIBIT 6.4   **Arguments For and Against Multiple-Supplier Approach**

Source: Adapted from Mathur and Hayes, "Teaching Note: Intel-PED," Harvard Business School Publishing, 1994b.

Pros of a Multiple-Supplier Approach	Cons of a Multiple-Supplier Approach
Competition motivates suppliers to improve and be more responsive, and provides the buyer with financial leverage in pricing negotiations.	Increases the complexity of vendor relationships, spare parts, and service contract management.
Reduces the impact of supplier failure.	Requires duplicate engineering and development efforts to integrate two vendors' technologies.
Increases the flexibility to change technologies as the life cycle evolves and allows more ready experimentation with alternative technologies.	Vendors have less trust and loyalty, making influence over and access to them more difficult.
	Makes ramp-up of new facilities, transfer of production among facilities, and operations logistics more complicated.
	Can reduce learning curve effects, if there are multiple technologies to learn and volume is shared among them.
	Can increase training and equipment maintenance costs.

performance, in which case multiple vendors may be used. Automobile manufacturers, for example, use multiple vendors for items such as tires even for a single vehicle model. Intel, on the other hand, aims for as much consistency as possible across its fabs, which drives it to minimize the number of equipment vendors it uses.

Viability and Reliability of Suppliers

There are a number of risks a company must recognize and manage in its relationship with any supplier: Is the supplier financially healthy, and will it be in business in the foreseeable future? Is the supplier located in a region with high risk of natural disaster, labor strife, and so on? Does the supplier have a viable and reliable supplier network itself? Does the supplier perform reliably against the company's cost, quality, availability, features and innovativeness, and environmental performance standards?

Having a supplier go out of business is not a high-probability event, but disruptions such as labor strikes, fires, and floods at suppliers happen with some frequency, and performance lapses even more frequently. Vacuum cleaner manufacturer Oreck's manufacturing facility in Long Beach, Mississippi, was shut down for 10 days when Hurricane Katrina hit. Flash devices for Internet Appliance products were in short supply when manufacturers underestimated demand and were unable to meet their customers' requirements. Whenever risk of failure is high along any of these dimensions, it is practical to consider having multiple sources. While it is not trivial to move work among suppliers in the event of the failure of one, having contracts already in place with backup sources can speed the process.

Stability of Technology Associated with Sourced Item

When a firm's competitiveness relies on using the most current process, information, or product technologies, and it procures that technology from suppliers outside the firm, the stability of the technology dictates whether or not it should use more than one supplier. If the technology is stable, then barring motivators to do otherwise, it can source from a single supplier. This assumes that if the technology changes or evolves, it does so at a rate with which the supplier can keep pace. On the other hand, if technology is changing rapidly, the capabilities of the single source could possibly be overtaken by another supplier. Having multiple sources in such a case increases the likelihood that the newest technology is available from a current supplier. If the firm is using leading-edge technology, however, it may find that there is only one qualified supplier, particularly if aspects of the technology are proprietary.

General Electric, Pratt & Whitney, and Rolls Royce all make aircraft engines. Boeing and Airbus design their new aircraft with flexibility to handle an engine from any one of these manufacturers. They do so partly because their customers, the airlines, like to have choices, but also because they want to keep all three suppliers in business. Each aircraft program Boeing and Airbus undertake is large, and they generally contract with more than one engine manufacturer on these programs. Without competition, the aircraft manufacturers figure, they cannot be assured that there will be pressure to invest in the development of the latest engine technologies. They multisource not only to have access to the latest technologies, but to encourage their suppliers to invent those new technologies.

A firm does not have to multiple source to be assured of getting access to the latest technologies. Keeping an eye on developments across the supply base, in the sourced technology as well as in alternative technologies that might fulfill the same need, can provide the firm with assurance that its single relationship is current. The firm doesn't have to have contracts with all suppliers in the network to access such information, although it might get more ready access if it did.

Proportion of the Buyer's Purchases to the Total Business of the Supplier

If the amount of business a firm does with a specific supplier represents a very small part of that supplier's business, then the supplier may hold a relative position of power that makes single sourcing risky. The supplier is likely to view the business as less important than that from other customers that procure larger quantities and to be less responsive to the firm's requests. In this case, multiple sources can both mitigate risks and provide a lever in the relationship. If the supplier thinks that it can gain more volume, or risks losing the work it has because its competitors are providing better service, then it may be more motivated to perform. In general the negotiation power of the customer goes up with the number of suppliers from which it sources a particular item.

On the other hand, if the amount of business the firm does with a specific supplier represents a very large part of that supplier's business, there are risks of a different type. A significant change in the buyer's requirements of the supplier will radically change the supplier's business. If demand decreases dramatically, the supplier may not be able to sustain a viable business. If demand increases dramatically, or if the mix of items required changes significantly, the supplier may not be able to respond in a reasonable time. Some companies set limits on the amount of any one supplier's business they want to make up, as they don't want to be responsible for the well-being of the supplier should demands shift. Instead, they spread their demand across multiple suppliers. Other companies manage their supplier relationships by, for example, smoothing orders to the supplier as much as possible or providing longer-term contracts, so that the suppliers do not face undue risks.

Branding Implications of Sourcing Decision

Sometimes the item being sourced is a key branding mechanism of the product or service ultimately being marketed. Computer marketing, for example, is often based on the microprocessor and uses the "Intel Inside" slogan, bicycles focus on the particular brand of components (e.g., Shimano), and cars emphasize the brand of the entertainment system (e.g., Kenwood, JVC). When branding is an important part of the product or service design and marketing and a single brand is sought, the buyer will be driven to use a single source. Branding, however, need not be unique, thus supporting a multiple-source strategy. The airframe manufacturers, for example, market multiple engine brands for a given aircraft model.

Competitiveness of Market

When the market for the item being sourced is highly competitive, multiple suppliers will compete for business from the sourcing company, offering incentives on cost and delivery or performance improvement over time. Competitiveness tends to reduce the uniqueness of offerings, but in general increases the performance of suppliers across the board.[5] In these situations, the use of multiple sources may increase the buyer's negotiation power and drive vendor performance improvements. A single supplier faces the risk that the buyer will shift its entire volume to an alternative source, but such a shift is risky for the buyer. A buyer

---

[5] One can view the performance improvement as an economies of scale effect with the number of suppliers.

with multiple sources, on the other hand, can more readily move volume among them creating greater risk for the suppliers. Ultimately, the task for the company is to balance the performance of suppliers with the difficulty of coordinating additional suppliers.

Choosing the Right Number of Suppliers Summary

Companies today limit the total number of suppliers with which they choose to engage, often creating hierarchical networks of suppliers in which first-tier suppliers perform larger (now outsourced) chunks of work and direct the lower-tier suppliers that formerly reported directly in to the top-level buyer. They form closer relationships with their top-tier suppliers, often collaborating on new designs and sharing critical cost and scheduling information.

At each level in the hierarchy, companies must decide how many suppliers they want to have in total, but also how many suppliers they want to have for each item or group of items (commodity groups) they purchase. There are a number of considerations to be made, including whether or not the sourced item is unique, how viable or reliable a supplier is, how rapidly the underlying technology is changing, what portion of the supplier's business the firm wants to be, whether or not the supplier's brand is important to selling the buyer's product or service, and how competitive the market is for the item being sourced.

Structuring Supplier Relationships

We have talked about how a firm might decide how many suppliers to have in total and for any given item. Now we turn to the more complex question of how the relationships with the suppliers that are in the network should be structured. Answering this question requires that we address

- *Supplier roles:* Is the supplier providing a component, module, or complete product? Is it providing process technology to support production or service delivery? Or is it providing a service or completing part of the service process of the firm? Does it have a particular role in the firm's international supply network?
- *Supplier relationships:* How should the supply network be organized? What type of governance structure should be used in managing each type of supplier in that network?
- *Incentives and contracts:* How does a firm create a mechanism for suppliers to improve performance over time? Can the members of a supply network be motivated to work for the betterment of the network overall, perhaps by sharing the investments and the gains?

Roles of Suppliers

The role of a supplier is dictated in part by the vertical integration strategy of the firm, as described in Chapter 2, and by the facilities strategy of the firm, as described in Chapter 5. The vertical integration strategy dictates how many of a firm's activities it wishes to retain internally and how many it wishes to outsource. A product firm may outsource the design and manufacture of a complete product, the manufacture of the complete product, or just modules or components of the product. A service firm may outsource raw materials production (as McDonald's generally does beef and potatoes), just one task (as McDonald's does in outsourcing drive-through order taking to call centers), or an entire process. How much it outsources will determine the roles its suppliers play.

The facilities strategy dictates whether or not a supplier is responsible for accessing a specific market, accessing certain capabilities (skill sets, technologies), or accessing low factor costs. It also may dictate whether the supplier is of "low competence," meaning that it simply provides the required access and feeds that information back to the parent organization, or it is of "high competence" and plays a more significant role developing its own products or services to serve the local market. Chapter 5 describes these roles in more detail and summarizes them in Exhibit 5.11.

The specific role that a supplier plays impacts the way the supplier is engaged. One might, for example, develop a different type of relationship with a supplier performing design services than with a supplier providing components. The design supplier is likely to be more core to the firm, and the firm runs the risk that the design it purchases may also be sold to its competitors; it may want to structure a relationship or contract that disallows such sharing. Further, it is likely to have a more collaborative, information-sharing relationship with that supplier. A commodity part supplier, on the other hand, by definition offers something that is exactly like that offered by its competitors. The relationship the firm has with a commodity provider might be more arm's length.

We turn now to a more detailed discussion of the types of relationships from which the firm might choose.

Types of Supplier Relationships

There is a spectrum of possible relationships from which a firm might choose (Exhibit 6.5). On one end is an arm's-length relationship, which is appropriate when a firm is procuring a

EXHIBIT 6.5
Spectrum of Relationships with Suppliers or Customers

Type of Relationship	Description	
Arm's-length relationships	Traditional, cost-based, free-market, short-duration, purchase-order-driven relationships	
Modified vendor relationships	Value-added services (e.g., supplier managed inventories)	
Long-term contracts	Long-term supply contracts	
Nonequity-based collaboration	R&D consortia (e.g., Sematech) Cross-marketing agreements Cross-production agreements Joint purchasing activities	
Minority equity investments	Invest in supplier	More toward vertical integration
Licensing arrangements	Provide license to supplier in technology that host firm develops, but in which it wants to limit investments	
Investment integration	Coordinate investment jointly	
Joint ventures or strategic alliances	Allow firms to exchange certain goods, services, information, or expertise while maintaining a formal trade relationship on others	
Asset ownership	Host firm retains ownership for critical assets in adjacent stages of the industry chain but contracts out all other aspects of ownership and control	
Full ownership	Host firm fully owns activity	

commodity from an established market and has no need for close interaction on scheduling, quality, or other areas of performance. At the other end of the spectrum is full ownership, which is used (as described in Chapter 2) when the activities or processes being performed are core, there is not an established outside market so the firm must complete the job internally, the economics of ownership are compelling, or there are product or technology reasons to integrate. Full ownership has a number of risks as well: The internal process may not be able to achieve economies of scale; it may not be able to afford investments to keep up with rapidly changing technologies; it may detract from the company's focus on its core activities; and it may not be motivated to perform as well as it would if it were a stand-alone organization.

Clearly companies today have moved away from the ends of the spectrum, engaging with suppliers in a number of different ways. Those seeking some of the benefits of vertical integration without full ownership may engage in asset ownership, where some of the critical assets of the business are owned, or in joint ventures or strategic alliances, where both parties have a vested interest in a shared outcome. Those seeking more coordination, collaboration, information sharing, or interaction than implied by an arm's-length relationship but not interested in any form of ownership might work with vendors to provide more value-added services, such as vendor-managed inventory, or engage in long-term contracts that imply a greater commitment than does arm's-length commodity trading. These relationships allow the firm to engage in more than just price negotiation and extraction of concessions as is typical of arm's-length relationships. Unless the purchase is a true commodity, cooperation can be very important, and firms may seek more than an arm's-length relationship.

Other possible arrangements include nonequity-based forms of collaboration such as the many R&D consortia that are formed among multiple firms and sometimes governmental agencies, nongovernmental organizations (NGOs), national labs, and university researchers (Ring et al. 2005) to do collaborative research and minority equity investments. Cisco, for example, lists 19 minority equity investments in such companies as CyberCash that makes software to handle secure transactions over the Internet.[6] These investments do not necessarily imply a long-term relationship; CyberCash was subsequently purchased by VeriSign.[7]

JIT II manufacturing is another way of structuring supplier relationships with the goal of reducing the lead time from design through delivery of a product or service (Pragman 1996). Bose Corporation based the JIT II approach on a number of concepts from Japanese supplier management. In JIT II, a sales representative from the supplier works full time at a customer's firm while being paid by the supplier. The supplier representative works as a member of the customer's procurement team, focuses on planning and materials needs, and is authorized to purchase materials from his or her supply organization. From the customer's point of view, the supplier is always available, develops a deep understanding of the customer's needs, and has access to all the information needed to reduce lead times, cut costs, and improve quality. JIT II allows concurrent engineering and value analysis to be performed on an ongoing basis and may include having on-site, supplier-owned and operated inventory stores. Suppliers who support JIT II relationships usually see an increase in the volume of work they do for the supported customer over time.

The type of relationship a firm chooses to engage in with any particular supplier depends upon what role it wishes that supplier to play and how critical the sourced item is to the firm. For most companies, sourcing encompasses a range of different relationships. Some suppliers,

[6] http://www.cisco.com/warp/public/750/invest.html, July 22, 2006.
[7] http://www.cybercash.com/, July 22, 2006.

such as those of major subassemblies or service process chunks, represent very strategic relationships. Others, such as commodities suppliers, do not require the management attention or structure that a more strategic relationship does. Given knowledge of the different roles of suppliers and of the spectrum of supplier relationships from which the firm might choose, the next logical question is what type of relationship best fits what supplier role. Which supplier roles warrant a more strategic relationship with increased interaction and which require less? In other words, which supplier roles require relationships towards the arm's-length end of the spectrum, and which require relationships towards the total ownership end?

Matching Relationship Types with Supplier Types

In general, the choice of relationship to have with a supplier depends upon the criticality of the item being sourced and the volume purchased, as shown in Exhibit 6.6 (Handfield et al. 2000). The criticality of the item sourced is a function of the importance of the item to the delivery of the firm's product or service and of the risk associated with obtaining that item. In this framework, a critical strategic supplier is one that provides something for which it is difficult to find a substitute or alternative supplier and that is critical to creating the firm's output. Critical strategic suppliers are likely to rate a relationship on the full ownership end of the spectrum. Noncritical suppliers, on the other hand, provide standard items that are easily substituted and have adequate availability. These relationships can likely be managed with arm's-length or close to arm's-length relationships.

Bottleneck suppliers and leverage suppliers fall somewhere in the middle. Bottleneck suppliers provide critical items, but those items are only required in low volume. It is difficult to find substitutes for these items, and the suppliers operate in monopolistic markets with high entry barriers, often in a critical geographic or political situation. Leverage suppliers, on the other hand, supply noncritical items, but in high volumes. Like noncritical suppliers, there is adequate supply from a number of alternative suppliers of items that meet standard specifications, and substitution is possible. To lock in a relationship with a bottleneck supplier, the firm may need some investment of equity or capital. Leverage suppliers, on the other hand, can likely be managed with modified vendor relationships or long-term contracts.

Thus, one can choose a position on the spectrum of supplier relationships in Exhibit 6.5 based on how critical the item being sourced is to the firm and the volumes in which it is purchased.

EXHIBIT 6.6   Types of Suppliers by Criticality and Volume and Likely Types of Relationships

	Item Purchased in Low Volume	Item Purchased in High Volume
Item Being Sourced Is Critical to the Firm	**Bottleneck Suppliers** Nonequity-based collaboration Minority equity investments	**Critical Strategic Suppliers** Investment integration Joint ventures Strategic alliances Asset ownership
Item Being Sourced Is Not Critical to the Firm	**Noncritical Suppliers** Arm's length Modified vendor contracts	**Leverage Suppliers** Modified vendor contracts Long-term contracts

EXHIBIT 6.7 Buyer-Supplier Relationships Based on Level of Investment in One Another

Source: Reprinted from Bensaou, "Portfolios of Buyer-Supplier Relationships" *MIT Sloan Management Review,* 1999, pp. 35–44, by permission of publisher.

	Low Supplier-Specific Investment	High Supplier-Specific Investment
High Buyer Specific-Investment	Captive buyer	Strategic partnership
Low Buyer Specific-Investment	Market exchange	Captive supplier

Mutual Investment Relationships

As more and more relationships fall in the middle of the spectrum of relationships in Exhibit 6.5, suppliers and buyers alike increasingly face the question of whether or not they should invest in each other's businesses and under what conditions. Exhibit 6.7 describes the four combinations created by low or high investment by the buyer in the supplier and low or high investment by the supplier in the buyer. In a strategic partnership, both parties have investments that tie them together. At the other extreme, in market exchanges, neither party has a significant investment in the other and can readily switch to another customer or supplier. The captive buyer and supplier quadrants represent asymmetric relationships where one party has leverage over the other. The market exchange relationship falls near the arm's-length relationship end of the types of relationship spectrum, while the strategic partnership relationship is closer to the full ownership end. Interestingly, Japanese and U.S. firms have roughly the same percentage of strategic partnership and market exchange relationships, but the United States has a much higher percentage of captive buyer relationships, while Japan has a much higher percentage of captive supplier relationships (Bensaou 1999).

Empirical research shows that each type of relationship is characterized by a different set of product/service, market, and supplier characteristics as summarized in Exhibit 6.8 (Bensaou 1999). What this chart provides, then, is guidance as to when each type of relationship might be most appropriate. Strategic partnerships, for example, should be used when the item being sourced is a highly customized or integrated subsystem that requires strong engineering and technical capabilities, is being applied to a high-growth and competitive market, and relies on proprietary technology or processes at the supplier. Market exchange relationships, on the other hand, are more relevant for highly standardized items that leverage simple, mature technologies and are relatively stable.

Not surprisingly, each type of relationship has different requirements for information-sharing mechanisms, the task characteristics of the boundary spanner (which describe how the parties in the relationship interact), and the climate and process characteristics of the interaction as shown in Exhibit 6.9 (Bensaou 1999). Strategic partnerships require greater information sharing, higher-skilled boundary spanners who can deal with the ambiguity and uncertainty inherent in the relationship, and a climate of mutual trust and commitment. Suppliers in these partnerships are likely to be involved early in the buyer's design processes and engage in joint decision making. Market exchanges, on the other hand, require limited information exchange except during contract negotiation, little if any nonroutine work on the part of the boundary spanners, and little integration between buyer and supplier during design or otherwise. Market exchanges might well be handled through web-based auctions and information systems that allow for scheduling, billing, and payment. (Such information systems are the subject of Chapter 9.)

EXHIBIT 6.8   Contextual Profiles for Different Relationships

Source: Reprinted from Bensaou, "Portfolios of Buyer-Supplier Relationships" *MIT Sloan Management Review,* 1999, pp. 35–44, by permission of publisher. Copyright © 1999 by Massachusetts Institute of Technology. All rights reserved.

	Low Supplier-Specific Investment	High Supplier-Specific Investment
High Buyer-Specific Investment	**Captive Buyer** *Product characteristics* Technically complex Based on mature, well-understood technology Little innovation and improvements to the product *Market characteristics* Stable demand with limited market growth Concentrated market with few established players Buyers maintain an internal manufacturing capability *Supplier characteristics* Large supply houses Supplier-proprietary technology Few strongly established suppliers Strong bargaining power Customers heavily depend on these suppliers	**Strategic Partnership** *Product characteristics* High level of customization required Close to buyer's core competency Tight mutual adjustments needed in key processes Technically complex part of integrated subsystem Based on new technology Innovation leaps in technology, product, or process Frequent design changes Strong engineering expertise required Large capital investments required *Market characteristics* Strong demand and high-growth market Very competitive and concentrated market Frequent changes in competitors due to unstable or lack of dominant design Buyer maintains in-house design and testing capability *Partner Characteristics* Large multiproduct supply houses Strong supplier-proprietary technology Active in research and innovation (i.e., R&D costs) Strong recognized skills and capabilities in design, engineering, and manufacturing
Low Buyer-Specific Investment	**Market Exchange** *Product characteristics* Highly standardized products Mature technology Little innovation and rare design changes Technically simple product or well-structured complex manufacturing process Little or no customization to buyer's final product Low engineering effort and expertise required Small capital investments required *Market characteristics* Stable or declining demand Highly competitive market	**Captive Supplier** *Product characteristics* Technically complex products Based on new technology (developed by suppliers) Important and frequent innovations and new functionalities in the product category Significant engineering effort and expertise required Heavy capital investments required *Market characteristics* High-growth market segment Fierce competition Few qualified players Unstable market with shifts between suppliers

(continued)

(continued)

Many capable suppliers
Same players over time

Supplier Characteristics
Small "mom and pop" shops
No proprietary technology
Low switching costs
Low bargaining power
Strong economic reliance on industry
  sector business

Supplier Characteristics
Strong supplier-proprietary technology
Suppliers with strong financial capabilities and
  good R&D skills
Low supplier bargaining power
Heavy supplier dependency on the buyer and
  economic reliance on the specific industry

Thus, one approach to determining the appropriate role to give a supplier is to assess the degree to which either the buyer or supplier must make investments specific to the relationship. Cisco provides another example of a means of determining whether to outsource an activity and how to manage it if outsourced. Cisco classifies activities (Exhibit 6.10) as to whether the activity is core and whether the activity is what it calls *mission critical*. A core activity is consistent with what we describe as core in Chapter 2 and is an activity that contributes directly to competitive advantage. An activity that is not core is called *context*. A mission-critical activity is one whose shortfall risks the company's operations. Examples of the different classifications include new product introduction, which is both core and mission critical; assembly, which is context and mission critical; manufacturing training, which is nonmission critical but core; and desktop support, which is context and nonmission critical. Exhibit 6.10 presents the outsourcing and supplier management strategies for each of the four classifications. For example, the context and mission-critical tasks require outsourcing with tight control. As is the case for all these frameworks, the more important relationships, based on what is core and mission critical, require more control and partnership arrangements that are closer to the ownership end of the spectrum.

Matching Roles and Relationships in Design Outsourcing

There are a number of different roles dictated by the firm's vertical integration strategy that design suppliers may play, from designing complete products or services to providing design services for an internal product or service development organization, to designing the equipment or processes to be used in the production or service delivery process. And there is a spectrum of relationships, similar to that described in Exhibit 6.5, that might be adopted to manage suppliers in these roles (Vakil 2005). The buyer can

- Procure an existing design for a complete product or service, for a component or module of a product or service, for a process methodology, or for a piece of equipment.
- Engage the design supplier in making minor revisions to an existing design.
- Hire the design supplier to perform a specific service or piece of an internal design process.
- Specify the characteristics of the item to be designed and hand them off to the design supplier to execute the design:
  - For a complete product or service.
  - For a component or module of a product or service to be integrated with a design being completed by the buyer.

EXHIBIT 6.9   Management Profile for Each Contextual Profile

Source: Reprinted from Bensaou, "Portfolios of Buyer-Supplier Relationships," *MIT Sloan Management Review*, 1999, pp. 35–44, by permission of publisher. Copyright © 1999 by Massachusetts Institute of Technology. All rights reserved.

	Low Supplier-Specific Investment	High Supplier-Specific Investment
High Buyer-Specific Investment	**Captive Buyer**	**Strategic Partnership**
	Information-sharing mechanisms "Broadband" and important exchange of detailed information on a continual basis Frequent and regular mutual visits	*Information-sharing mechanisms* "Broadband," frequent and "rich media" exchange Regular mutual visits and practice of guest engineers
	Boundary spanner's task characteristics Structured task, highly predictable Large amount of time spent by buyer's purchasing agents and engineers with supplier	*Boundary spanner's task characteristics* Highly ill defined, ill structured Frequent unexpected events Large amount of time spent with supplier's staff, mostly on coordinating issues
	Climate and process characteristics Tense climate, lack of mutual trust No early supplier involvement in design Strong effort by buyer toward cooperation Supplier does not necessarily have a good reputation	*Climate and process characteristics* High mutual trust and commitment to relationship Strong sense of buyer fairness Early supplier involvement in design Extensive joint action and cooperation Supplier has excellent reputation
Low Buyer-Specific Investment	**Market Exchange**	**Captive Supplier**
	Information-sharing mechanisms "Narrowband" and limited information exchange, heavy at time of contract negotiation Operations coordination and monitoring along structured routings	*Information-sharing mechanisms* Little exchange of information Few mutual visits, mostly from supplier to buyer
	Boundary spanner's task characteristics Limited time spent directly with supplier staff Highly routine and structured task with little interdependence with supplier's staff	*Boundary spanner's task characteristics* Limited time allocated by buyer's staff to the supplier Mostly complex, coordinating tasks
	Climate and process characteristics Positive social climate No systematic joint effort and cooperation No early supplier involvement in design Supplier fairly treated by the buyer Supplier has a good reputation and track record	*Climate and process characteristics* High mutual trust, but limited direct joint action and cooperation Greater burden put on the supplier

- For the product or service itself, while retaining internal design of certain components of the design (e.g., retaining design of print cartridges for printers).

To procure an existing design, the buyer likely engages in a contract similar in nature to an arm's-length contract, perhaps with some modifications or a licensing agreement. At the other

EXHIBIT 6.10   Cisco Approach to Activity Classification and Supplier Management Strategy

Source: Data provided by Miller, Cisco Systems, Inc., 2005.

	Core	Context
Mission Critical	*Example:* New product introduction *Strategy:* Perform in house	*Example:* Assembly *Strategy:* Outsource with tight control
Nonmission Critical	*Example:* Manufacturing training *Strategy:* Outsource with some control	*Example:* Desktop support *Strategy:* Outsource and control specifications

end of the spectrum, hiring a designer to design a reasonable amount or all of a product or service requires much more collaboration, perhaps reaching the stage of a joint venture or strategic alliance.

If the design supplier is designing and delivering the complete good or service, it is referred to as an *original design manufacturer (ODM)*. (There is no well-known name for the parallel concept in service design, so we use this term generically.) These design suppliers engage in the full range of activities including design and development tasks such as development of prototypes and workable designs, testing, and qualification of parts suppliers, as well as the ramp-up and production tasks. They may start with a specification from the buyer or may develop their own products or services to be supplied to more than one firm. In the latter case, the buyer is simply branding the product or service as its own and focusing on sales and marketing. The many store-branded grocery products are a good example. C&H Sugar Company, for example, packages sugar under many different brand names including Safeway's store brand and Costco's Kirkland brand.

If the design supplier is developing only part of the product or service, then it may enter into a joint design manufacturer (JDM) relationship with the buyer. In this case, there could be a collaborative design, or the JDM could be asked to design certain components or modules. Joint design may be the correct strategy when the OEM views design as critical strategically, but there is a viable market in design services for some of the components.

Design outsourcing involves risks that go beyond manufacturing or service delivery outsourcing (Vakil 2005). First, if the ODM can use the design with other customers (or the design was developed by the ODM for sale to a range of customers), the buyer could lose any competitive advantage and so may want guarantees on some level of exclusivity. Second, since there is even more of the value chain being outsourced, there could be some loss of power and control. Third, there may be loss of intellectual property if the ODM owns the design. Finally, component and supplier selection may be controlled by the ODM, lessening the ability of the buyer to achieve its design for supply chain goals. While outsourcing design provides many advantages, these risks have to be assessed and managed in the structure of the supplier relationships.

Incentives and Contracts

Incentives and contracts are the formal means by which supplier relationships are structured and thus should be chosen to match the requirements of the type of relationship desired. They define how information is exchanged, who has responsibility for quality management and whether and how inspection is done, where design responsibility lies, how much information is shared for planning and scheduling purposes and how integrated the schedules are, and what goals or targets are set for improved performance. Longer-term relationships, such as strategic partnerships, require contracts and incentives that focus on process improvement and sharing of economic gains. The incentives can be in the form of shared savings, changes in share of the business, longer-term commitments, and so forth. From the buyer's point of view, incentives for price reductions are often important over the longer term. Short-term relationships, such as market exchanges, have very different contract requirements that reflect their arm's-length nature. These contracts focus much more on short-term performance against a relatively clear set of objectives.

Incentives and contracts can have a major effect on the success of a supplier relationship. A carefully structured arrangement, such as in a revenue-sharing or buy-back arrangement, for example, can be useful in creating incentives to procure volumes that can improve the overall performance of an entire supply chain and of each of its members. A well-structured set of incentives between a firm and it suppliers can smooth variations in ordering and limit over-ordering when multiple customers are competing for supply. The types of incentives and contracts that one might consider include revenue sharing, buy-backs, consignment, and vendor-managed inventory.

Incentives to Improve Flexibility

Contracts and incentives can play a major role in reducing risk in supply chain planning and inventory management. In these situations, a contract might allow flexibility for both the buyer and the supplier. When demand fluctuates substantially and a buyer places highly varying orders on its suppliers, it is very difficult for suppliers to respond efficiently and effectively. Incentives can also play a useful role when multiple customers are competing for a limited allocation from a supplier. If customers over-order to ensure allocation and then cancel when they receive a larger than expected allocation, suppliers have difficulty in managing their supplies efficiently. Incentives to limit orders, such as discounts or priorities on future orders, can then be very helpful (Hsu 2006). Structured flexibility contracts are beneficial in highly uncertain environments in providing minimum guarantees to the supplier for certain volumes, higher prices for changed orders, broader guarantees for flexibility over the longer time horizon and, in general, some risk sharing among the two parties (Schmidt 2003, and Tsay and Lovejoy 1999).

Another incentive structure employs vendor-managed inventories (VMIs). Under VMI arrangements, the supplier fully manages the inventory at the retailer or customer location under the assumption that the supplier is in a better position to make inventory management decisions. Buyers leave all the details of decisions on reorder points, reorder frequencies, and reorder quantities to the vendor. The supplier is in a position to do this more efficiently and, by having information from multiple customers, will likely develop policies that are better for the supply chain as a whole. In addition, the vendor can avoid possible double marginalization effects, which we discuss shortly. VMI is often used in the grocery industry.

Incentives to Optimize Inventory and Stockout Trade-Offs

In a typical retail setup, such as that pictured in Exhibit 6.11, the retailer makes a guess at what customer demand will be and, using the newsvendor model described in Chapter 4,

EXHIBIT 6.11
A Typical Supplier-Retailer-Consumer Relationship

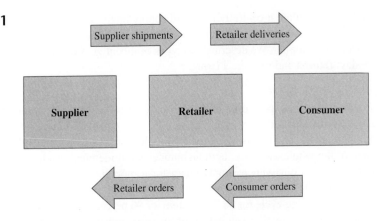

trades off the cost of having excess inventory with the cost of having shortages to determine how much to order. Consumers then arrive at the retail outlet and either find what they are looking for or experience a stockout. At the end of a selling cycle, the retailer is either left with excess inventory or experiences lost sales upon running out of inventory. Suppose that the retailer were removed from this scenario, and the supplier were to sell directly to the consumer. It is possible that the economic performance of the combined supply chain could be greater with this direct relationship than with the retailer involved.

Let's look at an example with numbers to make this point clear. A supplier makes a widget for a cost of $5 and sells it to a retailer for a wholesale price of $7.50. The retailer in turn sells it to the consumer for $10 and at the end of the selling cycle sells excess units for $3.75. Suppose that the demand for this widget is uniformly distributed from 15 to 20 units and the retailer can order anywhere from 15 to 20 units. If the retailer orders only 15 units, it will receive a total profit of $37.50. The supplier also makes $37.50 so the total supply chain profit is $75. (The total profits associated with the supply chain are the sum of the supplier's profits and the retailer's profits.[8]) If the retailer orders 20 units and demand is only 15, then its profits sink to $18.75, as it loses money on the excess units it purchased. The supplier, on the other hand, makes $50, and the total supply chain profit is $68.75. If we do these calculations for all possible retailer order quantities and demand outcomes, we find that the retailer optimizes its profits by purchasing 17 units, the supplier optimizes its profits when the retailer buys 20 units, and the supply chain profits are maximized when the retailer purchases 19 units. In economic terms, this is a form of double marginalization; a single engagement based on the supplier cost and the retail price would provide greater economic profit than having the supplier work through the retailer without shared incentives to maximize the performance of the supply chain. Detailed calculations for all of our widget examples can be found in the appendix to this chapter.

Typically, in situations such as that pictured in Exhibit 6.11, the amounts procured by the retailer for sale to the customer are not as great as those in direct supplier-to-customer arrangements. The question then becomes how to coordinate the supplier and retailer

---

[8] We simplify the transaction and focus only on cost to illustrate this principle. Quality and other factors would also be relevant.

incentives to simulate a centrally managed supply chain that could overcome the dynamics of the two separate engagements. In short, the retailer needs an incentive to procure more from the supplier. We describe two types of incentive programs that are used in practice today: returns and revenue sharing.

Supplier Allows Returns

A common means of providing an incentive for a retailer to order more is to allow the retailer to return unsold items at the end of the selling cycle. A supplier could either take back a percentage of the unsold items at full wholesale price, or all of the items at a percentage of the wholesale price; both techniques yield identical results.

Let's return to our widget supply chain for a moment and see how such an incentive might play out. In this case, we assume that the retailer can return all unsold inventory at the end of the selling cycle for $6.75 per item, or 90 percent of the wholesale price. Further, we assume that the supplier can get rid of the excess inventory for the same salvage value of $3.75, perhaps by selling it through another location. Under this arrangement, the retailer is motivated to order 19 units, which maximizes its profits as well as those of the supplier and of the overall supply chain. Total supply chain profits are optimized and are the same as in the situation described above where the supplier sells directly to the customer.

Allowing returns increases the profits to all players in the supply chain. With returns, the costs of excess inventory are reduced from the retailer point of view, increasing the optimal amount to purchase from the supplier, and despite the likelihood of returns, the overall economic effect for the supplier improves. Many suppliers allow such buybacks, particularly in industries such as cosmetics and greeting cards where the marginal costs are low compared with the retail prices, variety is high, and the physical costs of returns are low (or nonexistent, as in some cases the goods are simply discarded).

Consignment arrangements are similar but have a different effect on the timing of cash flow.[9] A supplier operating on consignment owns the goods until they are sold and continues to own them when they are not sold. In essence, consignment is a return or buyback arrangement in which the returns value is the same as the wholesale price to the retailer. In other words, the supplier buys back unsold inventory from the retailer for the wholesale price at which it sold it to the retailer originally. If all other assumptions remain equal in our widget example, this leads as expected to the retailer ordering the maximum possible demand of 20, while the supplier still wants to provide only 19 units and total supply chain profits are still maximized at 19 units. Usually in consignment arrangements, a limit is placed by the supplier on the amount of inventory it wishes the retailer to carry, as the retailer would otherwise wish to order more than the supplier wants to supply.

Revenue Sharing

The second method of coordination is revenue sharing. There are many variants of revenue-sharing contracts, but in general they involve reducing the wholesale price from the supplier to the retailer and then sharing the revenues from the consumers.

We return once again to our widget example. Let's assume in this case that the wholesale price the supplier received is equal to its cost of $5 but that it receives 25 percent of the revenue of $10 for each unit the retailer sells. Like a returns policy, this motivates the

---

[9] Consignment has to do with ownership of inventory. VMI has to do with who manages the inventory. While vendor-managed inventory may be on consignment, it is not required to be.

retailer to order up to 19 units, thus maximizing profits for the supply chain overall and providing greater returns to both the supplier and retailer. In this revenue-sharing arrangement, the supplier takes on more risk, as it is now selling the widgets at cost, but by doing so, it motivates the retailer to order more.

The double marginalization effect that these incentives are designed to address is due to the way that the supplier and retailer behave given the probability distribution of demand. We turn to the example of Blockbuster and a stylized example of revenue sharing in the video rental world. When Blockbuster first instituted revenue sharing with its suppliers, the wholesale prices of videos dropped substantially and Blockbuster, along with other video retailers, earned a significant amount of revenue from the agreements. Ultimately, though, Blockbuster discontinued its revenue-sharing arrangement and wound up in court with one of its suppliers. The lack of success was partially due to the advent of lower-cost DVDs but also illustrates some of the pitfalls and challenges of such cooperative incentive arrangements: costs of returns, the importance of a clear arrangement, the need for each party to gain something significant from the arrangement, and the need to share in the overall improvement.

The following example using data from the video rental business clearly shows the effect of a revenue-sharing arrangement (Narayanan and Brem 2003). While Blockbuster rents its products more often than selling them, the effects are quite similar. Consider the following costs and usage for a video purchase and rental:

Video purchase price to the retailer: $45

Average rental income: $4

Marginal cost to produce the video: $2

Average number of rentals per video: 35

Average revenue per video lifetime $= 35 \times \$4 = \$140$

Purchase price under revenue sharing: $5

Revenue sharing: 50%

We can then use the newsvendor formulation presented in Chapter 4 to determine stocking policies under a straight purchase arrangement, a revenue-sharing arrangement, and a centrally controlled supply chain. If we assume that salvage values are low and that one party is going to manage the supply chain to optimize total supply chain profits, then we have

$$C_u = \text{Cost of underage} = \text{Revenue} - \text{Marginal cost} = \$140 - \$2 = \$138$$

$$C_o = \text{Cost of overage} = \$2$$

$$C_u/(C_o + C_u) = 138/140 = 98.6\%$$

which suggests a very high service level. Suppose, however, that the video store is managing the decision of how many videos to buy. With a purchase price of $45, the cost of underage is $140 − $45 = $95 and the cost of overage is $45, yielding an optimal percentile of 95/140 and a service level of only 67.9%. More important, the stocking levels are well below optimum for the supply chain as a whole, yielding lost profits for a high-demand situation.

With revenue sharing, however, the incentives are such that the retailer will purchase an amount that is closer to the supply chain optimum. If the purchase price to the retailer of the video under revenue sharing is reduced to $5, and the retailer shares the $4 per rental income 50/50 with the supplier, the following results:

$$C_u = (35 \times \$2) - \$5 = \$65$$

$$C_o = \$5$$

$$C_u/(C_o + C_u) = \$65/(\$65 + 5) = 92.9\%$$

The service level is much higher than the 69.7 percent of the straight purchase agreement but still lower than the supply chain optimum of 98.6 percent. Thus the total supply chain profits will be closer to optimal. We also note that the video supplier will realize more revenue per tape ($5 purchase plus $2 per tape times 35 rentals, or $75) than it did before ($45 per tape). The video store will realize lower revenue per tape, which suggests that it should look for more favorable revenue-sharing terms. The example shows how revenue sharing and buybacks can increase overall supply chain performance.

This effect is illustrated graphically in Exhibit 6.12. The curve represents the total costs of inventory based on a standard inventory management model. The two classes of costs in such models are (1) costs of holding inventory—capital, rent, and so forth—which increase as inventories increase and (2) costs of shortages—penalties and lost sales—which decrease as inventories increase. The result is a curve that first decreases and then increases. The optimal inventory level is found where the two costs are balanced at the lowest point on the curve, A. However, the retailer faces its own considerations and might order less than this optimum, which is indicated by point B, to the left and up from optimal point A. If the manufacturer allows returns or shares revenue, this in effect increases its inventory costs and shifts the curve up as indicated by the dashed line in Exhibit 6.12. With the new cost structure, the retailer will be motivated to order more. With the revenue-sharing arrangement, the optimum point, C, on the new cost curve becomes feasible and is optimal for the manufacturer. Even though the new optimum point, C, is more costly than the optimum of the old curve, it is still better than point B for the manufacturer, indicating the desirability of allowing returns or revenue sharing. While the specifics of the numbers need to be analyzed for any given case, a company will want to allow at least a partial return

EXHIBIT 6.12

Economics of Revenue Sharing or Returns with Retailers

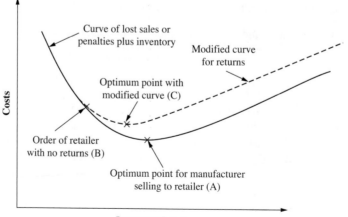

Curve of lost sales or penalties plus inventory

Modified curve for returns

Optimum point with modified curve (C)

Order of retailer with no returns (B)

Optimum point for manufacturer selling to retailer (A)

Costs

Inventory Level

allowance so that the customer will procure an amount representing a point on the high end of demand feasibility. Thus, revenue sharing is an important incentive for encouraging behaviors that jointly optimize the performance of a supply chain.

We have addressed a number of options for structuring incentives to achieve supply chain coordination (e.g., eliminating double marginalization), supply chain control (e.g., through vendor-managed inventories), and supply chain flexibility (e.g., by using structured flexibility contracts).

Sourcing Overseas and from Other Countries

Companies source a great deal from overseas locations or other countries[10] with significantly lower factor costs. These factor costs include labor, material, capital, and energy, although labor is usually the factor cost that results in most overseas sourcing. While the savings from factor costs can be obtained when a company places its own assets in the other country (offshoring), often it is more effective to gain those advantages through an outside supplier (outsourcing). Chapter 2 discusses the vertical integration decision that leads to outsourcing, and Chapter 5 the facilities strategy decisions that lead to offshoring. Here we address the use of suppliers to gain access to factor cost reductions overseas, or the combination of outsourcing and offshoring.

Sourcing overseas entails significant risks and management challenges. Many companies have staffs that focus on nothing but the companies' overseas relationships, addressing legal, tax, and administrative issues. Other companies engage partners that are skilled not only in supplying products or services but in managing the overseas sourcing relationship. Foxconn, for example, which supplies a number of multinational companies such as Dell and Motorola, provides a wide range of components and often complete products for its customers, as well as services in supply network coordination and logistics management, both inbound and outbound. In doing so, it makes it easier for companies that wish to enter into a sourcing relationship in China. Li & Fung is a Hong Kong company that coordinates the manufacturing and supply chain activities of a large number of Asian sources in apparel and a number of other industries. The success of Li & Fung suggests the value of using an intermediary in coordinating foreign sources. Here are some important principles for firms choosing to engage in sourcing overseas.

Offshore or Be at a Major Disadvantage

For many products and services, the factor cost differences obtainable by sourcing overseas are too significant to stay in a developed market and remain competitive. The media reports documenting both plant closings and white-collar layoffs in developed countries have been ongoing for a number of years and such events will continue far into the future. It is nearly impossible to stop or slow down globalization forces. Companies have to adapt to such trends. Even in businesses with large capital costs, labor costs can be significant

---

[10] We distinguish overseas from other countries for the cases such as Mexico, which is technically not overseas from the United States. Throughout this section, we refer to the combination of overseas and other countries as sourcing overseas.

when one considers the entire value chain and the activities and supplies that feed any one source. Labor costs include not only direct labor, but also the overhead labor that designs new products or services, procures materials and services, and manages production or service delivery. Obtaining engineering resources from China and India, for example, can be far less expensive than sourcing the same resources in the United States or Europe. Thus, outsourcing and offshoring may be a necessity.

Sometimes Advantage Can Be Gained Without Outsourcing and Offshoring

Despite the obvious and sometimes significant advantages that can be gained in factor cost reductions by sourcing overseas, there are advantages to sourcing in a developed country: proximity and innovation. Thus, local sourcing in a developed country is recommended when the company's products or services (1) come in a wide variety; (2) entail high transportation costs; or (3) are innovative or in the early stages of their life cycles.[11] We discuss each of these in the following paragraphs.

For Wide Variety

It is expensive to offer a wide variety of products or services from an overseas or long lead-time source. Either expedited transportation (e.g., air freight) or large inventory investment must be made. Local sources provide shorter lead times, which in turn reduce the amount of safety stock inventory required. As long as customer-required lead times are less than the lead times associated with sourcing overseas, high variety dictates a local strategy. Dell uses local sourcing in its customization approach, and New Balance Shoes uses local sourcing to support high variety in an industry that is otherwise nearly all offshore. When a product or service can be completely customized, then local sourcing becomes even more compelling.[12]

For High-Transportation-Cost Products

For products that are expensive to transport, local sourcing clearly has a transportation cost advantage. If a local source can maintain the present and future factor cost differential below the transportation cost differential, then local sourcing becomes imperative. Products such as automobiles, coal, and cement that have high transportation costs relative to inventory costs or a relatively high weight per unit value fall in this category. For the U.S. market, it is not so much importing cars from outside the United States that led to the loss of market share for GM and Ford, but the performance of foreign manufacturers within North America itself.

For Innovative or Early Life-Cycle Products and Services

When products or services are in the early stages of their life cycles where designs are unstable and change rapidly, local sourcing in a developed country may be an advantage. Similarly, if the more innovative customers reside in a developed country, locating close to them may be an advantage. That said, many low-cost locations have developed impressive design skills and apply them to develop a wide range of products and services, not

---

[11] These advantages of proximity and cost can sometimes be obtained for developed economies by sourcing in a location that is close by. Sourcing in Mexico for U.S. companies and sourcing in Eastern Europe from Western European countries gives some advantages of proximity and cost.

[12] Some services such as IT can be customized offshore and these are exceptions.

just low-end or simple commodities. The advanced economies in general can generate an innovation advantage, but such an advantage is only relevant for certain types of products. Typically, a high-margin, low-manufacturing-cost product, such as pharmaceuticals, will see little advantage through offshoring its production to a low-cost location. Indeed such a company may want to produce in one high-cost location because of scale considerations and proximity to its R&D organization.

Temporary Sourcing Advantages Require Flexibility

Offshoring advantages are temporary. The histories of Japan, Korea, Taiwan, Singapore, and Hong Kong illustrate that internal pressures and changes in wage rates and standards of living lead to a reduction in the cost advantages of low-cost locations over a number of years. (See, for example, Exhibit 5.6, showing fluctuations in labor rates.) Thus, a sourcing strategy focusing on a particular overseas location, such as China, may need to change. Companies must be prepared to modify their sourcing strategies and contractors may need to think about how to manage their assets as these changes take place. For a buyer, this may simply mean looking for other sources or using multiple sources in the long term. For a contractor who has made a sizable investment in a particular location, it may mean thinking about how to keep such a location competitive as factor costs go up, or how to be flexible to move to other locations. Contractors such as Flextronics and Foxconn have made major investments in southern China, partly in capital equipment but also in the infrastructure to support complexes of over 100,000 workers. It is not clear how flexible such investments will remain in the future.

Offshoring Summary

In summary, outsourcing and offshoring are extremely powerful, and companies that do not recognize the trade-offs can be ruined. However, there are some situations where sourcing within a local market can be advantageous. A firm must also recognize the temporary aspect of some offshoring situations.

Managing Suppliers

We have talked at a strategic level about the roles of suppliers, the types of relationships a firm might have with its suppliers, how to match roles to relationships, and the special case of sourcing overseas. We now turn to the task of implementing the supplier relationships and managing them over time. We address the things that have to be done in managing the supplier network and then the infrastructure that is needed to get those things done. We close this section with a discussion of the management of contract manufacturers in particular.

The Task of Collaborating With and Integrating Suppliers

Collaborating with and integrating suppliers to achieve competitive performance of an entire supply chain requires coordinating production or service delivery plans, quality management, and design and development.

To coordinate production and service delivery plans, buyers and suppliers up and down the supply chain must share information about forecasts, production or service delivery capacities and schedules, and inventory availability. This information must be shared in close to real time in supply networks that have implemented lean thinking, as suppliers respond in short lead times with relatively small quantities. There are a number of ways of creating the required level of information sharing:

- Co-location of highly interdependent stages of the process facilitates rapid and face-to-face exchange of information.
- Vendor-managed inventories (VMIs) concentrate information management at the vendor.
- Incentives such as buybacks and revenue sharing reduce double marginalization to achieve better, if not perfect, coordination.
- Electronic communication and coordination of schedules when orders are based on an automated pull system prevents generation of a constant stream of purchase orders.
- Streamlined authority for ordering, such as in a JIT II arrangement, reduces the amount of information that must be communicated.

Implementing these techniques and smoothly sharing planning and scheduling information, however, is not trivial. Collaborative forecasting relationships, for example, have proven difficult to implement in many cases. The most successful implementations have been between companies that already had an established relationship and were willing to spend time hashing out differences in their forecasting methods and definitions of demand.

The coordination of quality performance throughout a supply chain is often done through relatively extensive inspection and testing at each stage. Quality problems are best identified at the source, so should be found and fixed at the supplier's rather than at the buyer's facility. Organizations with advanced quality programs limit inspection and achieve quality through process control based on dynamic collection of process data and worker-based problem-solving methods. These organizations often provide quality training for their suppliers and even engage in joint problem solving around supplier quality issues. Some processes, such as wafer fabrication, though, have inherent quality issues that are best handled by testing. And yet others find that it is more cost-effective to inspect all items received from a supplier, discard the ones that do not meet specifications, and tell the supplier to improve or lose the business.

The amount of interaction and collaboration required to coordinate design and development depends on whether or not the outsourced design is clearly specified and has well-defined interfaces with other elements of the design. When specifications are clear, little interaction or communication outside the specification statement is required. When specifications are less clear, far more interaction is required. In extreme cases, members of the design supplier's staff may reside at the buyer's site to engage in ongoing conversations about the design. Information technologies such as product data management (PDM) systems can be used to coordinate design, but creating firewalls around the proprietary information in these systems so that the design supplier sees only what is necessary can be difficult.

In general, the more strategic the relationship, the more critical communication and information sharing is. Collaborative relationships are not always successful. To create a strategic partnership both parties need to see the value of collaboration, make the investment, and then realize the gains from the relationship. Toyota is held up as an exemplar in the development of an infrastructure and set of interorganizational processes to facilitate transfer of tacit and explicit knowledge throughout its supplier network (Dyer and Hatch 2004). It uses three key processes to do so:

1. Supplier associations provide a forum in which Toyota can share information with and elicit information from its suppliers. At regular meetings suppliers share information about market trends, production plans, and policies and have more extensive interactions about cost, quality, and safety performance. The association focuses on achieving very specific targets as well as on training and development of members of the supply network.

2. Consulting services run out of Toyota's Operations Management Consulting Division (OMCD) actively work with suppliers to teach about and implement the Toyota Production System (TPS). Suppliers in turn are expected to share what they learn with other suppliers in the network.

3. Voluntary learning teams, also organized by the OMCD, bring together groups of suppliers to work together on productivity and quality improvements. The teams are encouraged to explore new ideas and applications of the TPS together.

Use of these three mechanisms has improved the performance of Toyota's supplier network by passing along TPS techniques from Toyota itself and by allowing suppliers to form tighter relationships with one another that allow them to share knowledge and problem solve together.

Not all companies are as sophisticated as Toyota in its ability to develop its supplier network. Nonetheless, production and supply chain planning, quality, and design and development are three areas where companies have developed successful collaborative relationships, even though the challenges are often significant.

Critical Success Factors in Supplier Management

Managing suppliers in today's highly dispersed and networked business environment is a far greater challenge than it ever has been. Most companies outsource more of their work, making them more reliant on their suppliers and creating complex and difficult integration problems. The role of the procurement function in most companies has evolved significantly as a result, requires far more senior management attention, and employs more highly skilled personnel than it has in the past. Here we address two of the factors—executive leadership and management controls—buyers and suppliers up and down the supply chain find are critical to managing procurement in today's world.

Leadership, at both the individual and executive levels, is critical to managing supplier relationships (Useem and Harder 2000). Executives must signal the importance of the procurement function to the organization, act as advocates for it, be involved in establishing the appropriate supply chain structure, and proactively design the supplier management process to be successful. In short, they must do much of the strategic thinking described earlier in this chapter and lead the organization in implementing those strategies, keeping a long-term focus while managing day-to-day execution (Handfield et al. 2000).

Supplier management also requires management controls in the form of a strong procurement team, information technology support, and performance measurement (Quinn 1999). The status of procurement organizations has changed significantly as companies have reduced the number of suppliers they engage and have placed greater responsibility on the remaining suppliers. Procurement personnel are no longer responsible solely for price negotiation and boilerplate contract administration. Instead, individuals in the organization must be able to think strategically in the assessment of suppliers, development of supplier relationships, negotiation of incentives and contracts, and integration of the suppliers into the firm (Useem and Harder 2000).

Information technology to manage supplier networks is also becoming increasingly sophisticated. Private eHubs or extranets use what some call "metaprise" software to create a common platform for automating transactions and sharing information. These eHubs integrate with firm-specific enterprise management systems; allow the unsophisticated members of the network to automate their processes; provide visibility to inventories, forecasts, point-of-sale data, and production plans throughout the network; integrate sourcing tools such as those to support requests for quotation (RFQ) and auctions; and aggregate demand for purposes of price negotiation.[13]

Management controls also include performance measurement systems that link the performance of procurement to the rest of the company and provide clear guidance for suppliers. Supplier performance improvement relies on determining cost of ownership, setting short-term improvement goals, and then measuring long-term performance (Handfield et al. 2000). Suppliers are frequently measured along the same lines we have talked about in characterizing a business strategy: cost, quality, availability, features and innovativeness, and environmental performance. They are also evaluated on the basis of the capabilities they have and can offer to the buying firm.

When executive leadership and management controls are not sufficient to gain required improvements in supplier performance, there are a number of approaches that the organization can undertake to remedy the situation (Handfield et al. 2000). If the supplier lacks commitment to the relationship, the buyer might make clear to the supplier where it stands, tie the supplier relationship more closely to performance improvement, concretely illustrate the benefits of the relationship, and ensure follow-up by assigning a supplier champion. If the supplier lacks sufficient resources to meet the buyer's needs, the buyer might simplify improvement requirements, draw on its own resources to offer personnel support, and offer training for the supplier's staff.

Often the issues that arise in a buyer-supplier relationship are not so one-sided, and the buyer must reflect on its own role in the relationship (Handfield et al. 2000). If the buyer finds a lack of trust, it may assign an ombudsman to work through the situation, or it may just minimize its legal involvement, protecting its own confidential information and spelling out the requirements of the situation clearly. If it finds that there is a mismatch of organization cultures, it may have to adapt itself to the supplier's culture or create an expectations roadmap that allows the two cultures to interact. If it finds that there are insufficient inducements to the supplier to improve its performance, it can offer better financial incentives, offer repeat business, or design motivation into the contract in other ways, such as providing the supplier an opportunity to develop its own capabilities.

Despite all the firm's efforts to create healthy and effective supplier relationships, even the strongest relationships can deteriorate (Anderson and Jap 2005). To avoid this "dark side" of supplier relationships, the firm can reevaluate older relationships, develop backups, develop common goals, and not allow conflicts to linger. Some organizations are better than others at managing their supplier relationships. Exhibit 6.13 shows the five levels of procurement organization maturity from beginner to world class.

Becoming a world-class supplier management organization that provides competitive differentiation for the firm requires active executive leadership, highly skilled procurement personnel, well-constructed performance metrics, integrated information systems, and constant attention to the many ways in which supplier relationships can fail.

---

[13] http://logistics.about.com/library/weekly/uc010101b.htm, July 17, 2006.

EXHIBIT 6.13 Procurement Organization Maturity Model

Source: Adapted from Billington & Horenstein, e3 associates, inspired by Software Capability Maturity Model developed by the Software Engineering Institute at Carnegie Mellon University, http://e3associates.com/images/procurement%20maturity%20model.pdf, August 11, 2006.

Level of Maturity	Role	Typical Activities	Procurement Organization Value Measured By:	Results for the Organization
Beginner	Administrator	Issue POs. Make it safe and easy to buy things. Reactive environment.	Tolerable level of complaints.	Understand total spend. Price at or above market.
Basic	Advisor	Shop the world. Have basic commodity knowledge. Understand costs and technology. Make good, but primarily reactive, decisions aligned with enterprise needs.	Period-to-period price takedowns.	Understand total spend and market opportunities. Price at or below market.
Competitive	Process enabler	Influence suppliers to get preferred treatment. Understand costs, availability, market trends, and risk. Primarily reactive environment.	Period-to-period price takedowns.	No surprises. Excellent price—better than market—and assurance of supply.
Leader	Contributing partner	Process focused, tool-enabled environment. Worldwide access to suppliers for materials and services. Decisions are well thought out and holistic in context. Primarily proactive environment.	Total economic value.	Better total costs.
World Class	Competitive differentiator	Create clear and defined competitive advantages for enterprise enabled by automated tools and processes. Proactive environment.	Total economic value created.	Leader in market.

The Special Case of Contract Manufacturing in the Electronics Industry

Contract manufacturing began to be used heavily in the 1990s as computer and other electronics manufacturers identified and focused on their core competencies and outsourced production. (See Chapter 2 for a description of Hewlett-Packard's transition.) At first, they just outsourced printed circuit board assembly. Then they began contracting out assembly and test of entire products and eventually began outsourcing the services associated with production, including process engineering and a variety of procurement functions. While this allowed many OEMs to improve their cost structures and in some cases quality and availability as well, it also exposed them to increased risk. In particular, allowing contract manufacturers (CMs) to manage the procurement activities associated with production—from supplier selection through contract negotiation to supplier management—creates significant vulnerabilities for the OEM.

There are three flows that procurement functions handle: physical flows of goods and materials; information flows of instructions, reports, and data; and financial flows.

Associated with each flow are planning, execution, and management activities. When responsibility for any one of these activities is ceded to a CM, the CM gains power that it can exploit in ways that are unfavorable to the OEM. Exhibit 6.14 provides examples of ways in which CMs can take advantage of these vulnerabilities.

There are a number of tactical solutions for dealing with these risks as shown in Exhibit 6.15. More importantly, there are alternative means of structuring the relationships with contract manufacturers to mitigate the risks. OEMs may choose among the following types of relationships:

- Turnkey procurement: CM performs the full procurement function, negotiating and buying directly from suppliers.
- Turnkey procurement with audits: CM performs the full procurement function, but OEM audits prices and quantities.

EXHIBIT 6.14   Examples of Risks Associated with Subcontracting Procurement Activities to Contract Manufacturers

Source: Adapted from Amaral et al. "Outsourcing Production Without Losing Control," *Supply Chain Management Review,* 2004. Reprinted with permission.

	Physical: Efficient and effective movement of goods and materials	Informational: Timely, clear, and secure communication of instructions, reports, and data	Financial: Improved cash-to-cash performance and compliance with legal and regulatory requirements
Planning: Robust determination of future requirements	When the CM is given authority to determine the capacity and materials required, it can guide the choices of whom and how much to its own advantage.	The CM may not be as concerned about providing good-quality forecasts to suppliers as the OEM would be, thus jeopardizing the OEM's relationship with the suppliers.	If the CM is allowed to choose suppliers and negotiate contracts with them, it can make self-serving or myopic decisions that could lead to unexpected damage to the OEM's brand should the supplier not perform.
Execution: Reliable and responsive completion of current actions	When the CM controls physical inventories, it can divert materials flows to unintended uses.	When the CM decides how much to order from each supplier, it may or may not follow OEM guidelines for sharing the work, possibly pocketing differences in costs or creating ill will between the OEM and suppliers.	When the CM controls cash flows to and from suppliers, it can obscure visibility into individual transactions or leverage agreements for its own benefit.
Management: Resolution of issues and continuous improvement of performance	If the CM supervises the rebalancing of inventory across locations, it can optimize its own profit and pass along expediting costs to the OEM.	If the CM is in charge of monitoring the performance of suppliers, it can manipulate data and hide negligent actions.	If the CM is in charge of monitoring costs and developing suppliers, it can retain financial benefits, create charges, and underinvest in support.

EXHIBIT 6.15
Approaches to Safeguard against Risks of Outsourcing Procurement Functions to Contract Manufacturers

Source: Amaral et al., "Outsourcing Production Without Losing Control," *Supply Chain Management Review,* 2004. Reprinted with permission.

	Physical	Informational	Financial
Planning	• Make path preferences clear and explicit • Track and audit purchases by part and supplier	• Monitor and help reduce forecast errors • Communicate forecast ranges and flexibility requirements • Share the cost of inventory liability or shortages with the CM	• Establish codes of conduct for all suppliers and investigate compliance • Maintain "veto" power regarding which parts and suppliers are used • Obtain warranties from CMs protecting against poor quality or patent violations
Execution	• Track and audit part quantities and usages (including "defective" and "scrap") • Request OEM-specific stocking locations	• Make part and supplier preferences clear and explicit • Track and audit transactions by part and supplier • Maintain relationships with suppliers and meet with them periodically	• Employ price-making mechanisms to prevent disclosure of OEM-specific supplier prices • Refuse to accept summary invoices • Audit transactions for accuracy • Maintain relationships with suppliers and ensure that CMs are making timely payments
Management	• Retain ability to transfer parts to alternative locations, even to those of alternative CMs • Require preapproval of expediting over a certain limit • Share responsibility of expediting costs to better align incentives	• Jointly collect, manage, and interpret performance data and metrics • Request detailed transactions data, not simply summary reports • Collaboratively decide on root causes and corrective actions • Audit data for discrepancies that could indicate potential errors or manipulation	• Make contract terms explicit, such as the speed of cost increases/reductions and liability for engineering changes and excess inventory • Monitor and audit these contract terms • Appropriately compensate service providers for risk-sharing, quality-of-support, and other desirable behavior

- Supplier rebates: CM buys parts on behalf of the OEM at a standard list price and then rebates the difference between the list price and the OEM's privately negotiated price to the OEM.
- Buy-sell: OEM buys directly from the supplier at a private price and sells to CM at a different rate, but all inventory is drop-shipped to the CM.
- Consignment: OEM buys and owns the inventory, which is stored at the CM.
- In-house: OEM buys directly from suppliers, managing storage and transit to CMs.

Each of these structures mitigates the risks described in Exhibit 6.14 to a different degree, as shown in Exhibit 6.16. Turnkey procurement is the most risky of the structures,

EXHIBIT 6.16 How Procurement Models Deal with Procurement Risks

Source: Amaral, et al., "Outsourcing Production Without Losing Control," *Supply Chain Management Review,* 2004. Reprinted with permission.

Where OEMs Can Be Exploited	Turnkey	Turnkey with Audits	Supplier Rebates	Buy-Sell	Consignment	In-house
1. Planning - Physical — The CM can guide the "who" and "how much" decisions to its own advantage	not mitigated	not mitigated	not mitigated	fully mitigated	fully mitigated	fully mitigated
2. Planning - Informational — The CM can hide the questionable intent or quality of its forecasts within the "errors" that will inevitably occur	not mitigated	not mitigated	not mitigated	partially mitigated	fully mitigated	fully mitigated
3. Planning - Financial — The CM controls the preferential treatment and can make self-serving supplier selection decisions	not mitigated	not mitigated	partially mitigated	fully mitigated	fully mitigated	fully mitigated
4. Execution - Physical — The CM gains physical possession of materials and can divert them toward unintended uses	not mitigated	not mitigated	not mitigated	not mitigated	partially mitigated	fully mitigated
5. Execution - International — The CM can place actual orders that differ from the OEM's guidelines	not mitigated	partially mitigated	partially mitigated	fully mitigated	fully mitigated	fully mitigated
6. Execution - Financial — The CM can obscure visibility into individual transactions or charges and negotiate similar supplier pricing for itself	not mitigated	partially mitigated	partially mitigated	fully mitigated	fully mitigated	fully mitigated
7. Management - Physical — The CM can rebalance inventory to optimize its own profit while passing along expediting costs	not mitigated	not mitigated	not mitigated	partially mitigated	partially mitigated	fully mitigated
8. Management - International — The CM can manipulate performance data and hide negligent actions	not mitigated	partially mitigated	partially mitigated	partially mitigated	partially mitigated	fully mitigated
9. Management - Financial — The CM can retain financial benefits, create charges, and underinvest in support	not mitigated	partially mitigated	partially mitigated	partially mitigated	partially mitigated	fully mitigated

KEY: = hazard is fully mitigated   = hazard is partially mitigated   = hazard is not mitigated while maintaining procurement in house is the least risky. OEMs must assess the extent to which each of the risks exists and then structure its relationships accordingly. Once structured, the OEM must use the tactical tools of Exhibit 6.15 to further reduce the risks inherent in the chosen structure.

Summary

In this chapter we have covered the major strategic questions that a company must answer in establishing its sourcing strategy: How many suppliers should it have in all, and how many for each item purchased? What roles should its suppliers play, and how should the relationships with those suppliers be structured? How should suppliers be motivated? Under what conditions should a company source overseas? How should the procurement function be structured and managed, and how should the risks of outsourcing be mitigated? We close with a brief example of how United Technologies Corporation (UTC) manages its supplier relationships and a six-step process for creating a sourcing strategy.

A Closing Example

United Technologies maintains a large number of sourcing relationships across its variety of businesses. Managing suppliers across these businesses requires a significant amount of discipline and structure. The corporation set up a central group to address the common challenges and to implement the structure. Exhibit 6.17 presents the eight-step approach that it developed. Each of the steps also required a set of formal documentation, and there were major reviews at the end of steps one, three, and seven.

Seven-Step Sourcing Strategy Development Process

In this chapter we have emphasized the importance of sourcing strategies in companies that engage in a considerable amount of outsourcing. But companies that are highly vertically integrated must pay attention to their sourcing strategies as well. The way in which a company's suppliers are organized and managed can play an important role in helping that company achieve competitive advantage. So, regardless of a company's level of vertical integration, it needs to consider the following steps in developing a sourcing strategy:

Step 1: Determine the Critical Components, Products, or Services to Be Outsourced
Using the vertical integration strategy development framework described in Chapter 2, decide which materials, components, products, services, and processing equipment will be

EXHIBIT 6.17 **UTC Eight-Step Procurement Process**

Source: United Technologies. Reprinted with permission.

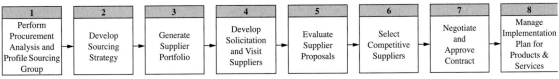

outsourced. Outsourced services may include procurement, design, information technology management, and various human resources functions. Generally the items to be outsourced are those that are not core to the business or critical to the mission of the business. All others are outsourcing candidates.

Step 2: Identify Which Products or Services Should Be Sourced Overseas

Identify the products and services for which factor costs are critical and consider alternatives for offshoring and possibly outsourcing them. Identify the products and services—those with high variety, those with high transportation cost, and those early in their life cycles—and consider sourcing them in developing countries with higher factor costs but better access and lower transportation costs. Determine where these products and services should be sourced in conjunction with the facilities and supply chain strategies.

Step 3: Determine the Number of Suppliers

Decide how many suppliers in total the company wants to work with, which will in turn dictate the structure of the resultant supplier network and the architecture of the firm's products or services. Working with a small number of suppliers implies a hierarchical network with a few first-tier suppliers that have responsibility for major modules of the product or subtasks of the service.

For any given outsourced item, decide how many suppliers to support. Use a single supplier when the item being sourced is unique, when the technology underlying the item is relatively stable, when using that item is critical to the company's brand, and when the volume purchased is not too large a proportion of the supplier's business. When in doubt about a supplier's viability or reliability, when competition among suppliers is beneficial, or when suppliers are too small to reasonably support the company's volume, consider a larger number of suppliers. Unless procuring a commodity where arm's-length relationships are acceptable, a limited number of suppliers is best.

Step 4: Determine the Organizational Relationship

Choose a role for each of the suppliers based on what is being sourced from the supplier as well as the supplier's position in the supply network (e.g., providing market access with low competence). Evaluate where on the spectrum of supplier relationships—arm's length to near full vertical integration—to place the supplier, given its role and criticality to the organization.

Step 5: Determine the Levels of Engagement and the Risk Management Methods

The volume of purchases and criticality of the items purchased to the organization suggest the importance of the relationship to the company. Based on the importance of the relationship, buyers and suppliers both determine the amount of investment they wish to have in one another. They may maintain a market exchange relationship with no investment in one another, invest heavily in each other, or have an asymmetrical relationship in which only one invests heavily. The level of investment in turn suggests the characteristics of the relationship. Based on those characteristics and the specific tasks being outsourced, a company can then develop a set of risk management methods.

Step 6: Determine Any Contracts and Incentives for the Relationship

Basic contracts include pricing as well as other terms and conditions for how issues such as changes in demand, quality problems, and various contract breaches will be handled. More sophisticated contracts provide flexibility to both parties to deal with uncertainty, and others allow for the parties to work together to optimize the performance of the supply chain overall. Such incentives include buybacks, revenue sharing, returns, and other financial incentives.

Step 7: Establish the Appropriate Procurement Management Structure

Provide strong executive leadership, hire appropriate talent in the procurement organization, set up performance metrics to measure both suppliers and the performance of the procurement organization itself, and implement information systems to support internal decision making and communicate appropriate information with suppliers.

Cisco's supplier relationships are absolutely critical to its success. It clearly understands which suppliers are most important to achieving competitive success and structures its relationships with them to ensure they share the same vision and objectives for performance as Cisco. This chapter has covered a number of the tools and techniques Cisco might have used in doing so.

Appendix **A**

Revenue-Sharing Calculations[14]

The following revenue-sharing calculations make the following assumptions:

- Supplier cost to make the widget = $5.00
- Wholesale price to the retailer = $7.50
- Retail price to the consumer = $10.00
- Salvage value at the end of a selling cycle = $3.75
- Demand for the widget is uniformly distributed from 15 through 20, meaning that any value of demand from 15 through 20 inclusive is equally likely
- The retailer can order anywhere from 15 through 20 units

The full set of calculations for this case is shown in Exhibit 6.A1. Here is how the calculations for each cell are performed. In the case in which the retailer orders 15 units, it will receive a profit of $2.50 (retail price at which the item is sold less wholesale price at which the item was purchased) for each of the 15 units it sells for a total profit of $37.50. The supplier also makes $2.50 per unit, so also makes $37.50, and the total supply chain profit is $75. If the retailer orders 20 units and demand is only 15, then its income will be the revenue from the 15 units that were sold ($2.50 × 15 = $37.50) minus the cost of the remaining 5 units less their salvage value [($7.50 − $3.75) × 5 = $18.75] for total profit of $18.75. The supplier in this case will make $50 (20 × $2.50), and the total supply chain profit is $68.75. The best choices for the retailer, supplier, and supply chain are highlighted in Exhibit 6.A1. The retailer maximizes its profits by ordering 17 units, while the supplier maximizes its profits when the retailer orders 20 units. Total profits for the supply chain are maximized when the retailer orders 19 units.

[14] Methods drawn from Narayanan, "Supply Chain Close-Up: The Video Vault," Teaching Note. Harvard Business School Publishing, 2003.

EXHIBIT 6.A1   Supply Chain Profits–Based Case without Revenue Sharing

Source: Methods drawn from Narayanan, "Supply Chain Close-Up: The Video Vault," Harvard Business School Publishing, 2003.

		Number of Units to Stock					
Demand (units)		15	16	17	18	19	20
	15	$37.50	$33.75	$30.00	$26.25	$22.50	$18.75
	16	$37.50	$40.00	$36.25	$32.50	$28.75	$25.00
	17	$37.50	$40.00	$42.50	$38.75	$35.00	$31.25
	18	$37.50	$40.00	$42.50	$45.00	$41.25	$37.50
	19	$37.50	$40.00	$42.50	$45.00	$47.50	$43.75
	20	$37.50	$40.00	$42.50	$45.00	$47.50	$50.00
Expected retailer profits		$37.50	$38.96	$39.38	$38.75	$37.08	$34.38
Supplier profits		$37.50	$40.00	$42.50	$45.00	$47.50	$50.00
Expected supply chain profits		$75.00	$78.96	$81.88	$83.75	$84.58	$84.38
Expected fill rate		86.54%	91.20%	94.82%	97.46%	99.17%	100.00%

EXHIBIT 6.A2   Supply Chain Profits with Retailer Returns

Source: Methods drawn from "Narayanan, "Supply Chain Close-Up: The Video Vault," Harvard Business School Publishing, 2003.

Demand (units)	15	16	17	18	19	20
Expected retailer profits	$37.50	$39.46	$40.88	$41.75	$42.08	$41.88
Supplier profits	$37.50	$39.50	$41.00	$42.00	$42.50	$42.00
Expected supply chain profits	$75.00	$78.96	$81.88	$83.75	$84.58	$84.38
Expected fill rate	86.54%	91.20%	94.82%	97.46%	99.17%	100.00%

EXHIBIT 6.A3   Supply Chain Profits under Consignment

Source: Methods drawn from Narayanan, "Supply Chain Close-Up: The Video Vault," Harvard Business School Publishing, 2003.

Demand (units)	15	16	17	18	19	20
Expected retailer profits	$37.50	$39.58	$41.25	$42.50	$43.33	$43.75
Supplier profits	$37.50	$39.38	$40.63	$41.25	$41.25	$40.63
Expected supply chain profits	$75.00	$78.96	$81.88	$83.75	$84.58	$84.38
Expected fill rate	86.54%	91.20%	94.82%	97.46%	99.17%	100.00%

EXHIBIT 6.A4   Supply Chain Profits under Revenue Sharing

Source: Methods drawn from Narayanan, "Supply Chain Close-Up: The Video Vault," Harvard Business School Publishing, 2003.

Demand (units)	15	16	17	18	19	20
Expected retailer profits	$37.50	$39.38	$40.63	$41.25	$41.25	$40.63
Supplier profits	$37.50	$39.58	$41.25	$42.50	$43.33	$43.75
Expected channel profits	$75.00	$78.96	$81.88	$83.75	$84.58	$84.38
Expected fill rate	86.54%	91.20%	94.82%	97.46%	99.17%	100.00%

When the supplier allows the retailer to return unsold inventory at the end of the selling season for 90 percent of the wholesale price, or $6.75 per widget, and the supplier can still sell the items at the salvage value of $3.75, the calculations are as shown in Exhibit 6.A2. With this policy, both retailer and supplier are motivated to move 19 units through the system to optimize supply chain profits.

If the supplier provides the widgets to the retailer on consignment with no limitation on inventory levels, in essence promising to take all unsold items back at wholesale price, the results are as shown in Exhibit 6.A3. Now the retailer wishes to order 20 widgets, but the supplier still wants to operate at the supply chain profit maximizing point of 19 units.

Finally, when the supplier and retailer forge a revenue-sharing agreement under which the supplier provides the widgets to the retailer at cost but recovers 25 percent of the $10 income per widget sold, the calculations are as shown in Exhibit 6.A4. Now the retailer wishes once again to get 20 units, while the supplier prefers the supply chain optimizing number of 19 widgets. Various adjustments to the revenue-sharing arrangement can be made to entice both retailer and supplier to choose the optimal 19 units.

References

Amaral, Jason, Corey A. Billington, and Andy A. Tsay. "Outsourcing Production Without Losing Control." *Supply Chain Management Review,* 8, no.8 (November–December 2004), pp. 44–52.

Anderson, Erin, and Sandy D. Jap. "The Dark Side of Close Relationships." *MIT Sloan Management Review* 46, no. 3 (Spring 2005), pp. 75–82.

Bensaou, M. "Interorganizational Cooperation: The Role of Information Technology. An Empirical Comparison of U.S. and Japanese Supplier Relations." *Information Systems Research* 8, no. 2 (1997), pp. 107–124.

Bensaou, M. "Portfolios of Buyer-Supplier Relationships." *MIT Sloan Management Review* 40, no. 4 (Summer 1999), pp. 35–44.

Bensaou, M., and N. Venkatraman. "Configurations of Interorganizational Relationships: A Comparison between U.S. and Japanese Automakers." *Management Science* 41, no. 9 (1995), pp. 1471–1492.

Bhote, K. *Strategic Supply Management—A Blueprint for Revitalizing the Manufacturer Supplier Partnership.* New York: American Management Association, 1989.

CIO Magazine. "What Went Wrong at Cisco." August 1, 2001, http://www.cio.com/archive/080101/cisco.html.

Clark, Kim B., and Takahiro Fujimoto. *Product Development Performance: Strategy, Organization, and Management in the World Auto Industry.* Boston, MA: Harvard Business School Press, 1991.

Dyer, Jeffrey, and Nile W. Hatch. "Using Supplier Networks to Learn Faster." *MIT Sloan Management Review,* 45, no. 3 (Spring 2004). pp 57–63.

Galbraith, Jay R. *Designing Complex Organizations.* Boston, MA: Addison Wesley, 1973.

Handfield, Robert B., Daniel R. Krause; Thomas V. Scannell, and Robert M. Monczka. "Avoid the Pitfalls in Supplier Development." *MIT Sloan Management Review* 41, no. 2 (Winter 2000), pp. 37–49.

Hsu, Mindy. "Improving Customer Service Levels through Centralized Supply Flexibility." MIT master's thesis, 2006.

Krause, D.R. "Supplier Development: Current Practices and Outcomes." *International Journal of Purchasing and Materials Management* 33, no. 2 (1997), pp 12–19.

Krause, D.R., R.B. Handfield, and T.V. Scannell. "An Empirical Investigation of Supplier Development: Reactive and Strategic Processes." *Journal of Operations Management* 17, no. 1 (1998), pp. 39–58.

Mathur, Gita, and Robert Hayes. "Intel-PED." Harvard Business School Publishing, 693-056, 1994a.

Mathur, Gita, and Robert Hayes. "Intel-PED." Teaching note. Harvard Business School Publishing, for instructors only, 1994b.

McFarlan, F. Warren, and Brian J. Delacey. *Outsourcing IT: The Global Landscape in 2004.* Boston, MA: Harvard Business School Publishing, 2004.

Miller, James. "MIT/LFM Panel Discussion: Outsourcing and Global Competitiveness." Cisco Systems Inc., October 21, 2005.

Narayanan, V.G. "Supply Chain Close-Up: The Video Vault." Teaching note. Harvard Business School Publishing, for instructors only, 2003.

Narayanan, V.G., and Lisa Brem. "Supply Chain Close-Up: The Video Vault." Harvard Business School Publishing, 102-070, 2003.

Nolan, Richard L., Kelley Porter, and Christina Akers. "Cisco Systems Architecture: ERP and Web-Enabled IT." Harvard Business Publishing, 301099, 2005.

Pragman, Claudia H. "JIT II: A Purchasing Concept for Reducing Lead Times in Time-Based Competition—Just-in-Time Management." *Business Horizons* 39, no. 44 (1996), pp. 54–58.

Quinn, James Brian. "Strategic Outsourcing: Leveraging Knowledge Capabilities." MIT *Sloan Management Review* 40, no. 4 (Summer 1999), pp. 9–21.

Quinn, James Brian, and Frederick G. Hilmer. "Strategic Outsourcing." *MIT Sloan Management Review* 35, no. 4 (Summer 1994), pp. 43–55.

Ring, Peter Smith, Yves L. Doz, and Paul M. Olk. "Managing Formation Processes in R&D Consortia." *California Management Review* 47, no. 4 (Summer 2005), pp. 137–156.

Schmidt, Stephan. "Impact on Order Fulfillment Process Costs of Bounding Demand-Side Uncertainty through Structured Flexibility Contracts." MIT master's thesis, 2003.

Tsay, Andy A., and William S. Lovejoy. "Quantity Flexibility Contracts and Supply Chain Performance." *Manufacturing and Service Operations Management* 1, no.2 (1999), pp. 89–111.

Useem, Michael, and Joseph Harder. "Leading Laterally in Company Outsourcing." *MIT Sloan Management Review* 41, no. 2 (Winter 2000), pp. 25–36.

Vakil, Bindiya. "Design Outsourcing in the High-Tech Industry and Its Impact on Supply Chain Strategies." MIT master's thesis, 2005.

Watts, C., and C. Hahn. "Supplier Development Programs: An Empirical Analysis." *International Journal of Purchasing and Materials Management* 29, no. 2 (1993), pp. 11–17.

Womack, James P., Daniel T. Jones, and Daniel Roos. *The Machine That Changed the World.* New York: HarperCollins, 1990.

7

Business Process–Focused Strategies and Organizational Design

Introduction

In 1975, Amancio Ortega lost a large lingerie order from a German wholesaler. In desperation, he opened a shop to liquidate the excess inventory and called it Zara. Today Zara is the flagship brand of the Spanish fashion group Inditex and boasts over 720 stores in 54 countries. Between 1991 and 2003, Inditex's sales—more than 70 percent of which are accounted for directly or indirectly by Zara—grew more than 12-fold and its net profits 14-fold. In recent years, while many of its competitors have performed poorly, Zara's sales and net income have continued to grow at an annual rate of over 20 percent (Ferdows et al. 2004). What is the secret to Zara's success? It identified an unmet market need—high-fashion clothing sold at low prices—and filled that need using well-integrated and highly responsive product generation and order fulfillment processes that broke all the rules of supply chain management in the fashion industry.

Ortega believed that consumers regarded clothes as a perishable commodity to be consumed quickly just like yogurt, bread, or fish, so went about building a retail business that provided "freshly baked clothes" (Dutta 2002). Further, Ortega's early scare with the German wholesaler provided him with a valuable lesson: To be successful, "you need to have five fingers touching the factory and five touching the customer" (Ferdows et al. 2004). This translated into the creation of a vertically-integrated business model covering design, just-in-time production, marketing, and sales that allows the company to design, produce, and deliver a new garment and put it on display in its stores worldwide in six weeks. In contrast, the average high-fashion retailer spends nine months planning and delivering each season's collection. Twice-a-week deliveries to stores not only deliver the new items, but replenish old styles so stores can carry low inventories, assured that they will be able to replenish them quickly. As a result, Zara's inventory is only about 10 percent of its sales, while its rivals' average 14–15 percent.

This highly integrated process starts at the design center in La Coruña, where over 200 twenty-something designers sit together with product, procurement, and production-planning managers in the midst of Zara's centralized design and production complex. They gather suggestions daily for new cuts, fabrics, or entire product lines from store managers around the world both by phone and PDA. They weigh the inputs, decide what to make (only one-quarter of their ideas make it to production), and draw up the ideas on their computers. Completed drawings are communicated by intranet to Zara's factories where, within days, they are cut, dyed, stitched, and pressed. Three weeks later, the designs are on display in Zara's stores worldwide. Zara introduces 11,000 new garments in a typical year, many of which will only be available for a matter of weeks before being replaced (Helft 2002).

Zara's production and distribution management is centralized at La Coruña in a four-story, 5-million-square-foot building. (That's about nine times the size of Amazon.com's warehouse in Fernley, Nevada, or about 90 football fields [Helft 2002].) In stark contrast to the rest of the industry, which outsources virtually all of its production, Zara produces about half of its clothing in house using sophisticated just-in-time systems learned from Toyota. Three principles are key to the smooth performance of its supply chain: tightly integrated communications, facilitated both by a very simple, but effective information system and a very flat and highly linked organization structure; adherence to a strict schedule of orders from and shipments to its retail outlets that makes its work relatively predictable; and practical investment in capital assets, such as production lines dedicated to men's, women's, and children's clothing, that provide significant flexibility. Zara also sources most of its fabric and dyes from other Inditex companies, thus extending its supply chain control within the group.

The efficiency with which Zara's supply chain works allows it to offer a large variety of the latest designs quickly and in limited quantities, and thus collect 85 percent of the full ticket price on its retail clothing versus the industry average of 60–70 percent. Retail stores can rapidly adjust orders to respond to customer demand, so less than 10 percent of Zara's stock remains unsold, compared to an industry average of 17–20 percent. The rapid turnover of items in Zara's stores attracts significantly more customer visits, thus allowing Zara to spend only 0.3 percent of its revenues on advertising, compared to competitors that spend 3–4 percent (Ferdows et al. 2004).

In short, Zara found an unoccupied space in the market and designed its key business processes—product generation and order fulfillment in this case—to respond efficiently and effectively to the needs of that market. In doing so, it developed and fine-tuned a set of operations capabilities that made it a highly successful competitor in the fashion industry. In doing so, it answered these questions:

- On which business processes should the company focus to achieve success in this market?
- How should the company align its resources and capabilities to optimize the performance of those business processes?

In this chapter, we explore the concept of process management as a means of achieving competitive advantage and then describe three primary business processes important to many organizations: product or service generation, order fulfillment, and service and support. For each process, we discuss the importance of integrating management, process, organization, and information technology to achieve optimal process performance. We close with a section on organizational design and human resource management in operations, as these, along with information technology (described in Chapter 9), are critical cornerstones of each of the business processes. These areas represent the major infrastructural foundations of operations.

Business Process Management

The question of whether or not a firm can gain sustainable competitive advantage from investment in operational process excellence lies at the heart of the debate described in Chapter 1 between strategists, who argue that positioning is most critical, and those who argue that capabilities development is most critical (Porter 1996). There is strong empirical evidence that companies can and do achieve competitive advantage through their investments in business process excellence, often because they are much farther down the learning curve for those processes than are their competitors (Hayes and Upton 1998, Hayes and Pisano 1994). At its heart, achieving process excellence requires understanding the basic workflows in the organization and how those workflows can best be organized, structured, and managed to achieve the desired results.

Emergence of the Process-Based View

The notion of examining the workflows in an organization to streamline them or make them more effective is not new. In the early 1900s, industrial engineers Frederick Taylor and Frank and Lillian Gilbreth proposed breaking work down into small increments (tasks) that might make the work easier and more efficiently done (Taylor 1911, 1967). Known as the scientific method, some of the basic ideas underlying their thinking survive to this day in various quality management and business process reengineering (BPR) approaches. Continuous improvement and quality management methods, particularly as embedded in the well-known plan-do-check-act cycle, based on work by Walter A. Shewhart and popularized in the 1950s by W. Edwards Deming,[1] entail workflow or process analysis. Today these steps are embedded in the five-step define-measure-analyze-improve-control (DMAIC) process that is at the heart of Six Sigma programs. These methods, discussed in Chapter 10 in the context of quality management, are important to understanding and improving workflows.

Business process reengineering (BPR), popularized in the 1990s in the book *Reengineering the Corporation* (Hammer and Champy 1993), also emphasized workflow analysis. It argued that continuous improvement of existing processes was insufficient, and that sometimes radical redesign and reorganization of an enterprise was necessary to lower costs and increase quality of service. Instead of starting with existing processes and improving them over time, BPR recommended wiping the slate clean and designing new processes with revised assumptions about technology, people, and organizational goals. In particular, BPR emphasized the role that new information technologies might play in a redesigned process.[2] Seven principles underlie the BPR approach:

1. Organize around outcomes, not tasks.
2. Prioritize all of the processes in the organization in order of redesign urgency.

---

[1] http://www.balancedscorecard.org/bkgd/pdca.html, August 2, 2006.
[2] http://www.prosci.com/intro.htm, August 2, 2006.

EXHIBIT 7.1

**Process versus
Functional
Views**

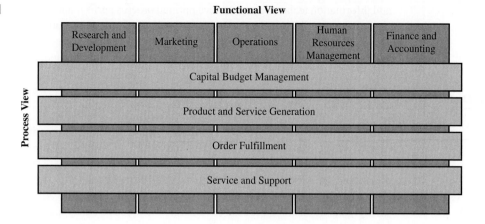

3. Integrate information processing with the work that produces the information.

4. Treat geographically dispersed resources as though they were centralized.

5. Link parallel activities in the workflow instead of just integrating their outputs.

6. Move decision making to where the work is performed, and build control into the process.

7. Capture information once and at the source.[3]

The approach forced companies to take an integrated view of their processes, examining in detail how information flows were managed and then simultaneously designing the process flow, organizational structure, and information systems to support the most efficient information flow possible. Progressive Insurance, for example, completely reinvented how it did claims processing, reducing the time for its adjustors to inspect a damaged vehicle from 7–10 days to 9 hours (Hammer 2004).

The process view that emerged from BPR examines businesses in terms of the processes they perform, such as product generation, order fulfillment, and service delivery, instead of in terms of the functions in which most firms are organized: operations, marketing, research and development, human resources, and finance and accounting (Exhibit 7.1). The BPR methodology can be applied at the level of the major processes shown in Exhibit 7.1 or for subprocesses such as procurement, which is subsumed in order fulfillment, or service prototyping, which is included in product and service generation. The business process view focuses on what matters to the customer and forces the organization to examine those activities with a cross-functional view to optimizing their performance.

In sum, business process reengineering built upon well-understood concepts of process analysis and design but raised the application of those concepts to a new level. It caused firms to shift their focus from operational improvement to operational innovation, thus developing a capability for process redesign that offered them the prospect of sustainable competitive advantage (Hammer 2004). In doing so, it has shifted the focus of the firm from functional excellence to customer-driven process excellence.

---

[3] http://searchcio.techtarget.com/sDefinition/0,,sid19_gci536451,00.html, August 2, 2006.

EXHIBIT 7.2
Transformation Process with Inputs and Outputs

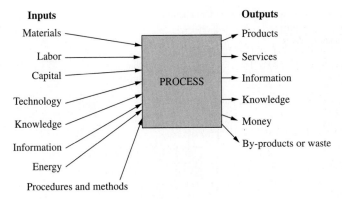

Process and Value-Stream Mapping

In simplest terms, a process flow shows the inputs to the process, including materials, labor, energy, knowledge, information, and capital, and the outputs from the process, including the desired product, service, or transaction, as well as knowledge or information generated and other by-products (Exhibit 7.2). There are two widely used tools that support process analysis: process mapping, which is generally used in applications of business process reengineering and Six Sigma, and value stream mapping, which is used to map physical flows, particularly in applications of lean operations.

Process Mapping

Process mapping is a hierarchical method to describe how a transaction is processed. It is a visual representation of a workflow that shows the stream of activities involved in converting a set of inputs to a desired set of outputs. High-level process maps, or "30,000 foot overviews," are used to scope new projects and set boundaries around the portion of the process to be examined, while detailed process maps are used to analyze the process, identify potential causes of problems, and suggest improvements.[4]

Exhibit 7.3 shows a highly simplified and generic process map for a nine-step process that involves five people. The process is initiated by the customer who may place an order or submit an inquiry to the company. To fulfill the customer's request, four people within the company get involved, three of them more than once, in completing the eight remaining steps of the process. The process map quickly shows people who work within the process as well as others who may be less familiar with the process what the entire flow looks like and where critical interactions within it lie. Often, upon examination of such a process map, changes to make the process more efficient become obvious. In this stylized example it may make sense to consolidate some of the work so that fewer people are involved in the process, thus entailing fewer handoffs, fewer opportunities for communications errors, and a shorter throughput time (Exhibit 7.4). Such a change requires both redesign of the process as well as reallocation of tasks in the organization. There are a number of software tools that support the generation of process maps, including Microsoft Visio, SigmaFlow, and iGrafx.

[4] http://www.isixsigma.com/dictionary/Process_Map-101.htm, August 2, 2006.

EXHIBIT 7.3
Generic
Process
Mapping
Example

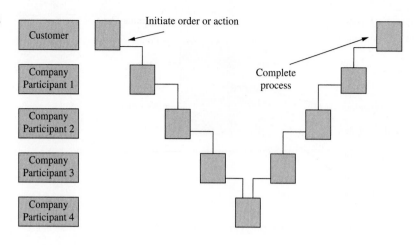

An Example of Process Mapping

A more detailed example of a real-world process mapping exercise is illustrative. A multi-billion-dollar manufacturer of electronic equipment learned that some of its competitors were able to fully install new systems at their customers' sites in less time than it took just to schedule the order. It decided that it needed to look at the order-to-invoice process flow and to significantly reduce the lead time associated with that flow. It developed the "as-is" process map in Exhibit 7.5 to learn more about the steps in the process, who was executing them, and why it was taking so long. In this chart, the partner places an order with the company, which launches a process that includes sales, finance, operations, and suppliers in some manual and some automated activity to complete the order. Finance personnel, for example, must book the order in the Oracle information system and later are triggered to send an invoice once the order is shipped.

EXHIBIT 7.4
Generic
Process Map
with
Improvements

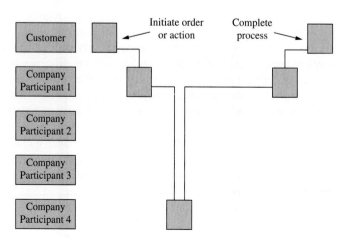

EXHIBIT 7.5 As-Is Process Map

Shaded boxes indicate a process step that is completed manually. Unshaded boxes indicate steps that are automated.

Source: Printed with permission from PRTM, a global management consulting firm, based on work performed at Network Appliance, Incorporated. Copyright 2006 PRTM, Inc.

"As-Is" Quote to Invoice Process Flow Diagram

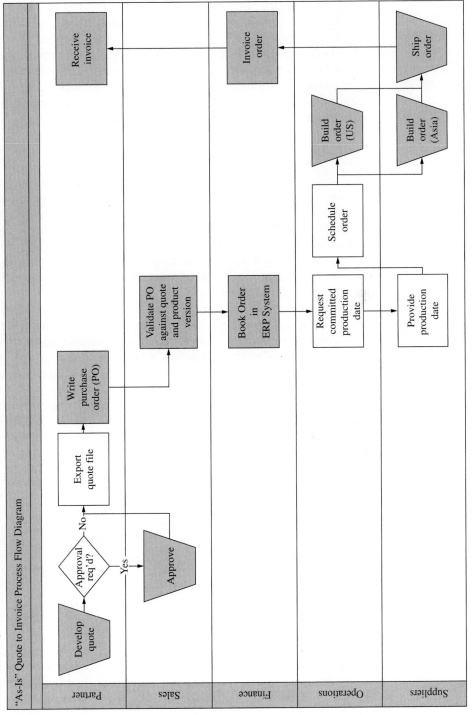

After studying the process and identifying the steps that took the most time, the company invested in information systems that will allow it to automate many of the internal steps in the quote-to-invoice process, thus reducing the order and invoice processing time from five days to five minutes, and also provide its partners with increased visibility into what is happening with their orders. In the new process, shown in Exhibit 7.6, the sales organization only manually handles those quotes that require approval, and the finance organization no longer manually handles the order at all. The partner, too, completes more work automatically and receives additional notifications as to the status of its orders—e.g., purchase order confirmation, order status, and advance ship notice.

Value Stream Mapping

Value stream mapping (VSM) is used to visualize and understand the flow of material and information as a product or service makes its way through the value stream. It tends to be applied more broadly to, for example, the entire process from receiving raw material through delivery of the product or service to the customer. It is typically used to map the physical flow rather than the transactional flow and can be used in efforts to make operations leaner. VSM gathers a broader range of information than process mapping and is often used to identify where to focus improvement or change projects.[5] We discuss VSM in more detail and provide an example in Chapter 10.

In sum, process mapping and value stream mapping are useful to illustrate how both business and physical processes can be as effective as possible and to aid in developing the cross-functional organizational forms needed for effective business processes. Process maps in particular clearly illustrate how a business process is performed, highlight the cross-functional relationships that are involved, and suggest places where the process might be improved.

Operations-Related Business Processes

There are three business processes that are important to most companies: product or service generation, which is the process of creating new products or services and delivering them to the market; order fulfillment, which starts with taking a customer order and ends with delivering the desired good or service to the customer; and service and support, which starts with a customer inquiry or support request and ends with fulfilling that request. Many companies manage these processes with cross-disciplinary processes, metrics, organizational structures, and information technology to make them run as smoothly as possible in the eyes of the customers. We explore each of them in turn to provide some sense of what the processes entail, how firms manage them, and the ways in which they contribute to gaining competitive advantage.

Product and Service Generation

In Chapter 5, we highlighted the importance of the new product and service generation process to companies: On average, companies derive roughly 30 percent of their revenues and profits from products or services introduced in the past five years; service companies derive slightly less, while high-tech companies derive slightly more. In short, new product

---

[5] http://www.isixsigma.com/dictionary/Value_Stream_Mapping-413.htm, August 2, 2006.

EXHIBIT 7.6   Proposed Process Map

Shaded boxes indicate a process step that is completed manually. Unshaded boxes indicate steps that are automated.

Source: Printed with permission from PRTM, a global management consulting firm, based on work performed at Network Appliance, Incorporated. Copyright 2006 PRTM, Inc.

B2B E-Commerce "To-Be" Quote-to-Invoice Process Flow Diagram

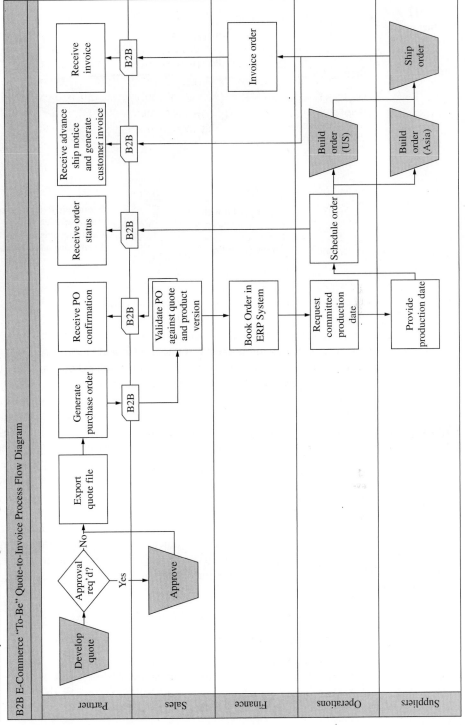

EXHIBIT 7.7
Product or Service Development Funnel

Candidate Projects:
Advanced development
Breakthrough
Extensions or derivatives
Improvements

Strategy Screen for Fit with:
Target market segments
Brand priorities
Competitive position
Platform strategy
Customer life-cycle
  management

Technical Feasibility Screen:
Technology strategy fit?
Technology exist?
Technology work?
Manufacturing or service
  delivery process?
Supplier capabilities?

Market Acceptance Screen for Fit with:
Target customer set
Brand image
Channel priorities

Ecomomic Return Screen:
Risk assessment
Capital requirements
Engineering resource requirements

Product or Service Portfolio

and service generation is crucial to the growth and financial well-being of most companies. That makes managing the cross-functional process of generating those new products and services an important focus in most organizations.

At the highest level, product and service generation is a process of creating new ideas, filtering them to the few that should be developed for delivery to the market, and then executing the development and delivery process for those few. This process is often depicted as a funnel (Exhibit 7.7) to show that the firm must start with a wide range of product or service ideas and then apply a number of screens—strategic fit, market acceptance, technology feasibility, and economic viability—to those ideas to select the ones that will be developed and delivered to the market. Portfolio planning, typically executed by the senior management team in an organization, is at the core of the funneling process. The product or service development process, with which the firm executes the chosen ideas, starts with a planning phase that links the objectives of the project to the corporate strategy and then refines the product or service through a series of iterative and increasingly more detailed steps until it is ready for delivery to the market (Exhibit 7.8).

EXHIBIT 7.8 **New Product or Service Development Process**

Source: Adapted from Ulrich and Eppinger, *Product Design and Development,* 3rd ed., McGraw-Hill/Irwin, 2004, Exhibit 2.2.

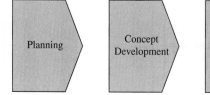

Planning → Concept Development → System-Level Design → Detailed Design → Testing and Refinement → Production or Service Delivery Ramp-up

EXHIBIT 7.9
Overlapped Phases of Product or Service Generation Process

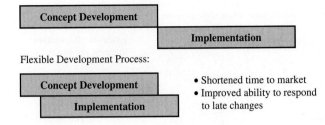

Traditional Linear Development Process:

Concept Development

Implementation

Flexible Development Process:

Concept Development

Implementation

• Shortened time to market
• Improved ability to respond to late changes

Each industry, and indeed each company in an industry, depicts its process in a slightly different way, but all processes generally contain the same steps. For example, in the pharmaceutical business, product generation focuses on research into new drug compounds and is a long process as the drugs go through many trials to prove their efficacy and safety. Fashion businesses, such as toys, athletic shoes, and apparel, must develop a wide range of concepts and then select the right ones and bring them to the market all within a one-season cycle. (Zara, of course, is an exception in that it does not adhere to the seasonal cycles of the industry.) The automobile industry emphasizes styling and design for manufacturability in an attempt to balance customer needs with the ability to consistently build high-quality products.

Although we have drawn these processes in linear representations for the most part, the steps of the process are rarely executed linearly. To reduce the length of time the entire process takes, the steps of the process are often overlapped (Exhibit 7.9) or executed in fast iterative cycles (Exhibit 7.10). The classic spiral model of software development (Exhibit 7.11), for example, shows the highly iterative nature of the software development process as it goes through several rounds of development and testing to zero in on what the customer wants. The more iterative the process, the more cross-functional interaction is required.

EXHIBIT 7.10   **Iterative Model of Product Development**

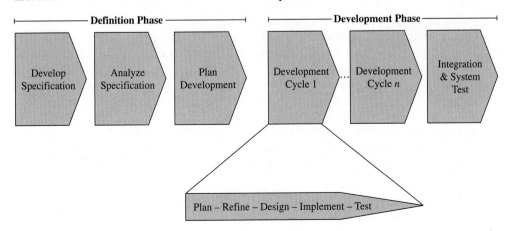

EXHIBIT 7.11 Spiral Model of Software Development

Source: Boehm, "A Spiral Model of Software Development and Enhancement," *IEEE Computer,* 1988. Printed with permission.

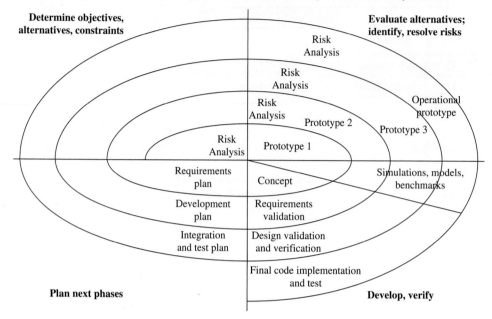

This new product or service development process resides within a larger new product or service generation system (Exhibit 7.12).[6] That system is driven by a senior management team responsible for strategic planning (i.e., the management of the funnel), for allocating resources among the product or service development projects in the firm's portfolio, and for measuring the performance of the system. The senior management team oversees execution of a set of projects, often employing what is known as a *stage-gate* (Cooper 2001) or *phase-review process* to check in with the project teams on a regular basis, monitor their progress, ensure ongoing fit with the strategic plan, and reallocate resources as needed. Each development project typically follows a defined process for managing the stages of the product or service development process and is executed by a cross-functional core team responsible for managing the day-to-day work of the broader development team. The entire new product or service development system is supported by a set of information systems that range from computer-aided design (CAD) and simulation systems used by the designers themselves to portfolio management systems used by the senior management team, to product data management (PDM) systems that integrate data from across the functions. Integrative information systems are particularly critical for geographically dispersed teams (Eppinger and Chitkara 2006).

As we will see, all of the cross-functional processes we discuss in this chapter require an integrated management system such as the one shown in Exhibit 7.12, including top management guidance, a defined process, supportive cross-functional organizational structures, and integrative information technology. One of the key drivers for managing

---

[6] Thanks to Jane Creech of Strategic Business Systems for a variety of inputs to the development of this model over the years.

EXHIBIT 7.12
New Product or Service Development System

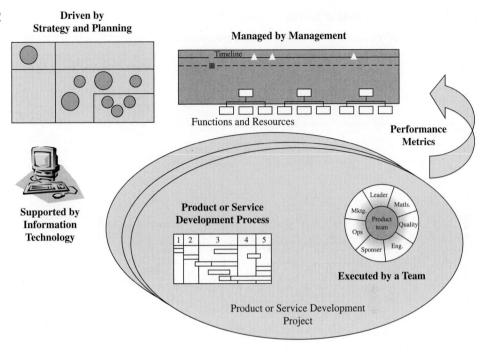

Driven by Strategy and Planning

Managed by Management

Timeline

Functions and Resources

Performance Metrics

Supported by Information Technology

Product or Service Development Process

Leader · Matls. · Mktg. · Product team · Quality · Ops · Eng. · Sponser

Executed by a Team

Product or Service Development Project

such integrated systems is a set of metrics that relate the performance of the process to customer needs and desired business outcomes.

Product and Service Generation Metrics

The commonly cited adage "Tell me how I'm measured, and I'll tell you how I'll act" suggests the importance of performance metrics in process management. Product and service generation efforts are generally measured on time, budget, and meeting of customer requirements for features, quality, and cost. The specific choice of metrics in these categories can drive very different behaviors on the part of the product or service generation team.

Many firms measure time-to-market (TTM), or the length of time from original concept development to the time when the first product or service is delivered to the market. TTM metrics, however, allow the development organization to focus on just getting the product or service to the market and not worry about what happens after launch. Other firms look at time-to-volume (TTV), which measures the length of time from original concept to when it can be produced or delivered at volume. TTV metrics force the development organization to concern itself with how the product will be manufactured or how the service will be delivered and to make ramp to volume as smooth as possible.

Yet other organizations use a break-even time (BET) metric, which measures the amount of time from concept development until the product or service breaks even, paying back the investment in its development (Exhibit 7.13). BET metrics force the development team to fully integrate all the functions to ensure that not only is the product or service developed and ramped quickly, but that it is something that customers really want and will pay for. In the 1990s, Hewlett-Packard set a stretch objective to cut its BET in half,

EXHIBIT 7.13   **Product or Service Generation Metrics**

Source: House and Price, "The Return Map," *Harvard Business Review,* 1991. Printed with permission.

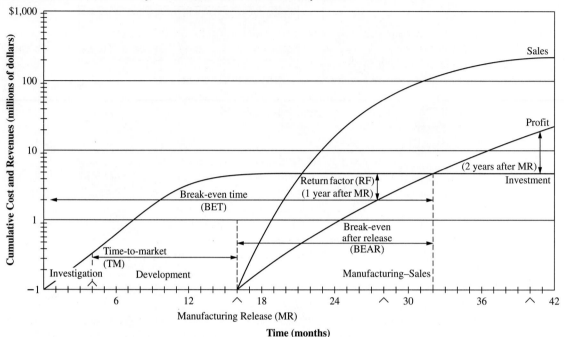

which forced radical redesign of its new product development process with significantly more cross-functional integration.

While most firms have metrics for time, budget, and customer satisfaction, the emphasis they place and the targets they set for each vary by the importance of performance along that dimension to the organization. In the automobile industry, companies vary in the extent to which they strive to develop new products more frequently or to include the latest new technologies and create the newest features. BMW, for example, has a reputation for innovative vehicles that perform at a level above its competitors. Its product development process strives to incorporate the latest technology and develop vehicles with outstanding performance. Thus, while time-to-market is important for BMW, meeting customer expectations for new features is required. In the fashion industry, on the other hand, Zara is less concerned about technology integration and more concerned about capturing the very latest in customer trends. By linking its product generation process to a flexible and responsive manufacturing system, Zara brings a large number of concepts to its stores far more quickly than can its competitors. For Zara, rapid time-to-market is essential; it can quickly adjust product features if needed.

Organizing for Product and Service Generation

Product or service generation is inherently an information processing exercise (Eppinger 2001). Each step of the process requires information from other steps of the process and generates information to be used by other steps of the process. In the ideal world, information would flow in only one direction, and no iteration among steps would be required.

In the real world, there is no choice but to iterate, as people throughout the development process must share information with one another to achieve timely product or service introductions that satisfy customers. Scientists in the laboratories of pharmaceutical companies work closely with technology specialists on the generation and testing of compounds. Marketing and product specialists at athletic shoe companies work closely with each other on communication of consumer trends and customer needs. Automobile companies, known historically for "throwing designs over the wall" between engineering and manufacturing, have learned to collaborate on design for manufacturing guidelines to ensure fast manufacturing ramp-ups and consistent quality production. Thus, product or service development organizations must be structured so they can efficiently and effectively resolve problems and conflicts among the functions and work together to integrate the output of the subtasks to which they have been assigned (Hayes et al. 1988).

The organizational design that best supports a new product or service generation process optimizes information flows among the players. Often those information flows are dictated by the architecture and design of the product or service. Consider, for example, the design of a large commercial aircraft engine (Sosa et al. 2004). The engine consists of eight systems—six modular and two integrative—and each system contains five to ten components, for a total of 54 components in the entire engine. The design interfaces among the components of the engine can be represented in a design structure matrix (Eppinger 2001) such as that depicted in Exhibit 7.14. Here a W represents a weak design interface and S a strong design interface. Notice that most, but not all, of the interfaces among components are contained within the system in which they reside. How, then, should the organization be structured to manage the information flows suggested by these design interfaces? In this case, there are 60 design teams dedicated to the development of the engine, 54 of them focused on the individual components, and six of them dedicated to a handful of system integration tasks such as rotor dynamics and secondary flow. The design structure matrix showing the communications among these teams is depicted in Exhibit 7.15 where an O represents a relationship between two teams. If one matches the entries in the design structure matrices (Exhibit 7.16), where the symbols show matched, unmarked and aligned, not surprisingly one finds that there is fairly strong alignment between the two. In other words, the organizational structure supports the information flows required by the product architecture and design. Mismatches between the two suggest opportunities for organizational redesign. (See Sosa et al. 2004 for further discussion of the implications of mismatches.)

There is a range of organizational designs that can be used to support the optimal information flows. (In Exhibit 7.17 there are three functions with different shapes for different functions, and three projects). In the classic functional organizational structure, information is passed up and down the hierarchy as needed to communicate between the functions. Very few organizations today work completely in this mode, as it is generally slow and unresponsive to change. At the other extreme, the project organization is structured entirely around product or service generation projects, and each team has the requisite functional members. While this organizational structure allows focus on specific projects, it can lack flexibility for sharing resources across projects and for development of functional skills. More common structures are matrix forms that vary from those with "lightweight" project managers to those with "heavyweight" project managers (Hayes et al. 1988). In heavyweight project organizations, the project managers have complete control over their projects and the resources assigned to them from the functions. In lightweight project organizations, the project managers have less direct control, and the functions play a stronger role.

EXHIBIT 7.14 **Design Structure Matrix Showing Design Interfaces for Pratt & Whitney Engine**

Source: Sosa, et al., "The Misalignment of Product Architecture and Organizational Structure in Complex Product Development," *Management Science,* 2004. Printed with permission.

		Modular systems						Integrative systems	
		Fan system	LPC system	HPC system	CC system	HPT sys.	LPT system	Mech. comps.	External and controls
Modular systems	Fan system (7 components)	• s s w s • s s s • s w w s s • w w w w w • w w w • w s w w •	s s s s s w w w w w w w				w	s s w w	w w w s w w w
	LPC system (7 components)	w s w w w s w w s w w w s w w s s s	• s s w s s s • s w s s s s • w w • s s • w s s s w • w s s s w •	s w s w w s w s w w. s s s w w				 s	w w w s w s s w w w w w s
	HPC system (7 components)	w w w w w w w w	w w w w w w	w s • w s s s w s s w w • s s w w s s • s w w w s s s • s w w w w w s • w s w w w • s s w s •	 w w w	 w		 w s w	w w w w w w w w w s w

	CC system (5 components)		w
			s w
				w
				s s
				w s • w
				s
				w s
					• s w s
					s • s s s
					w s • w
					s •
					   •
						s
						w w
						w w
						
								w w w
								w
								
								s
									w w w
									w w w w w w w
									   w
									w s s
									      w w w w

	HPT system (5 components)			w w
				
				w
				
				w
					w
					s w s w
					   w
					   w
					s s
						• w w s w w w
						w • w w s
						w w • s s w
						s w s • w w
						w s s w • s w w
								w w
								w s
								w
								w s
									w w
									
									w w
									w w w

	LPT system (6 components)	s			w w	w w s w s • s s s w w w s s s w s • s	• s • w s w s s • s w s w s s • s w s w w s • s s w s w •	s s w	s s w w s w
Integrative systems	Mech. components (7 components)	w w s w w	w s s w w w	w w w w w	w s w s w s w s w	w w	w s w w	• w w w s w w • s s s w w • w w w s • w s • w s • w w w w w w w •	w w w w w w w w w w w w w w w w w w w w
	External and controls (10 components)	w w s w w w w w w w	s w w s s w w s w w s w	s w s w s s w s w w s s s w s s w	s s s s w w s w s s s w w w w w	s w s w s s w w s s w w w	s s s s s w w s s s	s s s s s s s s s w s s w s w s s s w s s s s w s	• s s s s s • w s s s • w w s s s s s s w s • s s w s s w s s s • • s w s s • s w s w s s s s s s • s s s s s w w s • • s s s s s s • w s w s s s w s s w •

W = WEAK design interface; S = STRONG design interface

There is a wide range of structures between these ends of the spectrum. Many organizations form a "core team" of representatives from each functional area that is charged with making key decisions about the product or service. Core team members in turn are responsible for working with the functions from which they come to get the needed work done. Choosing among the various organizational approaches depends on the importance of the project to the organization, how critical cross-functional integration is to execute the project, how highly utilized individuals assigned full time to a project will be, and how important it is to execute the project quickly (Ulrich and Eppinger 2004). In general, the more important the project, the more critical cross-functional integration, and the more speed required,

EXHIBIT 7.15   Design Structure Matrix Showing Organizational Interactions

Source: Sosa, et al., "The Misalignment of Product Architecture and Organizational Structure in Complex Product Development," *Management Science*, 2004. Printed with permission.

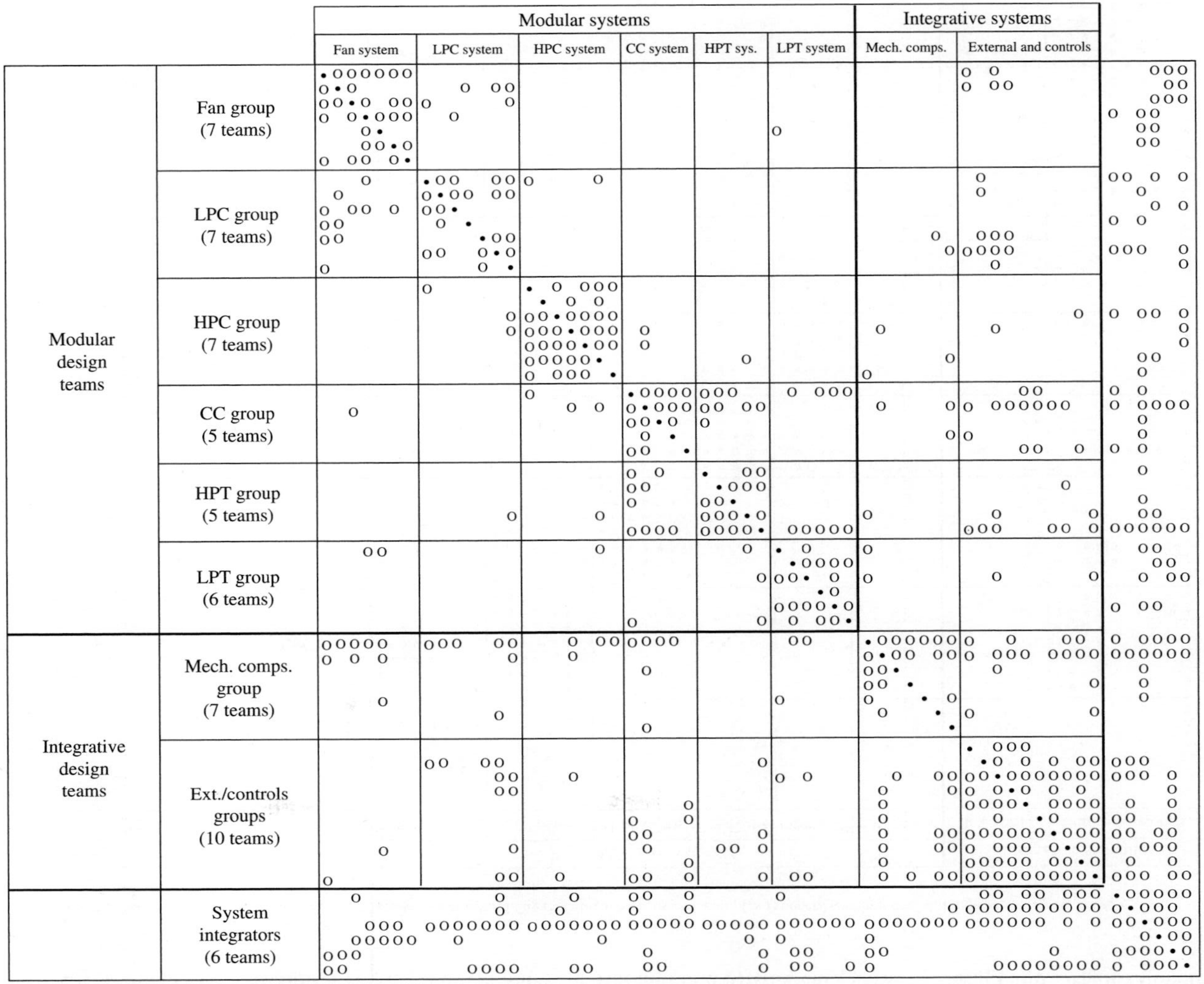

O = Relationship exists between two teams

EXHIBIT 7.16 Design Structure Matrix Showing Matches and Mismatches between Design and Organizational Interfaces

Source: Sosa et al., "The Misalignment of Product Architecture and Organizational Structure in Complex Product Development," *Management Science,* 2004. Printed with permission.

		Modular systems						Integrative systems	
		Fan system	LPC system	HPC system	CC system	HPT sys.	LPT system	Mech. comps.	External and controls
Modular	Fan	• # # # O O O # • # # # • # w # # O # • # # # w # • w # # • # O # # # •	s # s # # # w w # # w w				#	s s w w	# # # s # # w
	LPC	w s # w # s w w O # # w O # # w # # # #	• # # w # # # • # # # # # # • w # • s # s • # # # # # • # s s # w •	# w s w w O s w s w w s s s w w				O #	# # # # # # # # # w w w #
	HPC	w w w w w w w w	# w w s w w w w # w w w # w w	• w # s # # # w • s # # # # • # # # O # # # • # # # # O # # • O O # # # # O • s # O # O s •	# O w	#		# s # #	w w w w # w # w w
	CC	O		O w # #	• # # O # # • # # # # # • # # • # # •	O # O O # O # O w w	O O O O	w # # w #	# # w # # # # # # # w w # s s # # # w
	HPT		O	w w w #	O # # # s w O w # # O O	• w w # # w • # # # # # • s s # # # • # # # # # •	w w w w w # O # O #	#	w w O w s # # # O # # # #
	LPT	O #		# w	O	# w s O w w w #	• O s • # # # # # # • s # w s • # w # # # # • # # w # # •	# # w	s s w # s w O
Integrative	Mech. comps.	O O O # # # O O # w	O O # O # # w # w	O # O # w w	O # # # w # w # w	w	w O # # w	• # # # # O # # • # # # # # O • w w w O # • w # • # # • w w w w w w w •	# w # O # # # # # # # O w O w w O # w w # w w w w w
	Ext./ ctrls.	w w s w w w w w # # w	s w O # # # # # O # w s s s w w # w w # #	s s # w w s w s s #	s s s s # # w # # # # w # # O #	s O s # O # # #	s s O s # s s w s # #	s s s s # s # # # s # # # # # # # # # # s # O # O	• # # # s s s • # # # # # # O • # # # # # # # # • # # w # s # # # # • # # # # # • # w # # # # # # # • # # # # # # # # • O # # # # # # O O • # # # # # # # # # # •

W = Unmatched WEAK interface; S = Unmatched STRONG interface; O = Unmatched team interaction; # = Aligned presence of interface and interaction; (Blank) = Aligned absence of interface and interaction; • = Diagonal elements (meaningless)

EXHIBIT 7.17
Organizational
Designs for
Product or
Service
Generation

Source: Ulrich and
Eppinger, 2004, as
adapted from Hayes,
et al., 1998. Printed
with permission.

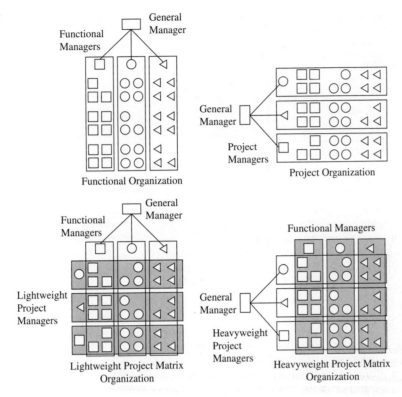

the closer the organization will move to a heavyweight structure. Designing the new product or service generation team gets more complicated for large development projects where integration is needed across the many subtasks involved. The auto industry, for example, uses platform teams to bring together all the teams developing subassemblies or modules of the car in a formal organizational structure (Clark and Fujimoto 1991).

Information Technology Supporting Product and Service Generation

Organizational design alone cannot accommodate the many and sometimes complex interactions that must take place to develop a new product or service. Information technology plays an important role as well. Product data management (PDM) systems, sometimes known as engineering data management or engineering document management systems, manage engineering data, perform version control and configuration management, and facilitate workflow through the product or service generation process. They store all of the data related to a product and to the processes that will be used to design, manufacture, deliver, and support the product. Much of the data that populates the PDM system comes from other computer-based tools such as computer-aided design (CAD), computer-aided manufacturing (CAM), computer-aided engineering (CAE), and various simulation tools. Data also come from procurement information systems that supply information about preferred parts or suppliers and from marketing systems that provide forecasts and other customer-related information.

PDM systems started as stand-alone systems to support the product generation process, but today are fully integrated with enterprise resource planning (ERP) systems, allowing

EXHIBIT 7.18
Order Fulfillment Process

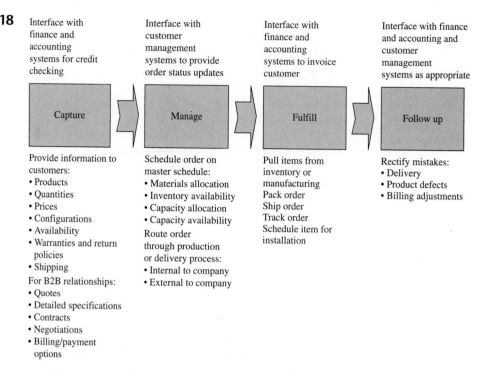

Interface with finance and accounting systems for credit checking

Interface with customer management systems to provide order status updates

Interface with finance and accounting systems to invoice customer

Interface with finance and accounting and customer management systems as appropriate

Capture → Manage → Fulfill → Follow up

Provide information to customers:
• Products
• Quantities
• Prices
• Configurations
• Availability
• Warranties and return policies
• Shipping
For B2B relationships:
• Quotes
• Detailed specifications
• Contracts
• Negotiations
• Billing/payment options

Schedule order on master schedule:
• Materials allocation
• Inventory availability
• Capacity allocation
• Capacity availability
Route order through production or delivery process:
• Internal to company
• External to company

Pull items from inventory or manufacturing
Pack order
Ship order
Track order
Schedule item for installation

Rectify mistakes:
• Delivery
• Product defects
• Billing adjustments

integration of the product or service generation task with the supply chain for efficient new product or service introduction. Integration of systems across organizational and geographic boundaries facilitates development of products and services by globally dispersed teams (Eppinger and Chitkara 2006).[7]

Product and Service Generation Summary

The product or service generation process is critical to most organizations. By definition, it is a process that involves all functional areas in the firm—product or service design, production or service delivery, marketing and sales, and finance and accounting. A well-defined process for managing product or service generation developed with senior management support and a strong process owner, a clear set of metrics for the performance of the process, cross-functional organizational designs, and integrated product data management software are all critical to developing firmwide competence in product or service generation.

Order Fulfillment and Processing

The order fulfillment process starts with an interaction with the customer that results in capturing an order and ends when that customer's order has been fulfilled (Exhibit 7.18). Each step of the process entails a number of activities, many of which require cross-functional interaction. Orders may be "captured" by phone, fax, e-mail, or in various different online formats. Even before submitting their orders, customers expect to be informed about the products or services, including not only features, but prices, availability, warranty policies, shipping options, and the like. This information is likely to come from design, marketing,

---

[7] For more information on PDM systems see http://www.npd-solutions.com/bok.html, August 3, 2006.

quality, and operations. In a business-to-business setting, the order capture process may entail receiving a proposal, generating a quote, reviewing detailed specifications, negotiating contracts, and setting up a billing and payment system.

In the management phase of the order fulfillment process, the order must be scheduled for manufacturing or delivery, which involves coordination across the supply chain with both internal and external operations as needed. Information from the management phase about materials and capacity availability is required in the capture phase to let the customer know whether or when the product or service is available. In the fulfillment phase, an item is pulled from inventory or production, packed, shipped, tracked, and ultimately received by the customer, or a service is generated and delivered. Inevitably, there are errors that occur in the order fulfillment process that must be rectified in a follow-up phase. The customer may have ordered or received the wrong product or service, there may be billing adjustments needed, or the product or service received may be defective.

In most cases, the customer's experience of the order fulfillment process provides him or her little view into the mechanics behind it. When the process goes wrong, however, the customer doesn't want to hear that marketing promised something on the website that operations cannot supply in time, or that quality is responsible for handling defective products, but not for ensuring that accounting refunds the customer's money. The entire order fulfillment process must work smoothly across functional boundaries to serve the customer. The order-taking function cannot take orders without considering delivery constraints, interfacing with production on what a reasonable delivery date might be, or checking component or product availability. A customer must be given a realistic delivery date. New orders must be considered in production or inventory planning, so component procurement and other such actions may be taken in time.

Order Fulfillment Process Metrics

According to the Supply-Chain Operations Reference-model (SCOR) established by the Supply-Chain Council, there are two general measures of order fulfillment:[8]

1. *Perfect order fulfillment* is defined as the "percentage of orders 1) delivered 'on time and in full' to request date and/or to commit date; 2) that meet the customer's three-way match (invoice, purchase order, and receipt); and 3) have no product quality issues."[9] There are two metrics commonly used to measure "on time and in full":

   a. Line fill rate—percentage of lines on an order filled in full.
   b. Order fill rate—percentage of orders filled in full.

2. *Order fulfillment cycle time* is "a continuous measurement defined as the amount of time from customer authorization of a sales order to the customer receipt of product. The major segments of time include order entry, dwell time for future dated orders, manufacturing, distribution, and transportation."[10]

These metrics all focus on things that customers care about. Other internal-facing metrics that can help diagnose problems in the order fulfillment process include order picking and assembly times and delivery performance.

Just as with the product and service generation process, it is impossible to achieve significant gains in performance on any of these metrics if the functions in the organization don't work

---

[8] http://www.supply-chain.org/page.ww?section=SCOR+Model&name=SCOR+Model, August 3, 2006.

[9] http://www.scelimited.com/perfectorderfulfillment.html, August 3, 2006.

[10] http://www.scelimited.com/orderfulfillmentcycletime.html, August 2, 2006.

together. The process mapping example we provided earlier in this chapter (Exhibits 7.5 and 7.6) makes this clear. Sales, finance, operations, and suppliers to the company all had roles to play in completing the order fulfillment process, and improvements in the process were only possible through cooperation among them to develop appropriate and efficient information flows.

Organizing for Order Fulfillment

A typical order fulfillment process consists of a number of parties performing separate steps. For example, sales may initiate contact with the customer, receive a set of specifications, interact with marketing or engineering to see whether or not the order is feasible, interact with operations to see when the order might be delivered, and work with finance and accounting to determine what to charge. Once the order is entered into the system, production or service delivery personnel may work with various internal and external suppliers to coordinate production or delivery, with engineering for any redesign work that needs to be done, with marketing to ensure full understanding of what is to be delivered, and possibly with the customer to provide progress updates. There are many opportunities for errors in the handoffs among the functions, and inevitable delays created in passing work around among them.

To create an integrated order fulfillment process that performs well against the customer-focused metrics described earlier, the steps of the process must be linked and intermediate queuing between them limited. While the project-based work of product and service generation lent itself well to a variety of team-based structures, the transaction-oriented work of order fulfillment does not. The functions that perform the steps of the order fulfillment process have other activities they must perform as well, making it more difficult to dedicate them to specific order fulfillment teams. Organizations thus take a couple of different approaches to organizing to improve the process.

First, they form teams or task forces with representatives from each of the relevant functions to look at the process, often using Six Sigma or business process reengineering (BPR) approaches. The participants on these teams are expected to communicate back to their functions about the process redesign work that is being undertaken, giving their colleagues a processwide perspective and gaining buy-in to changes needed to streamline the process. Thus, the organization increases understanding of what needs to be done to better serve the customer and forces some amount of communication across functional boundaries in the task force setting. Second, companies sometimes name a champion or leader for the order fulfillment process who is measured on the performance of that process (perfect order fulfillment) and, often with no direct reports, is expected to influence those involved in the process to work together or change their own behaviors in ways that will improve the process.

Very often, however, the easiest way to achieve integration of the order fulfillment process is through the development and implementation of information technology that allows information to flow readily among the functions and in many cases makes decisions without human intervention. The design and implementation of such systems may well be the recommendation of a task force chartered to look at the process.

Information Technology Supporting Order Fulfillment

Historically, the information systems that support order entry have been separate from those that support the production or service delivery process. Today, while part of the same enterprise resource planning system, they are still in different modules of the system and are often implemented by different organizations. A process map of the front end of U.S. Power Technologies' order fulfillment process shows the many different databases and systems that are involved in taking an order (Exhibit 7.19). Some of these reside out in the field sales force, others in the

EXHIBIT 7.19 Front End of the Order Fulfillment Process at U.S. Power Technologies

Source: Printed with permission from ABB Inc.

Management of Processes: U.S. Power Technology Sales Order Process

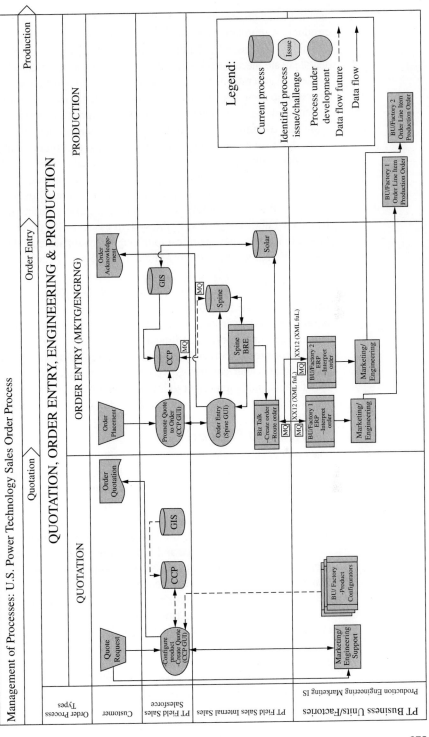

internal sales organization, and yet others in the business units charged with delivering the product. A number of issues arise in managing the interfaces among these systems (Exhibit 7.20). Issue C, identified in the middle section of Exhibit 7.20, for example, suggests that there are inaccuracies in matching up quotations to orders when order entry takes over the process. In general, information about the status of production, service delivery, and/or inventory is needed to accurately estimate order delivery times for customers. Conversely, the production or service delivery and inventory systems must receive information about incoming orders that allows for dynamic updating of forecasts, inventories, back orders, and so forth.

In more sophisticated systems, like Dell's direct model that involves direct delivery to customers without the intermediate step of a retailer or wholesaler, there is a feedback loop from the production-inventory system to the order processing system that structures what options are available to customers at any given time. Orders may be shifted to a product for which there is favorable component status, thus assuring rapid delivery, or orders may be delayed until congestion in the system eases. Dell's production tracking system is also linked to its customer relationship management software so that customers may track their orders throughout the assembly and delivery cycle (Kraemer and Dedrick 2001).

Order Fulfillment and Processing Summary

For a company such as Dell, "perfect" order fulfillment is a cornerstone of its competitive advantage. To deliver its customized, build-to-order products with reasonable lead times, it has invested in an order fulfillment process, order fulfillment management and organizational structure, and order fulfillment software that support its achievement of world-class performance. Other companies with different strategies (e.g., build-to-stock, direct delivery) may find it equally important to invest in a fully integrated order fulfillment system but may choose different processes, organizational designs, and information technology to do so.

Service and Support

The product and service generation and order fulfillment processes are widely understood to be critical to business performance, but service and support is frequently ignored or given less attention. Often, these processes are viewed as peripheral, not contributing to competitiveness and even a burden. Yet, the process by which customers access spare parts, on-site service, service through a central repair facility, technical support by web or phone, and so forth is often the most visible and thus frustrating when it goes wrong.

The structure of the service and support process varies widely by the types of service and support offered. Some companies offer on-site service and repair, others expect the customer to come in to a service or repair facility, and yet others simply send out replacement units and don't bother with repair. Some provide call center support 24 hours a day, while others expect the customer to find answers on the web. Some solve complex problems, like the high-end electronics company whose high-level process is depicted in Exhibit 7.21 and sometimes takes months to diagnose a problem with the customer's equipment due to the extreme technical complexity of the products. Others, like Comcast, provide phone support to help customers get their modems running again in minutes.

As with the other business processes, many functions can be involved in service and support. Engineering may be involved in defining service routines or in working with service personnel to diagnose problems. Operations may run repair depots, supply spare parts, or use quality data that comes from support phone lines. Marketing may design the warranty,

EXHIBIT 7.20 Issues in the Front End of the Order Fulfillment Process at U.S. Power Technologies

Source: Printed with permission from ABB Inc.

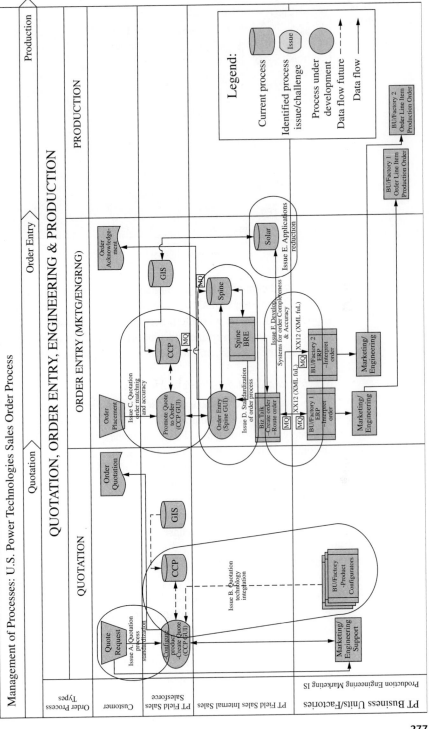

EXHIBIT 7.21
Repair Process

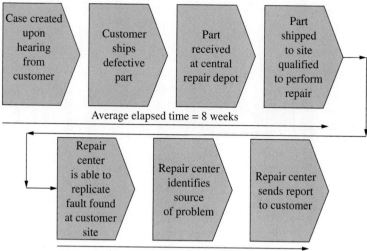

Case created upon hearing from customer

Customer ships defective part

Part received at central repair depot

Part shipped to site qualified to perform repair

Average elapsed time = 8 weeks

Repair center is able to replicate fault found at customer site

Repair center identifies source of problem

Repair center sends report to customer

Average elapsed time = 20 weeks

service, and support packages and sell them along with the product or service to the customers. A separate organization may be responsible for actually delivering the service or support itself. So, as with the other business processes, there is a need for a shared set of metrics to assess the service and support process, for cross-functional organizational efforts to manage the process, and for information technology that integrates the effort.

Service and Support Process Metrics

The primary metrics for assessing service and support functions from a customer's point of view are the speed and quality of the service. Customers want their issues resolved quickly, accurately, and permanently. Thus, companies measure the length of time it takes to resolve a customer's issue—whether on the phone, by e-mail, or in person—and the customer's satisfaction with the end result. Customer satisfaction surveys evaluate various aspects of the service, such as the knowledge, professionalism, and communications skills of the person providing the service, the outcome of the service, the speed with which it was provided, and the influence of the experience on what the customer thinks of the company and the probability of making a repeat purchase.[11]

Organizing for Service and Support

As for the other two business processes we've discussed, service and support requires integration among functional areas. As for order fulfillment, it is rare to find cross-functional teams dedicated to service and support, as it is an ongoing set of transactions with the customer that needs to be managed. Instead, task forces may be deployed to set metrics for the process and to study it to find ways in which it might be improved. A leader may be given responsibility for seeing that the process is executed smoothly but have to do so with no direct authority for all the responsible functions.

---

[11] http://www.supportindustry.com/kstorm/2005surveygraphs.htm, August 4, 2006.

Information Technology Supporting Service and Support

Information technology, once again, is often the best way to integrate the service and support functions. Spare parts management systems include modules for parts demand planning (e.g., forecasting for both current and planned products), parts inventory planning (e.g., determining how much of each part to maintain in inventory), parts supply planning (e.g., determining distribution requirements and managing purchase orders), parts distribution planning (e.g., pushing inventory into distribution centers or pulling it from those centers), and parts monitoring (e.g., monitoring shortages).[12] The service module of a customer relationship management (CRM) system may cover service order management, service contract management, complaints and returns, in-house repair, case management, installed base management, warranty management, and resource planning.[13] Other software is used to run call centers and web interfaces that provide service and support. The data to populate these systems are gathered throughout the organization and must be integrated to show a common perspective to the customer throughout the service and support process.

Service and Support Summary

How a company performs service and support can have a major effect on its competitive position, in either a positive or negative way. If a company develops a reputation for poor service, it can experience a loss of short-term buyers as well as long-term customers. On the other hand, a company can develop a reputation for outstanding service, thereby enhancing its competitive posture. Caterpillar Inc., a $36 billion manufacturer of construction and mining equipment, diesel and natural gas engines, and industrial gas turbines, makes spare parts and repair services a core part of its strategy.[14] Caterpillar promises rapid service anywhere in the world, using a combination of inventory management, transportation, and information technology to fulfill this goal. Saturn Corporation, spawned by General Motors, became known early in its history for its service management methods. Through a new type of dealer network, Saturn reduced the tension that often accompanies the buying and servicing experience.

Choosing a Business Process Focus

A firm chooses the business processes on which it wishes to focus based on what competitive advantage it seeks in the marketplace. A company competing on innovativeness and features might depend on the superiority of its product or service generation process. A company competing on availability might invest in developing its order fulfillment capability. A company competing on quality might want to ensure the best end-to-end customer experience with strong service and support processes. Whatever processes the company chooses to showcase, it will have to invest in developing the metrics, process, organizational structure, and information technology to develop the process to the level at which it can provide competitive advantage. Process mapping and other methods from the quality management and business process reengineering toolboxes can be helpful in moving an organization down this path.

---

[12] http://www.sap.com/solutions/businessmaps/C79D913A7E43449C9592E55B20A92973/index.epx, August 4, 2006.
[13] http://www.sap.com/solutions/businessmaps/84418B92F7B44629895E506E63C20669/index.epx, August 4, 2006.
[14] http://www.cat.com/cda/layout?m=38028&x=7, August 4, 2006.

Organizational Design of Operations

The basic nature of work today has changed radically from what it was as little as 20 years ago. Today, work is: "more cognitively complex, more team-based and collaborative, more dependent on social skills, more dependent on technological competence, more time pressured, more mobile, and less dependent on geography" (Heerwagen et al. 2006). In today's more global and competitive world, that work is done in organizations that are "leaner and more agile, more focused on identifying value from the customer perspective, more tuned to dynamic competitive requirements and strategy, less hierarchical in structure and decision authority, less likely to provide lifelong careers and job security, and continually reorganizing to maintain or gain competitive advantage" (Heerwagen et al. 2006).

In this new and ever-changing environment, organizational design has become an increasingly prominent part of senior management's work. Organizational design requires first understanding the company's strategic direction and then integrating the elements of an organizational design to support that strategy. Those elements include (Galbraith 2002):

- *Organizational structure:* who reports to whom; where decision-making power is located.
- *Decision-making processes:* how information flows around the organization and how decisions get made.
- *Human resources:* what skill sets are needed in which positions; how they are hired, trained, fired.
- *Rewards:* how people are measured, motivated, and rewarded both intrinsically and extrinsically.

Choices made for each of these elements together form the design of the organization. It is helpful to think of organizational design as the way in which managers design and control the flow of information in that organization.

Information Processing View of an Organization[15]

The fundamental problem in organizational design is the difficulty of coordination among multiple groups within a company. In a large organization that employs a number of specialist groups and resources, the task that the organization is chartered with accomplishing must be divided into subtasks to be executed by each specialty. Once the work is divided up, it must then be integrated once again for completion. The executors of the individual subtasks cannot communicate with all of the other executors with whom they are interdependent, so the organizational design must provide mechanisms that permit coordinated action across these many interdependent actors. When uncertainty is relatively low, there are three mechanisms that can be used to coordinate the work of the organization:

- *Rules or programs:* To the extent that the required subtasks and the relationships among them can be described in advance, rules and programs can be used to dictate how the work should be done.

---

[15] This section is based on Jay Galbraith, "Organization Design: An Information Processing View," *Interfaces* 4, no. 3 (May 1974).

- *Hierarchy:* When there are exceptions to those rules and programs, inquiries or conflicts may be sent up the hierarchy for resolution.
- *Targets or goals:* When there is a moderate amount of uncertainty in the system, decision making can be pushed to lower levels as long as everyone is working toward a shared set of goals or targets.

When uncertainty gets too great, however, shared goals are no longer sufficient and the hierarchy cannot handle the amount of communication required to resolve uncertainties. In that case, the organization must be redesigned in one of the following ways:

- *Create slack resources:* Slack can be built into the system—time/schedule, budget, inventory—to reduce the interdependence among the subtasks and thus reduce the information processing required.
- *Create self-contained tasks:* By regrouping the subtasks around shared outputs (e.g., a specific subassembly or subprocess), information processing can be localized in smaller groups.
- *Invest in vertical information systems:* Budgeting and planning systems that allow senior management to clearly set priorities and thus push decision making as low as possible in the organization, or that allow for rapid replanning as needed, reduce exception processing workload.
- *Create lateral linkages or relationships:* Where subtasks are inherently interconnected, a number of options exist for creating communication linkages among them:
  - Direct contact between individuals who share a problem or task.
  - Liaison roles between two groups who share a problem or task.
  - Task forces to integrate the inputs of multiple people who represent a variety of subtasks.
  - Teams, which evolve from task forces and are more permanent structures.
  - Managerial linking roles higher up in the hierarchy assign responsibility to a manager for integrating a set of subtasks.
  - Matrix organizations with dual reporting relationships allow integration and communication in multiple directions.

Today, organizations work under a high degree of uncertainty and cannot afford to introduce much slack into their systems, so are left with three options for organizing: (1) cluster to the extent possible into self-contained tasks; (2) increase investment in planning systems that allow senior management to set direction for the company and quickly alter that direction in response to the competitive marketplace as needed; and (3) develop various forms of lateral linkages using organizational design and information systems. Organizational design issues were apparent as we addressed the three business processes: Metrics are at the core of planning systems, organizational structures connect critical decision-makers in the process, and information technology moves information fluidly to all involved in the process. We turn now to an examination of the organizational design elements involved, leaving further discussion of information technology to Chapter 9.

Organizational Structure

Organizational structures become more complex as business strategies evolve. A business that is focused on a single product, service, or market can be structured simply with the

EXHIBIT 7.22
Organizational
Structure for
a Typical Firm
Today

Source: Adapted from
Galbraith, http://www
.jaygalbraith.com/
resources/aomhawaii
2005-2.pdf, August 6,
2006.

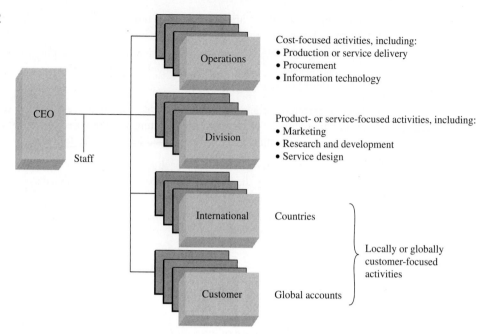

Cost-focused activities, including:
• Production or service delivery
• Procurement
• Information technology

Product- or service-focused activities, including:
• Marketing
• Research and development
• Service design

Countries

Locally or globally customer-focused activities

Global accounts

classic functional silos (manufacturing or service delivery, marketing and sales, research and development or service design, human resources, and finance and accounting) reporting in to the chief executive officer (CEO). As the business grows and diversifies, it forms divisions that focus on the different sub-businesses but continues to organize functionally within those divisions. When the company expands internationally, it may create organizations that are focused on each of the countries in which it is developing presence, while retaining the divisional structure for the core business. Finally, as the company increases its focus on customers, it may develop organizations such as global account management teams to provide consistent service to large customers globally. The result is often an organizational design with a complex mix of functional, divisional, and customer-focused structures, and the operations function increasingly stands alone in support of the product- or service- and customer- focused groups (Exhibit 7.22).[16]

The new, more complex organization structures create new integration challenges. How, for example, is the newly isolated operations function to serve its many masters in the product- and customer-focused groups? There are a number of structural solutions to the integration problem.[17] At a relatively informal level, the operations group may build its informal networks throughout the organization, co-locate personnel in or rotate them through the other groups, or host interdepartmental events that bring various groups together. More formally, it may choose to designate liaisons to the other groups, insist on joint membership in partner organizations, or identify project or program managers to manage important cross-cutting processes or outcomes. The more formal the mechanism

[16] http://www.jaygalbraith.com/resources/aomhawaii2005-2.pdf, August 6, 2006.
[17] http://www.marshall.usc.edu/ceo/teleconferences/2003_orgdesign/mohrman.pdf, August 5, 2006.

used, the greater the decision-making power vested in the people involved, and the more robust the linkages that are created.

Operations managers play two roles in structuring their organizations. At the highest level, they work with executive management in the company to determine where the operations function fits. Should it stand alone as a functionally focused organization, or should it be more integrated with the other groups within the company? Where cost is most important to the company's performance, it may be best to have operations stand alone to minimize overhead and aggregate volumes for minimum cost. Where availability and responsiveness are most important, it may be best to have smaller units to support the product- or customer-focused groups that can react quickly to needs within those groups. Once a decision has been made as to where operations reports in the company, the operations manager must decide how relationships with the other groups in the company will be managed. Where speed is of the essence, more formal integrative roles may be required. Otherwise, development of an informal network may suffice.

Organizing in Teams

As predicted by the information-processing view of organizations, teams have become the basic building blocks of organizations today. Teams in essence form self-contained tasks. Communication needs are focused within the team, leading to faster decision making, effective integration of subtasks, and more effective performance. Cross-functional product development teams, for example, may be formed to integrate knowledge from manufacturing and engineering in design for Six Sigma (DFSS) efforts. Application of lean thinking requires cross-functional groups to identify improvement opportunities and form cellular structures among people previously separated by inventory or other buffers. Six Sigma quality improvement efforts use strictly defined teams, including sponsors, team leaders, project champions, black belts, green belts, and other team members to engage in problem-solving efforts.

The fundamental issue in organizational design—that of balancing the autonomy of the subtask teams with the need to integrate their work to complete the organization's overall task—is rife in team-based environments. Empowering employees and giving them the autonomy to work in teams has been shown to lead to superior performance, but within a large multinational company the work of the many individual teams must be reconciled and integrated. In some cases, teams can be collected into larger groups to form self-contained tasks within which most required information exists to do the work. Other times some degree of centralized control may be required. The determination of when to centrally control the work of teams is in part based on the extent to which there is commonality in the products, processes, markets, or customers being served by the individual teams (Exhibit 7.23). When there is a good deal of commonality, or the different tasks are highly interdependent, a global process managed either in a centralized or a collaborative way works best. When the work the teams are doing is unique and there is little task interdependency, then it is best to let them run independently with little central coordination or control (Klein 1991).

Organizational structure, and the choice of a team structure within it, is but one of the factors in an organizational design, though. Information flow and decision making, reward systems, and the abilities of the people in the organization are important as well.

EXHIBIT 7.23
**Coordination of
Autonomous
Teams**

Source: Reproduced
with permission from
Klein, "Re-Examination
of Autonomy in Light
of New Manufacturing
Practices," *Human
Relations,* 1991, by
permission of Sage
Publications Ltd.

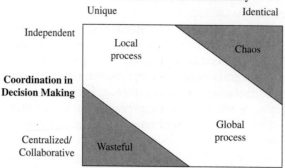

Product/Process Commonality

Unique   Identical

Independent

Local
process   Chaos

**Coordination in
Decision Making**

Global
process

Centralized/
Collaborative   Wasteful

Decision-Making Processes

To make a matrix organization work well, shared work and business processes are required. All units, whether vertical or lateral, need clear charters with integrated strategic leadership from the top. That implies that there are clear and flexible planning processes that engage managers from all the cells in the matrix structure. Decision-making processes must be supported by well-integrated information systems that deliver appropriate and accurate information to decision-makers as they need it.

Rewards

We have discussed metrics throughout this chapter as a means of focusing an organization on the outcomes it is to achieve. (We discuss metrics in more detail in Chapter 11.) To be effective, the metrics must be embedded in the reward systems of the organization. Metric setting starts at the top of the company with the strategic plan and then drives through the product and service plans, which must take into account the requirements of the various customers and geographies that the product or service is to serve. Operations plans are often constructed to support a particular product plan but may also have to support individual geographies as well. Through an iterative development process, the strategic plan emerges that dictates the high-level metrics for the organization.

Shared metrics and goals alone support creation of a shared vision about what needs to be accomplished by a cross-functional team but have the most leverage when they are embedded in the performance measurement system. Thus, individual performance evaluations must include the important metrics and goals, and ultimately both intrinsic and extrinsic rewards must be based on them as well. New product development teams are often given a bonus *as a team* for achieving time-to-market metrics. Participants in the order fulfillment process, on the other hand, may be rewarded individually for their specific contributions (e.g., order-picking rate) to the performance of the overall process.

Human Resources

The skill sets required to work in the types of organizations we are describing are different from what they used to be. Leaders in matrix organizations wear two hats, so must have the flexibility to readily switch roles as needed. They must be strong communicators to help the people in their organizations understand how they fit into the larger organizational system, and what their goals and objectives are. They must keep those working for them from feeling the tension of working for two groups by maintaining clarity around both goals and constraints. They must know how to raise and resolve issues both vertically and laterally in the organization.[18]

Many of the jobs in these organizations require what some call "knowledge workers," or people who are able to cope both with complexity as well as ambiguity, people who are in a continuous learning mode, and people who are able to think outside the narrow bounds of their educational training to integrate concepts from across disciplines (Heerwagen et al. 2006). In addition to this set of cognitive skills, workers in today's organizations need to be able to work on teams, sharing and collaborating to complete their jobs, and learning from one another. While all operations jobs don't require these knowledge worker skill sets, an increasing number do.

Operations managers thus have to be able to define new types of jobs, many that require people to work across organizational boundaries in liaison-type roles like those described earlier. They then need to recruit to those positions, train new employees to come up to speed quickly in their new jobs, manage them while there, and fire them if needed. A larger portion of the operations workforce is now made up of temporary, part-time, or contract employees, making the ability to bring new workers on board quickly and help them exit gracefully even more important.

In short, human resources management requires determining needed skill and staffing levels and recruiting, training, retaining, and firing employees. It requires designing jobs (including degrees of autonomy and dependence), setting performance targets, and structuring the jobs into appropriate work units. It requires providing employees with needed information, communication, and knowledge resources to do their jobs. Human resource policies can create competitive advantage for a company. *Fortune,* for example, chooses the 100 best places to work in the United States each year in large part on the basis of personnel policies at the companies and the company culture.[19]

Organizational Design Summary

Organizational design is a task of understanding the critical information flows in an organization, breaking the work to be done into digestible chunks that maximize the amount of information to be communicated within the chunk, and then integrating the work once again to complete the overall task of the organization. There are four dimensions of organizational design to be considered: (1) the structure of the organization itself; (2) the decision-making and communication processes; (3) the reward and evaluation system; and (4) the skill sets of the employees themselves. When decisions about these four dimensions are made cohesively to support the strategic direction of the organization, they can provide powerful competitive advantage.

Summary

Today, customer-centric organizations are replacing the product-centric organizations of the past. Customer-centric organizations require different structures, approaches to thinking, reward structures, and skill sets (Exhibit 7.24). The resulting organizational structures are more complex than we have known in the past, including some functional-focused, some product-focused, and some customer-focused activities (Exhibit 7.22). Integrating the critical processes in these organizations is a complex task, but one that organizations must accomplish

[18] http://www.marshall.usc.edu/ceo/teleconferences/2003_orgdesign/mohrman.pdf, August 5, 2006.
[19] http://money.cnn.com/magazines/fortune/bestcompanies/full_list/, August 6, 2006.

EXHIBIT 7.24   Product-Centric versus Customer-Centric Organizations

Source: Adapted from Galbraith, "Organizing to Deliver Solutions," *Organizational Dynamics,* 2002.

	The Product-Centric Company	The Customer-Centric Company
Goal	Best product for customer	Best solution for customer
Value Creation Route	Cutting-edge products, useful features, new applications	Customizing for best total solution
Mental Process	Divergent thinking—how many possible uses of the product?	Convergent thinking—what combination of products are best for this customer?
Organizational Concept	Product profit centers, product reviews, product teams	Customer segments, customer teams, customer profit and loss statements
Most Important Process	New product development	Customer relationship management
Measures	Number of new products Percentage of revenue from products less than two years old Market share	Share of most valuable customers Customer satisfaction Lifetime value of a customer Customer retention
Culture	New product culture—open to new ideas, experimentation	Relationship management culture: searching for more customer needs to satisfy
Most Important Customer	Most advanced customer	Most profitable, loyal customer
Priority-Setting Basis	Portfolio of products	Portfolio of customers, customer profitability
Power to Employees	Who develop products	With in-depth knowledge of customer's business
Rewards	Highest reward is working on next most challenging product Manage creative people through challenges with a deadline	Highest rewards to relationship managers who save the customer's business
Sales Bias	On the side of the seller in a transaction	On the side of the buyer in a transaction
Pricing	Price to market	Price to value and risk share

to be competitive. Thus, most organizations must focus some effort on explicitly managing their product or service generation, order fulfillment, and service and support processes.

In this chapter, we have discussed these three business processes and what firms do to manage and improve them and have specifically addressed the dimensions of organizational design that must be considered in business process management. We close with an example of a company that has used its organizational design to gain competitive advantage, and then a couple of frameworks for thinking about and implementing business process focus and organizational design.

A Closing Example

W. L. Gore & Associates, Inc., is roughly a $2 billion privately held company that is perhaps best known in consumer markets for its Gore-Tex® fabric products, although it has many other products in markets as diverse as electronic and electrochemical materials, cable and cable assemblies, filtration, and geochemical services. It has about 7000 associates who work in more than 40 plants and sales locations worldwide.[20] Gore's organizational design has won acclaim for creating "a culture that is as imaginative as its products."[21] The various elements of the design are clear in the company's own description of its corporate culture:

> How we work sets us apart. We encourage hands-on innovation, involving those closest to a project in decision making. Teams organize around opportunities and leaders emerge.
>
> Our founder, Bill Gore, created a flat lattice organization. There are no chains of command or pre-determined channels of communication. Instead, we communicate directly with each other and are accountable to fellow members of our multi-disciplined teams.
>
> How does all this happen? Associates (not employees) are hired for general work areas. With the guidance of their sponsors (not bosses) and a growing understanding of opportunities and team objectives, associates commit to projects that match their skills. All of this takes place in an environment that combines freedom with cooperation and autonomy with synergy.
>
> Everyone can quickly earn the credibility to define and drive projects. Sponsors help associates chart a course in the organization that will offer personal fulfillment while maximizing their contribution to the enterprise. Leaders may be appointed, but are defined by 'followership.' More often, leaders emerge naturally by demonstrating special knowledge, skill, or experience that advances a business objective.
>
> Associates adhere to four basic guiding principles articulated by Bill Gore:

> - Fairness to each other and everyone with whom we come in contact.
> - Freedom to encourage, help, and allow other associates to grow in knowledge, skill, and scope of responsibility.
> - The ability to make one's own commitments and keep them.
> - Consultation with other associates before undertaking actions that could impact the reputation of the company.[22]

In this description are all the elements of an integrated organizational design: The structure works with the information processing, communications, and decision-making processes and the human resource policies to create a coherent package. Although a private company, Gore rewards its employees with stock, thus encouraging them to see themselves as members of the overall Gore team.[23] Gore's strategy of being a highly innovative company is played out in all of the choices made.

Developing a Business Process Focus

Adoption of a business process focus has allowed many organizations to streamline critical processes and gain at least short-term competitive advantage from those processes. Firms, such as Progressive, that have internalized the capability to do operational innovation regularly derive sustainable competitive advantage from that capability. There are six steps to successful operational innovation (Hammer 2005):

Step 1: Scope the effort. Identify the business process to be improved. Start at the level of the full enterprise and make sure the defined scope is broad enough to allow for more than just incremental innovations.

---

[20] http://www.gore.com/en_xx/aboutus/fastfacts/index.html, August 5, 2006.

[21] http://www.fastcompany.com/magazine/89/open_gore.html, August 5, 2006.

[22] Source: http://www.gore.com/en_xx/aboutus/culture/index.html, August 4, 2006, reprinted with permission.

[23] http://www.fastcompany.com/magazine/89/open_gore.html, August 5, 2006.

EXHIBIT 7.25   Example of a Design Team Structure

	General Manager	Section Manager	First Line Manager	Individual Contributor
Operations	Team member 1			
Marketing		Team member 2		
R&D				Team member 3
Finance and Accounting			Team member 4	
Human Resources				Team member 5

Step 2: Assign a process owner. Operational innovation requires radical change that cuts cross organizational boundaries. To be successful, the change effort must be led by a senior executive or manager who has the authority to make change happen across the organization and the personal leadership skills to get people outside his or her own organization to cooperate.

Step 3: Establish a cross-functional design team. It is often said that those who create take ownership. The team that works through the design of the new process must fully represent the points of view of all levels of the organization as well as all functions. When Hewlett-Packard undertook major organizational redesign efforts, it made sure to select at least one representative from each row and column of a chart like Exhibit 7.25, thus ensuring all perspectives were heard. People assigned to the design team must be given enough time and must know that they will be evaluated on the outcome of their work. They, and their managers, must understand that the redesign work is high priority.

Step 4: Do the process design. The tools of Six Sigma and business process reengineering, and in particular the use of process maps, are prominent in operational innovation efforts. In short, the team must answer the following questions:[24]

- What are the expected outcomes of the process?
- What work has to be done to complete the process? Are there any activities that don't need to be done at all? How thoroughly does each aspect of the work need to be performed?
- Where should the work be done?
- When should the work be done?
- Who should do the work?
- What information must be provided to those doing the work?

By answering these questions, the new business process and associated organizational and information systems requirements become clear.

Step 5: Build buy-in at both management and working levels. Throughout the design work, members of the design team should be working with their counterparts in the organization to not only gather data as to what the current process entails, but to communicate the thinking of the design team so that both the people who will lead the new process, as well as those who will execute it, can make their inputs to the design and learn about it as it develops. Having that buy-in considerably accelerates the implementation process.

[24] http://www.infomanagementcenter.com/enewsletter/200408/feature.htm, August 6, 2006.

Step 6: Act. Don't get stuck in "analysis paralysis" or with a sense that the design has to be fully complete before implementation. Just as new product and service development teams prototype their ideas and try them out so that they can learn more about their designs, so the design of new business processes is an iterative one. Implement, measure, and adjust the process to fine-tune it over time rather than trying to fine-tune it before implementation.

Operational innovation almost inevitably leads to organizational redesign at some level. When a process gets radically restructured, there are many people throughout an organization who are affected. Thus, doing operational innovation goes hand in hand in many cases with organizational design. We summarize an approach for doing this next.

Developing an Organizational Design

Just as vertical integration, process technology, capacity, facilities, and sourcing strategies must be decided in the context of the overall business strategy, so must the organizational strategy for operations. Exhibit 7.26 depicts the steps in a process to develop and assess an organizational design:

Step 1: Identify key stakeholders and their interests. What outcomes do they want from the company? How do they measure those outcomes? What weight should each of their interests carry in the organizational design?

Step 2: Understand the business context. What is the business strategy? How is the firm positioned competitively? What capabilities does it wish to develop? What is management's philosophy about how to run the business? What are the characteristics of the workforce? Is it primarily knowledge workers?

Step 3: Identify the key dimensions of organizational focus. Along which dimensions does the company need to be focused to accomplish its work? A functional orientation?

EXHIBIT 7.26
Developing an Organizational Design

Source: Drawn in part from Beer, et al., *Managing Human Assets,* The Free Press, 1984.

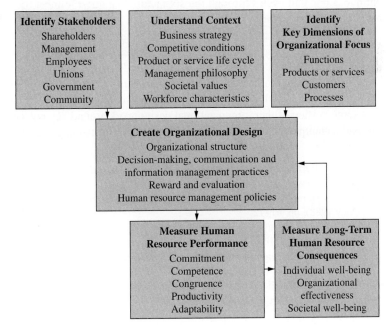

Identify Stakeholders	Understand Context	Identify Key Dimensions of Organizational Focus
Shareholders	Business strategy	Functions
Management	Competitive conditions	Products or services
Employees	Product or service life cycle	Customers
Unions	Management philosophy	Processes
Government	Societal values	
Community	Workforce characteristics	

Create Organizational Design
Organizational structure
Decision-making, communication and information management practices
Reward and evaluation
Human resource management policies

Measure Human Resource Performance	Measure Long-Term Human Resource Consequences
Commitment	Individual well-being
Competence	Organizational effectiveness
Congruence	Societal well-being
Productivity	
Adaptability	

A product or service focus? A customer focus? Which processes are most critical to the company's customers? What emphasis should be placed on them?

Step 4: Create an organizational design and implement. What structure—hierarchical, matrix, something in between—will best serve the company? How should decision making and communication be handled, in particular to integrate the organization around its important processes and tasks? How should both vertical and lateral information processing be managed? What types of skill sets are needed, and what hiring, training, and retention programs are needed to develop and support those skill sets? What mix of full-time, part-time, and contract employees should be used? How will people be evaluated and rewarded? To what extent should tangible compensation be used, and where are intangible rewards more beneficial?

Step 5: Measure human resource performance for that design. How effective is the chosen design? How committed are the employees to the organization? How well does the organization attract and develop employee competence? How productive is the organization? What levels of absenteeism and employee turnover does the organization sustain? How well aligned are the employees' goals to the company's? How adaptable is the organizational design to change?

Step 6: Measure the long-term impacts of the design. There are also longer-term consequences of an organizational design, including the effect on the well-being of the individuals who work for it, the effectiveness of the organization in reaching its overarching goals, and the extent to which the organization contributes to the well-being of the broader society in which it operates.

Step 7: Adjust the organizational design. Based on the measurements, there may be some adjustments needed to cause the organizational design to better align with the objectives of the business, or there may be changes in the business environment that suggest modifications to the design. Thus, the process of developing the organizational design is a continuous one that cycles through the six factors in a quest to meet the needs of an ever-changing business strategy.

Full treatment of the topic of organizational design is well beyond the scope of this book, and there are many good resources available to those thinking about it, some of which are listed at the end of this chapter. As is clear in the Gore example, however, organizational design plays a critical role in accomplishing the firm's objectives and requires attention by all functional areas including operations. Today's complex organizations find they must focus some portion of their organizational design work around key business processes. The tools and techniques in this chapter should help in understanding both of these issues.

References

Beer, Michael, Bert Spector, Paul Lawrence, D. Quinn Mills, and Richard Walton. *Managing Human Assets.* New York, NY: The Free Press, 1984, p. 16.

Boehm, B. "A Spiral Model of Software Development and Enhancement." *IEEE Computer* 21, no. 5, (May 1988), pp. 61–72.

Clark, Kim B., and Takahiro Fujimoto. *Product Development Performance: Strategy, Organization, and Management in the World Auto Industry.* Boston, MA: Harvard Business School Press, 1991.

Cooper, Robert G. *Winning at New Products: Accelerating the Process from Idea to Launch.* Cambridge, MA: Perseus Publishing, 2001.

Dutta, Devangshu. "Retail @ the Speed of Fashion." 2002, published at http://3isite.com/articles/ImagesFashion_Zara_Part_I.pdf, August 23, 2005.

Eppinger, Steven D. "Innovation at the Speed of Information." *Harvard Business Review,* 79. no. 1 (January 2001), pp. 149–158.

Eppinger, Steven D., and Anil R. Chitkara. "The New Practice of Global Product Development." *MIT Sloan Management Review* 47, no. 4 (Summer 2006), pp. 22–30.

Ferdows, Kasra, Michael A. Lewis, and Jose A.D. Machuca. "Rapid-Fire Fulfillment." *Harvard Business Review* 82, no. 11 (November 2004), pp. 104–110.

Galbraith, Jay. "Organization Design: An Information Processing View," *Interfaces* 4, no. 3 (May 1974), pp. 28–36.

Galbraith, Jay. "Organizing to Deliver Solutions." *Organizational Dynamics* 31, no. 2 (2002), pp. 194–207.

Hammer, Michael. "Deep Change: How Operational Innovation Can Transform Your Company." *Harvard Business Review* 82, no. 4 (April 2004), pp. 84–95.

Hammer, Michael. "Six Steps to Operational Innovation." April 2005, http://hbswk.hbs.edu/archive/4927.html, (accessed August 5, 2006).

Hammer, Michael, and James Champy. *Reengineering the Corporation.* New York: Harper Business, 1993.

Hayes, Robert. H., and Gary P. Pisano. "Beyond World Class: The New Manufacturing Strategy." *Harvard Business Review* 72, no. 1 (January–February 1994), pp. 77–86.

Hayes, Robert H., and David M. Upton. "Operations-Based Strategy." *California Management Review* 40, no. 4 (Summer 1998), pp. 8–25.

Hayes, Robert H., Steven C. Wheelwright, and Kim B. Clark. *Dynamic Manufacturing: Creating the Learning Organization.* New York, NY: The Free Press, 1988.

Heerwagen, Judith, Kevin Kelly, and Kevin Kampschroer. "The Changing Nature of Organizations, Work, and Workplace." February 8, 2006 *Whole Building Design Guide,* http://www.wbdg.org/design/chngorgwork. php?print=1, (accessed August 5, 2006).

Helft, Miguel. "Fashion Fast Forward." *Business 2.0,* 3, no. 5 (May 2002), pp. 61–66.

House, Charles H., and Raymond L. Price. "The Return Map: Tracking Product Teams." *Harvard Business Review,* 69, no. 1 (January–February 1991), pp. 92–101.

Klein, Janice A. "Re-Examination of Autonomy in Light of New Manufacturing Practices." *Human Relations* 44, no. 1 (1991), pp. 21–38.

Klein, Janice A., and Betty J. Barrett. "One Foot in a Global Team, One Foot at the Local Site: Making Sense of Living in Two Worlds Simultaneously." *Virtual Teams* 8 (2002), pp. 107–125.

Kraemer, Kenneth, and Jason Dedrick. "Dell Computer: Using e-Commerce to Support the Virtual Company." Center for Research on Information Technology and Organizations, June 2001, http://www.crito.uci.edu/GIT/publications/pdf/dell_ecom_case_6-13-01.pdf, (accessed August 3, 2006).

Poppendieck, Mary. "Principles of Lean Thinking." 2002, http://www.poppendieck.com/papers/Lean Thinking.pdf, (accessed August 2, 2006).

Porter, Michael E. "What Is Strategy?" *Harvard Business Review,* 74, no. 6 (November–December 1996), pp. 61–78.

Sosa, Manuel E., Steven D. Eppinger, and Craig M. Rowles. "The Misalignment of Product Architecture and Organizational Structure in Complex Product Development." *Management Science* 50, no. 12 (December 2004), pp. 1674–1689.

Taylor, Frederick W. *The Principles of Scientific Management,* New York: HarperCollins, 1911, and New York: W.W. Norton, 1967.

Ulrich, Karl T., and Steven D. Eppinger. *Product Design and Development,* 3rd ed. Burr Ridge, IL: McGraw-Hill/Irwin, 2004.

Chapter 8

Coordinating the Supply Chain

Introduction

In 1984 as an undergraduate at the University of Texas, Michael Dell started to sell computer components directly to his customers from his dormitory room. He then left college and started to build and sell PC clones directly to customers.[1] This was the beginning of Dell Computer Corporation and later Dell, Inc. The concept of the company was to deliver to customers the computers that they ordered directly from Dell. This concept was fairly simple. By selling computer systems directly to customers, Dell could best understand their needs and efficiently provide the most effective computing solutions to meet those needs. This approach eliminates retailers that add unnecessary time and cost, or can diminish Dell's understanding of customer expectations.[2] Product could not be obtained through retailers and could only be ordered by telephone or fax and later through the Internet.

This approach to marketing and selling and distributing the company's products was known as the *direct model*. The model led to significant growth and success, as Dell became the world's largest computer company in a relatively short amount of time (Exhibit 8.1). The direct model is still the basis of Dell's operations today. Dell deals directly with its customers without the use of retailers, distributors, or other third parties except its transportation agents. It has developed a sophisticated network of its own plants, along with the subcontractors that build complete systems such as laptops, modules for its other products, and peripherals and that provide transportation services to support its direct model. While Dell has encountered some business challenges at times and personal computers have become more of a commodity, the direct model and the systems that support it became the basis of Dell's strategy.

---

[1] http://www.hoovers.com/globaluk/sample/co/history.xhtml?COID=13193, September 3, 2006.

[2] http://www.dell.com/content/topics/global.aspx/corp/background/en/facts?c=us&l=en&s=corp&~section=000, September 3, 2006.

EXHIBIT 8.1

Dell's Annual Revenue and U.S. Personal Computer Share

Source: Data drawn from http://www.dell.com/content/topics/global.aspx/corp/investor/en/history?c=us&l=en&s=corp, September 3, 2006.

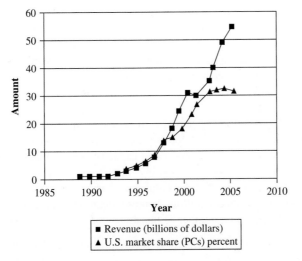

The direct model can be viewed as a system of marketing, sales, and distribution. It can also be viewed as a system of information management for order processing and a sophisticated system of distributing finished goods. These are certainly important parts of the Dell system, but, in terms of operations, Dell's capabilities in coordinating the supply chain have enabled Dell to execute the direct model. The direct model is an integrated system for responding to customers in a very short amount of time. This system includes several characteristics:

- First, the system requires carefully monitored inventory (typically owned by suppliers) so that the company will have everything it needs to build computers.
- Second, it requires a set of production lines that can assemble computers quickly.
- Third, it requires enough capacity in assembly to handle peak short-term assembly requirements. Assembly capacity is managed in such a way that it can be increased or decreased quickly, as with temporary workers, but at peak it is enough to respond to all orders.
- Fourth, it requires the information systems to process the custom built orders and coordinate the kitting, building, and delivery of these orders.
- Finally, it requires a product development and management system that emphasizes the product variety that the system is capable of but limits variations that the system cannot fulfill.

Dell has utilized a system that is referred to as *postponement* that we will describe in more detail later in the chapter. What Dell does is build-to-order from a specific point in the value chain, but up until that point the system uses a traditional build-to-stock system. In that sense the value added is postponed until the order arrives and the computer is built. The advantage of the system is that the lead time from the point of postponement is relatively short compared with the lead time for the components and modules that are part of the machine. Thus, Dell can build the computer and customize it in a relatively short amount of time.

While Dell markets a build-to-order system, it is only build-to-order for part of the value chain. In addition, the range of variation available to customers is limited within certain guidelines. The chassis (the computer case), for example, is standardized with only a small number of chassis variations so that the assembly process can be standardized. The strategy is thus limited customization with rapid order fulfillment. At the same time, Dell has developed a cost advantage since inventories are reduced and distribution does not include any retailing steps.

The skills needed to develop this strategy encompass a number of areas. They include the inventory management for the components and parts, the coordination of suppliers, and the coordination of the custom production and capacity management systems. They also include the information systems for assembly, distribution, capacity management, and order processing. The skills that Dell has emphasized are in the areas of logistics and supply chain management, and its capabilities in these areas are a large part of its success.

The Dell example suggests a number of questions about supply chain management:

- How does a company determine where to locate inventory and what inventory service levels to support, and how do these inventory decisions support strategy?
- How do decisions in transportation and distribution, flow patterns with suppliers and distributors, and other related questions affect the strategic position of the firm?
- Can the outcomes of the decisions improve a company's performance cost, quality, availability, features/innovativeness, or environmental performance?
- How do supply chain decisions affect availability and the subdimensions of availability such as lead times, breadth of product line, and so on?
- What are the trade-offs inherent in the logistics and supply chain system? For example, is there a trade-off between cost and service?
- What are the key factors in general that dictate logistics and supply chain design?
- Which factors support strategies such as customization or rapid or direct delivery?

This chapter explores these questions and the general question of how to design the supply chain.

Supply Chain Decisions

We first attempt to understand and clarify the use of the term *supply chain management*. The term has acquired a great deal of significance in recent years, but its meaning is subject to some ambiguity. Supply chain management has traditionally encompassed such issues as supply chain structure and number of distribution locations, assignment of customers to plants and warehouses, inventory management, supply chain metrics, forecasting, reverse logistics, demand management, and relationship management. As the era of outsourcing and dealing with multiple partners has evolved, the term supply chain often has come to imply a much broader definition and, in some minds, now includes strategies for vertical integration, outsourcing, and supplier management. Some consider the supply chain strategy to be virtually the entire operations strategy. While our definition of the supply chain is fairly broad and includes such concepts as supply chain structure, we do not include vertical integration or supplier management. These issues were addressed in Chapters 2 and 6, respectively.

Logistics and supply chain decisions, even using the narrower range that we include, encompass a number of areas:

- *Inventory management:* Inventory management includes two separate decision areas. The first is *inventory levels*. In particular what levels of inventory for make-to-stock goods should be considered? How will this vary by item? The second is *inventory positioning*. Specifically, at what locations in the supply chain will inventory be positioned?

- *Production planning and materials management:* At the production level, how does a company plan inventory and schedule production? While these decisions affect strategic positioning, they can also be the basis of unique capabilities through lean operations. The question of lean capabilities is treated more extensively in Chapter 10.

- *Forecasting and demand management:* This includes the methods for forecasting demand, so that inventory policies and methods for managing demand in response to uncertainty can be set.

- *Transportation modes and policies:* How will goods be transported to customers or final inventory points? Will high-speed modes such as air be used, or will lower-cost modes such as truck or rail be used? What modes are used for the range of products and customers? How much air transportation should be used? Should air transport supplement ocean freight for expedited orders? For certain classes of items? Should it be used exclusively?

- *Reverse logistics:* How does the supply chain deal with returns and flows back from customers?

- *Supply chain structure:* Supply chain structure specifies the number of stages of supply and the locations of value-added work. It also describes to what extent demand is pulled and configured to order. A personal computer may be built to order at one of several locations, with component inventories that are procured on a build-to-stock basis from a series of first- and second-tier vendors.

- *Distribution structure:* How many distribution centers and warehouses should be used, both regionally and globally? Where should they be located? These decisions will affect both service in terms of proximity and cost in terms of efficiency. Strategies that distinguish between smaller and larger numbers of distribution centers can affect the strategic posture of the firm.

- *Distribution flow patterns:* Which location is each customer zone serviced from? Alternatively, will customers be served directly at their homes and businesses? If so, how will such distribution be handled?

- *Metrics:* How is the supply chain evaluated? What metrics best fit the strategic objectives?

- *Outsourcing of supply chain activities:* To what extent should supply chain activities such as transportation, distribution, and warehousing be outsourced? Serving customers directly often requires contracting a company such as UPS to deliver. In general the framework of Chapter 2 can be used to address this issue.

- *Supplier selection and coordination:* There are major supply chain choices even after the outsourcing decision is made. Different supplier options and how they are coordinated will have major effects on material flow, and these options can change dynamically. Some apparel companies will use a wide range of contractors and manage these contractors on an ongoing basis, and the choices of contractors might change periodically.

With increased outsourcing, the challenges of coordination have become more significant. Mechanisms for coordination such as vendor-managed inventories, discussed more in Chapter 6, can help address some of these challenges.

Logistics and supply chain decisions will have their major impacts on availability. But there are a variety of subdimensions of availability. These dimensions include delivery time, percentage of demand satisfied from stock, breadth of product line, and customization capability. Logistics and supply chain issues can also affect other strategic dimensions. Efficient management of inventories, for example, in a postponement type of system can provide significant cost advantages. The variety of dimensions of availability suggests an expanded set of tools for logistics and supply chain decisions, which we explore further in the next section.

A variety of technologies have increased the impact of supply chain decisions. These technologies include information technology, transportation, and warehousing and have led to new supply chain forms and concepts. Some of these concepts revolve around direct customer delivery. Others reach the other end of the spectrum through large centralized warehouses such as the warehouse club. How does one evaluate the applicability of these concepts?

While developments in technology have enabled major improvements in logistics and supply chain performance, companies still face major pitfalls in making decisions:

- *Lead times:* Lead times for many components are quite long, particularly in the age of globalization.
- *Offshore sourcing and production:* Dealing with offshore sourcing and production can significantly complicate management of the supply chain.
- *Lack of visibility:* Despite the advancement in information technology, many businesses do not have the visibility into the activities of all parts of their supply chains.
- *Multiple moves:* Because of the advent of outsourcing and multiple stages of production, we see material move many times before the ultimate arrival at the customer. The personal computer is a classic example. A typical microprocessor might be produced by Intel in Arizona, packaged as an individual microprocessor in Malaysia or the Philippines, attached to a motherboard in Taiwan, and assembled in a PC somewhere in the United States or Europe.

These factors can lead to adverse results in supply chains and logistics. When multiple procurements from various far-flung locations in the world are required, both significant inventories and out-of-stock situations can result. Long lead times and lack of visibility can create the same result. The strategic task is to develop structures and systems that overcome these problems and support the operations strategy.

To address these issues, we present in the next two sections a set of tools and approaches for making supply decisions.

Tools for Supply Chain Decisions

We first present a number of tools for making supply chain decisions and evaluating trade-offs.

Input and Output Framework

Supply chain decisions need to address both the multiplicity of supply chain decisions and the range of strategic outputs. Decisions will have major impacts on cost, availability, and environmental performance and, indirectly, on quality and features/innovativeness. Cost is significantly affected by the efficiency of the logistics system and supply chain. With lower levels of inventory and shorter lead times, major advantages of cost can be gained. Availability has a number of subcategories:

• *Delivery or service time:* How long does it take to deliver to customers? Under a make-to-stock system, this would be transit time. Under a make-to-order system, it would be assembly plus transit time.

• *Service level:* What percentage of demand is satisfied from stock in a make-to-stock system? In a make-to-order system, what percentage of component demand is satisfied from stock? In general, what is the service performance of inventory?

• *Variation of service level or delivery time:* In most logistics systems and supply chains, service level will vary according to a number of dimensions such as customer class, order priority, item type, and item demand. For very slow-moving items, for example, companies might choose to have a lower level of service. Since a given service level requires a higher percentage of safety stock for slow-moving items (Magee et al. 1985), the lower service level will allow for better use of inventory investment. For slower-moving items in a national distribution network, a single-stock location may allow service level to be comparable to other items, but this may cause longer lead times.

Other criteria to allow differentiated service include different classes of customers and orders. For example, a price premium may dictate faster delivery. Product characteristics may also dictate differentiated service.

Lighter-weight, higher-value products can be stocked in a single location with a high service level and low delivery time. The reason for this is that lighter-weight, higher-value products do not, on a relative basis, incur a great deal of transportation costs. On the other hand, they do incur more inventory costs because of their value, so keeping inventory in a single location makes sense. The ratio of the value to weight, which dictates the relative value of inventory and transportation cost, is what we call the *value density*. Whatever the criterion, differentiation on service can have different meanings.

• *Customization and breadth of product line or service:* A great deal of breadth in the product line requires an extensive inventory to support the larger range of items. Customization requires a strategy of readily available components, production capacity to handle customization, and possibly quick-response transportation capabilities.

Mapping Tools

The logistics and supply chain strategy involves mapping decisions to the various strategic outputs. The major decisions that we noted in the last section will have direct effects on the subcategories noted above.

Exhibit 8.2 presents the table for mapping strategic outputs to the major supply decisions. Ideally, it could be used for a planning mechanism for developing a strategy. The exhibit also presents an example of how some of the inputs might affect some of the outputs. In any application, the inputs are a combination of many factors, and the example shows the effects of some of these factors. For the case of transportation modes, we might consider how the use of air compared with ocean freight might affect things. We would expect the use of air transport to improve delivery time and decrease variation.

A company can use the mapping tool to identify potential strategies. For example, if the strategy is based on customization or fast delivery, the chart can be used to identify policies

EXHIBIT 8.2   Strategic Inputs and Outputs for Logistics System and Supply Chain

N denotes neutral, arrows denote effect

	Delivery or Service Time	Service Inventory Level	Variation of Service Level	Customization and Breadth of Product Line
Transportation Modes	Air ↑	N	Air ↓	N
Inventory Levels	Higher ↑	↑	↓	↑
Inventory Position	Closer ↑	N	↑	↓
Supplier Selection and Coordination	Diverse, remote ↓	N	↑	Diverse ↑
Distribution Structure	Locations ↑	N	↑	↓
Planning and Scheduling	Customization ↓	↓	↑	↑

for each of the major supply chain decisions. Faster delivery time would entail more use of air and/or more locations.

We explore two of these inputs—distribution structure and inventory positioning—further.

Distribution Structure

Distribution structure focuses on the number of facilities and locations. Additional locations provide closer proximity to customers, but with increased costs. As an approximation, total inventory costs increase with the square root of the number of locations, while distance to customers decreases inversely with the square root. (See, for example, Magee et al. 1985 or Pendrock and Rosenfield 1980).

Thus

$$C = En^{1/2} \quad \text{and} \quad D = Fn^{-1/2}$$

where

C = Cost
D = Distance to customers
n = Number of warehouses
E and F are constants.

These approximations are based on a number of assumptions plus some features of single-station inventory models; the rationale is presented in the appendix to this chapter.

Often times, supply chain and logistics performance can be significantly improved by increasing the number of locations despite the increase in facilities costs. With any make-to-stock system with finished goods inventory, this is often the case. As a general rule, one can use these relationships to get an approximate idea of the trade-off between cost and service and thereby establish the number of distribution points in the system.

Information technology has often been cited for enhancing supply chain performance. The great improvement in transportation systems in the United States has also had a significant impact. With modern transportation methods, a company can have five strategically placed warehouses and still reach nearly all the population of the country with one day of ground travel time. The same is true in Europe. Exhibit 8.3 presents a

EXHIBIT 8.3
Example of Five Warehouses Covering Nearly all the U.S. Population within One Day of Travel

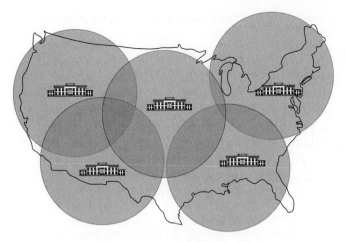

scenario for the United States with five warehouses covering the country. Similar improvements have been realized in material handling and warehousing technologies.

Distribution structure also includes the strategy for material flow from source to destination. This will often require a network flow model. Such a model often uses optimization procedures, and models flow through factories, warehouses, and distribution centers. Typical issues addressed include which warehouses service each set of customers, where the warehouses are located, and what the required flow from factories to warehouses is. These types of models were presented in Chapter 5 as important tools for developing a facilities strategy. They are also important tools for developing a supply chain strategy.

Inventory Positioning

Positioning indicates where in the supply chain inventory is located. With many possible inventory locations, the company needs to choose the locations for buffer inventories. Other locations would have little or no buffer inventory. A good approximation rule is to limit the number of such buffer locations to as few as possible. In particular, with multiple stages of production and distribution and multiple sites at each stage, placing stock at all or most locations can significantly increase inventory since so many locations are in the network. A company can eliminate stock at some stages (except for stock in transit or cycle stock) without adversely affecting service by assuring that any reserves cover the lead time to the next upstream location that has buffer stocks. (See, for example, Willems 2000.) While the buffer point closest to the customer is a particularly important location (treated later as the push-pull delimiter), other locations are also important strategically. Some guidelines in determining buffer locations are:

- Buffer before the high value-added steps.
- Buffer after variable lead times.
- Buffer before significant increases in product variety.

While these are just general guidelines, they can be helpful when the supply chain has a large number of steps.

Item limitation is an additional factor in inventory location and positioning decisions. One may not want to store all items in all locations. The reason for this has to do with economies of scale in inventory management. Faster-moving items require a lower amount of inventory (on a proportional basis) to meet a given level of service. The general relationship is as follows (see Rosenfield 1994):

$$C = AS^{-B}$$

where

C = percent inventory cost
A = a constant
S = item sales
B = a constant between 0 and 0.5 (typically 0.3 or 0.4)

The appendix presents the rationale for this.

Since it is more expensive to stock slower-moving items, strategies for storing these items include providing lower levels of service or, more typically, stocking them in fewer locations. Since inventory also increases with the number of locations, as noted before, stocking in fewer locations mitigates the expense of supporting a slow-moving item. This type of strategy is used effectively for slow-moving but expensive spare parts and by mail-order companies for their slow-moving items.

Amazon.com, as a national retailer with a wide variety of products, illustrates this possibility. While the company has a national network of warehouses, it has the capability of stocking very slow-moving items at single locations. In fact, one of Amazon's competitive advantages is that it has the scale to stock very-slow-moving items at individual locations.

Item consolidation is an example of economies of scale in supply chain operations. Scale arises in transportation, inventory management, and warehousing. In transportation, more volume allows more frequent full loads. Alternatively, if transportation is either partially or completely outsourced, then economies can be gained through volume pricing or bringing consolidated loads directly to an outside carrier facility. Amazon.com follows this strategy, which it calls *carrier injection,* by delivering large consolidated loads to locations of the postal service and other carriers at locations that are relatively close to the customer. In warehousing, higher volumes allow for higher efficiency. Finally, in inventory management, the relationship between inventory and sales volumes indicates that higher volumes require less inventory on a percentage basis. Companies with larger volumes due to market share or national consolidation, such as Amazon.com, can capitalize on such economies.

Cost-Service Trade-Offs

Often, the choices in supply chain decisions can be the basis of trade-offs in strategic outputs. For example, by increasing inventory costs to carry additional items, service (through a wider range of items) can be improved. Cost and service show a trade-off in a number of ways. For example, while additional warehouses can increase costs, service is improved because product is held in closer proximity to customers. Alternatively, faster transportation can provide faster service but at higher costs. Analysis of such trade-offs can be useful in making supply chain decisions.

Rosenfield et al. (1985) explore the cost-service trade-off curve where service is represented as delivery time. They present models to develop the curve and discuss its importance as a tool for developing a logistics and supply chain strategy. Strategically it can

EXHIBIT 8.4
Typical Cost-Service Trade-Off Curve

Source: Rosenfield et al., "Implications of Cost-Service Trade-offs on Industry Logistics Structures," *Interfaces,* 1985. Reprinted with permission.

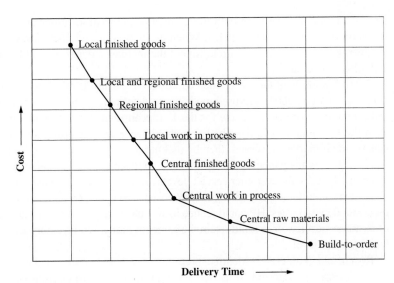

clearly present to a company the range of trade-offs available in making decisions on inventory positioning. For example, it can illustrate the range of cost premiums needed for improvement in service.

Exhibit 8.4 shows a typical cost-service trade-off curve. Exhibit 8.5 shows an example from a consumer products company. The interesting aspect of this example is that cost and

EXHIBIT 8.5
Sample Cost-Service Trade-Off Curve for a Consumer Products Company

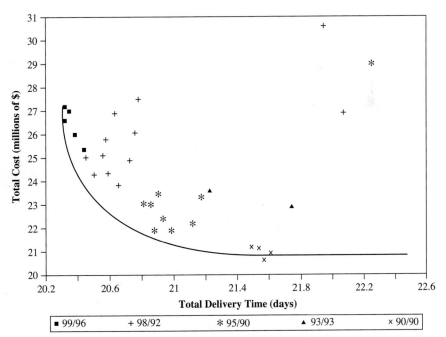

Specific scenarios varied locations and number of warehouses. First number (e.g., 99 in 99/96) represents service on A items, second number represents service on B and C items. A items are fast movers, and B and C items represent moderate and slow movers, respectively.

service variations arise from both the number of physical locations and inventory service levels on different classes of items. When an item is out of stock at the nearest location, the average service time goes up to reflect the increased delivery time from the factory or next closest source.

A good example of the use of such curves is HP's analysis of its DeskJet printer business (Kopczak and Lee 2004). HP used modeling to determine (a) whether or not to use a facility in Europe to customize products for the European market rather than continue to serve it from the U.S. facility and (b) whether it should redesign the printer to use a power supply generic to all markets it served (thereby making the customization for the European market and inventory management easier operations). In this case, the models focused on trading off inventory levels with customer service levels, and the output is shown in Exhibit 8.6. The benefits of undertaking any one of the proposed strategies or a combination of them can be understood in two ways: HP could reduce its inventory investment and achieve the same level of customer service, or it could retain the same investment in inventory and increase its customer service level.

Rosenfield et al. (1985) identify three sets of factors that dictate the shape of the curve. These factors are referred to as demand and variety, transportation economics, and the value-added chain. The demand and variety factor reflects demand stability and predictability; stability increases with higher demand, lower variability, and lower product variety. With more stability, the inventory investment required to reach a desired service level is much lower. It thus becomes feasible to position inventory at more locations while still

EXHIBIT 8.6
Cost-Service
Trade-Offs for
HP Example

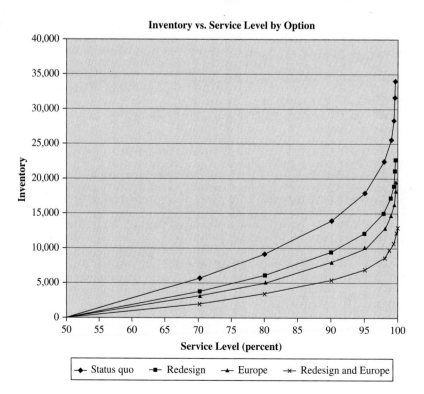

maintaining a moderate investment. With more stability it is hence easier to get better service through more inventory locations. The transportation economics factor is determined by the ratio of value to unit weight (or value density, which we discuss shortly). As value per unit weight increases, it becomes more cost-effective to provide higher service through faster transportation alternatives. The value chain parameter explores how much value is added as delivery time is increased. This dictates the cost and service alternatives for stocking inventory at various points of the value chain. In the next section we will also use these factors to generalize the types of logistics and supply chain strategies that might be appropriate in different circumstances.

Strategic options for the models that Rosenfield et al. (1985) propose include transportation modes, number of inventory positions, inventory service level, and degree of postponement of final inventory position. The authors also discuss the competitive implications of different shapes of curves.

While the curve may not be fully constructible in all situations, the strategic task is to understand the range of cost and service alternatives available to a company. This can help the company articulate its logistics and supply chain strategy.

Matching Structure to Product and Market Characteristics

In the process technology chapter (Chapter 3) we introduced the concept of matching the process technology to the characteristics of the product and markets. The product-process matrix was one of the methods presented in that chapter. A similar approach can be developed for the supply chain. By examining product characteristics and market factors, we can design the supply chain to best fit the needs of these products and the markets of which they are part. Rosenfield et al. (1985) suggest three such factors. Based on these factors, a company can often suggest the type of logistics and supply chain strategy that might be appropriate.

The first factor is the magnitude of transportation costs. In evaluating this, the organization needs to determine how to measure such costs or, put another way, what other costs transportation costs are being compared with. The important comparisons are to procurement costs, production costs, and inventory costs. The general factor dictating relative delivery cost is *value density,* which is the value per unit weight. This measure has always been important in logistics and supply chain decisions. With high value density, the importance of inventory costs due to higher values outweighs the importance of transportation costs due to low weights. Strategies that emphasize reduced numbers of inventory locations are advisable here. An example might be a single centralized location with expedited transportation. With low value density, a strategy with multiple locations closer to customers to reduce transportation costs might make more sense.

A second factor is demand uncertainty. This is typically related to the volume of sales or movement of a typical product. For fast-moving products, there are economies of scale in inventory in that demand uncertainty is relatively low.[3] For fast-moving products, it is thus feasible to stock goods at many locations, as the inventory required will not be significant

[3] It is not always true of course that faster-moving items have less demand uncertainty (on a relative basis) than slower-moving items. However, on an empirical basis, this is typically the case when one examines multi-item data at most companies. There are also statistical models that suggest that faster-moving items have less uncertainty.

even with multiple locations. Slow-moving items have higher demand uncertainty and thus require larger inventories on a percentage basis. These in turn are best stocked at a limited number of locations because of the high inventory costs. The importance of volume of demand as a proxy for demand uncertainty depends on the assumption that volume of sales correlates with predictability of demand. While this is in general true, there may be counter examples where it is not, such as for newly introduced products in a growing market.

The concept that different levels of demand uncertainty warrant different supply chain designs is in some sense not a complicated one, and a number of observers emphasize this. Fisher (1997) suggests that *functional products with predictable demand* should be handled with efficient supply chains that focus on minimizing inventories and costs. He suggests that *innovative products with uncertain demand* should be handled with responsive supply chains with excess capacity and buffer stocks. For product sets with a wide range of uncertainty, it is important to maintain different supply chain structures or at least have different treatments of the different sets of products.

A third factor is product variety. This factor is closely tied in with product volume, as significant variety is closely correlated with low volumes. With large product variety, volumes are typically low, demand uncertainty is usually high, and inventory is more expensive on a relative basis. In these cases, a company might follow the same types of strategies that work with high demand uncertainty, such as stocking inventory only at a limited number of locations. Alternatively, a firm might employ a postponement strategy by limiting variety to later in the process.

Simchi-Levi et al. (2003) have attempted to classify strategies according to the value density (referred to as relative delivery cost) and demand uncertainty, two of the three key factors noted above. They developed a chart that presents logistics and supply chain strategies as a function of the four combinations of demand uncertainty and value density (Exhibit 8.7). For low value density and low demand uncertainty, transportation costs are relatively high, inventory costs are relatively low, and the low demand uncertainty allows efficient inventory usage. In this case, which would apply to high-volume commodities, one would use multiple stock locations with high service levels. With high-value density and high demand uncertainty, transportation costs are low and inventory costs are high. In this case, one is less concerned with transportation costs, but inventory costs must be

EXHIBIT 8.7
**Supply Chain
Strategies as
a Function of
Key Variables**

Source: Adapted
from Simchi-Levi
et al., *Designing and
Managing the Supply
Chain,* 2nd ed.,
McGraw-Hill/Irwin,
2003.

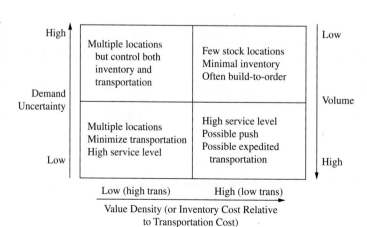

carefully managed. One minimizes stock locations and should consider build-to-order. These two cases comprise the lower-left and upper-right corners of the table. The two other corners represent more complicated combinations. The upper left involves high uncertainty and hence difficult-to-manage inventory costs, but also high transportation costs. Both of these sets of costs must be managed. (Simchi-Levi et al. 2003 suggest that furniture falls in this category and that it is best distributed on a fixed schedule.) The lower right involves low transportation costs and high value density, but demand uncertainty is low. In this case, one may not have many stock locations, at least for some items, but a relatively high service level may be possible, regardless. Simchi-Levi et al. (2003) suggest a push system in this situation and note that books and CDs fit this profile.

Supply Chain Tools Summary

The input-output framework, cost-service trade-off curve, and product-market matching tools can all be useful in determining supply chain choices. Decisions such as number of inventory locations, service levels, and transportation modes can all be supported by these types of tools. We now present some specific approaches that serve as the basis of supply chain strategy.

Approaches for Managing the Supply Chain

We review a number of approaches for managing the supply chain. These include the use of information technology to better coordinate the supply chain, use of a postponement system to better manage lead time and product variety, and focusing on customization and direct delivery. For the particular case of postponement, we discuss the difference between what we call internal and external postponement. Such approaches can be the basis of competitive advantage as in the case of Dell.

Using Information Technology to Coordinate the Supply Chain

Modern supply chains often have a large number of steps and they are often owned by different companies. A poorly coordinated supply chain can lead to poor service, frequent stockouts, redundant inventories, or a combination of such problems. In coordinating a supply chain, information technology can take on a major role. Coordinating a supplier and manufacturer in a JIT environment, for example, will require frequent exchange of information. While we treat information technology issues more extensively in Chapter 9, we discuss the information technology issues that affect supply chain management and coordination issues here.

To illustrate the issues in coordination, we describe one of the most common problems that can occur in multistage supply chains, either within a single organization or across a multicompany supply chain. This problem, the bullwhip effect was illustrated in Exhibit 1.1 (see, for example, Lee et al. 1997). The bullwhip effect is the amplification of variation from the end of the supply chain (with the customer) to the upstream suppliers and wholesalers. This amplification in variability creates the need for significant extra capacity and inventory and causes difficulties in planning. The bullwhip effect is illustrated in Exhibit 8.8 for a four-stage system.

EXHIBIT 8.8
Demand Variation by Supply Chain Location under the Bullwhip Effect

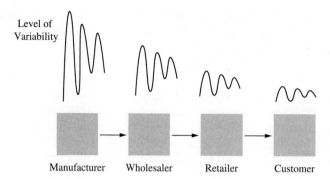

The bullwhip effect is a strategic issue since it can have a significant negative impact on cost and service. Supply chain and logistics performance is often closely linked with the degree that the bullwhip can be controlled. Since many, if not most, supply chains are multiple stages, the effect can be a major issue. As we will suggest, management of the bullwhip effect is often an information technology issue.

Lee et al. (1997) point out four causes of the bullwhip effect. These include (1) demand forecasting updating, (2) order batching, (3) price fluctuation, and (4) rationing and shortage gaming. How each of these causes the bullwhip effect is straightforward. Demand updating from a perceived increase in the forecast might cause one player in the supply chain to increase orders, resulting in a bigger variance to the next party upstream. When customers or particular stages of the supply chain order in batches upstream, demand is again distorted. Finally, pricing changes and perceived shortages will cause players to increase orders, thereby increasing the variance of demand upstream. Since the mathematical variance increases, additional stocks must be maintained to protect against the increased variance.

An additional cause of the bullwhip effect that Lee et al. (1997) does not include is what we call *decentralized policies*. Since each player in the supply chain formulates inventory policy based on inventory at its position, the set of policies cannot be optimal. If a great deal of inventory exists downstream of a position, then it may not make sense for the position to order less, even if it has very low inventory. The best policies should be based on all the information for all the positions. One strategy that has proven to be effective looks at what is called the *echelon inventory*, which is the inventory at a position as well as the entire inventory downstream of that position.

In our view, the major cause of the bullwhip effect is filling the pipeline (Lee et al. 1997 refer to it as *demand forecasting updating*). When the forecast changes, the work in process must reflect that change. If the demand forecast changes from 100 to 200 units per week and the lead time is four weeks, for example, then work-in-process inventory must change from 400 units to 800 units, a change that causes a major burden on all stages of the supply chain.

Approaches for Dealing with the Bullwhip Effect

To some extent, the bullwhip effect is unavoidable. However, information technology and other approaches can be useful in dealing with the effect. Strategies for mitigating the bullwhip effect consist of forecasting improvements; structural approaches such as incentives, alignment of metrics, and pricing; coordination or centralization of information and policy; and supply chain visibility. The first strategy, forecasting improvements, can reduce the effects of filling the pipeline, particularly by reducing lead times. Structural approaches such as incentives were described in Chapter 6.

The general idea of the third approach, the coordination or centralization approach, is to manage the supply chain in a coordinated manner in the way that a single party could manage it. The single party would have information available on all of the stages of the supply chain, including inventories, orders, and, most important, customer demand. Decisions can then be made that are responsive to customer demand while inventory is still managed within the entire supply chain. Vendor-managed inventory, for example, allows one party (the supplier) to coordinate the supply chain for more than one partner. Collaborative mechanisms such as collaborative planning forecasting and replenishment (CPFR), while not centralizing information and policy, allow multiple parties to work together and thus help to achieve the same goal. These types of approaches have resulted in better managed supply chains in some industries.

The information technology role in addressing the bullwhip effect is *supply chain visibility*. Information about demand and inventory must be visible to all players in the supply chain. The most important part of this information is customer demand. To some extent, visibility of customer demand is the holy grail of logistics and supply chain management. If information can be captured at the point of sale and shared by all the supply chain partners, the bullwhip effect can be reduced and, more generally, the performance of the logistics system and the supply can be greatly improved.

There can be countervailing forces that create barriers to supply chain visibility and better coordination. Promotions can lead to amplification of the bullwhip effect. A supplier may view the customer or the customer may view the supplier as a competitive threat that may move vertically within the supply chain and assume additional market power. In absence of a mutually beneficial relationship, the partner could be viewed as a threat.

Examples of Coordination and Information Systems Issues

Some examples illustrate the coordination and the information systems issues—both the advantages that can be gained as well as the negative effects that result when there is a lack of coordination. An instructive example is the traditional distribution model for the automobile industry. While automobile companies are attempting to implement more direct methods of ordering and replenishment, dealers historically have ordered most cars. With some exceptions, the manufacturers do not observe customer demand, but only the orders that the dealers place. In addition, true demand may not be the same as actual sales, since the latter is distorted by showroom inventory. (For example, a customer may buy a vehicle that has a set of options different from what he or she desires.) This creates a number of problems. The production is not geared to actual demand, but to a filtered demand based on what dealers think customer demand is going to be. In addition, the manufacturers undergo a bullwhip effect in that the filtered demand they see has a higher variance and is subject to the "filling the pipeline" effect. Furthermore, to the extent that demand must be partially forecast, the forecasting is being done independently by the set of dealers. The result is increased inventories that often include specific vehicle models that are infrequently ordered.

In addition to these effects, which are primarily due to the two-stage manufacturer-dealer system, custom orders take a great deal of time, and the entire system is burdened with large amounts of inventory because of the number of dealers. Some of the effects of this are large numbers of dealers in major metropolitan areas and option packages in dealer inventory that do not quite reflect customer demand.

The automobile manufacturers are struggling to make improvements in the system and are trying to find alternatives. Saturn, when it was first established, developed systems to better monitor customer demand and limit dealer options. All the automobile manufacturers are identifying ways to reduce lead times on custom orders. The example illustrates the ways in which information technology can support supply chain and logistics strategies.

E-commerce applications represent additional ways that information systems can be used together with logistics and supply chain improvements. While auction sites have been the application most publicized (and oversold), we have seen e-commerce applications that have made more effective use of supply chains. Amazon.com can use its position as a national retailer to gain an advantage in supplying low-demand items. It needs to stock such items at one location only. While other concepts, such as grocery delivery, have foundered, e-commerce technology does suggest the possibility of innovative supply chain concepts.[4]

A number of companies now use information technology to provide advantages in the operation and coordination of the supply chain, which in turn give a major competitive advantage in operations and service. Wal-Mart has used information systems to develop a number of operations advantages. By capturing and monitoring customer demand and using this information to better control orders and inventory, Wal-Mart can gain a cost advantage. The company carefully manages store inventories with this information. This control is extended throughout the distribution system, as Wal-Mart uses its information technology capabilities to coordinate the flow and inventories through its distribution centers.

Through the use of information systems, Cisco has developed capabilities for coordinating its orders through its group of suppliers. Cisco outsources nearly all of its production and uses what it refers to as a *loosely coupled supply chain.* (See Hagel and Brown 2002.)

Postponement and Customization

A second approach for managing the supply chain is postponement. The postponement concept has served as a major method of innovation in the use of supply chains. (See Zinn and Bowersox 1988 and Lee et al. 1993.) Postponement is stocking of goods *before* final configuration or customization (see Exhibit 8.9), with final configuration and customization pulled from the postponement portal. In the well-known example of postponement implemented by HP (Kopczak and Lee 2004) cited earlier in the discussion of trade-off curves, the company would make printer "engines" for the entire world in one location, and the localization materials (labels, power supplies, manuals, etc.) would be added subject to local demands in various markets. The point of the postponement was chosen so that the company would be able to carry inventories of printer engines to handle the entire world market in one location, while reducing final inventories of the configured printers within each country.

Postponement can either be *internal* or *external.* In an externally focused postponement system, the final assembly or configuration is not completed until the final customer makes an order. Thus, Dell stocks motherboards, disk drives, and other PC components

---

[4] Amazon has implemented a number of information technology concepts that have given it advantages in supply chain performance. These include order processing and fulfillment, logistics, and inventory management (Wilke 2002). Some of the applications include how to set inventory levels, how to fill orders from inventory, and where to locate inventory. Its use of information technology is further explored in the next chapter.

EXHIBIT 8.9
A Postponement
System

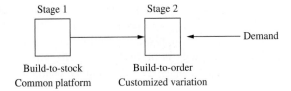

Stage 1

Stage 2

Demand

Build-to-stock
Common platform

Build-to-order
Customized variation

and then assembles to order. By doing this, it gains advantages from stocking only generic components from which orders are drawn. The components represent the change from a push system (inventory is anticipatory stock) to a pull system (systems are built to order). In an internally based system, finished goods inventories are still used to satisfy demand, but postponement limits such inventories. HP still kept stocks of printers for each market, but the lead times were much smaller because of the inventory of in-process engines.

Postponement can lead to significant advantages whether it is internally or externally focused. Inventory can be consolidated where there is less product variety (thereby reducing inventory due to economies of scale), and lead times can be reduced for any configuration step that is postponed since there is a shortened lead time to a previous inventory step. When a system is externally focused, we have the possibility of customization to customers with a relatively short lead time.

The factors that enter into postponement decisions are similar to the inventory positioning question discussed earlier. The issue becomes not only where to place inventory, but also what form, in terms of component and subassemblies, should be stored. So the factors for the various steps in the value chain are the value added at each step, lead times, variability of lead times, and changes in product and component variety. Postponing internally implies stocking components or subassemblies at a particular step. Ideally, this is before a great deal of value is added or product variety greatly increases, but also before short and deterministic lead times.

Postponement strategies are often referred to as push-pull strategies, where production or distribution is pushed to a particular point in the supply chain based on forecasted demand. (See, for example, Simchi-Levi et al. 2003.) From that point on, demand is pulled based on actual demand. The point at which inventory is positioned and from which orders are pulled we will refer to as the *push-pull delimiter* or *boundary*. In a classical warehousing system, the push-pull delimiter is the warehouse where merchandise is stocked. Demand is then pulled from the warehouse. The innovative concept of postponement is that the push-pull delimiter or boundary is often before the final production of a product.

The externally based postponement system is illustrated by Dell, which builds and configures personal computers from components and subassemblies. Some of the factors in inventory positioning and internally based postponement are relevant here. The lead time for assembly and configuration is quite short, enabling Dell to fulfill orders to customers in just a few days. Product variety increases a great deal between the components and final configuration, and value added for final configuration is high. The conditions for postponement are ideal for placing inventory at the component level, and Dell has used this to develop an entire operating system.

Postponement strategies have made customization viable to a much greater degree than previously envisioned. Even in situations where postponement opportunities are not possible or are limited, it is still possible to customize products and services to individual customers. Costs will increase but they may be worth the trade-off. One needs to design the manufacturing system and supply chain to do this as efficiently as possible. We explore customization as a strategy in more detail in Chapter 10. The point is that customization is often associated with specialized supply chain capabilities such as component availability.

Implementing Externally Based Postponement Systems

The implementation of an externally based postponement system and the location of the push-pull delimiter or boundary suggest questions of both production and distribution. Simchi-Levi and Simchi-Levi (2002) suggest that the boundary should consider the entire length of the value chain (See Exhibit 8.10). If a distribution center, warehouse, or retail store is a boundary, then in our view this is essentially a push system, as the final product is still being produced to stock. In this case, the location of the boundary is largely a question of distribution economics. Transportation and inventory economics determine the right number of locations. For the purposes of this discussion, if items are stocked in a form before the final configuration for the customer, then we view it as a push-pull system or, equivalently, an externally based postponement system. The boundary is the point from which orders are taken.

The push-pull system and the boundary raise two questions:

1. What factors determine whether a push-pull system or an externally based postponement system can work and how well it can work?
2. What are the factors that dictate the location of the boundary or delimiter?

We first consider some of the factors that dictate whether such a system can work at all:

• *Assembly or configuration capacity:* Since the pull part of the system needs to be able to respond to any variations of customer demand, the capacity of any operations that assembles, builds, or configures to order must be large enough to handle short-term variations. Alternatively, in a push system, production capacity need only be large enough to handle average demand over an intermediate horizon.

• *Assembly or configuration lead time:* Since orders are pulled from the push-pull boundary or delimiter, the assembly and configuration time after the boundary must be as short as possible to satisfy customers in a reasonable lead time.

EXHIBIT 8.10
The Push-Pull Boundary

Source: Simchi-Levi and Simchi-Levi, "The Effect of e-Business on Supply Chain Strategy," MIT working paper, 2002. Reprinted with permission.

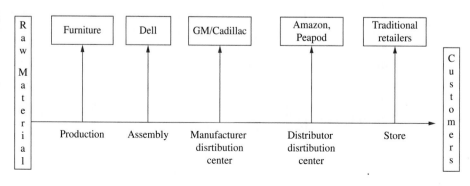

- *Assembly modularity:* The degree to which assembly can be a relatively simple operation of modular components dictates the simplicity and shortness of the lead time. With modular assembly or configuration, one can design a system to build in the short lead times to make a push-pull system work.
- *Value added at distribution:* In some value chains, distribution centers add value to the product in terms of minor configuration. This is in effect a postponement system with a push-pull boundary at the value-added point of the distribution system.
- *Demand uncertainty:* If demand is relatively stable, then the capacity needed to satisfy demand in the pull part of the system will not need to be significant, more easily enabling a push-pull system. As noted previously, demand is typically more stable at higher volumes.
- *Product variety and product proliferation:* With a great deal of product variety it becomes a great deal more difficult for a business to stock finished product. A postponement system with the push-pull boundary just before the final product proliferation becomes more feasible.
- *Economical delivery costs and value density:* With relatively low delivery costs, it becomes more feasible to pull product from a centralized location. If centralization is feasible, then it also might be feasible to configure or assemble from this central location. Value density thus becomes relevant. High value density implies economical delivery costs, at least in a relative sense, which allows for pulling from a single central location, which in turn allows configuration of assembly-to-order at this central location.

Economical delivery costs and low value density by themselves do not suggest an externally based postponement system. They simply favor a centralized inventory or a system with a few locations. Since assemble-to-order or configure-to-order is often a relatively expensive operation, a centralized system becomes an enabler. In cases where assemble- or configure-to-order capacity is relatively inexpensive, it is possible to do this on a decentralized basis, and value density and transportation costs become less important. An example of this is the one-hour photo lab. Its services are customized for each order, yet are located in many locations.

Dell Computer's assemble-to-order system capitalizes on the range of factors that support a postponement system. In particular:

- Dell has developed a short lead-time assembly system.
- Final assembly capacity is relatively inexpensive (and Dell has managed its assets in such a way as to ensure relatively low costs).
- Assembly is a simple operation using preassembled modules.
- Product variety (in Dell's system) is very high, but component variety is much lower.
- PCs have relatively low distribution costs, allowing for a centralized system.

Dell designed its system to facilitate the postponement system. The company has emphasized short lead times and simple assembly and offers very high product variety. Not all factors support the postponement system. For example, demand is uncertain and volatile, so Dell makes every effort to manage this demand. The result is a system that favors and leverages postponement. (The Dell system can also have some negative impacts. If certain components are out of stock, Dell will offer free upgrades. A challenge for Dell is to properly manage this against component inventory costs.) Overall, by setting up the externally focused postponement where the push-pull boundary is before final configuration and assembly, and by managing inventories of components and managing demand, Dell has developed competitive advantages in both cost and delivery time.

In an externally based postponement system the general approach is to have final assembly or configuration as the push-pull boundary. It is possible to have this boundary further back in the value chain. Deciding whether to do this depends on the same factors that dictate inventory positioning. These again are:

- *Product proliferation:* The boundary should be before significant proliferation and after low proliferation.
- *Lead time:* The lead time after the boundary needs to be relatively short.
- *Value added:* Ideally, value added after the boundary is high.
- *Variability of lead time:* Lead-time variability after the boundary should be low.

When product proliferation is large and the business is by nature custom, then the system *must* build- or assemble-to-order. In this case the advantage of a postponement system is that it can reduce lead times by moving the boundary (component inventory) closer to final assembly. Certain types of furniture are a good example of this.

A configuration- or assembly-to-order using postponement can be the basis of competitive advantage. At the same time, the variety offered must not cause difficulties in this final step. In other words, the variety offered needs to be easily handled by the systems. Options that complicate production, add a great deal of cost, or lengthen lead times could compromise the system.

Rapid Response and Direct Delivery

A third approach to manage the supply chain is through methods of rapid response and direct delivery. By developing combinations of inventory positions and expedited transportation, companies competing on service have developed systems of meeting very aggressive service goals. Caterpillar, on its service operations, promises very fast service on replacement parts and has used this to gain a competitive advantage. Sport Obermeyer (see Hammond and Raman 1994) used early sales data to rapidly replenish styles that were in high demand. In general, the use of early sales data to provide accurate response can mitigate high uncertainty situations. This is combined with information sharing, replenishment coordination, and shorter delivery times to provide the rapid response capability. The systems of efficient consumer response (ECR) and quick response (QR) have been used to implement some of these concepts in the grocery and apparel industries.

The ultimate in service is direct delivery. Direct delivery for some companies is the core of their business, and the degree that they can execute the routing and scheduling tasks is a key part of their competitive position. While direct delivery may involve higher logistics costs, the savings in other supply chain costs, such as the amount of stocking costs at multiple outlets, can make up for such costs. Often, the direct delivery strategy may be linked to other strategies, such as direct-to-customer distribution channels and centralized distribution channels.

Direct delivery is similar to customization in that it is a customer-specific service that provides something beyond the usual product and service. Many competitive situations today have given rise to both direct delivery and customization. We have seen this trend through the explosion in mail order and electronic commerce businesses for many retailers. Some of this activity is for companies with a single distribution center. Hence, deliveries

EXHIBIT 8.11
Spectrum of
Products and
Strategies

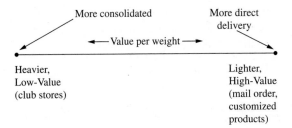

are being made from a single location to customers all over North America. This in turn is based on technological advances in distribution and information technology.

In particular, a number of trends have made direct delivery (along with customization) more feasible today. These include:

- Lower costs of scope and variety in manufacturing.
- More capabilities and lower costs in information technology, allowing for more sophisticated manufacturing and delivery approaches.
- Changing economics of transportation.
- Better material handling capability.

These capabilities have allowed companies to develop more sophisticated approaches in areas such as vehicle routing and distribution. However, the so-called last mile[5] still remains a major challenge for competing in this area and should remind everyone that not all items need to be customized or delivered directly to the customer.

In considering the strategic options in terms of direct delivery, we can consider some of the parameters relating to products and markets that we covered earlier. At one end of the spectrum we would have high-value products that are relatively compact and low-weight and would not require a great deal of customer interaction before purchase. (That is, the customer would not feel the need to touch or feel the product.) At the other end of the spectrum, you would have heavier, low-value products.

Exhibit 8.11 presents the spectrum. At the right end of the spectrum, we will see more and more direct customer delivery. This is based on the changes in economics and capabilities that are driving businesses toward improved service and direct customer delivery. However, this trend is limited, and it will be difficult and impractical for direct delivery to encompass all types of products, particularly those of high weight and low value. In addition, the advent of large stores such as warehouse clubs has led to a different type of improved service—a single location where customers can procure a wide variety of products. This comprises the left side of the spectrum. These types of facilities can serve as an alternative to direct customer delivery. There will always be the need for the traditional retail outlet, but in many cases, these will be larger, more consolidated facilities. Such large facilities are more efficient in terms of both inventory and distribution. The strategic imperative is to match the delivery system to the type of product and to optimize delivery as much as possible.

---

[5] The last mile refers to the final part of the direct delivery. It is relatively inexpensive to ship products in consolidated loads to locations that are close to the customer. The final delivery of the product or service is relatively more expensive.

The growth of delivery services and the advent of delivering directly to customers have provided opportunities to a number of companies. UPS and FedEx have used logistics and information capabilities as well as advantages of scale to develop leadership in this area.

Example, Approach, and Summary

We offer a number of conclusions of supply chain strategy. First, strategy should address the five strategic outputs as well as the expanded outputs that comprise availability. Second, the advent of improved information technology and transportation capabilities has increased the leverage of supply chain decisions. But the use of these is still subject to trade-offs. There are trade-offs in using expedited transportation and in implementing customization and delivery even if the economics of those trade-offs are different. Third, strategies for logistics and the supply chain need to address a set of questions that are particular to these decisions such as: How many inventory locations should be used and where should inventory be stored? At what locations in the value chain should inventory be stored? What transportation modes should be used? To what degree should customization and pull strategies be used? If a customization or pull strategy is used, what are the locations that demand is being pulled from or customized at?

Example of the Use of Supply Chain Capabilities

We close this chapter with an example and a step-by-step approach to develop a strategy. The example is based on a concept we call the *storefront* and illustrates how an innovative use of the supply chain can be the source of competitive advantage.[6]

The basis of the storefront method relates to the range of tasks performed by a service organization and the tension between the marketing and operational sides of any business. Many service organizations perform a large number of tasks. For example, a full-scale automobile dealership is an inventory location, a spare parts location, a service location, and a marketing and sales location. These various functions can be classified as either marketing or operational. From an operational point of view, it can be advantageous to centralize certain operations and limit the number of locations. For example, a service operation will reduce cost by limiting the number of spare parts locations. Direct delivery to customers will be more efficient if dispatching is done on a centralized basis. On the other hand, marketing and sales will want as much customer contact as possible and will thus want a large number of decentralized locations. Depending on the structure of the organization, this can create a tension between the two parts of the organization.

The logistics and supply chain goal in this situation is to separate the different functions, creating the concept of a storefront, which is a customer contact location with reduced operational tasks. The concept is illustrated by a project that one of the authors completed for what was then the Linde (now Praxair) division of Union Carbide Corporation (Rosenfield 1989), which handled Carbide's packaged gas business.

[6] Some of the example that follows is excerpted from Rosenfield, "Storefront Distribution for Industrial Products," *Harvard Business Review,* 1989. Reprinted with permission.

Linde made and delivered gases through regional distributors around the country. Customers also could obtain "hard goods"—supplies for use with the gases, such as welding rods. Linde shipped nitrogen, oxygen, and other gases from central points to branch locations in large tank cars, as well as in smaller steel cylinders loaded on tractor-trailers. These cylinders were then put on trucks and delivered to customer sites.

At one time, the branches were full-service establishments with operational, marketing, and administrative duties. When Linde was looking for ways to consolidate the various parts of its gas-filling business, it proposed curtailing some full-service outlets. In particular, it wanted the branches to distribute cylinders to its customers from central sites, and it designated some branches as *storefronts*—locations that would only take orders, initiate customer contacts, and maintain inventories of gas cylinders and spare parts for the walk-in trade.

Linde would deliver packaged gases from the central plants, thereby saving both the costs of maintaining inventory and hauling cylinders and the fixed-facilities costs arising from storing secondary inventory. Storefront operating costs would be low, as would the costs of carrying a moderate amount of cylinder and hard-goods inventory.

Customers would still get the same service; delivery would just be from a different location. The company could eliminate all its branches and install an 800 number in their place, since routine transactions were usually carried out over the telephone. But such a move would have meant a loss of contacts for the sales force. Moreover, a customer occasionally found it necessary to come into a branch office to inspect a new product or converse with a salesperson.

The validity of the storefront idea depended on meeting the service and marketing needs from less-than-full-function branches and, more importantly, on allaying the concerns of subsidiary management. The experiment, slated for two of the subsidiaries, drew a good deal of attention throughout the company.

The key to the different approach was the economics of centralized delivery. Centralization would reduce some of the logistics, double handling, and inventory levels at the branches. In particular, centralization would largely eliminate the costs of steps 2, 3, and 4 of the current systems, summarized below.

1. Filling and storing cylinders at the central point.
2. Loading cylinders and parts on tractor-trailers and delivering them to secondary locations.
3. Unloading and storing cylinders and hard goods at the branches.
4. Warehousing and handling activities at the branches.
5. Loading goods on route trucks and delivering them to customers.

Step 5, however, would grow because of the initial and final travel times. For example, with eight hours a day available for driving and an hour's driving time to reach a customer zone, six hours would be available for service calls and time between stops. This situation would be 75 percent as efficient as the old one, in which a branch is located at the center of a particular driver's customer zone. Hence, the new arrangement would require more drivers.

The savings would depend on the distance of the branch from the central point and the sales volume it covered. As volume rises, of course, the amount of inventory necessary to support a unit of sales declines. For the packaged gas operation, the larger the branch office, the more efficient its required cylinder and spare parts inventory would be.

EXHIBIT 8.12
Storefront Savings for Industrial Gas Example

Source: Rosenfield, "Storefront Distribution for Industrial Products," *Harvard Business Review*, 1989, pp. 44–48. Reprinted with permission.

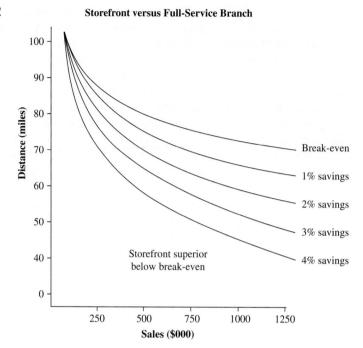

Branch efficiency came down to this: The closer one was to a central site and the lower its sales volume, the more desirable its conversion to a storefront. Linde constructed a set of trade-off curves to help in the decision making (Exhibit 8.12).

The company operated some branches within 50 miles of the central sites, and these units were costing a surprising 6 percent extra in distribution outlays. Consequently, they were targeted for conversion. Some more distant branches also turned out to be good candidates for conversion because they were small and weren't realizing any economies of scale. Based on the results for two subsidiaries, the company rolled out a national storefront program that covered many branches.

Many different industries have realized some economies using storefronts or concepts very similar to storefronts. The U.S. Postal Service has consolidated some of its routing and delivery functions, while operating some units as retail outlets only. In the authors' view, a major possibility for this concept is the auto industry. There is no real reason why automobile dealers have to be major inventory and service centers as well as sales offices. Distribution and inventory could theoretically be centralized on a regional basis. While sales could be established on a different scale, a customer might test-drive a vehicle at a local dealer, but the actual vehicle he would purchase might be a short drive away. Sales offices could then be set up at other types of locations, such as a mall. While the auto companies have developed systems to swap inventory for customers, only GM has experimented with something similar to a storefront, when it developed a system for Cadillac. The system was not successful as designed, possibly because GM was not able to create a system of incentives for the different levels of dealers. While it discontinued the experiment, it did develop improved systems for custom orders and for understanding customer demand.

Summary   The various considerations of this chapter suggest a somewhat structured methodology for developing a strategy for logistics and the supply chain. The steps of the approach are as follows:

Step 1: Operations strategy and supply chain choices. Based on the operations strategy, develop options for each of the decision choices for the supply chain. This includes inventory policy, transportation modes, and so on. Determine how each of the decisions affects the strategic outputs, including the subdimensions of availability.

Step 2: Mapping and supply chain tools. Develop options for each of the key inputs (inventory policy, transportation mode, etc.) and understand how they affect strategic outputs. Use the product and market matching tools to develop basic supply chain choices and then use the mapping tools to suggest alternative strategies.

Step 3: Feasibility of postponement and other approaches. Determine if any of the approaches for supply chain management, such as postponement, are appropriate. Determine if enhanced information technology tools or customization or direct delivery can play a role in strategy.

Step 4: Inventory and supply chain analysis. Complete any supply chain analyses that are necessary. First develop an understanding of inventory management options, such as positioning and location. Then determine any alternatives inherent in any network flow options using appropriate models.

Step 5: Cost-service trade-offs. Based on the analyses, develop any trade-off curve that is subject to strategic decision making.

Step 6: Finalize the strategy. Based on the mapping and matching tools, the review of approaches, any detailed network or inventory analyses, and trade-off curves, finalize the supply chain strategy. The strategy will specify policies for each of the subdecisions described earlier in the chapter.

Appendix A

The Square-Root Relationships in Inventory Management

The square-root relationships relate inventory cost to sales at a single location and system inventory and distance to the customers as a function of the number of facilities. These relationships can be very useful in understanding the relationship between cost and service and supply chain design choices. The key relationships are:

$$P = AS^{-1/2}$$

$$C = En^{1/2}$$

$$D = Fn^{-1/2}$$

where

C = Cost

P = Percent cost

S = Sales at a single location

D = Distance to customers

n = Number of warehouses

and

A, E, and F are constants.

These approximations are based on a number of assumptions plus some features of single-station inventory models. First is the feature of economies of scale in inventory. When inventory is stored at a single location, inventory increases with demand but with decreasing returns. A square-root relationship is a reasonable approximation to this and is based on the statistical concept that the standard deviation of the sum of independent variables varies as the square root of the number of terms in the sum and hence the mean of the sum does. The argument for this is as follows:

Suppose demand is based on the sum of independent random variables (arising, say, from different geographical regions of a larger market). That is, if demand increases, then there are more terms in the sum. Suppose we have a sum of k independent random variables. So,

$$Y_k = X_1 + X_2 + \ldots + X_k$$

Then the relationships for the mean and standard deviation are

$$\text{Mean } (Y_k) = k\text{Mean}(X_i)$$

$$\sigma(Y_k) = \text{Sqrt}(k)\sigma(Y_i)$$

Thus the standard deviation increases as the square root of k as the mean goes up by k. As a first-order approximation, inventory is proportional to the standard deviation of demand.

On a percentage basis we get the following:

$$P = \text{Percent cost} = \text{cost}/S = (AS^{1/2})/S = AS^{-1/2}$$

This establishes the first relationship.

If we increase the number of facilities, each station covers a smaller portion of demand. Suppose that we increase the number of facilities by four. Then each one covers one-fourth of the demand and thus has half the inventory (by the single-station relationship). But the sum of inventory for all four would have four times one-half or double what one large one would have. Similarly, if we have n times as many

storage locations, each one would have $1/n^{-1/2}$ of the single large location, but the n total would have n times $n^{-1/2}$ or $n^{1/2}$ in total inventory times the single large one. This establishes the second relationship.

If we next assume that demand is distributed uniformly among the facilities, then the service area of each one would be $1/n$ times the area of a single large one. The linear dimension of this service area (which would be proportional to the average distance to the customer) would be the square root of this area. This establishes the third relationship.

Empirically, however, inventory does not vary as the square root of demand, but as a power of demand between .5 and 1. The reason for this is that there is usually correlation of demand among different geographical regions or physical locations. This will modify the relationship between inventory and the number of locations since each location's relationship with its demand level is changing.

It will also modify the relationship between percent cost and sales at a single location. This relationship becomes

$$P = \text{Cost}/S = (AS^G)/S, \text{ where } G \text{ is a constant between .5 and 1.}$$

Combining powers of S, we then get $P = AS^{G-1}$ or $P = S^{-B}$ for a power of B between 0 and 0.5.

Finally, one can combine these types of relationships to develop a relationship between cost and distance to the customer as the number of warehouses changes. The reader is referred to Rosenfield et al. (1985) for the details of this.

References

Fisher, Marshall. "What Is the Right Supply Chain for Your Product?" *Harvard Business Review* 75, no. 2 (1997), pp. 105–117.

Greis, Noel P., and John D. Kasarda. "Enterprise Logistics in the Information Era." *California Management Review* 39, no. 4 (Summer 1997), pp. 55–78.

Hagel, John, III, and John Selley Brown. "Orchestrating Business Processes—Harnessing the Value of Web Services Technology." JohnHagel.com, 2002.

Hammond, Janice, and Anath Raman. "Sport Obermeyer, Ltd." Harvard Business School Publishing, 695–022, 1994.

Hayes, Robert, and Steven Wheelwright. *Restoring Our Competitive Edge: Competing through Manufacturing.* Hoboken, NJ: John Wiley & Sons, Inc., 1984.

Hill, Terry. *Manufacturing Strategy: Text and Cases.* 3rd ed. Burr Ridge, IL: McGraw-Hill/Irwin, 2000.

Kopczak, Laura, and Hau Lee. "Hewlett-Packard Company, DeskJet Printer Supply Chain (A)." Stanford Graduate School of Business, Case GS-3A, 2004.

Lee, Hau L., Corey Billington, and Brent Carter. "Hewlett-Packard Gains Control of Inventory and Service through Design for Localization." *Interfaces* 23, no. 4 (July–August 1993), pp. 1–11.

Lee, Hau L., V. Padmanabhan, and Seungjin Whang. "The Bullwhip Effect in Supply Chains." *Sloan Management Review* 38, no. 3 (1997), pp. 93–102.

Magee, John F., William C. Copacino, and Donald B. Rosenfield. *Modern Logistics Management: Integrating Marketing, Manufacturing and Physical Distribution.* Hoboken, NJ: John Wiley & Sons, Inc., 1985.

Pendrock, Mark, and Donald B. Rosenfield. "The Effects of Warehouse Configuration Design on Inventory Levels and Holding Costs." *Sloan Management Review* 21, no. 4 (1980), pp. 21–33.

Pine, B. Joseph, II. *Mass Customization: The New Frontier in Business Competition.* Boston, MA: Harvard Business School Press, 1999.

Rosenfield, Donald B. "Storefront Distribution for Industrial Products." *Harvard Business Review* 67, no. 4 (July–August 1989), pp. 44–48.

Rosenfield, Donald B. "Demand Forecasting." In *Logistics Handbook,* eds. J. Robeson and W. Copacino. New York: The Free Press, 1994.

Rosenfield, Donald B., Roy D. Shapiro, and Roger Bohn. "Implications of Cost-Service Trade-Offs on Industry Logistics Structures." *Interfaces* 15, no. 6 (1985), pp. 47–59.

Simchi-Levi, David, and Edith Simchi-Levi. "The Effect of e-Business on Supply Chain Strategy." MIT working paper, 2002.

Simchi-Levi, David, Philip Kaminsky, and Edith Simchi-Levi. *Designing and Managing the Supply Chain.* 2nd ed. Burr Ridge, IL: McGraw-Hill/Irwin, 2003.

Wilke, Jeffrey. Presentation at MIT annual e-Business conference, April 30, 2002.

Willems, Sean P., and Stephen C. Graves. "Optimizing Strategic Safety Stock Placement in Supply Chains." *Journal on Manufacturing and Service Operations Management* 2, no. 1 (2000), pp. 68–83.

Zinn, Walter, and Donald J. Bowersox. "Planning Physical Distribution with the Principle of Postponement." *Journal of Business Logistics* 9, no. 2 (1988), pp. 117–136.

Chapter 9

Information Technology

Introduction

Amazon.com has been one of the few companies of the dot.com era to survive and develop a competitive advantage over traditional businesses. While many companies developed Internet-based businesses as an extension of either a retailing business or a mail-order business, few companies successfully started stand-alone Internet-based retailing businesses without an existing brand or business on which to build. Amazon.com was launched in 1995 as an online bookstore by Jeff Bezos, who was still president, CEO, and chairman in 2007. It soon diversified into a broad range of items including DVDs, music CDs, computer software, video games, electronics, apparel, furniture, and groceries. It has separate websites to serve Canada, the United Kingdom, Germany, Austria, France, China, and Japan and ships selected products globally. The company's net sales grew at 66 percent, compounded annually, from about $148 million in 1997 to $8.5 billion in 2005 (Exhibit 9.1). Amazon's financial performance was not always stellar, however; its operating income did not turn positive until 2002 (Exhibit 9.2).

What is the basis of Amazon.com's advantage and growth? When Amazon presents to the investment community,[1] it argues that its competitive advantage comes from:

- *Capital efficiency:* Amazon limits its capital investment to its headquarters facilities and warehouses, while its primary competitors in the retail space must also support retail stores. Further, it generates cash through working capital management, as it receives payment from its customers on average 17 days before it has to pay its suppliers for the same items.

- *Inventory velocity:* Amazon's inventory turnover has averaged 16.5 times per year since 1997 (Exhibit 9.3), which translates directly into a cash benefit in, for example, reduced obsolescence. For comparison purposes, in April 2006 when Amazon's inventory turns were 14, Costco's were 12, Best Buy and Wal-Mart's were 8, Home Depot's were 5, and Barnes & Noble's were 3. At the same time, Amazon's gross margin was 24 percent, while Costco's was 12 percent.

---

[1] http://phx.corporate-ir.net/phoenix.zhtml?c=97664&p=irol-presentations, August 14, 2006.

EXHIBIT 9.1 **Amazon Net Sales from 1997 to 2005**

Source: Data drawn from http://phx.corporate-ir.net/ phoenix.zhtml? c=97664&p=irol-reportsAnnual, August 14, 2006.

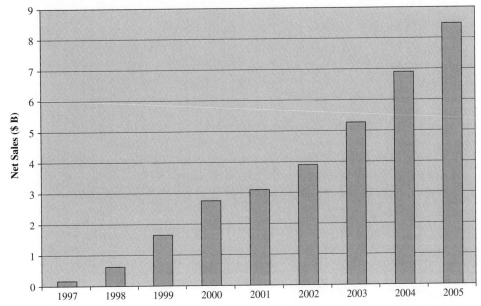

EXHIBIT 9.2
Amazon Operating Income as a Percentage of Sales

Source: Data drawn from http://phx .corporate-ir.net/ phoenix.zhtml?c=97664 &p=irol-reports Annual, August 14, 2006.

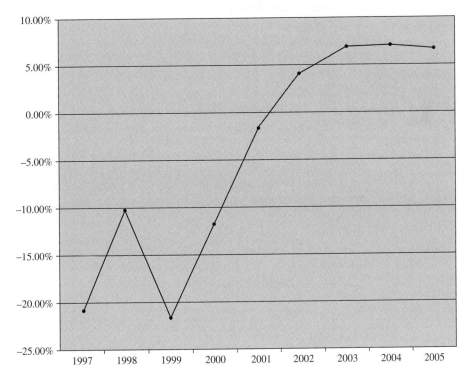

EXHIBIT 9.3
Inventory Turnover at Amazon (1997–2005)

Source: Data drawn from http://phx .corporate-ir.net/ phoenix.zhtml?c= 97664&p=irol-reports Annual, August 14,. 2006.

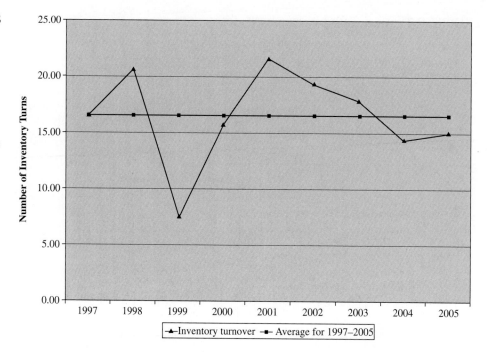

- *Technology:* Amazon sees technology as its "ally" and advances in bandwidth and Internet penetration as supporting its ability to grow both its base of customers as well as its base of third-party sellers. Jeff Bezos says "What gets us up in the morning and keeps us here late at night is technology. From where we sit, advanced technology is everything."[2]

Amazon uses information technology to execute supply chain management on a large scale, making its gains in capital efficiency and inventory velocity possible. Here are some specific ways in which Amazon employs information technology to its advantage:

- Information technology allows Amazon to sell to a national market, which in turn allows it to realize economies of scale in inventory management. The inventory for a low-demand book, for example, can be located at a single warehouse but used to efficiently serve an entire national market.
- Information technology allows Amazon to run its warehouses as efficiently as possible. In fact, Amazon's warehouses are so high-tech "they require as many lines of code to run as Amazon's website does."[3] Complex algorithms, for example, analyze relationships among the items customers purchase to find groupings that can be co-located in the same warehouse, thus reducing shipping costs.[4] Amazon even has a

[2] http://businessweek.com/print/magazine/content/03_51/b3863115_mz063.htm?chan=mz, August 14, 2006.

[3] http://www.mutualofamerica.com/articles/Fortune/May03/fortune.asp, August 19, 2005.

[4] http://seattlepi.nwsource.com/business/158315_amazon28.html, August 15, 2006.

"chief algorithms officer" to take on tough problems like these. As a result of such investments, Amazon dropped the cost of operating its warehouses from 20 percent of revenues to less than 10 percent.

- Information technology embedding sophisticated dispatching and distribution rules and customer management software optimizes delivery performance and enhances the company's service reputation. Making fewer distribution mistakes allowed Amazon to reduce its customer service contacts per order by 50 percent between 1999 and 2003.

- Information technology allows Amazon to offer its retailing and supply chain management services to other large retailers such as Target, myriad small booksellers, and a number of other retailers. It is in part due to the 1.1 million sellers Amazon supports that the selection of goods it offers went up by 42 percent in 2005, in turn providing additional economies of scale.

- Information technology allows Amazon to support one of the first truly worldwide communities, created originally around sharing book reviews and the like and enhanced later with increasingly sophisticated search capabilities. As of 2006, Amazon had over 57 million active customers participating in some way in that community.[5] The company's website and order entry system are the gold standard for Internet customer retail interaction, and Amazon continues to build its community through new services. A program called ScoutPal, for example, allows a bookseller to type or scan the ISBN number for a book into any type of wireless web device and instantly see what the book is selling for on Amazon. Shoppers, thus, can wander through garage sales or used bookstores and immediately determine the value of a prospective purchase.

In short, the heart of Amazon.com's business model is information technology (IT). Amazon invests heavily in "technology and content" development (Exhibit 9.4). Over the past nine years it invested 7 percent of its sales on average in IT, more in its earlier years and less recently as its technology has stabilized. In 1998 it won first place in Business and Related Services in the Computerworld Smithsonian Award competition, a prize given to those who demonstrate "vision and leadership in the innovative use of information technology."[6]

Amazon's information technology development is far from over. In 1999 it purchased a search company, Alexa, and in 2002, it invested in an internal start-up, A9.com, and hired a pioneer in online information retrieval to head it up, with the charter of creating a "search engine with memory."[7] Some argue that Amazon has built "a stack of software on which thousands or millions of others can build businesses that in turn will bolster the platform in a self-reinforcing cycle."[8] Amazon strives to be "earth's most customer-centric company," focusing on selection, availability, and price to do so. Its information technology investments are at the core of achieving this strategy.

[5] http://media.corporate-ir.net/media_files/irol/97/97664/2006_Shareholder_Meeting_Final_Web.pdf, August 15, 2006.

[6] http://phx.corporate-ir.net/phoenix.zhtml?c=97664&p=irol-newsArticle&ID=233843&highlight=, August 15, 2006.

[7] http://www.nytimes.com/2004/09/15/technology/15search.html?ex=1252900800&en=63 edc8f5d6ce2fc6&ei=5090&partner=rssuserland, August 15, 2006.

[8] http://businessweek.com/print/magazine/content/03_51/b3863115_mz063.htm?chan=mz, August 14, 2006.

EXHIBIT 9.4

Technology and Content Investment as a Percentage of Sales at Amazon

Source: Data drawn from http://phx .corporate-ir.net/ phoenix.zhtml? c=97664&p=irol- reportsAnnual, August 14, 2006.

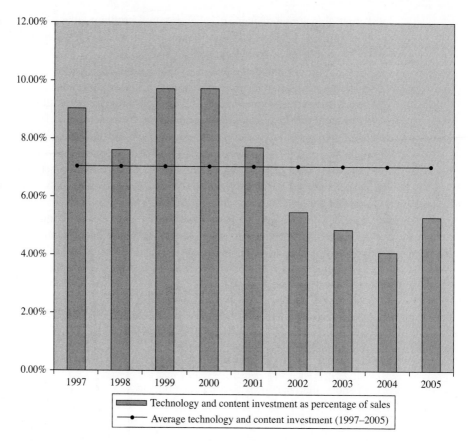

Technology and content investment as percentage of sales

Average technology and content investment (1997–2005)

Not all companies can achieve the competitive advantages Amazon has with investments in information technology. Some investments only allow a company to achieve parity with its competitors. In either case, to develop an information technology strategy a company must answer the following questions:

- Can the company derive a competitive advantage from its investments in information technology? If so, along which dimensions (e.g., cost, quality, availability, features/ innovativeness, or environmental performance) or with which capabilities?

- How much should the company invest? Does that investment have to be sustained over time, or, as with Amazon, can it be reduced as the company grows and becomes more established?

- Where should the proposed investment in information technology be focused? How should the investment be distributed across projects?

- Should the company invest in purchasing standard information technology applications or developing custom applications? In what balance should it use standard and custom information technology?

- How should information technology development, implementation, and maintenance be organized? How will projects be implemented? How should performance of the information technology management function be measured?

This chapter focuses on how to develop, evaluate, and implement information technology strategies that provide either competitive advantage or just competitive parity. We start by defining information technology and enterprise resource planning (ERP) systems in particular. We then highlight some of the strategic applications of information technology within operations and finally examine the specific information technology strategy questions just raised.

Information Technology Investment Choices

In the past several years, many companies focused their information technology investments in enterprise resource planning (ERP) systems. Today, in many companies, these systems continue to form the backbone around which companies make their IT investments. It is thus important to understand what ERP systems are, what benefits companies sought from them, and how they are evolving today.

An ERP system ideally supports organizations in planning, allocation, and management of the resources required to execute all of the organization's basic functions, including new product or service development, production, service delivery, marketing, sales, human resources management, and finance and accounting.[9] The purpose of an ERP system is to integrate all of the data and processes of the organization into a single, unified system, often by using a single, unified database that stores the data for the collection of system modules needed to run the individual processes. ERP systems integrate what formerly would have been stand-alone applications such as manufacturing resource planning, accounts receivable management, and payroll processing. ERP systems today are found in all types of organizations including nonprofits and governmental agencies, as well as all types of for-profit businesses.

IT investments can be in ERP systems, application modules that are separate from ERP, or customized applications. While the well-known vendors of ERP software, such as Oracle and SAP, would like their customers to buy complete packages from them to support all their operations, most companies do not do so. Instead, companies are likely to invest in the database management software and core applications (such as accounting and human resource management functions) from one supplier, but then supplement that software with some combination of applications purchased from a variety of vendors and custom-developed software. Thus, companies pick and choose from among the many software packages that are available to suit the particular processes or applications in which they are interested. The key to creating a successful ERP implementation is to integrate all the modules through shared database software. To better understand ERP systems, it is helpful to understand their origin and some of the key processes they cover.

The Evolution of Enterprise Resource Planning (ERP) Systems

ERP systems grew out of manufacturing resource planning (MRP II) systems, which in turn developed from materials requirements planning (sometimes known as little MRP) systems. MRP II systems offered the promise of integrated planning of production and purchasing and the coordination of the steps of the internal manufacturing process with upstream suppliers. When MRP II on its own failed to meet expectations, and just-in-time

---

[9] Some information in this section drawn from http://en.wikipedia.org/wiki/Enterprise_resource_planning, August 15, 2006.

EXHIBIT 9.5
Manufacturing
Resources
Planning System
Example

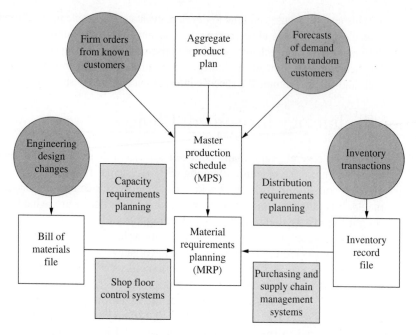

and lean thinking approaches emerged, the notion of an integrated enterprise and, further, of an integrated supply chain developed, which in turn led to the notion of ERP systems.

Manufacturing Resource Planning (MRP) Systems

A basic (little) MRP system (Exhibit 9.5) starts with a master production schedule (MPS), which collects together actual orders from customers and forecast demand, and explodes that MPS using a bill of materials (BOM), which tells how many of each type of part are needed to make an end item, and information about inventory balances to create a materials requirements plan. That plan in turn is used to schedule production orders on the shop floor and purchase orders with vendors. Suppose, for example, that there is demand for 10 widgets (represented on the MPS) and that each widget requires two of subassembly X (given by the BOM). Further, suppose that purchased subassembly X takes four weeks to acquire. With this information, the MRP system calculates that there are 20 Xs required and schedules the release of a purchase order for four weeks prior to when the widget is to be assembled. The MRP system then repeats this computation for every level of subassembly and component, properly accounting for the lead times and product structures. It is these computations that are at the heart of many ERP systems. For those unfamiliar with how MRP works, see the sidebar "The Mechanics of MRP" on page 327.

Information Systems to Support Just-in-Time and Lean Thinking

The limited success of MRP systems does not imply that IT investments in planning are of little value or not important. Instead, many companies invest in IT that either integrates elements of MRP with elements of just-in-time (JIT) and lean techniques or focuses fully on facilitating JIT and lean operations. While MRP "pushes" work through a system, exploding the master production schedule and then coordinating the work of suppliers with that

The Mechanics of MRP

Suppose we are building tables. The bill of materials (BOM) for the table is shown in Exhibit 9.6. The table requires four legs, each of which needs two screws and one caster, and two top pieces, each of which needs three screws and two brackets. The lead times associated with doing final assembly of the table and sub-assembly of the legs and top pieces, and ordering the screws, casters, and brackets are shown in Exhibit 9.7. Suppose that there is demand for 100 tables in week 10. Because it takes one week to assemble the tables, we have to place an order for the 100 tables in week 9 (Exhibit 9.8).

In order to assemble 100 tables during week 9, we must have available 400 table legs and 200 top pieces. It takes two weeks to get table legs, so we must release a production order to the shop floor for 400 legs in week 7 (Exhibit 9.9). Similarly, we need to place an order for 200 top pieces in week 8. Finally, we calculate demand for the components. We need two screws for each table leg for a total of 800 in week 7 and three for each top piece for a total of 600 in week 8. The full MRP explosion that will be used to schedule both production and purchase orders is shown in Exhibit 9.10.

The MRP system has some challenges. First, it assumes that there is unlimited production capacity in the manufacturing facility, that there is an unlimited supply of materials available from suppliers, and thus that any schedule it calculates is feasible. Clearly these are not correct assumptions in most circumstances.

Second, MRP systems work best under conditions of reasonable stability. Small changes in the master production schedule can cause major changes in the order profiles for lower level subassemblies or components in a phenomena referred to as *MRP nervousness.* Newer MRP systems address some of these issues by taking into account constraints on utilization (e.g., with capacity requirement planning modules), batching, and so forth, but users still need to be aware that these systems cannot always be flexible enough to meet all scheduling requirements.

Indeed, because they need stability and regularity in production to work well, MRP systems have not had the strategic impact that was originally envisioned. Today, MRP systems are used more for long-term materials planning and purchasing, and other systems such as just-in-time are used for short-term production planning and scheduling.

EXHIBIT 9.7 Lead Times for a Table

Item	Lead Times
Table	1 week
Leg	2 weeks
Top piece	1 week
Screw	3 weeks
Caster	4 weeks
Bracket	1 week

EXHIBIT 9.6 Bill of Materials for a Table

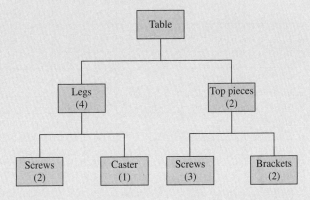

(continued)

(continued)

EXHIBIT 9.8
Lead-Time
Offsetting
Demand for
a Table

	Week:	1	2	3	4	5	6	7	8	9	10
Table	Required										100
LT = 1	Order Placement									100	

EXHIBIT 9.9
Exploding
Demand for
Legs and Lead-
Time Offsetting

	Week:	1	2	3	4	5	6	7	8	9	10
Table	Required										100
LT = 1	Order Placement									100	
Leg	Required	0	0	0	0	0	0	0	0	400	0
LT = 2	Order Placement	0	0	0	0	0	0	400	0	0	0

EXHIBIT 9.10
Full MRP
Explosion

	Week:	1	2	3	4	5	6	7	8	9	10
Table	Required										100
LT = 1	Order Placement									100	
Leg	Required	0	0	0	0	0	0	0	0	400	0
LT = 2	Order Placement	0	0	0	0	0	0	400	0	0	0
Top Piece	Required	0	0	0	0	0	0	0	0	200	0
LT = 1	Order Placement	0	0	0	0	0	0	0	200	0	
Screw	Required	0	0	0	0	0	0	800	600	0	0
LT = 3	Order Placement	0	0	0	800	600	0	0	0		
Caster	Required	0	0	0	0	0	0	400	0	0	0
LT = 4	Order Placement	0	0	400	0	0	0	0			
Bracket	Required	0	0	0	0	0	0	0	400	0	0
LT = 1	Order Placement	0	0	0	0	0	0	400	0	0	

on the shop floor, JIT "pulls" work through the system. JIT systems dictate one-for-one replenishment of inventory and, to the extent possible, a leveling of demand. The IT systems needed for such a system can be fairly simple. The original Toyota system, for example, used paper "kanban" cards that were sent back and forth between stations to signal replenishment.[10]

The systems can also involve much more sophisticated applications. In automobile manufacturing, for example, sophisticated software sequences vehicles to level workload in the factory as well as on suppliers, smoothing out the variable needs of assembly. Tasks that are varied, such as the need to install four doors instead of two, and the intermittent need for sunroofs, are placed into the schedule according to a repeating pattern. This way, sunroof installers are not faced with the task of installing several in a row, and suppliers do not receive sporadic demand for large quantities. The vehicle production schedule is transmitted electronically to suppliers so that they can supply the assembly lines directly. Many companies have successfully implemented IT applications that are targeted at focused activities such as these.

Lean manufacturing and JIT systems had major strategic impact on a number of industries, as we discuss in more detail in Chapter 10, that went well beyond reduced direct costs and inventory levels, although these savings have been significant. In many situations, JIT and lean implementations were the impetus for deeper strategic change in inventory management and schedule development. For instance, JIT and lean systems emphasize that inventory is wasteful and should be reduced, which in turn allows problems in the material delivery system to be identified and addressed. Companies use these systems to gain competitive advantage and to create changes in their own organizations. While the focus of these changes has been the business process, the accompanying information systems have been a key part of the changes as well.

ERP Systems Today

The impact of MRP, JIT and lean systems, and the accompanying IT infrastructure led to the promise of enterprisewide systems. ERP systems were designed to link data from all parts of the corporation, use that data to streamline information flows and decision making, and facilitate better decisions based on real-time data. For example, an ERP system could use an order inquiry to trigger a contract, generate a production schedule, make appropriate modifications in planning and inventory, and notify both internal operations and suppliers of the changes. In addition, it could update the balance sheet, accounts payable, and accounts receivable. In short, the enterprisewide system could coordinate a required set of activities across functions in the organization and across formerly separate software packages. In addition, the system could be linked to advanced planning tools to make scientifically better, if not optimal, decisions. A capacity-planning tool, for example, could be used to intelligently schedule production if the system was given hard capacity constraints and the cost of temporarily increasing capacity.

---

[10] JIT systems, as we describe in more detail in Chapter 10, employ "kanbans" to signal the need for production from an upstream operation. Kanbans can take many forms, from paper to electronic. The use of kanban cards in some organizations replaces the need for more sophisticated information systems, as the required information is either carried directly on the product or is built into the process.

EXHIBIT 9.11
ERP System
Modules

Source: Adapted from
Davenport, "Putting
the Enterprise into the
Enterprise System,"
*Harvard Business
Review,* 1998.

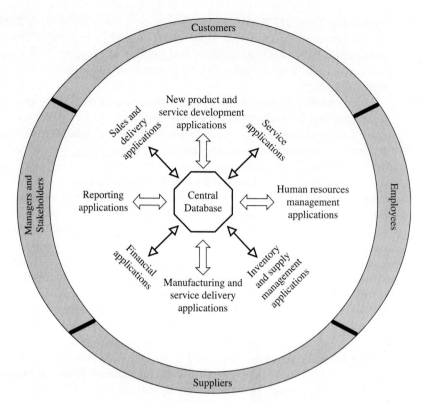

The heart of an ERP system is a central database that coordinates data from the different parts of the organization (Exhibit 9.11). The data managed by the ERP system come from and are used by all areas of the organization, from research and development to manufacturing and service delivery to sales and marketing, and by support functions such as human resources management and finance and accounting. The functions included in enterprise systems, now called *enterprise application suites (EAS),* from two of today's major providers, SAP and Oracle, are shown in Exhibit 9.12. Some of the specific activities that might be covered in those modules are shown in Exhibit 9.13.

It is rare for a company to purchase and implement all of the modules of an ERP system, and even rarer for a company to use modules only from one ERP provider. More common are installations of core modules from one provider (e.g., all of the financial and human resources management modules) supplemented by specialized modules from specialized suppliers for other critical functions. Unique functions might be performed by customized software applications. Where these are to be integrated with the ERP system, they are written to work on the shared ERP database.

Challenges in Implementing ERP Systems

The primary reasons why companies undertake ERP implementation include:

- To integrate their financial information and develop a common picture of what is going on throughout the company.

EXHIBIT 9.12
ERP System Models Offered By SAP and Oracle

Source: http://www .sap.com/usa/solutions/ index.epx, August 15, 2006, and http://www .oracle.com/applications/ e-business-suite.html, August 15, 2006.

Modules in mySAP Business Suite	Modules in Oracle E-Business Suite
mySAP Customer Relationship Management	Advanced procurement
mySAP ERP	Contracts
mySAP ERP Financials	Corporate performance management
mySAP ERP Human Capital Management	Customer data management
mySAP ERP Operations	Customer relationship management
mySAP ERP Corporate Services	Financials
mySAP Product Lifecycle Management	Human resources management
mySAP Supply Chain Management	Intelligence
mySAP Supplier Relationship Management	Interaction center
	Learning management
	Logistics
	Maintenance
	Manufacturing
	Marketing
	Order management
	Product lifecycle management
	Projects
	Sales
	Service
	Supply chain execution
	Supply chain management
	Supply chain planning
	Transportation management

- To integrate customer order information and smooth the flow from order through delivery.
- To standardize and speed up manufacturing processes across dispersed business units.
- To reduce inventory across the supply chain.
- To standardize human resources information.[11]

While ERP offers all these potential advantages, it has its limitations. In the late 1990s, in the heyday of ERP adoption, there were a number of newsworthy failures. Hershey Foods issued profit warnings in November and December 1999 after experiencing massive distribution problems following a flawed implementation of SAP's R/3 ERP system. Its shipments to stores in the peak Halloween and pre-Christmas sales periods were significantly affected, and Hershey shares ended the year down 27 percent from the year's high. In November 1999, Whirlpool also blamed shipping delays on difficulties associated with its SAP R/3 implementation, causing its share price to nosedive as well. Pharmaceutical distributor FoxMeyer Drug actually collapsed following an SAP R/3 implementation, and its bankruptcy trustees subsequently filed a $500 million lawsuit against SAP, and another $500 million suit against co-implementer Andersen Consulting.[12] The pitfalls encountered in implementing enterprise systems should be well understood by anyone developing a strategy for information systems in an operations setting. They include:

- *Training.* Successful implementation depends on the skills and experience of the workforce in using enterprise systems correctly. This means not only training people in the

[11] http://www.cio.com/research/erp/edit/erpbasics.html, August 15, 2006.
[12] http://www.cio.com/archive/060100_erp.html, August 15, 2006.

EXHIBIT 9.13 Sample Activities in Each ERP Module	Financials	General ledger Cash management Accounts payable Accounts receivable Fixed asset management
	Human Resources	Payroll Training Benefits Hourly time-card management
	Customer Relationship Management	Marketing Sales (e.g., lead management) Service e-Commerce Channel management Call center operations
	Manufacturing	New product introduction Bills of materials Global, multifacility production planning Materials requirements planning Shop-floor scheduling and control Scheduling Capacity planning Quality control Cost management Manufacturing process flow Environmental, health, and safety
	Supply Chain Management	Inventory Order entry Purchasing Product configuration management Supply chain planning Supplier scheduling Distribution requirements planning
	Product Life-cycle Management	Project management Specification, bill of materials, technical documentation management Collaborative engineering tools Quality management

technical aspects of the system and how they are to use the system to do their jobs, but also in helping them understand the entire process and how what they do fits in. Until people understand the big picture and their roles in it, they find it hard to appreciate the value of entering their own data properly and the adverse effect if they don't. The performance of enterprise systems is only as good as the weakest link in the system. Overcoming the natural resistance in some organizations to sharing information across organizational boundaries is an important part of the training.

- *Data integrity.* Any planning system relies on the quality of data and information given to it. If there are problems with data entry or forecasting, then the modules of the system will give flawed answers. Forecasting, in particular, is a difficult exercise for most companies, yet as is clear with our MRP example, forecasts can drive the entire system. To the extent that lean thinking reduces lead times, forecast accuracy becomes somewhat less critical, but data accuracy—bills of materials and inventory records, for example—remains important.

- *Reengineering associated business processes.* Implementation of enterprise systems almost always requires changes in the fundamental ways in which a company does its business. JIT and lean manufacturing systems, for example, are predicated on level production, minimal changes, and consistency. MRP systems, similarly, don't work well under conditions of high variability. When an ERP system is implemented to facilitate a move to MRP or JIT or some combination thereof, it requires that the company understand and take on the required process changes as well. Often such reengineering blurs organizational boundaries and changes lines of responsibility, so attention to organizational design issues is important in implementation as well.

- *Balancing flexibility and uniformity.* ERP systems promise uniformity and the use of consistent procedures across different parts of the organization. For some companies this may be a great advantage. However, with varying local conditions, others may find such uniformity undesirable and require some adaptation in the application of selected ERP modules. It can be a major challenge to find the correct balance. A "federalist" approach in which different versions of the same system are rolled out in different regions may be optimal (Davenport 1998), but may require significant human and financial resources to execute.

- *Customization.* Many companies need custom versions of specific ERP applications. ERP software vendors, for example, often customize planning and scheduling software to capture the intricacies of a specific industry. Sometimes tailored software can be purchased off the shelf, and other times the company will have a package customized prior to implementation. Companies thus need to determine what type of application is needed and whether or not a standard package is appropriate. On one hand, purchasing standard software is likely to be easiest, but requires the company to change its business processes to fit the requirements of the software. On the other hand, using the same software as other companies in the industry offers no distinct advantage. Companies must be thoughtful, though, about where and when they want to use customized applications. Choosing to use custom software so that the company doesn't have to change its business processes can be dangerous, unless it is clear that the process in question can offer competitive advantage.

- *Complexity versus simplicity.* Operations management in many environments is quite complex. Although business process reengineering and lean thinking strive to reduce complexity, there is a limit to how simple operations in a company with thousands of products and millions of customers can be made. In general, attempts to develop software to solve all the problems that arise in such complex environments ultimately fail, just as the original implementations of MRP failed. Well-managed companies simplify their operating systems so that the necessary software tools can be used effectively, but at the same time understand the limitations of the systems. In general, ERP systems focus on solving the problems that are most common across companies and rarely deal with the full complexity or with the specific nuances of a given business.

A company must be aware of many issues in selecting and investing in ERP systems. Take, for example, a major consumer goods manufacturer that implemented an ERP system with the objective that it would be standardized across the company's multiple facilities. In the end, the implementation was successful in areas such as human resources, finance and accounting, purchasing, and order management, but not in manufacturing planning and scheduling. Because the company viewed cost as its strategic driver, it focused on process utilization and materials management and did not fully implement the scheduling functionality of the ERP system. Consequently, ERP was used mainly as a transaction management system and had little impact on decision making and optimization.

This situation is not unusual. ERP has been instrumental in many areas such as accounting, human resources management, order management, and purchasing. Planning and scheduling have been a bigger challenge. Many of the same challenges confronting MRP arise: General planning and scheduling systems cannot adapt to all situations; there are constraints in staffing, materials, or equipment; and planning and scheduling require stability and consistency. Companies must look at the key drivers of their businesses and from those derive their IT needs. They can then carefully select the right ERP systems and applications modules to fit those needs rather than letting the ERP systems dictate their business strategies.

ERP systems are not only expensive and complex, but they are available to everyone. As such, they are a "leveling" technology that drives everyone toward parity. Any strategic use of ERP systems must address whether the implementation is designed to provide parity with other organizations in the area of information technology or whether it is to provide a competitive advantage. To gain competitive advantage, a company must be doing something truly novel and using ERP and its data management capabilities to enhance the novelty. We turn now to the ways in which IT can provide competitive advantage.

Information Technology as Competitive Advantage

With the advent of more powerful computers and networks, a great deal of hype and misunderstanding has arisen about ERP and information technology in general. On one hand are companies like Amazon.com that have used IT to great advantage. On the other hand are companies that have fruitlessly spent millions of dollars that they later viewed as investments of only limited utility. Some view IT as one of the critical capabilities of leading companies and one needed to augment other core competencies (Bauer et al. 2001). In this view, IT decisions can be made with the goal of developing a competitive advantage by providing some kind of unique service. An alternative view suggests that IT investments are made largely to provide parity and prevent IT from having a negative impact. ERP implementations, for example, allow a wide range of advantages, including seamless visibility of information among different parts of the organization, sharing of supply chain and production information within the company and among partners, and coordination of production and procurement schedules given lead time and capacities. However, if others are also embracing ERP, it may only be a leveling technology (Davenport 1998) that provides parity with others rather than any distinctive advantage.

Information technology often requires associated changes in business processes to make the productivity and strategic gains promised upon its purchase. In this way, it is similar to the introduction of electric power in the late 19th century (*The Economist* 2003) when productivity gains did not materialize until companies completely reorganized their plants. To use water as a power source, machines needed to be in a line and directly connected together. With electric power, these machines no longer needed to be connected, but could be placed wherever they best fit in the flow through the facility. But, with early use of electric power, facilities did not reflect this newfound flexibility. It was only later, with new layouts, that larger gains in productivity appeared. Similarly, IT productivity gains did not appear in a significant way until many years after companies started investing in IT. They only showed when a significant lag time was built into the measurements, and when investments in other capabilities were considered simultaneously (Brnjolfsson and Hitt 2003, Brynjolffsson 2003). In short, IT investment typically requires that the organization undertake changes in its business processes at the same time that it is implementing the new systems. When companies do so, they achieve the productivity gains they seek and can potentially gain competitive advantage, but doing so may take some time after the original investment.

Information technology has arguably facilitated major changes not only in the processes used by companies to run their individual businesses, but in the structure of industry at large. Originally, information technology investments were viewed as facilitators for the flow of information and materials within the firm. As information and communications technologies advanced, it became more and more reasonable to share information with organizations outside the firm. Information technology thus facilitated the effective creation of global multifacility networks and multicorporation enterprises by enabling different corporate entities to work together. A supply chain made up of multiple organizations can replace a supply chain of one or a small number of organizations. Indeed, information technology is facilitating a general trend toward more outsourcing, less vertical integration, and smaller firms.

Information Technology and the Virtual Organization

The ultimate extension of the outsourcing and vertical disintegration trends is the virtual corporation or virtual supply chain, where different organizations or groups of individuals come together, often temporarily, for a particular task, project, business, or short-term endeavor (Malone and Laubaucher 1998). Advanced information technology allows the creation of these extended enterprises, letting them act as a single entity. These "Internet-connected supply chains" (Exhibit 9.14) integrate hard assets with virtual organizations that perform the required exchange functions. The exchange functions are websites that allow different entities to interact within a marketplace to process transactions. The exchanges cover interactions of a number of different parties including suppliers, logistics providers, and customers (Lapide 2000). They work in a much more networked fashion than conventional supply chains (Exhibit 9.15) that operate without virtual functions or exchanges and perform their tasks in a more serial manner. Conventional supply chains often forge their information-sharing links separately among the various pairs in the chain, potentially with different information systems and different data definitions and standards.

Internet-connected supply chains require "extended outsourcing strategies" that move beyond the simple outsourcing models we've discussed elsewhere in this book. In extended outsourcing strategies, which are feasible only using advanced information technology, the company interacting with the end customers acts as an agent for the virtual corporation. Cisco, for example, supplies its customers with roughly $35 billion in goods and services a year but often doesn't physically touch the goods it causes to be delivered to them. In Cisco's network, a customer order may be automatically placed with one outside contractor,

EXHIBIT 9.14
The Internet-Connected Supply Chain

Source: Reprinted from Lapide, "The Innovators Will Control the E-Supply Chain," AMR Research report, 2000. Printed with permission.

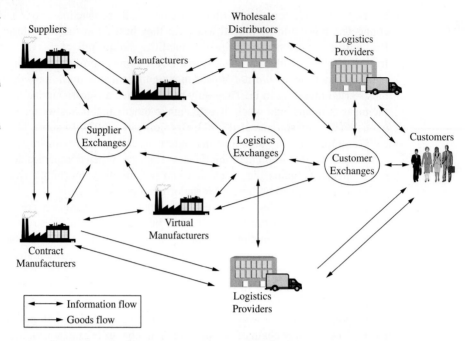

produced and tested by another contractor, and shipped by yet a third contractor. First- and second-tier suppliers are linked directly to the order process, and all suppliers in the network have visibility to all required data. Cisco's information network facilitates not only fulfillment of a customer order, but product development and new product introduction as well. Cisco can implement this strategy only through advanced information technology that processes orders and manages the virtual supply chain.

EXHIBIT 9.15
Conventional Supply Chain

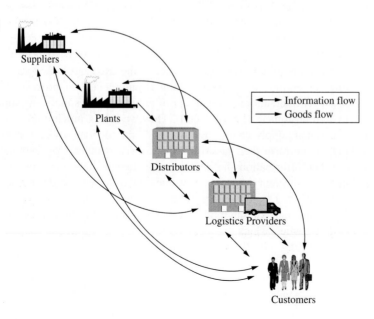

Internet-connected supply chains can more readily ameliorate the bullwhip, or "beer-game," effect, in which variability in observed demand increases upstream in the supply chain, as they provide visibility to true customer demand rather than batched orders from downstream partners. Information technology also facilitates the reconfiguration of the supply chain as needed. If a company's business requires it to bring together different sets of players for the different activities it must perform over time, like a consulting firm might bring together different skill sets for each assignment, information technology can be critical to track the activities of the suppliers and manage the interactions and the project outcomes.

The concept of a virtual corporation does have limitations. Operations work best under conditions of stability. While the virtual corporation offers the potential of flexibility, it is misleading to consider the possibility of unlimited flexibility. Some of the networked partners may not be able to meet requirements with large variations. The better networked enterprises offer some flexibility, but recognize the limitations of their network partners and allow the different players to focus on and hone their skills in specific tasks.

Information technology facilitates the networked enterprise or virtual corporation. As companies structure themselves more and more along these lines, they must determine where in the supply chain or value chain to position themselves and what information technologies they need to support that position.

Opportunities for IT-Based Competitive Advantage in Operations

IT investments, particularly when implemented as a standard ERP package, are rarely the source of competitive advantage as a whole. Instead, strategic advantage is derived from the business process redesign that accompanies implementation, or more likely from the customization of select pieces of the ERP system. Effective use of IT enables a company to implement strategic business concepts. Because of this, IT can drive operations strategy, but usually only in conjunction with other operational concepts such as lean manufacturing. In this section, we highlight potential uses of IT within operations to gain competitive advantage in the categories depicted in Exhibit 9.16. The IT applications in these cases may be standardized, but are often customized. As depicted in the exhibit, sometimes competitive advantage is derived by applying IT to specific locations within the value chain and other times it entails orchestrating activities that span the value chain.

New Product Development: Use of Workgroup Technologies

Today, information technologies enable individuals to work together under different circumstances than in the past. For example, people in geographically distant locations can now work together in product development teams through the advanced use of information technology. The IT systems that allow scattered workgroups to be effective include (Graban et al. 1999 and PricewaterhouseCoopers 1998)[13]:

1. *Groupware:* Enables the exchange of information, making communication in groups easier. It facilitates product development tasks as well as management of other major projects. Not only

---

[13] For more information on product life cycle management systems, see http://www.plmic.com/ (accessed August 15, 2006).

EXHIBIT 9.16
Strategic Uses of IT in the Value Chain

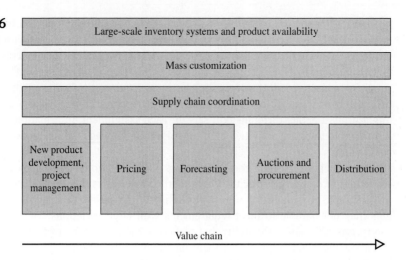

Large-scale inventory systems and product availability

Mass customization

Supply chain coordination

| New product development, project management | Pricing | Forecasting | Auctions and procurement | Distribution |

Value chain

does groupware make communication easier, but by doing so enables improved execution of tasks such as those involved in bringing a new product to market.

2. *Workflow management:* Enables the tracking of processes, facilitating information exchange and helping to define the process. Workflow software, for example, communicates milestones and timing performance on a product development process.

3. *Documentation management:* Enables integrity of unstructured data and allows groups to organize documentation by certain attributes so that the information is easily searchable and therefore widely accessible.

These three systems underpin the implementation of most product data management (PDM) systems.[14] Because this technology is fairly standard today, it cannot by itself create competitive differentiation. Companies that implement it wisely and thoughtfully reengineer their product development processes, however, may obtain competitive advantage, particularly on a global scale (Eppinger and Chitkara 2006).

Forecasting

Forecasting will always be subject to significant errors, but use of more sophisticated approaches, such as those described in Rosenfield (1994), can reduce the variability of forecasts compared to true demand. This, together with reduced lead times, can greatly reduce the impact of forecast errors. In Internet-connected supply chains, forecasting is collaborative. Collaborative planning, forecasting, and replenishment (CPFR) is recognized as important among retailers and manufacturers. While the value of collaboration in planning and replenishment is fairly self-evident, forecasting also benefits from collaboration to incorporate market intelligence in developing consensus-based forecasts and a range of possible outcomes.

Improved forecasting techniques take advantage of advanced information technology that integrates time series information on past demand for individual items and groups of items with a number of external factors that could affect demand. These factors may

[14] See, for example, the elements of Agile's Agile 9 product at http://www.agile.com/solutions/agile9/index.asp, (accessed August 15, 2006).

include, for example, industry data, demand for related products, the company's and competitor's promotions, external data such as weather information, and macroeconomic data. The approaches use statistical analysis of these data sources as well as models that relate the different factors to each other. The better approaches use more data and more extensive and sophisticated models and thus rely more on IT resources and capabilities.

Pricing

Information technology offers the promise that pricing decisions can be optimized for specific market and operational conditions. Revenue management, a concept pioneered by the airlines, optimizes revenue given assessments of demand and capacity. Use of information technology allows a firm to make pricing decisions and implement them rapidly. A company that sells directly to customers, for example, can dynamically change prices to reflect product availability (reducing prices when availability is high and vice versa), relative demand in recent periods, measured price elasticity, and competitor pricing. All of these require information availability and technology capabilities.

Pricing and repricing are integral to Dell's direct model. Dell's frequent promotions are often based on parts availability and inventory; the company has the information systems capabilities to translate these inventory positions into pricing decisions. Indeed, Dell is a very good example of how information technology in general can enhance operational effectiveness. Its capabilities allow it to process orders and schedule them into the factory, price products, reserve inventory, schedule distribution, and communicate with the customer. It also uses IT to manage demand in response to changes in supply as it did during the shutdown of West Coast ports. While Dell's capabilities rest largely in supply chain management, they depend heavily on information technology.

Auctions and Procurement

One of the phenomena of the e-commerce era has been the advent of electronic marketplaces or exchanges that behave as automated price-clearing markets. Exchanges enable matches and determine appropriate prices between potential buyers and sellers. While public industry exchanges have not been extremely successful, a number of large companies created private exchanges that significantly reduced costs for certain types of items. The chemical industry, for example, has benefited from the use of exchanges.[15] Within the auto industry, Covisint, an attempt to facilitate an online business-to-business marketplace, failed when the partners in the exchange could not agree on a shared set of objectives and when the technology proved more difficult than expected to integrate with each of their individual enterprise management systems.[16]

Mitchell (2000) identifies four types of trading exchanges, shown in Exhibit 9.17. They are differentiated by the ownership roles taken and by the purpose of the exchange. The exchange owner may be a third party, or the traders may jointly own the exchange. The exchange may be set up to make the market more efficient or to simply enhance the trading process with a standardized approach. Four stylized types of exchanges result:

1. An independent vertical exchange (IVX), typically set up by a third-party owner, links buyers and sellers within a specific industry.

[15] http://webreprints.djreprints.com/907660072246.html, August 15, 2006.
[16] http://www.forbes.com/personaltech/best/2004/1004/001.html, August 15, 2006.

EXHIBIT 9.17
Trading
Exchanges

Source: Reprinted
from Mitchell,
"Trading Exchange
Infrastructure: 13-Stop
Shopping," AMR
Research report,
2000. Reprinted with
permission.

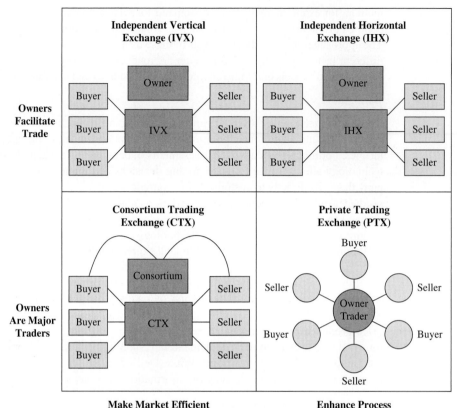

2. An independent horizontal exchange (IHX), also set up by a third-party owner, is not limited to a single industry, although the goods involved may have some similarities or commonalities. An IHX is similar to an IVX in that a third-party owner links buyers and sellers.

3. A consortium trading exchange (CTX) connects players within an industry and is directly organized by the buyers and sellers.

4. A private trading exchange (PTX) is developed by a single company to deal with its trading partners.

There are also hybrids of the four approaches shown. The most common type of exchange is the private trading exchange, which allows individual companies to develop better processes and efficient markets with their suppliers and customers. Such exchanges are usually used for commodities where price is the key purchase criterion.

In general, information technology facilitates price reductions by consolidating purchasing at a single location and then allowing all parties to view the same relevant information (Swaminathan and Tayur 2003). While auctions allow efficient pricing on commodities, the e-business firms and consortia that facilitate auctions (e.g., eBay) also allow companies to sell excess inventory and capacity, which in turn allows companies to more effectively manage their operations.

Supply Chain Coordination and Information Sharing

The Internet-enabled supply chain goes well beyond the use of point-of-sale (POS) data throughout the supply chain, but conventional supply chains have to update their approaches to information sharing as well if they want to optimize performance. In the traditional view of the supply chain (Exhibit 9.15), information is exchanged through orders, deliveries, and other two-way exchanges. The growing need to coordinate information and share more types of data suggests, however, that the flow of information and the organizational links cannot be simple two-way flows and relationships. Instead, supply chains are now sharing information using one central hub structure (Exhibit 9.18) that keeps data in a common format and allows it to be accessed and updated by all tiers of the supply chain (Hewitt 2001). The types of information that are being shared include:

- Sales data, ideally point-of-sale data.
- Inventory positions.
- Supply constraints.
- Production and delivery data for different stages of the supply chain.
- Both long- and short-term forecasts so that each stage can plan.
- Production plans and delivery schedules and any limits on how these can change.

In addition to sharing more information in these hub networks, many companies are also using collaborative tools. Collaborative planning, forecasting, and replenishment (CPFR), for example, not only fosters information sharing but also includes automated tools and other processes for forecasting and replenishment. CPFR efforts have had varying levels of success that often depend on the quality and extent of information sharing. Effective use of information sharing should be an important goal.

Information technology can support the performance of the supply chain in additional ways beyond information sharing, coordination, and inventory management. Many businesses have

EXHIBIT 9.18
Information Sharing Structure

Source: Adapted from Hewitt, "After Supply Chains, Think Demand Pipelines," *Supply Chain Management Review*, 2001.

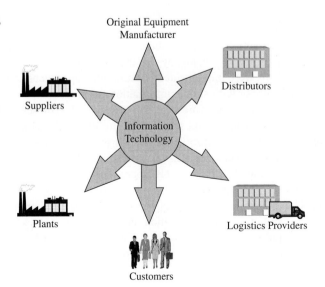

complex supply chains involving large numbers of facilities, multiple distribution centers, and a variety of product classes. Optimizing the flow of products from plants to distribution centers and then to markets can be extremely complicated. Chapter 5 presented some models used in facilities rationalization in a supply chain. Investment in information technology enables companies to use such models on a regular basis, helping to gain efficiencies and service improvements as well as possible strategic advantages.

Distribution

Information technology enables a number of improvements in distribution systems. Better routing algorithms, load consolidation, cross-docking methods at transit hubs, flow optimization, package tracking, and supply chain event management all enable significant improvements, more efficiency, and growth in direct customer delivery. Some of these are enabled by newer tools such as hand-held devices for recording distribution actions (e.g., picking up a package). Amazon.com, for example, uses dispatching software and what it calls *injection,* which is introducing loads at different postal locations to optimize total distribution.

Distribution improvements also significantly enhance the possibilities for companies to rapidly respond to orders and customize products. By having the capability of distributing individual orders to individual customers in a cost-effective and rapid manner, customization becomes more feasible.

Large-Scale Inventory Systems and Product Availability

The use of IT to develop sophisticated inventory systems enhance companies, such as Wal-Mart and Amazon.com, to gain competitive advantage in cost, availability, or both. The use of information technology for inventory management has the obvious effect of improved efficiency and inventory turns, which reduces cash-to-cash cycle times. But it also allows for increased variety. Here are some specific applications of information technology to improve inventory management.

Better Management of Individual Item Inventories   Many companies use generic approaches to setting inventory and safety stock levels such as holding a fixed number of weeks of reserve. These simplistic approaches typically do not tie directly to customer service and often result in the company having too much or too little inventory. Historically, such systems were implemented because other approaches were too complex to manage either manually or with simple information systems.

Today, more sophisticated systems are used. Silver et al. (1998) presents a number of theories on how to set inventory levels and safety stocks for individual items. Such techniques usually involve measuring and monitoring variations in demand and supply so that both individual and aggregated inventories can be optimized using mathematical approaches based on required service levels. Alternatively, approximations for demand variation based on item movements (e.g., Rosenfield 1994) can be used. In the application of these more advanced approaches, the IT system tracks variations of actual demand from forecast, builds a statistical distribution for the variation, and sets reserve stocks on an item-level basis to optimize overall inventory performance. The combination of forecasting, tracking demand and forecast error, and optimizing inventory performance requires a significant level of information technology investment.

Better Management of Inventory in Multistage Systems   When a supply chain consists of multiple production and inventory management stages, locating the inventory efficiently within the chain can be very complicated. Sophisticated approaches that take advantage of information systems' capabilities enable much better performance (e.g., Graves and Willems 2000). Generally, these approaches examine different locations, both those serving the customer directly and those serving other locations in the network, and determine the inventory resources required at each depending upon the lead time to move items between locations and the company's desired service level. Good systems limit inventory reserves to a minimum number of potential locations so that overall inventory investment is minimized. They also enable postponement strategies such as those described in Chapter 8 that allow for customization without significantly increasing inventory costs.

Inventory Strategies for National Markets   Many large companies pool national demand to achieve a significant advantage in economies of scale. They can efficiently maintain an inventory of low-demand items, which in turn allows them to carry a wider variety of items than a company serving only a local market. Suppose, for example, a potential customer is interested in a book that is infrequently purchased. It is unlikely that he or she will find it at a local bookstore, because it is costly for the bookstore to stock the book. Even a special order may be difficult, as the retailer may not stock it at its regional warehouse either. Amazon.com, on the other hand, aggregates demand for such low-volume items across a national market and can afford to carry a small inventory of the items to serve the market from a single location.

It is not enough, however, for Amazon.com to have scale and national markets to make such a strategy work. It must also have the information systems to set inventory targets, the ability to deliver from anywhere in the supply chain, and the ability to identify the best number of warehouses in which to stock each item. (The last determination is made as a trade-off between the higher cost of more stocking locations and the lower transportation cost obtained by being closer to the customer.) This collection of abilities allows Amazon.com to deal, for example, with a network of rare book vendors to procure copies of rare books, which increases the size of the library available to its customers by a factor of five. The increased variety offered by Amazon.com has been studied in terms of its economic effect on consumers. Amazon's reduced prices and the increased variety of online book sellers enhanced consumer welfare by close to $1 billion in 2000 (Brynjolfsson et al. 2003).

Successful Use of Point-of-Sale Data   Today's information systems allow companies to capture real-time sales data, share that data across the supply chain, and use the data to optimize inventories. Point-of-sale data allow companies to (1) produce more accurate forecasts and have shorter lead times, since both demand and current inventory positions are more up-to-date; (2) optimize inventory decision making systemwide instead of through functionally separate groups; and (3) overcome the bullwhip effect depicted in Exhibit 1.1. The bullwhip effect (e.g., Lee et al. 1997), further described in Chapter 8, is a phenomenon seen in many industries, where variation increases as the orders propagate up the supply chain. A relatively small change in demand or in the sales forecast causes the retailer to increase its order so as to adjust its reserve and in-transit inventories. The wholesaler or distributor in turn adjusts its orders, and the factory responds in kind. While improved forecasting helps, it is not nearly as effective as improved supply chain visibility achieved by sharing true demand throughout the supply chain. Capturing point-of-sale data and sharing it among all parties in the supply chain is theoretically possible for almost any company; however, the track record is limited and suggests that the quality of implementation is often a differentiator.

Mass Customization[17]   Mass customization, discussed in detail in Chapter 11, offers significant advantages in the area of availability. Mass customization tailors products and services to individual customers' desires, while achieving the efficiencies of mass production with high overall volumes. Because mass customization entails managing a huge number of product and process configurations, it requires management and coordination of much data and many parties. Information technology is thus an important enabler of mass customization. It is used to develop and analyze detailed customer profiles to be able to provide for each of these profiles; it facilitates efficient configuration of orders; and it coordinates the supply network to deliver against those orders. We address the first two of these—customer profiles and order configuration—in more detail here, having already addressed supply chain coordination.

The use of IT to build and analyze detailed customer profiles is well recognized and developed. A customer profile goes beyond simply tracking a customer's historical purchases. Instead, "learning relationships" with each customer are central to the ability to mass customize (Pine 1996). Developed through ongoing, interactive feedback, these relationships improve the manufacturer's understanding of customer needs. "The more the customer teaches the company, the better it can provide exactly what the customer wants—when, where, and how it is wanted . . ." (Pine 1996). In many industries, web-based applications are used to automate this ongoing dialogue. An editorial manager at Individual Inc., a Burlington, Massachusetts, company that publishes a mass-customized electronic newspaper, discusses the customers' interests with them before generating their first issue, and then uses a search engine to scan over 600 sources and select and send articles aligned with each individual's interests. Each week individual customers are asked to rate the relevance of the received articles. This data is fed back to the search engine to further tailor the search (Pine 1996). Clearly IT has made it much easier to collect and use customer feedback.

Perhaps one of the most customization-specific applications of IT has been in product (or service) configuration. The objective of a product configurator is to coordinate customer needs with modular product features and production processes to create a tailored product. Software applications automate the task of soliciting customer needs and developing specifications for manufacturing. For example, Andersen Corporation in Bayport, Minnesota, developed a multimedia system that allows customers and distributors to design, cost, and specify window systems from 50,000 components (Pine 1996). Between 1980 and 1994 the number of unique window configurations shipped by Andersen increased from 10,000 to over 160,000. A similar system is used to customize clothing, such as a pair of jeans, by delivering measurements to the manufacturer and automatically scheduling production, thereby reducing lead time and costs and making the overall value proposition viable to the customer.

The concept of configuring customer interfaces also applies in services. Interfaces can be configured in banking, professional services, or hotels through the analysis of customer profiles and preferences and tailoring the service to the individual profile.

---

[17] Drawn from Kandare et al. 1999.

New Information Technologies

Emerging information technologies will enable further development of some of the capabilities discussed in this chapter. RFID (radiofrequency identification) tags, for example, can potentially allow even better inventory tracking, higher efficiencies in material handling and movement, better supply chain visibility, and improved forecasting. However, as for any other new technology, the cost and effort for implementation should be assessed and compared with those of other, possibly less expensive, options to achieve the desired goals. Payment technologies such as PayPal and micropayment technologies, which allow for the electronic processing of relatively small payments on a day-to-day basis, will allow more efficient use of the web for order management and processing.

As such technologies advance, the strategic issue of parity versus advantage will continue to arise. When the technology is new, advantage can be gained. As the technology matures, new players will need to adopt the technology just to maintain parity.

Information Technology Investment Decisions

We have described ERP systems, what they do, and the advantages and disadvantages of investing in and using them. We have described ways in which a company might derive competitive advantage from investment in IT to support particular activities—new product development and introduction, pricing, forecasting, procurement, and distribution. We have described the use of IT to achieve overarching strategies such as supply chain coordination, large-scale inventory and product availability management, and mass customization. In the end, while any one of the approaches we described may work, each company must make its own choices about how much to invest in IT and how to allocate that investment.

IT strategy, as for all of the other decision categories we discuss in this book, starts with an understanding of the business strategy and what the company wishes to accomplish, either in the cost, quality, availability, features/innovativeness, or environmental performance position it wants to take in the market or in the capabilities it wants to develop. A company focused on low-cost availability of a wide variety of items, like Amazon, might invest in developing integrated order management, inventory control, and delivery systems. A company focused on features and innovativeness might invest more in systems to collect information about customers, share that information across the product development team, and connect members of the supply network for fast production and delivery ramp-up. A company wishing to excel in the application of lean thinking might invest in information systems that allow it to identify and minimize waste in its processes.

We should be clear, however, that IT strategy does not and should not focus entirely on the operations function. IT systems span not only all of the functions that reside within the company, but reach out to suppliers and customers as well (Exhibit 9.19). Thus, IT strategy is developed with a broad view across the organization and into the marketplace in which it operates.

> The essence of IT strategy is making choices, and the constantly co-evolving worlds of IT capabilities and institutional needs impose many choices on IT leaders. These choices are often situated in the path dependencies of prior choices (e.g., existing systems), and more importantly, they project path dependencies onto future choices (Wheeler 2003).

EXHIBIT 9.19
Scope of IT Strategy

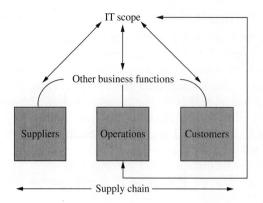

While it used to be that IT leaders could simply align their IT structures and spending to the business, today IT strategy and business strategy must co-evolve and mutually adjust to the constant changes in the external environment. We now address the fundamental questions the firm must ask in developing an IT strategy.

How Much Should the Company Invest?

The approach to determining how much to invest in IT and how to allocate that investment among projects is quite similar in many ways to the parallel decisions made for research and development (R&D). Companies typically express their aggregate R&D spending as a percentage of sales, just as we showed Amazon's "technology and content" spending as a percent of sales in Exhibit 9.4. They decide how much to spend on R&D in part based on competitive benchmarks and in part on the basis of their position in the industry. A company positioned as an innovator of leading-edge products and services, or a company in start-up mode, might spend more on R&D as a percentage of sales than a company positioned as a follower or competing in commodity markets on low cost. IT budgets can be determined using similar logic. The company's competitive strategy dictates where the company should be in its IT development spending relative to its competitors.

This top-down approach to setting an IT budget is typically complemented by a bottom-up review of the projects the company has under way and those it proposes doing. For a major strategic initiative, such as supply chain optimization, the company must also gather data on what IT support will be required to execute the strategic initiative and how much it will cost to develop that support. In the case of supply chain optimization, for example, the company might need basic ERP functionality complemented by investment in a set of custom-developed optimization models and supply network coordination tools. A long-range plan, or roadmap, for the development of all of the required functionality to accomplish the strategic initiative would provide information on investments as well as expected performance improvements required by the IT strategic plan.

In Which IT Projects Should the Company Invest?

Let's return for a moment to our R&D analogy. Once a company knows how much it wants to spend on R&D, it allocates that spending among R&D projects, forming an investment portfolio. It may allocate the funds to the projects that have the largest return on investment (ROI), it may choose projects that are strategically important, or it may use a mixed set of criteria to evaluate the projects. It is important to view breakthrough, platform, and derivative projects differently in the allocation process. Breakthrough projects play a critical role in the company's long-term strategy, as they provide new technologies, processes, or potential market opportunities, but it can be difficult to prove their ROI. Derivative projects, on the other hand, milk existing technologies and platforms by introducing relatively minor modifications that give them additional life or allow them to be sold in different markets. The ROI for a derivative project is usually much easier to estimate with some accuracy than an ROI for a breakthrough. When breakthrough and derivative projects are compared on the basis of their ROI, breakthrough projects often lose, as their ROI numbers are harder to assess and less certain. Thus, pools of funding for breakthrough, platform, and derivative projects should be separated from the overall R&D budget and then projects within each group compared to one another.

The same logic applies to the allocation of IT funds. The company must first decide which business processes are core and which are, as Cisco calls them, context (Chapter 6). Which business processes does the firm wish to optimize to gain competitive advantage, and which only provide a support function? Amazon clearly decided that its web interface with the customer, and the underlying search function, is core and invests heavily in its development. Accounting and human resources management, on the other hand, may simply be context for Amazon. Wal-Mart gained competitive advantage through superior inventory management, enabled by its investments in sales and inventory tracking IT. Again, accounting and human resources management may be context for Wal-Mart. Companies in the hospitality industry, however, for whom employees are the front line with the customers, might emphasize human resources management systems as core and make inventory management context (Prahalad and Krishnan 2002). Care must be taken in the determination of what is core and context to take a broad view of the business. IT offers the opportunity to integrate internal functions with one another, as well as internal operations with external suppliers and customers. The most important business processes, as discussed in Chapter 7, may be cross-cutting processes such as order fulfillment, large-scale inventory management, or rapid new product introduction. IT investments must be viewed accordingly.

The company must also understand which business processes are stable and which are evolving (Prahalad and Krishnan 2002). Knowledge about how a business process operates and what users expect from it is clear for stable processes, whereas for evolving processes that knowledge is still developing. Evolving processes are generally the most immediate source of competitive advantage. We now have two dimensions along which to think about IT investment: (1) Is the business process core or context and (2) is it stable or evolving (Exhibit 9.20)? IT to support business processes that are both context and stable should consist largely of standard, off-the-shelf packages that the company may not even choose to upgrade regularly if they are serving their purpose. Business processes that are both core and evolving, on the other hand, may require development of custom software either in house or by a third-party developer. It may make sense for the company to fully outsource business processes that are context but evolving to an organization that considers the process core and will invest in custom IT support as needed. Stable business processes that are core may be supported with standard packages, but care must be taken not to let the potential rigidity of such packages affect the ability of the company to adapt to the needs of the evolving core processes.

EXHIBIT 9.20   Categories of IT Investment

	Core Business Process	Context Business Process
Stable	Modify standard packages, ensuring support with the evolving core	Implement standard packages
Evolving	Build custom software in house or with a third-party developer	Consider outsourcing the process to an organization for which it is core

The categorization shown in Exhibit 9.20 suggests where IT spending should be focused. To obtain competitive advantage, a large chunk of the firm's IT budget should be spent on evolving, core business processes and relatively little on context processes. Projects to implement or modify standard packages in support of stable, context business processes should be justified on the basis of an ROI or other such cost/benefit calculation. Investments in evolving, core processes, on the other hand, may be justified by a strategic objective of the organization. For Amazon, for example, becoming the "earth's most customer-centric company" drives much of its IT investment.

This matrix provides a link between the top-down IT investment allocation process and the bottom-up aggregation of ongoing and proposed projects. By mapping the set of proposed projects into the matrix, the organization can see how much it is spending on the processes that are important to it, and can make adjustments to that spending based on its strategic direction. If it finds that most of the proposed projects, and thus IT budget, are being spent on maintenance of stable, context processes, when its future competitive advantage lies in development of systems to support an evolving, core process, then it will know that it has to shift some investment.

Should the Company Buy Standard or Build Custom Software?

We briefly touched upon the reasons a company might choose to buy standard software packages or to develop custom software in house or with a third party. There is another option: "borrow" open source software. Open source software has become a viable option in both the infrastructure and application software domains as software applications have become more modular, the technical barriers to sharing software have eroded, and quality of the software has increased (Wheeler 2003). In addition to considering stable versus evolving business processes addressed above, companies need to consider a number of other issues in choosing among standard, custom, and open source software (Exhibit 9.21). Firms must take into account not only the fit of the IT systems with their business requirements, but also the acquisition and maintenance costs, how the systems will be supported, and to what extent the systems provide future flexibility. Customizing a standard ERP package can be very expensive and complicated as many ERP packages are not designed to support extensive customization. As a result, most businesses implement the best practices that are embedded in the ERP system. Minor customization, however, is required to adapt the highly generic inquiries, reports, and other parameters of the ERP systems to the specific business setting. In short, the company trades off the costs of acquiring, maintaining, and supporting the software with the ability to control what the software can do and customize it to the company's needs.

EXHIBIT 9.21   **Considerations in Choosing Among Build, Buy, Borrow Options for Acquiring Software**

Source: Adapted from Wheeler, "Aligning IT Strategy to Open Source, Partnering, and Web Services," Educause Center for Applied Research, research bulletin, 2003.

	Fit with Requirements	Acquisition Cost	Maintenance Cost	Support Options	Control of Destiny
Build	Customized to specific business requirements	Full development cost Possibly requires hiring permanent staff	Full cost for changes Spending at level firm wishes	Company must provide its own support either internally or through a contractor	High, as company owns the code
Buy	Standardized across the industry May be tailored via built-in settings or use of add-ons	Development cost shared across multiple customers of the vendor Vendor profit built into price	Mandatory support costs Costs shared across multiple customers	Vendor provides support through warranty and service-level agreements	Very low Limited or no access to modify code Extensive add-ons or customization may complicate upgrades
Borrow	Assembled from standardized components and tailored in house	Minimal or shared cost	Discretionary Minimal, shared or full cost	Company For-fee vendors Partners Open source community	High, as company has access to the source code

Sometimes there is no software on the market to meet a company's needs: Amazon, for example, had to build a custom dispatching system to handle the volume and complexity of its orders. Other times there is software available, but that software forces adoption of a particular business process. Thus, the question of whether to standardize or customize is a nuanced and difficult one. On one hand, a standard system installation could bind the company in ways that significantly compromise its competitive advantage, yet on the other hand, a customized approach may be far too costly to be justified. In short, the company must find a balance between the need for efficiency, which suggests standardization, and the need for innovation, which suggests flexibility and some degree of customization (Prahalad and Krishnan 2002).

The IT application portfolio scorecard shown in Exhibit 9.22 highlights some of the important considerations in thinking through the customization-standardization trade-offs. The areas of potential IT investment are shown across the top of the matrix, and the key questions down the side. Each potential investment is evaluated against what role the IT is to play strategically, whether the underlying business process is evolving or stable, what degree of change will be needed to cause the software to support the process, where the application is presently sourced or will be sourced in the future, and what the estimated required budget is. We illustrate this evaluation for two areas of investment in Exhibit 9.22. For example, the procurement system is important in ensuring product availability, but it is a stable process for which an SAP module is used, and it requires little change and thus little budget. The supply chain management process, however, is important to the company's

EXHIBIT 9.22 **Scorecard to Assess Investment in IT Applications**

Source: Adapted from Prahalad and Krishnan, "The Dynamic Synchronization of Strategy and Information Technology," *MIT Sloan Management Review,* 2002.

	Information Technology Application Area							
	New Product Development	Pricing	Forecasting	Procurement	Supply Chain Management	Distribution	Finance and Accounting	Human Resources Management
Strategic Role				Availability	Mass customization			
Evolving or Stable				Stable	Evolving			
Degree of Change Needed				Small	Considerable			
Application Source				SAP	In-house			
Budget				Maintenance only	Development			

mass customization charter, is an evolving process, and is a candidate for custom software development.

A company must also consider the capability of the internal IT function in making a choice between buying standard packaged software and building custom software or customizing open source software (Exhibit 9.23). A highly capable IT function can potentially cause standard applications to provide competitive advantage, as standard tools *used well* can give superior performance. But the highly capable IT function contributes most in the

EXHIBIT 9.23
Strategic Potential as a Function of IT Capability and IT Application Type

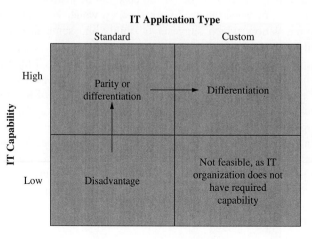

development of customized applications that provide differentiation and advantage. If the IT quality at a company is poor and the company is using standard applications, IT must improve its performance for the company to compete effectively. If it can improve its performance, it can usually compete at a level of parity. Note that the capability of the internal IT function may be in project management, not in the development of code per se; it may outsource much of the code development, but it must understand how to manage the outsourced work to achieve the desired ends.

Arguably, to obtain competitive advantage an organization must either customize selected IT applications, or it must excel at integrating and implementing standard software packages. Customization offers a distinct advantage that is hard to copy, as the application is not available to purchase. Integration can offer an advantage when it is done in clear support of a business process or competitive position, but remains responsive to changes in that strategy and evolves over time. Both approaches require highly capable IT organizations.

To What Extent Should Software Used Inside the Company Be Standardized?

The pros and cons of standardizing IT applications across a company are quite similar to those of standardizing process technology across the company (Exhibit 9.24). Standardizing offers benefits in reduced purchase, implementation, and support costs, while not standardizing allows local units to adapt their IT applications to their own needs. Note that the applications that are standardized across the company may be custom applications that each entity is required to use. Similarly, the nonstandard applications used by each entity may be standard off-the-shelf software, but each entity is allowed to make its own choice. Clearly the choice of whether or not to standardize across the company depends on just how different the businesses of the individual entities in the business are. Minor differences in how the entities choose to execute their processes probably do not merit allowing them to choose their own applications.

The choice of whether to standardize applications or not indicates the resulting structure of the IT organization and the role that a corporate IT function will play. If standardized systems are used across the company, the role of the central IT organization is to identify those systems, roll them out to the entities, and support them. If IT applications are not standardized across

EXHIBIT 9.24 **Benefits of Standardized versus Nonstandardized IT Applications across a Company**

Standardized IT Applications	Nonstandardized IT Applications
Reduces implementation costs, as each site can learn from those that have gone before it	Allows the local site to respond to site-specific conditions such as:
Facilitates cross-facility learning as sites share a common IT infrastructure	Market differences
Speeds the implementation process as bugs can be ironed out in the early implementations and then shared at later ones	Labor differences Supplier differences
Enables movement of products and other activities among sites, as there is no need for translation of the information among them	Allows local sites to develop competitive advantages that best fit their businesses
Minimizes support costs	May not impede data sharing if there is still a common data definition and structure at the corporate level

the organization, there must be more IT resources at each local entity, and the corporate role becomes one of managing common data definitions so that companywide reports (e.g., accounting reports) can be generated and so that entities can readily share data among their disparate systems.

How Should the IT Organization Be Designed?

The focus of many IT organizations in recent years has been on purchase, installation, and maintenance of ERP systems. Today, many companies are moving beyond ERP implementation and the establishment of the central databases at the core of those systems. They are now in a position to consider developing some of the custom applications we have been discussing. A number of lessons that are applicable to any large-scale systems efforts, especially for large multinational companies, have been learned from undertaking ERP implementation. These efforts often involve not only internal company personnel but a number of outside consultants, and work at three levels:[18]

1. *Top-level systems architecture:* Designs the overall dataflow for the enterprise, including the future dataflow plan.
2. *Business process reengineering:* Studies the organization's business processes and matches them to the corresponding processes in the planned system, identifying needed changes in both organization and systems.
3. *Technical programming and tool configuration:* Makes the appropriate modifications to the software to suit the identified business needs.

There are three stylized ways in which companies tend to undertake large-scale information systems implementation, each with its own implications for how the IT function is structured and works:[19]

1. *The Big Bang:* As its name suggests, in this approach companies jettison all of their legacy systems at once and install a single new system across the entire company. A number of companies took this approach to prepare for the year 2000 changeover, but few opt to do it if they have a choice. This "cold turkey" approach requires that personnel throughout the company get on board with using the new system quickly, and that they give up systems they may have home-grown and to which they have become accustomed. A very strong central IT organization with a clear mandate from the CEO is required to make the big bang work.
2. *Franchising strategy:* For large or diverse companies whose business units have little in common, independent systems may be installed in each unit that are connected for those common processes, such as accounting roll-ups, that cut across the enterprise. This is the most common approach to implementing large-scale systems changes. The corporate IT organization in this case might find an open-minded entity with which to run a pilot implementation, and then use its success with the first implementation to roll it out to other entities. The challenge for corporate IT management in this case is determining just how many different versions of the system are required and ensuring that data that needs to be shared across the company can be.

---

[18] http://en.wikipedia.org/wiki/Enterprise_resource_planning, August 15, 2006.
[19] http://www.cio.com/research/erp/edit/erpbasics.html, August 15, 2006.

3. *Slam dunk:* The goal of a slam dunk is quick installation with little or no process reengineering. The company might choose core modules of the system and implement them
without changing its internal processes much. This approach is generally used by smaller
companies that expect to grow into broader systems implementations. It yields few
competitive advantages, but provides the company with a toehold for future implementation. The role of the IT organization in this case is fairly rote.

In today's world, as we have highlighted throughout the chapter, IT is a critical cornerstone
of most companies' strategies. As a result, the roles of the chief information officer (CIO)
and of the IT organization have gained importance and prominence. CIOs make decisions
about the vision for the IT systems for the company, the structure of the IT organization,
specifically, how centralized it is, and the metrics by which the IT organization's performance
is measured. We address each decision briefly here.[20]

IT Vision

The primary role of the CIO is to jointly develop an information technology strategy in
conjunction with the other C-level executives in the organization. Today, IT strategy co-
evolves with the business strategy in many organizations, so the CIO must be able to both
communicate the latest technology trends so that other executives understand them and see
their potential, and understand the needs of the individual functions and business units as
well as those of the overall business. The IT department should be able to map out the company's entire software ecosystem in a visual display that makes the flow understandable,
clear, and logical to those outside the IT organization. The CIO's job is both to make that
flow relevant to the rest of the organization and to get the people within the IT organization on board with keeping it clear and focused on real business objectives. The vision the
CIO develops and communicates should revolve around accomplishing the business goals
of the company rather than around a specific software package. Implementation, for example, of Tigerpaw's CRM+ inventory control software suite should not be the vision; providing the company a chance to gain a competitive advantage in product variety through
inventory management might be a vision.

IT Organizational Structure

At the core of the question of how the IT function should be structured is the discussion
about how standardized IT systems need to be across the company. When the systems are
highly standardized, a strong central organization is needed to oversee their selection,
implementation, and support. When the systems are not standardized, the central IT
organization may be tasked with structuring companywide databases to facilitate companywide processes, or may have a more extensive role in supporting the individual business units or entities in the company as they seek and implement their own systems. To
determine how centralized the IT structure should be, the CIO has to answer these questions: How centralized should IT decisions be? How responsive must information technology be to local needs? Should the level of IT centralization vary by functional area?
For example, a case can be made to centralize all IT support of HR, since there should be
one best practice. However, manufacturing may have very different environments that

---

[20] We are grateful for input from a conversation with Ron Drabkin, formerly of JRG Software Inc.,
recently bought by CDC Software, in 2002.

need different IT support, with no one best practice. Similarly, should the level of centralization vary by business unit? Are the business units comfortable that a central IT organization can meet their individual business needs?

Measuring Performance

As the IT organization moves from being tactically focused to being core to the strategic positioning of the company, the metrics used to measure it change. Historically, many IT organizations were seen as performing well when they didn't cause any problems. Today, they are measured more on how well they support the business goals or, better yet, on what competitive advantage they offer to the company. To execute against those goals, the CIO needs to know: How capable is the workforce in the area of information technology? Is there an organization in place to help make sure that information technology within operations is working smoothly? How have prior IT projects gone? What were the expected benefits, actual benefits, expected time required, and actual time required of ramping up a new IT system? In particular, what was the cost of the software compared to the cost to get it running? How are IT cost controls put in place? What does the organization do when IT projects run over budget?

We have covered both strategic and tactical issues in this section, as questions that seem tactical often affect strategic outcomes. The ability to deploy nonstandard applications throughout a company—a strategic decision—may depend on the availability of IT skills in each of the entities—a tactical decision. The ability of the IT organization to develop, or manage the development of, custom software may dictate the degree to which the company can build its strategy around custom software. The answers to the questions we have raised—how much should the company invest in IT, how should that money be allocated, how much software should be bought off-the-shelf and how much should be custom-developed, to what extent should the entities in the company use standard software, and how should the IT function be organized—all go together to form the company's IT strategy.

Summary

In this chapter we defined information technology. We highlighted ways in which IT may provide competitive advantage, particularly in the area of operations management. We described specific IT applications in new product development, pricing, forecasting, procurement, supply chain management, and distribution, as well as applications in product availability, inventory management, and mass customization. We provided examples of companies—Amazon.com, Dell Inc., Cisco Systems, and Wal-Mart—that use information technology to gain competitive advantage. We discussed the limitations of information technology, the challenges of implementing large-scale systems changes, and the rigidity that IT can create for business processes. We outlined the major considerations made in choosing IT applications and managing their development and implementation in an organization. We close with a brief example of IT strategy development at a bank and a three-step process for generating an IT strategy.

Closing Example

Consumer Bank (a composite example compiled from experience with a number of retail banks, Kaplan and Norton 2004) wanted to shift its strategy from one focused on individual products to one offering complete financial solutions and one-stop shopping. To prepare itself for the transition, it identified seven key business processes that it needed to execute well in order to achieve its business goals: minimize problems, provide rapid response, cross-sell the product line, shift to an appropriate channel, understand customer segments, develop new products, and diversify the workforce. It then examined three categories of intangible assets—human capital, information capital, and organizational capital—to identify places where it needed to make further investment. The results of its work for information capital are summarized in Exhibit 9.25.

Arrayed underneath the six critical business processes that the CIO felt IT could affect is the set of applications the IT organization thought were needed to support each process. In order to cross-sell the product line, for example, the IT organization believed it needed a transformation application that would allow customers to analyze and manage their portfolios by themselves, an analytical application that would allow internal assessment of a customer's profitability to the bank, a transaction processing application that would integrate all information about the customer in a single file, and some technology infrastructure projects that would create the base on which the other applications could build. Once the team identified all of the applications it felt were critical to achieving success in each of the process areas, it evaluated the current status of those systems with scores from 1 if the systems were OK to 6 if a new application were required. The resulting chart provides the organization with a quick sense of where it stands in achieving its strategic goals and where investment is needed.

A Three-Step Process for Generating an IT Strategy

The companies that succeed in their strategic use of information technology in operations have a clear understanding of strategic imperatives, of how information technology fits these imperatives, and of both the opportunities and pitfalls of IT usage. We offer a three-step process that such companies might go through to develop their IT strategies.

Step 1: Understand how the company wishes to gain competitive advantage. The business strategy of the company dictates where the company wants to be positioned in terms of cost, quality, availability, features/innovativeness, and environmental performance. It also suggests capabilities that the firm either should leverage or needs to develop, potentially around critical business processes such as new product development, order fulfillment or service, and support. Understanding these business objectives is an important first step in the IT strategy development process. But the rapid evolution of IT technologies these days suggests that a discussion of the new opportunities IT creates for the business must be held in this step as well. Web-based technologies opened up entirely new business opportunities for companies like Amazon. Web-based ERP systems and wireless technologies open other vistas.

The output of this step of the process should be a general direction for the business strategy, a list of the processes that the organization agrees must be optimized to achieve that strategy, and the set of assumptions that constrain the process.[21] The organization must also decide how much it wishes to invest in IT. Benchmarks against competitors and knowledge of whether or not the company wishes to distinguish itself through IT are inputs to that decision.

[21] See, for example, the overview of Sheffield University's IT strategy at http://www.shef.ac.uk/cics/about/report/itstrat/its_info1.html, August 15, 2006.

EXHIBIT 9.25   An IT Strategy Map for a Consumer Bank

Source: Reprinted from Kaplan & Norton, "Measuring the Strategic Readiness of Intangible Assets," *Harvard Business Review,* 2004. Reprinted by permission of the publisher.

	Operations Management		Customer Management		Innovation	
Strategic Processes	Minimize problems	Provide rapid response	Cross-sell the product line	Shift to appropriate channel	Understand customer segments	Develop new products
Strategic Job Families	Quality manager	Call center representative	Certified financial planner	Telemarketer	Consumer marketer	Joint venture manager
Strategic Information Capital Portfolio						
Transformational Applications		Customer self-help 4	Customer portfolio self-management 4			
Analytical Applications	Service quality analysis 2	Best-practice community knowledge management system 3	Customer profitability 3	Best-practice community knowledge management system 2	Customer profitability 3	Best-practice community knowledge management system 2
Transaction Processing Applications	Incident tracking 6; Problem management 2	Workforce scheduling 3; Problem management 2	Integrated customer file 2	CRM/lead management 6; CRM/order management 2; CRM/sales-force automation 4	Customer feedback 2	Project management 2
Technology Infrastructure	Web enabled 3; Computer telephony integration 4	Computer telephony integration 4; Interactive voice response 3	CRM packaged software 2; Web enabled 3	Web enabled 3; Computer telephony integration 4	CRM packaged software 2	
Combined Readiness Level	✗	✗	?	✗	✓	✓

Ratings

1 OK

2 Minor enhancements needed

3 New development under way

4 New development behind schedule

5 Major enhancements required

6 New application required

✗ = not ready

✓ = ready

? = need to monitor

Step 2: Identify the ways in which IT can be used to support those goals. With direction from the business strategy, and a proposed budget, a company must determine in which business processes and systems to invest. This choice depends upon understanding which processes are core and which are context, which processes are stable and which are evolving, and which processes are supported by standard packages and which require custom software development. If IT is to be a competitive differentiator for the organization, more investment in custom development to support core, evolving processes and less investment in standard packages to support context, stable processes is required. The ability to make such an investment, however, depends upon the capability of the IT organization to either execute or manage software development.

Step 3: Organize the IT function to accomplish the goals. The organization of the IT function depends in part on what it needs to accomplish, as determined in step 2, and in part on the homogeneity of the organization it serves. If there is a large number of diverse business units in the company, and each has different business and thus IT needs, the IT function might be decentralized, and each business unit might undertake this three-step process on its own. In an environment with more homogeneous needs, a more centralized IT function allows the company to leverage its IT investment across multiple installations and coordinate data requirements for shared business processes.

IT skill sets must be matched to the task at hand. The greater the customization required, the more skilled the IT organization must be. Metrics to assess the IT organization's performance should link clearly to the company's business strategy and ensure that individual projects are yielding the expected benefits on time and on budget.

Information technology is becoming an increasingly important source of competitive advantage for companies that choose to use it well. Like Amazon, these companies are integrating their information systems to smoothly execute critical business processes and are selectively choosing to custom-develop software to differentiate themselves in areas where standard software doesn't meet their needs. In doing so, they set themselves apart from their competition, even in the use of standard applications.

References

AMR Research. "Supply Chain Strategies Outlook: E-Business Is Morphing Supply Chains." *The Report of Supply Chain Management.* January 2000.

Bauer, Michael J., Charles C. Poirier, Lawrence Lapide, and John Bermudez. *E-Business, the Strategic Impact on Supply Chain and Logistics.* Council of Logistics Management, 2001.

Brynjolfsson, Erik. The IT Productivity Gap. *Optimize,* no. 21, July 2003. pp. 26–43.

Brynjolfsson, Erik, and Lorin Hitt. "Computing Productivity: Firm-level Evidence." *Review of Economics and Statistics* 85, no. 4 (November 2003), pp. 793–808.

Brynjolfsson, Erik, Michael D. Smith, and Yu (Jeffrey) Hu. "Consumer Surplus in the Digital Economy: Estimating the Value of Increased Product Variety at Online Booksellers." *Management Science* 49, no. 11 (2003), pp. 1580–1596.

Brynjolfsson, Erik, Thomas W. Malone, Vijay Gurbaxani, Ajit Kambil. "Does Information Technology Lead to Smaller Firms?" *Management Science* 40, no. 12 (December 1994), pp. 1628–1644.

Davenport, Thomas H. "Putting the Enterprise into the Enterprise System." *Harvard Business Review* 76, no. 4 (July–August 1998) pp. 121–133.

The Economist. "The New New Economy. How Real and Durable are America's Extraordinary Gains in Productivity?", September 11, 2003, pp. 61–63.

Eppinger, Steven D., and Anil R. Chitkara. "The New Practice of Global Product Development." *MIT Sloan Management Review* 47, no. 4 (Summer 2006), pp. 22–30.

Evans, Philip, and Thomas Wurster. *Blown to Bits: How the New Economics of Information Transforms Strategy.* Boston: Harvard Business School Press, 2000.

Graban, Mark, Jochen Linck, and Bing Wang. "Operations Management in the Internet Economy." Paper for MIT course 15.769, May 1999.

Graves, Stephen C., and Sean P. Willems. "Optimizing Strategic Safety Stock Placement in Supply Chains." *Manufacturing & Service Operations Management* 2, no. 2 (Winter 2000), pp. 68–83.

Heizer, Jay, and Barry Render. *Operations Management.* 6th ed. Upper Saddle River, NJ: Prentice Hall, 2001.

Hewitt, Fred. "After Supply Chains, Think Demand Pipelines." *Supply Chain Management Review,* 5, no. 3 (May–June 2001), pp. 28–38.

Kandare, Greg, Adam Kohorn, Carey Mar, and Michael Milby. "Operations Strategy in the 90s and Beyond: Mass Customization." Paper for MIT course 15.769, May 1999.

Kaplan, Robert S., and David P. Norton. "Measuring the Strategic Readiness of Intangible Assets." *Harvard Business Review* 82, no. 2 (February 2004) pp. 52–63.

Klein, J., and A. Kleinhanns. "Closing the Time Gap in Virtual Teams." In *Virtual Teams at Work: Creating Conditions for Virtual Team Effectiveness,* eds. C. Gibson, and S. Cohen. Indianapolis, IN: Jossey-Bass, 2003.

Konsynski, Benn R. "Strategic Control in the Extended Enterprise." *IBM Systems Journal* 32, no. 1 (1993), pp. 111–142.

Lapide, Larry. "The Innovators Will Control the E-Supply Chain." "AMR Research report, May 1, 2000.

Lee, Hau L., V. Padmanabhan, and Seungjin Whang. "The Bullwhip Effect in Supply Chains." *Sloan Management Review* 38, no. 3 (1997), pp. 93–102.

Malone, Thomas W., and Robert J. Laubacher. "The Dawn of the E-Lance Economy." *Harvard Business Review* 76, no. 5 (September–October 1998), pp. 144–152.

Mitchell, Pierre. "Trading Exchange Infrastructure: 13-Stop Shopping." AMR Research report, August 1, 2000.

Pine, Joseph B. "Serve Each Customer Efficiently and Uniquely" In Network Transformation: Individualizing Your Customer Approach. Supplement to *Business Communications Review* 26, no. 1, (January 1996), pp. 2–5.

Prahalad, C.K., and M.S. Krishnan. "The Dynamic Synchronization of Strategy and Information Technology." *MIT Sloan Management Review* 43, no. 4 (Summer 2002), pp. 24–33.

PricewaterhouseCoopers. *Technology Forecast,* 1998.

Rosenfield, Donald B. "Demand Forecasting." *The Logistics Handbook.* James F. Robeson and William C. Copacino (ed.). New York, NY: The Free Press, 1994.

Silver, Edward A., David F. Pyke, and Rein Peterson. *Inventory Management and Production Planning and Scheduling.* 3rd ed. Hoboken, NJ: John Wiley & Sons, Inc., 1998.

Swaminathan, Jayashankar M., and Sridhar R. Tayur. "Models for Supply Chains in E-Business." *Management Science* 49, no. 10 (October 2003), pp. 1387–1406.

Szkutak, Tom. "Amazon.com." Credit Suisse First Boston Annual Technology Conference, December 2003.

Wheeler, Bradley C. "Aligning IT Strategy to Open Source, Partnering, and Web Services." Educause Center for Applied Research, Research Bulletin, vol. 2003, issue 24 (November 25, 2003).

Chapter 10

Cross-Cutting Capabilities: Lean Operations, Quality, and Flexibility

Introduction

Toyota Motor Corporation is one of the world's major corporate success stories. It is a clear leader in the world car industry by any number of metrics. Its net profits are more than double those of its next closest competitors, Nissan and Honda, and nearly triple those of GM and Ford (Exhibit 10.1). Its market capitalization is more than three times that of Honda or Nissan and larger than that of the "Big Three" U.S. automakers—GM, Ford, and DaimlerChrysler—put together (Exhibit 10.2). It regularly receives the highest customer satisfaction rating from J.D. Power and Associates; its cars took 4 of the 10 top spots in individual car ratings in 2004. Between 2000 and 2005, when the global output of the car industry grew by 3 million vehicles, half came from Toyota. Its global manufacturing presence grew from 11 manufacturing facilities in 9 countries in 1980 to 20 plants in 14 countries in 1990, to a total of 46 plants in 26 countries today. Toyota has truly become a global force in the car industry.

How has Toyota achieved its unique success? Most point to the Toyota Production System (TPS), Toyota's homegrown approach to eliminating waste, producing consistently high-quality output, and coordinating materials flows with just-in-time (JIT) techniques. Others note that the principles underlying the TPS, applied to Toyota's product development process, allow Toyota to bring new car models to market in about two years. With that product development lead time, not only can Toyota respond quickly to new market trends or to competitors' moves, but it can also generate and support a wide range of models to serve the global marketplace. Its secret to rapid product development and delivery is part reuse; two-thirds of the parts in a new model were used on previous Toyota models. But, in their zeal to understand the specific tools and techniques of the TPS and rapid product development cycles, observers often miss the core of Toyota's competitive advantage: its customer-focused, problem-solving, relentless pursuit-of-excellence culture. Even as Toyota grows globally, it maintains strict adherence to these basic principles, investing significantly in training and development to ensure that its culture is shared around the world.

EXHIBIT 10.1   Net Profit of Major Automobile Producers 2004 ($ billions)

Source: Data drawn from *The Economist,* "The Car Company in Front," 2005.

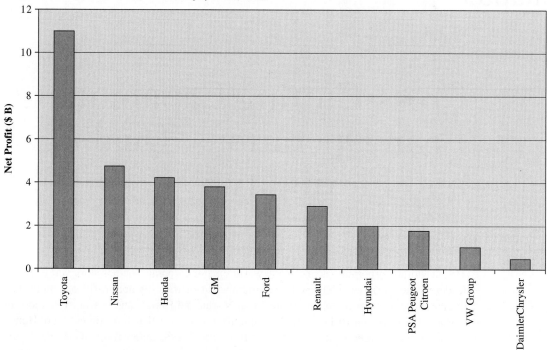

A brief history of the development of just-in-time, the Toyota Production System, and lean manufacturing at Toyota make clear that these programs are not just collections of tools but are capabilities that are deeply entrenched in the very core of the organization.[1] Three men are credited with creating the foundations of the TPS: Sakichi Toyoda, the founder; Kichiro Toyoda, his son; and Taiichi Ohno, a production engineer influenced by the teachings of W. Edwards Deming. In 1902, well before he founded the Toyota Group, Sakichi Toyoda designed a device that automatically stopped a weaving loom if any of the warp or weft threads broke. The invention reduced defects and increased yields, as it prevented a loom from producing more imperfect fabric and using up thread once the error was caught. The invention also facilitated an entirely new shop floor management system. Before the invention each machine required the attention of a single worker to watch for the occurrence of defects. With the device, a single worker could watch over multiple machines, rethreading and restarting those that were stopped. One of the fundamental principles of the TPS today, *jidoka*, requires that production be stopped at the first sign of a problem and that the problem be resolved before production starts again.

In the 1930s, when the Toyota Group was established, Kichiro Toyoda paid a visit to see Henry Ford's great invention, the assembly line. Inspired by what he saw and determined

[1] Materials for this section were drawn from http://www.toyotageorgetown.com/history.asp, http://www.tpca-cz.com/en, and http://www.strategosinc.com, October 15, 2006.

EXHIBIT 10.2 **Market Capitalization of Major Auto Manufacturers**

Source: Data drawn from Glauser, "The Toyota Phenomenon," The Swiss Deming Institute, www.deming.ch/downloads/E_Toyota.pdf, 2006.

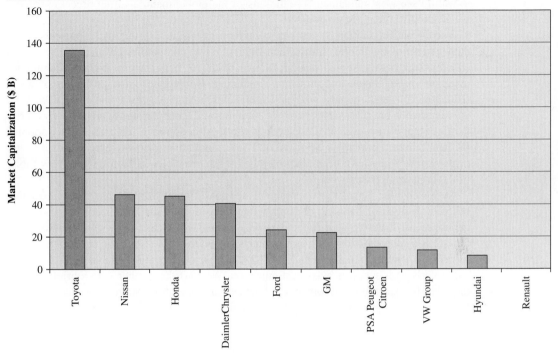

to figure out a way to make it work at much, much lower production volumes in Japan, he conceived of the basic notion of just-in-time (JIT) whereby the materials needed at the assembly line would arrive there in just the right quantities at just the right time. Taiichi Ohno, also inspired by Ford's assembly line process and impressed by how U.S. super-markets worked, conceived of the notion of "pulling" materials through the production process. In effect, he reversed the flow of materials so that later processes pulled materials from earlier processes just as a supermarket restocks its shelves when they are empty. Thus, the pull system and the use of kanban cards were born. This kind of fundamental rethinking of the production process is a core value of the TPS to this day.

In 1945, Kichiro Toyoda issued a challenge to Toyota employees to catch up with the American car industry in the next three years. Taiichi Ohno took this challenge to heart. He reasoned that the American workers were producing about nine times as much as the Japanese, so to catch up in three years would require figuring out how to get the work of 100 people done by just 10. Convinced that American workers were not exerting 10 times more effort than Japanese workers, he concluded that there must be a great deal of waste in the Japanese system and set about creating programs to eliminate that waste. He estab-lished a flow system, formulating the fundamental principles underlying cellular manu-facturing today, and realized the value of level production, today known as *heijunka*. The fundamental questioning of why things were done the way they were, combined with the ambitious target of catching up with the Americans, set the standard for a culture of lean thinking. Today's ambitious target is to win 15 percent of the global car market, and thus surpass General Motors to become the largest car manufacturer in the world. We will have to wait to see what fundamental rethinking of the global manufacturing process precedes the accomplishment of that goal.

The Toyota Production System, as its name suggests, is a system that represents a fundamental set of capabilities from which Toyota derives competitive advantage. The system encompasses organizational design, human resource management, process technology, materials management, and production planning. It integrates basic principles of waste reduction, consistent quality, and just-in-time materials management and applies them not only internally, but across its network of suppliers and other partners to create an enterprise that far outperforms even its closest competitors. Although many companies have adopted the lean thinking principles espoused by Toyota, including to some degree all of its competitors, few if any have been able to embed those principles as firmly in the very fabric of the organization as Toyota.

In this chapter, we take an approach somewhat different from the one in the preceding chapters. Instead of focusing on a particular decision that the firm needs to make (e.g., about process technology or capacity management), we discuss the development of capabilities as a source of competitive advantage. We address three specific capabilities in the world of operations management: lean operations, quality management, and flexibility particularly as it supports mass customization. We start the chapter with a brief recap of the role of capabilities development in business and operations strategy. We then describe lean operations, quality, and flexibility capabilities in some detail.

Cross-Cutting Capabilities

In Chapter 1, we discussed the basic premise of the resource-based view of strategy, which is that competitive advantage is derived from the firm's development of its resources and capabilities. In this view, firms occupy different market positions because they possess unique bundles of resources and capabilities that are valuable, rare, and inimitable. Resources include observable assets that can be valued and traded such as brands, patents, and licenses, while capabilities are intangible assets embedded in the people and practices of the organization. Collectively, these intangible assets facilitate performance of a coordinated set of tasks, utilizing the organization's resources, for the purpose of achieving a particular end result.

Some argue that investment in capabilities development of the sort we are discussing in this chapter provides only temporary competitive advantage, and that the tools and techniques associated with achieving operational excellence can be readily copied, placing companies at best at par with their competitors (Porter 1996). Others argue that the ability to continually push the "productivity frontier" out, and to keep it just out of reach of competitors, can indeed be a source of competitive advantage (Hayes and Pisano 1994). There is no doubt that Toyota's ability to regularly redefine the way in which manufacturing is done and supply networks are managed provides it significant competitive advantage.

It is on the basis of this belief that we dedicate this chapter to three cross-cutting capabilities that provide some companies competitive advantage today: lean operations, quality management, and flexibility. We distinguish capabilities development from business process management, the topic of Chapter 7, in that capabilities development entails embedding routines and ways of thinking deeply in the organization. Business process engineering may well lead to the development of new capabilities but need not necessarily do so. It may simply result in streamlining a process by eliminating steps in the process or reducing the time required at those steps. The development of capabilities, such as lean manufacturing at Toyota, requires changing the fundamental ways in which the organization thinks and acts.

Capabilities may be applied to take a given position in the marketplace. Toyota, for example, has a superior position in the marketplace on the quality dimension that leverages its capabilities in high-quality, consistent manufacturing. Increasingly, it is excelling along the features and innovativeness dimension as well due to its capability in rapid product introduction. As discussed in Chapter 1, this ability to leverage capabilities into a position in the marketplace permits us to reconcile the resource-based view with the positioning view of strategy.

We have discussed Toyota and its capabilities in lean manufacturing. Developing capabilities in quality management requires enterprisewide change in fundamental thinking as well. Although almost all organizations use quality management tools, very few embed them deeply enough in the culture, routines, and decision making of the organization to create a differentiating capability. Most organizations strive to improve the quality of their products and services as the *external* customer perceives it. Organizations that have strong quality management capability, on the other hand, focus on developing the *internal* processes that lead to high-quality output. The deep knowledge of their processes that they gain can then be leveraged to develop new products and services.

The third unique capability we discuss in this chapter is flexibility. Many view flexibility as a strategic output of an organization, but people do not buy a good or service because of the organization's flexibility. They buy because of the cost, quality, availability, features and innovativeness, or environmental performance of that good or service. While flexibility may well be the source of superior performance, it is an internal capability that helps fulfill strategic goals.

The fields of operations and manufacturing have experimented with many different approaches to performance improvement, including lean operations, total quality management, Six Sigma, and business process management. Many organizations attempt these improvement efforts by copying the visible and documented tools and techniques associated with the approach and fail because they lack deep understanding of the thinking behind the approach. The approaches thus come across as fads or the business equivalent of "flavors of the month." What we are talking about in this chapter is not the rote application of a set of tools or techniques, but the much deeper adoption of philosophies and ways of thinking that create sustainable sources of competitive advantage. In short, we address three unique capabilities that:

- Cut across different parts of the organization.
- Represent methods and approaches for the entire organization and not for a single customer process.
- Are internal capabilities and not strategic goals by themselves.

We now explore the three capabilities most associated with operations management today: lean operations, quality management, and flexibility.

Lean Operations

Lean manufacturing[2] has had a major influence on the competitive structure of a number of manufacturing industries, and its broader counterpart, lean thinking, is influencing a range of industries outside the manufacturing sector. In this section we describe some of the underlying principles of lean operations, and just-in-time manufacturing in particular. We explore four of the tools used to achieve lean operations, and close with a discussion of the ways in which lean operations can be used to obtain competitive advantage.

Lean operations had its beginnings in the development of just-in-time production and inventory management approaches in the automotive and electronics sectors. Originally conceived as an inventory management system, lean operations was later, and properly, understood to be an entire system of manufacturing management. There are a number of principles of lean manufacturing (Womack et al. 1990), but the general overriding principle is waste elimination. Waste, often referred to by the Japanese term *muda,* is any activity that "absorbs resources but creates no value" (Womack and Jones 1996, p. 15). Waste can be part of a production and distribution activity and can also appear in related activities, such as design, inventory management, and worker assignments. Exhibit 10.3 presents the different types of waste that can exist in a manufacturing or service system. Waste elimination not only reduces costs, it also provides a clearer view of how quality can be improved and fosters reduced lead times.

While the concepts of lean operations were originally applied to manufacturing systems, they can also be applied to service operations in areas such as capacity management, process flow, and materials support. Some of the specific concepts applied in lean operations are to:

- Produce at any location only when demanded by downstream users.
- Maintain production at a constant level to the degree possible.
- Reduce lot sizes as much as possible, preferably to a size of one.
- Achieve short, predictable lead times between steps.
- Strive for a linear flow of production to the extent possible. Use cellular flow for different product lines.
- Position suppliers to resupply frequently and in small lots as dictated by specific assembly requests.
- Limit number of suppliers and fully interact with them in materials management (schedule interactions), quality (limiting inspection), and design.
- Integrate design cycles fully with manufacturing, using concurrent engineering and reducing development lead times as much as possible.
- Reduce variability as much as possible, improving supplier consistency, machine reliability, and demand predictability.
- Reduce demand variation by managing it (e.g., encouraging demand in off-peak times or timing model releases in multiple markets) or by leveling it using strategically placed buffers. Understand that some degree of demand variability is unavoidable.

---

[2] Today the notions of lean manufacturing have been broadened to what some call the lean enterprise and others think of as lean thinking. See Womack and Jones (1996) for a current perspective on lean thinking.

EXHIBIT 10.3 Types of Waste

Source: Adapted from Ohno, *The Toyota Production System: Beyond Large-Scale Production,* Productivity Press, 1988, and Womack and Jones, *Lean Thinking: Banish Waste and Create Wealth in Your Corporation,* Simon and Schuster, 1996.

- Overproduction ahead of demand
- Unnecessary processing steps
- Waiting for the next processing step
- Unnecessary transport of materials
- Excess inventories
- Unnecessary movement of workers
- Production of defective parts or services
- Production of goods or services that do not meet customer needs

- Fully engage the workforce in the process by, for example, encouraging workers to suggest and manage quality improvements and providing them the power to stop the line if defects are occurring (e.g., with an andon cord system such as is used in the Toyota Production System).

In short, the essence of lean thinking is reducing waste and making operations as efficient and as consistent as possible. Large lot sizes, extra inventory, and increased complexity in the process flow are all forms of waste. The implementation of lean principles and approaches affects the entire organization from supplier management to product design, to human resources, to scheduling and materials management. Inventory reduction, which was the original focus of JIT and the basis of lean thinking, is the most prominent and visible of these areas of waste reduction. To make the principles of lean operations come alive, we briefly describe its precursor, just-in-time systems.

Just-in-Time Systems

JIT is a one-for-one replenishment system where production is initiated only when requested by a downstream operation. Exhibit 10.4 illustrates a three-step process that employs JIT. Suppose that there is a demand for one unit of product from this process. Operators at step 3 are then triggered to begin production of a new unit using materials from Cart B at the top of the diagram. Upon completing step 3, the operator returns Cart B to the flow at the bottom of the diagram, signaling to the operator at step 2 that more materials are needed. The step 2 operator will thus initiate production to fill a new Cart B. In turn, when step 2 starts production it uses material from its input Cart A. When the step

EXHIBIT 10.4

A JIT System

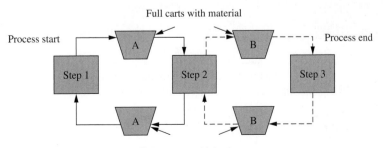

Full carts with material

Process start

Process end

Empty carts with kanbans

2 operator empties Cart A, he or she returns the empty Cart A to the operator at step 1, initiating production at that step. The full carts flow left to right across the top of Exhibit 10.4, and return empty from right to left across the bottom of Exhibit 10.4.

In Toyota's implementation of JIT in the Toyota Production System (TPS), Toyota developed a concept called a *kanban,* which is a card found at the bottom of each lot of material that signals the need for replenishment. Kanban refers to a simple signaling mechanism, which can take the form of a card, a plastic marker, a golf ball, or any number of other items. Alternative kanban mechanisms include spaces on a floor (often used in a distribution environment, where an empty space signifies the need for replenishment); a pallet, empty cart, or other container; or, in a computerized environment, a computer signal.

In a combined production-distribution environment, there can be JIT signals for both the production and distribution steps, as shown in Exhibit 10.5. In this picture, a production request is transmitted to the distribution system, which triggers a movement from inventory into production. The movement out of distribution then triggers a production request on another downstream operation. In this situation, one might use a dual-kanban system with different types of kanban mechanisms, one for production and one for distribution or conveyance. The distribution or conveyance kanban, shown as a paper document in Exhibit 10.5, replaces the empty cart used in the single kanban system in Exhibit 10.4. In Exhibit 10.5, carts still carry the inventory forward through the system, while paper kanbans signal the need for replenishment. Inventory management in a JIT environment requires determining how many carts (or their equivalent) should be used. The number of carts (or kanbans) times the cart size is the total amount of inventory (work-in-process plus safety stock) at each step of the process.

The objective in a true lean environment is to reduce the number of carts and the cart sizes as far as possible while still recognizing the need for some safety stock. In discrete manufacturing for less expensive parts, a lot size greater than one is common, while for more expensive parts (e.g., engines for automobiles), lot sizes of one are delivered to the assembly point in the order that they are needed.

A variation of JIT is constant work in process, or CONWIP (e.g., Hopp and Spearman 2001). CONWIP uses JIT replenishment over multiple steps in the production process, as

EXHIBIT 10.5
A Dual-Kanban System

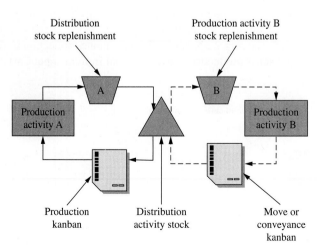

Distribution stock replenishment

Production activity B stock replenishment

A

B

Production activity A

Production activity B

Production kanban

Distribution activity stock

Move or conveyance kanban

EXHIBIT 10.6
A CONWIP System

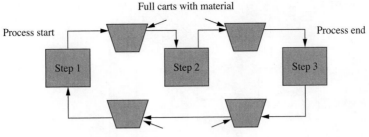

shown in Exhibit 10.6, keeping the total number of carts in the system constant. Lots flow through the multiple steps from left to right as they complete each step, and replenishment carts flow from right to left. However, the completion of step 1 or step 2 does not trigger any replenishment. Only final step 3 triggers replenishment. When a lot of finished goods is completed at step 3 and leaves the system, a replenishment cart is sent to request more input. This variation of JIT preserves the principle of only starting work on a lot when one is demanded through a completion.

JIT is often compared with MRP systems. (See Chapter 9.) While JIT initiates, or pulls, orders only when demanded, MRP is viewed as pushing orders through the system to meet the needs of a schedule. Some argue that these approaches are incompatible, but in reality many companies blend them using an MRP system to plan material purchases to support a JIT-based production system. They do so because the lead times to acquire many materials are too long to support JIT. The MRP systems provide ample warning to vendors that materials will be needed, allowing them to plan and run their own production processes. In many cases, actual delivery of the materials against the MRP-based orders is done on a JIT pull system basis.

In a lean system where production is level and uncertainty is reduced, it is possible to carry a small amount of inventory. Often, however, companies reduce their inventories without sufficiently decreasing variability or smoothing demand. Shortages result, making the company believe that inventory reduction and lean implementation approaches are unachievable or the methods inappropriate. It is important to understand that inventory cannot be reduced unless the conditions that support inventory reduction are achieved: Variability reduction, production leveling, and lot size reduction are crucial to successful inventory reduction and thus lean implementation.

Benefits of Lean Operations

Lean implementation is designed to create an efficient operation. It also yields a number of other improvements, such as

- Reduced lead times through lower work-in-process inventory.
- Problem solving and quality improvement driven by needs to reduce waste and variability.
- Team building and cooperation by linking different steps.
- Cooperation with suppliers by examining the implications of lean operations on a systemwide basis.

EXHIBIT 10.7
Effects of JIT

Before JIT

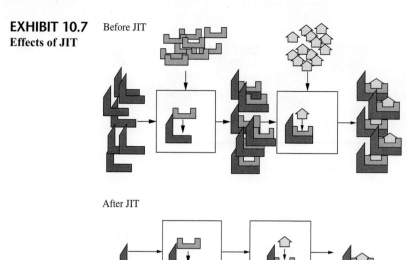

After JIT

The actual reduction of inventory and waste is in itself a significant aspect of lean operations. Exhibit 10.7 shows a two-step assembly process in which some simple shapes are put together. In the before-JIT environment, large piles of both component and subassembly inventory clutter the process flow, making it appear chaotic and jumbled. In the after-JIT environment, the process flow is clearer and easier to follow. Simply drawn, this depicts the benefits of inventory reduction.

JIT and lean operations engage the entire production system, including suppliers. Many manufacturers originally used implementation of lean operations in their own facilities as an excuse to push inventories back to their suppliers. In the end, the improvements they were seeking, however, depended on the full supply chain and thus required lean implementation at their suppliers as well. The conditions for including suppliers in a successful lean program are the same as for implementing at a single producer: Variation and lot sizes must be reduced across the entire supply chain, lead times must be shortened, and requirements must be leveled. Toyota's implementation of the TPS involved locating its suppliers close by to ensure short delivery lead times, frequent communication of schedules, and minimization of delivery lot sizes. The role suppliers played in the TPS was just as crucial as the invention of kanbans or andon cords.

Tools of Lean Implementation

Although JIT is a cornerstone of lean implementation, there are a number of other tools that are important as well, including:

- Cellular one-piece flow.
- Value stream mapping.
- Production leveling.
- Supplier rationalization.

We review these tools in the following sections.

Cellular One-Piece Flow

In production systems that have multiple product lines sharing work cells, it is sometimes hard to avoid a chaotic process flow with jumbled and even arbitrary movement of materials among shared resources. The result is long and wasteful material-handling movements, significant queue buildups as products wait for shared resources, and, as a result, long lead times and high inventories.

Cellular flow requires setting up dedicated lines for each different product family in a facility, as shown in Exhibit 10.8. Before the implementation of cellular manufacturing, products A, B, and C shared the same resources at steps 2 and 4 of the process. Implementation of cellular manufacturing split the resources used to accomplish steps 2 and 4 so that products A, B, and C each have their own complete production lines. The use of dedicated lines (1) minimizes flow time since dedicated work cells are closer to each other, (2) minimizes inventory through shorter lead times (since work cells are close together and synchronized), and (3) reduces set-up times and improves quality since each work cell is optimized for the product family it builds. Further, cellular flow facilitates reducing lot sizes, which, as our discussion of JIT highlights, is an important part of lean implementation. Since the work cells are optimized for a specific product family, lot size reduction becomes more feasible. In the Toyota Production System, lot size reduction, particularly through the development of techniques for "single minute exchange of dies" for stamping, was a major focus of the designers. In Exhibit 10.8, the cellular flow is linear, but in many cellular applications the flow is a U-shape, which often reduces space required and encourages interaction and problem solving among workers on the line.

Can all process be converted to cellular flow? The transition is not always easy and can involve trade-offs. Sometimes resources, because of scale or other reasons, must be shared among several product families. Other times, there may be limits to lot size reduction. In such cases, a product family's process flow may be partially completed in a dedicated cell and partially completed on a shared resource. Honeywell, a company that has made lean operations

EXHIBIT 10.8
Effects of
Cellular Flow

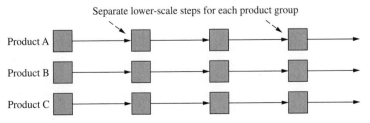

Before implementation of cellular production

Product A

Product B

Product C

Common steps 2 and 4

After implementation of cellular production

Separate lower-scale steps for each product group

Product A

Product B

Product C

a key part of its strategy, ran into this issue in some of its implementations in its aerospace group. However, by limiting the number of times a product family moved to a shared resource, Honeywell was able to implement cellular flows within much of its production.

Value Stream Mapping

Unlike cellular flow, which is a tool that is used to actually implement lean operations, value stream mapping it a tool that is used to plan lean operations. Value stream mapping is used to develop improved process flows by identifying and mapping each step in the process and is often used to develop cellular flows. It can identify wasted movements, unnecessary steps, and excess inventories. Even without a transition to cellular flow, value stream mapping has the potential to streamline processes and eliminate wasteful non-value-added steps.

Value stream mapping is closely related to the process-mapping tool presented in Chapter 7. Both methods aim to identify process improvements by graphically mapping out the process, with blocks representing physical steps in the process and arrows showing flows of information. The major difference between the tools is the type of process to which they are applied. Process mapping is used for business processes such as order fulfillment and emphasizes how tasks and information are passed among different parties. Value stream mapping is used for production or service creation processes, and depicts how value is created and added. In a production process, for example, value stream maps emphasize the physical flow of material. A value stream map can be used in a distribution operation, a customer service operation such as banking, or a service business such as a theme park to physically map out how transactions, products, or customers flow through the system.

It is easiest to see the use of value stream mapping through an example. Hamilton Sundstrand is a subsidiary of United Technologies Corporation and is one of the largest global suppliers of aerospace systems for commercial, regional, corporate, and military aircraft as well as for international space programs. Hamilton Sundstrand's value stream mapping efforts focused on streamlining and improving the flow of its manufacturing operations. Exhibit 10.9 presents the value stream map of different products through one of its operations on a board. The bottom set of paper notes depicts the set of discrete process steps in a process that flows from left to right. The top group of paper notes represents a set of action items to improve the process and flow. The company refers to these as *kaizen steps.* After a major redesign of the process, the company made a number of major improvements. The new process value stream for the product line is presented in Exhibit 10.10. The number of steps, represented by the major blocks in Exhibit 10.10, was greatly reduced, and the information flow, represented by the lines at the top of the exhibit, originated from only a few locations. This example, like other examples of value stream mapping, shows graphically how simplification can improve flow. In other applications, Hamilton Sundstrand sometimes split a large process flow into individual flows for different sets of products, creating cells for each.

Production Leveling

A key element of introducing lean processes is reduction in variation, but there are parts of all systems that are in the control of the designers and others that are less so. For example, a lean implementation can reduce variation in output (e.g., by reducing or eliminating process breakdowns), variation in supply (e.g., by having frequent supplier deliveries with short lead times), and variation in inventory (e.g., by reducing lot sizes). To some degree,

EXHIBIT 10.9 **Hamilton Sundstrand Value Stream Before Redesign**

Source: Reprinted with permission from United Technologies Corporation.

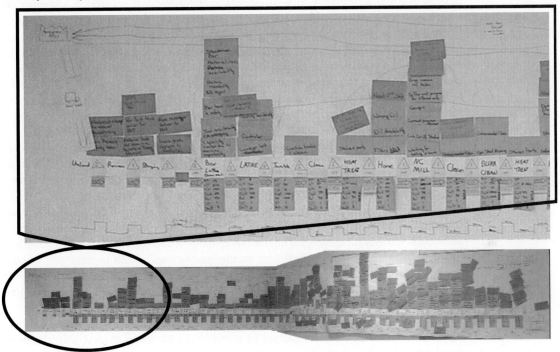

EXHIBIT 10.10 **Hamilton Sundstrand Future State**

Source: Reprinted with permission from United Technologies Corporation.

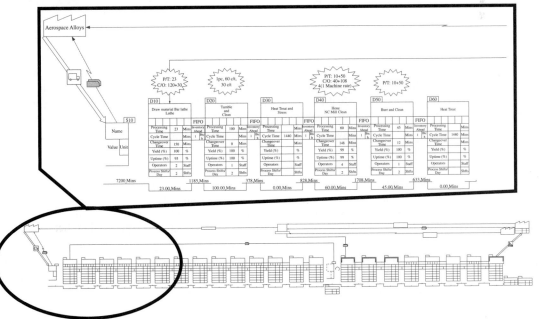

however, it is difficult to reduce variation in demand. Customer demand is always subject to some uncertainty. Despite this, there are tools to manage uncertainty and allow the core process to operate as evenly as possible. By keeping the process level, a company can reduce inventory in the center of the process and more easily maintain consistent quality.

One tool that helps keep the process level is demand management. While demand cannot be completely managed, it can be influenced. For example, promotions during off-peak periods can be used to reduce short-term variations. Across multiple markets, products can be managed in such a way as to level the mix and manage the life cycle at any given facility. For example, a Japanese company might delay introduction of a product in the U.S. market until the initial demand peak in Japan has passed. Mix in general can be leveled using promotions.

Smooth flow within the factory can also be obtained through production leveling, or *heijunka*, a critical aspect of the Toyota Production System. Heijunka is used to maintain some consistency in the production system even in the presence of some demand variation. It allows the company to fix the production schedule and order lead times and thus work on a consistent schedule within that given lead time. On a short-term basis, a manufacturer can smooth production of specific product features, such as cars with and without sunroofs and those with two or four doors. Over a longer horizon it can limit changes in aggregate production levels such as the total number of vehicles produced. Toyota uses time horizons of five days, one-and-a-half weeks, one month, and two-and-a-half months over which it allows different, but increasing, levels of changes to production plans (Mishina 1995). With the shortening of order lead times in the automobile industry, such strategies have been increasingly limited, but they can still be implemented on a short-term basis.

Although smoothing strategies strive to minimize demand variation, manufacturers inevitably need to carry some amount of post-process inventory to deal with remaining variability. Every lean system has some inventory but endeavors to limit its levels and the number of locations in which it is stored. By keeping inventory at the end of the process to deal with variation, inventory in the midst of the process can be minimized.

Supplier Rationalization

The final tool of lean implementation that we will address is the management of suppliers. We deal with supplier management extensively in Chapter 6, but it is worth commenting on some of the areas where lean operations affect supplier management. First, suppliers should be considered within the larger system in which the principles of lean and just-in-time are being implemented. Just as within the factory, the goals for supplier management include short lead times, frequent deliveries, and little inventory buffer. This may mean moving suppliers close by. By looking at the entire system, there is less of a tendency to simply push inventory back to the suppliers. Second, when quality is managed by the workers within the process, required inspection of supplier's products is minimal.

The principle of a limited number of suppliers described in Chapter 6 is an important aspect of lean operations. Before the advent of lean, large OEM manufacturers typically had hundreds and sometimes thousands of suppliers. Many companies reduced these by an order of magnitude. However, such changes have not been consistent, and some companies still struggle with the legacy of a large supplier base. The relationship of number of suppliers and the benefits of lean implementation is direct. With more suppliers, implementation of the full range of lean tools is more difficult. It thus becomes important to limit the extent of the supplier base.

The Impact of Lean Operations on Competitiveness

There is no doubt that the implementation of lean operations has had wide-ranging effects in a number of industries, even for companies that do not fully embed lean thinking as a capability or way of doing business as Toyota does. Applications of lean operations in the automobile industry in Japan have resulted in significant improvements in cost and quality (Womack et al. 1990), and, as fully described in the introduction to this chapter, Toyota continues to be a global leader with the sustained advantage it gained from deeply embedding lean thinking throughout its operations.

The significant reductions in inventory achieved through lean operations have a direct effect on improved performance along a number of dimensions. Inventory reduction, for example, translates directly into labor productivity improvements even across companies with very different starting points (Abegglen and Stalk 1985). Increasing inventory turns are directly related to overall financial performance of companies (Schonberger 1996). Thus, implementation of the tools and techniques of lean operations can lead to improved corporate performance.

It is the embedding of lean thinking throughout the company, however, that makes it a capability–something rare, inimitable, and valuable. Toyota clearly has this capability. A study of capabilities development in the automobile industry showed clearly that Toyota has the best inventory performance and best overall performance of any player in the industry despite attempts by all to adopt the techniques of lean operations (Lieberman and Dhawan 2005). Further, that superior performance has been sustained over 30 years. The study examined a number of factors including value added per employee, labor productivity, and inventory turnover. Toyota's performance far outstripped that of its competitors in measures such as the ratio of work in progress (WIP) to sales (Exhibit 10.11) and technical efficiency, which is related to labor productivity (Exhibit 10.12).

EXHIBIT 10.11

WIP/Sales Ratio for a Number of Auto Manufacturers

Source: Reprinted from Lieberman and Dhawan, "Assessing the Resource Base of Japanese and U.S. Auto Producers: A Stochastic Frontier Production Function Approach," *Management Science,* 2005, by permission of the publisher.

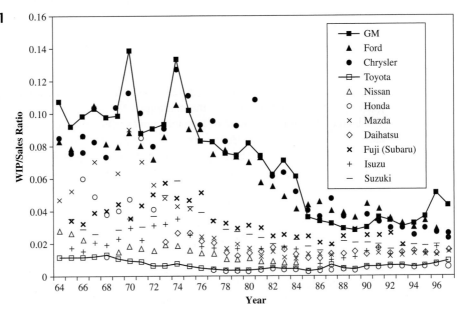

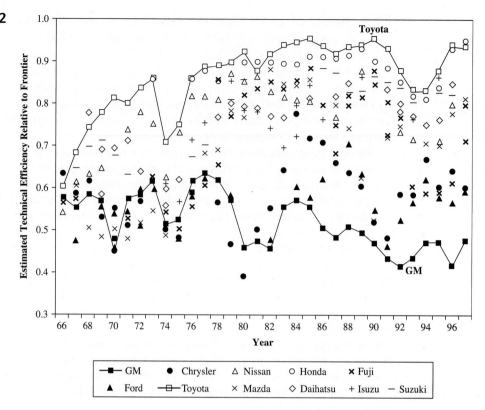

EXHIBIT 10.12
Technical Efficiency by Automobile Firm and Year

Source: Reprinted from Lieberman and Dhawan, "Assessing the Resource Base of Japanese and U.S. Auto Producers: A Stochastic Frontier Production Function Approach," *Management Science,* 2005, by permission of the publisher.

■— GM	● Chrysler	△ Nissan	○ Honda	✻ Fuji
▲ Ford	□ Toyota	✕ Mazda	◇ Daihatsu	+ Isuzu	— Suzuki

Given the power of lean operations, why is it not universally adopted? In short, it is very hard to fully develop and embed such capabilities. While many of the tools and techniques of lean operations are widely used, it is rare to find an organization like Toyota where lean thinking permeates its very core. This difference is at the heart of the argument between the positioning and the resource-based views of strategy. The act of deeply embedding lean thinking at Toyota has allowed it to differentiate itself from others, as it has a capability that most others cannot imitate. That said, the use of some number of lean tools and techniques, while not full development of a capability, can allow companies to position themselves differently in the marketplace.

Much of the implementation of lean techniques is in the areas of materials management and production scheduling. How a company manages materials and schedules production can directly relate to its strategic goals. The more a strategy is directed toward customization and build-to-order, for example, the more the production scheduling system plays a role in supporting its goals. Customization requires more capacity, greater parts availability, and closely linked order fulfillment and production scheduling systems. On the other end of the spectrum, companies that focus on achieving low cost through standardization emphasize a level schedule and predictability. They may focus on a limited line of products and use a scheduling system that seeks repeatability. These considerations are obviously closely tied in with the management of the supply chain as discussed in Chapter 8.

In summary, lean implementation can drive significant cost, quality, and lead time (availability) benefits for any organization, but deeply embedding lean thinking can allow an organization to achieve even more. The problem is that it is very difficult to take this additional step.

Thus, companies considering adopting lean operations may choose to simply use some of the lean techniques that are most relevant—just-in-time inventory management, production leveling, reduction in number of suppliers—or they may choose the more challenging task of developing a capability in lean operations that permeates the organization.

Quality Management

Quality management, like lean operations or lean thinking, can be a cross-cutting capability from which companies derive competitive advantage. Like lean operations, quality management consists of a set of tools, techniques, and methods, but it is also based on philosophies and values that, when firmly embedded in the culture of the organization, make it valuable competitively. Just as we did for lean operations, we provide a brief history of quality management, describe its current incarnation as Six Sigma, give an overview of major tools used, and close with evidence that quality management pays off.

In Chapter 1 we defined quality as one of the dimensions along which a customer assesses a company's products or services and the characteristics the customer evaluates as tangible (e.g., aesthetics, reliability, serviceability) and intangible (e.g., competence, access, security). In this chapter we focus less on the customer's perception of quality and more on the firm's internal capability to execute its processes using the philosophies and tools of quality management. There is clearly a relationship between the two: Firms that excel at quality management provide higher quality products and services as measured by their consistency and lack of defects. Toyota, where quality management is embedded along with lean thinking, plainly shows this relationship in the J.D. Power customer satisfaction ratings. Other companies, such as Quantum Corporation, have leveraged their internal process quality into higher reliability products.

Development of Total Quality Management

Many of the basic tools and much of the thinking that underpin Six Sigma today were developed by a handful of people—Shewhart (1931, 1986), Deming (2000), Juran and Gryna (1980), Ishikawa (1991), Ohno (1988), Shingo (1986), and Taguchi et al. (1984)—starting in the late 1930s. What has evolved since that time is our ability to use the tools together programmatically to achieve companywide benefit. Total quality management (TQM) wove process improvement tools together with team-based problem solving to create, in essence, learning organizations. Full TQM implementations involved all members of the organization in quality-driven efforts to satisfy customers and benefit the members of the organization and society at large.[3] The Japanese version of TQM includes:

- *Kaizen:* Develop a process that is visible, repeatable, and measurable.
- *Atarimae hinshitsu:* Examine the intangibles that affect the process and work to optimize their impact on the process.
- *Kansei:* Examine the way the product is used by the customer with an eye to improving both the product and the development process.
- *Miryokuteki hinshitsu:* Observe product use in the marketplace to uncover new product applications and identify new products to develop.[4]

[3] http://en.wikipedia.org/wiki/TQM, August 17, 2006.
[4] http://www.webizus.com/newsletter/oct02/software-quality.html, August 17, 2006.

EXHIBIT 10.13

Deming's Fourteen Foundational Points of TQM

1. Create constancy of purpose toward improvement.
2. Adopt the new philosophy of quality throughout the organization.
3. Cease dependence on mass inspection to achieve quality.
4. End the practice of choosing suppliers solely on price.
5. Identify problems and work continuously to improve the system.
6. Institute training on the job.
7. Teach and institute leadership.
8. Drive fear out of the workplace.
9. Break down barriers between departments.
10. Eliminate exhortations—without providing methods—from the workplace.
11. Eliminate work standards and numerical quotas for production.
12. Remove barriers to pride of workmanship—don't blame workers for system problems.
13. Institute and encourage vigorous programs of education, retraining, and self-improvement.
14. Act to accomplish the transformation.

TQM is defined as "a quality-centered, customer-focused, fact-based, team-driven, senior-management-led process to achieve an organization's strategic imperative through continuous process improvement."[5] Deming (2000) set forth a set of 14 principles (Exhibit 10.13) for companies to follow in the implementation of TQM. A number of his principles are similar to the lean principles we presented earlier. In general, while Deming encouraged the use of quality tools, his focus was primarily on getting both cross-functional and cross-level engagement in the collective learning and problem-solving process.

At the heart of quality management is identification and resolution of defects, a notion that was later broadened to the identification and elimination of waste. Quality programs centered around determining an appropriate level of allowable defects. On the one hand, there were the costs of finding the defects (appraisal costs) or better yet of finding the root causes of the defects and fixing them to prevent further defects (prevention costs) (Exhibit 10.14). On the other hand, there were the costs of having to remedy defects after they happened (internal failure costs) or, worse yet, of having them be found in the marketplace (external failure costs). To reduce the defect level to near zero required significant expenditures on appraisal and prevention, while allowing too many defects was costly in both internal and external failure costs (Exhibit 10.15). Later, in the "quality is free" era (Crosby 1979) arguments were made that the cost of poor quality in the marketplace was so large that virtually any internal efforts to prevent errors were worthwhile.

One of the continuous improvement tools most associated with TQM evolved from John Dewey's (1938, 1997) learning cycle—experiencing, reviewing, concluding, planning[6]—to become the plan-do-check-act (PDCA) cycle (Exhibit 10.16). The steps of the PDCA cycle require that the organization:

- **Plan:** Design or revise business process components to improve results.
- **Do:** Implement the plan and measure its performance.

[5] http://en.wikipedia.org/wiki/TQM, August 17, 2006.

[6] http://www.wilderdom.com/experiential/elc/ExperientialLearningCycle.htm, August 17, 2006.

EXHIBIT 10.14
**Categories
of Costs
of Quality**

Source: Based on
Juran and Gryna,
*Quality Planning
and Analysis: From
Product Development
through Usage,*
McGraw-Hill, 1980.

Internal Failure	**Appraisal**
Scrap and yield loss	Inspection
Rework and retest	Testing
Downtime	Testing equipment
Disposal	
External Failure	**Prevention**
Returns	Planning
Adjustments	Training
Goodwill	Process control
Warranty and repairs	Data analysis
Discounts	Testing before release

- **Check:** Assess the measurements and report the results to decision makers.
- **Act:** Decide on changes needed to improve the process.

The concept is that improvement in any process is accomplished by a combination of implementing new approaches and monitoring and measuring the results. The PDCA cycle allows for continual improvements through a series of smaller improvements. The steps are performed by teams for either an operational process such as a production process, or a business process such as product generation. In short, the cycle suggests that to improve a process the organization must understand the process, identify potential changes, implement those changes on a small scale, measure the results, and, if the results are effective, roll out the changes more broadly.

Six Sigma

The tools and philosophies of TQM evolved and were ultimately repackaged in the late 1980s as Six Sigma. In 1986 Bill Smith, then a vice president of quality of Motorola, conceived a metric for measuring defects in parts per million, and set a target for reducing defects below 3.4 parts per million by driving processes to operate within plus or minus six standard deviations (six sigma) of their means. From this was born a program that moved well beyond manufacturing defect control to a disciplined and data-driven process

EXHIBIT 10.15
**Trade-Offs
in Cost of
Quality**

Source: Based on
Juran and Gryna,
*Quality Planning
and Analysis: From
Product Development
through Usage,*
McGraw-Hill, 1980.

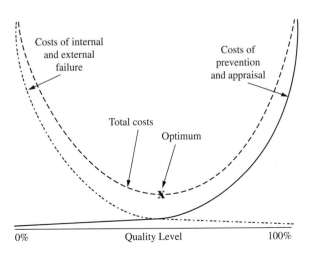

EXHIBIT 10.16
Plan-Do-
Check-Act
Cycle

for eliminating defects in any process. Motorola itself reports over $17 billion in savings from implementing Six Sigma. There are two methodologies—DMAIC and DFSS—and an approach to structuring problem-solving teams that make up Six Sigma programs.

DMAIC

Define-measure-analyze-improve-control, or DMAIC, is the most widely used of the Six Sigma methodologies and most closely resembles the original PDCA cycle. The specific steps of the process are detailed in Exhibit 10.17. The DMAIC methodology is used on existing products or processes that are not meeting customer specifications or are otherwise performing inadequately.

EXHIBIT 10.17 Steps in the DMAIC Process

Source: Adapted from http://www.isixsigma.com/dictionary/DMAIC-57.htm, August 2, 2006.

Define	Choose an issue on which to focus the quality improvement project
	    Identify the performance measures to be improved
	    Set some targets for improved performance
	Map the process flow
	    Identify the beginning and end of the process
	    Set boundaries around the portion of the process to be examined

Measure	Create a plan to collect appropriate data on the performance of the process
	    Types of defects to be analyzed
	    Outcome measures
	Collect the data
	Compare actual performance of the process to target performance to identify opportunities or gaps

Analyze	Seek root causes of defects Identify sources of variation List and prioritize improvement opportunities
Improve	Identify alternative solutions Choose a solution Develop an implementation plan Implement and measure results

Control	For improvements that achieve target performance:
	    Prepare an implementation plan
	    Roll the changes out throughout the organization
	Monitor the improvements after implementation
	Ensure that the improvements are institutionalized by changing:
	    Systems
	    Structures (staffing, training, incentives)

Some of the tools used by the DMAIC methodology are well known from the earliest development of quality management. They include:

- Process maps
- Run charts
- Histograms
- Stratification
- Cause and effects diagrams (sometimes called *fishbone* or *Ishikawa diagrams*)
- Regression
- Control charts
- Five whys (i.e., asking why five times to get to the root cause of a problem)

At the heart of most quality improvement efforts is an attempt to understand and reduce variation. Every process varies. Some of the variation is inherent in the process but can be maintained within predictable limits. This is referred to as *common cause* variation. Other variation occurs due to unusual events and is called *special cause* variation. The goals of quality management are to eliminate special cause variation and to reduce common cause variation to the greatest extent possible. See Brassard and Ritter (1994) for more detailed descriptions of the basic quality tools and how they are used to manage variation and improve processes.

DFSS and DMADV

While the DMAIC process is applied to existing products, services, or processes, design for Six Sigma (DFSS) and define-measure-analyze-design-verify (DMADV) and its variants are applied to the development of new products, services, and processes. A number of tools have been developed and used over the years to ensure rapid, on-time, reliable, consistent, and robust development of new products: Quality function deployment (QFD) (Hauser and Clausing 1988), failure modes and effects analysis (FMEA), and design of experiments (DOE), sometimes known as the *Taguchi method* (Taguchi 1987), are among the best known. QFD assists the development team in matching customer requirements to product specifications, and in understanding the many trade-offs that may be made in developing the product or service. FMEA identifies potential failures in a design before it is fully developed. DOE allows the design team to collect data on its design without testing every possible combination of factors and results in creating a design that is robust to variability in multiple factors.

DFSS integrates many of these tools in a process targeted at developing high-quality designs. By targeting Six Sigma performance for the new product or service, it forces early understanding of customer expectations and needs (the customers' "critical to quality" metrics). One of the approaches to achieving DFSS is DMADV, whose steps are shown in Exhibit 10.18. There are, however, a number of variations on this process (Simon 2006).

Thus, there are two primary approaches in Six Sigma quality programs. DMAIC is the most widely used and is applied to improving existing processes. DFSS is less standard across the industry but integrates the tools many companies already use to achieve quality in new product, process, or service development. Although these approaches are useful, it is in defining an approach to implementing quality programs throughout a company that the Six Sigma efforts have made the most difference from prior quality programs. Six

EXHIBIT 10.18
Steps in the
DMADV Process

Define the project goals and customer (internal and external) deliverables.
Measure and determine customer needs.
Analyze the process options to meet the customer needs.
Design the process to meet customer needs.
Verify the design performance and ability to meet customer needs.

Sigma adherents follow to a strict program by which problem-solving teams are created and managed to roll out Six Sigma tools in the organization.

Organizing for Six Sigma

Six Sigma identifies six key roles for successful implementation. The definition of these roles is not standard across the industry but typically includes something akin to the following:[7]

1. **Executive leadership** involves the CEO as well as a senior leader reporting to the CEO who has responsibility for implementing quality programs throughout the company. They establish the vision for Six Sigma implementation and empower others to explore new ideas for breakthrough improvements.

2. **Champions** are drawn from the upper management ranks to oversee the integrated implementation of Six Sigma across the organization.

3. **Master black belts** are often assigned to a specific area or function within a business and work with the owners of the processes within that area to set quality targets and plans and track progress. They act as in-house expert coaches, devote 100 percent of their time to Six Sigma, and assist and guide black belts and green belts. They are trained both to apply the rigorous statistical analysis associated with Six Sigma and to integrate deployment of Six Sigma programs across the organization.

4. **Process owners,** as the name implies, are responsible for individual processes in the organization. They work closely with the master black belts to implement identified process improvements.

5. **Black belts** devote 100 percent of their time to the application of the Six Sigma methodology to specific projects under the guidance of the master black belts. Champions and master black belts identify projects, while black belts execute them.

6. **Green belts** are trained in Six Sigma, but take it on along with their other job responsibilities. They operate under the guidance of black belts and support them in achieving the overall results. In organizations adopting Six Sigma as an organizationwide management approach, green belts eventually come to do all of their work using Six Sigma practices.

Unlike prior quality management programs, where the personnel to staff quality improvement projects was drawn from the ranks, black belts are specifically trained and engaged as change agents to drive Six Sigma throughout the organization. Just as in the days when there was concern that having a vice president of quality implied that no one else in the organization needed to be responsible for quality, there is concern today that black belts take on too much responsibility for quality, thus relieving management of accountability for

---

[7] See http://www.isixsigma.com/library/content/c010128a.asp and http://en.wikipedia.org/wiki/Six_sigma for more information on Six Sigma organizational design, (accessed October 27, 2006).

making the required change. As we discussed in Chapter 7, performance measurement and rewards must align with the desired outcomes of a Six Sigma implementation to ultimately make it work.

The Impact of Quality Management on Competitiveness

As with the implementation of lean operations, the implementation of quality improvement tools and techniques does not necessarily lead to a distinct competitive advantage. There are a handful of companies—General Electric, Motorola, Honeywell among them—that have undertaken companywide implementations. These companies claim cost savings of anywhere between 1 to 5 percent of revenues annually as a result.[8] If they are able to sustain this kind of savings over time and thus outperform their competitors, they may well have a distinctive capability.

Other companies, such as Toyota, have embedded quality improvement—by Six Sigma or by other names—in the very fabric of their organizations. These organizations are able to leverage the resulting organizational capability in new directions. Toyota, for example, says that it "makes things" and at some level does not care what it makes. It is just good at making things. Motorola found that, once it fine-tuned its processes, it was able to introduce new products that took advantage of its higher quality processes. Plus Development Corporation survived the large influx of competitors to the disk-drive-on-a-card market because of its investment in quality and became one of the market leaders in disk drive reliability as a result.

Few companies, however, take on quality improvement programs at this level. Nonetheless, there are advantages to be gained. Estimates of what a black belt can save a company range from $75,000 to $230,000 per project. Completing four to six projects per year yields savings per black belt of somewhere between $300,000 and $860,000.[9] And all of the quality tools and techniques can be applied at a local level in the organization to achieve some gains.

In short, quality management can be developed into a cross-cutting capability in an organization. But it is hard to do so. Most companies use quality management tools and techniques either because they have to in order to retain parity with their competitors or because they can improve their cost or quality position in the marketplace. Some use quality management techniques to improve their availability, innovativeness, and/or environmental performance as well. It is rare to find one like Toyota that lives quality management at its core.

We turn now to the last of the cross-cutting capabilities in which companies can invest to gain sustainable competitive advantage: flexibility.

Flexibility

Flexibility is a cross-cutting capability that allows an organization to be responsive or readily adjustable to changing conditions. Those changing conditions range from rapidly changing customer needs to fluctuating raw materials availability. Customers do not evaluate a firm's outputs based on the firm's flexibility, but the ability of the firm to achieve

---

[8] http://www.isixsigma.com/library/content/c020729a.asp, November 6, 2006.

[9] See for example http://www.isixsigma.com/library/content/c020729a.asp, November 6, 2006.

cost, quality, availability, and features/innovativeness targets that the customer does care about may require developing capabilities in flexibility. Burger King differentiated itself from McDonald's because it offered customers the opportunity to "have it your way," but still get the food quickly and at low cost. This required Burger King to develop flexibility, which it did by using a postponement strategy (see Chapter 8). It cooks the raw burgers, stores them in a steam table, and then assembles them to meet the needs of specific customer orders. Its operations infrastructure, from the information technology it uses to take the orders to the way it cooks the burgers, is set up to support flexibility.

In this section we first address flexibility in a general way, defining the types of variability in response to which firms might choose to develop flexibility, and then presenting a set of alternative means of achieving flexibility. We then turn to a specific type of flexibility that is developed in response to high product or service variability–customization.

The Need for Flexibility

Broadly speaking, the need for flexibility in operations settings stems from variability in the markets served, the resources utilized, and the technologies employed. There are many specific examples of such variability that can be usefully categorized into the following five types (Beckman 1987):

1. Demand variability
2. Supply variability
3. Product or service variability
4. Process variability
5. Workforce and equipment variability

Much of the variability originates outside the firm, and all five types may occur simultaneously. The particular mix of variability experienced varies for each company depending on its industry and competitive environment. We briefly define each type of variability.

Demand Variability

Perhaps the most obvious reason for developing flexibility is to enable an organization to respond to variations in demand for its products or services. The two principle components of demand variability are product or service mix variability and volume variability. Product or service mix variability occurs when a company supports multiple products or services, and the mix of products or services demanded varies over time. Mix variability may occur with or without changes in the total volume of products or services generated. Volume variability occurs when the total volume generated goes up or down, and can happen with or without shifts in mix.

Two examples illustrate how different demand variability can look. A publisher of children's books produces and sells thousands of different titles. In addition to product mix variability–some titles are growing in popularity, some are declining, some are relatively stable, some are erratic–the entire line is subject to strong seasonal fluctuations. Titles that are not available in warehouses a few weeks before the holidays are lost sales. In stark contrast, consider a manufacturer of networking products with two models of a particular product that are trivially different from a production perspective. Not only is there no seasonal fluctuation in demand, but customers will wait days to get what they want. The uncertainty for the networking products company is about how fast demand for these products will grow and how long the products will live.

Both the publisher and the networking products manufacturer are concerned about their ability to accommodate variability in either product mix or volume, but what that means and what it requires in terms of flexibility differ greatly between the two organizations.

Supply Variability

Demand variability is generated from the customer side. Supply variability comes from the other end of the supply chain and arises when there is variability in the quality and timeliness of materials deliveries and in industries where materials technologies are changing. Sugar refiners, for example, deal with large seasonal fluctuations in the availability of raw materials. Their choices for dealing with this variability depend upon whether they process sugar cane or sugar beets. Beet refiners are at the mercy of the harvest, for beets must be processed immediately or lose their sugar content. Cane refiners, however, have the choice of either completely processing incoming cane as it is harvested or partially processing it and then holding the raw sugar until it is needed.

In the electronics sector, companies like Dell regularly update their products with new technologies from their many suppliers. The companies selling disk drives, memory chips, microprocessors, and so on regularly develop new technologies or add new features to their devices, which Dell has to consider accommodating.

Product or Service Variability

Closely related to demand variability is product or service variability, which refers to variation in the product or service itself. This could include variety in the product or service itself at any given time or changes over time in the product or service. Rapidly shrinking new product development cycles over the past 10 to 20 years mean that companies are putting new products into the market at a much faster rate today than ever before. The sea change wrought by the Internet increasingly provides customers with what they want, when they want it, wherever they want it, which in turn forces companies to think about how to customize their products or services to individual customer needs. Today, the ability to offer a wide range of products or services is at the heart of what is known as *mass customization.* We will return to a more in-depth discussion of customization strategies later in this chapter.

Process Variability

Process changes, from the most technical hardware changes to the more behavioral changes associated with new managerial approaches, are among the most difficult to undertake. When new continuous-casting processes and furnace technologies were introduced in the 1970s, U.S. Steel chose to shut down some of its operations rather than change. Others, however, adopted the new technologies and stayed in business. Adoption of lean manufacturing techniques or of Six Sigma quality improvement programs often involves changes to both hardware and software, which means that taking on the change permeates the entire organization. Arguably, at the heart of the ability to respond to process change or to take on process changes is the ability of the organization to learn (Senge 1990).

Workforce and Equipment Variability

Even without changes in the overall process, the two resources an operation employs directly—labor and equipment—are also sources of variability. Variations in quality, output, and reliability are present at some level in every worker and piece of capital equipment. Unlike introduced process changes, variations in workforce and equipment often occur spontaneously and are only partially controllable. In integrated circuit manufacturing, process yields, particularly for new processes, are notoriously low, even though vast sums have been spent improving the technology. Labor turnover in many service industries runs as high as 50 percent a year.

Types of Variability Summary

Exhibit 10.19 summarizes the five types of variability with which a firm may contend. Although our discussion so far suggests that the sources of variability are independent, they not only occur simultaneously, but throughout the supply chain. Further, one event can trigger changes in multiple sources of variability simultaneously. As we discussed in Chapter 5, a facilities location decision might cause the company to choose a different production process, source from different suppliers, or even redesign a product to make it more manufacturable in the new location or of greater interest to local customers. Competitive moves may also trigger a series of changes in the sources of variability.

We turn now to the means by which a company might cope with variability or, in other words, how it might choose to be flexible.

EXHIBIT 10.19   Definitions of Five Types of Variability

Type of Variability	Description
Demand Variability	Volume variability: shifts in total volume generated over time Mix variability: shifts in the mix of products or services generated
Supply Variability	Quality variability: shifts in adherence to quality standards by suppliers Delivery timeliness variability: shifts in adherence to delivery commitments by suppliers New materials or technology New suppliers
Product or Service Variability	Introduction of new products or services Variations in products or services to meet specific demands of individual customers or groups of customers
Process Variability	Introduction of new process technologies Introduction of new managerial approaches (e.g., lean)

Workforce and Equipment Variability	Equipment performance against specification over time
	Equipment downtime
	Labor performance
	  Absenteeism
	  Turnover
	  Variable skill sets

Means of Achieving Flexibility

Traditionally, companies have tried to protect operations from the negative effects of variability. Operations are simply much easier to run if demand is stable, suppliers are reliable, products or services are unchanging, and the processes used stay the same. But there is more to it than just making operations easier to run. Companies that make major capital equipment investments to run their operations, or have a large number of production or service employees, are often under great pressure to use these resources efficiently. Efficiency is most easily achieved with constant or level output (thus the emphasis on heijunka in lean operations) and high equipment and labor utilization.

There are three methods of responding to variability. Two of these methods buffer operations from the effects of variability, and the third responds to variability through flexible operations. The first method is to reduce variability itself, which requires involvement of all the functions in the organization. The procurement organization might work with suppliers to ensure on-time delivery of as-specified materials. The marketing organization might work with customers, offering special deals, price promotions, and other such incentives for customers to procure products or services at a steady rate. Dell and Amazon.com are masters at monitoring their inventory positions and managing demand accordingly. The research and development organization might design products or services in a modular fashion so that the operations function sees little difference among them when producing or delivering them. The human resources management organization might develop programs to retain employees and encourage regular attendance.

The second method is to carry inventory. Finished goods inventory buffers operations from variability in demand. Raw materials inventory buffers operations from variability in supply. Work-in-process inventory buffers operations from workforce and equipment variability. Inventory may allow an organization to seem more flexible to a customer; the customer can order any product and receive it quickly. Both of these approaches, however, are really means of protecting the core operations activities of the firm from variability. They are not means of actually increasing the flexibility of those operations.

So, how might the firm engage in actually developing flexible operations? The third method, to develop flexibility as a cross-cutting capability, requires participation across the organization and even across the supply chain. Within the operations function itself, there are a few things that can be done to increase flexibility.

- *Acquire flexible technology.* One of the earliest "flexible manufacturing systems" was Allen-Bradley's motor starter plant in Milwaukee, Wisconsin, that made 125 different types of motor starters in batches as small as one. Because the technology could physically accommodate a range of sizes and shapes of motor starters and was computer controlled to quickly access assembly instructions, it could ship orders within 24 hours of receiving them. Modern manufacturing technologies such as CNC (Computer Numerical Control machines) and industrial robots facilitate flexible manufacturing systems by moving control from a rigid hardware basis to a readily modifiable software basis (Spira and Pine 1993).

- *Reduce setup and cycle times.* The less time it takes to change over from one product to another or from one service to another, the easier it is for the facility to quickly generate different products or services. Similarly, the less time it takes to produce an entire product or deliver an entire service, the more responsive the system can be to changes in end demand.

- *Cross-train the workforce so that any given individual can be called upon to perform a broad variety of tasks.* Historically, especially in union environments, workers were highly specialized and not allowed to perform functions outside their specific task. Not only did this limit the flexibility of the organization to use workers where they were needed, but it limited the ability of the workers to understand the entire process and their role in it. They were thus less able to respond when change was needed.

- *Maintain excess capacity.* As queuing theory shows, the more highly utilized an operation is, the less effectively it deals with variability. In fact, it suggests roughly that operations that are utilized more than 60 to 70 percent will suffer significant degradation in performance (wait times and queue lengths). Thus, an organization that wishes to perform in environments with high variability maintains excess capacity. McDonald's, for example, only utilizes its grill 30 to 40 percent of the time, even during peak hours. Why? It cannot reliably deliver "fast" without surge capacity (Rikert and Sasser 1980).

Some of these mechanisms may be applied outside the core operations function as well. Excess capacity across a facilities network, or throughout a supply chain, may allow the entire network or chain to respond more quickly to changes in demand. As we discussed in Chapter 5, for example, some companies maintain capacity to produce a single product at multiple facilities so that production can easily be moved around in the face of varying demand. This generally implies that there is excess capacity in the facilities network overall. Similarly, reducing the time it takes to move materials through a supply chain makes that supply chain more responsive to variability. It is for this reason that many companies choose to co-locate with their suppliers, thus minimizing transportation time.

Although it is clear from our discussion to date that all functions are involved in achieving flexibility in an organization, it is worth highlighting the highly cross-functional involvement required in managing product or service variability. Today's focus on mass customization requires integrated effort by product or service developers, marketing, and operations to determine what type of variety customers want and then to design products and services that produce that variety and the operations that can deliver them. Companies may choose to develop products that adapt themselves to customer needs over time, or they may choose to design modular products or services that allow customers to pick and choose, in effect designing a product or service to their specifications. Modular products provide more unique product designs for modest increases in the number of components, facilitating provision of a wide range of products or services at relatively low costs. (Postponement strategies, as described in Chapter 8, rely on modular designs.) We will explore more details of mass customization shortly.

Measuring Flexibility and Making Trade-Offs

Clearly, developing flexibility involves making trade-offs. Inventory investments are costly. Carrying excess capacity causes operations efficiency to decline. Equipment designed for flexibility may be less efficient than specialized equipment. Suppliers may charge more for providing increased variety. Multiplant networks may require more planning overhead to keep operations balanced. If not managed carefully, attempts to achieve flexibility can get out of hand and result in a chaotic environment. The fact that achieving flexibility comes at a cost suggests that being able to measure the flexibility of an operation could have some value.

Measuring flexibility, however, is difficult. There are three possible measures one might use (Upton 1994): (1) *range* measures the range of products or services an operation can provide by measuring the set of values the operation is able to deliver along a given dimension; (2) *mobility* measures the cost or effort of making a change within the range; and (3) *uniformity* assesses the ability of the system to provide consistent performance across the range. In short, one can measure flexibility of a system by the variety of items it can deliver, the cost of changing from one item to another, and the consistency of performance along the cost, quality, and availability dimensions across all items. While this information is helpful in assessing the flexibility of a system, it still requires translation into a set of benefits, either to the company or to the customer. These benefits can then be traded off against the costs of achieving the flexibility.

Flexibility and Customization[10]

Being flexible allows companies to achieve a number of benefits including lower-cost production or service delivery and higher availability. Perhaps the greatest benefit gained through investments in flexibility today is customization. Customization allows an organization to respond to customer needs for wider product or service variety. This section explores strategies for customization with particular emphasis on mass customization, which holds the promise of customization with the cost advantages of standardized or mass production.

Customization is the tailoring of product or service features for a particular group or individual. *Mass customization* is delivering a customized good or service while maintaining the low cost, quick delivery, and high quality associated with mass production. (See Chapter 3 for a fuller description of the types of processes and a comparison of mass customization and mass production.) Put another way, mass customization is about doing "different things for different customers at or below the same cost you once did the same things for everybody." Taken to an extreme, it is about doing "only and exactly" what each customer wants (Gilmore 1995). Previously, a company had to choose between a low-cost or high-differentiation strategy. Today, a company can provide both with a mass customization strategy (Spira and Pine 1993).

Some products, such as fine suits, fine jewelry, machine tools, and airplanes, have always been customized. But now, products once considered standard are being customized: Levi's is mass customizing jeans, Mattel is mass customizing the Barbie™ doll, and Dell is mass customizing computers. With increasing numbers of companies offering customized goods, customers have begun to expect personalized goods and services at low cost with quick response times.

The Role of Customers in Mass Customization

The starting point for developing a mass customization strategy is understanding the level of customization necessary to serve customer needs within the full range of customization possible. Doing so requires understanding the dimensions of the product or service that should be customized, the extent to which they are customizable, and how directly the customer should be involved in the customization process. There are six questions a firm can

---

[10] Some of this section is excerpted from Kandare et al. 1999.

ask to understand the dimensions of and extent to which the product or service should be customized (Pine 1993):

1. "Who needs my product or service and why? How can I provide it to whoever wants it?
2. What do customers do differently with my product or service? How can I provide whatever they want and need?
3. Where do customers need my product or service? What do I need to do to provide it wherever they want it?
4. When do customers need to shape my product or service to their needs? What can I do to provide it whenever they want it? Can I provide it instantly? Twenty-four hours a day?
5. Why do customers need my product or service? How can I add more value to meet their desired ends?
6. How do customers need my product or service? What can I do to provide it however they want it?"

Once the level of desired customization is known, the firm needs to decide how it wants to involve its customers in the process. When a firm adopts a mass customization strategy, it places the customer in control, allowing customer preferences to drive the production or service delivery and distribution processes. There are four different ways of involving customers (Gilmore and Pine 1997) that depend on the degree to which the product itself is customized and the degree to which the representation (e.g., packaging) of the product is customized. Exhibit 10.20 shows the four resulting approaches a firm can take, each of which is described briefly below:

1. **Collaborative approach.** In the collaborative approach, which involves changing both the product and its representation, the company "conducts a dialogue with individual customers to help them articulate their needs, identify the precise offering that fulfills those needs, and make customized products for them." Examples include Dell and Boeing, both of which actively engage each customer in configuring his or her product. Each product is then manufactured and distributed to meet specific customer's needs.
2. **Adaptive approach.** Companies using the adaptive approach, in which there is no change in either the product or its representation, offer one standard product that users can customize themselves. This approach allows the manufacturer to leverage

EXHIBIT 10.20
Four Approaches to Mass Customization

Source: Reprinted from Gilmore and Pine, "The Four Faces of Mass Customization," *Harvard Business Review,* 1997, with permission by the publisher.

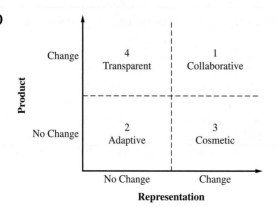

economies of scale throughout the supply chain but still meet customer needs for customization. In the automotive industry, for example, customers can customize seat and mirror positions, drive train performance, and suspension performance. Toyota's Scion brand is capturing the U.S. urban youth market with its ability to customize otherwise standard vehicles at its dealerships.

3. **Cosmetic approach.** Cosmetic customization, which involves no change in the product, but different representations, "presents a standard product differently to different customers." Coke, for example, can be bought in individual cans, six packs, cases, and one-liter and two-liter bottles. FedEx offers overnight delivery in different packages—large and small envelopes, different sized boxes, tubes, and so on. By identifying the different forms in which customers like to get their products or services, these companies are able to offer the sense of customization without changing the product or service itself.

4. **Transparent approach.** The transparent approach, which involves no change in representation but does change the product, "provides individual customers with unique goods or services without explicitly informing them that those products and services have been customized." Many modern automobiles, for example, have onboard computers that analyze an operator's driving habits and customize the performance of the drive train to suit the customer—all without the driver ever knowing it. Upscale hotels keep records of individual customer preferences, such as for a late-night snack, coffee first thing in the morning, or a softer-than-standard pillow. They deliver these services without making obvious to the customer that they have collected and analyzed the data.

Structuring Supply Chains for Mass Customization

Often, providing customized products or services to end users involves the entire value chain. Let's assume a continuum of strategies from full standardization to full customization, and a value chain that contains four steps: (1) detailed design of the overall product, (2) fabrication of the individual components or subassemblies, (3) assembly of the fabricated components into the finished product, and (4) distribution or delivery of completed product to the end user. Exhibit 10.21 shows five degrees of customization along a continuum and shows their effect on the structure of the value chain (Lampel and Mintzberg 1996). Each stage is described briefly below:

1. **Pure standardization.** The customers' needs or wants have no direct influence at any point in the value chain and customers are given only one choice. The classic example of pure standardization was the early Ford assembly line from which customers were allowed to choose cars that were black, black . . . or black. Companies adopting a pure standardization strategy choose a dominant design (Abernathy and Utterback 1978, Suarez and Utterback 1995) targeted to meet the needs of the broadest possible market.

2. **Segmented standardization.** The customers' needs influence the number and types of products or services offered, but differentiation occurs only at the point of distribution. McDonald's, for example, offers meals that range from Big Macs to Happy Meals in an attempt to serve a range of markets. Automobile producers offer color variation, family sedans, sports cars, trucks, and so on. Standard designs are offered to meet the needs of smaller market segments.

EXHIBIT 10.21

Implementing Customization across the Value Chain

Source: Reprinted from Lampel and Mintzberg, "Customizing Customization," *Sloan Management Review,* 1996, with permission by the publisher.

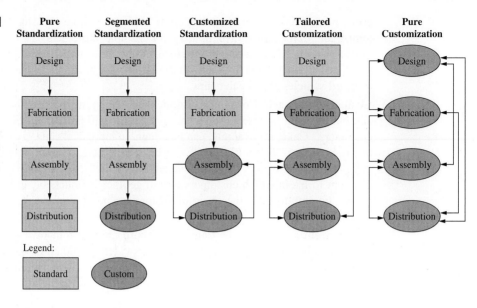

3. **Customized standardization.** The customer has direct influence over the assembly of standard components. Dell Inc., for example, allows customers to design computers to their needs. The ability to customize the computer, however, is limited to standard components as presented by the company. Burger King, similarly, "fabricates" standard burgers and then assembles them to customer needs. Customers can directly influence the assembly of the product but still have no influence on the fabrication of the components.

4. **Tailored customization.** The customer has direct influence over distribution, assembly, and fabrication of the product, influencing all but the fundamental design. Levi's, for example, scans or takes measurements of a customer's body and then resizes standard pattern designs to make jeans uniquely to the customer's dimensions. The current trend in upscale pre-fab housing is also leveraging tailored customization.

5. **Pure customization.** The customer directly influences every aspect of the value chain for a given product. Building designs, for example, require the client to describe his or her needs, an architect to design the building, and then a general contractor to execute the design. All members of the value chain are involved in delivering a unique solution to the customer.

The degree of customization the firm takes on suggests the extent to which it will involve its value chain in delivering that customization. Pure customization requires a highly vertically integrated supply chain, or well-developed supplier relationships that facilitate communication of complex and often tacit information up and down the chain. Pure standardization, on the other hand, allows vertical disintegration and relatively arm's-length supplier relationships.

Implementing Mass Customization

To perform mass customization, a firm must have:

- *The ability to understand customer needs and segment those needs into clusters around which products or services might be customized.* For a company to be good at customization, it must first understand the requirements for customization in its market. Does its market require collaborative, transparent, or cosmetic customization? Does its market require pure customization, pure standardization, or something in between? To answer these questions, the firm must be able to understand customer and user needs and then identify clusters of needs that go together. FedEx, for example, identified an overriding need to deliver packages overnight, but it also identified clusters of needs around the types of things—a single sheet of paper, a notebook, a rolled set of drawings—that needed to be delivered. While the output of a segmentation process may seem obvious, it is not always easy to reach.

- *The ability to design adaptive and/or modular products or services.* Once a company knows what types of customization its market requires, it engages in a collaborative effort among marketing, which understands customer needs and how those needs might be segmented; research and development, which understands the design parameters of the product or service and how they can be varied; and operations, which understands what it takes to cost-effectively deliver against the various design parameters to design the customizable products or services. The three functions interact to make a sometimes nontrivial set of trade-offs in determining just how customized a firm's products or services can be, and how to deliver the chosen level of customization. The design capabilities required vary by type of customization. Firms engaged in pure customization, for example, need to be able to work closely with customers and quickly design to their specifications. Firms that do partial customization (i.e., design standard products that are customized in fabrication, assembly, and/or distribution) need to be able to identify standard products or modules and all the different ways they can be assembled.

- *The ability to translate needs into a product or service specification and track custom orders.* Customization increases the number of possible product or service configurations, which in turn necessitates an order-taking process that accurately translates the customer's needs into a producible product or deliverable service. Order-taking processes, often automated like Dell's, must present the customer a clear set of options that provides sufficient choice but does not bewilder or overwhelm the customer. Once the needs are translated into a unique order, it must be tracked throughout the production or service delivery process to ensure that the customer's specific needs are met. Once the order is in process, substitution is no longer possible.

- *The ability to produce or deliver against custom orders.* Internal operations, and in many cases the entire supply chain, must be structured to deliver against the custom orders using the various approaches described earlier. Flexible technologies, reduced setup and cycle times, and excess capacity are all tools that might be used to make the processes themselves capable of delivering against custom orders.

Just as lean operations and quality management require integrated decision making and joint action across functions and across the decision categories we have covered in this book, so does the development of flexibility. The adoption of a customization strategy affects decisions about vertical integration, facilities, capacity, business processes, information technology, production processes, and supply chain coordination. Firms may choose to vertically integrate more or less depending upon whether they choose a pure standardization or pure customization strategy. Firms may structure their facilities networks with excess capacity to accommodate moving production or service delivery around the network. Business processes, particularly in design, facilitate translating needs into specifications and designing adaptive and modular products. Supply chain coordination smoothes the flow of parts to final product assembly. Information systems allow collecting customer needs, taking orders, and tracking orders throughout the process. Process technology allows low-cost production or service delivery.

When an entire organization works together to optimize its approach to achieving flexibility, it may develop a capability that is difficult to replicate. Dell has certainly done so in the computer industry. Its unique collection of abilities—in understanding customer needs, product design, online order taking, production, and delivery—allow it to stand apart from all of its competitors.

Summary

Lean operations, quality management, and flexibility are capabilities that can be the source of competitive advantage. They cut across the functions in an organization—operations, research and development, and marketing—and often integrate suppliers and customers across the supply chain. They integrate decisions from the categories we have discussed in this book, in particular, business processes, information technology, process technology, and supplier management. They embody new approaches to management and to executing systematic change in an organization. They represent a set of methods and approaches from which a company can select, even if it does not embrace the full program.

News about how the automobile industry is coping with the economic downturn of the early 2000s says it all:

> Dusted with an early snow, hundreds of brand-new Jeeps sit parked in neat rows in barbed-wire-fenced lots at Detroit's airport. All dressed up with plastic on the seats and bar codes on the windshields, the convoy-in-waiting has nowhere to go since Chrysler dealers are balking at taking on even more inventory. Since the mid-1980s, when Japanese automakers began making vehicles in large volumes in the United States, Detroit's automakers have talked of the need to better align production with demand and move to a model of just-in-time manufacturing.[11]

By mid-2006 GM had a 76-day supply of cars, Ford a 75-day supply, and Chrysler an 82-day supply excluding fleet sales. Toyota Motor Corporation's supply? About 30 days. Toyota's investment in lean operations is more than a passing fad. Through good times and bad, it continues to ply its capabilities to take market share and grow its business.

References

Abegglen, James C., and George Stalk, Jr. *Kaisha, the Japanese Corporation.* Cambridge, MA: Basic Books, 1985.
Abernathy, W.J., and J.M. Utterback. "Patterns of Industrial Innovation." *Technology Review,* 80, no. 7 (June–July 1978), pp. 40–47.

---

[11] http://news.moneycentral.msn.com/provider/providerarticle.asp?feed=OBR&Date=20061105&ID=6167525, November 7, 2006.

Beckman, Sara L. "Manufacturing Flexibility and Organizational Design." PhD thesis, Stanford University, 1987.

Beckman, Sara L., and James V. Jucker. "Achieving Flexibility in Manufacturing." Working paper. Stanford University, 1989.

Brassard, Michael, and Diane Ritter. *The Memory Jogger II: A Pocket-Guide of Tools for Continuous Improvement and Effective Planing.* Salem, NY: GOAL/QPC, 1994.

Crosby, Philip B. *Quality Is Free: The Art of Making Quality Certain.* New York: McGraw-Hill, 1979.

Deming, W. Edwards. *Out of the Crisis.* Cambridge, MA: The MIT Press, 2000.

Dewey, J. *Experience and Education.* New York: Simon and Schuster, 1938, 1997.

The Economist. "The Car Company in Front." March 11, 2007. www.economist.com/background/displaystory.cfm?story_id=E1_PVJJDDD.

Ford Motor Company Press Release, 2005. http://media.ford.com/newsroom/release_display.cfm?release=15645, September 10, 2005.

Gilmore, James H. "Understanding the Market of One." *U.S. Distribution Journal* 222, no. 6, (June 15, 1995), ISN:0897–1315.

Gilmore, James H., and Joseph B. Pine. "The Four Faces of Mass Customization." *Harvard Business Review,* 75, no. 1 (January–February 1997), pp. 91–101.

Glauser, Ernst C. "The Toyota Phenomenon." The Swiss Deming Institute, www.deming.ch/downloads/E_Toyota.pdf, October 17, 2006.

Hauser, John, and Don Clausing. "The House of Quality." *Harvard Business Review,* 66, no. 3 (May–June 1988), pp. 63–73.

Hayes, Robert H., and Gary P. Pisano. "Beyond World Class: The New Manufacturing Strategy." *Harvard Business Review,* 72, no. 1 (January–February 1994), pp. 77–86.

Hopp, Wallace J., and Mark L. Spearman. *Factory Physics: Foundations of Manufacturing Management.* 2nd ed. New York: McGraw-Hill/Irwin, 2001.

Ishikawa, Kaoru. *Introduction to Quality Control.* New York: Springer, 1991.

Juran, Joseph M., and Frank M. Gryna, Jr. *Quality Planning and Analysis: From Product Development through Usage.* New York: McGraw-Hill, 1980.

Kandare, Greg, Adam Kohorn, Carey Mar, and Michael Milby. "Operations Strategy in the 90s and Beyond: Mass Customization." Paper for MIT course 15.769, May 1999.

Lampel, Joseph, and Henry Mintzberg. "Customizing Customization." *Sloan Management Review* 38, no. 1 (Fall 1996), pp. 21–30.

Lieberman, Marvin B., and Rajeev Dhawan. "Assessing the Resource Base of Japanese and U.S. Auto Producers: A Stochastic Frontier Production Function Approach." *Management Science* 51, no. 7 (2005), pp. 1060–1075.

Mishina, Kazuhiro. "Toyota Motor Manufacturing, U.S.A., Inc." Harvard Business School Publishing, 693019, 1995.

Ohno, Taiichi. *The Toyota Production System: Beyond Large-Scale Production.* New York: Productivity Press, 1988.

Pine, Joseph B. "Mass Customizing Products and Services." *Planning Review* 21, no. 4 (July–August 1993), pp. 6–13.

Pine, Joseph B. "Serve Each Customer Efficiently and Uniquely" In "Network Transformation: Individualizing Your Customer Approach." *Business Communications Review* 26, no. 1, (January 1996), Supplement, pp. 2–5.

Porter, Michael. "What Is Strategy?" *Harvard Business Review,* 74, no. 6 (November–December 1996), pp. 61–78.

Rikert, David C., and W. Earl Sasser, Jr. "McDonald's Corporation." Harvard Business School Publishing, 681044, 1980.

Schonberger, Richard J. *World-Class Manufacturing: The Next Decade.* New York: The Free Press, 1996.

Senge, Peter M. *The Fifth Discipline: The Art and Practice of the Learning Organization.* New York: Doubleday, 1990.

Shewhart, Walter A. *Economic Control of Quality of Manufactured Product.* Princeton, NJ: D. Van Nostrand Company, Inc., 1931.

Shewhart, Walter A. *Statistical Method from the Viewpoint of Quality Control,* Mineola, NY: Dover Publications, 1986.

Shiba, Shoji, and David Walden. *Four Practical Revolutions in Management.* New York: Productivity Press, 2001.

Shingo, Shigeo. *Zero Quality Control: Source Inspection and the Poka-Yoke System.* New York: Productivity Press, 1986.

Simon, Kerri. "What Is DFSS?" http://www.isixsigma.com/library/content/c020722a.asp, October 28, 2006.

Spira, Joel S., and Joseph B. Pine. "Mass Customization: Manufacturing." *Chief Executive,* no. 83 (March 1993), pp. 26–29.

Suarez, Fernando F., and James M. Utterback. "Dominant Designs and the Survival of Firms." *Strategic Management Journal* 16, no. 6 (September 1995), pp. 415–430.

Taguchi, Genichi. *System of Experimental Design: Engineering Methods to Optimize Quality and Minimize Costs.* Louise Watanabe Tung (trans.). White Plains, NY: Quality Resources, 1987.

Taguchi, Genichi, Subir Chowdhury, and Yuin Wu. *Taguchi's Quality Engineering Handbook.* Hoboken, NJ: Wiley-Interscience, 1984.

Upton, David. "The Management of Manufacturing Flexibility." *California Management Review* 36, no. 2 (Winter 1994), pp. 72–89.

Womack, James P., and Daniel T. Jones. *Lean Thinking: Banish Waste and Create Wealth in Your Corporation.* New York: Simon and Schuster, 1996.

Womack, James P., Daniel T. Jones, and Daniel Roos. *The Machine that Changed the World.* New York: Simon and Schuster, 1990.

Chapter 11

Strategy Development and Practice

Introduction

In 1960 Alex d'Arbeloff and Nick DeWolf, who met when they were classmates at the Massachusetts Institute of Technology in the 1940s, recognized the need for automated testing in the fabrication of electronic components. At the time, testing was done largely manually by a bevy of technicians in a process that they knew would become a bottleneck as companies grew. So, they developed a business plan for a new breed of "industrial grade" electronic test equipment, rented space above a local hot dog stand in Boston, and started Teradyne. According to DeWolf, "Tera is the prefix for ten to the twelfth power, and dyne is the unit of force. To us, the name meant rolling a 15,000-ton boulder uphill."[1]

Like Axcelis (see Chapter 1), Teradyne's fortunes ebb and wane with those of the electronics industry, and it has grown and shrunk through acquisition and divestiture over the years. Although it reached just over $3 billion in sales in 2000 at the height of the dot.com boom, today it is roughly a $1 billion company (Exhibit 11.1) whose core business is to provide test equipment for complex system-on-chip (SOC) semiconductors. Teradyne expanded from its original focus on diode and integrated circuit testing to testing in related fields through both internal technology development and acquisition of related technologies (Exhibit 11.2).

From its inception, the company focused on developing superior technology solutions for testing problems. The company created an environment in which manufacturing and design worked closely together to foster innovative designs and deliver advanced technological solutions to the market. Both its acquisition strategy and its internal management strategies support gaining access to the best technology and developing advanced products using that technology. In recent years, the company has focused on testing electronic products given the "intersection of increasing complexity and the drive of consumer economics and performance."[2]

---

[1] http://www.teradyne.com/corp/history.html, September 8, 2006.

[2] Information on Teradyne is based on interviews with CEOs Michael Bradley and George Chamillard on November 16, 2006, and August 7, 2001, respectively.

EXHIBIT 11.1 Net Sales at Teradyne

Source: Data drawn from http://www.teradyne.com/invest/annual.html, November 7, 2006.

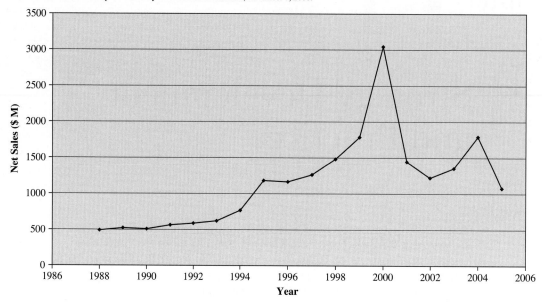

EXHIBIT 11.2
Percentage of Sales by Business Segment at Teradyne

Source: Data drawn from http://www.teradyne.com/invest/annual.html, November 7, 2006.

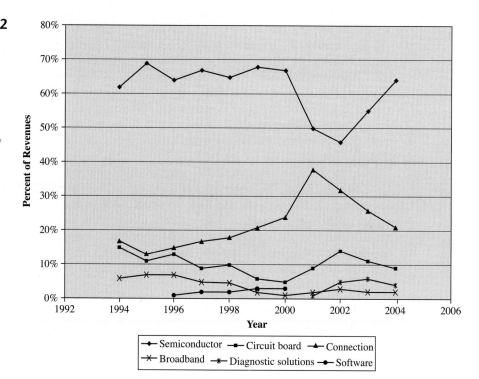

Today, Teradyne is about a $1.1 billion company. In addition to its core business of semiconductor test equipment, it has businesses in assembly test equipment (both board and system level), phone and cable networks, automotive diagnostics, and military aeronautics. As Teradyne has diversified its business and acquired a variety of companies, its challenge has been to implement a strategic planning process that supports its strategy of addressing the intersection of technological complexity and lower costs. Teradyne has also created a planning process that takes into account its heritage of electronic testing. Its strategy, which is reinforced in the planning process, focuses on organic growth in its core business of semiconductor testing. It will enter adjacent markets if there is a strong profit pool, there is technology or customer leverage, and the company has the ability to differentiate product offerings.

Each year Teradyne's formal strategic planning process starts at corporate with an examination of the external environment that results in setting performance targets and goals for each of its five businesses. It also lays out the steps in the planning process, including who is responsible, when the steps must be completed, and what they entail. The plan is fact-based, focuses on the vital few issues facing the company in the upcoming year, and establishes stretch goals for the company to accomplish. The executive committee oversees plan development.

The business units then develop their plans. They, too, assess their external environments, as well as gather information on their customers and competitors. They each generate a plan that serves as a strategic statement for the business unit, identifying a path forward that addresses underlying assumptions and changes from prior years. The business unit plans have four features: First, they are four-year plans that start in the middle of each year. Second, they state key assumptions for the current year. Third, they identify key obstacles. Fourth, they create a model for financial performance. In general, the businesses are given a great deal of flexibility, with few expectations for standardization or centralization of processes or sourcing strategies. The division plans are rolled up to the corporate level to ensure that in aggregate the corporate goals are achieved.

Teradyne's approach to strategy development grew out of a desire to have crisper goals to deliver growth and targeted financial performance. It discovered total quality management (TQM) techniques in the mid-1980s from the electronics industry in Japan and realized that application of plan-do-check-act cycles (see Chapter 10) would allow it to much better describe its strategy-making process. The resulting process is thorough and rigorous. The well-defined output comprises an annual plan and a four-year midterm plan that is long enough to stretch just beyond its two- to three-year product development cycles. The company reviews the annual plan during two meetings each quarter: The first is a strategy meeting that highlights the interaction between the annual plan and the four-year plan, integrating short-term reality with longer-term objectives. The second is a business review meeting at which it assesses how well it is doing at reaching key goals.

Despite the rigorous manner in which strategy is developed and implemented, Teradyne works hard to ensure a spirit of entrepreneurialism in its business. It only standardizes and creates central systems where appropriate: human resources, legal, finance, and information technology. Sales, product development, manufacturing, and marketing are managed at the division level. Much of Teradyne's manufacturing today is outsourced. It retains internal manufacturing functions primarily to support new product development and for final configuration and testing.

Responding to a sense that its strategic planning process needed more rigor, Teradyne developed a fact-based planning system. Not all companies follow a strategic planning process that is quite as analytically rigorous or thorough as Teradyne's. Some let their strategies evolve more organically through the patterns of decisions made on a day-to-day basis, particularly around the allocation of resources. Others focus on identifying best practices and imitating them under the assumption that operations philosophies and techniques should be driven by competitive benchmarks and business excellence models to improve competitiveness through the development of people, processes, and technology (Voss 1995). Whatever approach is taken, however, most share some basic elements of strategy-making—establishing metrics and benchmarking competitors or best-in-class operators.

This chapter closes the book with an integrative look at the decision categories—vertical integration, process technology, capacity, facilities, sourcing, business processes, supply chain management, information technology, and capabilities development—we have addressed in the last nine chapters. It starts with a look at a couple of the tools that are integral to strategy-making in many firms: performance metrics and benchmarking. It then examines each of the five bases of competition—cost, quality, availability, features/innovativeness, and environmental performance—and the ways in which companies integrate choices in the decision categories to perform competitively along that dimension. It closes with a recap of how companies develop and implement operations strategy.

Metrics and Benchmarking

As we described in Chapter 1, companies may develop their operations strategies from the top down, driving decisions about operations activities and investments from their business objectives, or from the bottom up, learning about the capabilities of the company and identifying business opportunities in which to apply them. In reality, many companies are like Teradyne. They integrate both approaches, establishing top-level objectives, collecting information throughout the organization—particularly from those on the front lines with customers—and then integrating the information to create a strategic focus for the company. Some (e.g., Acur and Jorgensen 2003) argue that there is yet a third approach to making operations strategy, which is to examine, or benchmark, and then imitate others. Whatever the approach, most companies engage in a process of establishing performance metrics against which they can measure strategic outcomes, and many companies do some form of benchmarking to learn about how other companies work. We highlight these important activities in this section.

Performance Metrics

Performance measurement requires establishing the metrics that will be used to perform periodic quantitative assessment of a process and the procedures that will be used to carry out the measurement and interpret the data in the light of previous or comparable assessments.[3] For better or worse, a company's choice of metrics guides the behaviors of its employees and directs its outputs. In recent years, it has become increasingly apparent that firms must be managed with more than just financial metrics (Kaplan and Norton 1996 and 2001). Financial metrics that focus on answering the question "To succeed financially,

---

[3] http://en.wikipedia.org/wiki/Metrics, November 7, 2006.

EXHIBIT 11.3
Balanced
Scorecard
Model

Source: Adapted from
http://www.balanced
scorecard.org/basics/
bsc1.html, retrieved
November 7, 2006.

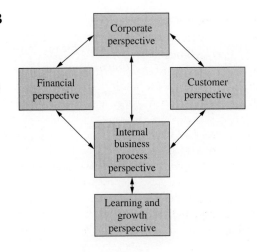

how should we appear to our shareholders?" are important, but there are three other sets
of metrics with which they must be balanced.[4] Customer-focused metrics answer the question "To achieve our vision, how should we appear to our customers?" and force the company to adopt a customer's perspective of its performance, which financial metrics alone
do not necessarily accomplish. Internal business processes metrics address the question
"To satisfy our shareholders and customers, what business processes must we excel at?"
and get at the heart of many of the questions we have raised in this book. Finally, learning
and growth metrics answer the question "To achieve our vision, how will we sustain our
ability to change and improve?" which speaks to capabilities development.

The balanced scorecard that integrates these four sets of metrics (Exhibit 11.3) leverages basic total quality management (TQM) principles to create feedback around internal
business process outputs but adds feedback around the outcomes of business strategies to
create "double loop" learning (Argyris and Schön 1996). Proponents of the balanced
scorecard emphasize the importance of data and metrics to an organization as they provide
a factual basis to examine the status of the organization from different perspectives, engage
in continuous improvement of business processes, highlight trends in performance over
time, supply quantitative data for decision support systems, and allow feedback systems
themselves to be updated over time.[5]

We have structured this book around performance along five customer-focused
dimensions—cost, quality, availability, features/innovativeness, and environmental
performance—each of which implies a set of potential metrics. Exhibit 11.4 lists possible metrics for each dimension.

In addition to identifying performance metrics for the objectives the organization
wishes to accomplish, it is also important to identify targets for the metrics.[6] Performance
targets are often the means by which an organization communicates a strategic initiative.

---

[4] Questions taken from http://www.balancedscorecard.org/basics/bsc1.html, November 7, 2006.

[5] http://www.balancedscorecard.org/basics/bsc1.html, November 7, 2006.

[6] Information on target setting in part drawn from http://www.2gc.co.uk/pdf/2GC-MB0603.pdf,
November 7, 2006.

EXHIBIT 11.4 **Performance Metrics for Five Customer-Focused Dimensions**

Dimension	Metrics to Measure Internal Performance	Metrics to Measure Effect on Customer

Cost	Cost of materials
	Cost of labor
	Cost of energy
	Factor productivities (labor, material, energy)
	Cost of good sold (COGS)
	Fully delivered product or service cost
		Cost to the customer
		  Purchase price
		  Cost of ownership

Quality	Cost of quality
	  Appraisal costs
	  Prevention costs
	  Cost of failure internally
	  Cost of failure externally
	    Warranty costs
	    Lost customers
	Defect rates
		Defect rates
		Mean time between failure
		Service costs

Availability	Time-to-market of new products or services Break-even time for new products or services Order fulfillment time Delivery or service time Variation in service time Service level on inventory Variation in service level Number of variations offered	Time from order placement to order receipt Product or service availability "off the shelf" Availability of common variations
Features/ Innovativeness	Innovation capabilities Number of new features, products, technologies Customization or breadth of product line or services in new features	Advanced features or technologies Measurable product or service performance
Environmental Performance	Environmental violations Pollution emissions (NOx, SO2, CO2) Hazardous waste production Recycling rate Toxic release inventory Resources used in production and use	Percentage of recycled materials used Resources consumed in usage

John Young, then CEO of Hewlett-Packard, made clear his interest in improved quality performance throughout the company when he announced the stretch goal of reducing warranty defects tenfold during the decade of the 1980s. Other times performance targets describe a competitive benchmark to be achieved. Fast food outlets are well aware of the order turnaround times they are expected to accomplish to continue to be "fast" food. Other targets encourage particular employee behaviors. Wells Fargo Bank sets targets for employee contributions of time outside the workplace to community causes.

The target-setting process entails not only determining what the targeted value of a performance metric is, but how progress toward that target will be measured. How will data be collected and presented? Will managers be alerted whenever performance deviates from the target or only when it deviates by a preset amount? Are the targets set milestones that have to be reached, or is there a linear scale along which performance is gauged? Are there multiple measures for a given target or only one? What actions will the organization take if the target is not reached? What will it do when it is reached? Just as TQM underlies the development of the balanced scorecard, it provides methodologies (e.g., the seven-step methodology from Shiba and Walden 2001) for meeting performance targets.

Target setting and performance monitoring are an integral part of implementing an operations strategy. We turn now to a specific exploration of target setting in the area of cost.

Target Costing[7]

Historically, many organizations priced their products using a cost-plus approach. They estimated direct materials and labor costs, increased those costs by some percentage that represented overhead costs, and then added a standard margin for profit, all based on information and variables internal to the company. Then, depending on the competitive environment, customers could either accept the price or not. Value-based pricing, on the other hand, attempts to determine the value provided by a product or service to the customer and charge customers accordingly.[8] Value-based pricing may or may not result in the firm making profit on the product. Competitive benchmarks can also be used to establish a price position in the marketplace.

Target costing involves designing a product or service with a specific cost target in mind. The target cost might be set by the market price of existing competitors, by knowledge about customer satisfaction with the prices of the company's own products in the marketplace, by interest in adding products or services at a different price point than others in the current portfolio, or by an internal goal to increase profitability. For new products or services, target costs may be derived from marketing projections of customer behavior and willingness to pay. In general, the target cost is generated with information from outside the company, and the organization adjusts as needed to meet it.

When the target cost must be significantly lower than current market prices, companies may set stretch goals, which are aggressive targets established without a clear roadmap of how to reach them. Often stretch goals can only be met if the organization finds different ways of working. It might, for example, find that it has to engage in concurrent engineering where product development and manufacturing work hand in hand to deliver a product that is significantly cheaper. New platform products in particular must be designed by cross-functional teams with representation from manufacturing, procurement, and marketing to balance priorities and achieve the right combination of cost and features for the market. It might find that it has to use technologies that come from sources other than its own internal development organizations. It might find that it has to facilitate increased cooperation across the supply chain—beyond four-wall thinking—to accomplish the goals.

Designing products around a target cost is often far more efficient and faster than the "over-the-wall" mentality of marketing handing engineering requirements, engineering handing manufacturing a design, manufacturing handing marketing a finished product out of which it has squeezed as many costs as possible, and then marketing making the best of the result in the marketplace. Target costing encourages cooperation from the outset.

---

[7] Parts of this section and the section on competing on costs are based on the work of Tom Blake and Gary Tarpinian, former MIT students.

[8] It is also possible to do rate-of-return pricing in which the firm seeks a specific return on its products or services. This is usually only possible under monopolistic conditions.

Intel provides an example of the comprehensive change that can be achieved through target costing. In the late 1990s, Intel was struggling to make a profit in the flash memory business. While its margins on high-performance microprocessors were high, margins on memory chips were limited by commodity prices set in the market. Intel's manufacturing costs were initially much higher than those needed to produce memory chips profitably. Intel set an aggressive cost target for memory chips and mobilized manufacturing to meet the targets. Targets for all cost categories (even such seemingly irrelevant items as clean room gowns) were established, and cost teams reported progress toward the targets to factory management weekly. Not only did the costs for memory chips fall, but many of the cost reductions applied to the microprocessors as well. Aggressive cost cutting during a time of flat revenues helped Intel fuel a strong recovery in late 1998 and early 1999.

Target costing offers several advantages over conventional cost management. It is proactive and encourages breakthrough process innovation in order to meet goals. It spans supply chain and engineering disciplines. It is market-driven, so ensures a balance between price and features. A drawback of target costing when implemented throughout the supply chain is that it tends to push suppliers toward commoditization, competing only on price and not product innovation.

Activity-Based Costing

Target costing requires an organization to know its cost structure well and be able to track the costs of delivering a product or service relatively closely. Activity-based costing (ABC) is a means of doing so. Developed in the mid-1980s (Kaplan and Cooper 1998 and Cooper and Kaplan 1988), ABC replaced accounting approaches in which overhead was spread across products or services on the basis of the direct labor they consumed (Exhibit 11.5). Historically, direct labor was a large portion of the cost of making a product, so allocating overhead cost based on the number of hours of direct labor it took to make the product was

EXHIBIT 11.5
Traditional Approaches to Costing Products and Services

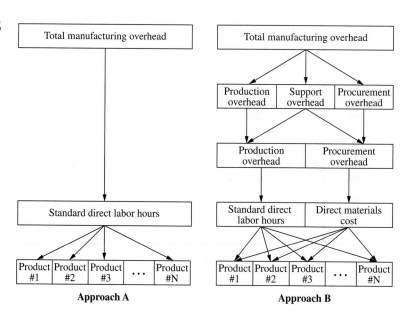

Approach A   **Approach B**

reasonable (Approach A in Exhibit 11.5). As the portion of direct labor in products declined and direct materials costs rose, some companies chose to split overhead into that associated with production and that associated with procurement. They then split support overhead between production and procurement, and allocated resulting production overhead on the basis of direct labor, and procurement overhead on the basis of direct materials costs (Approach B in Exhibit 11.5). The next step was to distribute overhead into even narrower activities and then allocate it based on how the products being built consumed the resources employed by those activities. Thus, ABC was born.

ABC is a means of collecting and classifying cost data to make better strategic decisions (e.g., Brimson 1997). Direct costs, like direct materials and direct labor, are still allocated directly to the products or services that consume them, while the fixed, or indirect costs, including support overhead costs, are allocated by activity using cost drivers (Exhibit 11.6). (Not all of the indirect costs are fixed per se; costs such as shipping and receiving might track longer-term capacity requirements and thus not vary directly with volume.) Cost drivers describe the relationship between the activity and the product or service, or more precisely, describe the means by which the product or service consumes the resources

EXHIBIT 11.6
Activity-Based Costing for a Printed Circuit Board Assembly Operation

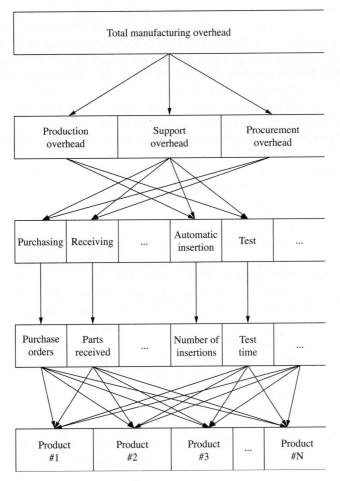

associated with the activity. For example, the cost driver for a shipping activity might be the number of packages shipped. Shipping costs might be assigned to each product based on the number of packages of that product that are shipped, regardless of the size of the packages or the dollar amount of their contents. The supporting logic for choosing this cost driver is that the shipping person has to go through just as much time and effort to ship a large package as he or she does to ship a small package.

ABC allocates based on *standard cost,* the cost per activity assuming full capacity. If, for example, the shipping activity is capable of handling 3,000 shipments per month and costs $12,000 per month to operate, the standard cost is $4 per shipment. If product X required 40 shipments in a given month, it would then receive an allocation of $160 from the shipping activity for that month. If, at the end of an accounting period, only 2,200 shipments were made, the remaining 800 shipments (or $3,200) might be assigned to "unused capacity." Unused capacity information could in turn be used to plan future shipping capacity. Standard costs should be calculated infrequently to avoid reacting to minor statistical fluctuations in volume. Standard costs can then change when capacity changes or operating costs change, and good (but not perfect, real-time) estimates of spending can be reflected in product or service costs.

It is important to choose an appropriate set of cost drivers when implementing ABC. Cost drivers should be few in number but be a strong indicator of the actual consumption of resources within the company. This limits additional record keeping but increases cost accuracy. Cost drivers should emphasize those activities where the company might differentiate itself from its competitors. If materials costs are a large portion of product or service costs, a company might perceive little value in spending time allocating the other costs. But if its competitors have the same materials costs, the remaining costs may be its only point of distinction. In general, ABC systems should be designed with clear goals in mind. Does the company want to better understand its product or service costs? Does the company want to reduce the costs of its service delivery activities? Does the company want to understand the profitability of individual customers? Choice of cost drivers should relate to the goals the ABC system is designed to achieve.

ABC, and its inherent ability to classify costs in a number of different ways, offers a number of benefits:

- *Insight on profitability of products, services, and/or customers due to more accurate cost allocation.* With improved profitability information, marketing and sales can push the company in directions of greater profitability.
- *A consistent view of costs that results from using a standard cost, rather than share of actual spending.* By charging a product the cost based on the cost drivers instead of some type of average cost, profitability and pricing strategies can be better aligned.
- *Ability to better forecast resource demands and costs from more accurate data on expected consumption.* For example, if the customer is demanding smaller shipments, then more shipments will be required and the capacity for shipping must be increased. This insight falls out as a by-product of ABC but would not be obvious from looking at sales projections alone.
- *Finally, ABC is holistic and can address indirect expenses outside operations that are often large yet unassigned.* ABC can be applied to the supply chain, inventory management, and corporate functions like legal and personnel, as well as operations activities.

Benchmarking and Best Practices

Benchmarking, as defined by the American Productivity & Quality Center (APQC), is the process of identifying, understanding, and adapting outstanding practices and processes from organizations anywhere in the world to help your organization improve its performance.[9] The outstanding practices that provide the benchmark to be achieved are often referred to as best practices. Benchmarking goes well beyond performance measurement and beyond target setting, as it allows a company to improve its business processes by learning about and exploiting best practices. A study by APQC found that organizations achieved paybacks from their most successful benchmarking projects of between $76 and $189 million in the first year.[10]

An organization might choose to benchmark its strategies against those of its competitors, its business processes against those who are thought to have best-in-class processes, or performance against selected metrics. Cost metrics suitable for benchmarking might include manufacturing cost, labor productivity, and line yield. Availability metrics might include order fulfillment time and inventory availability. Quality metrics might include initial product defects. Features and innovativeness metrics might include the technology performance of a product, or inclusion of features in a service. Environmental performance metrics might include use of recycled content or emissions. Benchmarking data is attractive because it is quantitative and fairly easy to interpret. A cursory review of benchmarking data can tell an organization where its strengths and weaknesses lie for the given competitive dimension.

Although benchmarking is often conducted with competitors or other companies outside the industry, many firms have made considerable gains by benchmarking internal divisions. Lucas Automotive, a British automotive parts manufacturer that is now part of TRW, used a five-stage process to identify and disseminate best practices among 20 sites in its own organization (Helliwell 1992): topic selection, enquiry and analysis, discussion, conclusions, and communication. The focus of the initial review was on payment systems, but this was extended to many other parts of the organization including manufacturing. By capturing and disseminating best practices from all 20 sites, Lucas was able to improve performance across the board without singling out specific sites as good or bad and identified savings ranging from 2 to 25 percent depending on the cost category. While the study did not result in overwhelming improvement at any one site, all of the best practices were found to be practical and easy to implement because they were already in use elsewhere in the organization.

Internal benchmarking was also important to Intel's implementation of its Copy Exactly! strategy. Copy Exactly! sites are designed to run essentially identical manufacturing processes using the same equipment with the goal of processing wafers exactly the same way regardless of location. (See Chapter 3 for more detail on the program.) Despite this disciplined approach, Intel still found significant cost differences across factories. Exhibit 11.7 presents the 1999 costs for three different fabrication facilities: D2 in Santa Clara, California; F11 in Rio Rancho, New Mexico; and F12 in Chandler, Arizona. F12, for example, provided the benchmark for cost of spare part consumption, so was expected to share its (best) practices to help the other facilities reach the same low consumption levels.

---

[9] http://www.isixsigma.com/offsite.asp?A=Fr&Url=http://www.apqc.org/portal/apqc/ksn?paf_gear_id=contentgearhome&paf_dm=full&pageselect=include&docid=112421, November 7, 2006.

[10] http://www.isixsigma.com/offsite.asp?A=Fr&Url=http://www.apqc.org/portal/apqc/ksn?paf_gear_id=contentgearhome&paf_dm=full&pageselect=include&docid=112421, November 9, 2006.

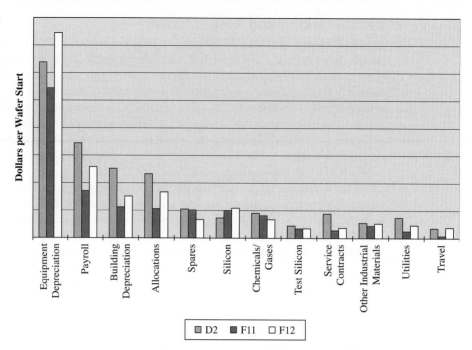

EXHIBIT 11.7
Costs by Category for Three Different Intel Manufacturing Sites

Source: Tarpinian, "Cost Reduction Methodology and Management," MIT master's thesis, 1999.

Intel factories use the ample and timely data from Intel's massive manufacturing information system to benchmark each other on a weekly basis.

Benchmarking in general does not place any limits on where to look. Companies often search the world to find best practices, best technology, or best processes. While the examples of Lucas and Intel focus on internal benchmarking, external benchmarking is often more important. Henry Ford got his inspiration for assembly-line manufacturing by watching production at a Chicago slaughterhouse. Toyota derived just-in-time from grocery store inventory management. GTE studied an elevator company to improve its field service, and the Ritz-Carlton redesigned its housekeeping process after benchmarking one of its competitors.[11] Before a company can engage in benchmarking, however, it must fully understand the technology, process, or practice it is studying within its own organization.

Benchmarking identifies where significant differences exist between organizations, and best practices explain the root causes for the difference. Armed with this knowledge, an organization can adapt its own technologies, practices, or processes to reach the "best in class" level. Benchmarking information is easy to collect, interpret, and implement, and the exercise of benchmarking forces an organization to look beyond itself for solutions and learn from others. Unfortunately, though, best practices do not provide breakthrough innovations. At best, an organization can only get as good as everyone else. As one manager stated, "Whatever is best practice today will almost certainly not be tomorrow." So, while benchmarking has great value, it should not be used as a substitute for other types of strategic planning that allow the company to rethink its position in a marketplace and the potential uses of its capabilities.

[11] http://www.isixsigma.com/offsite.asp?A=Fr&Url=http://www.apqc.org/portal/apqc/ksn?paf_gear_id=contentgearhome&paf_dm=full&pageselect=include&docid=112421, November 9, 2006.

Taking a Position in the Marketplace

In Chapter 1 we introduced five dimensions along which a firm might choose to position itself or compete: cost, quality, availability, features/innovativeness, and environmental performance. In the subsequent eight chapters we addressed eight decision categories: vertical integration, process technology, capacity, facilities, sourcing, business processes and organizational structures, supply chain management, and information technology. In each chapter we discussed the ways in which decisions in that category might affect positioning along each of the dimensions. Here we pull all of that discussion together and talk about the integrated set of decisions a firm might make in taking a position along one of the dimensions. Recall that one of the characteristics of a good strategy is that the decisions made across the categories are consistent with one another and work together to support the business strategy. We emphasize understanding of the interactions among decisions in the following discussion.

We will address each dimension of competition in turn, knowing that firms rarely position themselves along just one dimension. Effective strategies typically emphasize one or two of the five dimensions of performance; it is very difficult to be the leader in all five. Part of the strategy development process is selecting which subset to emphasize. We return to a discussion of competition along multiple dimensions at the end of this section.

Developing a strategy for a given dimension involves choosing among the multiple ways in which that dimension might be characterized or measured and may entail making trade-offs among those measures. Along the cost dimension, for example, a company might choose to focus on purchase cost to the customer, or it might choose to focus on total cost of ownership. Along the availability dimension it might choose to focus on time-to-market for new products, on having products available within a promised lead time, or having services available upon demand. Exhibit 11.4 lists sets of possible metrics one might use along each dimension.

We now turn to an examination of each of the five dimensions of performance. For each dimension we briefly define the alternative measures an organization might use, highlight some of the strategic choices it might make in each of the decision categories, and then describe ways in which those decisions work together to support the performance goals. Our discussion is by definition a simplified version of what one would find in reality, as we cannot fully represent those complexities here.

Competing on Cost

A company competing along the cost dimension might choose to compete on the basis of purchase cost to the customer, or it might worry more broadly about the full cost of ownership for the customer. As we discussed earlier, target costing, which focuses on the internal cost to build a product or deliver a service, is one way of connecting the customer's cost with internal cost structures. Activity-based costing is a way of collecting and analyzing internal costs. Benchmarking allows a firm to understand where it stands in terms of cost. Cost metrics can be used to achieve cost benchmarks inside a firm. ABC and benchmarking are useful tools in making some of the decisions we now discuss.

Vertical Integration

Firms will choose to outsource if the supplier markets provide lower costs (Chapter 2). If the global market supports off-shoring (Chapter 6), then off-shoring may be best accomplished through an outsourcing relationship. On the other hand, if internal operations provide lower costs, a vertical integration relationship may be preferred.

Process Technology

Process technology allows cost advantage to be gained through scale, scope, and experience. As we note in Chapter 3, learning and experience provide cost advantages through economies of scale and scope, labor efficiency improvements, and product and process standardization. Oftentimes the learning or experience curve itself reflects these factors. For example, if market volume increases and a firm maintains more share than its competitors, then its scale alone can provide advantage. With a varying product line, economies of scope can provide a similar cost advantage. Exploitation of the experience curve and the development of cost advantages often require a sequence of process improvements. These may not be simple incremental improvements but significant process changes to capture new efficiencies, increased scale, or both.

A cost reduction strategy may also benefit from standardization of processes in a cost-competitive environment. Process standardization, such as that achieved in Intel's Copy Exactly! program, allows efficiencies in process costs from location to location.

Capacity

A cost-based strategy suggests tightly controlled capacity with very little excess. In those cases where capacity is flexible to address short-term fluctuations, the company would attempt to develop economic means of adding temporary capacity rather than incur the expense of more permanent excess capacity.

Facilities

In a cost-based strategy, facilities decisions are usually linked to technology choices through standardization and appropriate scale at each location. Facilities-focus questions (Chapter 5) are also relevant. While it is difficult to generalize, a process focus for the facilities network is often appropriate for a cost-based strategy.

Sourcing

When pursuing a cost-based strategy, particularly in a global environment, managing suppliers is critical. Globalization provides more options, as complex products that were once available from a single supplier are now available from many suppliers in all corners of the globe. As more suppliers become available, competition increases and products become commodities.

This does not mean that companies move successively from source to source chasing the lowest cost, but it does mean that a company may make significant investments in different parts of the world to access low costs. It also means that companies will make fairly sophisticated analyses to optimize the total global flow.

Business Process Focus

The key business process for a cost-based strategy is product or service design and development. New product or service development is often cited as the source of advantages in quality and innovativeness but has a significant impact on costs as well. Good designs can result in products and services that are efficient to build or replicate. When design is done in conjunction with operations, key considerations such as cost can be incorporated in the design.

The literature offers evidence of this. For example, Womack, Jones, and Roos (1990), in their landmark study of automobile plants, show that plants that perform well on quality (assembly defect frequency) also perform well on labor efficiency, suggesting that similar factors drive quality and efficiency. The study also showed enormous ranges in efficiency (13.2 hours per vehicle in the best Japanese plants to 57.6 in the worst U.S. plants and 78.7 in the worst plants in newly industrializing countries [NICs]). While the NIC figure may be due to the use of more labor-intensive methods in NICs, the range of efficiencies suggests that there are factors beyond plant design and worker issues that are driving the difference. The ability to achieve low defect frequencies and high labor efficiencies is rooted in the company's ability to design for producibility.

Good design capabilities require integration of design and operations. Various techniques introduced in recent years, such as design for manufacturing, concurrent engineering, coordinated engineering, and so forth, help companies integrate these functions. As one manager stated when asked if designs are still "thrown over the wall,"

> 15 years ago (designs) got thrown over the wall, but that doesn't happen much any more. There are some groups who take life cycle management very seriously. Generally speaking, cost is clearly taken into account as the product is designed. There is a group that is constantly looking at it in volume production to take advantage of other opportunities. The life cycle people are part of manufacturing, sit between design and manufacturing, and follow it through its life for continuity. They are always looking at the market as well to make changes on the fly.

Organization and Human Resources

While it is difficult to generalize, firms pursuing cost minimization might choose a process-based strategy and will not utilize a labor force with higher factor costs than necessary. Cost metrics will be used to a significant degree in measuring both firm performance as well as the performance of individuals within the firm.

Supply Chain Management

Managing the supply chain can yield significant advantages in cost. Dell is a good example. While Dell has emphasized its capabilities in customization and rapid delivery, it has also achieved cost advantages. Some of this is due to in-plant process design, but effective supply chain management has also increased inventory turns and reduced supplier costs. By managing the supply chain, a company can reduce inventory (both reserve and transit), component, and handling costs.

The importance of supply chain coordination in the management of costs is not unrecognized among managers. As one manager stated:

> This is where the saving will come from, rather than the process. I am not separating manufacturing out as a subset, because it is a vital link, but the look must be across the entire chain. The focus has always been on four-wall manufacturing, and that maybe there is another 10% we can get here, but what can we get across the whole chain? You are always looking at continuous improvement within manufacturing processes, but there are less and less breakthroughs within those walls. Manufacturing will look at inventory. This is not new, but the cost of carrying the inventory will become greater and greater. With standardization, prices will become competitive and you will push the supply base to carry the inventory rather than you. We will pay for products when we ship them; we won't pay in advance. We will continue to look to our suppliers to manage their inventory and help them do that.

We will go back to the subassembly level to help efficiencies. We're big enough, and if you want to do business with us, we want the supply within a certain distance and delivered like we want it. Industry is moving toward paying for product only after it is shipped. Suppliers carry their own inventory until the end user pays for it. We're actually looking to let our suppliers into our own computer system for access to orders. We're also looking at giving suppliers free access to the plant, and telling them, "Here's the bin, make sure it never runs out."

Information Technology

Firms will invest in information systems that provide accurate information on costs and all the activities of product or service generation, production or service delivery, and sales and support.

Summary and an Example

So which of these decisions are key to a cost-based strategy?

- Scale, scope and experience (process technology)
- Design capabilities (business processes)
- Supply chain management

Finally, *standardization,* both of process and product, can be the basis of a cost-based strategy. We noted the advantages of process standardization above. Product standardization can also foster reduced manufacturing costs through process scale, reduced complexity and materials, and increased experience. With increased demands for product variation and customization, standardization may be difficult. However, even with significant product variations, there may be opportunities for standardization of components and subassemblies and modular design. One approach is to allow a variety of customer options but to control the scope of these in order to be as efficient as possible. While it is preferable to design products that can be customized easily, this may not always be possible.

We close this section with an example of a cost-based strategy. Southwest Airlines gained significant market share and profits by becoming a low-cost producer. Its cost per seat mile was greater than 25 percent below that of the major carriers (Heskett 2003). Southwest achieved this performance through a number of strategies. It used a standard technology of only Boeing 737s, and it further standardized its processes through limited service offerings (no reserved seats, limited snacks and drinks). It tightly managed its capacity, both in terms of its fleet and the workforce. Its location strategy limited it to alternative low-cost, smaller airports when feasible. Its human resources strategy focused on open-ended job specifications, allowing it more flexibility in turning planes around at airports, and team measures, fostering teamwork. Its adoption of a point-to-point model, rather than hub and spoke, allowed more consistency and less variability in workload at airports as it eliminated the peak periods when waves of planes arrive and depart. Many of these approaches allowed it to significantly reduce the time at the airport to turn the plane around from arrival to departure, which was the key to its lower costs.

Competing on Quality

In Chapter 1 we defined the quality characteristics the customer evaluates as tangible (e.g., aesthetics, reliability, serviceability) and intangible (e.g., competence, access, security). In Chapter 10 we described the cross-cutting capability a firm might develop to execute its processes using the philosophies and tools of quality management. We also described the relationship between the two: Firms, such as Toyota, that excel at quality management provide higher quality products and services as measured by their consistency and lack of defects. Quality as a means of competition is different from quality management as a capability. However, a quality capability, and the quality tools associated with developing that capability, can be the basis for competing on the quality dimension. A firm that chooses to gain competitive advantage through quality may choose a particular focus from among the various tangible and intangible characteristics, or it may choose to develop quality as a companywide capability. Most likely, if it develops quality as a capability, it will choose to position itself competitively to take advantage of that capability.

The definition of quality that we have used throughout this book focuses on particular attributes of a product or service. Other definitions tie quality more directly to how well a product or service meets different types of specifications and customer needs, including the following six dimensions of conformance (Shiba and Walden 2001):

1. *Fitness to standard* deals with how well the product or service meets internal specifications of the company.
2. *Fitness to use* specifies how well the product or service meets needs as perceived by the customer.
3. *Fitness of cost* specifies how well the product or service meets customer needs, but with the additional stipulation that it does so economically.
4. *Fitness to latent requirements* addresses needs that the customer does not articulate. The Sony Walkman, for example, created a new market for portable music, fulfilling the unspoken need to be able to carry music wherever one goes. Huggies Pull-Ups fulfilled an unexpressed need to help children and parents negotiate the trials of toilet training.
5. *Fitness of corporate culture* emphasizes how products and services are consistent with the corporate principles of the company producing the product or service. This enables the company to quickly develop products in a rapidly changing business environment.
6. *Fitness for society and the global environment* implies that products and services are supportive of people, their work, and the surrounding environment.

This definition of quality is quite broad, encompassing the cost, features, and environmental performance of the product or service as a part of its quality. Indeed, as we discovered in our discussions of quality as a cross-cutting capability, quality management can reach across the organization and affect all elements of the organization's performance.

Different organizations may choose to compete on different dimensions of quality. A budget hotel chain and a luxury hotel chain may both compete on quality, but the budget hotel will emphasize consistency and standards while the luxury hotel will emphasize high standards of service. Automobile manufacturers might emphasize original defects or reliability, but more upscale automobile brands might also emphasize fit and finish and durability. The remainder of this section discusses the possible choices a firm might make in the eight decision categories to compete on quality given this breadth in the definition of quality.

Vertical Integration

If its suppliers cannot meet quality standards, a firm might choose to vertically integrate; it may outsource when suppliers can. If the firm outsources, it may have to invest in education and other supplier management oversight programs to ensure quality performance. When these programs become too expensive, the firm may consider vertically integrating to reduce costs of achieving quality. A firm might also choose to vertically integrate if the quality programs it teaches its suppliers are being leveraged by its competitors.

Process Technology

Technology can be the basis of quality by providing control and consistency. Automation is often chosen over manual methods, as it provides both consistency—machines behave more or less predictably over time—and control—machines can be instructed more easily than humans. Automation also allows the organization to collect data about the performance of its process and to analyze the variables that contribute to quality outcomes. Process standardization also contributes to consistency, as processes are the same within or across facilities. Standardization allows for more rapid learning about the process, if information is shared across installations, and allows for greater control when work is moved from site to site. Thus, a firm seeking high-quality performance might choose to invest in process automation and to standardize technologies within and across facilities.

Capacity

Capacity strategy might not have a direct impact on quality, but a firm must manage any short-term or long-term expansion so that quality is consistent and does not suffer in comparison to the baseline.

Facilities

Quality-based competitiveness could be supported by a number of facilities-focus strategies—product, process, or market. A firm might choose to standardize processes across different facilities to increase consistency. The firm needs to locate where it can access process improvement technology and the skilled labor to support such access.

Sourcing

With the amount of work that is outsourced today, achieving competitive differentiation on the basis of quality is increasingly dependent on the quality performance of suppliers. The challenge for differentiation, of course, is that a firm's competitors can all access the same supply base and, thus, the same quality performance. Companies work with their vendors to ensure quality performance by:

- Coordinating parts and components acceptance, with or without inspection. Supply chains that still emphasize inspection may suffer quality problems. A customer that accepts product without significant inspection can fulfill quality goals at reduced costs.
- Educating suppliers in quality management techniques to improve their performance.
- Engaging in joint design efforts to design quality into a product or service from the start.

Business Process Focus

As we noted in the section on cost competition, good design capabilities are the source of high quality, low cost, and more features and innovation. Quality derives from designs that are durable and are not subject to problems and defects. In addition, the integration of design and manufacturing allows the development of products and services that are easy to produce.

Complexity is often the source of problems; tight linkages between design and manufacturing or design and service operations facilitate complexity reduction.

Order fulfillment and service and support, because they are directly observable by customers, are also important for quality.

Organization and Human Resources

Managerial commitment is necessary to develop a strategy based on quality. Workers need to believe that management supports quality goals even when they conflict with efficiency goals. Will management, for example, allow shipment goals to suffer if there is a quality issue? While it is often said that cost and quality do not need to be traded off, management decisions do not always suggest that this is the case. Management commitment is necessary to create a culture of quality throughout the organization. A culture of quality exists when the entire organization understands the importance of quality and the goals and metrics reinforce quality. Only then can quality become a capability.

Supply Chain Management

While different supply chain structures are compatible with a quality focus, firms need to coordinate with suppliers on quality of materials and components.

Information Technology

Information technology supports a quality strategy in a number of ways. IT systems need to provide information on quality metrics and performance. Data needs to be collected on process and product performance. These include not only direct process or service performance such as yield or defects, but also operational parameters that might be related to performance.

Summary and an Example

So which decisions are important for a quality-based strategy? In our view, the most important categories are:

- Business processes (product generation and design)
- Process technology
- Sourcing
- Organization (management commitment and culture)

No discussion of quality is complete without emphasizing *scientific approaches* such as statistical quality control and quality function deployment. The development of scientific approaches requires coordinated investments across a number of decision categories including process technology, information technology, and human resource skill development.

Toyota is a benchmark for quality. As we discuss in Chapter 8, its development of lean manufacturing created a culture of quality and also allowed it to continually realize superior performance on vehicle quality measures such as initial defects. As part of its lean system, the scheduling of materials and management of its supply chain were based on just-in-time principles. Its process technology was continually improved and tested to create consistency and predictability. Its sourcing strategy emphasized working with suppliers to achieve quality and consistency. Its design processes were integrated with manufacturing and resulted in both lower assembly times and fewer defects. Human resource policies and management structures were geared to waste and defect reduction and process improvement. The information systems were geared toward process knowledge and quality measures and included emphasis on scientific approaches.

Competing on Availability

Competing on availability implies having products or services available when customers want them. But when customers want things depends on the context: In the grocery industry, customers expect products to be on the shelf; in the airplane industry, customers expect to wait months for delivery of their products; in a fast food restaurant, customers expect to be waited on quickly; in the insurance industry, before Progressive's reinvention (see Chapter 7), customers expected to wait days before seeing a claims adjuster after an accident. Customers worry not only about the time it takes to get an existing product but also about the time it takes for new products to come out. In general, competing on the timeliness dimension of availability requires taking time out of the process, whether internal or external. Competing on availability also means giving the customer access to a variety or range of products or services, which draws upon an organization's ability to be flexible.

Here are some decisions a firm might make to improve its performance along the availability dimension. As we noted in Chapter 8, supply chain management decisions are the most influential along the availability dimension and directly affect different measures of availability, including delivery time, delivery time variation, service level, service level variation, and variety.

Vertical Integration

Firms will vertically integrate when it allows them to gain control over a process and then reduce the time it takes to execute that process. They will vertically disintegrate if having multiple suppliers of a component or service allows them more flexibility in moving demand around to access the shortest delivery times. They will vertically integrate to control the design process when they want to be able to rapidly respond to changes in customer demand or to fully customize products or services.

Process Technology

Firms will invest in process technologies that have short cycle times. When they are providing a broad variety of products or services, they will invest in reduced setup times so that changeover time from product to product or service to service is short, facilitating rapid delivery of the product or service.

Capacity

Firms will carry excess capacity to handle surges or variations in demand. They will pay particular attention to their bottleneck activities, ensuring that they are operating efficiently.

Facilities

Firms may choose to locate multiple small facilities in local markets to rapidly meet demand in those marketplaces. They may also choose to co-locate facilities that feed one another to minimize transportation time between them.

Sourcing

Firms will work with their suppliers to reduce lead times throughout the supply chain. They may co-locate with suppliers to minimize transportation time. They may ask suppliers to carry inventory and excess capacity to be prepared for surges or variations in demand.

Business Process Focus

If a firm is concerned about getting new products or services to market quickly, it will focus on reducing time-to-market through the product or service generation process. If a firm is trying to meet availability requirements on existing products, it will focus on shortening the order fulfillment cycle. If it is focused on rapid response to customer inquiries or repair problems, it will focus on shortening the sales and support cycle.

Organization and Human Resources

Firms seeking high availability need to move information around the organization and make decisions quickly. They will push decision making as low in the organization as possible and form self-contained groups that can rapidly respond to new situations.

Supply Chain Management

Firms competing on availability will focus on inventory management material flows, scheduling, and other supply chain management decisions. They might use rapid transportation to improve delivery time and tailored inventory policies to achieve service levels on specific items or classes of items.

Information Technology

Firms will invest in information technology that makes information available at the point of use to streamline decision making. It will connect all points of the supply chain to the greatest extent possible, communicating sales information back to the front of the chain so that the earliest stages can respond as quickly as possible to changes in demand.

Summary and an Example

The flexibility capability can be important to meeting availability goals, particularly the variety and customization goals. Flexibility generally requires taking decisions to carry excess capacity, invest in flexible technologies, cross-train the workforce, design facilities to handle a variety of activities, source from multiple or flexible suppliers, and tightly integrate design and operations. Burger King competes on variety, and does so by postponing differentiation of its burgers until it receives a customer order. Its information systems support taking custom orders, as does its flexible sandwich assembly process.

McDonald's competes on a different dimension of availability—service time to the customer. It trains its workers to move in as efficient a path as possible to collect a customer's order. It builds inventory to meet surge demand in the shortest amount of time. It standardizes its products so there is little or no setup time in the process. It produces burgers in batches to maximize throughput. Its information systems predict demand and tell the person at the grill when to start cooking burgers. It outsources order taking in the drive-thru lines to minimize the amount of time it takes. The operations decisions it makes collectively allow McDonald's to have one of the fastest order delivery times in the fast food industry.

The Burger King and McDonald's contrast illustrates the two primary facets of competing on availability and how the decisions made in pursuing those two different directions differ.

Competing on Features and Innovativeness

Competing on features and innovativeness implies having superior products or services in terms of what they do and how they perform. BMW offers superior performance in power and handling. A rare Bordeaux fine wine offers a set of intangible attributes that delights the consumer. Cisco offers the latest technologies in its high-end networking products. What decisions might a firm competing on features and innovativeness make?

Vertical Integration

A firm offering features that require redesigning a product or service to each customer's individual needs might fully vertically integrate so as to gain control over the process from design through delivery. Alternatively, a firm wishing to access a variety of different technologies to put into its new products might vertically disintegrate so it has the freedom to change technologies at will.

Process Technology

Firms will invest in process technologies that support innovation and rapid new product or service introduction. Where necessary, they will invest in concurrent development of products or services and processes, as Intel does in the development of microprocessors and Bank of America does in design of new consumer banking services.

Capacity

Firms regularly introducing new products or services, or supporting a variety of features, will carry excess capacity. Some, like Bank of America, build excess capacity into everyday operations for prototyping and testing new products or services. Others set aside capacity for that purpose.

Facilities

Firms will locate in regions where they can access both the talent required to generate new products and services as well as the technologies they need from external suppliers. They may choose to co-locate new product development with manufacturing or service design with service delivery to facilitate sharing between them.

Sourcing

Firms will have tight relationships with those suppliers that provide critical technologies, components, or processes. They may form joint ventures or other such partnerships that facilitate sharing detailed product or service design data and making joint decisions to achieve a shared outcome.

Business Process Focus

Companies with reputations for superior products and services often have superior design and development processes. They manage the interface between new product development and manufacturing, or service design and service delivery, closely so that the development, prototyping and testing, and product or service introduction go smoothly.

Organization and Human Resources

A company that strives to offer feature-laden and innovative products or services will hire strong engineering and technical talent to staff its new product or service development teams. It will have team-based evaluation and reward systems to encourage cross-functional engagement on new product or service development teams.

Supply Chain Management

A firm offering feature-laden or innovative products will design a supply chain to support not only its product or service delivery but also the product development or service design supply chain. It will also create a supply chain with sources in those parts of the world that are on the forefront of development.

Information Technology

Firms will invest in project-based information systems applications that allow them to manage the complex data associated with new product or service development. The systems bridge the functions in the organization to collect data as needed and integrate with the transaction-based systems to ensure smooth introduction through production or service delivery to the market.

An Example

BMW achieves its reputation for well-designed, high-performance vehicles through significant investment in both design and technical talent. It has information technology, such as computer-aided styling, that supports rapid iteration on new designs. A recent partnership with HP yielded simulation capability that allows it to reduce car design time 15-fold.[12] It locates design teams in both Germany and the United States to access knowledge from both markets and recently sequestered a cross-functional design team at Elizabeth Taylor's former home in Malibu, California, for six months to redesign its SUV. BMW's chief of design sometimes assigns up to six teams to compete on the design of a new car.[13] Information technology, organizational design, and facilities location work together to facilitate BMW's competing on features and innovativeness.

Competing on Environmental Performance

Environmental performance is an increasingly important dimension on which companies compete. Being proactive on environmental management can preempt costs that might be incurred as the result of new regulations and can save costs associated with complying with regulations. But, increasingly, environmental management is also about accessing new market opportunities (Hartman and Stafford 1998) and capturing consumers who consider environmental performance in their purchasing decisions (Kleiner 1991). Today, proactive

---

[12] http://www.hp.com/hpinfo/newsroom/press/2003/030305a.html, November 10, 2006.

[13] http://www.fastcompany.com/online/62/bmw.html, November 10, 2006.

environmental management policies can provide competitive advantage (Porter and van der Linde 1995, Sharma and Vredenburg 1998, and Greenlaw 2004).

There are two dimensions along which a firm might consider its environmental performance (Hart 1997):

1. *Controlling pollution and eliminating waste.* This entails reducing emissions from existing processes and considering alternative technologies that are cleaner.
2. *Product stewardship.* This requires taking responsibility for all aspects of a product or service from design through delivery and directly engages the product or service design team to minimize the effects of the product or service on the environment. Life-cycle analysis (LCA) is commonly used to understand the impacts of a product from design through production through use and then recovery and recycling.

A sustainability vision is an all-encompassing view of the organization—its technologies, markets, products or services, and processes—and their collective impact on the environment. In the long run, sustainability implies minimizing that collective environmental impact.

The remainder of this section discusses the pattern of decisions for an environmentally based strategy.

Vertical Integration

A firm will choose to vertically integrate if increased control over the supply chain will allow it to improve environmental performance. Alternatively, it may choose to outsource activities that are less environmentally sound so as not to have to directly manage those activities. Increasingly, consumers are forcing companies to take responsibility for the environmental performance of their entire supply chain, so outsourcing to avoid responsibility is less effective than it might have been in the past.

Process Technology

Process technology is, of course, the source of most emissions from a production or service delivery facility. Firms seeking outstanding environmental performance will invest in clean technology that minimizes the use of natural resources. They may work closely with equipment suppliers, as Intel does (Chandler 2004), to encourage development of increasingly cleaner technologies over time.

Capacity

Excess capacity can be a source of waste, particularly if the capacity is consuming resources even as it is not being used. Thus, in general, an environmentally sound company would choose to minimize investment in excess capacity.

Facilities

Facilities location decisions may be driven by environmental considerations. Intel, for example, must locate where it has ready access to a large supply of water or must create a supply when not readily available. Firms may choose to locate near suppliers or customers to minimize the environmental effects of transportation. Firms interested in managing their environmental images must be careful about locating in regions with lax environmental regulations, even if they plan to comply with higher standards or, at the very least, carefully manage publicity about their activities in the region.

Sourcing

Managing suppliers for environmental soundness is critical to most companies today (Rosen et al. 2000, Beckman et al. 2000), and more so for those seeking to compete on that dimension. They must engage in setting environmental performance standards, and monitoring performance against those standards as an active part of supplier management programs. Deeper relationships are formed when firms wish to co-design a product or service for environmental soundness.

Business Process Focus

The business process most affected by environmental management is the new product or service generation process. To fully engage in product stewardship, the product development or service design function must have knowledge of environmental impacts and have the tools required to assess environmental impact. They must be chartered to take environmental impact into account along with other design variables and to make appropriate trade-offs.

Organization and Human Resources

As for competing on features and innovativeness, there are technical skills required to compete on environmental performance. The firm may need people who can read and interpret regulations and then assess the potential effects on the firm. Or it may need engineers who can do the analytical work required to assess and minimize the environmental effects of a particular product or service design.

Supply Chain Management

Environmentally aware firms concern themselves with how efficiently their supply chain uses resources. For example, does producing a product from wood have minimal net effects on forests? Does fast food packaging make good use of recycled inputs? Does the automobile minimize consumption of resources in use? Do the firms recycling computers release toxic waste into the environment? By understanding the effects of a product or service throughout the supply chain, from raw materials production to customer use and ultimately to recovery and recycling, a company can better understand how it should design that product or service.

Information Technology

There is an increasing number of IT applications that help a firm assess its environmental impact. Life-cycle analysis (LCA) packages, for example, evaluate the impact of a product from "cradle to grave."[14] Information from LCA can be used to work with suppliers to redesign products, processes, or services with lower environmental impact.

---

[14] http://www.howproductsimpact.net/, November 11, 2006.

An Example

Global Garage Sale, one of the largest eBay drop-off consignment stores in the country, is located in Winooski, Vermont, where it was recognized in 2006 by the Department of Environmental Conservation for its environmental performance. Global Garage Sale's business itself focuses on recycling by helping people place unwanted items into the hands of others who can use them, instead of into the landfill. But it goes beyond that to adopt environmentally sound practices throughout its operations by:[15]

- Utilizing a cargo van that runs on compressed natural gas, resulting in 90 percent cleaner emissions when compared to using a gasoline engine.
- Encouraging its employees to carpool.
- Installing new thermo-pane windows to become more energy efficient.
- Reusing much of the packing material and shipping boxes it receives from customers and helping other businesses by reusing their unwanted packing material (like styrofoam peanuts and bubble wrap) and cardboard boxes.
- Donating leftover, unsold merchandise to a nonprofit that manages reuse operations, giving the items another chance to be reused.
- Recycling much of its solid waste, including unusable cardboard, paper, plastic, and glass.
- "Closing the loop" by purchasing recycled products like office paper and other paper products.
- Adopting an environmentally preferable purchasing policy whereby environmental impacts are considered during purchasing decisions.

Thus, Global Garage Sale integrates facilities, process technology, sourcing, supply chain, and business process decisions to structure an organization that competes on environmental performance.

Making Positioning Decisions Summary

We have provided a sense for what types of decisions a firm competing along one of the five customer-focused performance dimensions might make. Clearly, firms compete along more than one dimension, so must make trade-offs in the decision-making process. Exhibit 11.8 summarizes the decisions that might be made for each dimension and thus highlights potential conflicts. It provides a somewhat simplified view of the complexities we have presented throughout the book and should not be taken out of that deeper context. But it also illustrates some of the guiding principles that might be used in thinking about operations strategy design.

Most firms compete along at least two of the performance dimensions. When they do so, they must make appropriate trade-offs and then make choices that are consistent across the decision categories in supporting their objectives. Dell, for example, provides a wide variety of features at low cost with availability as promised. It does so by standardizing the components it uses to build its products, which in turn allows it to minimize its materials costs and minimize the inventory it carries. Minimizing inventories allows it to reduce its cycle times, so it can respond relatively quickly to custom orders, which in turn keeps its costs

[15] http://www.vermontguardian.com/dailies/102006/102706.shtml, November 11, 2006.

EXHIBIT 11.8 Possible Decisions in Each Decision Category by Performance Dimension

	Cost	Quality	Availability	Features/ Innovativeness	Environmental Performance
Vertical Integration	Integrate to control costs Disintegrate when suppliers can achieve greater economies of scale	Integrate to control quality Disintegrate when suppliers can afford to invest more in quality improvement	Integrate to control availability Disintegrate when flexibility to choose alternative suppliers is needed to respond to variable needs	Integrate to collaborate on design Disintegrate when flexible access to alternative technologies is desired or when new designs can be made with standard parts	Integrate to control performance or do joint design-for-environment efforts Disintegrate when suppliers can afford to invest more in reducing environmental impact
Process Technology	Capitalize on scale and experience Procure special-purpose equipment that can be fine-tuned to operate at low cost when making standardized output Procure general-purpose equipment with low changeover time for variety	Invest in process engineering and quality improvement processes to optimize process performance	Invest in equipment with short cycle times, and when producing high variety with low setup times	Invest in general-purpose equipment that can be easily reconfigured to handle new products or services or a variety of features	Invest in equipment that has low resource consumption and produces few emissions
Capacity	Minimize investment in excess capacity to the extent possible understanding trade-offs (e.g., if there is not enough capacity, the firm may have to carry more inventory)	Invest in excess capacity if it allows the process to be run with higher quality (e.g., if running a machine and making a person work faster reduces quality, then increase capacity)	Invest in sufficient excess capacity to handle fluctuations in demand without increasing delivery times	Invest in sufficient capacity to handle customization or variety in advanced features	Minimize investment in excess capacity if it consumes additional resources or creates addition emissions
Facilities	Locate facilities to access low-cost materials, labor, and technologies	Locate facilities to access process improvement knowledge and sufficiently skilled labor to run a quality process	Locate facilities near the market or near suppliers to minimize lead times and delivery times	Locate facilities to access technologies important to new product or new service development Locate facilities near the research and development function to smoothly introduce new products and services	Locate facilities in regions with high environmental performance standards

(continued)

(continued)

	Cost	Quality	Availability	Features/Innovativeness	Environmental Performance
Sourcing	Work with suppliers to minimize costs, perhaps by multiple sourcing and having them bid against one another	Work with suppliers to maximize quality, perhaps investing in education programs to help them learn quality methods	Work with suppliers to reduce lead times, perhaps co-designing products, services, and processes with them	Work with suppliers to access a variety of technologies, components, products, or services Engage in joint development efforts	Work with suppliers to improve environmental performance, perhaps co-designing products and/or processes to minimize environmental impact
Business Processes and Organizational Structure	Streamline all critical business processes to remove non-value-added tasks Focus on design for cost	Analyze and improve critical business processes to minimize errors Focus on design that supports quality Align managerial goals to support culture of quality	Streamline critical business processes to reduce time	Structure business processes to deal with variety, likely through investment in supporting information technology	To the extent that business processes have environmental impact, identify sources of impact and reduce them (e.g., impact of commuting)
Supply Chain Management	Streamline and standardize supply chain operations to minimize cost	Collaborate with supply chain partners, offering education programs, or working on joint design programs to increase quality	Structure supply chain and policies to meet availability goals Reduce lead times and inventory throughout the supply chain to make it more responsive	Forge close relationships with first-tier and other critical suppliers to work on joint product or service development Provide integrating information technology to suppliers to manage advanced features	Perform life-cycle analysis on environmental effects throughout the supply chain, and engage partners in environmental impact reduction efforts
Information Technology (IT)	Invest in the minimal amount of IT needed to support the organization	Invest in IT that provides feedback to each process on its performance and means of improvement Invest in IT to support scientific approaches to quality	Invest in IT that links the members of the supply chain with information that allows rapid decision making and response	Invest in IT that handles the complexity of variety (tracks components, products, services, customers throughout the supply chain)	Invest in IT that facilitates collection and analysis of information needed to reduce environmental impact

EXHIBIT 11.9   **Relationship between Capabilities and Performance Dimensions**

	Cost	Quality	Availability	Features/ Innovativeness	Environmental Performance
Lean Operations	Reduces costs by eliminating waste	Improves quality by focus on continuous improvement	Improves availability by reducing lead times	Allows for higher variety through reduced setup times	Improves environmental performance by reducing waste
Quality Management	Reduces costs through less scrap and rework and lower warranty costs	Improves quality as a primary objective	Improves availability by increasing yields	Increases opportunities for new product or service development that leverages better understood processes	Improves environmental performance by reducing waste
Flexibility	May reduce costs through reduced setup times	May improve quality through better understood processes	Improves availability by adapting to changes in demand	Improves the ability of the organization to provide product and service variety	May improve environmental performance by only making what customers want

down as it often receives payment for a new computer before it has paid for the components to make that computer. Thus, Dell has found a happy balance among cost, availability, and features that pleases its customers and distinguishes it from its competition.

Capabilities-Based Strategy

We have focused the last section largely on positioning strategies, but capabilities-based strategies are equally important. As we described in Chapter 10, a company may develop capabilities in lean operations, quality, and flexibility, although there are many other capabilities an organization might develop. These capabilities may be used to support a positioning strategy as described in Exhibit 11.9. More likely they will be used to support a position that is a combination of the dimensions. Toyota, for example, is positioned well along almost all of the dimensions relative to its competition as a result of its investments in lean operations.

Strategy Implementation

We have focused much of this book on the development of operations strategy, but the fact is that strategy execution or implementation is equally important. When Ernst & Young asked 275 portfolio managers what was most important in shaping their management and corporate valuations, strategy execution topped the list.[16] The ability to execute strategy, rated number one, was more important than the quality of the strategy itself, which was rated number three. An analysis of why CEOs fail suggested that some 70 percent of the failures were due

---

[16] http://www.corporatesunshine.org/measuresthatmatter.pdf, November 11, 2006.

not to poor strategies, but to poor execution.[17] Other studies suggest that fewer than 10 percent of effectively formulated strategies are successfully implemented (Kaplan and Norton 2001). Why do organizations fail at strategy execution (Hrebiniak 2005)?

- Managers are trained to plan, not execute. Planning is taught in school and in innumerable books, but execution is learned "on the job."
- Some senior managers believe that implementation is best left to lower-level employees, that planning should be distinguished from doing. Thus, when they have completed their strategic plans, they turn them over, abdicating further responsibility for their execution.
- Execution usually takes longer than strategy formulation. Conditions change over time, derailing implementation efforts. Management turns over, so knowledge of a given strategic plan disappears.
- Strategy implementation involves more people than does strategy formulation, so communication becomes vital. But communication in and coordination of a large organization is complex and difficult.

So, although this book is focused on the development of operations strategies, we acknowledge that strategy execution is equally important and address a few critical implementation issues here.

In Chapter 1 we discussed the notion that a strategy can be defined as the pattern of decisions an organization makes. If this is the case, then implementing a new strategy requires changing the patterns of decisions the organization makes. It requires changing how resources are allocated to business units, departments, projects, and people. It requires changing how performance is measured. It requires changing, perhaps, not only the decisions that people make, but the way in which they make those decisions. The change management effort required to implement new strategies can be wide-ranging and daunting to even the most experienced manager.

Successful programs to implement strategy cut across the organization, involving everyone from top to bottom, from design through operations to sales. Strategy implementation requires aligning skills, resources, and organizational culture. It may require building new capabilities or changing the organizational culture. It requires running short-term operations in a way that is consistent with achieving the long-term strategy. It requires communication and coordination up and down the organizational hierarchy, across business and functional units, as well as outside the company with suppliers and customers. It requires carefully managing and overcoming resistance to change that can come from any corner of the organization.

There are five principles for effectively implementing strategy (Kaplan and Norton 2001):

1. Mobilize change through executive leadership.
2. Translate the strategy to operational terms.
3. Align the organization to the strategy.
4. Make strategy everyone's everyday job.
5. Make strategy a continual process.

We now address each principle in turn.

---

[17] http://money.cnn.com/magazines/fortune/fortune_archive/1999/06/21/261696/index.htm, November 11, 2006.

Mobilize Change through Executive Leadership

Whether a strategy is planned from the top down, or developed from the bottom up, senior leadership for its execution is critical. Some argue that ownership and active involvement of the executive team in strategy execution is the single most important condition for success. Just as for implementation of any other major change program (e.g., Six Sigma quality), the behavior of senior managers sets the tone for behavior throughout the organization. When senior managers are rigorous in their thinking, ask the right questions about strategy implementation, and lay out a logical order for the execution of decisions and actions, it is easier for lower-level employees to follow suit.

Management focus in a strategy implementation effort starts with mobilizing the organization, creating momentum for the change. Then it shifts to governance, establishing the organizational infrastructure for rolling out the change. This likely entails structuring a number of teams from the executive level through the ranks that convert the strategy into action plans and oversee their execution, and establishing tight communications linkages among them. Finally, management must oversee the institutionalization of the new structures, culture, and values associated with the strategic change.

Translate the Strategy to Operational Terms

Top-level corporate objectives—e.g., increase shareholder value, take market share from the competition, improve productivity—must be translated into operational terms to be actionable. Over the years there have been many approaches to the translation process. *Hoshin planning,* a top-down strategic planning and execution system that originated in Japan, entailed seven steps: (1) identify critical business issues, (2) establish business objectives to address those issues, (3) define the company's overall goals, (4) develop strategies to support the overall goals, (5) define subgoals or tactics to support each strategy, (6) establish metrics or indicators of process performance, and (7) establish business fundamental measures. The first three steps were done by senior management and the others by the rest of the organization as the plans were rolled out.[18]

Strategy maps are another means of linking strategy to execution (Kaplan and Norton 2001). Strategy maps, an example of which is shown in Exhibit 11.10, start with the overriding objectives of the organization (e.g., sales growth, productivity improvement, increased return on capital employed) and connect them to key drivers. This effort is not dissimilar to that of putting together a DuPont chart (Exhibit 11.11), but places more focus on nonfinancial measures. DuPont charts show the relationships among financial measures and can be used to determine how a change in performance in one measure affects another. Return on total assets, for example, is the product of margin on sales and investment turnover, and margin on sales in turn is the ratio of net income before taxes to sales. Return on total assets can be increased by increasing the sales margin, which in turn can be increased by increasing sales. Although this particular example is perhaps simplistic, understanding the many relationships in the chart is more complex.

Once financial objectives are established they can be connected to a customer value proposition. What will the organization do for its customers that will allow it to achieve its financial objectives? Here is where the strategy map connects to the five dimensions of

---

[18] http://www.siliconfareast.com/hoshin.htm, http://www.qualitydigest.com/may97/html/hoshin.html, November 11, 2006.

EXHIBIT 11.10 **Strategy Map**

Source: Drawn from Kaplan and Norton 2001.

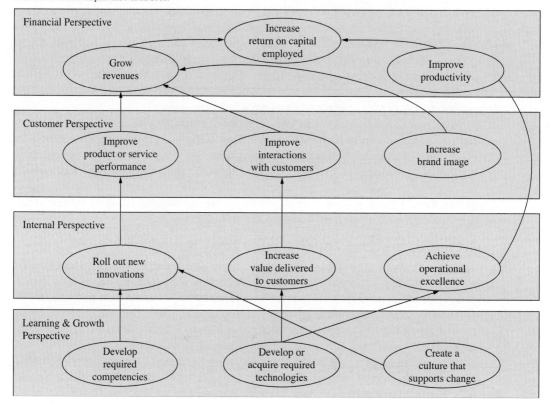

competitive performance—cost, quality, availability, features/innovativeness, and environmental performance. How does the firm want to differentiate itself in terms of the attributes of its products or services, the types of relationships it has with its customers, or in its brand image?

The map then shifts from an external view of the organization—through the lenses of its shareholders and customers—to an internal view of the organization and the activities in which it will engage and capabilities it will develop. The internal perspective layer of the strategy map speaks to the programs or activities that will be undertaken either to achieve the financial objectives (e.g., operational excellence to improve asset utilization) or to meet the customer value proposition (e.g., rolling out new product programs to increase quality to the customer). The learning and growth perspective of the strategy map addresses the competencies, technologies, and organizational alignment needed to achieve its goals.

The graphic depiction of the layers of the strategy map—the overall company objectives, the financial perspective, customer perspective, internal perspective, and learning and growth perspective—allows the organization to see the relationships among the activities it is undertaking to execute its strategy.

EXHIBIT 11.11 DuPont Chart

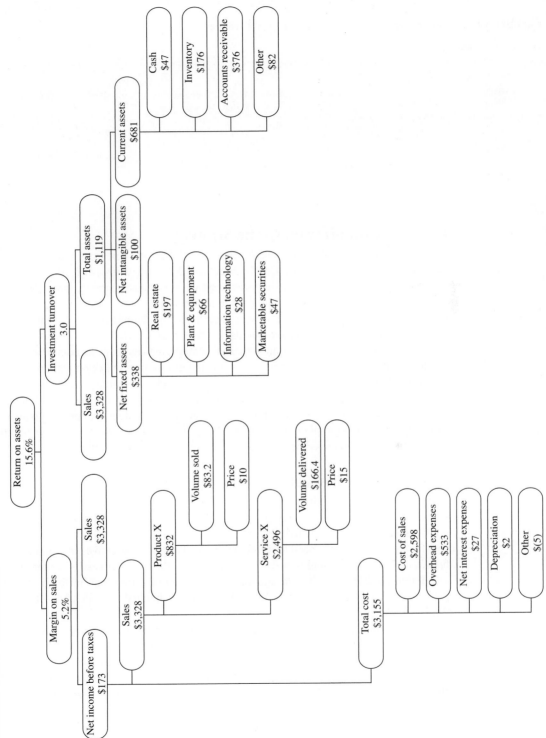

EXHIBIT 11.12   Role of Personal Objectives in Strategy Execution

Source: Drawn from Kaplan and Norton 2001.

| **Mission:** Why the organization exists | **Core Values:** What the organization believes in | **Vision:** What the organization wants to be | **Strategy:** The game plan for achieving the vision | **Initiatives:** The individual efforts that make up the game plan | **Personal Objectives:** What the individual needs to do on an initiative | **Outcomes:** Objectives the organization wishes to accomplish |

Align the Organization to the Strategy

In Chapter 7 we talked about the classic elements of what is sometimes referred to as the *star model*[19] of organizational design (Galbraith 2002): strategy, structure, process, people, and rewards. Strategy execution requires creating congruence among them (Hrebiniak 2005). It must define the role of the corporate function, identify and leverage synergies among the business units, and clarify which activities (e.g., human resources management) should be shared among the business units and functions.

Some organizations establish an office of strategy management to coordinate implementation efforts across the organization, including: aligning the organization around a shared set of goals, conducting strategy reviews, overseeing the strategy planning process, effectively communicating strategy throughout the organization, integrating and monitoring the individual initiatives being undertaken toward the strategy, connecting budgeting activities to the strategic plan, aligning workforce incentives to the plan, and facilitating best practice sharing across the organization (Kaplan and Norton 2005).

Make Strategy Everyone's Everyday Job

To implement strategy, individuals throughout the organization must be able to link their personal objectives to the strategy (Exhibit 11.12). This means that not only do they need to understand the strategy, which requires that it be communicated clearly and completely from the top, but they also need to develop their own personal objectives in alignment with that strategy and be measured for performance against those objectives. When the strategy is communicated holistically throughout the organization, rather than in the hierarchical fashion suggested by hoshin planning, it allows each individual to respond and feel a part of achieving the overall strategy.

Incentives must be established that fuel and guide motivation, are tied to strategic objectives or to short-term objectives that are derived from the strategy, and reward the doers and performers. Responsibility and accountability must be clearly established and controls put in place with timely and valid information (Hrebiniak 2005). When objectives, responsibility, performance metrics, controls, and incentives are aligned, individuals are clear about what they are to accomplish and can do so.

[19] http://www.jaygalbraith.com/star_model.asp, November 11, 2006.

Make Strategy a Continual Process

Strategy making is an ongoing process in today's rapidly changing business environment (Brown and Eisenhardt 1998). It requires constantly scanning the external environment for changes in customer preferences, available technologies, and competitive position. So, strategy implementation must be ongoing as well. It must be embedded in the budgeting and planning processes and supported by information technology and analytical tools. Research shows that 85 percent of management teams spend less than one hour per month discussing strategy (Kaplan and Norton 2001). But they devote entire monthly meetings to reviewing performance against plan, analyzing variance against past performance, and developing action plans to deal with variances.

To continually update and implement strategy, organizations need a mechanism such as the strategy map to link strategic and financial performance. They need to set aside time to talk about strategy and to share results of performance against strategy widely throughout the organization. Finally, they need a means of adjusting the strategy when market conditions or other opportunities suggest that they do so. Allowing all members of the company to see performance information, and then share their responses to it, makes the entire company more flexible in response to needed change.

Implementing Operations Strategy

Operations is clearly just one of the players at the table in the implementation of corporate and business strategy. Some of the decisions we have discussed in this book fall into the internal perspective on the strategy map. They are internal initiatives that may be undertaken in support of financial objectives or customer value propositions. Other decisions we have discussed in this book fall into the learning and growth perspective on the strategy map. They provide for the development of capabilities—skills, processes, or technical capabilities—that in turn support the internal initiatives. Operations also represents the supply chain in the strategy-making and implementation process and must ensure that it closely aligns the objectives of suppliers with those of the firm.

Often the operations function manages the largest capital investments the firm has to make, so it is responsible to see that those investments are made in line with the overall strategy (Mills et al. 2002a). Operations must be an equal player at the table in strategy making and implementation, compromising as needed to meet the overall objectives of the organization. If, for example, the corporate strategy asks for improved product or service availability, operations may have to compromise its efficiency to ensure the availability objective can be met. Working with the other functions, it can determine where and when such trade-offs are needed.

Empirical Reviews of Strategy Development

In Chapter 1 we presented approaches to strategy development (Exhibit 11.13) that involved understanding competitors, customers, and complementors and then either choosing a position in the marketplace that differentiated the firm along one or more of the cost, quality, availability, features/innovativeness, and environmental performance dimensions or developing a distinctive set of capabilities. In this chapter we presented approaches to strategy

EXHIBIT 11.13
Integrated
Strategy-
Making
Framework

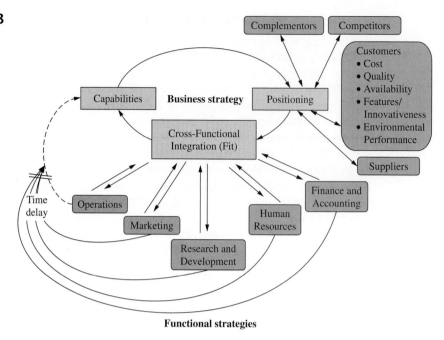

Functional strategies

implementation that involve top management leadership, organizational alignment, and high involvement of employees through personal objective setting and appropriate incentives. These are all ideal approaches to strategy development and implementation.

In this section of the chapter, we examine how firms actually plan and implement strategy. We briefly review evidence that available literature has on the topic, and then present findings from our own work in the area. The International Manufacturing Strategy Survey, conducted in more than 20 countries, has provided data for a number of studies. Here are some of the important things these studies have learned. A formalized manufacturing strategy enhances and facilitates the translation of competitive criteria via manufacturing improvement goals into action programs (Acur et al. 2003). However, only half of the European companies in the survey develop formal strategies. Manufacturing is a significant competitive force in many of these companies, though not as influential in the development of business or market strategies and goals as many would like to see. It is apparently easier for business and marketing goals to influence manufacturing than the other way around. This may imply that manufacturing is still a secondary consideration in strategy formulation and manufacturing strategy a derivative of corporate and market strategy. Better-performing companies in the survey tend to implement action plans such as total quality management (Laugen et al. 2003) and most companies seek strategic flexibility, or the ability to evolve one type of strategy into another (Cagliano et al. 2003). The most stable strategies are based on differentiation.

In order to further understand actual strategy implementation practice, we conducted interviews with senior executives—vice presidents of operations or supply chain—about strategy practice in a number of major companies. Exhibit 11.14 lists the companies. We also interviewed two CEOs and one president of North American operations, so were able

EXHIBIT 11.14
Companies
Interviewed
on Strategy
Implementation

Amazon.com	Genzyme
Axcelis Technologies	Intel
Cisco Systems	Kyocera
Dell	Polaroid
Flextronics	Qualcomm
General Motors	Teradyne

to gain insight into strategy development at a very high level. The questions we explored in these interviews included:

- How formal is the business strategy development process?
- What approach is taken to strategic thinking? Market positioning? Capabilities development? Others?
- What role does operations play in the process?
- Does the process encompass all decision categories? How are specific decision categories addressed?
- How do outsourcing, globalization, and other recent trends drive strategy development?
- What is the relationship between strategies and action plans?

Based on these discussions we developed some hypotheses on the process of developing a strategy. The specific areas in which we tried to develop conclusions were the general approach to developing a strategy, the formalization of the process, the integration and role of operations, and the major issues that get incorporated in the process. We were particularly interested in whether companies follow a formal process with careful consideration of all operations decision categories and whether the use of this ideal has any impact on performance.

Positioning- or Capabilities-Focused Strategy

The first question we examined is whether managers view the two means of strategy development—positioning versus capabilities—as a source of tension. As we noted in Chapter 1, there has been a debate about the two views. The competitive strategy view or positioning view (Porter 1998) suggests finding an explicit position in the marketplace based on market dynamics and competitive factors. Based on this position, a business identifies the appropriate activities that must be executed to take that position. The positioning view argues that capabilities are not sufficient, that operations approaches can be duplicated, and that operational excellence can be achieved by one's competitors, so capabilities are not a defining source of advantage. The resource or capabilities approach (Hayes and Pisano 1996) suggests that strategy is based on the capabilities in operations, whether in lean operations, quality management, flexibility, or some other domain. Capabilities are the strategic consequence of functional execution and cannot be easily bought or copied. Thus, new capabilities can be the source of competitive advantage. As we emphasize in Chapter 1, we believe that strategy is an iterative process that takes into account both perspectives. So, one significant question for practicing managers is whether they see this as a source of tension and whether companies employ both viewpoints.

Our interviews suggest that this tension is less apparent in actual practice than one might anticipate from discussions in the literature. Most companies are well aware of their capabilities and think about exploiting them as they develop their business and operations strategies. At the same time, most companies believe that they must choose a position in the marketplace in which to compete. In effect, these companies integrate the two approaches to thinking about strategy, as we have prescribed (Exhibit 11.13). Operations can be the source of competitive advantage, and strategy development must take into account a firm's operations capabilities. At the same time, the process must also consider the external environment and market position.

Consistency among Decision Categories

The next topic that we explored is the consistency of decisions made in the defined decision categories. Most experts believe that operations strategy should be developed by making consistent and integrated decisions in the structural and infrastructural categories outlined in this book. The reality, at least for the companies we worked with, was that the ideal process is not always followed for two reasons. First, not all categories were seen to be relevant or equally important in the process. Second, often an overriding strategic goal or principle supplants decision making in a particular category. For example, a company's overriding goal to be on the so-called bleeding edge of technology might dictate the choices of process technology in operations. Or a company's strategy to be the lowest-cost producer similarly might dictate different technology choices. A corporate imperative to outsource would obviate an operations decision around vertical integration.

However, even when all categories are not rigorously analyzed in the formal strategic development process, certain key categories generally are. The most addressed and analyzed areas include vertical integration decisions, capacity decisions, and facilities decisions. Vertical integration decisions are viewed as major strategic decisions, while capacity and facilities decisions are viewed as the major capital decisions. In each of these cases, decisions are viewed as having major strategic impact and frameworks of the types in this book are used for evaluation.

Given the significant increase in outsourcing in recent years, vertical integration is treated carefully and seriously by nearly all of the companies. However, there are situations (not among this sample of companies) where outsourcing decisions were made that were called into question afterward. There was some view that perhaps decisions were made on a short-term basis and overly influenced by the outside environment in which much outsourcing was being done. Within the sample of companies cited here, there were some suggestions that supplier capabilities are often a source of disappointment. These situations underscore the need to make all decisions in a rigorous, integrated manner.

Formality of Strategy Planning Process

The next area we examined was the formality of the strategy development process. While our implication is that the strategy development process be a very formal process, the reality is that a mix of methods ranging from very formal planning methods to very informal processes is used. This is consistent with the results of Acur et al. (2003). The informal processes are typically ad hoc with little documentation and irregular meetings. Decisions are made on an as-needed basis. Formal methods are based on regularly scheduled meetings, often annually but sometimes more frequently, with formal checklists and procedures. The annual or periodic processes are supplemented by a series of regular meetings with subgroups to help the process.

In addition, when methods are formal, the actual methods vary. Some companies base their processes on top-down goals such as growth or financial performance benchmarks, or operational goals such as quality and speed. Other organizations use a combination of top-down goals in conjunction with a process in which the lower parts of the organization identify major issues from the bottom up. Acur et al. (2003) analyzed 378 companies to understand how the formalization of manufacturing strategy affects the design of manufacturing strategy decisions (e.g., the bottom-up versus top-down approach). Their results indicate that formalization of manufacturing strategy and the process of designing the manufacturing strategy (top-down versus bottom-up approach) are closely related. A formalized strategy is more likely to employ a top-down rather than a bottom-up approach. However, all combinations are possible. Intel, although it uses a formal approach, uses a bottom-up approach, as it did to develop the "Intel Inside" campaign. Other companies use a specific method to formalize their approach. For example, Teradyne heavily uses total quality management methods and adapts these methods to the strategic planning process.

Role of Operations in Strategy Making

The next area we examined was the role of operations and how integrated operations is in the strategy development process. The ideal is full involvement, but in reality the extent of operations involvement in the strategy development process varies. Business strategy development is often more formal than operations strategy development. At a few companies, operations is fully integrated in the strategy development process. We found that this is typically the case when investments are large—as is the case with Intel, where semiconductor fabrication fabs require billions of dollars of investment, and Genzyme, where investments in biotech manufacturing are also large—or when process capabilities are critical to gaining competitive advantage. At many other companies, operations makes decisions within a broad framework developed by senior management that provides limits on operations strategy decisions. In these cases, some of which represent very successful companies, the full integration of operations in the planning process does not occur.

While operations may not always be a full part of the process, it can still drive strategy and be the basis of competitive advantage. This varies by company and also by decision category. Exhibit 11.15 presents an overview for some of the decision categories of the level at which decisions are typically made and of the strategic importance of the category. For example, vertical integration decisions are usually made at the corporate level and are considered a major strategic issue. Sourcing decisions are made jointly among corporate and operational groups and are not viewed as being as strategic as vertical integration is. The case of information technology is particularly interesting. For some of the companies interviewed, information technology was not a major critical factor. Many of these companies follow in technology implementation. For others, such as Cisco and Amazon.com, information technology is critical; these companies lead implementation.

EXHIBIT 11.15
Importance
and Decision-
Making
Level for Key
Strategic
Categories

Decision	Level	Strategic Importance
Vertical integration	Corporate-level decision	Considered a major strategic issue
Sourcing	Shared between corporate and operational groups	Increasingly considered a major strategic issue
Capacity/facilities	Major investments are jointly made	Strategic when large investments are involved
Process technology	Often made at operational level	Infrequently a major strategic issue
Information technology	Driven from corporate level	Not clearly seen as a strategic issue
Organization and human resources	Corporate-level for consistency	Not clearly seen as strategic

Strategy as a Set of Guiding Principles

At some companies, there are guidelines and principles that are the basis of the business and operations strategies. Decisions for each of the major functions and the various decision categories are then made to be consistent with the guidelines and principles. The principles and guidelines are typically based on management's assessment of the external environment and the company's capabilities. These principles can be very simple concepts that may or may not be adequate bases of strategy. But perhaps that is their strength. For example, Cisco outsources as much as possible. On the other hand, Genzyme tries to build in-house. Intel bases part of its strategy on the Copy Exactly! approach. For Intel, Copy Exactly! is the output of the strategic process rather than a driving principle but, as a practice, has been a source of competitive advantage.

Perhaps the most interesting example of this approach is the Dell "direct" model by which Dell commits to deliver directly to customers. Much of its strategy seems to be driven by the direct model, and marketing and operations decisions, for example, are consistent with the direct model. Thus, a fairly simple concept—one that is difficult to practice, as Dell's competitors have learned—can be the basis of strategy.

Summary So what do the empirical results imply? We see a number of patterns:

- While formal methods are important, some companies succeed with less formal practices.
- The concept of consistency is important, between the business and operations strategies, among the functions, and among decision categories.
- Decisions in some categories are more important than those in others. But it is important to consider all categories in developing a well-thought-out strategy.
- While the roles of all functions are critical to the process, manufacturing and operations sometimes follow strategy development rather than being equal partners in the process. The evolution of operations strategy suggests that this pattern is not ideal, but only time will tell.

We hope that this book has convinced you that formal processes and full integration of operations are important. But, at a minimum, the key operations categories need to be analyzed in a rigorous and integrated manner. Sometimes a fairly simple concept can be the basis of strategic competitive advantage if it is carefully developed and implemented.

Business has undergone many changes in recent years and will undoubtedly undergo many more in the years and decades to come. It is as clear now as in the past that operations is important—whether in the manufacturing or in the service sector. Today, information technology, outsourcing, and globalization have become driving factors that require careful assessment and analysis in the development and implementation of operations strategy. We have introduced the concepts and analyses relevant to some of these factors. We have also introduced concepts that have been newly enabled by some of these trends— e.g., Internet-based information applications, integrated product and service development, and various supply chain management techniques.

The general approaches and principles of operations strategy are as applicable today as they were yesterday and will be tomorrow. While there may be new techniques or technologies, business leaders will still need to think about the strategic implications of these techniques or technologies. Whatever the driving factors or decision areas in the future, operations can be the source of competitive advantage and needs to be integrated within a coherent process for developing a business strategy. We hope that this book has made clear the potential strategic impact of operations and the techniques for finding, planning, and gaining competitive advantage through operations.

References

Acur, N., and H. Jorgensen. "Three Perspectives on Manufacturing Vision Development." Proceedings, 17th International Conference on Production Research. Blacksburg, VA. ed. M.P. Deisenroth. Paper 0075. (2003).

Acur, N., F. Gertsen, H. Sun, and J. Frick. "The Formalisation of Manufacturing Strategy and Its Influence on the Relationship between Competitive Objectives, Improvement Goals, and Action Plans." *International Journal of Operations and Production Management,* 23, no. 10 (2003), pp. 1114–1141.

Ahuja, Gautum, and Stuart L. Hart. "Does It Pay to Be Green?" *Business Strategy and the Environment* 5, no. 1 (1996), pp. 30–37.

Argyris, C., and D. Schön. *Organizational Learning II: Theory, Method and Practice.* Reading, MA: Addison Wesley, 1996.

Beckman, Sara L., Christine Rosen, and Janet Bercovitz. "Environmentally Sound Supply Chain Management: Implementation in the Computer Industry." In *Handbook of Environmentally Conscious Manufacturing,* ed. Christian Madu. Boston, MA: Kluwer Academic Publishers, 2000.

Blake, Thomas, and Gary Tarpinian. "Cost Management." Paper for MIT course 15.769, May 1999.

Brimson, James A. *Activity Accounting: An Activity-Based Costing Approach.* Hoboken, NJ: Wiley, 1997.

Brown, Shona, and Kathleen Eisenhardt. *Competing on the Edge: Strategy as Structured Chaos.* Boston, MA: Harvard Business School Press, 1998.

Cagliano, Raffaella, Nuran Acur, and Harry Boer. "Manufacturing Strategy Configurations: Stability and Trends of Change." Proceedings. Europa-POMs Conference, Lake Como, Italy. eds. Spina G., A. Vinelli, R. Cagliano, M. Kalchschmidt, P. Romano, and F. Salvador, vol. 1, (June 2003), pp. 53–63.

Chandler, Thomas. "Program Management Systems for the Semiconductor Processing Capital Equipment Supply Chain," MIT master's thesis, June 2004.

Cooper, Robin, and Robert S. Kaplan. "Measure Costs Right: Make the Right Decisions." *Harvard Business Review* 66, no. 5 (September–October 1988), pp. 96–103.

Eppinger, Steven, and Karl Ulrich. *Product Design and Development.* 3rd ed. Burr Ridge, IL: McGraw-Hill/Irwin, 2004.

Frosch, Robert A., and Nicholas E. Gallopoulos. "Strategies for Manufacturing." *Scientific American,* Special Edition, September 1989, pp. 144–152.

Galbraith, Jay. "Organizing to Deliver Solutions." *Organizational Dynamics* 31, no. 2 (2002), pp. 194–207.

Garvin, David A. *Managing Quality: The Strategic and Competitive Edge.* New York: The Free Press, 1988.

Ghemawatt, P. "Sustainable Advantage." *Harvard Business Review* 64, no. 5 (1986), pp. 53–58.

Gilmore, James H. "Understanding the Market of One." *U.S. Distribution Journal* 222, no. 6, (June 15, 1995). ISSN: 0897–1315.

Gilmore, James H., and Joseph B. Pine. "The Four Faces of Mass Customization." *Harvard Business Review* 75, no. 1 (January–February 1997), pp. 91–101.

Greenlaw, Tamara. "Cross-Functional Environmental Initiatives: Addressing Restriction of Hazardous Substance (RoHS) Technical Challenges at Sun Microsystems." MIT masters thesis, June 2004.

Hart, Stuart L. "A Natural-Resource-Based View of the Firm." *Academy of Management Review* 20, no. 4 (1995), pp. 986–1014.

Hart, Stuart L. "Beyond Greening: Strategies for a Sustainable World." *Harvard Business Review* 75, no. 1 (January–February 1997), pp. 66–76.

Hartman, Cathy L., and Edwin R. Stafford. "Crafting 'Enviropreneurial' Value Chain Strategies through Green Alliances." *Business Horizons* 41, (March–April 1998), pp. 62–72.

Hayes, Robert H., and Gary. P. Pisano. "Manufacturing Strategy: At the Intersection of Two Paradigm Shifts." *Production and Operations Management* 5, no. 1 (Spring 1996), pp. 25–41.

Hayes, Robert H., Steven C. Wheelwright, and Kim B. Clark. *Dynamic Manufacturing: Creating the Learning Organization.* New York: The Free Press, 1988.

Hayes, R., G. Pisano, D. Upton, and S. Wheelwright. *Operations, Strategy, and Technology: Pursuing the Competitive Edge.* Hoboken, NJ: Wiley, 2005.

Helliwell, James. "Best Practice: A Technique for Reducing Cost." *Accountancy,* 110, no. 1190 (October 1992), pp. 115–116.

Heskett, James L. "Southwest Airlines—2002: An Industry under Siege." Boston, MA: Harvard Business School Publishing, 803-133, 2003.

Hrebiniak, Lawrence G. *Making Strategy Work: Leading Effective Execution and Change.* Indianapolis, IN: Wharton School Publishing, 2005.

Kaplan, Robert S., and Robin Cooper. *Cost and Effect: Using Integrated Cost Systems to Drive Profitability and Performance.* Boston, MA: Harvard Business School Press, 1998.

Kaplan, Robert S., and David P. Norton. *The Balanced Scorecard: Translating Strategy into Action.* Boston, MA: Harvard Business School Press, September 1996.

Kaplan, Robert S., and David P. Norton. *The Strategy-Focused Organization: How Balanced Scorecard Companies Thrive in the New Business Environment.* Boston, MA: Harvard Business School Press, September 2001.

Kaplan, Robert S., and David P. Norton. "Creating the Office of Strategy Management." *Harvard Business Review,* 83, no. 10 (October 2005), pp. 72–80.

Kleiner, Art. "What Does It Mean to Be Green?" *Harvard Business Review* 69, no. 5 (1991), pp. 38–47.

Laugen, Bjorge Timenes, Nuran Acur, Harry Boer, Jan Frick, and Frank Gertsen. "The Best Performing Companies' Practices." Proceedings. Europa-POMs Conference, Lake Como, Italy. eds. Spina G., A. Vinelli, R. Cagliano, M. Kalchsmidt, P. Romano, and F. Salvador, vol. 1 (June 2003), pp. 179–189.

Mills, John, Ken Platts, Mike Bourne, and Huw Richards. *Competing through Competences.* Cambridge, UK: Cambridge University Press, 2002a.

Mills, John, Ken Platts, Andy Neely, Huw Richards, and Mike Bourne. *Creating a Winning Business Formula.* Cambridge, UK: Cambridge University Press, 2002b.

Neely, Andy, Mike Bourne, John Mills, Ken Platts, and Huw Richards. *Getting a Measure of Your Business.* Cambridge, UK: Cambridge University Press, 2002.

Porter, Michael. *Competitive Strategy: Techniques for Analyzing Industries and Competitors.* New York: The Free Press, 1998.

Porter, Michael, and C. van der Linde. "Green and Competitive: Ending the Stalemate." *Harvard Business Review* 73, no. 5 (September–October 1995), pp. 120–134.

Rosen, Christine, Janet Bercovitz, and Sara Beckman. "Environmental Supply Chain Management in the Computer Industry: A Transaction Costs Economics Perspective." *Journal of Industrial Ecology* 4, no. 4, (2000), pp. 83–103.

Sharma, Sanjay, and Harrie Vredenburg. "Proactive Corporate Environmental Strategy and the Development of Competitively Valuable Organizational Capabilities." *Strategic Management Journal* 19, no. 8 (1998), pp. 729–753.

Shiba, Shoji, and David Walden. *Four Practical Revolutions in Management.* New York: Productivity Press, 2001.

Tarpinian, Gary. "Cost Reduction Methodology and Management." MIT master's thesis, 1999.

Voss C. "Alternative Paradigms for Manufacturing Strategy." *International Journal of Production and Operations Management* 15, no. 4 (1995), pp. 5–16.

Womack, James P., Daniel T. Jones, and Daniel Roos. *The Machine That Changed the World.* New York: Simon and Schuster, 1990.

Name Index

Subject Index

Page numbers followed by n indicate notes.